ROUTLEDGE HANDBOOK OF SPORT AND CORPORATE SOCIAL RESPONSIBILITY

As the role of sport in society becomes ever more prominent and as sports organizations become increasingly influential members of the global community, so it has become more important than ever for sport to consider its wider social responsibilities.

The *Routledge Handbook of Sport and Corporate Social Responsibility* is the first book to offer a comprehensive survey of theories and concepts of CSR as applied to sport, and the social, ethical and environmental aspects of sport business and management. It offers an overview of perspectives and approaches to CSR in sport, examines the unique features of the sport industry in relation to CSR, explores the tools, models, common pitfalls and examples of best practice on which managers can draw, and discusses how CSR and corporate citizenship can be integrated into the sport management curriculum.

The book covers every key issue and functional area, including implementation, strategic benefits, communication and corporate image, stakeholder engagement, and the measurement and evaluation of CSR policies and practices, and includes detailed international case studies, from the NBA and the Olympic Games to Japanese soccer. The *Routledge Handbook of Sport and Corporate Social Responsibility* is important reading for any student, researcher, manager or policy maker with an interest in sport business, management, ethics or development.

Juan Luis Paramio-Salcines is a Senior Lecturer in Sport Management at Universidad Autónoma de Madrid, Spain. His principal scholarly interests include sport facilities and event management, commercial development and accessibility provision of stadiums, the economic impact of sport events and CSR in Sport. His work has been published in *Sport and Society*, *Soccer and Society*, *American Journal of Economics and Sociology*, *Urban Affairs* and *Sport Management Review*.

Kathy Babiak is an Associate Professor of Sport Management at the University of Michigan, and Co-Director of the Michigan Center for Sport Management and the Sport Health and Activity Research and Policy Center for Women and Girls. Her research focuses on the intersection between sport and society – particularly as it relates to social responsibility and the professional sport industry. Her work in this area has appeared in *Journal of Business Ethics*, *Journal of Sport Management*, *Corporate Social Responsibility and Environmental Management* among others.

Geoff Walters is a Senior Lecturer in Management at Birkbeck, University of London and Director of the Birkbeck Sport Business Centre. His research interests include board-level governance and corporate responsibility, with a particular focus on the sport industry. He has published numerous articles in journals such as *Business Ethics: A European Review*, *Journal of Management and Organization*, the *Journal of Corporate Citizenship*, and *Sport in Society* among others.

Foundations of Sport Management

Series editor:
David Hassan, University of Ulster at Jordanstown, UK

Foundations of Sport Management is a discipline-defining series of texts on core and cutting-edge topics in sport management. Featuring some of the best known and most influential sport management scholars from around the world, each volume represents an authoritative, engaging and self-contained introduction to a key functional area or issue within contemporary sport management. Packed with useful features to aid teaching and learning, the series aims to bridge the gap between management theory and practice and to encourage critical thinking and reflection among students, academics and practitioners.

Also available in this series:

ROUTLEDGE HANDBOOK OF SPORT AND CORPORATE SOCIAL RESPONSIBILITY

Edited by Juan Luis Paramio-Salcines, Kathy Babiak and Geoff Walters

LONDON AND NEW YORK

First published 2013
by Routledge
2 Park Square, Milton Park, Abingdon, Oxon OX14 4RN

First published in paperback 2016
by Routledge
2 Park Square, Milton Park, Abingdon, Oxon OX14 4RN

Simultaneously published in the USA and Canada
by Routledge
711 Third Avenue, New York, NY 10017

Routledge is an imprint of the Taylor & Francis Group, an informa business

British Library Cataloguing in Publication Data
A catalogue record for this book is available from the British Library

Library of Congress Cataloging in Publication Data
Routledge handbook of sport and corporate social responsibility / edited by Juan Luis
Paramio-Salcines, Kathy Babiak and Geoff Walters.
pages cm
1. Sports--Management. 2. Sports--Finance. 3. Sports administration. 4. Social responsibility
of business. I. Babiak, Kathy.
GV716.R69 2013
796.06'9--dc23
2013001478

ISBN: 978-0-415-78305-7 (hbk)
ISBN: 978-1-138-12162-1 (pbk)
ISBN: 978-0-203-74753-7 (ebk)

Typeset in Bembo by
GreenGate Publishing Services, Tonbridge, Kent

CONTENTS

PART II
Implementing CSR in sport 77

PART III
Stakeholder engagement in CSR in sport 183

ILLUSTRATIONS

Figures

Tables

BIOGRAPHIES

Editors

Juan Luis Paramio-Salcines is a Senior Lecturer in Sport Management and Leisure Studies at Universidad Autónoma de Madrid, Spain. He has a PhD in Sport Management from the University of Loughborough after completing an MA in Sport Management at Complutense University of Madrid. His principal scholarly interests include sport facilities and event management, commercial development and accessibility provision of stadiums, the economic impact of sport events and CSR in sport. His work has been published in *Sport and Society*, *Soccer and Society*, *American Journal of Economics and Sociology*, *Urban Affairs* and *Sport Management Review*.

Kathy Babiak is an Associate Professor of Sport Management at the University of Michigan, and Co-Director of the Michigan Center for Sport Management and the Sport Health and Activity Research and Policy Center for Women and Girls. Kathy has a PhD in Sport Management from the University of British Columbia, Vancouver, Canada after completing an MA in Sport Studies-Sport Administration at the University of Ottawa. Her research focuses on the intersection between sport and society – particularly as it relates to social responsibility and the professional sport industry. Her work in this area has appeared in *Journal of Management and Organization*, *Corporate Social Responsibility and Environmental Management*, *Journal of Business Ethics*, *Journal of Sport Management*, *Sport Marketing Quarterly* and *International Journal of Sport Management and Marketing*.

Geoff Walters is a Senior Lecturer in Management, Department of Management, at Birkbeck, University of London and a Director of the Birkbeck Sport Business Centre. He has a PhD in Management from the University of Birkbeck, London after completing a BSc in Management at Lancaster University and an MA in Labour Studies at the University of Manchester. His main research interests are corporate responsibility in sport, governance and regulation in sport and stakeholder theory in the sport industry. He has published widely on CSR in sport, including in *Journal of Management and Organization*, *Soccer and Society*, the *Journal of Corporate Citizenship* and *Management Decision*.

Authors

Christos Anagnostopoulos is a Lecturer within the Sport and Event Management department at Coventry Business School, and an associate member of the Centre for International Business of Sport (CIBS). He holds a degree in sport management and an MA in the business of football. His doctoral dissertation (2008–2013) looks at managerial decision-making processes within the charitable foundations of the English football clubs. His key teaching and research interests lie in organizational behavior with a focus on issues such as decision-making, influence tactics, passion at work and interpersonal trust associated with the concept of corporate social responsibility in and through sport. His work has been published in *Soccer and Society* and *Social Responsibility Review*. He is also the co-author of the first textbook in Greek literature that explicitly examines the organization and management of Greek football.

Cheri L. Bradish (PhD, Florida State University) is an Associate Professor in the Department of Sport Management at Brock University, Canada. Her area of interest is with regards to sport marketing, sport sponsorship as well as CSR in sport. Among a number of conference proceedings and publications, her research has appeared in the *Journal of Sport Management, International Journal of Sport Management and Marketing, Sport Management Review* and *Sport Marketing Quarterly*. Cheri also has significant experience in the sport industry, including work with the Florida Sports Foundation, Nike Canada Inc., Florida State University Department of Athletics (NCAA), the Vancouver Grizzlies (NBA), and, most recently, as a Sponsorship and Sales Specialist with the Vancouver Organizing Committee for the 2010 Olympic and Paralympic Games (VANOC). In 2011, she was chosen as the Canadian Olympic Committee's representative to attend the International Olympic Academy (IOA) Session for Educators of Higher Institutes of Physical Education in Ancient Olympia, Greece.

Cristiana Buscarini is an Associate Professor of Corporate Strategy and Business Administration at University of Rome 'Foro Italico' and since 2004 has been a member of the Italian Association of Sport Management and also has been member of Italian Academic Council (CUN). Her current research interests include business ethics, corporate social responsibility and sport management and sport governance. Recent publications include *New Features of CSR for Italian Sport Federation (Azienda Publica)* and *Entrepreneurship and Strategic Behaviour (Aracne, Rome)*. She has also been the coeditor of *CSR and Social Report in Sport Organizations (Franco Angeli)*.

Carlos Campos is an Associate Professor of Sports Management in the Department of Business Administration at Universidad de Extremadura, Spain. Prior to this, he obtained a Bachelor's degree in Business Administration at Universidad Autónoma de Barcelona and a PhD in Business Administration at Universidad de Cadiz in Spain. His current research interests include sports marketing, fitness management, sport sponsorship and turnaround strategies in professional sport. He is also Director of www.managingsport.com.

David Carson is a Professor Emeritus of Marketing in the Department of Marketing, Entrepreneurship and Strategy, University of Ulster. His research interests lie in marketing for SMEs and quality of marketing in services industries, especially in tourism. He has published widely in both of these areas. He has wide businesses experience both in consultancy and directorship roles including contemporary companies such as Walt Disney World, Stena Line Ferries Europe, Belfast Harbors and Titanic Quarter Belfast as well as providing advice to numerous SMEs in a variety of industries. Alongside he has been editor of the *European Journal of Marketing*, President of the Academy of Marketing UK and was elected Fellow of the Chartered Institute of Marketing (CIM).

Jonathan Casper (PhD, University of Northern Colorado) is an Associate Professor and Sport Management Program Coordinator at the North Carolina State University. His research interests include social and psychological aspects of youth and adult sport participation, sports' role within active living and quality of life, and participant and fan consumer behavior. His work has been published in journals including *Journal of Sport Management, Sport Management Review, European Sport Management Quarterly, Journal of Physical Activity and Health, Journal of Park and Recreation Administration* and *Leisure Sciences.*

Jean-Loup Chappelet is a Professor of Public Management and Dean of the Swiss Graduate School of Public Management, University of Lausanne. He specializes in sport management and sport policy with a particular emphasis on the organization of Olympic Games and the governance of the Olympic System. He has written several books and many articles in these domains and he sits on the editorial boards of two main sport management journals. For 12 years he was the director of the MEMOS program, an executive masters in sport organization management supported by Olympic Solidarity.

Packianathan Chelladurai (PhD in Management Science, University of Waterloo) is currently a Professor at Troy University, Alabama after moving from the Ohio State University. Widely recognized as a leader in the field of sport management, he has specialized in human resource management in the sport and recreation for the past 30 years. He is the author of three books and his research has been widely published in major journals. In 1991, he was the editor of the *Journal of Sport Management* and was also the first recipient of the North American Society for Sport Management's (NASSM) prestigious Earle F. Zeigler Award.

T. Bettina Cornwell (PhD in Marketing, The University of Texas) is the Edwin E. and June Woldt Cone Professor of Marketing in the Lundquist College of Business at the University of Oregon. She is also Director of Research for the Warsaw Sport Marketing Centre at the University of Oregon. Prior to joining the University of Oregon, she was Professor of Marketing and Sport Management at the University of Michigan. Her research focuses on marketing communications and consumer behavior and typically includes international and public policy emphases. Bettina's research has recently appeared in *Journal of Advertising, Journal of Advertising Research, Journal of Consumer Research, Journal of Experimental Psychology: Applied, Journal of the Academy of Marketing Science* and *Journal of Public Policy & Marketing.*

Phil Downs (Member of the British Empire, MBE, since 2004 for services to disabled people) is the secretary of the Manchester United Disabled Supporters Association (MUDSA) and the Disability Liaison Officer at Manchester United Football Club since 1989. He also founded MUDSA regarded as the first organization of its kind in Europe. Alongside, Phil was a founder member and Chair (2002–2007) of the National Association of Disabled Supporters (NADS) which is a body by all the official bodies in football to represent the views and needs of disabled football supporters where he was instrumental in developing and producing the "Accessible Stadia" guide. Alongside he has been instrumental in different nationwide disability awareness campaigns, including the Level Playing Field. He has wide businesses experience in consultancy to a number of public and private bodies, including UEFA, NADS, Scope or 2012 London Olympic Games. Furthermore, he has been co-author on several publications related to the disability provision in European stadia within a Corporate Social Responsibility framework.

Barry Drust completed his undergraduate degree in Sport Science in 1993 at Liverpool John Moores University and then obtained his PhD with a project entitled 'Metabolic Responses to Soccer-Specific Intermittent Exercise' in 1997. He then lectured at The University of Teesside and The University of Durham before returning to Liverpool in 2002. Barry is now the Head of the Football Exchange, an internal organization that directs all of the football-related activity within the School of Sport and Exercise Sciences. Barry's specialist research area is the physiology of intermittent exercise. Within this area is a particular interest in the sport of football.

Kevin R. Filo is a Lecturer at Griffith University. His research interests are focused on the synergy that exists between sport and charity. This research examines the antecedents and outcomes of charity sport events. He has published his research in *Journal of Sport Management, Sport Management Review, Tourism Management, Journal of Leisure Research* and *Sport Marketing Quarterly*, amongst others. From 2004–2005, Kevin was the Merchandising Coordinator for the Lance Armstrong Foundation, managing the supply chains for the highly successful **LIVESTRONG** wristband campaign, a cause-related marketing campaign between Nike and the LAF, which has raised over $70 million for the LAF.

Daniel C. Funk is a Professor of Sport and Recreation Management at Temple University's School of Tourism and Hospitality Management (STHM). In addition, he is also a Washburn Senior Research Fellow and directs research and PhD programs for STHM. He is a member of Temple's Sport Industry Research Center. Funk also holds an adjunct appointment as the Professor of Sport Marketing in the Griffith Business School at Griffith University in Australia. Funk has written a refereed scholarly book, an industry book and a sport marketing textbook. He has authored or contributed to more than 75 articles published in a variety of journals, including *Sport Marketing Quarterly*.

Munehiko Harada is a Professor of Sport Management at the Osaka University, Japan since 1987. He received his PhD from Pennsylvania State University in 1984. He has published widely on the sport and leisure industries. He was working as a member of the 2008 Osaka Olympic Bid Committee and currently is also involved in the 2020 Tokyo Olympic Bid Committee. Alongside, he is also currently the President of the Japanese Association for Sport Management (JASM).

Dae Hee Kwak (PhD in Sport Management, University of Maryland) is an Assistant Professor of Sport Management in the School of Kinesiology, University of Michigan. Prior to joining the University of Michigan, he was Assistant Professor of Sport Marketing at Indiana University. His research focuses on sport consumer behavior, with an emphasis on how both emotional and cognitive factors derived from sport-related stimuli influence consumers' decision and behavior in a variety of sport consumption contexts. His work has recently appeared in the *Journal of Sport Management, International Journal of Sports Marketing and Sponsorship, Journal of Gambling Studies, International Journal of Sport Management, Recreation and Tourism, Sport Marketing Quarterly, International Journal of Sport Communication, Journal of Management* and *Organization and Management Decision*.

Bob Heere is an Assistant Professor at the University of Texas at Austin. His research interests are focused on the relationship between sport and society and how we can manage or leverage sport for to benefit society. Of particular interest within this matter are issues related to identity and community development. His work has been published in many management, ethics and sport management journals such as *Journal of Sport Management, Journal of Marketing Theory and Practice, Sport Management Review, Journal of Business Ethics* and *European Sport Management Quarterly*.

Kate Heinze (PhD in Management and Organizations, Northwestern University) is an Assistant Professor of Sport Management in the School of Kinesiology, University of Michigan. Her research uses cultural and institutional analyses to understand organizational and institutional change, with an emphasis on values-based entrepreneurship. She studies these issues primarily in the contexts of wellness and sport. Her research has appeared in *Administrative Science Quarterly.*

David Hindley is an Academic Team Leader at Nottingham Trent University where he combines the challenging task of managing academics with teaching sport sociology and the politics of sport. His doctoral thesis concerned the utility of governance in a sporting context, focusing on football, cricket and swimming. From this, and later work looking at supporter democracy and the community role of football clubs, he has published and presented widely. David is currently working with Notts County Football in the Community, where he is also a Trustee, on developing a toolkit for enhancing the schemes' monitoring and evaluation processes.

Yuhei Inoue is an Assistant Professor at the University of Memphis. He has a PhD in Business Administration at Temple University where he wrote his doctoral thesis titled "Investigating the Role of Corporate Credibility in Corporate Social Marketing: A Case Study of Environmental Initiatives by Professional Sport Organizations." His current research interests include the application of strategic management to the sport context in general and to the study on CSR of sport in particular. He has published widely on this topic in journals such as *Journal of Sport Management*, *Sport Management Review* and *Tourism Management.*

Liyan Jin is a doctoral student majoring in sport management at the University of Florida. Her research interests focus on the social responsibilities of sport event host organizations and their impacts on consumer behavior. She has published in such journals as *European Sport Management Quarterly* and *the International Journal of Sport Marketing* and *Management*. She is a frequent presenter at international and national conferences.

Matthew Juravich (PhD in Sport Management, University of Michigan) is an Assistant Professor in the Department of Sport Science & Wellness Education in the College of Education at the University of Akron. His primary research applies upper echelons theory and institutional analyses to understand variations in organizational performance in the North American professional sport context. His research has appeared in the *Journal of Sport Management.*

R. Aubrey W. Kent is an Associate Professor of Sport Management at Temple University. Dr Kent joined the Temple sport management program in 2008 after serving for the past 9 years as director and graduate coordinator of the sport management program at Florida State University. He is also currently serving as past-president of the North American Society for Sport Management (NASSM). At Temple, he serves as acting-program director and is the head of the newly established Sport Industry Research Center (SIRC), while directly overseeing research in the area of sport and social responsibility. Over his career, he has focused in the area of industrial/organizational psychology, and more recently in the area of corporate social responsibility. His work has been published in numerous journals, including articles in *Journal of Sport Management*, *European Journal of Sport Management*, *Sport Marketing Quarterly*, *Journal of Park and Recreation Administration*, *International Journal of Coaching Science*, *North American Journal of Psychology*, *Management Decision*, *Journal of Education for Business*, *International Sports Journal* and *Journal of Applied Sport Psychology.*

Lisa A. Kihl is an Associate Professor (2010–present), Sport Management, School of Kinesiology at the University of Minnesota. Her main research interests lie in the intersections of ethics and sport policy. Specifically, she is interested in how corruption impacts organizational stakeholders who were not involved in a corrupt acts; the role of athletes in the governance of sports organizations; and the development of elite athletes' civic agency and civic identities in relation to addressing social issues. She has published extensively in journals, including *Journal of Sport Management*, *European Sport Management Quarterly*, *Sport Management Review*, *Journal of College & Character*, *Journal of Issues in Intercollegiate Athletics* and *International Journal of Sport Policy*.

Chiyoung Kim is currently a doctoral candidate at the University of Texas at Austin. She focuses her research on corporate social responsibility and its effects on consumer attitudes, particularly in an international context. She has published in *Sport Marketing Quarterly*, *Journal of Sport Management* and *Sport Management Review* and won the best case study award at EASM in 2009 on the globalization efforts of the NBA.

Minhong Kim is currently a doctoral student majoring in sport management at the University of Georgia. He received a BSc in physical education from Yonsei University in 2008 and earned his MSc in sport management from the University of Florida in 2011. His research goal is to improve and expand the understanding of sport philanthropy, especially professional and collegiate sport donor behavior and corporate social responsibility effectiveness in sport-related organizations. He has published his master's thesis on corporate social responsibility in *European Sport Management Quarterly* and is also a frequent presenter at international and national conferences.

Mark Langhammer is Director of the Association of Teachers & Lecturers (ATL) in Northern Ireland and is ATL's representative on the Northern Ireland Teachers Council. Mark previously worked as Director of the University for Industry/learndirect program, as CEO of North Belfast's urban regeneration Partnership and as Director of the Dunanney Centre, a social enterprise center in the Rathcoole housing estate. He is a current member of the Ministerial Group on Higher Education under Sir Graeme Davis and served previously on the CCEA's Ministerial curriculum working group on 'Learning for Life and Work'. Mark was previously Chair of the Northern Ireland Association of Citizens Advice Bureaux, 1994–1998, and of Playboard NI, 1998–1999. Mark is a Trustee on Monkstown Amateur Boxing Club and is a life member of Crusaders Football Club. He is currently engaged in efforts to build a cross community stadium and sports village in North Belfast, Northern Ireland's most polarized and segregated constituency.

Hai Li is a Professor of Sport Management and serves as an Associate Dean in the School of Economics and Management at Shanghai University of Sport. He focuses research on sport marketing, sports lottery administration and sport representation, in which corporate social responsibility has often been a topic of inquiry. He has published extensively in such journals as *Journal of Gambling Studies*, *Journal of Shanghai University of Sport* and *Journal of China Sport Science*. He has been granted a number of funded projects, including a project on social responsibility of China sports lottery administration funded by the Chinese Academy of Social Science.

Roger Levermore is currently Visiting Associate Professor and Interim Director of MA programs at the Hong Kong University of Science and Technology. He has worked at the University of Liverpool Management School since 2001. He lectures on CSR from a range of situations; in international development, strategy and the sports industry. His main research interests are in the interaction of business, the sports industry, sport fandom, international development and international relations. He has published widely in these areas for journals in management, international development, geography and sport science. He has edited two books: *Sport and International Relations* (Routledge, 2004) and *Sport and International Development* (Palgrave Macmillan, 2009, 2012).

Cheryl Mallen has been an Associate Professor in Sport Management since 2002 at the Department of Sport Management at Brock University, St Catharines, Ontario, Canada. Cheryl has an EdD from the University of Southern Queensland, an MA from the University of Western Ontario and a BHK from the University of Windsor. Her work has been widely published in *Sport Management Review, Sport in Society, Journal of Sport Management, European Sport Management Quarterly* and *Journal of Management & Sustainability*.

Daniel S. Mason is a Professor with the Faculty of Physical Education and Recreation and an Adjunct Professor with the School of Business at the University of Alberta, Edmonton, Canada. Dr Mason's research takes an interdisciplinary approach and focuses on the business of sport and the relationships between its stakeholders, including all levels of government, sports teams and leagues, the communities that host teams, agents and players' associations. His research has been funded by the Social Sciences and Humanities Research Council of Canada and Alberta Gaming Research Institute and published in *American Behavioral Scientist, Contemporary Economic Policy, Current Issues in Tourism, Economic Development Quarterly, Economic Inquiry, Journal of Management and Organization, Journal of Sport Management, Journal of Sport Tourism, Journal of Urban Affairs, Managing Leisure* and *Tourism Management*. In 2004 he was named a Research Fellow by the North American Society of Sport Management.

Laura Misener is an Assistant Professor in the School of Kinesiology at the University of Western Ontario. Dr Misener's research focuses on how sport and events can be used as instruments of social change. Her work critically examines numerous ways that sport events have been purported to positively affect community development, social infrastructure, social inclusion and healthy lifestyles of community members. Dr Misener's current research programme is focusing on the role of sport events for persons with a disability in influencing community accessibility and community perceptions of disability. Her work on events and urban community development has been published in scholarly outlets such as *Journal of Sport Management, Journal of Organization and Management, Managing Leisure* and *Journal of Sport and Social Issues*.

Simon Morgan has been at the Premier League since June 2007 working as Head of Community Development. Simon oversees the Premier League's domestic good cause strategy with responsibility for working with the League's 20 member clubs and key community partners including Sport England, Nike, Government Departments, the Professional Footballers' Association, the Football Association, the Prince's Trust, the Football Foundation and the Metropolitan Police. Before joining the Premier League he worked for Fulham FC Community Sports Trust as Head of Community. From 1985 to 2001 Simon was a professional footballer playing for Leicester City, Fulham FC and Brighton and Hove Albion, and made two England under-21 appearances.

Rita Mura is a Lecturer on Sport Strategy and Business Administration at the University of Rome "Foro Italico." She received her PhD in Economics and Finance at University of Rome "Sapienza" in 2011. Her research interests are nonprofit governance, sport governance and CSR. She is the author of *Governance in Nonprofit Organization: Motivation and Performance* (Rirea, 2012).

Danny O'Brien is an Associate Professor in the School of Health Sciences at Bond University, Gold Coast, Australia. His research in sustainable surf tourism, event leverage and organizational change in sport has been published in *Journal of Sport Management*; *Sport Management Review*; *European Sport Management Quarterly*; *Annals of Tourism Research*; *European Journal of Marketing*; *International Journal of Culture*; *Tourism and Hospitality Research*; *Journal of Hospitality & Tourism Research*; and *Journal of Leisure Research*.

Milena M. Parent is an Associate Professor in the School of Human Kinetics at the University of Ottawa, Canada, and Norwegian School of Sport Sciences, Oslo, Norway. Her primary research area relates to organization theory and strategic management within major sporting events. She is also interested in stakeholder and partnership governance issues. She has published articles in *Journal of Sport Management*, *Journal of Business Ethics*, *Corporate Reputation Review*, *European Sport Management Quarterly*, *International Journal of Sport Management and Marketing*, *International Journal of Sport Finance* and *Event Management*. She has also published many book chapters, and is the co-author of *Understanding Sport Organizations: The Application of Organization Theory* (2nd edn) (Human Kinetics, 2006, with Prof. Trevor Slack) and of *Managing Major Sports Events: Theory and Practice* (Routledge, 2012, with Sharon Smith-Swan).

Dan Parnell is a Program Leader for the Sport and Exercise Science degree at the University of Derby. His primary research interests are in sport, health and management. Dan's current projects concern the role of sport as a vehicle for social change, health intervention evaluation and organizational development, with a specific focus on football. Dan has worked with a host of English Premier League and Football League Clubs. Dan is now working with a range of football clubs and sport-based social change projects to help them capture, understand and subsequently enhance their effectiveness.

Michael E. Pfahl is an Assistant Professor of the College of Business at Ohio University. His research is primarily conducted from a qualitative perspective and includes the convergence of media, technology and sport, the relationship between the natural environment and sport, and human resource issues in sports organizations. His work has been published in journals such as *Sport Management Education Journal*, *Journal of Sport Management* and *the Athletics Administration*. He is also the author of *Sport and the Natural Environment: A Handbook for Sport Managers* (Kendall Hunt, 2011).

Seung Pil Lee is a Research Fellow in Sport Management at the Department of Sport Management at University of Michigan. He has a PhD in Sport Management from the University of Michigan, after completing an MA in Sport and Exercise Management at the Ohio State University and a BA in Economics with major in statistics at Korea University. His principal scholarly interest includes sponsorship, partnerships and corporate social responsibility through sports and leisure activities for community development and sustainable development of business and society. His work has been published in *Journal of Sport Management*, *Journal of Advertising* and *American Journal of Health Behavior* (forthcoming).

David Richardson is the Assistant Director of the School of Sport and Exercise Sciences at LJMU and a principal lecturer in sport social science. David's research and consultancy specialist areas include youth development, organizational culture and community. David has worked with numerous top- and lower-tier football clubs across Europe, including England,

France, Portugal, Spain and Sweden. David has led, and co-ordinated, the development of a unique partnership between Everton Football Club and LJMU. This work examines the role of football as a vehicle for positive behavioral change with respect to the social, environmental and lifestyle aspects of day-to-day existence.

Stacy-Lynn Sant holds a Master of Science degree in Business Management with a specialization in International Marketing from the University of the West Indies, St. Augustine Campus, and is currently a PhD candidate in the Faculty of Physical Education and Recreation at the University of Alberta, Canada. Her research interests include sport tourism and sport management and her doctoral dissertation explores the legacies of the Olympic Games with particular emphasis on prospective hosts' bid strategies and the leveraging of these events for long-term tourism benefits in the host city and region.

Berit Skirstad is an Associate Professor in Sport Management at the Department of Society and Culture at the Norwegian School of Sport Sciences (NSSS). She founded the study of sport management at the NSSS in 1986. From 2005 to 2009 she was the president of the European Sport Management Association. Her research field is sports organizations, leadership and volunteers. She has edited *Who is Who in Norwegian Sports* (Universitetsforlaget, 1986) and co-edited *Worldwide Trends in Youth Sport* (Human Kinetics, 1998) and *Pain and Injuries: Social and Ethical Analysis* (Routledge, 2006). Since launching *European Sport Management Quarterly (ESMQ)* in 2001, she has served as a reviewer and co-editor of two special issues.

Richard Smith is the founder and project manager of Unify Global Sport where he conceives and delivers conferences and community sport events in the UK and oversees. His interests lie in the economic impact of major events to a country/region/city as well as "Moving The Nation," getting more public, private and third sector stakeholders to work together to get more people, more active, more often. In addition to his experience in consultancy at major sport events in the UK he is also been involved in the development of Craigavon Intercultural Program's long-term strategy of assisting migrants that arrive and live in the Craigavon Borough, Northern Ireland. He has completed a Masters in Marketing and Entrepreneurship at the University of Ulster.

Gareth Stratton is currently the Director of the Applied Sports, Exercise Technology and Medicine Research Centre since early 2012. Previously, he spent over 20 years developing his discipline in paediatric and health-related research at Liverpool John Moores University. Gareth has chaired a number of national groups responsible for producing evidence-based guidance on young people, physical activity and health. Gareth has two main areas of academic interest: child maturation and physical activity, and physical activity fitness and health. Gareth has published over 100 peer reviewed papers and book chapters, holds numerous competitive grants and has been invited to speak at many international conferences and workshops.

Steve Sutherland started his career in professional football in 1988 and is now a freelance sports marketing consultant and an ambassador of the Charlton Athletic Community Trust (CACT). During his tenure as Commercial Director of Charlton Athletic FC Steve played a role in establishing CACT when the Trust was created to build on the Club's highly successful "Football in the Community" program. CACT is the largest football-related charity in the UK by turnover and is regarded as one of the most innovative corporate social responsibility programmes of any English football club. He left Charlton Athletic in 2009 to establish Steve Sutherland Sports Marketing.

Richard Tacon is currently undertaking a PhD at Birkbeck, University of London in which he is examining social capital in voluntary sports clubs and how realist evaluation can be used to assess the social impact of sport and inform sport and social policy. He previously completed an MSc in Sport Management and the Business of Football at Birbeck in 2004, prior to which he received a BA Hons in Classics at the University of Cambridge. Richard also worked as a researcher at the Central Council of Physical Recreation, the umbrella body for the national governing and representative bodies of sport and recreation in the UK. Recently, with Geoff Walters he has written a report on *Corporate Social Responsibility in European Football* for the football governing body, UEFA. Richard's main research areas are the social impacts of sport, evaluation within sport and CSR in sport.

Scott Tainsky (PhD, University of Michigan) is an Assistant Professor of Sport Management and Co-Director of the Tourism and Sport Management Laboratory, University of Illinois. His research interests in a broad sense are to recognize the unique aspects of sports and the sport industry, and understand their disparate effects on sport organization and sport fan typologies. The specific goal of his research is to increase the total utility created by major sports leagues. He has published articles in *Journal of Sport Management, International Journal of Sport Management and Marketing European Sport Management Quarterly, International Journal of Sport Management and Marketing, Journal of Sports Economics, Review of Industrial Organization* and *Social Science Quarterly*.

Sylvia Trendafilova is an Assistant Professor at the University of Tennessee. Her research focuses on environmental management in and through sport. Her work explores varies activities under the umbrella of corporate social responsibility and the relationship of those activities to environmental sustainability. Her work is informed by theories from political economy, sociology and behavioral analysis. She has published many articles in *Journal of CSR and Environmental Management and Sport Science Review* and the *Cyber Journal of Applied Leisure and Recreation Research*. She has also published many book chapters on the area of sport and CSR.

Ivan Waddington is Visiting Professor at the Norwegian School of Sport Sciences, Oslo and the University of Chester. He is the author of *Sport, Health and Drugs* (Spon, 2000) and a co-author of the British Medical Association report, *Drugs in Sport: the Pressure to Perform* (British Medical Journal Books, 2002). He has also co-edited *Fighting Fans: Football Hooliganism as a World Phenomenon* (University College Dublin Press, 2002); *Sport Histories: Figurational Studies of the Development of Modern Sports* (Routledge, 2004); *Pain and Injury in Sport: Social and Ethical Analysis* (Routledge, 2006); and *Matters of Sport: Essays Presented in Honour of Eric Dunning*, Routledge 2007). His most recent book (with Andy Smith) is *An Introduction to Drugs in Sport: Addicted to Winning?* (Routledge, 2009). He is currently editing for Routledge *Handbook of Drugs in Sport* (with Verner Møller and John Hoberman).

Matthew Walker is at the School of Human Performance and Recreation at the University of Southern Mississippi. His primary interests lie in the areas of CSR and citizenship practices of organizations in the sport industry, but more generally in the fields of organizational strategy and theory. More specifically, his work has focused on the strategic impact of CSR with regard to the attributions consumer assign to sports organizations. In addition, he has worked on projects examining social identity, social capital, brand communities and social impact. He has published in *Journal of Sport Management, Sport Management Review, Journal of Business Ethics, Sport Marketing Quarterly, Journal of Marketing Theory and Practice, International Journal* *of Sport Management, Management Decision International* and *Journal of Sport Finance*. He is also co-author of several books, including most recently *Internships in Sport Management* (2011).

Doug Williamson is currently a Visiting Fellow at Nottingham Trent University. His research interests center on sport and disability, and in particular the development of special Adapted Games for severely disabled young people via his Project Adapted. These games include Polybat, Table Cricket and Zone Hockey. These are all currently being used in the School Games for 2012. More recent research has focused upon developing the concept of 'technical equity' with regards social inclusion in sport, and developing a new adapted form of tennis.

Richard Wolfe is Professor of Strategic Management and a Winspear Fellow at the Peter B. Gustavson School of Business, the University of Victoria. Dr Wolfe holds degrees in organization theory, business administration and physical education. Much of Wolfe's current research focuses on using sport as a lens through which we can learn about various types of organizations: e.g. by studying innovation, leadership, communication, teamwork and strategy in sport; about those phenomena in a general sense and, thus, apply learnings from sport to other organizational settings. Using this perspective, Wolfe has conducted studies of innovation, the determinants of team success, corporate social responsibility and emotion in sport, with a focus on how findings of each phenomenon can be generalized to various organizational settings. Wolfe is the past editor of *Journal of Sport Management* and has published in such journals as *Journal of Sport Management, Journal of Management, Organizational Science, Human Resource Management, Academy of Management Executive* and *European Sport Management Quarterly*.

Eli Wolff is Program Director of the Sport and Development Project at Brown University, United States. His work focuses on the intersection of research, policy and practice to advance sport and human rights, development and social change. Wolff coordinated efforts to include sport within the United Nations Convention on the Rights of Persons with Disabilities. He has also been active in Olympism and Olympic education, as well as in the area of athlete activism. Wolff has contributed to advancing sport and development through research, policy and practice. His main areas of interests are human rights, Olympism, disability, social change and athlete activism.

James J. Zhang is a Professor of Sport Management in the Department of Kinesiology at the University of Georgia, where he serves as the Director of the International Center for Sport Management (ICSM). His primary research interests are conducting studies in the areas of sport consumer behavior and sport organization behavior, and he has published in all major journals in the discipline of sport management.

PREFACE

Corporate social responsibility (CSR) has become a key managerial trend over the past 30 years as business organizations are increasingly expected to demonstrate a commitment and contribution to society through a range of activities. It has also become a field of scholarship that has attracted a significant amount of interest amongst academics from a variety of disciplines in which the role and contribution that organizations make within society and the nature of their social responsibilities are fundamental questions underpinning the field. These questions also feature prominently within the context of the sport industry. This is in part due to the growth in commercialism, particularly in professional sports, but also reflects the perception that sport has the potential to realize positive impacts within society. In addition, concerns surrounding the transparency and accountability of sports organizations also raise questions about their role. For these reasons, many sporting organizations have become involved in a variety of activities that can be considered within the context of CSR. At the same time, there has been an increase in scholarly attention that has sought to better understand the nature of CSR within the sport industry, which we have gathered in this volume.

The underlying aim of this *Handbook of Sport and Corporate Social Responsibility* is to provide an introduction to the different ways in which the sport industry is addressing the issue of CSR. More specifically it aims to ground CSR in sport within the context of mainstream business and management literature by using key managerial issues associated with CSR as a framework to structure and analyze CSR in sport. The book contains 26 chapters that are split into five parts. Part I will introduce a range of different theoretical issues within CSR and consider the implications on the sport industry. Part II focuses on the implementation and integration of CSR into the organization's culture and strategy in a variety of sports organizations. Part III considers aspects related to stakeholder engagement in CSR in sport programs and projects and how different types of sports organizations, including professional sports leagues in the US and Europe, the International Olympic Committee (IOC), and professional teams and athletes, manage their stakeholder relationships in practice. Part IV looks at the ways in which sports organizations, including professional leagues and clubs and sport federations, communicate their CSR activities, while the final part of the handbook focuses on the issue of measurement and considers how sports organizations identify different criteria and indicators that may assess the impact of their CSR activities.

This is the first dedicated textbook to the issue of CSR in the sport industry and, as such, it aims to provide an introduction to the field of study for both undergraduate and postgraduate students on sport management courses. It should also be of interest to those from a broader range of subjects, both within leisure, sport and recreation programs and general management/ corporate responsibility programs. The case studies throughout the book will also serve as a resource for staff involved in teaching modules on CSR in sport as well as modules relating to ethics and sport, and the role of sport in society. The case study nature of the handbook will also mean that it is both accessible and useful to practitioners working with the professional sport and leisure industries.

CSR WITHIN THE SPORT INDUSTRY

An overview of an emerging academic field

Juan Luis Paramio-Salcines, Kathy Babiak and Geoff Walters

Overview

This introductory chapter sets the scene for the textbook. It places corporate social responsibility (CSR) within its historical context, considering the emergence of CSR within organizations as well as tracing the development of academic literature around the subject. It then draws on recent academic research within business and management literature to set out managerial challenges that organizations face when addressing CSR. It is these challenges that are used to provide the framework for this handbook and the corresponding chapters deal with these issues. This introduction concludes by providing a background as to why CSR is a relevant issue for sport organizations.

Introduction

In the twenty-first century, business organizations have increasingly been expected to demonstrate a greater commitment and contribution to society through social and environmental activities. CSR, the term most commonly used to refer to these types of responsibilities of business, has become the means through which organizations seek to demonstrate this commitment and contribution to society. The increasing prominence of CSR can be explained by a range of endogenous factors, including high-profile failures in corporate governance that have concentrated attention on issues of corporate responsibility, accountability, transparency and the short-term basis upon which corporate performance is measured (Clarke, 2004). There has been a focus on issues of corporate excess, particularly following the financial crisis that began in 2008 in which the public sector in the US and the UK has been required to "bail out" a number of private sector banks. Examples of corporate irresponsibility, such as the Deepwater Horizon oil spill in the Gulf of Mexico in 2010, also lead to concerns surrounding the negative impacts that business can have within society.

At the same time, a number of exogenous factors also place further importance on CSR. There has been a drive to promote responsible corporate behavior through the development of international and national CSR standards, frameworks and guidelines (the United Nations Global Compact, Global Reporting Initiative and the ISO 26000 are three prominent examples), whilst CSR has also been of increasing interest to governments. For example, CSR officially entered the discourse of the European Union at the Lisbon Summit of the European Council in 2000 where social responsibility through lifelong learning, work organization, equal opportunities,

1

social inclusion and sustainable development were considered important components of the ten-year Lisbon strategy to promote sustainable economic growth and greater cohesion (De Schutter, 2008). Crane *et al.* (2008) also point out the rise in socially responsible investment funds and the increased media attention that have helped to raise further awareness of CSR.

These factors have encouraged organizations to consider their role within society (Blowfield and Murray, 2008) and, as a result, CSR has become a key management trend over the past 30 years with an increasing number of organizations creating separate CSR departments, appointing individuals to CSR-specific roles and putting in place budgets dedicated to CSR activities. At the same time, academic research on CSR has gathered pace with CSR becoming an issue which scholars from a range of disciplines have considered. This multi-disciplinary approach has meant that CSR is not dominated by an overarching theoretical approach, a set of strictly defined assumptions, or agreed-upon methods of inquiry (Lockett *et al.*, 2006). Indeed, despite a proliferation in scholarly inquiry, there are a variety of theories that can be used to explain what is meant by CSR and therefore fundamental debates on the role of organizations in society and the nature of their social responsibilities continue. For this reason, it has been argued that, rather than consider CSR as a construct, theory or discipline, it should be considered as a field of scholarship with permeable boundaries as suggested by Lockett *et al.* (2006).

The growth of CSR within the corporate sector has been paralleled by an increase in CSR behavior within the sport industry. Over the past 30 years sport organizations have been involved in a range of initiatives that can be considered within the field of CSR such as philanthropy, community involvement, youth educational activities and youth health initiatives (Babiak and Wolfe, 2009; Walker and Kent, 2009). This is in part due to the potential benefits that involvement in sport is said to bring about including improved physical health and psychological health, a reduction in crime, and improvements in community cohesion, social capital and education. However, these benefits are by no means automatic; indeed, the evidence is inconsistent and the processes through which sport is presumed to result in benefits are not well understood (Coalter, 2007) (issues that are discussed in detail in Chapters 2 and 3). Despite the different CSR activities, in recent years academic research on sport and CSR has been a growing field of inquiry (e.g., Babiak and Wolfe, 2006; Smith and Westerbeek, 2007; Breitbarth and Harris, 2008; Breitbarth *et al.*, 2011; Walters, 2009; Bradish and Cronin, 2009; Godfrey, 2009; Walker and Kent, 2009; Dolles and Söderman, 2010; Ferkins *et al.*, 2010; Misener and Mason, 2010; Sheth and Babiak, 2010; Walters and Tacon, 2010; Walters and Anagnostopoulos, 2012; Athanasopoulou *et al.*, 2011; Inoue *et al.*, 2011; Walker *et al.*, 2012). In part, the growing prominence of CSR within sport has been argued to reflect the unique features of the sport industry (Westerbeek and Smith, 2005; Smith and Westerbeek, 2007; Trenberth, 2011). At the same time, as the authors mentioned above noted, there have also been arguments that as the role of contemporary sport has become more commercial and sport organizations have become increasingly influential members of the global community, similar concerns of responsibility, transparency and accountability that are evident within the corporate world have made the transition to sport leading some to suggest that sport organizations cannot ignore CSR and that they have to implement it (Babiak and Wolfe, 2009).

Given that CSR is an issue that cuts across a range of disciplines and can be viewed from multiple perspectives, conceptualizing CSR as a field of scholarship is particularly appealing. This handbook takes this approach and considers CSR to be a broad field of scholarship. More specifically, it focuses on the different ways in which the sport industry is addressing the issue of CSR, and in doing so, becomes the first text within this particular subset of the broader field of CSR. It draws on key managerial issues identified in the CSR literature to provide the framework for the analysis of the dynamic relationships between sport organizations and society in different contexts and how it has been applied in a plethora of countries and cultures. In this introduction we briefly provide a historical overview of the development of CSR from both empirical and theoretical perspectives. This is kept brief as more in-depth reviews exist (e.g., Carroll, 1999, 2008; Frederick, 2006). We then consider the key managerial challenges that organizations face when addressing CSR. This part provides the background to the managerial issues identified in mainstream academic research that we have used to structure this handbook and the corresponding chapters. We then provide a background as to why CSR is a relevant issue for sport organizations to address before providing an overview of the structure and the chapters within this handbook. It is hoped that this handbook will serve as a guide to understanding what a wide spectrum of sport organizations do within society beyond their on-pitch performance.

The historical development of CSR

Within the context of the US, Windsor (2001) traces the development of CSR to the Progressive Reform movement in the late 1800s and early 1900s, arguing that a sense of responsibility was evident within the approach taken by some early business leaders towards improving the working and living standards of employees. Similar examples of a commitment towards employee welfare can be seen with the co-operative and mutuality movements in the UK where progressive business owners such as Robert Owen at New Lanark implemented welfare schemes (Clarke, 1998). Although improving worker productivity also demonstrates a business motive, it is certainly the case that improving employee conditions suggests an adherence to responsible business practice (Carroll, 2008). During this period corporate philanthropy, however, was limited. Whilst individual philanthropy has a history dating back to the mid-nineteenth century, the dominance of laissez-faire capitalism and the reluctance to use funds for anything other than business needs restricted corporate giving (Sharfman, 1994). However, legislative changes in the US in 1917 and the growth in the number of charitable organizations were two key reasons for the increase in corporate philanthropy as Sharfman (1994) suggested. By the 1920s therefore, business leaders were aware of social obligations (Windsor, 2001). The establishment of organizations such as the International Labor Organization was also a factor that forced business executives to consider the societal impact of their organizations (Blowfield and Murray, 2008). Carroll (2008) termed this period one of "trustee management" in which businessmen believed in the need to balance profit maximization with the needs of other stakeholders.

The development of CSR as a new field with academic literature on management only really began in the 1950s. Up until this point there had been little discourse that explicitly considered the role that business organizations played within society. It was the publication of *The Social Responsibilities of the Businessman* by Howard Bowen, regarded as one of the first generation of scholars in the field, in 1953 that has been considered as the birth of academic writing on CSR and the beginning of scholarly debate about the role of business in society (Carroll, 1999; Frederick, 2006). At that time, Bowen (1953: 6) defined CSR as "the obligations of businessmen to pursue those policies, to make those decisions, or to follow those lines of actions which are desirable in terms of the objectives and values of our society." This seminal text reflects a period in which business executives were comfortable with the idea of CSR but, despite an increasing awareness of the issue of CSR, organizations did not really progress beyond philanthropic activities and were unmotivated by a return on their activity (Carroll and Shabana, 2010; Frederick, 2006).

During the 1960s and 1970s, literature on CSR expanded as researchers sought to further define what CSR was and what it meant for business and society (Carroll and Shabana, 2010). For example, Frederick (1978, 2006) argued that CSR represented a company taking a socially responsible position, while in a seminal article, Carroll (1979) maintained a broad definition of CSR to include the economic, legal, ethical and discretionary expectations that society has of business organizations. It was during this period that contrasting views on CSR also emerged, most famously with the position taken by Friedman (1970). He took a classical economic approach and considered that business organizations had an economic and legal responsibility, arguing that the social responsibility of business was to increase profits, but that anything more than this (ethical or discretionary activities) meant that CSR was in fact a subversive doctrine.

The differences between the Friedman (1970) perspective and the definition given by Carroll (1979) demonstrate key arguments on the nature of business and the role it has to play within society. While Friedman considers that certain types of initiatives (e.g., welfare) fall outside the responsibilities of a company and are therefore incompatible with the objectives of a business, others feel that these types of activity are part of the responsibility that a company has in addition to profit maximizing. However, these types of CSR activity are not necessarily incompatible with business objectives. During this period Carroll (2008) and Porter and Kramer (2002) argue that some organizations began to take a managerial approach towards CSR that involved institutionalizing CSR within organizational policy and strategy. Academic research during this period also began to consider whether there was a relationship between CSR and financial performance.

During the 1980s, alternative themes, including stakeholder theory, business ethics theory, corporate social performance and corporate citizenship, emerged as contrasting ways of conceptualizing the social responsibilities of an organization (Carroll, 1999). Indeed, CSR was viewed as "the base-point, building block, or point-of-departure for other related concepts and themes, many of which embraced CSR-thinking and were quite compatible with it" (Carroll, 1999: 288). This illustrates that CSR had become increasingly complex due to these additional constructs which often are used to describe the same or similar things (Matten and Crane, 2005). Because of this, Carroll (2008) argues that in the 1990s there was little academic development of CSR although in practice more organizations began to institutionalize CSR through formalized CSR policies. This was in part due to media reports on poor organizational practices (e.g., Nike and the use of sweatshops) although it was also a period in which more ethically minded companies began to emerge (such as the Body Shop and others), as argued by Porter and Kramer (2006), where there was a clear belief that ethical behavior could align with profitability. It was during this period therefore that there was a shift in justifying CSR on normative grounds to a more instrumental, performance-oriented motivation (Lindgreen and Swaen, 2010; Kotler and Lee, 2005). Academic literature has kept pace: increasingly there have been attempts to understand how organizations seek to implement CSR leading to a large body of empirical research with an emphasis on linking CSR with corporate financial performance; CSR is increasingly seen as a way to add value to the business and to add real value to the society (Porter and Kramer, 2002, 2006; Kotler and Lee, 2005).

The above discussion (very briefly) charts the development of CSR and demonstrates that it has a long history, both in regard to the way in which it has been addressed by organizations and the way in which it has developed within academic literature. However, Crane *et al.* (2008: 4) argue that it is unusual for a topic that has such prominence to lack consensus over a definition or set of principles. This has the potential to leave CSR open to interpretation: different perceptions could therefore constrain the development of CSR both academically and within organizations (Dahlsrud, 2008). For example, while there is general consensus that CSR is concerned with the societal responsibilities that a business has, recent debates consider whether this should refer to activities and motivations that extend *beyond* an organization's direct economic interest and legal obligations or whether it should *include* these. Some have argued that as society's fundamental expectation of business is that it performs an economic function, this should form a key part of any definition of CSR (e.g., Carroll, 1999). Others have argued that a business's economic component ought to be regarded as the reason for its existence, rather than a responsibility to society (Daft, 2003). In this latter view, definitions of CSR should exclude the economic component of a business organization's activities. What both the early and more recent debates on the nature of CSR demonstrate is that CSR can be interpreted in different ways by different people at different times and that it can still be considered a social construct (Dahlsrud, 2008; Okoye, 2009). Indeed, Smith and Langford (2009) and Okoye (2009) argue that CSR will mean different things, but not always the same thing to different stakeholders. This underpins the difficulties in developing a succinct definition of CSR with Godfrey and Hatch (2007) claiming that the failure to achieve a common language with which to develop the concept has meant that CSR has become a tortured concept within academic literature.

Managerial challenges

Whether motivated by a belief that business has a responsibility and an ethical commitment to society or whether CSR activities are seen as a strategic, business-driven tool that can add value to a business (Porter and Kramer, 2002, 2006) and to the society, what is clear is that CSR is a key management trend that organizations in the twenty-first century cannot ignore. With this in mind, Lindgreen and Swaen (2010) identified five key managerial issues related to CSR. These are communication, implementation, stakeholder engagement, measuring CSR and the business case for CSR. While considered distinct it is clear that they are closely inter-related. For example, measuring CSR outcomes and determining the link, if any, between CSR and business performance may support a business case for CSR: this may increase the likelihood that CSR initiatives will be implemented and sustained to have greater impact. These five issues are looked at in turn below.

It has been argued that organizations need to consider ways in which to communicate their CSR activities. There is evidence that many organizations do undertake and report CSR activities: in 2005, more than 80 of the FTSE 100 listed companies in the UK produced a CSR report separate from the annual report (Owen, 2005). Similarly, "more than 80% of Fortune's Top 50 companies are developing reports that will enable international audiences to know their CSR efforts. Furthermore, 96% of them had a website section, a formal report, or both" (Wenhao and Kaufmann, 2011: 11636). CSR reports are just one mode of communication. Nevertheless, it has been argued that many organizations are unclear on how to report CSR and have difficulties in developing a strategy given the lack of consensus and terminology surrounding CSR leading to inconsistent communications (Ellerup Nielsen and Thomsen, 2007). A more strategic perspective on CSR suggests that CSR communicating is a way for an organization to position its brand, although organizations need to be aware that this can be interpreted in a cynical manner and that consumers may perceive it to be little more than a marketing or public relations exercise (Mohr *et al.*, 2001).

The second key managerial issue is the implementation of CSR into the activities of an organization, although it has been argued that this is an area that lacks empirical and theoretical support (Lindgreen and Swaen, 2010). For many organizations, the adherence to codes of conduct is seen as a way to implement CSR. Nevertheless, CSR implementation is a complex and multifaceted aspect: CSR can relate to many different types of organizational activity, including leadership, workforce activities (e.g., fair remuneration; employee communication), supply chain activities, community activities (e.g., sponsoring social causes, financial donations, employee volunteering) and environmental activities (resource/energy use, pollution and waste management) (Blowfield and Murray, 2008) (issues that are most explicitly analyzed in Babiak and Wolfe's Chapter 1). The wide variety of organizational activities that can come under the umbrella of CSR, as a number of authors such as Walters and Tacon (2011), Rahbek Pedersen (2006) and Maon *et al.* (2009) concur, demonstrates that there is no one overarching framework, nor set of guidelines on CSR implementation, and as such it can be perceived as an issue that requires a tailor-made approach (see Downs and Paramio-Salcines, Chapter 8).

The third managerial issue associated with CSR is engagement with stakeholders. Stakeholder theory itself emerged in the 1980s and 1990s as an alternative theme to CSR although it has been recognized that with the nature of the relationship between business and society and how this is defined and acted upon being a fundamental issue of CSR (Freeman, 1998; Freeman *et al.*, 2004; Blowfield and Murray 2008) stakeholder theory is intimately bound up with CSR (Campbell, 2007; Carroll, 1999; Maignan and Ferrell, 2004; Pava and Krausz, 1997). For example, Carroll (1991: 43) observed that "there is a natural fit between the idea of corporate social responsibility and an organization's stakeholders" and that a stakeholder approach is useful, from an organizational perspective, in that it "puts 'names and faces' on the societal members or groups who are most urgent to business, and to whom it must be responsive." The prioritization of stakeholder demands and pressures in the name of CSR by the different stakeholder groups a company might have, and how companies make decisions about these pressures and demands, is still not clear (O'Riordan and Fairbass, 2008). For sport organizations in particular, the engagement with and perception by stakeholders is essential for effective operations, and therefore should be a matter of significant managerial and theoretical interest.

The fourth issue is measurement and evaluation of CSR activities. The key questions are how should CSR be measured, what criteria should be used, and how can we best understand the impact that CSR activities have on both the organization and those stakeholders that are involved with the CSR initiatives? The fact that CSR relates to many different organizational activities means that measuring CSR and determining impact is complex. This is reflected in the fact that there are different types of methods used to measure CSR (Turker, 2009). First, there are reputation indices and database, of which the Kinder, Lydenberg and Domini (KLD) database in the US is a well-known example. These types of measurements rank companies on several attributes, presumed to be related to CSR. However, there are several problems with using such databases to "measure" CSR, including the restrictiveness of the attributes on which companies are rated and the ways in which companies are screened out of the databases (Van Oosterhout and Heugens, 2006: 15–18). Second, academic studies have sought to measure CSR through single- and multiple-issue indicators such as environmental pollution control or efforts to recall sub-standard products. However, this kind of measurement decision is often made because such data is easily available, rather than because the issues examined genuinely reflect a clear theoretical understanding of CSR. A third way in which CSR has been measured has been through the analysis of corporate publications that allows for a comparison between the types and extent of CSR activities that organizations are involved in. There are clear limitations with such an approach as it ultimately relies on how different companies report their activities and as such, it is difficult to measure impact but what it can do is provide a comparative analysis of how companies communicate their responsible behavior. The final method for measuring CSR relies on questionnaire surveys, containing a number of items. These have previously been administered to individuals within organizations, attempting to measure CSR at either the individual, or organizational, level. What this shows is that despite both academics and business practitioners having made considerable attempts to measure corporate social responsibility, there is no single best way in which to do so.

The fifth managerial issue within CSR is presenting the business case for undertaking CSR activities. We have seen the complexity in defining and understanding what constitutes CSR activity and the fact that, for some, CSR is seen as a part of a strategic management strategy. This has created a need to demonstrate that CSR activity improves business performance. While CSR has been argued to benefit organizations in a number of ways, including through improved corporate reputation, competitor differentiation, brand loyalty development and improved financial performance (Mullen, 1997; Porter and Kramer, 2006), there is a need for a robust evidence base to support these claims: as such the need for rigorous forms of measurement (the fourth managerial issue) is important. Certain aspects of CSR, in which there are clear efficiency gains that can translate into cost savings (such as environmental efficiency) or new revenues (via cause-related marketing efforts) are more tangible examples of where there is a clear business case.

Corporate social responsibility in sport: the status of the field

As was previously mentioned, CSR in sport is a growing field of academic study that as yet, is not as advanced as more mainstream research and understanding of CSR more generally. However, many sporting organizations have been involved in a range of activities that can be considered within the context of CSR for many years. In the US for example, teams within the major leagues have been involved in philanthropic and community activities for many years, whilst there has been a long-standing commitment to CSR in the UK professional football industry through the *Football in the Community* schemes that were set up in the 1980s (see Morgan, Chapter 18). More recently there has been an increase in CSR activities across a range of different types of sport organizations. For example, it has become common for high-profile, wealthy individual athletes to set up charitable foundations that provide funding to worthy causes, such as the Lance Armstrong Foundation, **LIVESTRONG**, (see Filo, Funk and O'Brien, Chapter 5) that funds cancer research. However the recent developments that place Lance Armstrong at the centre of a sophisticated doping scheme raise pertinent questions about the social responsibility activities of high-profile athletes and whether the creation of charitable foundations are in part a way to deflect attention from the behavior of individual athletes within a sport. CSR is also firmly on the agenda of many sport-governing bodies. UEFA (Union des Associations Européennes de Football), the governing body for European football, has developed a social responsibility partnership portfolio and is working with a number of charity partners to address specific issues including racism, reconciliation and peace, football for all, violence, health and humanitarian aid. UEFA has also made a commitment to allocate 0.7 percent of annual revenue to social projects – in line with the commitment made by the developed nations of the world to donate 0.7 percent of gross national product (GNP) to development assistance as part of the Millennium Project (Walters and Anagnostopoulos, 2012). There has also been increasing demand for sport events to consider their overall impact and to implement CSR through a variety of initiatives. At both the 2006 Winter Olympics in Turin and the 2006 Super Bowl in Detroit there were a range of CSR initiatives (Babiak and Wolfe, 2006), while FIFA launched the "Win in Africa, With Africa" program in 2006, a CSR initiative aimed at supporting social developments within the African continent drawing on the 2010 FIFA World Cup in South Africa (Walker *et al.*, 2012).

It has been argued that sport organizations offer a particularly appropriate context for CSR with a recent academic review highlighting seven key features of sport CSR (Smith and Westerbeek, 2007). First, the popularity and global reach of sport can ensure that sport CSR has mass media distribution and communication power. That is, the prominence of sport within the media helps to promote and communicate CSR activities to a wide audience. Second, sport CSR has youth appeal: children are more likely to engage in a CSR program if it is attached to a sport organization or a sport personality – this has the potential for greater influence and impact. Third, sport CSR can be used to deliver positive health impacts through programs and initiatives designed around physical exercise – particularly relevant for countries facing growing obesity rates in children and youth. Fourth, sport CSR will invariably involve group participation and therefore aid social interaction. This can also lead to a fifth benefit, which is improved cultural understanding and integration. Sixth, particular sport activities may lead to enhanced environmental and sustainability awareness. Finally, participating in sport CSR activities can also provide immediate gratification benefits. Despite these perceived benefits that arise from sport organizations' involvement in CSR, it is important to understand that these benefits are not guaranteed or routine. It has been argued the need for more research and evidence that helps to better understand the processes through which sport is presumed to lead to various social benefits. Nevertheless, the seven factors make clear the potential for sport organizations to engage effectively in CSR.

Despite the growing propensity for sport organizations to address CSR, and in light of the significant growth in mainstream management literature on CSR over the past 30 years, it is somewhat surprising that academic analysis of the role of sport and social responsibility is a relatively recent trend. However there is an increasing impetus to develop understanding of this field demonstrated through the growing number of research articles published in academic journals and the fact that there have been special issues of academic journals dedicated to sport and CSR (e.g., *Journal of Sport Management* (vol. 23, no. 6), *International Journal of Sport Management and Marketing* (vol. 10, no. 1–2) and *the Journal of Management and Organization* (vol. 16, no.4)). These examples reflect the growing interest and demand for CSR research within the sport industry.

The contributions in this handbook

This is the first dedicated textbook on the subject of CSR and sport management and, as such, the underlying aim is to provide an introduction to the different ways in which the sport industry is addressing the issue of CSR. More specifically, it aims to ground CSR in sport within the context of mainstream business and management literature by using key managerial issues associated with CSR as a framework to structure and analyze CSR in sport. While Part I sets out some theoretical issues, the remaining chapters in the following four parts present examples that demonstrate different ways that reflect the managerial concepts outlined in the introductory chapters.

One important contribution of this handbook is that it has an international appeal, bringing together contributions from a good mix of high quality academic and practitioner's backgrounds from Australia, Bulgaria, Canada, China, Greece, Italy, Japan, New Zealand, Norway, Spain, Switzerland, the United Kingdom and the United States. This geographic diversity of authors and contributors also reflects the global spread of CSR in sport as well as helping to illustrate the commonality and differences of approaches to CSR in sport worldwide. As stated above, Part I will examine different theoretical perspectives to the analysis of CSR and sport while the subsequent four parts look at particular managerial issues involving sport organizations. Chapter 1, by Babiak and Wolfe, frames CSR in professional sport by identifying the main pillars of CSR activities. This chapter explores labor relations, environmental sustainability, community relations, philanthropy, diversity and corporate governance as primary activities in which a professional sport organization might engage in CSR. Chapter 2 by Waddington,

Chelladurai and Skirstad considers the contested nature of CSR and the variety of competing approaches to understanding CSR. It seeks to examine some of the outcomes for sport organizations which adopt CSR policies, but also critically considers the issue of who benefits from CSR policies. Chapter 3 by Levermore takes a critical perspective to the analysis of CSR in sport, arguing that, despite increasing prominence of CSR initiatives, they fail to address weaknesses in the structure and governance of sport, particularly within the context of professional sport. Chapter 4 by Bradish, Mallen and Wolff examines how CSR is becoming more accepted in undergraduate and postgraduate sport management programs in North American, European and Asian countries. As part of this review, they provide some guidelines for innovatively integrating lessons of CSR into the pedagogy for the sport management curriculum and speculate about the future of CSR in sport management programs.

Part II focuses on the implementation and integration of CSR into the organization's culture and strategy in a variety of sport organizations. Despite the recent controversy over the doping scandal within the sport of cycling, Chapter 5 by Filo, Funk and O'Brien addresses the setting, the range of programs promoted and types of partnerships developed by cyclist Lance Armstrong's LIVE**STRONG** Foundation. Chapter 6 by Anagnostopoulos provides a historical account of English football and its relationship with the concept of CSR and considers key issues associated with implementation. With environmental sustainability a prominent issue, it is also important for sport facilities and events to consider minimizing their negative impact on the environment. With this in mind, Chapter 7 by Trendafilova, Phfal and Casper addresses how and why sport organizations analyze the implicit and explicit motives driving environmental practices within the context of the National Collegiate Athletic Association (NCAA) and member schools in North America. Chapter 8 by Zhang, Jin, Kim and Li will explain how the issue of environmental CSR has been addressed within the context of Asian sport events, particularly in the context of the Beijing Olympics in 2008. Chapter 9 by Downs and Paramio-Salcines provides a case study of the ways Manchester United Football Club has integrated the issue of accessibility into the culture and management of the organization and analyzes the strategic relevance of this as a way to enhance the image of the club as a socially responsible organization. In Chapter 10 Smith, Langhammer and Carson will explain how sport was used as the strategic tool for a non-profit organization in order to integrate ethnic minorities within an area of Northern Ireland. Chapter 11 by Campos provides a case study of an indoor football club in Spain and how it has marketed the launch of an education, sport and integration program. Chapter 12 by Harada is the final chapter in Part II, and presents a case study of the Japan Professional Football League (J League). In particular, the chapter examines sport–related CSR from the perspectives of how companies connect their support of sports to fulfilling their CSR, and how professional teams and the J League are enhancing their value by promoting and implementing CSR activities.

Part III considers aspects related to stakeholder engagement in CSR in sport programs and projects and how different types of sport organizations, including professional sport leagues in the US and Europe, non-profit organizations such as the International Olympic Committee and their major global event such as the Olympic Games, professional teams and athletes, manage their stakeholder relationships in practice.

This part begins with Chapter 13 by Kihl and Tainsky which examines Major League Baseball's Reviving Baseball in Inner Cities program: a program run between MLB clubs and non-profit organizations specifically focusing on urban community stakeholders. The chapter highlights some of the challenges and offers practical considerations in managing these types of partnerships. Chapter 14 by Misener, Sant and Mason considers the impact of sport organizations on local communities in the context of mega events. Using the 2010 Vancouver Winter

Olympic and Paralympic Games as the research context, they seek to demonstrate how sustainable development is being adopted as a means of social responsibility and corporate community involvement in the Games. Chapter 15 by Parent and Chappelet explores how Olympic stakeholders affect the IOC in its CSR activities and how they are impacted by the IOC's activities. They examine the relationships between the IOC, the organizing committees of Olympic Games, and other stakeholders in relation to the IOC's CSR activities. Chapter 16 by Babiak, Heinze, Lee and Juravich examines the phenomenon of athlete philanthropy (in particular the formalization of these practices through the establishment of charitable foundations) and considers how athletes in particular enact their socially responsible initiatives, what motivates them to be charitable and the perceived benefits they offer society as well as those that they themselves receive. This part finishes with Chapter 17 by Walters and Tacon which presents the results of survey research looking at corporate responsibility in European football and details the extent and manner in which professional football clubs across Europe engage with stakeholders.

Part IV discusses the ways in which sport organizations communicate their CSR activities. The part begins with Chapter 18 by Morgan which provides a comprehensive overview of the variety of CSR programs at the Premier League and how they are communicated. Chapter 19 by Sutherland takes a football club perspective and considers the ways in which the community foundation at Charlton Athletic Football Club has communicated one of its key CSR initiatives. This part concludes with Chapter 20 by Buscarini and Mura that highlights recent trends in the field of social accounting and reporting involving Italian sport federations.

The final part of the handbook focuses on the issue of measurement and considers how sport organizations identify different criteria and indicators that may assess the impact of their CSR activities. Chapter 21 by Kwak and Cornwell considers the benefits and drawbacks of cause-linked marketing within the sport context. In Chapter 22, Inoue and Kent identify the growing importance placed on measuring and evaluating CSR and present a framework for assessing the impact of CSR initiatives. This is an important aspect given that Chapter 23, by Walker, Heere and Kim, argues that many sport organizations have developed a fear of program evaluation and as such, shy away from evaluating the effectiveness of CSR, instead relying on generic public relations and marketing messages to convey CSR strategies. Chapters 24 and 25, by Hindley and Williamson, and Parnell, Stratton, Drust, and Richardson, respectively, consider the challenge of measuring and evaluating the impact of community projects delivered by the community schemes at Notts County Football Club and Everton Football Club.

The handbook closes with a chapter by the editors discussing the implications for theory and practices of CSR in sport as well as outlining where the CSR in sport agenda is going to be in the near future. As this is the first dedicated textbook to the issue of CSR in the sport industry, it aims to provide an introduction to the field of study for both undergraduate and postgraduate students in sport management courses. It should also be of interest to those from a broader range of subjects, both within leisure, sport and recreation programs and general management/corporate responsibility programs. The examples and cases throughout the book will also serve as a resource for staff involved in teaching modules on CSR in sport as well as modules relating to ethics and sport, business ethics, sociology of sport, policy studies in sport and the role of sport in society. The cases and examples in the handbook will also mean that it is both accessible and useful to practitioners, working with the professional sport and leisure industries.

References

Athanasopoulou, P., Douvis, J. and Kyriakis, V. (2011) 'Corporate social responsibility (CSR) in sports: Antecedents and consequences', *African Journal of Hospitality, Tourism and Leisure*, 1 (4), 1–11.

Babiak K. and Wolfe, R. (2006) 'More than just a game? Corporate social responsibility and Super Bowl XL', *Sport Marketing Quarterly*, 15 (4), 214–222.

Babiak, K. and Wolfe, R. (2009) 'Determinants of corporate social responsibility in professional sport: Internal and external factors', *Journal of Sport Management*, 23, 717–742.

Blowfield, M. and Murray, A. (2008) *Corporate Responsibility: A Critical Introduction*. Oxford: Oxford University Press.

Bowen, H. (1953) *Social Responsibilities of the Businessman*. New York: Harper & Row.

Bradish, C. and Cronin, J. (2009) 'Corporate social responsibility in sport', *Journal of Sport Management*, 23, 691–697.

Breitbarth, T. and Harris, P. (2008) 'The role of corporate social responsibility in the football business: Towards the development of a conceptual model', *European Sport Management Quarterly*, 8 (2), 179–206.

Breitbarth, T., Hovemann, G. and Walzel, S. (2011) 'Scoring strategy goals: Measuring corporate social responsibility in professional European football', *Thunderbird International Business Review*, 53 (6), 721–737 (Online). Available at: http://onlinelibrary.wiley.com/doi/10.1002/tie.20448/abstract (accessed: August 15, 2012).

Campbell, J. (2007) 'Why would corporations behave in socially responsible ways? An institutional theory of corporate social responsibility', *Academy of Management Review*, 32 (3), 946–967.

Carroll, A.B. (1979) 'A three-dimensional conceptual model of corporate performance', *Academy of Management Review*, 4 (4), 497–505.

Carroll, A.B. (1991) 'The pyramid of corporate social responsibility: Toward the moral management of organizational stakeholders', *Business Horizons*, 34 (4), 39–48.

Carroll, A.B. (1999) 'Corporate social responsibility: Evolution of a definitional construct', *Business and Society*, 38 (3), 268–295.

Carroll, A.B. (2008) 'A history of corporate social responsibility: concepts and practices', in Crane, A., McWilliams, A., Matten, D., Moon, J. and Siegel, D. (eds.) *The Oxford handbook of corporate social responsibility*. Oxford: Oxford University Press, pp. 19–46.

Carroll, A. and Shabana, K. (2010) 'The business case for corporate social responsibility: A review of concepts, research and practice', *International Journal of Management Reviews*, 12 (1), 85–105.

Clarke, T. (1998) 'The stakeholder corporation: A business philosophy for the information age', *Long Range Planning*, 31 (2), 182–194.

Clarke, T. (2004) 'Cycles of crisis and regulation: The enduring agency and stewardship problems of corporate governance', *Corporate Governance: An International Review*, 12 (2), 153–161.

Coalter, F. (2007) *A wider social role for sport: Who's keeping the score?* London: Routledge.

Crane, A., McWilliams, A., Matten, D., Moon, J., and Siegel, D. (2008) (eds.) *The Oxford Handbook of Corporate Social Responsibility*. Oxford: Oxford University Press.

Daft, R. L. (2003) *Management*. Thomson South-Western, USA.

Dahlsrud, A. (2008) 'How corporate social responsibility is defined: an analysis of 37 definitions', *Corporate Social Responsibility and Environmental Management*, 15 (1), 1–13.

De Schutter, O. (2008) 'Corporate social responsibility European style', *European Law Journal*, 14 (2), 203–236.

Dolles, H. and Söderman, S. (2010) 'Addressing ecology and sustainability in mega-sporting events: The 2006 Football World Cup in Germany', *Journal of Management & Organization*, 16 (4), 587–600.

Ellerup Nielsen, A and Thomsen, C. (2007) 'Reporting CSR – what and how to say it?' *Corporate Communications: An International Journal*, 12 (1), 25–40.

Ferkins, L., McDonald, G. and Shilbury, D. (2010) 'A model for improving board performance: The case of a national sport organisation', *Journal of Management & Organization*, 16 (4), 601–621.

Freeman, R. E. (1998) 'A stakeholder theory of the modern corporation', in Pincus, L.B. (ed.) *Perspectives in business ethics*. Singapore: McGraw-Hill, pp. 171–181.

Freeman, R. E., Wicks, A.C. and Parmar, B. (2004) 'Stakeholder Theory and "The Corporate Objective Revisited"', *Organization Science*, 15 (3), 364–369.

Frederick, W.C. (1978) 'From CSR1 to CSR2: The maturing of business and society thought', Working Paper no. 279. Graduate School of Business, University of Pittsburgh.

Frederick, W.C. (2006) *Corporation, be good! The story of corporate social responsibility*. Indianapolis: Dog Ear Publishing.

Friedman, M. (1970) 'The social responsibility of business is to increase its profits', *New York Times Magazine*, September 13, 32–33; 122–126.

Godfrey, P. (2009) 'Corporate social responsibility in sport: An overview and key issues', *Journal of Sport Management*, 23 (6), 698–716.

Godfrey, P. and Hatch, N. (2007) 'Researching corporate social responsibility: An agenda for the 21st century', *Journal of Business Ethics*, 70 (1), 87–98.

Inoue, Y., Kent, A. and Lee, S. (2011) 'CSR and the bottom line: Analyzing the link between CSR and financial performance for professional teams', *Journal of Sport Management*, 25 (6), 531–549.

Kotler, P. and Lee, N. (2005) *Corporate social responsibility: Doing the most good for your company and your cause.* Hoboken, NJ: John Wiley & Sons.

Lindgreen, A. and Swaen, V. (2010) 'Corporate social responsibility', *International Journal of Management Reviews*, 12 (1), 1–7.

Lockett, A., Moon, J. and Visser, W. (2006) 'Corporate social responsibility in management research: Focus, nature, salience and sources of influence', *Journal of Management Studies*, 43 (1), 115–136.

Maignan, I. and Ferrell, O.C. (2004) 'Corporate social responsibility and marketing: An integrative framework', *Journal of the Academy of Marketing Science*, 32 (1), 3–19.

Maon, F., Swaen, V. and Lindgreen, A. (2009) 'Designing and implementing corporate social responsibility: A framework grounded in theory and practice', *Journal of Business Ethics*, 87, 71–89.

Matten, D. and Crane, A. (2005) 'Corporate citizenship: Toward an extended theoretical conceptualization', *Academy of Management Review*, 30 (1), 166–179.

Misener, L. and Mason, D. (2010) 'Towards a community centred approach to corporate community involvement in the sporting events agenda', *Journal of Management & Organization*, 16 (4), 495–514.

Mohr, L.A., Webb, D.J. and Harris, K.E. (2001) 'Do consumers expect companies to be socially responsible? The impact of corporate social responsibility on buying behavior', *The Journal of Consumer Affairs*, 35, 45–72.

Mullen, J. (1997) 'Performance-based corporate philanthropy: How "giving smart" can further corporate goals', *Public Relations Quarterly*, 42 (2), 42–49.

Okoye, A. (2009) 'Theorising corporate social responsibility as an essentially contested concept: Is a definition necessary?', *Journal of Business Ethics*, 89, 613–627.

O'Riordan, L. and Fairbrass, J. (2008) 'Corporate Social Responsibility (CSR): Models and theories in stakeholder dialogue', *Journal of Business Ethics*, 83 (4), 745–758

Owen, D. (2005) 'CSR after Enron: A role for the academic accounting profession', Working Paper n. 33, International Centre for Corporate Social Responsibility, University of Nottingham.

Pava, M.L. and Krausz, J. (1997) 'Criteria for evaluating the legitimacy of corporate social responsibility', *Journal of Business Ethics*, 16 (3), 337–347.

Porter, M. and Kramer, M. (2002) 'The competitive advantage of corporate philanthropy', *Harvard Business Review*, December, 57–68.

Porter, M. and Kramer, M. (2006) 'Strategy and society: The link between competitive advantage and corporate social responsibility', *Harvard Business Review*, 84, 78–92.

Rahbek Pedersen, E. (2006) 'Making corporate social responsibility (CSR) operable: How companies translate stakeholder dialogue into practice', *Business and Society Review*, 111 (2), 137–163.

Sharfman, M. (1994) 'Changing institutional rules: The evolution of corporate philanthropy, 1883–1953', *Business & Society*, 33 (3), 236–269.

Sheth, H. and Babiak, K. (2010) 'Beyond the game: Perceptions and practices of corporate social responsibility in the professional sport industry', *Journal of Business Ethics*, 91 (3), 433–450.

Smith, A. and Westerbeek, H. (2007) 'Sport as a vehicle for deploying corporate social responsibility', *Journal of Corporate Citizenship*, 25, 43–54.

Smith, V. and Langford, P. (2009) 'Evaluating the impact of corporate social responsibility programs on consumers', *Journal of Organization and Management*, 15 (1), 97–109.

Trenberth, L. (2011) 'The sport business industry', in Trenberth, L. and Hassan, D. (eds.) *Managing sport business: An introduction.* London: Routledge, pp. 3–16.

Turker, D. (2009) 'Measuring corporate social responsibility: A scale development study', *Journal of Business Ethics*, 85 (4), 411–427.

Van Oosterhout, J. and Heugens, P. (2006) 'Much ado about nothing: A conceptual critique of CSR', *ERIM Report Series Research in Management* (Online). Available at: http://repub.eur.nl/res/pub/7894/ERS-2006-040-ORG.pdf (accessed: September 29, 2012).

Walker, M. and Kent, A. (2009) 'Do fans care? Assessing the influence of corporate social responsibility on consumer attitudes in the sport industry', *Journal of Sport Management*, 23, 743–769.

Walker, M., Kaplanidou, K., Gibson, H., Thapa, B., Geldenhuys, S. and Coetzee, W. (2012) 'Win in Africa, With Africa: Social responsibility, event image, and destination benefits. The case of the 2010 FIFA World Cup in South Africa', *Tourism Management*, 34, 80–90 (Online). Available at: http://www.sciencedirect.com/science/article/pii/S026151771200060X (accessed: October 10, 2012).

Walters, G. (2009) 'Corporate social responsibility through sport. The community sports trust model as a CSR delivery agency', *Journal of Corporate Citizenship*, 35, 81–94.

Walters, G. and Anagnostopoulos, C. (2012) 'Implementing corporate social responsibility through social partnerships', *Business Ethics: A European Review*, 21 (4), 417–433.

Walters, G. and Tacon, R. (2010) 'Corporate social responsibility in sport: Stakeholder management in the UK football industry', *Journal of Management and Organization*, 16 (4), 566–586.

Wenhao, C. and Kaufman, K. (2011) 'Corporate social responsibility in fortune magazine's top 50 companies: State of action and salient trends', *African Journal of Business Management*, 5 (29), 11636–11651.

Westerbeek, H. and Smith, A. (2005) *Business leadership and the lessons from sport*. London: Macmillan.

Windsor, D. (2001) 'The future of corporate social responsibility', *The International Journal of Organizational Analysis*, 9 (3), 225–256.

PART I

THEORETICAL PERSPECTIVES ON CSR IN SPORT

1

PERSPECTIVES ON SOCIAL RESPONSIBILITY IN SPORT

Kathy Babiak and Richard Wolfe

Overview

Corporate social responsibility (CSR) has become an area of increasing importance for many corporations. Organizations in the sport industry, also, are increasingly engaging in socially responsible activities. Along with its increased diffusion, CSR has received growing attention in the academic literature (Babiak and Wolfe, 2009). Our objective in this chapter is to provide a broad overview of CSR in sport. To do so, we: (1) provide an overview of the *CSR* and *CSR in sport* constructs; (2) present conceptual rationale for the adoption of CSR initiatives; and (3) describe the essential types of CSR in sport initiatives, which we refer to as *CSR in sport pillars*. Our focus in the chapter is on professional sport in North America. While we focus on keeping the "territory" covered somewhat manageable, as we will address in the chapter's final section, the manner in which we frame CSR in sport is also generalizable geographically, and to other types of sports organizations (e.g., major events; sports federations; intercollegiate sport).

An overview of the *CSR* and *CSR in Sport* constructs

CSR

As the copious literature in the area suggests, social responsibility is an ethical ideology or theory that an entity, be it an organization or individual, has an obligation to act in a manner that contributes to and benefits society at large. This responsibility can be passive, by avoiding engaging in socially harmful acts, or active, by performing activities that directly advance social goals. These ideas have experienced substantial growth over the past two decades, as evidenced by the adoption of practices that aim to benefit society by an increasing number of entities (businesses, nonprofit organizations, and individuals) as well as by the academic exploration of this phenomenon. The academic social responsibility literature has focused on examining activities that promote positive social change; how such initiatives improve the well-being of communities on local and global levels; and what efforts are being made to address gaps in the areas of health, education, race relations, the environment, and economic development. CSR represents a set of actions that: are intended to further some social good, extend beyond the explicit pecuniary interests of the firm, and are not required by law (McWilliams and Siegel, 2000). It "refers to company activities – voluntary by definition – demonstrating the inclusion of social and environmental concerns in business operations and in interactions with stakeholders" (Van Marrewijk, 2003: 97). Similarly, Ullmann (1985: 543) defines CSR as "the extent to which an organization meets the needs, expectations, and demands of certain external constituencies beyond those directly linked to the company's products/markets."

Over the past 60 years, the justifications and positioning of the social responsibility of businesses has been wide ranging. In 1962, Friedman compellingly argued that a corporation's responsibility is to its shareholders – to maintain financial viability (through the development and sale of products and/or services) (Friedman, 1962). Others held opposing perspectives, including the view that organizations are not responsible solely to shareholders but also to other stakeholders that can affect or be affected by an organization (Donaldson and Preston, 1995; Freeman, 1984). This thinking then extended to the use of CSR as strategic response/good business practice (Hess and Warren, 2008; Porter and Kramer, 2006) or as "insurance" for future misdeeds (Gardberg and Fombrun, 2006; Godfrey, 2005). More recent work has positioned the use of doing good as a means to market and/or to help brand a business and the cause it supports (Gupta and Pirsch, 2006; Irwin *et al.*, 2003; McGlone and Martin, 2006; Roy and Graeff, 2003).

Carroll's (1979, 1991) framing of CSR is inclusive and instructive. Carroll conceptualized CSR as being composed of four elements: economic (the basic responsibility to make a profit and, thus, be viable), legal (the duty to obey the law), ethical (responsibility to act in a manner consistent with societal expectations), and discretionary (activities that go beyond societal expectations). Godfrey (2009) suggests that Carroll's framing is useful for two reasons. First, Carroll characterizes and deconstructs a business' non-economic responsibilities to differentiate between those that are enforced (legal responsibilities), contextual (ethical norms), and voluntary (discretionary). Second, Godfrey argued that the hierarchical nature of Carroll's framework provides a prescriptive model of the circumstances where tradeoffs (among competing demands) may be appropriate (e.g., firms struggling to make profits should not focus on discretionary CSR activities).

CSR in the sport context

Until the early 1990s, CSR did not play a significant role in sport (Kott, 2005; Robinson, 2005). Currently, however, professional sports organizations are entering into various socially responsible initiatives at a rapid pace. In our 2009 publication in *Journal of Sport Management*, we described a broad array of activities professional sports organizations (e.g., leagues, teams, and even individual athletes who are brands/businesses in and of themselves) engage in (Babiak and Wolfe, 2009). Prior to addressing the *CSR in sport pillars*, we address a seminal matter: given the well-established literature on CSR, one might wonder whether there is a need to address CSR in sport. In what follows, therefore, we highlight what we believe to be the unique aspects of sport as it relates to CSR.

Is sport unique with respect to CSR?

The four features that make sport unique with respect to CSR, and thus merit making CSR worthy of investigation in the professional sport context are: passion, economics, transparency, and stakeholder management (Babiak and Wolfe, 2009). Below, we review how CSR may affect or be affected by these factors.

Passion

The formative attribute which differentiates sport from other industries is the emotion, the devotion, and passion that the product (the athlete, team, game) generates among fans/consumers (Cashman, 2004). Given the strong emotions generated by sport, we suggest that teams or athletes promoting, for example, healthful living, will yield a larger, more attentive audience than would businesses or employees from other industries. Further, it has been suggested that the passion and identification that sports teams generate can be beneficial to communities as a whole by encouraging and strengthening community integration (Wakefield and Wann, 2006; Wilkerson and Dodder, 1987).

Economics

Given the unique economic elements of the sport industry, such as their monopoly power, the special protections they receive from governments via antitrust laws, and the public support they receive for constructing arenas and stadia, there are often different expectations and perceptions of the role and responsibility of professional sports teams and leagues to provide social benefit and give back to the community (Swindell and Rosentraub, 1998).

Transparency

Almost everything achieved by the leadership of a sport team (e.g., player signings, player salaries, who plays, who sits, trades, changes in strategies), as well as team outcomes (i.e., wins/losses), and contributions to good causes, is open knowledge (Armey, 2004). In addition, off the court/field behavior of a team's employees (e.g., players, coaches), invariably, becomes open knowledge (Armey, 2004). Organizations in other industries typically do not face the same type of scrutiny of their business practices or of their employees' behaviors.

Stakeholder management

Success in the sport industry necessitates the ability to work with a complex set of stakeholders (e.g., various levels of government, sponsors, fans, local communities, minor leagues, media, players). We suggest that each of the features addressed just above, passion, economics, and transparency, contribute to the complexity of stakeholder relationships. Strong relations with stakeholders can benefit from CSR activities (Wallace, 2004).

Recognizing these four unique elements of professional sport and how each is related to CSR provides the rationale for addressing CSR in sport as a phenomenon different from CSR in other domains – though there certainly are areas of overlap. Moreover, from a more applied perspective, addressing these differentiating factors allows practitioners to more strategically position CSR initiatives and increase the potential impact CSR in sport can have.

The rationale for the adoption of CSR initiatives

Recent academic writing has considered the strategic integration of CSR with corporate objectives; by linking the company's core strategy and its CSR efforts, the potential of contributing to both societal beneficiaries and to business performance is increased (Bruch and Walter, 2005; Porter and Kramer, 2006). In addition, such a strategic approach to CSR is considered to be more sustainable (Porter and Kramer, 2006). Responding to pressures external to the organization is, of course, important for businesses success (Hess *et al.*, 2002; Hess and Warren, 2008; Marquis *et al.*, 2007). Pressures related to CSR could emanate from various stakeholders: e.g., customers (Vogel, 2005), activist groups (Den Hond and De Bakker, 2007), legislators (Dawkins and Lewis, 2003), or local communities (Boehm, 2005). Internal drivers such as the values, ethics, and moral priorities of top management, owners, employees, and athletes, and other internal variables (e.g., knowledge, skills, expertise) are also important determinants of CSR adoption and implementation (Babiak and Wolfe, 2009; Beliveau *et al.*, 1994).

Given the increasing focus on strategic CSR (i.e., broadening the concept to dual – organizational and social – benefits), it is worthwhile to consider the approaches and areas in which a business might engage in CSR. While an explicit link between CSR and financial performance has yet to be established, many of the intangible benefits a business may attain are dependent on the type of CSR practiced (i.e., social responsibility in labor relations may lead to greater employee commitment, or social responsibility in corporate governance may lead to more effective relations with regulatory institutions or legislative bodies; see literature on these intangible benefits of CSR: Campbell, 2007; Jensen, 2002; Turban and Greening, 1996; Vogel, 2005).

Stemming from the above conceptual arguments, four prevailing justifications for CSR have been identified (Porter, 2008; Porter and Kramer, 2006):

- *Moral obligation*: a business should achieve commercial success in ways that honor ethical values and respect people, communities, and the natural environment. This justification supports the idea that companies need to be good citizens and "do the right thing."
- *Sustainability*: businesses should avoid short-term behavior that is socially detrimental or environmentally wasteful; this justification emphasizes environmental and community stewardship. As per the World Business Council for Sustainable Development this justification implies: "meeting the needs of the present without compromising the ability of future generations to meet their own needs";
- *License to Operate*: every company needs tacit or explicit permission from governments, communities, and numerous other stakeholders to do business;
- *Reputation*: CSR initiatives are justified on the grounds that they will improve a company's image, and thus, strengthen its brand, enliven morale, and potentially raise the value of its stock.

As argued by Porter and Kramer (2006), however, the above justifications focus on the tension between business and society rather than the interdependence and do not provide direction, guidance, or priority for a company's actions. Because CSR priorities are often reactive, unfocused, and driven by public relations (PR) and image concerns, the impact to the organization and to society is often not measured or maximized. Porter (2008) suggests that the competitiveness of a company depends on the surrounding environment and the community in which it operates. Given their concerns, Porter and Kramer (2006: 5) suggest that to "advance CSR, we must root it in a broad understanding of the interrelationship between a corporation and society while at the same time anchoring it in the strategies and activities of specific companies." Organizational decisions concerning CSR, then, need to be made related to the synergistic use of organizational resources and core competencies to address key stakeholders' interests to achieve both organizational and social benefits (McAllister and Ferrell, 2002).

While as described above, the rationale for addressing CSR in sport is strong, given its unique traits, the essential framing of the construct, as per the extant literature, holds; i.e., in considering CSR in sport, Carroll's model, which includes economic, legal, ethical, and discretionary components, appears to fit. Another way to frame CSR in sport is to consider the focal organization – i.e., whether it is an organization directly in the sport industry as sport may be used as a means to be socially responsible by non-sport organizations. We term this use of sport as a vehicle for non-sport companies as *Social Responsibility Via Sport*. Some authors such as Smith and Westerbeek (2007) and Lee and Cornwell (2011) identify the unique aspects of sport that might benefit a company engaging in *Social Responsibility Via Sport* (mass appeal of sport, youth orientation, media attention (see Smith and Westerbeek (2007) for a more thorough description)). Sports organizations themselves also engage in socially responsible activities and we refer to CSR of a sport organization as *Social Responsibility of Sport*. We describe these distinctions next.

Organizations involved in *Social Responsibility Via Sport* partner with sport teams or other sport organizations to leverage the unique elements of sport addressed above (e.g., passion, stakeholder relationships) to enhance their own brand identity (Lee and Cornwell, 2011; Smith and Westerbeek, 2007). Examples of *Social Responsibility Via Sport* include Barclays Bank's Spaces for Sport program which brings specialist coaching and training projects to disadvantaged communities; KPMG's support and sponsorship of "Reviving Baseball in the Inner Cities" – a MLB initiative to encourage underserved youth to participate in baseball – and get physically active in inner cities; Vodafone's longstanding relationship with the Homeless World Cup, an annual football tournament held in different cities around the world and which brings together homeless people from around the world; and Coca-Cola's support of the Special Olympics to help support athletic participation and competition for special needs children.

Social Responsibility of Sport refers to socially responsible activities and initiatives engaged in by professional sport businesses and organizations. This category encompasses for-profit sports organizations such as Nike or Adidas who are increasingly drawing attention and awareness to environmental sustainability issues in the manufacture of their products and have also adopted extensive regulations concerning labor relations. Also in this category are non-profit sport oriented organizations such as the Women's Sports Foundation or the Homeless World Cup which exist to ameliorate social issues such as homelessness, obesity, equity, and access for underrepresented populations using sport as a tool and vehicle. Many social responsibility of sport initiatives are enacted by sports teams and leagues (e.g., the NBA, NHL, NFL, MLB); examples include the NHL's "Hockey Fights Cancer" and "NHL Diversity" programs; the NBA's "Read to Achieve" and "Basketball without Borders" initiatives; the PGA Tour's charitable giving; and the Vancouver Canucks Mindcheck initiative. *Social Responsibility of Sport* also includes social responsibility initiatives of individuals (e.g., athletes, coaches, executives) in the industry engaging in charitable efforts (such as establishing charitable foundations (Babiak *et al.*, 2012) (see also Chapter 5, Filo, Funk and O'Brien).

CSR in sport initiatives – CSR pillars

The types and focus of socially responsible initiatives vary considerably. Our attention now turns to the six areas in which sports organizations practice socially responsibility. We refer to these as the "Pillars of Social Responsibility in Sport." These areas were culled from CSR indexes that were designed for identifying trends in CSR performance for social investing. A number of ratings and investment indices (DJSI, Ethibel, FTSE4Good, Domini400, KLD, Calvert, and CGQ) have devised commonly referenced CSR indicators. By and large, these are based on assessments of corporate reputation, content analysis of annual reports, and survey questionnaires (Turker, 2009). A comparison of the indices indicated that each has neglected criteria included in others (Fowler and Hope, 2007). Moreover, it is argued that indicators be tailored, by industry, in formulating a CSR index (Giannarakis and Theotokas, 2011).

Given this call for industry-specific indicators, we have adapted and synthesized the indices listed above to six professional sport relevant pillars: labor relations, environmental management and sustainability, community relations, philanthropy, diversity and equity, and corporate governance. These pillars reflect the complexity and scope of actions that sports organizations can incorporate in their CSR initiatives. Below, we describe the pillars, and offer examples.

Labor relations

This pillar of social responsibility concerns how a business treats its employees. A firm's employees determine its success. In addition to this instrumental view of employees, it is argued the employer has a moral obligation to make business decisions in a manner that considers the welfare of employees. The importance of this pillar is emphasized by Skibola (2010, para 4):

> While corporate responsibility is often used in reference to the organization's interaction with outside communities, it also touches upon how members of the organization are actually treated and valued. How they are treated determines both self-perception and performance within the workplace.

Treatment of employees is increasingly recognized as a component of socially responsible business. For example, the UN Global Compact (a self-reporting system that certifies organizations willing to commit to socially oriented principles) identifies responsibility to labor as one of its categories (the others being human rights, transparency, and environment). This Compact is symbolic, however, as it sets general aspirational standards with no strict enforcement or obligation. Interactions with employees can span dimensions that are legal and ethical/moral. Aspects of this pillar include paying workers fairly, providing a safe work environment, prevention of harassment (climate of support), health and retirement benefits, fair and equitable recruitment, hiring, promotions, and training and development for employees (Perez-Batres *et al.*, 2012).

Prevalent examples of how labor relations contribute to discourse concerning CSR were the labor practices of suppliers to sportswear companies such as Nike and Reebok (Yu, 2007). The outcomes of related manufacturing practise exposés have led both organizations to adopt stringent policies concerning labor relations. The Nike experience in particular focused attention on CSR in labor relations.

In professional sport, a number of unique factors emerge with respect to labor relations. Considerable attention has recently been given, for instance, to the issue of concussions and head injuries (Chronic Traumatic Encephalopathy) among athletes in both the NHL and NFL. Due to increasing media attention, emerging lawsuits, and a moral and ethical imperative, this issue has become a major concern for players, team management, and league executives. The long-term effects of head injuries on athletes are unknown, and leagues are beginning to actively engage with researchers and equipment manufacturers to examine the sport's rules and regulations in efforts to reduce this danger. Recently the NFL committed $30 million to examine such matters in an effort to address player safety concerns. Roger Goodell, the Commissioner of the NFL stated:

> Our goal is to aggressively partner with the best scientists to understand more about the brain and brain injuries, to make things safer for our athletes and for others. If we can learn more about the brain, we can not only make football safer, but make things safer for other sports and other walks of life. We want players to enjoy long and prosperous careers and healthy lives off the field. So we focus relentlessly on player health and safety, while also keeping the game fun and unpredictable.
>
> (Maske, 2012, para 2).

Another example of efforts in professional sport to address issues related to labor relations is the establishment and growth of player development and education programs. Professional athletes have been reported to experience high levels of bankruptcy post-playing career. In 2009, an article in *Sports Illustrated* reported that 78 percent of NFL players are bankrupt or facing serious financial stress within two years of ending their playing careers and 60 percent of NBA players are broke within five years of retiring from the game (Torre, 2009). Other social challenges face athletes as well, such as high divorce rates (Torre, 2009), and high rates of gambling (Kreidler, 2006).

In order to support athletes in facing such challenges, professional leagues such as the NBA and the NFL have developed programs to help athletes make transitions into the leagues as well as out (after retirement). Many athletes come to the NBA with one year of college, and thus, without having developed the personal and professional skills necessary for them to succeed, and the league, therefore, has begun to view it as their concern to help the athletes in this dimension with various programs (Sheridan, 2006). For instance, the NBA's Rookie Transition Program includes an assortment of educational and developmental programs that outline the expectations, pressures, and demands of being a professional athlete. Other areas of support and education in the NBA include the following programs: *Professional and Life Skills* (addresses post career training finances, education), *Personal Development and Education* (addresses image and ethics, driving safety, drugs and alcohol, stress, and anger management), and *Legal Education* (addresses felony situations, gambling, gender violence, security, sexual harassment). Similarly, the NFL has off-field training and development programs for their athletes such as *NFL Prep*, *NFL Life*, and *NFL Next*. The NFL Player Engagement department "assists players in adjusting to life within the NFL, while challenging them to prepare for their next careers after their football-playing days are through" (NFL Player Engagement, 2012).

Environmental management and sustainability

This pillar of social responsibility is related to environmental management and sustainability. In recent years, environmental sustainability has grown in importance and has been placed on the agendas of most firms (Bird *et al.*, 2007; Kassinis and Vafeas, 2006; Welford *et al.*, 2007). Ecological initiatives can be related to legal, ethical, or discretionary responsibility (Carroll, 1979) and provide organizations opportunities for cost savings (economic responsibility; Carroll, 1979) and for the establishment of new, non-traditional partnerships.

Increasing emphasis has been placed on exploring this pillar in the sport management literature wherein environmental sustainability has been studied in relation to marketing/advertising practices (Kärnä *et al.*, 2001; Schmidt, 2006), building materials and facility management (Mallen *et al.*, 2010; McNamara and Gibson, 2008). In addition, the concept of environmental sustainability has been discussed in a number of sport contexts, including the Olympics and other sport mega-events (Belli, 2008; Lenskyj, 1998). Such work emphasizes the complexity of the relationship between sport and the environment and the challenges associated with this relationship. Environmental sustainability is a concern in other aspects of the sport industry as well, including intercollegiate athletics programs in the US, where Casper *et al.* (2012) found high levels of concern for the environment, but a disconnect between this concern and actions implemented. They speculated that this may be the result of a lack of communication between athletic departments and university leadership, concerns related to the cost of environmental implementation, and/or due to a lack of expertise or knowledge about sustainability initiatives.

Environmental initiatives in professional sport are also being empirically investigated. Babiak and Trendafilova (2011) examined the adoption of pro-environmental practices in several components of the value chain of professional sport teams and leagues (e.g., facility initiatives, in-game promotions, partnerships with vendors, etc.) and demonstrated rapid adoption of environmental initiatives. Other contributors to the literature in this pillar have taken a sport facility management focus. Kellison and Kim (forthcoming) examined this issue and found that the triple bottom line (TBL) of environmental, social, and economic benefits are considered by professional sport teams in particular as it relates to marketing their pro-environmental venues and facilities. Inoue and Kent's (2012) study indicates that messaging from sports teams influences consumers to internalize and to adopt pro-environmental behaviors in their actions both within a sport facility and in their lives – outside sport.

New sport facilities are being built (such as Target Field in Minneapolis, Minnesota) with state-of-the-art ecological programs. As examples, Target Field's recycling system conserves rain water which is then used for maintaining the field and minimizing water pollution, detailed attention was paid to energy efficient construction and maintenance, and to sustainable facility operations (e.g., lighting, heating, ventilation, air conditioning, and water flow). A new facility being built by the San Francisco 49ers will be an environmentally state-of-the-art stadium, including photovoltaic solar panels, a "green roof," water-conserving fixtures, recycled building materials, bicycle parking, and convenient access for public transit users and pedestrians (Green Sports Alliance, 2012a).

Teams (and some athletes) are considering the impact of their travel on the environment by purchasing carbon credits (Suzuki, 2009). The Houston Astros (MLB) and Philadelphia Eagles (NFL) engage in raising awareness of environmental concerns for example, by promoting their practice of planting a tree for every home run hit in the ball park (Astros). Additionally, teams are increasingly putting pressure throughout their value chain, on vendors (e.g., food services: composting, use of compostable plates and cups), contractors (e.g., waste management) and sponsors (e.g., Target Field's initiative with Pentair Water to highlight new water use standards). A recent trend is the emergence of ecological support groups focusing on sport. The Green Sports Alliance and National Resource Defense Council sport initiative monitor, support, educate and communicate matters related to the environment and professional sport. In summary:

> The sports industry is proving that greening is smart business. From cost savings and brand enhancements to new sponsorship opportunities and strengthening community ties, sports organizations are reaping the tangible economic benefits of greening which are essential to keeping their operations efficient.
>
> (Green Sports Alliance, 2012b)

Community relations

The third pillar, social responsibility in community relations, encompasses businesses' responsibility not to harm, and to make efforts to improve, their communities. Such initiatives can result in businesses having a better environment to operate in:

> Businesses engaging in community relations or community involvement typically conduct outreach to the community aiming to prevent or solve problems, foster social partnerships, and generally contribute to the community quality of life. They also participate in community relations to help improve their business by getting valuable community and other stakeholder input.
>
> (Industry Canada, 2012)

Maintaining positive relationships in their communities is a key priority for many organizations – including professional sports organizations. In taking an active interest and role in the communities in which they operate, sport teams can foster well-being, loyalty, support, and good will of community stakeholders.

Addressing important social issues in the community (e.g., homelessness, education, gang violence, obesity and health, after school programming) is a longstanding practice for professional sports teams and leagues. Such initiatives are a fundamental dimension of fostering the moral obligation, license to operate, and reputation rationales of CSR. The specific type and focus of a community outreach program vary, but generally involve leveraging organizational resources; the resources can include financial support, athletes, coaches, trainers, mascots, facilities, and logos. Increasingly, corporate sponsors and local non-profit organizations partner in such initiatives contributing to the visibility, expertise, and other support in executing the initiatives.

Some examples of well-established community relations efforts include the NBA's focus on intellectual development of disadvantaged youth. The NBA uses the power of sport to encourage youth to excel scholastically through their NBA Cares initiative which since its inception, has raised and distributed over $200 million across the US for social programming (NBA Cares, 2012). This program, which is implemented by each NBA team, concentrates on basic skills development, cultural awareness, community service, and teamwork. Another example of a community relations initiative is the Chicago White Sox (MLB Team) Volunteer Corp. According to the team,

> the White Sox Volunteer Corps was created by the Chicago White Sox in response to President Obama's call for Americans to better their communities through service. The team organized community service events that incorporated support from players, staff and members of the new volunteer group to serve shoulder to shoulder to make a positive and lasting impact in our community.
>
> (White Sox, 2012)

Activities of this initiative include refurbishing Boys and Girls Clubs facilities, coordinating blood drives, and food repacking sessions for local food banks.

Community relations are also a key focus of the NFL through their Play 60 program which is "a national youth health and fitness campaign focused on increasing the wellness of young fans by encouraging them to be active for at least 60 minutes a day" (NFL, 2012). This initiative employs the core competencies of the NFL and its teams and athletes (i.e., understanding of health, fitness, activity) in an effort to "tackle" childhood obesity via partnerships and collaborative arrangements with schools, corporate partners, and community organizations. In addition to addressing issues of health and wellness for children and youth, this program is used to engage youth in football and build skills and knowledge about the game itself. This has the strategic benefit of establishing loyalty, understanding, and interest in the game, and developing a potential future pool of talent and fans for the league.

Philanthropy

The fourth pillar in our framework is philanthropy. Currently, most large corporations engage in some type of philanthropy which has evolved in concept and practice. Corporate giving has advanced from donations to causes deemed worthy – typically by senior executives or owners of organizations – to a more strategic, formalized business practice (Porter and Kramer, 2006).

Giving priorities vary among organizations in areas such as the arts, education, environment, health, and social services. Brown *et al.* (2006) found that firms increasingly find philanthropic opportunities that complement their business. Consistent with this strategic orientation, "in the United States, corporate giving is about evenly split between *in kind* (e.g., product donations and pro bono work by corporate employees) and *monetary* (cash) giving" (Kiholm Smith, 2012: 341; original emphasis).

Many corporate philanthropy programs are administered through an independent corporate foundation. In some cases, funding for the foundation is provided by the for-profit parent, in some, fundraising is carried out independently by the foundation, and in other cases, the founder or owner may contribute to an endowment from which the foundation makes its donations (Kiholm Smith, 2012). In most cases, the foundations are legally separate entities.

Sport management research is beginning to address philanthropy. Some research has focused on how athletic performance influences donor behavior (e.g., in Intercollegiate Athletics (Strode and Fink, 2009)). However, there has been little empirical examination of the role philanthropy plays in professional sport. A few authors have addressed philanthropy in sport as part of broader CSR (e.g., Babiak, 2010; Babiak and Wolfe, 2009), and have demonstrated the rise of charitable foundations associated with professional sport teams. Inoue *et al.* (2011) examined CSR influences on traditional corporate outcomes of professional sport teams using charitable giving data as a proxy for CSR. These researchers did not find a link between CSR and attendance, though they found a negative relationship between CSR and financial performance; they explain these results as being due to stakeholders not being aware of team philanthropic activity.

As is the case in the corporate world more generally, increasingly, sport philanthropy has become a central and formalized function of a sport team's social responsibility efforts (Babiak and Wolfe, 2009). The formation of charitable foundations associated with a team or league offers the organization resource access, efficiency, and strategic advantages in a number of areas including the ability to secure additional resources (financial for example through fund raising initiatives), to coordinate strategically with outreach efforts of the team or league, to partner with organizations across sectors more effectively, to more efficiently and effectively organize and assign the costs of social responsibility.

One current example of the philanthropic initiatives in sport is that of the Tampa Bay Lightning of the NHL. The team owner Jeff Vinik has pledged to give out 25 grants of $50,000 each over the course of the season at Tampa Bay Lightning home games through the team's foundation (total giving of $1.25 million). In addition to the grants, Vinik has pledged that Lightning employees will contribute a total of four thousand hours of community service annually – all organized and managed through the foundation. "Owning a team allows Penny and [me] the visibility to give back," said Vinik. "It allows us to participate actively in the community and inspire others, hopefully, to do the same" (Foundation Center, 2012).

While the rise in philanthropy in professional sport has been documented and institutionalized through awards and recognitions (i.e., Beyond Sport, Steve Patterson Sport Philanthropy Award), such activity faces challenges. Cribb (2010), for example, found that the charities of Canadian professional sports teams distribute less than half of the money they raise, as substantial spending was on administration functions such as salaries, marketing, promotion, etc. Imbalances in ratios between expenditures and revenues are criteria upon which foundations are scrutinized, and often suggest ineffective management practices.

Diversity and equity

The fifth pillar of social responsibility in sports organizations is diversity and equity. Diversity is becoming a key item on the agenda of businesses as they grapple with demographic change, shifting social expectations, new employment practices and organizational structures, and increasingly diverse customers and other stakeholders. Creating a fair, equitable, and inclusive work environment is a fundamental objective of diversity management related to CSR. It is also, in many instances, a legislated area (e.g., in the US, the Americans with Disabilities Act of 1990).

The link between CSR and diversity occurs when a company seeks to ensure that its workforce reflects the society in which it operates, and/or when it creates a climate in which everyone's views, experiences, and perspectives are respected (Fenwick and Bierema, 2008). Related actions include employment of the disabled and offering access and facilities to this population, devising clearly articulated gay and lesbian policies, professional development, and institutional support in helping minorities advance in the organization, providing contracting opportunities to women and minority groups, offering work/life benefits, and programs to assist balancing family responsibilities and work.

Diversity issues in professional sport have been examined from a number of perspectives, but few have explicitly linked the issue to CSR. Lapchick and colleagues at the Institute for Diversity and Equity in Sport (TIDES) monitor trends in diversity in professional sport and intercollegiate athletics. Their yearly Gender Equity Report Card reports on the diversity of coaches, front office employees, senior management, ownership, and athletes. Findings from the most recent Report Card for the NBA (Lapchick, 2012), for example, indicate that African-Americans comprised 78 percent of all NBA players, and the number of female vice presidents increased by 6 in 2012 to 39 positions (18 percent total). Women also held 42 percent of all professional positions in the NBA league office, increasing one percentage point from the 2010–2011 season (Lapchick, 2012). The NBA received the highest scores in racial and gender diversity among front office employees and senior management of all of the professional sport leagues examined in the Report Card.

In practice, a growing emphasis has been placed on fostering equity and preventing discrimination in the professional sport industry. An example of these initiatives is the NFL's "Rooney Rule" which requires the league's teams to interview minority candidates for head coaching and senior football operations openings. The Rooney Rule has expanded opportunities for minorities in these positions since the rule was introduced in 2002. MLB has introduced a number of diversity initiatives including the Inaugural Civil Rights Game which was first played in Memphis on March 31, 2007. MLB's efforts rest on Jackie Robinson's vision to increase the percentage of African-American players as well as coaches and front office personnel. Diversity initiatives can also be community oriented; the NHL's diversity program is an attempt to augment interest and participation in the sport by offering economically disadvantaged and racially diverse youth opportunities to play hockey through their "Hockey is for everyone" program.

Other examples of efforts to integrate diversity into a sport business' CSR efforts are the Vancouver Canucks' Mindcheck initiative "dedicated to increasing awareness and understanding of mental illness in young people" (Schopf, 2012) and You Can Play "an advocacy program for lesbian, gay, bisexual and transgender athletes … with the aim to change homophobic attitudes on the ice and the field" launched, with support from the NHL, by Brian Burke, the General Manager of the Toronto Maple Leafs (CTV News, 2012).

Corporate governance

The final pillar of social responsibility is the broad, top management responsibility for corporate governance. Several significant corporate scandals and failures over the past years have refocused the attention of practitioners and academics to issues of effective governance, ethics, trust, and accountability in the management and oversight of their businesses. The rise in social activism and the emergence of new expectations have put a spotlight on, and increased the importance of, governance (Marsiglia and Falautano, 2005). Corporate governance is concerned with stewardship and emphasizes corporate ethics, oversight, and accountability; risk identification and management; external disclosure (transparency); and all essential responsible business practices (Jo and Harjoto, 2012). The underlying assumption is that effective governance will help prevent social irresponsibility (e.g., violation of rules, policies, and regulations) (Arora and Dharwadkar, 2011). Beyond simply being responsible by maintaining the viability of a business, governance entails the skillful consideration and balancing of the interests of all stakeholders, including employees, customers, partners, and the local community as well as engaging in the accurate and timely disclosure of clear, consistent, and comparable information in good and bad times (Jamali *et al.*, 2008).

Socially responsible governance in professional sport refers to the relationship among management, executives and owners, player associations, commissioners, and boards of directors, and is concerned with developing direction and policy for the business. Sport governance has received increasing scrutiny and emphasis due in large part to a number of ethical and moral scandals that have faced professional sports organizations, the repercussions of which have been felt widely and deeply. A number of governance practices have been called into question in sports organizations and linked to the call for more ethical and transparent business practices and decisions. For example oversight of the use of performance enhancing drugs among players in several US professional sport leagues has emerged as a serious governance concern and has attracted US congressional scrutiny and oversight. From BALCO to the Mitchell Report (2007), there is no doubt that few scandals have had as much of an impact on a sport, both in perception as well as in reality, as the steroid scandal that has touched Major League Baseball from a governance perspective.

Concern with banned substances in sport is based on fundamental principles of sport and fair play. The role governance plays is essential in extending and communicating the expected codes of conduct and values of sport. The dilemma faced by those governing sport in this case is that self-interests (profit, excitement, interest in the game – which all contribute to financial rewards) might run counter to integrity, ethics, and the development of the sport.

Other governance issues in sport relate to oversight and compliance with league and team policies. For instance the "Spygate" scandal of the New England Patriots, when Patriots' head coach Bill Belichick and his staff were accused of illegally videorecording the New York Jets' defensive play-calling signals in 2007. The NFL sanctioned the Patriots team because Commissioner Goodell found them to be in violation of league rules. The penalty was a $500,000 fine for Belechick, a $250,000 fine for the Patriots team, and the loss of a first round draft pick in the 2008 draft.

The 2007 gambling scandal by NBA referees also sheds light on governance and its link to an organization's social responsibility. In this case, an FBI investigation charged former NBA referee Tim Donaghy with betting tens of thousands of dollars on games that he officiated. Donaghy also admitted that he made calls that affected the outcome of games, so that he could manipulate the point spread and win his bets. Donaghy divulged that a number of NBA referees were involved in such behavior, and that directives sometimes came from league officials to extend playoff series to help increase TV ratings and ticket sales. Concerned about the integrity of the league, Commissioner David Stern stated:

> This is something that is the worst that could happen to a professional sports league. I want to say that we are going to make good on the covenant that we believe we have with our fans, and I pledge that my involvement will be as intense and complete as it can possibly be.
>
> (Associated Press, 2007)

As a result of this betting scandal, Stern revised the guidelines on the behavior of referees during the Board of Governors meeting. As indicated in the above examples, responsible governance integrates fiscal accountability, ethical behavior, legal compliance (as per Carroll, 1979, 1991), and organizational citizenship (Leonard and McAdam, 2003), as well as being related to the key dimensions of CSR in sport identified earlier, including stakeholder management, transparency, and the unique economics of sport.

Governance responsibility lies with top management. In US professional sport, the league commissioners, thus, have important governance duties – one of which is related to the image of their league. The commissioner typically creates rules, approves player contracts, engages in dispute resolution, and metes out disciplinary measures to owners and players, in efforts to act in the best interest of the game while adhering to the league's constitution and bylaws. An example of the role the Commissioner plays in ensuring ethical governance and maintaining integrity in the NFL is the personal conduct policy implemented in 2007. The development of this policy resulted from a range of violations and arrests of NFL players (such as former Atlanta Falcons quarterback Michael Vick who was charged with dogfighting and the Cincinnati Bengals whose team members were arrested 13 times between December 2005 and June 2007). Commissioner Roger Goodell introduced this personal conduct policy to help control the off-field behavior of players; the policy includes harsh penalties and suspensions for off-field misbehaviors. The ultimate intent was to preserve the league's public image, and to protect the players – the league's most valuable resource.

Conclusions

This chapter has positioned CSR within a particular context – professional sport in North America; as stated earlier we will address how our framing of CSR in sport is generalizable geographically, and to other types of sports organizations. We do so in this section. First, however, we provide a brief overview of our framing of CSR in sport. We suggest that CSR in sport builds on seminal elements of extant CSR literature. That is, CSR in sport has economic, legal, ethical, and discretionary *components* (Carroll, 1979, 1991) and it is based on moral obligation, sustainability, license to operate, and/or reputation *justifications* (Porter, 2008; Porter and Kramer, 2006). There are, however, four features that make *sport unique* with respect to CSR, these being: passion, economics, transparency, and stakeholder management (Babiak and Wolfe, 2009). Finally, we present the essential types of CSR in sport, which we refer to as CSR in sport *pillars*: labor relations, environmental management and sustainability, community relations, philanthropy, diversity, and corporate governance.

The above components, justifications, unique elements, and pillars are not meant to be considered independently. For example, a pillar (e.g., labor relations) can be related to each component, justification, and unique element of sport; moreover, pillars can overlap, as for example, a CSR initiative (i.e., the NFL's Rooney Rule) can include elements of the labor relations, diversity, and governance pillars. Addressing links among components, justifications, unique elements, and pillars in detail would take us beyond the purpose of this chapter; however, we do believe that it is a worthy endeavor for researchers (practitioners) to position their research questions (CSR initiatives) into a "pillar, component, justification, unique element" framework. Doing so will provide clarity to the focal research (practice) initiative.

Concerning generalizability to other contexts, we argue that the economic, legal, ethical, and discretionary *components* (Carroll, 1979, 1991), the moral obligation, sustainability, license to operate, and reputation *justifications* (Porter, 2008; Porter and Kramer, 2006); the passion, economics, transparency, and stakeholder management features that make *sport unique* with respect to CSR (Babiak and Wolfe, 2009); as well as the labor relations, environmental management and sustainability, community relations, philanthropy, diversity and equity, and corporate governance, CSR in sport *pillars* are as relevant to mega events and college sports, as they are to professional sports and are as relevant to Real Madrid as they are to the New York Yankees. The components, justifications, and features that make sport unique, and the CSR in sport pillars are also context specific, even within professional sport in North America. For example, the NFL's Rooney Rule has a very different "CSR profile" than does the NBA's Read to Achieve; that is they encompass different CSR components, can be justified with different rationales, and are related to different unique features of sport and to different pillars. Given such context specificity leads to different "CSR profiles" within professional sport in North America, surely the "CSR profile" of a CSR program implemented by the New York Yankees might be very different from that of a CSR program implemented by Real Madrid. However, our component, justification, unique features, and pillars framework is relevant to CSR in sport broadly, irrespective of its context. Ultimately, consideration of these elements of CSR in sport can enhance performance, save money, access new markets, serve new customers, enhance loyalty with existing consumers, strengthen employee relations, and help these businesses attain their pro-social objectives at the same time. An understanding of these CSR elements supports the ability of sport businesses to be more aware of their impacts, be more accountable for their actions, and demonstrate transparency in decision-making and processes – all hallmarks of social responsibility.

References

Armey, C. (2004) 'Inside and outside: Corporate America vs. the sports industry', in Falls, M. (ed.) *Inside the Minds: The Business of Sports*. Boston, MA: Aspatore, Inc, pp. 65–80.

Arora, P. and Dharwadkar, R. (2011) 'Responsibility (CSR): The moderating roles of attainment discrepancy and organization slack', *Corporate Governance: An International Review*, 19 (2), 136–152.

Associated Press (2007) 'Stern: Bet probe worst situation that I have ever experienced', *ESPN NBA*, July 25. Available at: http://sports.espn.go.com/nba/news/story?id=2947237 (accessed: November 25, 2012).

Babiak, K. (2010) 'The role and relevance of corporate social responsibility in sport: A view from the top', *Journal of Management and Organization*, 16 (4), 528–549.

Babiak, K. and Trendafilova, S. (2011) 'CSR and environmental responsibility: Motives and pressures to adopt sustainable management practices', *Corporate Social Responsibility and Environmental Management*, 18 (1), 11–24.

Babiak, K. and Wolfe, R. (2009) 'Determinants of corporate social responsibility in professional sport: Internal and external factors', *Journal of Sport Management*, 23 (6), 717–742.

Babiak, K., Mills, B., Tainsky, S., and Juravich, M. (2012) 'An investigation into professional athlete philanthropy: Why charity is part of the game', *Journal of Sport Management*, 26, 159–176.

Beliveau, B., Cottrill, M., and O Neill, H.M. (1994) 'Predicting corporate social responsiveness: A model drawn from three perspectives', *Journal of Business Ethics*, 13, 731–738.

Belli, B. (2008) 'Green Olympic dreams', *The Environmental Magazine*, February 29. Available at: http://www.emagazine.com/magazine-archive/green-olympic-dreams (accessed: May 1, 2013).

Bird, R.G., Hall, A.D., Momente, F., and Reggiani, F. (2007) 'What corporate social responsibility activities are valued by the market?', *Journal of Business Ethics*, 76 (2), 189–206.

Boehm, A. (2005) 'The participation of businesses in community decision making', *Business and Society*, 44 (2), 144–177.

Brown, W., Helland, E., and Smith, J. (2006) 'Corporate philanthropic practices', *Journal of Corporate Finance*, 12 (5), 855–877.

Bruch, H. and Walter, F. (2005) 'The keys to rethinking corporate philanthropy', *MIT Sloan Management Review*, 47 (1), 49–55.

Campbell, J.L. (2007) 'Why would corporations behave in socially responsible ways? An institutional theory of corporate social responsibility', *Academy of Management Review*, 32 (3), 946–967.

Carroll, A.B. (1979) 'A three-dimensional conceptual model of corporate performance', *Academy of Management Review*, 4 (4), 497–505.

Carroll, A.B. (1991) 'The pyramid of corporate social responsibility: Toward the moral management of organizational stakeholders', *Business Horizons*, 34 (4), 39–48.

Cashman, B. (2004) 'Winning on and off the field', in Falls, M. (ed.) *Inside the minds: The business of sports.* Boston, MA: Aspatore, Inc, pp. 7–26.

Casper, J.M., Pfal, M.E., and McSherry, M.W. (2012) 'Athletics department awareness and action regarding the environment: A study of NCAA athletics department sustainability practices', *Journal of Sport Management*, 26, 11–29.

Cribb, R. (2010) 'The high cost of sports charities'. *The Start.com*, April 24. Available at: http://www.thestar.com/news/investigations/article/800061--star-investigation-the-high-cost-of-sports-charities?bn=1 (accessed: October 27, 2012).

CTV News (2012) *Brian Burke, Son Launch Anti-homophobia Campaign.* Available at: http://www.ctvnews.ca/brian-burke-son-launch-anti-homophobia-campaign-1.777077#ixzz28GyX32BV (accessed: October 15, 2012).

Dawkins, J. and Lewis, S. (2003) 'CSR in stakeholder expectations: And their implication for company strategy', *Journal of Business Ethics*, 44 (2/3), 185–193.

Den Hond, F. and De Bakker, F. (2007) 'Ideologically motivated activism: How activist groups influence corporate social change activities', *Academy of Management Review*, 32 (3), 901–924.

Donaldson, T. and Preston, L. (1995) 'The stakeholder theory of the corporation: Concepts, evidence, and implications', *Academy of Management Review*, 20 (1), 65–91.

Fenwick, T. and Bierema, L. (2008) 'Corporate social responsibility: Issues for human resource development professionals', *International Journal of Training and Development*, 12, 24–35.

Foundation Center (2012) 'Vinik family pledges $10 million to Tampa Area Charities'. Available at: http://foundationcenter.org/pnd/news/story.jhtml?id=325600023 (accessed: October 27, 2012).

Fowler, S.J. and Hope, C. (2007) 'A critical review of sustainable business indices and their impact', *Journal of Business Ethics*, 76 (3), 243–252.

Freeman, E. (1984) *Strategic Management: A Stakeholder Approach.* Marshfield, MA: Pitman.

Friedman, M. (1962) *Capitalism and Freedom*, Chicago: University of Chicago Press.

Gardberg, N. and Fombrun, C.F. (2006) 'Corporate citizenship: Creating intangible assets across institutional environments', *Academy of Management Review*, 31(2), 329–346.

Giannarakis, G. and Theotokas, I. (2011) 'The effect of financial crisis in corporate social responsibility performance', *International Journal of Marketing Studies*, 3 (1), 1–10.

Godfrey, P.C. (2005) 'The relationship between corporate philanthropy and shareholder wealth: A risk management perspective', *Academy of Management Review*, 30 (4), 777–798.

Godfrey, P.C. (2009) 'Corporate social responsibility in sport: An overview and key issues', *Journal of Sport Management*, 23, 698–716.

Green Sports Alliance (2012a) '49ers new stadium shows commitment to environmental responsibility'. Available at: http://greensportsalliance.org/news-feed/49ers-new-stadium-shows-commitment-environmental-responsibility-fan-experience (accessed: October 27, 2012).

Green Sports Alliance (2012b) 'Game changer: How the sports industry is saving the environment'. Available at: http://greensportsalliance.org/news-feed (accessed: October 27, 2012).

Gupta, S. and Pirsch, J. (2006) 'The company-cause-customer fit decision in cause-related marketing', *Journal of Consumer Marketing*, 23 (6), 314–326.

Hess, D. and Warren, D.E. (2008) 'The meaning and meaningfulness of corporate social initiatives', *Business and Society Review*, 113 (2), 163–197.

Hess, D., Rogovsky, N., and Dunfee, T.W. (2002) 'The next wave of corporate community investment: Corporate social initiatives', *California Management Review*, 44, 110–125.

Industry Canada (2012) *Community relations*. Available at: http://www.ic.gc.ca/eic/site/csr-rse.nsf/eng/rs00592.html (accessed: October 27, 2012).

Inoue, Y. and Kent, A. (2012) 'Sport teams as promoters of pro-environmental behavior: An empirical study', *Journal of Sport Management*, 26 (5), 417–432.

Inoue, Y., Kent, A., and Lee, S. (2011) 'CSR and the bottom line: Analyzing the link between CSR and financial performance for professional teams', *Journal of Sport Management*, 25(6), 531–549.

Irwin, R., Lachowetz, T., Cornwell, T., and Clark, J. (2003) 'Cause-related sport sponsorship: An assessment of spectator beliefs, attitudes, and behavioral intentions', *Sport Marketing Quarterly*, 12 (3), 131–139.

Jamali, D., Safieddine, A.M., and Rabbath, M. (2008) 'Corporate governance and corporate social responsibility synergies and interrelationships', *Corporate Governance*, 16 (5), 443–459.

Jensen M. (2002) 'Value maximization, stakeholder theory, and the corporate objective function', *Business Ethics Quarterly*, 12, 235–256.

Jo, H. and Harjoto, M.A. (2012) 'The causal effect of corporate governance on corporate social responsibility', *Journal of Business Ethics*, 106, 53–72.

Kärnä, J., Juslin, H., Ahonen, V., and Hansen, E. (2001) 'Green advertising: Greenwash or a true reflection of marketing strategies?' GMI 33, 59–70.

Kassinis, G. and Vafeas, N. (2006) 'Stakeholder pressures and environmental performance', *The Academy of Management Journal*, 49 (1), 145–159.

Kellison, T.B. and Kim, Y.K. (forthcoming) 'Marketing pro-environmental venues in professional sport: Planting seeds of change among existing and prospective consumers', *Journal of Sport Management*.

Kiholm Smith, J. (2012) 'Corporate philanthropy', in Baker, K.H. and Nofsinger, J.R. (eds.) *Socially responsible finance and investing: Financial institutions, corporations, investors and activists*. New York: Wiley, pp. 341–358.

Kott, A. (2005) 'The philanthropic power of sport', *Foundation News and Commentary*, January/February, pp. 20–25.

Kreidler, M. (2006) 'Athletes and gambling: A longtime love affair', *ESPN*, May 5. Available at: http://sports.espn.go.com/espn/columns/story?columnist=kreidler_mark&id=2433819 (accessed: October 27, 2012).

Lapchick, R. (2012) 'The 2012 Racial and Gender Report Card: National Basketball Association', The Institute for Diversity and Ethics in Sport . Available at: http://www.tidesport.org/RGRC/2012/2012_NBA_RGRC[1].pdf (accessed: November 27, 2012).

Lee, S.P. and Cornwell, T.B. (2011) 'A framework for measuring the contributions of sport to society: Actors, activities and outcomes', in Kahle, L.R. and Close, A.G. (eds.) *Consumer behavior knowledge for effective sports and event marketing*, New York: Taylor and Francis.

Lenskyj, H.J. (1998) 'Sport and corporate environmentalism: The case of the Sydney 2000 Olympics', *International Review for the Sociology of Sport*, 33 (4), 341–354.

Leonard, D. and McAdam, R. (2003) 'Corporate social responsibility', *Quality Progress*, 36, 27–33.

Mallen, C., Adams, L., Stevens, J., and Thompson, L. (2010) 'Environmental sustainability in sport facility management: A Delphi study', *European Sport Management Quarterly*, 10 (3), 367–389.

Marquis, C., Glynn, M.A., and Davis, G.F. (2007) 'Community isomorphism and corporate social action', *The Academy of Management Review*, 32 (3), 925–945.

Marsiglia, E. and Falautano, I. (2005) 'Corporate social responsibility and sustainability challenges for a Bancassurance Company', *The Geneva Papers*, 30 (3), 485–497.

Maske, M. (2012) 'NFL donating $30 million to NIH for brain injury research', *Washington Post*, September 5. Available at: http://www.washingtonpost.com/blogs/football-insider/wp/2012/09/05/nfl-donating-30-million-to-nih-for-brain-injury-research (accessed: October 27, 2012).

McAlister, D.T. and Ferrell, L. (2002) 'The role of strategic philanthropy in marketing strategy', *European Journal of Marketing*, 36 (5/6), 689–743.

McGlone, C. and Martin, N. (2006) 'Nike's corporate interest lives strong: A case of cause related marketing and leveraging', *Sports Marketing Quarterly*, 15, 184–189.

McNamara, K.E. and Gibson, C. (2008) 'Environmental sustainability in practice? A macro-scale profile of tourist accommodation facilities in Australia's coastal zone', *Journal of Sustainable Tourism*, 16(1), 85–100.

McWilliams, A. and Siegel, D. (2001) 'Corporate social responsibility: A theory of the firm perspective', *Academy of Management Review*, 26 (1), 117–27.

Mitchell, G.J. (2007) *Report to the Commissioner of Baseball of an Independent Investigation into the illegal use of steroids and other performance enhancing substances by players in Major League Baseball*. Office of the Commissioner of Baseball.

NBA Cares (2012) *Overview*. Available at: http://www.nba.com/cares/overview.html (accessed: October 27, 2012).

NFL (2012) *NFL Play 60*. Available at: http://www.nfl.com/play60 (accessed: October 27, 2012).

NFL Player Engagement (2012) *Core Areas & Services Overview*. Available at: http://www.nflplayerengagement.com/CoreAreasAndServices.aspx (accessed: October 27, 2012).

Perez-Batres, L.A., Doh, J.P., Miller, V.V., and Pisani, M.J. (2012) 'Stakeholder pressures as determinants of CSR strategic choice: Why do firms choose symbolic versus substantive self-regulatory codes of conduct?' *Journal of Business Ethics*, 110, 157–172.

Porter, M.E. (2008) *On competition*. Boston: Harvard Business Press.

Porter, M.E. and Kramer, M.R. (2006) 'Strategy and society: The link between competitive advantage and corporate social responsibility', *Harvard Business Review*, December, 78–92.

Robinson, R. (2005) 'Sports philanthropy: An analysis of the charitable foundations of major league teams', Master's thesis, San Francisco, CA: University of San Francisco.

Roy, D.P. and Graeff, T.R. (2003) 'Consumer attitudes toward cause-related marketing activities in professional sports', *Sports Marketing Quarterly*, 12 (3), 163–172.

Schmidt, C.W. (2006) 'Putting the Earth in play: Environmental awareness and sport', *Environmental Health Perspectives*, 114, 286–294.

Schopf, D. (2012) 'Canucks launch Mindcheck program in memory of Rick Rypien', *The Hockey Writers*, February 11. Available at http://thehockeywriters.com/canucks-launch-mindcheck-program-in-memory-of-rick-rypien (accessed: October 15, 2012).

Sheridan, C. (2006) 'Stern dismayed by NBA player development system', *ESPN Insider*, June 9. Available at: http://sports.espn.go.com/nba/playoffs2006/news/story?id=2477110 (accessed: October 27, 2012).

Skibola (2010) 'The social responsibility to generate employee happiness' *Forbes. The CSR blog*, April 11. Available at: http://www.forbes.com/sites/csr/2010/11/04/the-social-responsibility-to-generate-employee-happiness (accessed: October 27, 2012).

Smith, A. and Westerbeek. H. (2007) 'Sport as a vehicle for developing corporate social responsibility', *Journal of Corporate Citizenship*, 25(7), 43–54.

Strode, J. and Fink, J. (2009) 'Using motivational theory to develop a donor profile scale for intercollegiate athletics', *Journal for the Study of Sports and Athletes in Education*, 3 (3), 335–354.

Suzuki, D. (2009) *For many NHLPA members, carbon offsets are just the beginning*. Available at: http://www.davidsuzuki.org/media/news/2009/03/for-many-nhlpa-members-carbon-offsets-are-just-the-beginning (accessed: October 27, 2012).

Swindell, D. and Rosentraub, M.S. (1998) 'Who benefits from the presence of professional sports teams? The implications for public funding of stadiums and arenas', *Public Administration Review*, 58 (1), 11–20.

Torre, P.S. (2009) 'How (and why) athletes go broke', *Si Vault*, March 23. Available at: http://sportsillustrated.cnn.com/vault/article/magazine/MAG1153364 (accessed: October 27, 2012).

Turban, D.B. and Greening, D.W. (1996) 'Corporate social performance and organizational attractiveness to prospective employees', *Academy of Management Journal*, 40, 658–672.

Turker, D. (2009) 'Measuring corporate social responsibility: A scale development study', *Journal of Business Ethics*, 85 (4), 411–427.

Ullmann, A. (1985) 'Data in search of a theory: A critical examination of the relationship among social performance, social disclosure, and economic performance', *Academy of Management Review*, 10, 540–577.

Van Marrewijk, M. (2003) 'Concepts and definitions of CSR and corporate sustainability: Between agency and communion', *Journal of Business Ethics*, 44(2–3), 95–105.

Vogel, D. (2005) *The market for virtue*. Washington, DC: Brookings Institution Press.

Wakefield, K.L. and Wann, D.L. (2006) 'An examination of dysfunctional sport fans: Method of classification and relationships with problem behaviors', *Journal of Leisure Research*, 38 (2), 168–186.

Wallace, C. (2004) 'An insider's look at – and love for – pro basketball', in Falls, M. (ed.) *Inside the Minds: The Business of Sports*. Boston, MA: Aspatore, Inc, pp. 27–48.

Welford, R., Chan, C., and Man, M. (2007) 'Priorities for corporate social responsibility: A survey of businesses and their stakeholders', *Corporate Social Responsibility and Environmental Management*, 15, 52–62.

White Sox (2012) *White Sox Volunteer Corps*. Available at: http://chicago.whitesox.mlb.com/cws/fan_ forum/volunteer.jsp (accessed: October 27, 2012).

Wilkerson, M. and Dodder, R.A. (1987) 'Collective conscience and sport in modem society: An empirical test of a model', *Journal of Leisure Research*, 19, 35–40.

Yu, X. (2007) 'Impacts of corporate code of conduct on labor standards: A case study of Reebok's athletic footwear supplier factory in China', *Journal of Business Ethics*, 81, 513–529.

2

CSR IN SPORT

Who benefits?

Ivan Waddington, Packianathan Chelladurai and Berit Skirstad

Overview

It is important to recognize at the outset that the concept of corporate social responsibility (CSR) is an essentially contested concept. Indeed, the contested nature of the concept of CSR – and more particularly the contested nature of the policies and practices which are conventionally subsumed under that name – constitutes both the starting point for, and the guiding thread of, this chapter. More specifically the chapter sets out to: (1) outline the contested nature of the concept of CSR and the variety of competing approaches to understanding CSR; (2) examine some of the possible outcomes for organizations which adopt CSR policies; (3) examine some of the possible outcomes for organizations within the wider society which are claimed to be beneficiaries of CSR; and (4) examine the socio-genesis of CSR, that is, the conditions under which organizations have developed CSR policies. Throughout this chapter, a central focus will be on the question "*cui bono?*" In other words, who benefits from CSR policies? The chapter will firstly draw on the general literature on CSR and will then apply the questions which have been raised in that context to the understanding of CSR within the sporting context.

CSR: a contested concept

As will become clear in reading chapters in this volume, definitions of the term CSR abound and there is no consensus on a definition of CSR. Bradish and Cronin (2009: 691), in their introduction to a special issue of the *Journal of Sport Management* which was devoted to CSR in sport, have noted that the concept of CSR "is both an ambitious and ambiguous concept in sport management." Godfrey, in his overview of key issues in social responsibility in sport, has noted that in terms of a definition, CSR is a "tortured concept, both theoretically and empirically" and he further points to the contested nature of CSR in his observation that the "legitimacy of CSR has been debated for the last 75 years" (Godfrey, 2009: 702–3). Breitbarth and Harris (2008: 189), in their examination of CSR in the football (soccer) business, cite Dow Votaw (1972) to the effect that CSR "means something, but not always the same thing, to everybody."

Given the situation described above, it is perhaps not surprising that a variety of definitions of CSR can be found both in the academic literature and among practitioners. One of the most widely accepted definitions appears to be that offered by McWilliams and Siegel (2001: 117), who suggested that CSR refers to "actions that appear to further some social good, beyond the interests of the firm and that which is required by law." In a positive – but also heavily value laden – comment on CSR, Bradish and Cronin (2009: 696) argue that at its core, "CSR mindset and practice is grounded in giving back to one's community, providing goodwill to others, and effectively bringing about change to important social causes while maintaining sound business strategies." However, not everyone takes such a sanguine view of CSR; indeed some authors have argued that it is the organizations which implement CSR policies which are themselves the major beneficiaries of those policies. For example, Jo (2011) has suggested that a "widely received view of CSR endorsed by the dominant groups of society – specifically, corporate executives, business and legal scholars, and the mainstream media – is that corporate managers may, can, and do 'sacrifice' corporate profits in the interests of society." However, in a hint of the radical critique of the concept and practice of CSR, he asserts that: "It should be noted that the private corporations do not 'sacrifice' profits. More often than not, short-term profits are utilized for a social purpose with the expectation of making more profits ... CSR decisions are made strategically. Profits are not sacrificed" (Jo, 2011: 2).

Such relatively involved statements – whether supportive of or against CSR as part of corporate strategy – do not help, we suggest, in trying to develop a more adequate understanding of CSR. For the purposes of this chapter we will adopt the definition of McWilliams and Siegel outlined above. However, we would emphasize the importance of the precise wording of that definition: that CSR refers to actions that *appear* to further some social good, beyond the interests of the firm. Thus we do not assume, as many authors appear to do, that CSR policies and practices necessarily have the beneficial effects for the wider society which the proponents of CSR claim; the question of the respective benefits of CSR to the wider society and to the organizations promoting and implementing CSR policies, as would be further discussed in other sections of the handbook, is a question which can only be adequately answered by a relatively detached examination of the empirical data. That is one of the objects of this chapter.

Approaches to CSR

As Broomhill (2007) has noted, within the management literature there are three discernible schools of thought about the policies and practices of CSR: neoliberalism, neo-Keynesianism and radical political economy.

Neoliberalism

Neoliberals hold that the *only* social responsibility of business is to increase its profits. A key statement of this position is that by Milton Friedman who, in an oft-quoted article in the *New York Times*, argued that:

> There is one and only one social responsibility of business – to use its resources and engage in activities designed to increase its profits so long as it stays within the rules of the game, which is to say, engages in open and free competition without deception or fraud.
>
> (Friedman, 1970)

And in a statement which will no doubt surprise many corporate executives whose companies have developed CSR policies, Friedman even suggested that business leaders who claim that business is not concerned "merely" with profit but also with promoting "desirable social ends" are "preaching pure and unadulterated socialism" and are "unwitting puppets of the intellectual forces that have been undermining the basis of a free society." Following the logical impli-cations of Friedman's argument, some neoliberals have argued that CSR is an unreasonable restriction on the primary objective of business – that is, making profits – and is therefore dam-aging to business, since the growing constraint on managers to undertake "socially responsible" actions removes managerial decisions "from their connections to the search for profit and the enhancement of stockholder value" (Younkins, 2000: 1). However, many neoliberals argue that, while Friedman was basically correct, the adoption by companies of CSR can be rational and profitable in the long run. As Younkins put it, "socially responsible actions such as chari-table contributions may be acceptable when the manager makes these in anticipation of effects that, in the long run, will be beneficial to business" (Younkins, 2000: 3).

Neo-Keynesianism

Neo-Keynesian writers, in contrast to neoliberals, argue that organizations have wider social responsibilities in addition to making profits and working within the law. There is an explicit recognition on the part of neo-Keynesians that market mechanisms work very imperfectly and that the activities of corporations can have what many people would consider negative consequences. Consequently, it is held, the interests not just of shareholders but of a range of stakeholders – for example employees, consumers, and members of the wider community – also need to be taken into account by developing CSR policies which address issues such as environmental sustainability, workplace practices, and the broader social and economic impact of corporation policy. A good example of this kind of approach is that of Carroll (1979) who suggests that, in addition to the economic and legal responsibilities identified by Friedman – that is the responsibilities to make profits and to obey the law – companies also have ethical responsibilities (to conform to generally accepted ethical norms) and discretionary responsibili-ties (to engage in activities that benefit the broader society even if they have no direct payback for the company). Specifically within a sporting context, CSR policies typically involve clubs, sports federations, or other sports organizations making charitable donations and/or using "star" players or coaches to support local community projects relating to such things as youth devel-opment, educational campaigns, health issues, or broader community development.

Radical political economy

Radical political economists disagree with those who see CSR as making a significant contribu-tion to relieving social problems and many suggest that the major beneficiaries of CSR are the very companies which adopt such policies. Thus, Jo (2011: 12) has suggested that corporations:

> may, can, and do utilize CSR for the sake of profits, survival, and growth. If a socially responsible action is inimical to profitability, not profitably but responsibility is likely to be abandoned. Suffice it to say that corporations strategically use their resources in order to reproduce themselves: ethical, humanitarian, or social concern is at most epiphenomenal.

As Godfrey (2009: 699) has also noted in his overview of CSR in sport:

> For critics, CSR represents an apology for socially negative byproducts, a palliative offered by corporations (or sport entities) to counteract a number of social harms … CSR can be viewed as blood money to atone for past sins, or as image production and projection that masks naked self-interest.

It might be noted that many international organizations, including some prominent sports organizations such as FIFA, have adopted CSR policies related to development issues in Africa and elsewhere, and elements of the radical critique outlined above can be found in the work of academics and in reports from some of the most respected international aid agencies working in these areas. For example, in 2005 *International Affairs* devoted a special issue to CSR in the developing world and the editors summarized the main conclusion of their contributors as follows: "Numerous claims have been made about the contribution CSR can make to poverty alleviation and other development goals. However, the contributors to this issue have reached the conclusion that current CSR approaches do not warrant such claims" (Blowfield and Frynas, 2005: 499). Christian Aid (2004: 5) was even more critical and suggested that

> corporate enthusiasm for CSR is not driven primarily by a desire to improve the lot of the communities in which companies work. Rather, companies are concerned with their own reputations, with the potential damage of public campaigns directed against them, and overwhelmingly, with the desire – and the imperative – to secure ever-increasing profits.

Although the above criticisms of CSR did not relate specifically to the CSR programs of sports organizations – Christian Aid's analysis, for example, focused on the activities of Shell, British American Tobacco and Coca Cola – the criticisms of CSR in the context of development are not without relevance for the sport context for, as noted above, a growing number of sports organizations have development-related CSR programs in Africa and elsewhere. One prominent example is the "Football for Hope" program of the Fédération Internationale de Football Association (FIFA), which is designed to promote public health, education and football in developing countries. We will return to this issue of sport, CSR, and development later.

Having outlined the major approaches to CSR, we are in a position to return to our key question: *cui bono?*

Cui bono? The bottom line

There has been a good deal of discussion in the general management literature – though very little discussion in the sport management literature – about whether or not CSR contributes to greater profitability. In a systematic review of 109 studies, Margolis and Walsh (2003) found that almost half of the results pointed to a positive relationship between CSR and corporate financial performance (CFP). Only seven studies found a negative relationship, with the other 48 reporting either non-significant relationships or a mixed set of findings. Further, Margolis and Walsh (2003: 277) note that a "simple compilation of the findings suggests there is a positive association, and certainly very little evidence of a negative association, between a company's social performance and its financial performance." A meta-analysis of 52 CSR–CFP studies reached a similar conclusion (Orlitzky *et al.*, 2003). However, Margolis and Walsh suggest such results should be treated with caution, since many of the studies were characterized by methodological and/or theoretical weaknesses; in this regard, they mention sampling problems, concerns about the reliability and validity of the CSR and CFP measures and omission of controls. Inoue *et al.* (2011) also note the problems involved in comparing data from many different industries. Studies within the sport industry may help to overcome this last-named difficulty since the data are, by definition, industry specific.

In the first of these sport-specific studies, Extejt (2004) sought to examine the relationship in the four US-based major professional leagues (MLB, NFL, NBA, and NHL) between teams' corporate philanthropy and business outcomes, as measured by financial performance and attendance. No significant relationship was found between charitable donations and financial performance, as measured by revenues and profits; neither was there any significant relationship between a team's philanthropic donation level and attendance.

Inoue and colleagues suggest that Extejt's results should be treated with caution because, although the study focused on a single industry, it simply studied the bivariate relationship between charitable activities and financial performance without including any control variables, while it was also based on data for a single year; the latter is problematic, they suggest, because there is likely to be a time lag between a firm's CSR involvement and its stakeholders' awareness. Accordingly in their own study, Inoue and colleagues sought to control several variables, including current and former team performance and stadium size, while the data covered all US-based professional teams in the MLB, NBA, NFL, and NHL between 2002 and 2006. The level of CSR involvement by the US pro teams was measured by the annual charitable contributions made by team-related foundations, while financial performance was measured by two indicators: attendance and operating margins.

Although Inoue and colleagues hypothesized, on the basis of stakeholder theory, the existence of a positive relationship between CSR and financial performance, their general conclusion was that CSR "had insignificant effects on both attendance and operating margin" (2011: 544). In seeking to explain this lack of significance, they suggested that there may have been a general lack of awareness of teams' CSR initiatives among fans or that teams had failed to use their CSR initiatives in strategic contexts. Perhaps more tellingly, they also suggested that these results may highlight "the unique nature of pro teams as privately held organizations." They note that existing frameworks of the relationship between CSR and financial performance are based on the analysis of publicly held corporations, the major objective of which is to maximize shareholder value. In contrast, they suggest, the goals of privately held corporations, such as US pro teams, may be much more varied due to the absence of shareholders. Thus, they suggest that

> owners of professional sports teams may have different objectives than financial gain, including winning, the protection of a community asset, and the trophy status of owning a team. Given this, for a wealthy owner, contributing to the community and satisfying his or her altruistic values through philanthropic activities could be a major goal … regardless of whether these activities generate any financial returns.
>
> (Inoue *et al.*, 2011: 547)

We agree with this latter point and we fully accept that the relationship between owners of teams and the team as a privately held corporation is different in many respects from the relationship between corporation executives and the publicly held corporations which they run. For example it is clear that, while a central objective of publicly held corporations is to generate profits for shareholders, many owners of private teams do not run them with a view to making profits. Indeed, in some cases they are prepared to run them at substantial losses in the hope that the expenditure of vast sums of money on star players will result in the winning of trophies. Chelsea Football Club, which is owned by the Russian billionaire Roman Abramovich, is a good example. Abramovich's personal fortune has enabled him to put huge amounts of money into the club for the purchase of star players. Largely as a consequence of this, Chelsea have, in recent years, won several trophies but in the first seven years of Abramovich's ownership, the club's total losses exceeded £500 million, with a record loss for a football club of £140 million in 2005 (Draper, 2010). It is difficult to imagine an entrepreneur running any other business in this way.

However, we would make a further point about the special character of sports teams. While Inoue and colleagues emphasize the fact of *private ownership* of many sports teams, we would wish to emphasize that the special character of these organizations derives not just from the fact of private ownership, but also from the fact that they are *sports teams*. While the emphasis of Inoue and colleagues on private ownership focuses attention on the relationship between the owner and the team and its CSR activities, an emphasis on the fact that they are *sports teams* focuses attention on the relationship between fans and the team. In this regard, it is important to note that, in many respects – and particularly in terms of their consumer behavior – the relationship between fans and their team is not just like any other relationship between a corporation which produces a product and the consumers of that product for, as Walker and Kent (2009: 746) have noted, "the level of affect displayed by its many consumers distinguish(es) the sport industry from most others."

One consequence of the strong affective connections of fans to their clubs is that the consumer behavior of sports fans is much less price sensitive than is the behavior of consumers of most other goods or services. Thus while someone may decide to purchase one car rather than another largely on the basis of price, fans of one team are not likely to transfer their allegiance to a rival team because the admission charges to the stadium are lower at the rival club; nor are fans of one club likely to purchase the replica team strip of a rival club because it is cheaper than that of their own team. In this regard, it is important to bear in mind that, while sports teams may be businesses, they are in many respects not just like other businesses. Being a fan of a club is not primarily about making rational economic decisions; it is, in large measure, about passion, which is not easily incorporated into traditional economic models.

This point was well made by Extejt (2004: 224) who, in seeking to explain the absence of any significant relationship between CSR and business outcomes in his own study, suggested that, in the context of sports teams, "win–loss records drive fan behaviour and attitudes in this industry; philanthropic behaviour has little, if any affect [sic]." That this is indeed the case is indicated in the study by Inoue *et al.* (2011), who found that although there was no positive relationship between CSR and financial performance there was, in the MLB, NBA, and NHL, a significant positive effect of team performance on attendance, which has obvious implications for financial performance. This suggests that the behavior of fans may be much more responsive to team performance than to teams' involvement in CSR activities; however, the peculiar features of sports teams as businesses suggest that the absence of any significant relationship between CSR and financial performance in the case of sports teams does not necessarily indicate a similar absence in the case of other organizations within the sports industry, such as manufacturers of sports equipment and clothing, which are likely to be much more overtly profit orientated. This is a matter for further research.

Finally, it should be noted that, if there is no clear evidence that CSR in sports clubs boosts profitability, expenditure on CSR is also unlikely to have any serious deleterious effects on profitability, since the amounts involved are, in relation to the incomes of professional sports teams, relatively small. Thus Extejt (2004: 220) has noted that among teams in the four US professional leagues, "the donation level is very low … 70 percent of the foundations associated with NBA and NFL teams donated less than one-half of 1 percent of their team's income, while MLB and NHL teams were only marginally more generous."

Cui bono? Other benefits to corporations

If the relationship between CSR and financial performance is unclear, are there other benefits which sports organizations might enjoy as a consequence of CSR policies? On this issue, the evidence seems clearer. As Babiak and Wolfe (2006: 215) have noted, engaging in CSR activities "can help a company in various ways." Babiak and Wolfe (2006, 2009) and Inoue *et al.* (2011) list these benefits as favorable impacts on firm reputation, consumer satisfaction, attractiveness of the firm as an employer, organizational commitment among employees, as well as creating a cushion for greater customer acceptance of price increases, greater acquiescence among key regulatory institutions or legislative bodies, and help in mitigating negative media scrutiny. But do these general advantages of CSR translate to the sport context?

In their study of CSR at Super Bowl XL, Babiak and Wolfe (2006: 214) discuss the ways in which the outreach efforts initiated by the NFL and the Super Bowl Host Committee "might help in building the NFL's image as a professional sport league that takes its social responsibility seriously." They describe the tree-planting effort designed to offset carbon emissions generated by increased vehicle traffic and suggest that, for the NFL, "being perceived as an organization that cares about the environment helped to create an image of an organization that is socially responsible." They also suggest that the awarding of contracts to firms that were at least 51 percent owned by minorities and/or women helped the NFL's "image as an organization that cares about minorities and women" (Babiak and Wolfe, 2006: 218). However, once again we have to add that these judgments should be treated with caution, since they appear not to be based on any systematic academic research into the impact of these initiatives on public perceptions of the NFL but rely, in the first example, on one journalistic report published a few days after the Super Bowl (and based largely on an interview with the NFL's environment program director) and, in the second example, on a statement on the NFL's own website. Clearly such sources of information should not be taken as indicative of a relatively detached analysis of the impact of the NFL's policies on the public perception of that organization. Broadly similar problems arise in a paper by Breitbarth and Harris (2008). They suggested:

> If implemented and managed rightly, these approaches can create specific sources of value among stakeholders, which can lead to significant benefits for the game itself: growing participation in football, increasing institutional relevance, (financial) profits, and thus strategic advantages in terms of competitiveness.
>
> (Breitbarth and Harris, 2008: 200)

However, it should be noted that, once again, these judgments are not based on any detailed empirical analysis of the actual consequences to date of CSR in football; rather, they are an optimistic statement of the beneficial consequences which, in the view of the authors, could follow if CSR policies are implemented and managed rightly. That they are not describing actual past consequences of CSR in football but hypothetical future consequences is clear when they try to set out the conditions which need to be met "in order to realize such healthy *future* development" (Breitbarth and Harris, 2008: 200; italics added).

However, a recent study by Walker and Kent (2009) offers more systematic data on the advantages of CSR for sports clubs. Those authors sought to analyze the influence of CSR on consumer attitudes – specifically in relation to reputational assessments and patronage intentions – towards clubs in the NFL. The consumers in this case are, of course, fans and fans display a high level of affect towards their clubs. Walker and Kent emphasize the importance of this in their suggestion that "it can be argued that in the sport industry, where cultivation of an affective connection to the organization is critical, CSR may provide 'secondary value' for the organization over and above those which have been seen in other industries" (2009: 744). In other words, because of the particular nature of the relationship between fans and clubs, there may be, at least in some respects, greater benefits from CSR in the sports sector than in other industries.

Further, Walker and Kent found that there was "a general positivity in sport consumers' responses" to the teams' CSR initiatives. More specifically, they found that CSR activities on the part of sports clubs had "a strong and positive impact on the organization's perceived reputation." They considered this to be a major benefit since "reputation is one of the most valuable intangible assets available to the company ... and cultivating relationships with consumers is an important objective of reputation-building activities for many companies" (Walker and Kent, 2009: 758).

They also found a significant positive relationship between CSR and two aspects of patronage intentions, with CSR being a "significant predictor of word of mouth and merchandise consumption behaviours." They suggest that these findings are particularly important because "when consumers perceive an organization as having a 'good' reputation they will speak favourably of them and as a result purchase their products to display their affiliation" (2009: 759). Their general conclusion is that "fans ... clearly value the socially responsible efforts of their teams and use this information especially when considering product selection and/or favourably speaking of the organization" and that CSR therefore has "an important strategic role to play for sport organizations" (2009: 763).

Cui bono? The intended beneficiaries

Margolis and Walsh (2003: 280–3) have noted a "preoccupation with instrumental consequences" in the literature on CSR. They add that if CSR policies are "evaluated only in terms of their instrumental benefits for the firm and its shareholders, we never learn about their impact on society, most notably on the intended beneficiaries of those initiatives." They suggest there is a need to reorientate analysis of CSR so that research "would ... focus on unearthing the effects that corporate actions to redress social ills actually have." We agree, though we would add a further point: the large number of studies of the impact of CSR on corporations – and in particular the impact of CSR on the profitability of corporations – coupled with the almost complete absence of studies of the impact of CSR on the wider society is, we suggest, indicative of the values and ideologies which have underpinned much of the research on CSR.

As noted earlier, CSR policies on the part of professional sports clubs typically involve a variety of activities, including programs in which players and/or coaches contribute time to particular causes and/or the club makes financial donations, often via charitable foundations. In addition, manufacturers of sports clothing may adopt CSR policies relating to such things as wages and labor relations in the factories in which their goods are manufactured, or to broader environmental issues. As Babiak and Wolfe have noted:

> Virtually all organizations within the sport industry, broadly defined, have adopted CSR programs. From Nike and Reebok to the NBA and NASCAR, examples abound of activities undertaken to bring messages and resources to underprivileged and other members of society who may not otherwise be the targets of socially responsible initiatives.
>
> (Babiak and Wolfe, 2009: 720)

Within the US, typical examples include the NBA's "Read to Achieve" program, designed to encourage young people to read and its "Basketball without borders" initiative, which involves a summer camp for young people designed to promote friendship, goodwill, and education through sport. In the UK a good example is provided by the "Football in the Community" schemes, which will be covered in more details by Morgan in Chapter 18, which are run by most professional soccer clubs and designed not just to increase community participation in football but also to use football as a means of promoting education and healthy lifestyles, developing life skills, and diverting young people away from anti-social behavior. But the critical question is: are such programs effective? In other words, do they have a significant impact in terms of reducing the social problems which they claim to address?

It may be useful, in trying to answer this question, to divide sport-related CSR policies into three broad areas: (1) schemes which involve clubs or sports organizations in simply making charitable donations or in helping to raise funds for good causes, such as the NHL's "Hockey Fights Cancer" campaign; (2) schemes which are designed to use sport or sports stars in local community projects relating to such things as educational campaigns, health issues or broader community development, such as the "Football in the Community" schemes in the UK; and (3) CSR policies adopted by international sports organizations such as Nike, Reebok, or FIFA, which may have important implications for social development in less developed countries. Let us examine each of these in turn.

Charitable donations

As Babiak and Wolfe (2009) have noted, nearly 90 percent of US pro teams have their own charitable foundations which provide charitable contributions, most usually in the form of cash donations, to local organizations involved in education, health, or youth work. For example, the NFL's Washington Redskins organization donated $250,000 to an 11 September relief fund; the charitable foundation of the Indiana Pacers has provided more than $6 million in donations over the last decade; and in 2005 the PGA passed the $1 million mark in charitable donations (Babiak and Wolfe, 2009; Extejt, 2004; Inoue *et al.*, 2011).

It is a reasonable assumption that those organizations which are the recipients of charitable donations will derive some benefit from those donations, since those donations would normally be used to fund the "good causes" in which those organizations are involved. Of course, there are theoretically limiting situations in which recipient organizations might conceivably be damaged by an increase in the receipt of charitable donations, for example if this resulted in a reduction in public funding equivalent to, or even greater than, the increase in charitable donations. However, this is a limiting case and it is reasonable to assume that recipient organizations, and those for whom they provide services, would normally benefit from charitable donations.

Using sport to support local community projects

The effectiveness of schemes of this kind – and therefore the question of whether local communities derive any significant benefits from such schemes – is much more difficult to judge. There are two key points to be made in this regard. The first is that such schemes are usually characterized by an absence of any built-in monitoring in terms of which their effectiveness can be judged. As Porter and Kramer (2006: 81) have noted in relation to CSR activities more generally, organizations typically describe their philanthropic activities in terms of dollars or volunteer hours spent, "but almost never in terms of impact." The second point is that grand claims are often made for the impact which such schemes can have on local communities. Consider, for example, the claims made on behalf of the Tottenham Hotspur Foundation, a charitable foundation established by the London soccer club, Tottenham Hotspur, which according to its website "is committed to providing the best sports, health, training and education programs for all our communities; creating opportunities, encouraging enterprise and innovation, promoting social cohesion and enhancing life skills" (Tottenham Hotspur Foundation, 2012). The foundation aims to:

> use sport and in particular football as a vehicle to create life changing opportunities for children, groups and individuals within communities … Activities are based on a belief that engagement through sport can result in far more than developing sports skills. It can harness a sense of mutual respect and trust, widen horizons, raise aspirations and provide opportunities to young people regardless of race, sex or age.
>
> (Tottenham Hotspur Foundation, 2012)

These are indeed very grand claims though there appears to be almost no systematic supporting empirical evidence. However, although there appears to be an absence of systematic

43

monitoring of community schemes run by, or in association with, sports clubs, there have been some attempts to evaluate similar claims made in relation to schemes – whether publicly funded or funded by charitable donations – which use sport as a means of seeking to promote health or education, to divert young people from drug use or antisocial behavior, or to promote aspects of community development such as social cohesion.

Within the UK, the most extensive review of such initiatives is probably that by Coalter (2007), who has examined the impact of sport-based community schemes on such things as social regeneration, educational performance, and crime prevention. The same author notes that ideological assumptions about the nature of sport and the effectiveness of sporting interventions have given rise to a number of presumed outcomes, though these have "rarely been articulated systematically, and even less frequently monitored and evaluated." For example, in an analysis of 180 programs on sport and social exclusion, only 11 had anything approaching rigorous evaluations, while a review of 120 programs for at-risk youth work in the USA found that only 4 percent undertook pre/post-evaluation of participation-related changes (Coalter, 2007: 21). And in an examination of sport-based community schemes designed to reduce drug use and anti-social behavior among young people, Smith and Waddington (2004) have pointed out that not only is there a general absence of supporting empirical evidence but also a number of theoretical reasons why one might be skeptical about the claims made about the effectiveness of such schemes.

One reason why such schemes have only rarely been subject to proper evaluation is that such schemes have frequently been initiated by those whom Lapchick (1989) has called "true believers" and whom Coalter (2007) has described as "sports evangelists." As Smith and Waddington (2004: 281) have noted, the ideological commitment of "true believers" leads all too often to an uncritical acceptance of the idea that sport is "unambiguously wholesome and healthy in both a physical and moral sense" and as a consequence, they find it difficult, in Coalter's words (2007: 7) "to think more clearly, analytically and less emotionally" about sport and its potential to deliver in relation to community based projects. However, a more analytical and less emotional approach is essential if we are to enhance our understanding of the impact of sport-based initiatives on the wider community.

Writing about CSR in professional sport, Babiak and Wolfe (2009) have proposed a framework which may be useful in studying some aspects of the relationship between sports organizations and the intended beneficiaries of CSR programs. They distinguish between corporate-centric CSR, stakeholder-centric CSR, and strategic CSR within the sport business. Corporate-centric CSR is largely internally driven and is based on and reflects the core strengths of the club or organization; they cite the example of the "Punt, Pass, and Kick" program which is designed to give boys and girls the opportunity to show their skills in NFL stadiums and to support the development of young athletes. Stakeholder-centric CSR is largely externally driven and involves sport clubs or organizations in responding to a broader social problem, as defined by groups within the wider society; they cite the example of the NBA's "Read to Achieve" program, aimed at encouraging young people to develop a love of reading. Strategic CSR initiatives draw upon an organization's core competences to deliver programs targeted at broader social problems. On the basis of this classification, they hypothesize differential impacts on the local community for different kinds of CSR. More specifically, they hypothesize: (1) given that corporate-centric CSR initiatives emphasize corporate competencies (for example in the NFL scheme, skills in football coaching) but tend to neglect broader societal needs, the impact of this type of CSR on the wider society will be limited; (2) given that stakeholder-centric CSR programs focus on broader societal needs, but do not draw upon the organization's core competencies (for example NBA players and clubs have no obvious competence in teaching or encouraging children to read), such initiatives will not serve external constituents as well as initiatives of organizations that have capabilities more directly related to the social issue being addressed. Furthermore, given that these programs are not based on organizational capabilities, they are unlikely to be sustained over a long period; (3) strategic CSR programs, which involve the use of an organization's core competencies in order to tackle a broader social problem, are most likely to have optimum benefits both for the target groups and for the company.

It may well be the case, as Babiak and Wolfe suggest, that the impact of CSR schemes will vary depending upon, among other things, the type of CSR scheme. However, that issue can only be adequately resolved by empirical research. As Godfrey (2009: 710) has noted, such empirical research "should focus on the real impacts of ... CSR initiatives by sport organizations" and he suggests that one research question, for example, would be "does community participation and support by athletes break down or reinforce existing gender, ethnicity, or racial roles and stereotypes?" Until such research has been undertaken, it is best to treat claims about the beneficial impacts of sport-based schemes on local communities with some skepticism. If the benefits of CSR to sports clubs are relatively clear, the benefits of CSR to local communities are much less clear.

CSR and international development

While the CSR programs of many sports clubs tend to have a local or community focus, the activities of international sports organizations such as FIFA, or of international sports manufacturing companies such as Adidas, Nike, and Reebok, may have important implications for broader processes of social development in less developed countries. And as we noted earlier, some of the most trenchant criticism of CSR has been made in relation to development issues. Particularly relevant in this regard are the comments of Peter Utting, Deputy Director and CSR research co-ordinator at the UN Research Institute for Social Development.

Utting (2004) has argued that, while CSR may provide some help in dealing with the worst symptoms of under-development, it may also be used to deflect criticism of corporations, reduce the demand for external regulation, and undermine the position of trade unions. Perhaps most importantly, he also suggests that there are a number of key political and economic mechanisms through which large international companies undermine the development prospects of poor countries and these do not figure in the CSR agenda of companies. In this regard, he cites the strengthening of global corporate property rights and corporate power, "perverse fiscal and pricing practices; and corporate lobbying for macroeconomic policies that can have negative developmental impacts" (Utting, 2004: 4). The implication of Utting's argument is that, in considering the impact of the activities of international organizations on development, we need to take into account not just those activities which are covered in their CSR policy statements, but the impact of their activities more generally. What light does such an approach throw on the development-related CSR policies of international sports organizations?

In 2005 FIFA become one of the first sports organizations to create an internal CSR unit (Bradish and Cronin, 2009: 691). The most high profile aspect of its CSR activities is its "Football for Hope" program, which it describes as "football's commitment to social development." In 2010 FIFA's World Cup was held in South Africa – the first time it had been held in Africa – and, in association with the World Cup, FIFA launched its "20 Centres for 2010" campaign with the aim of "achieving positive social change through football by building twenty Football for Hope Centres for public health, education and football across Africa." It is not clear how many centres have actually been built. At the time of writing (March, 2012) the FIFA website lists eight centres, two in South Africa and one each in Mali, Ghana, Namibia, Rwanda, Kenya, and Lesotho (FIFA, n.d). The activities of each centre are listed but no information is provided to suggest that the impact of these centers on health, education, or other aspects of development is being monitored.

However it is important also to take into account other aspects of FIFA's involvement in Africa via the 2010 World Cup. In 2010 the BBC revealed what it described as "the remarkable tax concessions that the world football authority FIFA demands of countries that wish to host a World Cup competition" (BBC, 2010). Details of these tax concessions were not made public until 2010 because FIFA requires all aspects of the technical bid document to remain confidential. However, in 2010 the Dutch government, which had made a joint bid with Belgium for the 2018 or 2022 World Cup, published on its website all the guarantees which FIFA had demanded, including a guarantee that FIFA would be exempt from all taxes in the host country (BBC, 2010). This involves, of course, a very substantial transfer of funds from the government of the host country – in the case of the 2010 World Cup, South Africa – to FIFA.

Szymanski (2010) has suggested that the 2010 World Cup in South Africa was "a bonanza for FIFA" and that, in economic terms, "only FIFA wins the World Cup." Towards the end of the 2010 competition, several media outlets produced highly critical reports which focused on the fact that while the economic benefits to South Africa were not clear, FIFA had "walk[ed] away with a reported profit of £2billion tax free" (*Observer*, July 11, 2010). A South African reporter, Rian Malan, writing in *The Daily Telegraph* (2010), concluded:

> South Africa winds up with 10 new stadiums, some smart new infrastructure and £450 million in tourist cash. FIFA walks off with about £2 billion in tax-free profits 50 percent more than it made at the last World Cup in Germany. The politicians who negotiated this deal clearly gave the farm away. Now they are laying down a smoke-screen, hoping we don't notice how thoroughly we've been diddled.
>
> (Malan, 2010)

Without belaboring the point, it is clear that, in order to understand the impact which FIFA has on social development in South Africa, it is important to take into account not just their "Football for Hope" program but also FIFA's demand for tax-free status in South Africa during the World Cup, which would almost certainly fall within Utting's description of a "perverse fiscal practice … that can have negative developmental impacts." More generally it might be said in relation to FIFA that, as Breitbarth and Harris (2008: 182) have noted, despite the establishment of FIFA's CSR unit, "the general moral integrity of the organization and a number of its 'goodwill' activities (e.g., the Goal Programme) remains doubtful."

The CSR policies of international companies which manufacture sports clothing raise rather different issues, central among which are those relating to wages and working conditions in the factories in which the goods are made. In the 1990s Nike was the subject of serious allegations relating to low wages, poor working conditions and the use of child labor in the factories in Pakistan in which Nike goods were manufactured. Nike responded to these criticisms by developing CSR policies which sought to address these issues. Today Nike, together with Adidas and Puma, have developed CSR policies and codes of conduct for their suppliers which state, among other things, that their suppliers must pay any national minimum wage, and must provide minimally acceptable working conditions. Notwithstanding the development of these CSR policies, however, it is clear that poor working conditions and illegal practices continue to characterize many of the factories in which these companies' sportswear is made.

As noted earlier most CSR schemes run by sports clubs are characterized by a lack of systematic monitoring. However, this is not the case with Nike, who has sought to monitor several aspects of their CSR programs and their code of conduct for their suppliers. However, Nike's own monitoring has highlighted a lack of progress towards their targets in several key areas. For example, in 2006, Richard Locke of the MIT School of Management examined Nike's own audit data and concluded that despite "significant efforts and investments by Nike … workplace conditions in almost 80 percent of its suppliers have either remained the same or worsened over time" (Levenson, 2008). Nike's own corporate responsibility report for 2007–09 indicated that excessive overtime working (above 60 hours per week) had taken place in 20 percent of the companies manufacturing its clothing in 2007, and that this had increased to 22 percent in 2008 and 24 percent in 2009 (Nike, Inc., n.d.).

Most recently, a detailed report published by War on Want (2012) and based on interviews with workers at six factories in Bangladesh which manufacture sportswear for Nike, Adidas, and Puma, documented continuing low wages, poor working conditions, and illegal practices. Although Bangladesh has the lowest minimum wage in Asia, five of the six factories did not even pay their workers this legal minimum wage. The average basic wage for all workers was £1.18 a day, while workers' total pay, including overtime, equated to just 16 pence per hour. As War on Want pointed out, it would take the average worker nearly 14,000 years to earn the equivalent of Puma's £5.1 million sponsorship package with Usain Bolt (War on Want, 2012: 4–5). To make up their incomes, workers worked excessively long hours, and all the factories supplying Nike, Adidas, and Puma broke the law by illegally employing staff for over 60 hours per week. War on Want also noted that many of the "impacts of exploitation within the clothing industry, such as long hours, hit women harder than men, given the entrenched cultural norms in which women are responsible for domestic work as well as taking care of their families" (2012: 8). The report noted that many women had not been given the full paid maternity leave to which they are entitled under Bangladeshi law, while it recorded that "sexual harassment and discrimination are also widespread within the factories we visited" (2012: 9). These data suggest that there have not been significant improvements in wages and working conditions, and that the development of CSR policies by these companies has had relatively little impact on those countries.

Interestingly, Nike's 2007–09 report indicates that it has had some success in meeting some environmental targets within its CSR program. For example, the report indicates a 19 percent reduction in waste in the manufacture of shoes between 2005 and 2009 and significant improvements in energy efficiency, with both a reduced energy use footprint and reduced costs. These data, taken together with the data about working conditions in Bangladeshi factories outlined above, suggest a conclusion which is not, perhaps, altogether surprising: that companies may be more likely to meet their CSR targets if these relate to green issues involving reductions in waste and energy cost savings and less likely to meet CSR targets in relation to issues such as wages, working conditions, workers' rights and health and safety at work, which might be seen as more likely to impact adversely on companies' profitability.

Blowfield and Frynas (2005: 499) noted that numerous claims have been made about the contribution CSR can make to poverty alleviation and other development goals, but they concluded that "current CSR approaches do not warrant such claims." This is perhaps also an appropriate conclusion in relation to the impact of CSR policies of international sports organizations. While more data are required, such data as do exist suggest that we should not assume that the CSR policies of international sports organizations produce significant benefits for developing countries.

The sociogenesis of CSR

Many scholars who have written about CSR have commented on what might be called the sociogenesis of CSR, that is, the social conditions under which companies have initiated CSR policies. Significantly, there appears to be a high degree of unanimity among scholars about what these conditions are. What is perhaps most surprising is that this unanimity is found among scholars representing all three wings of the debate identified by Broomhill, that is neoliberals, neo-Keynesians and radical political economists. For example Jo, who is a radical critic of CSR and who has charted the development of CSR or its forerunners from the mid-1800s, has noted that varieties of CSR "flourished during and after the crises of capitalism in [the] 1930s, 1970s, and 2000s" and he notes that the "recent surge in CSR researches corresponds to the growth in anti-corporate movement, environmental awareness, and shareholder/stakeholder pressure on corporate governance" (Jo, 2011: 2). Younkins (2000: 1), writing as a neoliberal, similarly suggests that the concept of CSR "can be traced to actions taken and pronouncements made by American business leaders as strategic responses to anti-business sentiments that developed during the late 1800s and early 1900s." And Broomhill himself has suggested that during periods "when corporations have become subject to public criticism and attempts at regulation, they have attempted to re-establish their legitimacy by adopting CSR-style strategies." He cites some telling examples: (1) in the late-nineteenth century the emergence of large corporations and the era of robber barons in the US led to the development of the anti-trust movement and, in response, corporations emphasized corporate responsibility as a way of avoiding government regulation; (2) in the late 1960s and 1970s a new wave of concern about the social and environmental impact of transnational corporations again led to increased attempts to regulate corporate activity and this, in turn, led a large number of US companies to adopt codes of conduct; (3) in the 1990s, criticism of corporate practices again escalated with criticisms from international trades unions, development NGOs and human rights organizations, and CSR discourse and programs emerged in part as a direct response to these pressures (Broomhill, 2007: 9–11). Walker and Kent (2009: 743–4) have similarly pointed out that in the early twenty-first century, consumer distrust of many corporations is high, "with the misdeeds of a few tainting the marketplace for the rest" and they add that many organizations "have responded to the mounting scrutiny and consumer demands by integrating elements of social responsibility into their business operations." The common thread in all these analyses is clear: the long-term development of CSR has occurred in a series of phases, or waves, each of which can be broadly understood as a response by corporations to criticism of what have been widely perceived as wrongful or socially irresponsible actions on their part.

Examples of CSR policies within sport which have been developed under these circumstances are not difficult to find. Perhaps most well known is the case of Nike, cited earlier. In 1996 Nike faced widespread criticism that factories which made its sportswear in Vietnam, Indonesia, and China failed to meet even the lowest standards of working conditions. Nike neither owned nor operated these factories and initially responded by saying it was not responsible for the conditions under which its clothing was made. That only fuelled more criticism, leading to a US television documentary entitled "Just do it – or else," which detailed the poor working conditions. Two years after the initial criticisms, and following protests and a strike of some 3,000 Chinese factory workers, Nike began to shift its approach to CSR by establishing a code of conduct and seeking to monitor its operations (Business China, 2008: 3). In similar fashion, FIFA's establishment of its CSR unit in 2005 followed several years during which FIFA's reputation had been badly damaged by persistent allegations of bribery and corruption (Jennings, 2006). In the US in 2007 there was a media frenzy as animal rights advocates demonstrated outside the NFL's headquarters to urge the league to suspend Atlanta Falcons quarterback Michael Vick, who had been indicted (and was later convicted) on charges related to dog fighting; the NFL responded by working with the American Society for the Prevention of Cruelty to Animals on public service announcements and programs to help educated players and the public (Battista, 2007). And Breitbarth and Harris (2008) correctly locate the development of "Football in the Community" schemes in England in the context of a growing number of problems associated with professional football – including governance at club and association level, treatment of supporters in terms of ticket prices and their recognition as stakeholders by the clubs, football hooliganism and crime, and racism in football – which had led to widespread criticism of clubs and the Football Association (FA) and to demands for the appointment of an independent regulator.

It is important to make clear that we are not suggesting that CSR initiatives *only* take place when organizations are subject to overt public criticism or demands for external regulation; such an argument would be patently false, for it is clear that organizations may, and do, initiate CSR policies under a variety of social conditions. However, there seems to be a clear consensus among scholars that they are more likely to initiate CSR policies under these conditions. Put briefly, the social pattern of CSR initiatives appears quite clear: phases, or spurts, in CSR initiatives have most typically followed widespread public criticism of corporate behavior.

In this regard it is interesting to note that almost all professional sports teams in the US have established team foundations and this has led Babiak and Wolfe (2009) to ask whether sport is unique with regard to CSR. One aspect of professional sport to which they point is of particular relevance in the context of the present discussion, namely its transparency. They point out that almost everything achieved by the team leadership (e.g., player signings, salaries, who plays, changes in team strategies) and their contributions to good causes, is open knowledge. Perhaps more importantly, so too is the off-field behavior of players. They note that organizations in other industries rarely face the same scrutiny of their activities and if an employee of a manufacturing company engages in immoral or illegal behavior, few people are likely to hear of it. However, they note that "if there is a parallel situation with an athlete or coach, it often leads to a media frenzy," and they cite the cases of Tank Johnson's probation violation, Michael Vick's involvement in dog fighting and Pacman-Jones's off-field issues. They conclude that sports organizations "may engage in CSR activities as insurance against negative reactions to such occurrences before the fact …or as an effort to improve their image after the fact" (Babiak and Wolfe, 2009: 722–3). In other words, they suggest that the high level of transparency of professional sport makes it particularly vulnerable to public criticism since there is a high probability that any wrongdoing by players or other team representatives will be picked up and amplified by the media.

This suggests that a key benefit of CSR to organizations, whether in the world of sport or elsewhere, is that it provides a means of countering negative media scrutiny; moreover, and perhaps more importantly, this in turn may be effective as a means of fending off external regulation. As we noted above, Broomhill has pointed out how CSR has developed at particular phases when corporations were subject to widespread public criticism and attempts at regulation; at such times, he suggests, corporations have emphasized corporate responsibility as a way of re-establishing their legitimacy and avoiding government regulation. Inoue *et al.* (2011: 535) have similarly pointed out that CSR may also generate public support for reduced government regulation, while Godfrey (2009: 702) also notes that advocates of CSR have suggested that it might "help limit increases in government regulation." Babiak and Wolfe (2009: 719) have noted that one of the intangible benefits of CSR may be that it generates "acquiescence among key regulatory institutions or legislative bodies" and, specifically in relation to sport, they note that sports teams

> do not face legal requirements to engage in community outreach efforts, but … [CSR] may be an effective way to stave off regulation in other areas. There have been governmental pressures on professional sport, most often related to the use of banned performance

enhancing substances and to antitrust legislation exemptions. When the threat of regulation exists, firms are more responsive to social needs.

(Babiak and Wolfe, 2009: 730)

Although most attention has been focused by researchers on the bottom line implications of CSR, it might be that the socio-political consequences, particularly in terms of averting external or governmental regulation, are of no less importance and are deserving of much more detailed analysis than they have received to date.

Conclusions

The central focus of this examination of CSR has been: who benefits? We have seen that while there are some data supporting the idea of a positive association between CSR and profitability, these data should be treated with caution, as the two relevant studies within sport found no supporting evidence of such a relationship. However, the evidence – both from the general management literature and from studies within sport – does suggest that CSR is associated with a wide variety of other benefits to companies.

The benefits of CSR to the wider society seem, however, much less clear. While it is reasonable to assume that recipient organizations and the activities which they promote benefit from direct cash donations, the evidence of wider social benefits from local community schemes in which sports clubs are involved are less clear, partly because there appears to be almost no monitoring of the outcomes of these activities; in this regard, we support the call of Margolis and Walsh for a reorientation of research on CSR towards a greater emphasis on the effects of CSR on the wider society. The impact of international sports organizations and sportswear manufacturers on development also appears problematic, for the currently available data suggest that we should not assume that the CSR policies of international sports organizations produce significant benefits for developing countries.

Finally, we examined the conditions under which CSR policies have been developed and suggested that perhaps the socio-political consequences of CSR may be of considerable importance and that these, too, merit more detailed examination.

References

BBC (2010) 'World Cup: to tax or not to tax?', *BBC news*, May 11 (online). Available at: http://www.bbc.co.uk/news/10091277 (accessed: March 22, 2012).

Babiak, K. and Wolfe, R. (2006) 'More than just a game? Corporate social responsibility and Super Bowl XL', *Sport Marketing Quarterly*, 15, 214–22.

Babiak, K. and Wolfe, R. (2009) 'Determinants of corporate social responsibility in professional sport: internal and external factors', *Journal of Sport Management*, 23, 717–42.

Battista, J. (2007) 'N.F.L. faces protests and pressure over Vick', *New York Times*, July 21 (online). Available at: http://nytimes.com/2007/07/21/sports/football/21vick.html (accessed: March 30, 2012).

Blowfield, M. and Frynas, J. G. (2005) 'Setting new agendas: critical perspectives on corporate social responsibility in the developing world', *International Affairs*, 81 (3), 499–513.

Bradish, C. and Cronin, J. J. (2009) 'Corporate social responsibility in sport', *Journal of Sport Management*, 23, 691–97.

Breitbarth, T. and Harris, P. (2008) 'The role of corporate social responsibility in the football business: towards the development of a conceptual model', *European Sport Management Quarterly*, 8 (2), 179–206.

Broomhill, R. (2007) *Corporate social responsibility: Key issues and debates*, Dunstan Paper no. 1/2007. Adelaide, Don Dunstan Foundation, University of Adelaide.

Business China (2008) 'Just doing it', March 31, pp. 3–4, *Economist Intelligence Unit. The Economics* (online). Available at: http://www.eiu.com/Default.aspx (accessed: August 29, 2012).

Carroll, A. B. (1979) 'A three-dimensional model of corporate social performance', *Academy of Management Review*, 4, 497–505.

Christian Aid (2004) *Behind the Mask: The Real Face of Corporate Responsibility*. London: Christian Aid.

Coalter, F. (2007) *A Wider Role for Sport: Who's Keeping the Score?* London: Routledge.

Draper, R. (2010) 'Chelsea in crisis after new £40 million loss as Abramovich continues funding freeze', *MailOnline*, December 25 (online). Available at: http://www.dailymail.co.uk/sport/football/article-1341591/Chelsea-crisis-new-40million-loss-Abramovitch-continues-funding-freeze.html (accessed: March 9, 2012).

Extejt, M. M. (2004) 'Philanthropy and professional sports teams', *International Journal of Sport Management*, 5, 215–228.

FIFA (n.d.) '20 Centres for hope' (online). Available at: http://www.fifa.com/aboutfifa/socialresponsibility/footballforhope/20centres/index.html (accessed: March 23, 2012).

Friedman, M. (1970) 'The social responsibility of business is to increase its profits', *New York Times Magazine*, September 13, pp. 32–3; 122–6.

Godfrey, P. C. (2009) 'Corporate social responsibility in sport: an overview and key issues', *Journal of Sport Management*, 23, 698–716.

Inoue, Y., Kent, A. and Lee, S. (2011) 'CSR and the bottom line: analyzing the link between CSR and financial performance for professional teams', *Journal of Sport Management*, 25 (6), 531–549.

Jennings, A. (2006) *Foul!: The Secret World of FIFA: Bribes, Vote Rigging and Ticket Scandals*. London: HarperSport.

Jo, T.H. (2011) *Heterodox critiques of corporate social responsibility*, Munich Personal RePEc Archive (online). Available at: http://mpra.ub.uni-muenchen.de/35367 (accessed: August 29, 2012).

Lapchick, R. E. (1989) 'For the true believer', in Stanley Eitzen, D. (ed.) *Sport in Contemporary Society: An Anthology*, 3rd edn, New York: St Martin's Press, pp. 17–23.

Levenson, E. (2008) 'Citizen Nike', *CNN Money*, 17 November (online). Available at:http://money.cnn.com/2008/11/17/news/companies/levenson_nike.fortune/index.htm (accessed: March 23, 2012).

Malan, R. (2010) 'World Cup 2012: the bill – £6.8 billion. The fantasy of success – priceless', *Daily Telegraph*, July 10, p. 46.

McWilliams, A. and Siegel, D. (2001) 'Corporate social responsibility: A theory of the firm perspective', *Academy of Management Review*, 26 (1), 117–27.

Margolis, J. D. and Walsh, J. P. (2003) 'Misery loves companies: rethinking social initiatives by business', *Administrative Science Quarterly*, 48 (2), 268–305.

Nike, Inc. (n.d.) *Corporate responsibility report FY07–09* (online). Available at: http://www.nikebiz.com/crreport/content/pdf/documents/en-US/full-report.pdf (accessed: March 20, 2012).

The Observer (2010) 'Only FIFA wins the World Cup', July 11, p. 48.

Orlitzky, M., Schmidt, F. L. and Rynes, S. L. (2003) 'Corporate social and financial performance: a meta-analysis', *Organization Studies*, 24, 403–41.

Porter, M. E. and Kramer, M. R. (2006) 'Strategy and society: the link between competitive advantage and corporate social responsibility', *Harvard Business Review*, December, 78–92.

Smith, A. and Waddington, I. (2004) 'Using "sport in the community schemes" to tackle crime and drug use among young people: some policy issues and problems', *European Physical Education Review*, 10 (3), 179–98.

Szymanski, S. (2010) 'Only FIFA wins the World Cup', *New Statesman*, July 5 (online). Available at: http://www.newstatesman.com/sport/2010/06/world-cup-south-africa-events (accessed: July 10, 2010).

Tottenham Hotspur Foundation (2012) *What We Do* (online). Available at: http://www.tottenhamhotspur.com/foundation/What+we+do/what-we-do.page? (accessed: April 5, 2012).

Utting, P. (2004) *Corporate Social Responsibility and Business Regulation*, UNRISD Research and Policy Brief 1, Geneva, United Nations Research Institute for Social Development.

Votaw, D. (1972) 'Genius becomes rare: A comment on the doctrine of social responsibility Pt. 1', *California Management Review*, 15 (2), 25–31.

Walker, M. and Kent, A. (2009) 'Do fans care? Assessing the influence of corporate social responsibility on consumer attitudes in the sport industry,' *Journal of Sport Management*, 23, 743–69.

War on Want (2012) *Race to the Bottom*. London: War on Want.

Younkins, E. (2000) 'Individual rights, social responsibilities, and corporations', *The Free Radical*, March/April (online). Available at: http://www.quebecoislibre.org/younkins22.html (accessed: February 8, 2012).

3

VIEWING CSR THROUGH SPORT FROM A CRITICAL PERSPECTIVE

Failing to address gross corporate misconduct?

Roger Levermore

Overview

This chapter has been written as a polemic to encourage debate on whether corporate social responsibility (CSR) through sport (especially that associated with the professional sport industry) can be considered to be "deep." This chapter emphasizes the weaknesses. It uses examples from publicly available documentation and relatively uncontroversial research conducted by the author. Whilst recognizing that some of the "strategic CSR" that accompanies the sports industry undoubtedly contains enough depth that ultimately alters the corporate governance of the industries they interact with (The World Anti-Doping Agency (WADA) arguably has achieved this), I feel that the majority of CSR through sport lacks sufficient substance, promotes too much greenwashing and distorts power relations. In short, the corporate governance of much of the professional sports industry is fundamentally bankrupt; CSR barely makes a dent in improving governance systems. Probably more contentious is my view that what is written in the main body here only touches the surface of the gross misconduct associated with how many sports industries operate. This includes allegations of corruption, bribery, money laundering, links with organized crime, prostitution, the historic alienation and disregard of fans and employees, being economically unsustainable, attempting to *grossly* distort the political decision-making process, racism, sexism and so on.

Introduction

This chapter draws upon empirical research conducted by the author (Levermore, 2010, 2011a, 2011b) and critical narratives of the nature of the sport industry expressed elsewhere, especially in the printed and Internet media. Its central argument is that CSR through sport is largely a "fig leaf" that regularly fails to seriously cover or address the serial weaknesses of the structural, governing foundations of sport encompassed by the term corporate governance. This is particularly so for CSR associated with professional sport.

There are three clear weaknesses associated with the "depth" of CSR through sport. First is the extent of "greenwashing" associated with CSR (Kallio, 2007: 165), whereby business largely uses CSR in an attempt to distract stakeholders (particularly the media and consumers) from its irresponsible actions. Part of the reason for this is the absence of serious measurement (and therefore evidence) that demonstrates sustained benefits for community recipients of CSR initiatives (see Waddington, Chelladurai and Skirstad, Chapter 2). What exists instead is an evaluation process that relates to a managerial, "top-down" political decision-making process where the scope of evaluation is determined by donors or those managing the program. Therefore, not only are the recipients of the program often ignored in the evaluation process, but the wider/deeper epistemology of the program is left unevaluated (Levermore, 2011a).

Second, corporations have been accused of "routine mobilization" in exploiting networks in the political process, strengthened further by CSR activity, to pervert decision-making in public policy to the detriment of civil society (Edward and Willmott, 2008). This manifests itself in, for example, the exclusion of grassroots communities and the disproportionate influence of businesses in shaping CSR (Prieto-Carrón *et al.*, 2006; Calvano, 2008) especially in avoiding more stringent regulatory accountability (Osuji, 2011). Third, the first two issues combined results in CSR having little substance, relevance or lasting impact for society (O'Laughlin, 2008; Hamann and Kapelus, 2004). A significant contributory factor is the irreconcilability in many CSR initiatives between short-term business objectives and longer-term societal ones (Newell, 2005). This is particularly the case for CSR that is conducted as a short-term action surrounding a one-off event (Muthuri *et al.*, 2009).

Prominent authors in this field have acknowledged these varying levels of paucity. For example, Babiak and Wolfe's (2009: 738) exploratory study notes that many studies fail to highlight corporate irresponsibility and other damaging aspects of CSR, suggesting that, "future work should consider such negative elements of CSR – and how they may influence 'saintly' behavior, that may be instituted to counter it."

However, what is written in the main body here only touches the surface of the gross misconduct associated with how the sports industry operates. Few academic books or articles really portray accurately the nature of the corporate governance of many sports industries – to incorporate the pervasive extent of forms of corporate immorality and irresponsibility; that include corruption, administrative malpractice, abuses of employment practice, perversions of unequal power relations, bribery, illegal betting, racism and sexism, to mention just a few. Corporate governance here is taken to mean the Western governance framework that accompanies all organizations and industries; that sets a balance between economic and social goals and a level of accountability and operating within accepted legal obligations. There are of course accounts written on some of these issues such as racism, sexism and corruption (see Jennings (2006) on malpractice at FIFA, Jarvie (1991) on racism and sport and Hargreaves (1994) on sexism in sport, for example). But my argument is that the reality of the levels of corporate irresponsibility are only touched upon and rarely publicly articulated in full detail. There is therefore a "disconnect" between the CSR through sport research and corporate governance literature. Why do I think this is? Partly because of the implicit and explicit threats/penalties incurred (legal, physical, loss of employment) from making specific articulation of examples. I say this from having researched and written on the global politics of sport for over a decade; this has included over 100 informal conversations on the nature of sports governance in my capacity as a lecturer/professor in management schools (particularly related to the running of the UK and European football industry).

Strategic CSR through sport

Despite the depth of analysis of CSR through sport becoming gradually more evident, particularly in articles that are moving away from mapping this relatively new territory in CSR expansion (see, for example, Smith and Westerbeek, 2007; Hamil and Morrow, 2011), I believe that part of the problem here is the way that most of the CSR through sport literature tends to be written from the "strategic CSR" viewpoint that has a tendency to either simply detail the perception that CSR through sport has increased significantly in the last decade or highlight the benefits that it brings to businesses, sport and society (the "win-win-win" perspective). This should not be too surprising with respect to reviews produced by, or for, sports organizations (Akansel *et al.*, 2010; Scottish Premier League, 2011), consultants/trade press (Sport Business, 2011) or by those employed as CSR directors (Morgan, 2010). Yet, a significant proportion of the scholarly work on the sport/CSR relationship also dwells primarily on its instrumental benefits (Ratten, 2010; Ratten and Babiak, 2010; Babiak and Trendafilova, 2010). Echoing the strategic CSR perspective in general, this literature posits that advantages to sport in employing CSR more explicitly and in a widespread manner can include enhancing commercial opportunities for sport businesses through positive brand identity and reputation management (Walters and Chadwick, 2009; Walker *et al.*, 2010; Walker and Heere, 2011), "unlocking" consumers within local communities (Westerbeek, 2010), ease tensions that might exist between sport enterprises and communities, and the ability to develop local authority partnerships (Walters and Chadwick, 2009). In some instances, such as Major League Baseball's social investment in the Dominican Republic (through widespread aid and tailored CSR projects) (as the many programs delivered by the Premier League in many parts of the world as explained in more detail in Chapter 18), "targeted CSR" makes general "good business sense" because it helps engender the development of athletes in fertile environments (Klein, 2009). Breitbarth and Harris (2008) offer a pertinent example of this perspective in their conceptual model that explains how sport can benefit strategically from engagement with CSR and applies empirical data from industrialized countries (England, Germany, Japan and US) to illustrate how this occurs.

Strategic benefits for the business community of CSR through sport (in other words, CSR that companies, especially multinationals, who use sport as their vehicle) starts with the recognition that sport is a "significant social institution" (Godfrey, 2009) that confers "unique" characteristics to CSR such as its communicative power, especially to a youth market, through mass media appeal, passion and interest generated because of its product (Babiak and Wolfe, 2009), and (especially contentious for critical CSR) its ability to influence the political process as it "presents a mechanism to legitimize political and economic systems" (Godfrey, 2009: 699).

Likewise, principally in wider sociological analyses that define CSR through sport broadly, sport assists societal development through its contribution to the functions and requirements of the welfare state in Europe (Heinemann, 2005), by increasing employment (Walters and Chadwick, 2009), the inherent assistance it provides to health and integrative initiatives (Smith and Westerbeek, 2007) and through striking improvements in social capital and economic development due to athlete remittances (Klein, 2009) (see also Levermore, 2010 and McGuire, 2008). This is particularly the case for CSR that surrounds sporting events as "corporations can make a greater contribution to civic and community development through strategic ties to a city's development agenda surrounding the hosting of sporting events" (Misener and Mason, 2010: 495) (see also Misener, Sant and Mason, Chapter 14).

Reinforcing the argument that the focus of CSR through sport is dominated by instrumental, integrative and normative stakeholder perspectives is the prevalence of stakeholder theory in assessing CSR through sport. Smith and Westerbeek (2007) use it as a "conceptual platform" and Hamil and Morrow (2011) apply it to evaluate a review of CSR in the Scottish Premier Football League. The application of stakeholder theory is more deeply embedded by Walters (2009) in an in-depth, qualitative examination of two community organizations linked to the English soccer industry. Babiak and Wolfe (2009: 717), in their review of internal and external factors concerning the determinants of CSR in professional sport, use stakeholder analysis at an agency level to predict "the types of CSR initiatives a sport organization is likely to adopt depending on its internal and/or external orientation" and present a research agenda based on the framework.

Whilst these examples present a demonstration of the predominant focus on the strategic aspect of CSR through sport, issues related to critical perspectives are occasionally referenced without analysis being taken forward. This includes a recognition that CSR through sport can be associated with "greenwashing," a proclivity to exclude communities (Breitbarth and Harris, 2008: 182–184) and a propensity for unethical practices by the rise in the commercialization of sport, through, for example, drug-taking, illegal payments and greed (Wheeler, 1994). This is partly due to the poor levels of transparency and accountability with sport decision-making structures (Godfrey, 2009). A deeper application of critical perspectives was undertaken by Khan *et al.* (2007) who drew attention to some of the problems with a Western-led awareness campaign relating to child labor in the manufacture of soccer balls.

Applying a more "critical CSR" approach to CSR through sport

Three of the core elements associated with critical CSR noted in the introduction (lack of long-term substance, "greenwashing" and unequal power relations) are applied to this analysis of CSR through sport.

Lack of substance to CSR through sport

Application of frameworks that attempt to assess the depth of CSR – such as that developed by Ponte *et al.* (2009) – gauge the depth of CSR through sport (both that by multinationals that use sport as a vehicle for CSR and professional sport doing CSR) as being one of the lowest or weakest forms of CSR. This is particularly the case for the 2010 FIFA's World Cup where a significant level of CSR through sport initiatives, notably those run by multinational corporations (see Levermore, 2011b) are "disengaged" and "distant." Examples of standalone CSR initiatives at the World Cup included Coca-Cola who listed their CSR attached to the tournament as funding a World Cup trophy parade through the African continent, awarding a prize to the best celebration by a player following the scoring of a goal and $1,500 towards the "Water for Schools" program every time a goal was scored. Similarly, McDonald's publicized as some of its CSR initiatives the Player Escort program (escorting players to the stadium) and a vague promise to unite customers through the thrill of football. Ponte *et al.*'s (2009) framework would most likely place these examples to be considered as distant and disengaged because the CSR is, at best, vaguely attached to the core objectives of the organizations and is weakly tied to its stakeholder aspirations of what CSR should be. Incidentally, in 2006, when the South African government established its annual measurement of the extent to which businesses operating in South Africa contributed to the transformation of society through CSR, it probably had such examples in mind in declaring that CSR through sport not be considered as a serious enough component of CSR in sport (Trialogue, 2007).

Particularly weak forms of CSR are thought to be awareness campaigns because they are often ill thought out and linked to sponsorship issues and lack substance (Chen *et al.*, 2008). A lack of substance in awareness campaigns was linked to the 2010 World Cup. For example, the 1Goal program (an initiative to raise international awareness about non-attendance of children at school) was criticized because "such high profile events are hard to reconcile with the realities of schooling in South Africa" (*Mail* and *Guardian*, 2010). It was therefore an example of a particularly poor fit; poorly thought out and misunderstood campaigning.

Deliberate "greenwashing"

The prevalence of "ethical blowback" (Shapiro *et al.*, 2010) in order to detract from negative publicity is implicitly recognized as a motive for engaging in CSR through sport (Walker and Kent, 2009). Taking a broader view, sport is afflicted with contrasting motives (Levermore, 2010); on the one hand it has a "virtuous" potential for promoting various forms of responsible business such as societal development, and on the other, the product of professional sport is heavily tarnished – associated with cheating, corruption and exclusionary practices. For instance, senior representatives of the world governing body of association football – FIFA – have long been accused of corruption and bribery by using its CSR and development funding in a manner to distort the electoral process (Levermore, 2008); such as in using money distributed through its GOAL program (primarily to strengthen the soccer infrastructure around the world but with secondary developmental aspirations) to ensure the re-election of President Sepp Blatter.

Examination of stakeholder groups in the English professional football (soccer) industry of the season 2011/12 highlights organizations that devote considerable energy to CSR through sport, but also have been tarnished by (quite often) staggering levels of corporate mismanagement. The argument being presented here is that these corporations use CSR in general (and sport as a significant vehicle of that CSR) as a means to present themselves in a responsible manner when their corporate governance actions are staggeringly irresponsible. This includes companies such as BSkyB, Deloitte, Npower and William Hill. A particularly apt example in 2012 (with financial institutions in the regular media glare for its unethical action) is Barclays Bank, which has been criticized of corporate irresponsibility, which significantly outweighs the impacts of its CSR initiatives in the sport industry. This includes financial support for the Zimbabwean government (Barnett and Thompson, 2007), accusations of violating international regulation on money laundering (Mollenkamp, 2010), large-scale tax avoidance and the well-publicized way in which it contrived to artificially fix the Libor exchange rate.

Distorting power relations

CSR through sport also stands accused of being largely driven by asymmetrical power relations, where initiatives are heavily influenced by aims infused with top-down, northern, competitive, heterosexual and masculinist traits. Variations of critical CSR – such as neo-colonial critiques (Sage, 1995; Bale and Cronin, 2003) – argue that modern, northern-dominated sports (such as football, baseball and basketball), perpetuate unequal economic and political relations, similar to extractive industries. The 2010 football World Cup, hosted by South Africa, provided an extensive array of examples where unequal power relations were evident. Before the start of the event, long-held concerns were expressed that World Cup strategies privileged elite football at the expense of grassroots soccer (Alegi, 2007). The tournament also witnessed specific examples of exclusion. Poor communities were forcibly evicted from tourist areas and stadia, especially in Cape Town and Durban (Al-Jazeera, 2010) and a pause in xenophobic attacks on African migrants was only temporary as they resumed soon after the World Cup final was played (*The Times of South Africa*, 2010), leading some to question the depth of unification with which the World Cup was credited, deriding it as being "fake nationhood" (Maseko, 2010). Issues around the 2010 World Cup are also discussed in Chapter 2.

Conclusions

This chapter has been written in a polemic nature to encourage debate on assessing the substance of CSR through sport and the ways in which CSR and corporate governance do and do not overlap, especially that associated with the professional sport industry. I want to reiterate that the examples used here on the weaknesses of CSR through sport are based on publicly available documentation and relatively uncontroversial research conducted by the author. This book, and other sources, state that CSR through sport is frequently regarded as being beneficial to business and communities/societies. For sport businesses, CSR can develop positive brand identity and reputation management, "unlock" consumers within local communities and ease tensions that might exist between sport enterprises and communities, whilst also developing local authority partnerships. Strategic benefits for the business community of sport CSR starts with the recognition that sport is a "significant social institution," that confers "unique" characteristics to CSR such as its communicative power, especially to a youth market, through mass media appeal, passion and interest generated because of its "product" and its (contentious) ability to "legitimately" influence political processes. Sport CSR is also said to assist societal development through its contribution to healthy living, anti-crime and other empowering initiatives as well as increase employment and through striking improvements in social capital and economic development due to athlete remittances.

Some of this "strategic CSR" undoubtedly highlights some CSR through sport that does contain enough depth that ultimately alters the corporate governance of the industries they interact with. The World Anti-Doping Agency (WADA) arguably has achieved this and FIFA's new structure on CSR (a two-chamber ethics committee was established in 2012 that investigates corruption allegations in an independent manner) might well deliver in the long-term too. It is too early to comment on their likely success as the process of the FIFA CSR committee was still being formulated at the time of writing this chapter. More contentious is my view that what is written in the main body here only touches the surface of the gross misconduct associated with how many sports industries operate. This includes allegations of corruption, bribery, money laundering, links with organized crime, prostitution, the historic alienation and disregard of fans and employees, being economically unsustainable, attempting to distort the political decision-making process, racism, sexism and so on. Quite often, determining whether CSR is "positive" or "negative" is down to personal judgment on what constitutes ethical behavior. To some, clubs cross the ethical line when altering names of stadia, being sponsored by a company that is deemed not to fit in with a family-friendly image, making an illegal approach for managers and players, or paying grossly inflated salaries for players (whilst paying non-playing staff a meagre salary). Other fans find this acceptable as long as it provides a competitive advantage on the pitch, secured through new player acquisitions and so on. Some of those involved in the management and administration of professional sports might publicly discredit such an argument but many researching and working in sports have privately supported such a viewpoint.

Bibliography

Akansel, B., Ates, E.B., Tapan, P. and Özden, Y. (2010) *Implementation of CSR at European Football Clubs*. FIFA/CIES Program in Sport Management, Report. Istanbul: Bahcesehir University.

Alegi, P. (2007) 'The political economy of mega-stadiums and the underdevelopment of grassroots football in South Africa', *Politikon*, 34 (3), 315–331.

Al-Jazeera (2010) 'Human cost of the World Cup', *Aljazeera*, March 8 (online) Available at: http://english.aljazeera.net/sport/2010/03/20103816395976656.html (accessed: October 22, 2010).

Babiak, K. and Trendafilova, S. (2010) 'CSR and environmental responsibility: Motives and pressures to adopt green management practices', *Corporate Social Responsibility and Environmental Management*, 18 (1), 11–24.

Babiak, K. and Wolfe, R. (2009) 'Determinants of corporate social responsibility in professional sport: Internal and external factors', *Journal of Sport Management*, 23 (5), 717–742.

Bale, J. and Cronin, M. (2003) *Sport and postcolonialism*. London: Frank Cass.

Barnett, A. and Thompson, C. (2007) 'Barclays' millions help to prop up Mugabe regime', *Guardian* (UK), 28 January, p. 1.

Breitbarth, T. and Harris, P. (2008) 'The role of corporate social responsibility in the football business: Towards the development of a conceptual model', *European Sport Management Quarterly*, 8 (2), 179–206.

Calvano, L. (2008) 'Multinational corporations and local communities', *Journal of Business Ethics*, 82 (4), 793–805.

Chen, J.C., Patten, D.M. and Roberts, R.W. (2008) 'Corporate charitable contributions: A corporate social performance or legitimacy strategy', *Journal of Business Ethics*, 82 (1), 131–144.

Edward, P. and Willmott, H. (2008) 'Dialogue. Corporate citizenship. Rise or demise of a myth?', *Academy of Management Review*, 33 (3), 771–775.

Godfrey, P.C. (2009) 'Corporate social responsibility in sport', *Journal of Sport Management*, 23 (5), 698–716.

Hamann, R. and Kapelus, P. (2004) 'Corporate social responsibility in mining in Southern Africa', *Development*, 47 (3), 85–92.

Hamil, S. and Morrow, S. (2011) 'Corporate social responsibility in the Scottish Premier League. Context and motivation', *European Sport Management Quarterly*, 11 (2), 143–170.

Hargreaves, J. (1994) *Sporting Females: Critical Issues in the History and Sociology of Women's Sport*. London: Routledge.

Heinemann, K. (2005) 'Sport and the welfare state in Europe', *European Journal of Sport Science*, 5 (4), 181–188.

Jarvie, G. (1991) *Sport, Racism and Ethnicity*. London: Routledge.

Jennings, A. (2006) *Foul!: The Secret World of FIFA: Bribes, Vote Rigging and Ticket Scandals*. London: HarperSport.

Kallio, T.J. (2007) 'Taboos in corporate social responsibility discourse', *Journal of Business Ethics*, 74 (2), 165–175.

Khan, F.R., Munir, K.A. and Willmott, H. (2007) 'A dark side of institutional entrepreneurship: Soccer balls, child labour and postcolonial impoverishment', *Organization Studies*, 28 (7), 1055–1077.

Klein, A. (2009) 'The transnational view of sport and social development. The case of Dominican baseball', *Sport in Society*, 12 (9), 1118–1131.

Levermore, R. (2008) 'Sport-in-International development. Time to treat it seriously?' *Brown Journal of World Affairs*, 14 (2), 55–66.

Levermore, R. (2010) 'CSR for development through sport. Examining its potential and limitations', *Third World Quarterly*, 31 (2), 223–241.

Levermore, R. (2011a) 'Analysing the extent to which evaluation of corporate social responsibility for development through sport is conducted', *Third World Quarterly*, 32 (3), 322–335.

Levermore, R. (2011b) 'Sport-for-development and the 2010 football World Cup'. *Geography Compass*, 5 (12), 886–897.

Mail and *Guardian* (2010) 'Giving education a sporting chance', *Mail* and *Guardian*, June 25, p. 47.

Maseko, Z. (2010) 'Rainbow-nation patriotism, pah!', *Mail* and *Guardian*, 21 June, p. 21.

McGuire, B. (2008) 'Football in the community: Still the game's best kept secret?' *Soccer & Society*, 9 (4), 439–454.

Misener, L. and Mason, D. (2010) 'Towards a community centred approach to corporate community involvement in the sporting events agenda', *Journal of Management & Organization*, 16 (4), 495–514.

Mollenkamp, C. (2010) 'Probe circles globe to find dirty money', *Wall Street Journal*, September 3, p. 1.

Morgan, S. (2010) 'Creating Chances: The Premier League's corporate social responsibility programme', *Journal of Sponsorship*, 4 (1), 15–25.

Muthuri, J.N., Matten, D. and Moon, J. (2009) 'Employee volunteering and social capital: Contributions to corporate social responsibility', *British Journal of Management*, 20 (1), 75–89.

Newell, P. (2005) 'Citizenship, accountability and community: The limits of CSR agenda', *International Affairs*, 81 (3), 541–557.

O'Laughlin, B. (2008) 'Governing capital? Corporate social responsibility and the limits of regulation', *Development and Change*, 39 (6), 945–957.

Osuji, O. (2011) 'Fluidity of regulation-CSR nexus. The multinational corporate corruption example', *Journal of Business Ethics*, 103 (1), 31–57.

Ponte, S., Richey, K.A. and Baab, M. (2009) 'Bono's product (RED) initiative: Corporate social responsibility that solves the problems of "distant others"', *Third World Quarterly*, 30 (2), 301–317.

Prieto-Carrón, M., Lund-Thomsen, P., Chan, A., Muro, A. and Bhushan, C. (2006) 'Critical perspectives on CSR and development: What we know, what we don't know, and what we need to know', *International Affairs*, 82 (5), 977–987.

Ratten, V. (2010) 'The future of sports management: A social responsibility, philanthropy and entrepreneurship perspective', *Journal of Management & Organization*, 16 (4), 488–494.

Ratten, V. and Babiak, K. (2010) 'Editorial. The role of social responsibility, philanthropy and entrepreneurship in the sport industry', *Journal of Management & Organization*, 16 (4), 482–487.

Sage, G. (1995) 'Deindustrialization and the American sporting goods industry', in Wilcox, R.C. (ed.) *Sport in the Global Village*. Morgantown, W.Va: Fitness Information Technology, 39–51.

Scottish Premier League (2011) *Football Clubs and the Community. SPL Community Report 2011*. Glasgow: Scottish Premier League.

Shapiro, S.L., Giannoulakis, C., Drayer, J. and Wang, C-H. (2010) 'An examination of athletic alumni giving behavior: Development of the former student-athlete donor constraint scale', *Sport Management Review*, 13 (3), 283–295.

Smith, A. and Westerbeek. H. (2007) 'Sport as a vehicle for developing corporate social responsibility', *Journal of Corporate Citizenship*, 25 (7), 43–54.

Sport Business (2011) *Sport and Social Responsibility. Planning, Implementing and Evaluating Effective Sport and CSR Programmes*. London: Sport Business.

The Times of South Africa (2010) 'Xenophobia redux', *The Times (of South Africa)*, July 8, p. 15.

Trialogue (2007) *The CSI Handbook*. 10th edn. Cape Town: Trialogue.

Walker, M. and Heere, B. (2011) 'Consumer attitude toward responsible entities in Sport (CARES): Scale development and model testing', *Sport Management Review*, 14 (2), 153–166.

Walker, M., Heere, B., Parent, M. and Drane, D. (2010) 'Social responsibility and the Olympic Games: The mediating role of consumer attributions', *Journal of Business Ethics*, 95 (4), 659–680.

Walker, M.B. and Kent, A. (2009) 'Do fans care? Assessing the influence of corporate social responsibility on consumer attitudes in the sport industry', *Journal of Sport Management*, 23 (6), 743–769.

Walters, G. (2009) 'Corporate social responsibility through sport: The community sports trust model as a CSR delivery agency', *Journal of Corporate Citizenship*, 35 (3), 81–94.

Walters, G. and Chadwick, S. (2009) 'Corporate citizenship in football: Delivering strategic benefits through stakeholder engagement', *Management Decision*, 47 (1), 51–66.

Westerbeek, H. (2010) 'Commercial sport and local communities: A market niche for social sport business?' *Sport in Society*, 13 (9), 1411–1415.

Wheeler, M. (1994) 'Ethics and the sports business', *Business Ethics*, 3 (1), 8–15.

Further reading

AT Kearney (2010) *The A.T. Kearney EU football sustainability study: Is European football too popular to fail?* Düsseldorf: A.T. Kearney.

Babiak, K. and Wolfe, R. (2006) 'More than just a game? Corporate social responsibility and Super Bowl XL', *Sport Marketing Quarterly*, 15 (4), 214–222.

Bradish, C. and Cronin, J.J. (2009) 'Corporate social responsibility in sport', *Journal of Sport Management*, 23 (5), 691–697.

Carroll, A. (1991) 'The pyramid of corporate social responsibility: Toward the moral management of organizational stakeholders', *Business Horizons*, 34 (4), 39–48.

Chand, M. (2009) 'Performance management practices and organizational strategy: A study of Indian leisure industries', *International Journal of Leisure and Tourism Marketing*, 1 (1), 12–28.

Chandler, A.D. (1962) *Strategy structure*. Cambridge, MA: MIT Press.

Dahlsrud, A. (2006) 'How corporate social responsibility is defined: An analysis of 37 definitions', *Corporate Social Responsibility and Environmental Management*, 15 (1), 1–13.

Detomasi, D.A. (2008) 'The political roots of corporate social responsibility', *Journal of Business Ethics*, 82 (4), 807–819.

Ede, F.O., Panigrahi, B., Stuart, J. and Calcich, S. (2000) 'Ethics in small minority businesses', *Journal of Business Ethics*, 26 (2), 133–146.

European Communities (EC) (2006) 'The new SME definition. User guide and model declaration', *European Communities/European Commission (2003/361/EG)*, Enterprise and Industry Publications: Luxembourg.

Fassin, Y. (2008) 'SMEs and the fallacy of formalising CSR', *Business ethics. A European review*, 17 (4), 364–378.

Fassin, Y., Rosse, A.V. and Buelens, M. (2011) 'Small-business owner-managers' perceptions of business ethics and CSR-related concepts', *Journal of Business Ethics*, 98 (3), 425–453.

Fitjar, R.D. (2011) 'Little big firms? Corporate social responsibility in small businesses that do not compete against big ones', *Business Ethics. A European Review*, 20 (1), 30–43.

Garay, L. and Font, X. (2012) 'Doing good to do well? Corporate social responsibility reasons, practices and impacts in small and medium accommodation enterprises', *International Journal of Hospitality Management*, 25, 662–682.

Garriga, E. and Melé, D. (2004) 'Corporate social responsibility theories. Mapping the territory', *Journal of Business Ethics*, 53 (1–2), 51–71.

Giardina, M.D. (2010) 'One day, one goal? PUMA, corporate philanthropy and the cultural politics of brand Africa', *Sport in Society*, 13 (1), 130–142.

Hoivik, H. von W. and Shankar, D. (2011) 'How can SMEs in a cluster respond to global demands for corporate responsibility?' *Journal of Business Ethics*, 101 (2), 175–195.

Irwin, R.L., Lachowetz, T., Cornwell, T.B. and Clark, J.S. (2003) 'Cause-related sport sponsorship: An assessment of spectator beliefs, attitudes, and behavioral intentions', *Sports Marketing Quarterly*, 12 (3), 131–139.

Jenkins, H. (2009) 'A "business opportunity" model of corporate social responsibility for small- and medium- sized enterprises', *Business Ethics. A European Review*, 18 (1), 21–36.

McCoy, D., Kembhavi, G., Patel, J. and Luintel, A. (2009) 'The Bill & Melinda Gates Foundation's grant-making programme for global health', *The Lancet*, 373, 1645–1653.

Morsing, M. and Perrini, F. (2009) 'CSR in SMEs. Do SMEs matter for the CSR agenda?', *Business Ethics. A European Review*, 18 (1), 1–6.

Niehm, L.S., Swinney, J. and Miller, N.J. (2008) 'Community social responsibility and its consequences for family business performance', *Journal of Small Business Management*, 46 (3), 331–350.

Ouchi, W.G. (1980) 'Markets, bureaucracies and clans', *Administrative Science Quarterly*, 25 (1), 129–141.

Palazzo, G. and Richter, U. (2005) 'CSR business as usual? The case of the Tobacco industry', *Journal of Business Ethics*, 61 (4), 387–401.

Phillips, R. (2008) 'European and American perspectives on corporate social responsibility', *Business Ethics. A European Review*, 17 (1), 69–73.

Porter, M.E. (2000) 'Location, competition and economic development: Local clusters in a global economy', *Economic Development Quarterly*, 14 (1), 15–34.

Russo, A. and Tencati, A. (2009) 'Formal vs. informal CSR strategies: Evidence from Italian micro, small, medium-sized and large firms', *Journal of Business Ethics*, 85 (2), 339–353.

Russo, A. and Perrini, F. (2010) 'Investigating stakeholder theory and social capital: CSR in large firms and SMEs', *Journal of Business Ethics*, 91 (2), 207–221.

Sheth, H. and Babiak, K. (2010) 'Beyond the game: Perceptions and practices of corporate social responsibility in the professional sport industry', *Journal of Business Ethics*, 91 (3), 433–450.

Slack, R. and Shrives, P. (2008) 'Social disclosure and legitimacy in Premier League football clubs: The first ten years', *Journal of Applied Accounting Research*, 9 (1), 17–28.

Spaaij, R. and Westerbeek, H. (2010) 'Sport business and social capital: A contradiction in terms?' *Sport in Society*, 13 (9), 1356–1373.

Spence, L.J. (2007) 'CSR and small business in a European policy context: The Five "c"s of CSR and small business research agenda 2007', *Business and Society Review*, 112 (4), 533–552.

Spence, L.J., Schmidpeter, R. and Habisch, A. (2003) 'Assessing social capital. Small and medium sized enterprises in Germany and the UK', *Journal of Business Ethics*, 47 (1), 17–29.

Supporters Direct (2010) *The Social and Community Value of Football*. Manchester: Substance (online). Available at: http://clients.squareeye.net/uploads/sd/Full_Report_singles_3C.pdf (accessed: August 22, 2012).

Trialogue (2010) 'Making CSI matter conference, May 2010' (online). Available at: http.//www.trialogue. co.za/conference2010_new.html (accessed: July 7, 2010; now offline).

Udayasankar, K. (2007) 'Corporate social responsibility and firm size', *Journal of Business Ethics*, 83 (2), 167–175.

Uhlaner, L.M., van Goor-Balk, H.J.M. and Masurel, E. (2004) 'Family business and corporate social responsibility in a sample of Dutch firms', *Journal of Small Business and Enterprise Development*, 11 (2), 186–194.

UNIDO and World Summit on Sustainable Development (2002) *Corporate Social Responsibility. Implications for SMEs in Developing Countries. UNIDO* (online). Available at: http://195.130.87.21:8080/dspace/bitstream/123456789/1169/1/Corporate%20social%20responsibility%20%20implications%20for%20small%20and%20medium%20enterprises%20in%20developing%20countries.pdf (accessed: August 22, 2012).

Walters, G and Tacon, R. (2010) 'Corporate social responsibility in sport: Stakeholder management in the UK football industry', *Journal of Management and Organization*, 16 (4), 566–586.

World Business Council for Sustainable Development (n.d.) *CSR. Meeting Changing Expectation*. Geneva. Switzerland, World Business Council for Sustainable Development.

Worthington, I., Ram, M. and Jones. T. (2006) 'Exploring corporate social responsibility in the UK, Asian small business community', *Journal of Business Ethics*, 67 (2), 201–217.

Wozniak, A. (2011) 'The missing subject found in the subject who does the thinking: Kierkgaard, the ethical and the subjectivity of critical theorists', *Business Ethics. A European Review*, 20 (3), 304–315.

Wulfson, M. (2001) 'The ethics of corporate social responsibility and philanthropic ventures', *Journal of Business Ethics*, 29 (1–2), 135–145.

4

TEACHING CSR

Considerations for sport management education

Cheri L. Bradish, Cheryl Mallen and Eli Wolff

Overview

As the field of sport management evolves, it is imperative that our discipline keeps pace of leading and crucial management concepts and practice. Of note the re-emergence of corporate social responsibility (CSR) in theory and practice in mainstream "business" has particularly important implications for sport management study. As such, CSR should be well-incorporated into educational offerings and expectations as we prepare the next generation of sport management professionals, as related concepts are crucial for sound sport management practice. This chapter approaches "CSR in sport" education from a holistic mindset, borrowing from accepted and common CSR business practice; while acknowledging the unique and important sport business landscape. Underpinning each concept and understanding, is the importance of sustainability and authenticity – in our related teaching, learning and application to the sport context. The objective of this chapter is to provide an overview of "CSR in sport" as related to educational programming and offerings for higher education programs worldwide. This chapter will review key definitions of the CSR concepts for undergraduate and graduate sport management and related students; will overview best practices for teaching related concepts; and will include recommended course requirements, materials and evaluation tools to maximize the related CSR concepts and learning for sport management study and practice.

Introduction

As is discussed broadly throughout this text, CSR subscribes to myriad definitions and interpretations, but at its core, can be broadly understood as the responsibility of organizations to be ethical and accountable to the needs of their society, as well as to their stakeholders (Bradish and Cronin, 2009). The concept of CSR also involves a movement from the "profits only" perspective to being concerned with "social well-being" (Hamann *et al.*, 2003: 39). This well-being involves sustainable practices and a value for all members of society along with the support that each member deserves a socially and culturally viable living environment, excellent natural environmental conditions and sustainable financial practices that support the community.

As the corresponding concepts and accountability here have been re-introduced to management practice and have received growing research attention and research, a number of important frameworks have been developed (Carroll, 1979, 1999) and research offered in this domain (Margolis and Walsh, 2003; Varadarajan and Menon, 1988), including recent and important sport inquiry and specialization (Breitbarth and Harris, 2008; Walker and Kent, 2009; Walker *et al.*, 2007) – this has re-entered the education domain as well. In particular, sport management programs have begun to include a number of concepts and offerings from within the CSR "umbrella" of responsibilities in their program offerings.

This chapter is concerned with the provision of CSR education to sport management students worldwide. The authors argue that higher education in sport management has a key role to play in terms of educating students to effectively enact CSR for the benefit of society and business. The foundations of this education include understanding the concept of what CSR means for sport, the principles and competencies for enacting CSR within sport, including understanding of the barriers and capabilities of CSR within the sport industry. This sport industry includes multiple spheres such as professional sport, amateur sport from the local to the international levels, including the Olympic Games, along with collegiate/university athletics. Further, given the unique nature of sport where, at the core, human performance and the personal – and often unpredictable – pursuit of athletic excellence occurs, social responsibility, accountability, and the value of being "good sports" is particularly important for athletes and sport managers alike. In addition, there is significant evidence that CSR and related topics under the umbrella of CSR, such as Sport for Development and sport philanthropy, particularly resonates with students (Mallen *et al.*, 2008) and a number of related courses and programs have recently emerged.

This chapter begins the discussion by outlining various manners encompassed under the umbrella of CSR and then examines sustainability and authenticity in CSR. Importantly, the discussion considers the role of citizenship in sport management and extends the concept of CSR to one of CSR and Accountability (CSR&A) (Hamann *et al.*, 2003). Next, principles and key concepts in CSR&A education are provided and extend to the concepts of Sport for Development, global sport development and community sport development. Then, another key component of CSR&A is introduced – environmental sustainability (ES), including its principles and activities. Finally, the topic of why CSR&A should be taught, along with concepts in providing this teaching in sport management programs is outlined. The conclusion includes a question on why be "good sports"? In addition, three debate questions are offered.

The umbrella of CSR

Perhaps one of the best approaches to reviewing and offering CSR in sport education is to consider the "umbrella" of responsibilities of CSR in general, and incorporate and adapt these to the sport context. Essentially, this mindset holistically considers "the various ways in which business' relationship with society is being defined, managed, and acted upon" (Bradish and Cronin, 2009). As such, a number of areas of inquiry and attention are related to the study of social responsibility, including the following:

- legal compliance (the responsibility of a company toward society to obey the law);
- philanthropy and community investment ("giving back" to society through philanthropic donations; includes cause-related or affinity marketing);
- environmental management (since the 1960s society has questioned the cost of growth to the environment; the environmental impact; and has spawned a greening revolution, including an emphasis on eco-efficiency use to highlight that there need not be a trade-off between business and environmental performance);
- animal rights (since the 1960s, in the context of a growing list of endangered species, the provision of rights for the welfare of animals from around the world has been promoted);

- human rights (since 1945, after World War II, the notion of a universal set of human rights shared by all people, and fundamental principles of freedom to all persons to lead a digni-fied life, free from fear or want, and free to express independent beliefs was established);
- workers' rights and welfare (during the 1990s a broader movement examining the glo-balized economy emerged, with a focus on the inequities of supply chains and workers' rights, came to light, such as the related concerns of "sweatshops" in third world countries for companies such as Nike, Reebok and Adidas, for example);
- market relations (throughout the 1950s and 1960s, faith-based and other organizations responded to unequal distribution of the wealth in the market with the creation of advo-cacy organizations, such as Oxfam);
- corruption (UN Global Compact; i.e., business such as mining, construction and defense have been criticized for paying commission to win business, especially in countries with limited transparency);
- corporate governance (including racial and gender diversity).

(adapted from *Corporate Responsibility* by Blowfield and Murray, 2008)

Thus, to understand, incorporate and communicate these nine areas of CSR responsibility, especially within a sport context with reflective practice and critical assessment, educators are well able to introduce the concept of – and set the groundwork for – CSR management and interpretation.

Underscoring CSR – sustainability and authenticity

Perhaps no better lesson – or course "theme" – should underscore the important of CSR education than that of sustainability and authenticity, specifically related to "sustainable and authentic programming and practice" of firms, associations and individuals engaged in any type of social responsibility work. Students need to be aware that CSR initiatives must be both sus-tainable and authentic in their commitment within a sport organization; meaning they should create a legacy, have in-depth programming, and, of particular importance, that a CSR mindset permeates and is embraced by all levels and layers of a sport organization. CSR, thus, needs to also be discussed in terms of organizational accountability.

Extending the concept of corporate social responsibility to include accountability

In this chapter, the concept of CSR is discussed broadly to include both Corporate Social Responsibility and Accountability (CSR&A), and, as such, CSR and CSR&A will be used interchangeably. This adaptation is important as it means that responsibility is inextricably linked to one's accountability for the sustainability of the social, cultural, financial and environ-mental aspects at the intersection of sport and our global societies.

In this chapter, responsibility is interpreted to mean that every member in sport management is an agent within the sport collective that is responsible for the enactment of socially responsible sport management decision-making. In addition, accountability is not intended as legislation that one must enact to ensure action has been taken; but, it is being personally accountable for the integration of socially responsible decision-making. Practitioners in sport management need to broadly serve as watchdogs for broad sustainability concerns throughout their industry, including accountability for the use of sport to counter social deterioration or financial inequalities as well as to promote and ensure the safeguarding of the natural environment.

CSR&A citizenship in sport management

Bateman and Organ (1983) coined the term "organizational citizenship behavior" and, since then, the term has been the focus of a variety of behaviors in a number of fields. An interpretation of this term by the authors is that a CSR&A citizen is an individual or group of individuals within an organization that embodies the care, concern and actions to generate policies, systems, processes, the use of technology, precautions, planning and spending for sustainability. An implication is that constituent sport management CSR&A citizens can be involved within any sport corporation, organization, counsel, government entity, facility, event or individual (including athletes) that encourage the implementation of sustainability within sport. Further, these citizens can be focused on any of the multiple sectors within the industry, such as sport marketing, law or finance as each sector may vary in terms of policies and directions taken for sport-ES (Environmental and Sustainability). It is noted that this citizenship has not been fully reflected upon and debated (Mallen and Chard, 2011). A question to stimulate debate on this topic has been included in the summary and future considerations section at the end of this chapter.

The principles in CSR&A

This chapter framed the definition of CSR&A education with Galvič and Lukman's (2007: 1876) position that principles are "fundamental concepts that serve as a basis for actions, and as an essential framework for the establishment of a more complex system." In this case, the principle of responsibility extends to having accountability within the four dimensions in sport outlined above, including the development of social, cultural, financial and environmental sustainability. This means that, fundamentally, actions in sport CSR&A include being accountable through elements such as transparency, reporting and developing capability, overcoming barriers and, overall, making progress concurrently in CSR&A and sport.

Further, the Brundtland Report (1987) presented to the World Commission on Environment and Development (WCED) stated that sustainable development involved action that "meets the needs of the present without compromising the ability of future generations to meet their own needs" (WCED, 1987: 1) (see Chapter 14, Misener, Sant and Mason). An interpretation of an application of this Brundtland Report concept to CSR&A is that one needs to act to encourage progress in sport in a manner that does not impede future generations from meeting their own needs for sport. Sustainability, thus, underscores all actions in sport.

The principle of social sustainability in CSR&A

One of the key concepts and links regarding CSR&A in sport education is related to Sport for Development, in other words, understanding the leading mechanism for sport to be accountable to society, at both the community and global levels. Sport for Development has been defined as "the use of sport to exert a positive influence on public health, the socialization of children, youths and adults, the social inclusion of the disadvantaged, the economic development of regions and states, and on fostering intercultural exchange and conflict resolution" (Lyras and Peachey, 2011: 1). One approach involves a Sport for Development framework designed by Schulenkorf (2012). This framework is promoted to "guide the strategic investigation of sport and event projects and their contribution to understanding and measuring direct social impacts and sustainable social outcomes for (disparate) communities" (Schulenkork, 2012: 1).

Key CSR&A in sport educational concepts
Sport for development

This form of intervention in sport and recreation addresses inequities inherent in mainstream sports provision (Hylton and Totten, 2008) as well as understood as organizations and governments that have adopted some sort of means of promoting, through sport, social inclusion to address the issues of disadvantaged groups and anti-social behavior. More universally, global sport development incorporates the concepts of globalization and international development, acknowledging the potential of sport as a tool to reach personal, community, national and international development objectives; sport can be used as a tool for addressing some of the challenges that arise from humanitarian crises and in conflict and post-conflict settings. There are a number of leading sport organizations doing Sport for Development work at the local and global levels, and these need to be incorporated in related CSR teaching and learning.

Global sport development

At its broadest interpretation, sport development on a universal scale has been recognized as an important tool in helping the United Nations achieve its objectives, in particular the Millennium Development Goals. By including sport in development and peace programs in a more systematic way, the United Nations can make full use of this cost-efficient tool to help us create a better world, and this was acknowledged in 2003 by the United Nations in declaring a "Sport for Development and Peace" working group, followed by 2005 being named the International Year of Sport and Physical Education. One of the industry leaders in global sport development is the humanitarian organization Right To Play. Right To Play (formerly Olympic Aid) originated through the Olympic movement, and serves as an international humanitarian organization with the goal of using sport and play programs for the development of the world's most disadvantaged communities and children, under the important global banner of "Sport for Development and Peace" (Right To Play, 2009). Other sport-related events and organizations have also successfully incorporated global giving into their corporate initiatives, including the National Basketball Association's (NBA) "NBA Cares" program, which encourages global outreach for key social issues (NBA, n.d.) (see Chapter 23, Walker, Heere and Kim) or the Fédération Internationale de Football Association's (FIFA) establishment of a "corporate social responsibility" unit within its organization, which gives a considerable percentage of their revenues to corresponding initiatives, including the Football for Hope program (FIFA, 2005). As such, FIFA has taken a most definitive lead in sport with regard to a strategic commitment to social development by being one of the first sport organizations to establish a "corporate social responsibility" unit within its organization (see Chapter 15, Parent and Chappelet).

Community Sport Development

Similar to global sport development, community sport development utilizes sport and related activities to support community development, and is regarded as a localized approach to community problem solving (Craig, 1998). Efforts in this area focus on building active and sustainable local communities based on social justice and mutual respect, and changing power structures to remove the barriers that prevent people from participating in the issues that affect their lives (Misener and Mason, 2010).

Case 1: Right To Play

One of the global leaders in global sport development, Right To Play is regarded as the leading international and humanitarian development organization using the transformative power of sport and play to build essential skills in children and thereby drive social change in communities affected by war, poverty and disease. Right To Play has been a pioneer in innovation for social change using sport and play and has a track record for creating programs that are both sustainable and replicable. Right To Play believes that self-confidence, self-esteem, respect for oneself and others, and overcoming adversity are some of many critical elements in the development of a child and must be fostered in order to create a safer, healthier and more productive society. Right To Play equips local community leaders with the necessary skills to transform their community – making lasting change, providing education, promoting health and preventing disease, developing local sport leaders, and via peace education encourages the prevention of conflict. Right To Play has recently also expanded their territorial reach, for example, establishing important programming in Canada's most disadvantaged aboriginal communities (see more details of the aims and activities of this organization in Right to Play, 2009).

Case 2: Homeless World Cup

The Homeless World Cup uses football – street soccer – as a catalyst for social change and provides an excellent example of local community development (in this case, demonstrated on a global stage). The Homeless World Cup is a social organization with the goal of ending homelessness through the sport of football. The organization hopes that engaging homeless people in football will encourage them to change their own lives and develop solutions to worldwide homelessness. The organization puts together an annual football tournament where teams of homeless people from each country compete.

Environmental sustainability

The principle of environmental sustainability in CSR&A

Understanding is needed between sport and the natural environment to ensure sport participation, events, infrastructure, etc. not only safeguards but also enhances the natural environment for future generations.

Activities to meet the principle of environmental sustainability

This principle can be met with actions that focus environmental management and operational performance systems (Mallen *et al.*, 2010). The environmental management systems include activities such as the development of sport environmental policies, targets, committees, funding, education and disclosure of environmental activities. Further, sport-oriented environmental programs could consider countermeasures against global warming (including using renewable energy, incinerating waste, saving electricity, purchasing energy saving equipment or environmentally friendly automobiles); countermeasures against environmental harm in sport event production (including reusing, recycling, reducing use of packaged material, implementing green purchasing and procurement, lifecycle assessment, environmental marketing and partnering with suppliers who support environmental products); and countermeasures against environmental risk (including a risk management system, reduction of chemical use, measuring discharge of toxic chemicals, reducing the use of chlorofluorocarbons, training for environmental emergencies, delegating environmental emergency responsibilities and sorting out related environmental laws and regulations) and environmental tracking (including tracking energy use, financial resource use, general wastes, water drainage, air and water pollution, greenhouse gases and compliance) (Mallen *et al.*, 2011).

Case 3: Olympic Games & Environmental Sustainability (ES)

Each set of Olympic Games since the mid-1990s has stated that they were "green." The Games used their communication ability to promote the safeguarding of the natural environment. Yet, despite the efforts, there has been incongruence between what was stated to happen at the Games concerning safeguarding the natural environment and what actually happened. Detrimental impacts have, thus, been realized (Paquette *et al.*, 2011). Importantly, a disconnect between who was responsible for environmental plans has been noted as the bid committee was a different group from the Games Organizing Committee. Incongruence means that while sport has begun to establish goals and objectives for ES, the meeting of these goals/objectives is not met. The incorporation of the ES, thus, does not meet with our understandings concerning how to enact ES. This means that ES is at the primary stage of development in sport and needs to be advanced.

This leads us to ask ourselves where do you stand on the debate concerning what elements in ES should be advanced within sport? A framework for debating the future of environmental sustainability specifically in the sport academy has been outlined by Mallen and Chard (2011). This debate encourages reflection on constraints within the natural environment (including what constraints on sport will occur due to ecological conditions by the years 2050–2060; how important these constraints will be to sport; and the consequences of responding, not responding or partially responding to the ecologically induced constraints) and actions that sport can enact to conserve the natural environment (including what actions are appropriate; and the relevance of these actions to sport for the future).

Why should CSR be taught globally within sport management programs?

Higher education has been declared an outstanding vehicle for creating sensitivity to a topic (Cordano *et al.*, 2003). The responsibility of educators can be viewed in the 2003 United Nations (UN) Resolution 57/254 at the 57th UN General Assembly that declared the years 2005–2014 as the "Decade of Education for Sustainable Development" (UN, 2003). The dedication of this decade encouraged concentrated effort to incorporate the concept of sustainable development within education, including corporate social, cultural, financial and environmental sustainability. Haigh (2005: 31–32) declared this decade as the "academe's best chance to date for making the deep and radical changes that will be necessary if the world's higher education institutions are to enact their responsibilities for creating a better and self-sustainable world." An interpretation in this chapter is that it is unlikely, however, that sport management education will completely fulfill this need to incorporate sustainable development by 2014. This is because, currently, all sport management higher education programs do not offer specific courses in CSR&A; albeit some courses are integrating this topic within modules of traditional topics (i.e., cause-related marketing in a marketing class; community relations in a strategy class) and in courses specifically related to business ethics, or community development.

Growth in CSR&A and related courses is necessary for sport management education to provide a forum for developing understandings concerning the directions, strategies, value and how to measure the impact of CSR&A within sport. Education in CSR&A can be multi-directional as it has been noted that "sustainability ... has no single blueprint" (Roome, 2005: 163); the teaching, however, requires the promotion of "an ability to judge the suitability of policies and approaches against a context" (Roome, 2005: 17). This context, as outlined by Wheeler *et al.* (2005: 173) is a need to "draw attention to the particularly pressing and linked issues of global insecurity, poverty and environmental stressors." It is imperative, thus, that this role for CSR&A be taught to sport management students. This need for CSR&A education follows Boucher's (1998: 80) argument that was made over a decade ago that in sport management "we definitely need to spend more time in our courses discussing, debating, and resolving some of the fundamental ethical and social problems involving the management of sport enterprise in our society."

Sport can play a role in CSR&A as it can be an equalizer in a world of unequal social, financial and environmental conditions. There is an urgent need to generate both stand-alone courses and to simultaneously incorporate CSR&A within courses due to what Roome (2005) described a rising number of organizational management personnel responsible for CSR&A. This joint strategy allows the topic to be fully interested within all educational aspects of sport management education. The authors of this chapter call for the development of student competencies for CSR&A to increase understandings and to underscore innovative solutions to enact CSR&A within the sport management industry. This necessitates the fostering of an awareness of the social, cultural, financial and environmental responsibilities within sport.

Teaching CSR&A in sport management programs

Incorporating CSR&A in the classroom is challenging for educators. The success of incorporating CSR&A has been found to be difficult due to the complexity of the topic (Murray and Murray, 2007), the lack of a priority status (Dahle and Neumayer, 2001; Thomas, 2005), the lack of faculty knowledge and a comfort level for working with the topic (Alabaster and Blair, 1996; Thomas *et al.*, 1999), along with constraints due to limited time and resources. Further, Calderhead (1996) and Marland (1998) indicated that decisions on incorporating topics and actions within the classroom can be driven by beliefs; this may include a lack of belief in CSR&A by higher education faculty or a lack of belief that it is their responsibility to ensure the provision of this education. In spite of the difficulties, Mathisen (2006: 111) has stated that: "As research institutions, they (universities) could and should develop much of the knowledge base for an ecologically enlightened society." Also, Thomas (2005: 187) called for "a commitment to education as a transformative learning process, in which students are challenged and given the opportunity to develop entirely new ways of understanding the role and behavior of the business enterprise." Cooper and Fava (2001: 13) encourage the development of students for the "growing need for those trained in industrial ecology." Geng *et al.* (2009: 987) promoted that "universities must bridge the traditional separation of an engineering school from a social sciences and humanities school to produce graduates who are able to contribute constructively to our society's future." Further, Springett (2005: 149) indicated that programs are striving "to introduce students to a dialectical discourse where problematic and opposing, even contradictory, views are incorporated into the discourses of sustainability."

The literature indicates that the topic has been introduced within business management and engineering education from various perspectives. For instance, strategies have included the case study method and observational learning theory (Allenby *et al.*, 2007) and the lifecycle assessment approach to advance decision making capacities (Cooper and Fava, 2001). It was stated by DesJardins and Diedrich (2003: 33) that "life-cycle cases in general are very helpful in revealing the full economic, ethical, and ecological consequences of product development, marketing, use, and disposal." Further, board games have been assessed as viable simulation tools to educate for the concepts of ecological thinking (Cushman-Roisin *et al.*, 1999) and hybrid lectures have been encouraged by Mulder (2004) to intertwine social issues with technical knowledge. In addition, Mathisen (2006) promoted interdisciplinary education with problem-orientations. Springett and Kearins (2005: 145) suggested that educators need to develop "interdisciplinary partnerships for education for sustainability in and between the institutions." Further, Thomas (2005: 186) stated the need to generate tools to develop understandings concerning the "degree to which students truly consider sustainability an integral part of the managerial decision-making process." Importantly in this chapter, an adaptation of Mallen *et al.*'s (2010) themes for sport management environmental education are applicable broadly to CSR&A education.

Theme 1 for developing CSR&A education involves a shift in thinking to incorporate CSR&A within sport management education. This shift involves a fundamental re-alignment to link decision-making and processes in ways that incorporate social, cultural, financial and environmental sustainability in course, project and research content. This theme requires understanding the state of current thinking (this will be discussed later in this chapter) and the development of approaches to advance sport linked to CSR&A. This theme gives rise to questions such as:

- What are the assumptions and values incorporated within sport-CSR&A thinking?
- What is the role of the leadership and grassroots groups in encouraging CSR&A thinking?
- How can CSR&A thinking be advanced within each sub-sector of sport management and what would be the impact?
- What theories underscore CSR&A thinking?

Course assignments can encourage an exploration of how CSR&A is viewed and implemented in sports organizations. Case studies are needed to support broader, interdisciplinary understanding of CSR&A.

Theme 2 for developing CSR&A education involves responsiveness in the managerial and operational performance strategies utilized within sport management. This includes applying CSR&A concepts to various strategies discussed in sport management, including schemes, tools, programs or methods and impact the human, technological and financial resources in sport management. This theme generates questions such as:

- What strategies can improve the success of CSR&A in sport?
- How can these strategies begin to generate understandings concerning the principles necessary in CSR&A?
- How can and should CSR&A be measured?
- What barriers impact the success of CSR&A and how can they be overcome?
- What competencies are needed to realize the options within CSR&A?

Classroom discussions can generate the top ten issues in CSR&A best practices and the competencies needed to overcome each issue. Much research is needed to support the discussions on issues, best practices and competencies as they are industry specific. Currently the best practices are unknowns in all of the areas encompassed within CSR&A. However, some criteria can be extracted from the philanthropy/charity awards, such as the Steve Patterson Award for Sport Philanthropy or the Beyond Sports awards. However, logically the key tenets would consider efficiencies in human resource, technology and financial resource management and processes to advance CSR&A. Further, it stands to reason that CSR&A competencies are needed by academics in sport management as well as the students and practitioners. These competencies are needed in strategic CSR&A management, along with issue management beyond ad hoc responses, and innovations for advancing the impact of sport within the social, cultural, financial and environmental spheres. Education is key to generating these competencies. This means that there is a need for tertiary or lifelong CSR&A education programs for sport managers, including students and their instructors and those already in the industry. Higher educational programs should play a role in the generation of understandings about CSR&A between the practitioners and those individuals studying, researching and teaching sport management. Further research in CSR&A is needed to support these sport-CSR&A educational programs.

Theme 3 involves the appropriate impact of CSR in sport. This theme involves visions of where sport is or should be heading in the future and what role CSR plays within this future. This theme raises questions such as:

- What is the appropriate level of CSR&A one generation of sport should be able to generate?
- What level of accountability should there be in sport-CSR&A for one generation of sport managers?
- When is the promotion of CSR&A only "greenwashing" or not true?
- What could sport look like if CSR&A is fully instituted within decisions and processes in sport management?
- What level of discretion does each sport manager have concerning CSR&A within the different sub-sectors of sport?

Assignments can ask students to determine how they could alter the direction of CSR&A in sport by the year 2025. The authors promote that educators develop a framework devised to establish *where* and *how* students can gain practical experiences specifically intended to develop CSR&A understandings.

Overall, a number of educational strategies can be encouraged for each sphere, including the social, cultural, financial and environmental aspects of CSR&A. For instance, Newman (2005) supported the use of an interdisciplinary approach for promoting environmental sustainability. Murray and Murray (2007) promoted open reflective practice on values to encourage acquired beliefs. Folke (2003: 227) supported the development of "understandings of the contexts that form, shape and reshape habits of thought and action." Springett (2005: 147, 154) emphasized reflective practice as providing "the power to guide people ... in action as they engage with the discourses of sustainability and sustainable development" and that students needed to be guided to critique sustainability and to consider multiple alternatives with "a pedagogy based in action methods." In this chapter we follow the work of Kagawa (2007) that there was no universally acceptable educational method which implies that CSR&A is context dependent and there is not a one-size-fits-all solution. Kagawa indicated, however, that "it is indeed vital to create a curriculum change process within which students' needs, aspirations, and concerns for sustainability are addressed" and that "higher education needs to play an increasingly significant role in helping students become active responsible citizens" (Kagawa, 2007: 335).

Why be "good sports"?

It is important to summarize this chapter with the importance of CSR&A in sport, and position this topic as one that is important for discussion in sport management education. CSR&A is, at the core, concerned with one's community, as well as key stakeholders. As such, sport business expectations are inherent in an ability to enact CSR&A. Business is not necessarily a "driver" of change for enacting CSR&A, but here again are a summary of key reasons why CSR&A is so important to sport and sport business management. CSR&A can:

- lead to increase sales and market share;
- strengthen brand positioning;
- improve corporate image and clout;
- increase the ability to attract, motivate and retain employees;
- decrease operating costs; and
- increase appeal to stakeholders.

Curriculum design and course evaluation: a 'giving' project

It is perhaps most important to position CSR&A in sport from a giving and/or philanthropic lens, hence lending to a generation of giving sensitive students. This, from a pedagogical perspective, would be aligned with the increase in "service learning" and/or experience learning. Therefore, any CSR&A in sport education or course work should strongly consider incorporating a means to simulate a "real" giving course-based experience. This would likely be interspersed with "real-world" sport philanthropy (case study, guest lectures, corporate documents) in a project assignment (presentation and/or case paper) where the students (in groups or individually) "pitch" a strategic "giving request" to their peers (in line with the sounds principles of CSR&A in sport, in particular authenticity and sustainability) for a "corporate give." This could and should include collective class input, via evaluation tools and measures (i.e., a CSR&A scorecard) as well as can include an interactive element of "fun money" whereby students allocate their "money" to the group that strategically presents the strongest.

Conclusions

The intent of this chapter has been to discuss and review, from a theoretical, applied and peda-gogical perspective, how sport management should consider teaching CSR, a most important concept and understanding for future sport management leaders. Throughout, we have dis-cussed a variety of CSR topics and concepts, including CSR and accountability, cause-related and social marketing, giving and philanthropy, and considerations for in-class discussions and projects. A number of questions for related debate can also be reviewed, including: 1) Should CSR be promoted from a corporate perspective or should the term "corporate" be removed from CSR and the educational focus be placed on social responsibility and accountability (SR&A)? How does this adaptation from CSR to SR&A change the implications of social, financial and the environmental aspects of sport management? 2) What should be included in a definition of a "corporate socially responsible citizen" compared to a "socially responsible and accountable citizen" in sport management? and 3) What visions can you conceive concerning what sport would be like if CSR was integrated within all decision-making and processes? In short, we trust that future sport management leaders will understand the breadth and depth of CSR for sport, and will embrace and incorporate related sound principles in their strategic planning. Being "good sports" is good for everyone.

References

Alabaster, T. and Blair, D.J. (1996) 'Greening the university', in Huckle, J. and Stirling, S. (eds.) *Education for sustainability*. London: Earthscan, pp. 86–104.

Allenby, B., Allen, D. and Davidson, C. (2007) 'Teaching sustainable engineering', *Journal of Industrial Ecology*, 11 (1), 8–10.

Bateman, T. and Organ, D. (1983) 'Job satisfaction and the good soldier: The relationship between affect and employee "citizenship"', *Academy of Management Journal*, 26, 587–595.

Blowfield, B. and Murray, A. (2008) *Corporate Responsibility: A Critical Introduction*. Oxford: Oxford University Press.

Boucher, R. (1998) 'Toward achieving a focal point for sport management: A binocular perspective', *Journal of Sport Management*, 12, 76–78.

Bradish, C. and Cronin, J.J. (2009) 'Corporate social responsibility in sport', *Journal of Sport Management*, 23 (6), 691–697.

Breitbarth, T. and Harris, P. (2008) 'The role of corporate social responsibility in the football business: Towards the development of a conceptual model', *European Sport Management Quarterly*, 8 (2), 179–206.

Brundtland Report (1987) *96th Plenary meeting*, United Nations General Assembly, Report to the World Commission on the Environment and Development. Available at: http://www.un.org/documents/ga/res/42/ares42-187.htm (accessed: November 24, 2012).

Calderhead, J. (1996) 'Teachers: Beliefs and knowledge', in Berliner, D.C. and Calfee, R.C. (eds.) *Handbook of educational psychology*. New York: Simon & Schuster Macmillan, pp. 709–725.

Carroll, A. B. (1979) 'A three dimensional conceptual model of corporate social performance', *Academy of Management Review*, 4 (4), 497–505.

Carroll, A. B. (1999) 'Corporate social responsibility: Evolution of a definitional construct', *Business & Society*, 38 (3), 268–295.

Cooper, J.S. and Fava, J. (2001) 'Teaching life-cycle assessment at universities in North America, II: Building Capacity', *Journal of Industrial Ecology*, 4, 11–15.

Cordano, M., Ellis, K. and Scherer, R. (2003) 'Teaching about the natural environment in management education: New directions and approaches', *Journal of Management Education*, 27 (2), 139–143.

Craig, G. (1998) 'Community development in a global context', *Community Development Journal*, 33, 2–17.

Cushman-Roisin, B., Rice, N. and Moldaver, M. (1999) 'A simulation tool for industrial ecology: Creating a board game', *Journal of Industrial Ecology*, 3 (4), 131–144.

Dahle, M. and Neumayer, E. (2001) 'Overcoming barriers to campus greening: A survey among higher educational institutions in London, UK', *International Journal of Sustainability in Higher Education*, 2 (2), 139–160.

DesJardins, J. and Diedrich, E. (2003) 'Learning what it really costs: Teaching business ethics with life-cycle case studies', *Journal of Business Ethics*, 48 (1), 33–42.

Fédération Internationale de Football Association (FIFA) (2005) *Football for hope: Football's commitment to social development*. Available at: http://www.toolkitsportdevelopment.org/mega-events/html/resources/22/22736AF1-DF5C-4F96-B3B5-F9380155F698/FootballforHope_E.pdf (accessed: November 15, 2012).

Folke, C. (2003) 'Social-Ecological resilience and behavioural responses', in Biel, A., Hansoon, B. and Martenensson, M. (eds.) *Individual and structural determinants of environmental practice*, 1, 226–242.

Galvič, P. and Lukman, R. (2007) 'Review of sustainability terms and their definitions', *Journal of Cleaner Production*, 15, 1875–1885.

Geng, Y., Mitchell, B. and Zhu, Q. (2009) 'Teaching industrial ecology at Dalian University of Technology: Toward improving overall eco-efficiency', *Journal of Industrial Ecology*, 13 (6), 978–989.

Hamann, R., Acutt, N. and Kapelus, P. (2003) 'Responsibility versus accountability? Interpreting the World Summit on sustainable development for a synthesis model of corporate citizenship', *Journal of Corporate Citizenship*, 9, 32–48.

Haigh, M. (2005) 'Greening the university curriculum: Appraising an international movement', *Journal of Geography in Higher Education*, 29 (1), 31–48.

Hylton, K. and Totten, M. (2008) 'Community sports development', in Hylton, K. and Bramham, P. (eds.) *Sports Development: Policy, Process and Practice*. 2nd edn. London: Routledge, pp. 77–88.

Kagawa, F. (2007) 'Dissonance in students' perceptions of sustainable development and sustainability: Implications for curriculum change', *International Journal of Sustainability in Higher Education*, 8 (3), 317–338.

Lyras, A. and Peachey, J. (2011) 'Integrating sport-for-development theory and praxis', *Sport Management Review*, 14 (4) 311–326.

Mallen, C. and Chard, C. (2011) 'A framework for debating the future of environmental sustainability in the sport academy', *Sport Management Review*, 14, 424–433.

Mallen, C., Adams, L., Stevens, J. and Thompson, L. (2010) 'Environmental sustainability in sport facility management: A Delphi study', *European Sport Management Quarterly*, 10, 367–389.

Mallen, C., Bradish, C. and MacLean, J. (2008) 'Are we teaching corporate citizens? Examining corporate social responsibility and sport management pedagogy', *International Journal of Sport Management and Marketing*, 4 (2/3), 204–224.

Mallen, C., Stevens, J. and Adams, L. (2011) 'A content analysis of environmental sustainability research in a sport-related journal sample', *Journal of Sport Management*, 25, 240–256.

Margolis, J.D. and Walsh, J.P. (2003) 'Misery loves companies: Rethinking social initiatives by business', *Administrative Science Quarterly*, 48 (2), 268–305.

Marland, P. (1998) 'Teachers' practical theories: Implications for preservice teacher education', *Asia-Pacific Journal of Teacher Education & Development*, 1 (2), 15–23.

Mathisen, W. (2006) 'Green utopianism and the greening of science and higher education', *Organization & Environment*, 19 (1), 110–125.

Misener, L. and Mason, D. (2010) 'Moving beyond economic impact: Sporting events as a community development tool', *Journal of Management and Organization*, 16 (4), 495–514.

Mulder, K. (2004) 'Engineering education in sustainable development: Sustainability as a tool to open up the windows of engineering institutions', *Business Strategy and the Environment*, 13 (4), 275–285.

Murray, P. and Murray, S. (2007) 'Promoting sustainability values within career-oriented degree programmes', *International Journal of Sustainability in Higher Education*, 8 (3), 285–300.

National Basketball Association (NBA) (n.d.) *NBA Cares: Bigger than basketball*. Available at: http://www.nba.com/caravan/caravan_nbacares.html (accessed: November 15, 2012).

Newman, A. (2005) 'Sustainable development, education and literacy', *International Journal of Sustainability in Higher Education*, 6 (4), 351–362.

Paquette, J., Stevens, J. and Mallen, C. (2011) 'The interpretation of environmental sustainability by the International Olympic Committee and the Organizing Committees of the Olympic Games from 1994 to 2008', *Sport in Society*, 14, 355–369.

Right To Play (2009) *History of Right To Play*. Available at: http://www.righttoplay.com/International/about-us/Pages/History.aspx (accessed: November 15, 2012).

Roome, N. (2005) 'Teaching sustainability in a global MBA: Insights from the one MBA', *Business Strategy and the Environment*, 14 (3), 160–171.

Schulenkorf, N. (2012) 'Sustainable community development through sport and events: a conceptual framework for Sport-for-Development projects', *Sport Management Review*, 15, 1, 1–12.

Springett, D. (2005) 'Education *for* sustainability in the business studies curriculum: A call for a critical agenda', *Business Strategy and the Environment*, 14 (3), 146–159.

Springett, D. and Kearins, K. (2005) 'Educating for sustainability: An imperative for action', *Business Strategy and the Environment*, 14 (3), 143–145.

Thomas, I., Kyle, L. and Alvarez, A. (1999) 'Environmental education across the tertiary curriculum: A process', *Environmental Education Research*, 5 (3), 319–337.

Thomas, T. (2005) 'Are business students buying it? A theoretical framework for measuring attitudes toward the legitimacy of environmental sustainability', *Business Strategy and the Environment*, 14 (3), 186–197.

United Nations (UN) (2003) *Resolution 57/254: United Nations decade for education for sustainable development.* UN General Assembly, February 2003, Agenda item 87(a) 02 55612. Available at: http://www. un-documents.net/a57r254.htm (accessed: October 22, 2008).

Varadarajan, P.R. and Menon, A. (1988) 'Cause-related marketing: A coalignment of marketing strategy and corporate philanthropy', *Journal of Marketing*, 52 (3), 58–74.

Walker, M. and Kent, A. (2009) 'CSR on tour: Attitudes towards corporate social responsibility among golf fans', *International Journal of Sport Management*, 11 (2), 1–28.

Walker, M. B., Kent, A. and Rudd, A. (2007) 'Consumer reactions to strategic philanthropy in the sport industry', *Business Research Yearbook: Global Business Perspectives*, 14 (2), 926–932.

Wheeler, D., Zohar, A. and Hart, S. (2005) 'Educating senior executives in a novel strategic paradigm: Early experience of the sustainable enterprise academy', *Business Strategy and the Environment*, 14 (3), 172–185.

World Commission on Environment and Development (WCED) (1987) *Our Common Future.* World Commission on Environment and Development. Oxford: Oxford University Press.

PART II

IMPLEMENTING CSR
IN SPORT

5

SOCIAL RESPONSIBILITY AND LIVE**STRONG**

Kevin R. Filo, Daniel C. Funk and Danny O'Brien

Overview

The Lance Armstrong Foundation (LAF) is an organization that has been highly successful leveraging sport and social responsibility. The LAF was founded in 1997 by professional cyclist Lance Armstrong, during his treatment for testicular cancer that had spread to his abdomen, lungs, and brain. The LAF was started based upon the idea of improving the lives of individuals affected by cancer. In its early years, the organization consisted of a small group of employees and volunteers working to raise money in the fight against cancer (*LIVESTRONG: Our history*, n.d.). Since those formative years, a number of factors have impacted the growth of the organization. First, cancer has emerged as the world's leading cause of death. Second, Lance's stature has expanded exponentially. Third, the resources available to the organization have increased significantly. Accordingly, the organization now reaches every corner of the globe. As an example, in 2010, over 1,100 grassroots LIVE**STRONG** days – a day/event founded by the organization in 2004 to celebrate the movement against cancer – were held in over 65 countries (*LIVESTRONG: Milestones*, n.d.).

The organization has been highly successful in advancing its mission to inspire and empower individuals living with cancer and in demonstrating social responsibility since its inception. This social responsibility has been augmented through cooperation from corporate partners and individual supporters. The development and guidance of the LIVE**STRONG** wristband campaign provided by Nike, as well as the dedication displayed by participants in LIVE**STRONG** events, provide excellent examples of this cooperation through social responsibility. This chapter presents information collected in a series of research projects on participants, employees, and the organization to provide a perspective on how social responsibility has been activated. Notably, all of the data and events presented below were collected and occurred prior to Lance Armstrong's fall from grace, which included the founder voluntarily resigning from the board for the charity in November 2012.

The LIVE**STRONG** wristband campaign: social responsibility through partnership

A major contributor to the growth of the organization was the LIVE**STRONG** wristband campaign, a cause-related marketing campaign between the LAF and Nike in which yellow silicone wristbands embossed with "LIVE**STRONG**" were sold for $1 each, with all proceeds benefitting the LAF. The campaign launched in May 2004 with wristbands made available online (in 10-packs, 100-packs, and cases of 1,200), as well as at select retailers from which wristbands could be purchased individually. The wristbands quickly became popular and demand overwhelmed supply. A substantial backorder ensued as the LAF began selling over 100,000 wristbands per day.

The LIVE**STRONG** wristband campaign was buoyed by exposure through a number of different channels. First, sport was a significant factor: Lance wore a wristband throughout his win in the 2004 Tour de France, and the wristband enjoyed near omnipresence during the 2004 Olympic Games as Nike athletes wore them with pride. Second, celebrity contributed as Sheryl Crow and Matt Damon were two of many luminaries seen wearing the wristband during public appearances early in the campaign. Third, the political stage provided exposure with John Kerry wearing a LIVE**STRONG** wristband throughout the 2004 US presidential campaign. Very quickly, the LIVE**STRONG** wristband became a phenomenon. In early 2005, Lance Armstrong appeared on the Oprah Winfrey Show as Oprah challenged her audience to break the single day sales record. The record was nearly tripled and website traffic was so high that Yahoo!'s servers were temporarily shut down. In 2005 alone, 55 million LIVE**STRONG** wristbands were sold (Carr, 2011).

Nike's efforts in helping to launch the LIVE**STRONG** wristband campaign provide one of the more successful examples of social responsibility activated through sponsorship. As a long time sponsor of the LAF, Nike financed the production of the first five million wristbands, and donated an additional $1 million to LIVE**STRONG** as an act of goodwill as the campaign commenced. When those first five million wristbands sold out, and the initiative took on a life of its own, Nike continued to provide advice, expertise, and novel marketing efforts while the LAF responded to the extraordinary demand. Despite concerns that the wristband represented a simple fad along with fears that the enormous amount of publicity generated would result in a backlash, the LIVE**STRONG** wristband campaign represents one of the most effective cases of CSR through cause-related marketing. Nike benefitted through the goodwill and positive associations generated via the media exposure highlighting Nike's role in launching and guiding the campaign, while the LAF drew enormous benefits in terms of attention and resources (McGlone and Martin, 2006).

Due in no small part to the success and ubiquity of the wristband, supporters of the organization began using LAF and LIVE**STRONG** interchangeably. In 2009, the LAF officially adopted the name LIVE**STRONG** for the organization (Salter, 2010a). Accordingly, the organization is referred to as LIVE**STRONG** throughout the remainder of this chapter.

Overall, in the 15 years since the organization began, LIVE**STRONG** has invested more than $275 million on cancer programs and initiatives. That figure of $275 million reflects 81 percent of every dollar raised by LIVE**STRONG** since its inception, as 81 percent of all funds raised by the organization go to mission activities, while the other 19 percent goes to administration costs (*LIVESTRONG: What we do*, n.d.). Beyond the vast success of the wristband campaign, the sport events managed by LIVE**STRONG** represent a significant fundraising initiative accounting for the money that has been raised and invested, and also reflect opportunities for LIVE**STRONG** to foster social responsibility through celebration of community. The Race for the Roses and LIVE**STRONG** Challenge represent the most prominent and successful examples of these events. As noted above, this chapter presents information collected in a series of research projects on participants, employees, and the organization to provide a perspective on how social responsibility has been activated. The social responsibility fostered through these multi-million dollar fundraising events is detailed next.

LIVESTRONG events: leveraging social responsibility through events

In its first year of existence, **LIVESTRONG** (then the Lance Armstrong Foundation) held the first annual Race for the Roses in Austin, Texas. The event was a cycling race developed to raise money for the organization's mission to inspire and empower individuals living with cancer. In this first year, the event generated a mere $130,000 for **LIVESTRONG** (M. Stoller pers. comm., May 5, 2004). In the years since that inaugural event, the Race for the Roses has grown to become a multi-million dollar fundraiser for **LIVESTRONG** and has evolved into a series of events – The Team **LIVESTRONG** Challenge – held annually in multiple cities across the United States.

In its current format, the team **LIVESTRONG** Challenge is held in Davis, California, Philadelphia, Pennsylvania, and Austin, Texas. Each event attracts thousands of participants relying upon dedicated volunteers and encouraging spectators to attend and cheer on participants. Participants are required to pay a registration fee, and are encouraged (and for some events, required) to raise additional funds. To promote additional fundraising, **LIVESTRONG** offers a variety of incentives and prizes including cycling gear and invitations to event-related dinners for individuals reaching set milestones. All proceeds beyond the operational costs associated with managing the event benefit **LIVESTRONG** directly. Participants can choose a ride between 10 and 100 miles, and walk and run options are also made available to participants. All participants are given a t-shirt and water bottle with their registration. As an example of the growth and success of the team **LIVESTRONG** Challenge, the 2011 team **LIVESTRONG** Challenge in Austin, Texas brought in nearly 4,000 participants and raised over $2.5 million for **LIVESTRONG** (*Team LIVESTRONG events*, n.d.).

As the team **LIVESTRONG** Challenge has succeeded and expanded, an assortment of academic inquiry has been conducted examining these events (e.g., Filo *et al.*, 2008, 2009, 2011). Specifically, a number of research projects have explored the nature of participants' relationships with these events; and social responsibility among participants through a strong connection to the cause has been shown to play a large part. First, qualitative data uncovered the motives driving event participation. Second, qualitative studies explored the sense of community present within the event. Finally, both qualitative and quantitative data have revealed the factors that contribute to the meaning participants hold for these events. These factors include recreation motive such as social and escape, along with motives for charitable giving including reciprocity and the desire to improve the charity, as well as camaraderie, cause, competency, and belief in making a difference. These research findings and their relevance to social responsibility are detailed below.

LIVESTRONG events and motivation

To uncover the motives driving individuals to participate in **LIVESTRONG** events, a series of four focus groups were conducted with participants in the 2005 Ride for the Roses and the 2006 **LIVESTRONG** Challenge in Austin, Texas (Filo *et al.*, 2008). The two focus groups with Ride for the Roses participants were held prior to the event during the event weekend, while the two focus groups for the **LIVESTRONG** Challenge were conducted three months prior to the event. Each focus group centred on discussing the motives and needs individuals were looking to satisfy through participation.

The focus groups revealed that motives tied to recreation participation and motives related to supporting a charity drove an individual to participate in the event. Specifically, seven motives were uncovered: intellectual, social, physical, reciprocity, self-esteem, need to help others, and

Table 5.1 Motives for LIVE**STRONG** event participants

Motive	Definition
Intellectual	The event as an opportunity to learn more about LIVE**STRONG**, its mission, and activities.
Social	The event as an opportunity to socialize with others, meet new people, reunite with past participants, and participate with friends and family.
Physical	The event as an opportunity to keep in shape, get healthy, and challenge oneself physically.
Reciprocity	Participating because one has benefitted from, or anticipates benefitting from, LIVE**STRONG**.
Self-Esteem	The event as an opportunity to enhance self-worth through supporting LIVE**STRONG**.
Need to help others	Participation as a reflection of a personal responsibility to improve the lives and well-being of those less fortunate.
Desire to improve the charity	The event as an opportunity to contribute to the success of LIVE**STRONG**.
Social X charity	The event as an opportunity to talk to others about their experience with cancer and their connection to the cause.
Physical X charity	Describing the physical challenge of the event in terms of the challenges faced by cancer survivors.

Source: Filo *et al.* (2008).

desire to improve the charity. With regard to the recreation motives, focus group participants described the event as an opportunity to learn more about the charity and its activities, to socialize with others through reuniting with past participants and meeting new people, and to keep in shape, get healthy, and challenge themselves physically. In terms of the motives for charitable giving, focus group participants highlighted having benefited from (or anticipating benefiting from) the charity, empowering themselves through supporting the cause, fulfilling a need to give back, and contributing to the success of LIVE**STRONG**, as factors that led them to participate in the events. Each of these motives not only contributed to event participation, but also contributed to the meaning participants ascribed to the event. Each motive is listed and defined in Table 5.1.

Notably, individual motives were not the only contribution to driving participation and meaning derived from the event experience. Rather, an interaction occurred between the recreation motives and the motives for charitable giving, leading to increased meaning held for the event. This interaction was most evident in how focus group participants described the social motive and the physical motive. As noted above, participants portrayed the event as a means to meet new people, reunite with past participants, and participate with friends and family. Terms such as "social affair" and "party" were used to illustrate this motive. However, the charitable component influenced this motive and focus group participants' expression of the motive. The event was depicted as an opportunity to talk to others about their experience with cancer, their connection to the cause, and the sense of individual responsibility to benefit society that brought participants together. As an example, Jack a five-year participant in the event stated the following:

For me personally, it's been meeting other survivors and having that common bond. It really helped me deal with it. I really, before I rode in the first Ride for the Roses, I somewhat blocked out my cancer experience, psychologically, I didn't want to deal with it. But participating really helped me kind of face it and deal with it. I guess it's really helped me talk to other people about it … I think it's a good thing, personally, to talk about it, and this event provides an outlet for this.

(Filo *et al.*, 2008: 516)

This point was further supported by the following explanation from Lee, another five-year participant:

And so much of what we do and when you read the paper and everything, you feel like our country and world is divided, everybody is attacking each other. Then you deal with all of these people at this event that you have this trust with, there are 10,000 people around and you know you can trust these people because you have this shared vision of what is good and what is right. And that's just an amazing feeling.

(Filo *et al.*, 2008: 517)

While expounding upon the physical motive, focus group participants mentioned the chance to "be active" and "keep in shape." Again, the charitable component influenced this motive. The physical challenge inherent to the training and completion of the event was described in terms of the challenges faced by cancer survivors. The following quote from Lee provides an example:

But the fact that it is a charity is significant, it's a real motivator when you're on the road and you're struggling past your normal capabilities, you think about the people you know who have cancer or MS and what they have to put up with. It makes the aches and pains and all that kind of stuff so trivial. And that empowers you to go on.

(Filo *et al.*, 2008)

Meanwhile, cancer survivors themselves provided a similar description, wherein the physical challenge was relayed in terms of the duress endured throughout their battle with cancer. For instance, Sarah drew a link between the determination required to beat cancer and the determination required to complete the event:

Going through chemo and all of that and I garnered strength through the organization, garnered strength through Lance's determination, and just, thought that, if I can do this, I can do anything … So it just became something that I wanted to do, and I'm fairly pitbullish with those things and I went after it.

(Filo *et al.*, 2008)

The findings derived from the focus groups, and the quotes provided above, demonstrate the influence of social responsibility on the motives driving participation in the **LIVESTRONG** events. That is, the benefit of the greater good, or in this case, the benefit of individuals living with cancer, influenced participants' respective decision to take part in the event. This influence is evident from the presence of the four motives for charitable giving that was uncovered. More importantly, the interaction between the recreation motives and the charitable component of the event provides further evidence of the importance of social responsibility. As with any sport event, recreation motives play a critical role for participants. In the case of the **LIVESTRONG** events, these recreation motives were affected by the greater good, or the philanthropic cause, tied to the events. This connection to the cause reflects a shared sense of social responsibility, and this shared sense of social responsibility underscores the sense of community present at LIVE**STRONG** events.

LIVESTRONG events and community

An additional finding to emerge from the focus groups was the creation of a sense of community, or communitas (Chalip, 2006) through the event. This communitas was touched upon throughout the focus groups as participants mentioned the sense of trust and connection felt towards other participants (Filo *et al.*, 2008). The sense of social responsibility embodied through the support of the charity, as well as the social aspects of the event, further facilitated this communitas.

The LIVE**STRONG** events have featured a number of opportunities for participants to gather, socialize, and celebrate. Over the years, these opportunities have included pre-event pasta dinners, cycling expositions, speaker events, a post-event party, and a volunteer appreciation party among others. The post-event party has been critical in fostering community. The post-event party features live music, food and beverage, merchandise tents, sponsorship activation, and an assortment of information booths allowing participants to learn more about the current activities of the charity. In addition, the party is hosted by an emcee who interacts with the crowd and invites participants onstage to share the story behind their participation and their experience with the event. Finally, each cancer survivor who completes the event is celebrated with a yellow rose presented to them as they transition from the finish line to the post-event party. Each of these features allows individuals to share their sense of social responsibility and celebrate their connection to the charity, creating communitas among participants.

To further explore sense of community within LIVE**STRONG** events, semi-structured interviews were conducted with participants in the 2009 LIVE**STRONG** Challenge in Austin, Texas at the post-event party, as well as over the phone. The purpose of these interviews was to analyze the sense of community derived from the event using Brint's (2001) six structural and cultural properties of Gemeinschaft (community). These six properties are: dense and demanding social ties; social attachments to and involvement in institutions; ritual occasions; small group size; perceptions of similarity with others; and common beliefs in an idea system, moral order, institution, or group.

The interview data supported the notion that a sense of community was present among event participants. This presence was reflected through the emergence of five of the six properties within the interviews. In describing each of these five properties, social responsibility was evident throughout the interviews.

Dense and demanding social ties are embodied in collective action networks in which individuals disseminate information and take action. Interview participants described the participant base as a like-minded collective from which participants could collect information (i.e., fundraising tips, training advice, advocacy initiatives) and draw inspiration. These ties existed both during and following the event as participants touched upon a sense of shared responsibility among participants to "spread the word" and continue to "support" LIVE**STRONG**. Social attachments to and involvement in institutions are reflected through empowerment and increased civic action among community members. Here, again, the support for LIVE**STRONG** provided the basis for this property as interview participants detailed their advocacy efforts and action taken on behalf of the charity to raise awareness and encourage support. This civic action was taken at both the individual and group level.

The property of ritual occasions serves to solidify group identity among community members. The event, and the various components of the event such as the post-event party highlighted above, provided a ritual occasion in which participants' identity and beliefs are re-energized. In particular, participants outlined strength in numbers emerging as a result of seeing everyone at the event. An additional aspect of the ritual occasion property is group symbols which served to reinforce the group identity. In this instance, the **LIVESTRONG** wristband and **LIVESTRONG** merchandise, along with the yellow rose given to participants upon completion of the event, provide examples of images and icons that reinforced the sense of community. The wristband and **LIVESTRONG** cycling gear were visible throughout the event and also provide a reminder of the cause when seen outside of the event parameters. This was mentioned frequently during the interviews. Small group size is based upon the idea that if a community becomes too large, accountability may diminish. This property did not emerge from the interview data as participants instead described the inspiration and reinforcement derived from the sheer size of the participant base and community.

Perception of similarity with others and common beliefs in an idea system, moral order, institution or group are closely linked together, and both properties were present. The perceived similarities mentioned by interview participants included a connection to cancer, as each interviewee was either a cancer survivor themselves or were a friend or loved one of a cancer survivor. An interest in and enthusiasm for cycling was another similarity demonstrated by participants describing love for cycling. Next, an overall dedication towards the event and cause exemplified within the properties described above was another similarity. Similarly, common beliefs were embodied in participants' commitment to both the charity and their fellow participants. Interviewees communicated their confidence and support for how **LIVESTRONG** was using the funds that had been raised, as well as the direction of **LIVESTRONG** overall. Meanwhile, their belief in each other to advance the mission of **LIVESTRONG** was also evident. The following quote from Peter at the post-event party summarizes the sense of community shared among event participants:

> I think you get enough of us together ... each of us individually, if each of us thinks we're just by ourselves then we can't do anything ... But then you see all these people, and I recognise the power of the collective.

> (Filo *et al.*, in press)

The sense of community described by the interviewees at the 2009 **LIVESTRONG** Challenge ties directly to social responsibility. Across each of the five properties, a greater good was apparent. This greater good included not only the charity and cause, but also the other participants. Moreover, this greater good was manifested in support, advocacy, and action on behalf of **LIVESTRONG** by the community of participants. The motives driving event participation, and the sense of community created through the event, represent factors that contribute to a meaningful event experience. This meaningful event experience again ties closely to social responsibility. The meaning ascribed to **LIVESTRONG** events is detailed next.

LIVESTRONG events and meaning

A recurring theme within the research on **LIVESTRONG** events is the meaning derived from the events by participants. As noted above, a number of factors contribute to this meaning. First, the motives that drive participation contribute to meaning. Second, constructs such as camaraderie, cause, and competency underscore this meaning. Third, a belief in making a difference shared among participants plays a part in creating a meaningful event experience. Once again, each of these contributing factors relates closely to social responsibility among participants.

The focus group data collected by Filo and colleagues (2008) suggested that the interaction between the recreation motives and the charitable component of the event leads to participant attachment to the event. Participant attachment to the event reflects that the event has taken on emotional, symbolic, and functional meaning (Funk and James, 2006). The influence of motives on attachment to the event has been confirmed quantitatively via a post-event questionnaire administered to participants in the 2007 LIVE**STRONG** Challenge in Austin, Texas (Filo *et al.*, 2011). The results from this study revealed that one recreation motive (social) and all four motives for charitable giving (reciprocity, self-esteem, need to help others, and desire to improve the charity) made a significant contribution to attachment to the event. Of particular note, this research compared the LIVE**STRONG** Challenge to a sport event with a less prominent charitable aspect, the 3M half marathon and relay, to determine if a difference existed in the relationship between motives and attachment. An important finding was that the charity-based motives made a stronger relative contribution to attachment for the LIVE**STRONG** event compared to attachment to the 3M half marathon and relay. This finding provides further evidence of the role social responsibility, embodied through the motives for charitable giving, in shaping participants' experience with the event and cause.

As a means to further investigate the emotional, symbolic, and functional meaning characterising attachment to an event, Filo and colleagues (2009) conducted interviews with participants in the 2006 LIVE**STRONG** Challenge. The interviews revealed three themes reflecting emotional, symbolic, and functional meaning. These three themes are: camaraderie, cause, and competency.

Camaraderie was revealed through the solidarity and friendship felt among event participants. Cause linked with the goals of supporting the charity and raising awareness shared by participants. Competency related to participants' enthusiasm for fitness and cycling. Each of these themes aligns closely with the properties of community described by the interviewees from the 2009 event (e.g., Filo *et al.*, in press). In addition, cause, camaraderie, and competency tied to emotional, symbolic, and functional meaning, respectively. Emotional meaning encompasses the event's capacity to allow an individual to connect with others as evidenced through the solidarity, friendship, and belonging inherent to camaraderie. Symbolic meaning involves a sport event taking on greater importance and facilitating self-expression as indicated by the greater good and inspiration within the cause. Finally, functional meaning corresponds with benefits derived from a sport event such as the health and fitness benefits underscoring competency. These three themes reflect the different aspects of the meaning held for LIVE**STRONG** events, and further demonstrate the social responsibility to the cause and the other participants exhibited at LIVE**STRONG** events.

In an additional investigation of attachment to LIVE**STRONG** events, and the meaning held for an event by participants, quantitative data were collected from participants in the 2007 LIVE**STRONG** Challenge (Filo *et al.*, 2012). The purpose of this study was to examine the influence of both motives and participant belief in making a difference on attachment to the event. The results revealed that belief in making a difference mediated the relationship between social and charity motives and the emotional, symbolic, and functional meaning held for the event (attachment).

These findings present two implications for social responsibility. First, the contribution of social and charity motives provides additional evidence of the role of these factors in creating a meaningful event experience. This supports the qualitative finding emerging from the focus groups, indicating that the social motive and charity motives drive participation and contribute to meaning held for the event. In addition, this aligns with the influence the charitable component of the event has on the social motive. Second, the mediating role of belief in making a difference upon charity motives suggests that the meaning derived from the event is influenced by participant desire to support a charity, and this meaning is strengthened when participants are confident in their own capacity to advance the mission of LIVE**STRONG**. The mediating role of this factor demonstrates the LIVE**STRONG** events represent a context in which participant belief that a difference can be made exists, and participation in the event can serve to reinforce this belief. Again, LIVE**STRONG** events have facilitated a sense of social responsibility among participants through satisfying a need to give back via supporting a charity. This finding demonstrates that this sense of social responsibility has been further activated through reinforcement that giving back will make a difference. LIVE**STRONG** has also leveraged social responsibility among individuals in the non-sport event environment.

LIVESTRONG and social media

The importance of engaging social responsibility among individuals is not lost on LIVE**STRONG** outside of the sport event context. Current LIVE**STRONG** CEO Doug Ulman has over one million followers on Twitter. This places him in the top 300 Twitter users in terms of followers overall, and among the highest ranking CEOs in the world (Salter, 2010c). The LIVE**STRONG** CEO Twitter handle is used as a means to hold an ongoing conversation with supporters and to communicate the daily activities of the organization. For example, Ulman has shared insights from his own battle with cancer, and also conducted a poll in which supporters could vote on how donations were to be used.

LIVE**STRONG**'s embrace of social media is reflected in the attention and resources allocated to these tools. LIVE**STRONG** has employed a full-time Online Community Evangelist who oversees social media. The LIVE**STRONG** blog serves as a center point for social media outreach sharing news, activism, and soliciting feedback from the online community. More than 60 percent of the traffic driven to LIVE**STRONG**'s official website comes from social media sites, and social media has been effectively used to generate attention for various LIVE**STRONG** initiatives (Hibbard, 2010). For instance, in 2009 and 2010, LIVE**STRONG** directed focus to ensuring individuals with cancer had access to the appropriate healthcare and created an action site featuring the Healthcare Reform Petition. The action site allowed individuals to create dedication pages for loved ones, share stories, and sign the petition. Twitter was the leading driver of traffic to the online petition and, in all, 70,000 signatures were collected online (Hibbard, 2010). Overall, LIVE**STRONG** has been applauded for the use of social media to sustain support. This includes having the largest Twitter following of any health care organization, as well as the development of a virtual LIVE**STRONG** wristband for individual's Twitter followers (Salter, 2010c).

Conclusions

LIVE**STRONG** has established itself as a successful non-profit organization in terms of both revenue and reach. In 2009, LIVE**STRONG** generated over $50 million in revenue across individual donations, cause marketing and licensing, merchandise sales, and other sources. In addition it attracted 260,000 visitors to its online support resources and over 1,800 local events were organized by volunteers on behalf of LIVE**STRONG** (Built Strong, 2010). The reasons for this success are myriad, and include factors such as excellent stewardship by various CEOs and the Board of Directors over the years, the publicity and resource windfall that occurred as a result of the rampant success of the LIVE**STRONG** wristband campaign, and the fact that LIVE**STRONG** supports a cause impacting everyone around the world. Collectively, all of these factors have made LIVE**STRONG**, "a force to be reckoned with" in the words of Leslie Lenkowsy, a professor at Indiana University's Center for Philanthropy (Salter, 2010b).

The research conducted on LIVE**STRONG** events has brought attention to an additional critical factor in this success: the capacity of these events to activate and leverage social responsibility among participants. The events attract thousands of participants, include a variety of surrounding activities, and take place across the United States. The findings of the research conducted on each event are presented chronologically in Table 5.2.

The research on the motives driving participants to these events revealed the traditional recreation motives that drive leisure and event participation played a role. However, motives for charitable giving also played a role, indicating that these events were viewed by participants as a means to demonstrate social responsibility through supporting the charity. More importantly, it was the charitable component of the event that shaped the way participants described the needs satisfied through participation, as exemplified by the meaning taken on by motives such as social and physical.

An additional finding to emerge from the investigation of motivation was the creation of community through these events. Communitas was identified as an outcome of the event facilitated in part by a shared connection among participants. This sense of community was examined further through an analysis of its properties. This analysis provided additional evidence of the sense of community fostered within these events. This sense of community was not only based upon the notion that participants understood they were giving back, but also their collective belief in each other and the institution to which they were giving back. The participants described the community as a like-minded collective brought together by similar interests and a conviction towards LIVE**STRONG**. The event serves as the vehicle to bring this community together and reinforce their beliefs.

Table 5.2 The findings of research on LIVE**STRONG** events

Event	Findings
2005 Ride for the Roses & 2006 LIVE**STRONG** Challenge	Seven motives contribute to participation and meaning held for the event. The charitable component of the event influences the social and physical motives.
2006 LIVE**STRONG** Challenge	Three themes: camaraderie, cause, and competency underscore the meaning held for the event.
2007 LIVE**STRONG** Challenge	One recreation motive and four motives for charitable giving contribute to meaning held for the event.
2007 LIVE**STRONG** Challenge	Belief in making a difference mediates the relationship among motives and attachment to the event.
2009 LIVE**STRONG** Challenge	A sense of community is facilitated through the event based upon participants' collective belief in their fellow participants and LIVE**STRONG**.

Source: Filo *et al.* (2008).

Finally, the meaning participants ascribe to these events is largely based upon engaging social responsibility. The motives for charitable giving make a significant contribution to the emotional, symbolic, and functional meaning held for the event. That emotional, symbolic, and functional meaning is tied to the themes of camaraderie, cause, and competency, each with a direct link to the social responsibility exhibited among participants. Lastly, participant belief in making a difference plays an important role in creating a meaningful event experience. Participants not only perceive the events as a mechanism to display social responsibility (and satisfy the motives for charitable giving), but the meaningful event experience is further enhanced by the belief that displaying social responsibility through participation advances social change on behalf of LIVESTRONG. The events of LIVESTRONG, more specifically, the activation of participants' social responsibility through these events, have been critical to the success of LIVESTRONG. Meanwhile, the LIVESTRONG wristband provides a symbol and social media provides additional tools to communicate and reinforce social responsibility. As the fight against cancer continues, LIVESTRONG will continue to provide an excellent case study of leveraging social responsibility to advance social change.

A number of opportunities exist within the context of social responsibility and charitable organizations, as well as for the investigation of social responsibility and LIVESTRONG. For charitable organizations overall, a number of challenges must be confronted with regard to fundraising. The strategies employed by charitable organizations in response to these challenges reflect can be examined by researchers. For instance, as charity sport events have gained in popularity, further emphasis is placed upon distinguishing an event to attract participants. The marketing and management initiatives implemented by charity sport event managers to differentiate events can be evaluated through academic enquiry. Meanwhile, the sheer number of events dilutes the fundraising base for the different events and causes, and charitable organizations may consider alternate forms of involvement beyond fundraising (i.e., volunteering, advocacy, lobbying) as critical outcomes derived from event participation. Similarly, the emergence of social media has allowed charity sport event participants to connect with potential sponsors and donors more frequently. This ease of connection is not always viewed positively (Rigby, 2011), and reflects an additional consideration for charitable organizations attempting to advance social responsibility through participatory events. These trends and challenges represent timely and important areas for academic exploration, while LIVESTRONG reflects an intriguing context for the examination of social responsibility.

Next, with regard to LIVESTRONG, a number of issues and questions surround the organization in the aftermath of the United States Anti-Doping Agency (USADA) revealing the evidence against LIVESTRONG's founder, Lance Armstrong. Following this revelation, Lance Armstrong voluntarily resigned from the board of the charity, and LIVESTRONG severed all ties with the founder. Lance subsequently confessed in a live television interview to the use of performance-enhancing drugs while winning the Tour de France seven straight years. As a result of these incidents, the organization has been confronted by a number of challenges concerning legitimacy and the association between the founder and the charity. In response, LIVESTRONG has continued to emphasize the importance of its mission, activities, and constituents, while also communicating that the organization has never been about one individual, but instead focuses on the millions of cancer survivors worldwide. It is far too early to assess the impact of these events and challenges on the organization, but the strategies implemented and consequences to follow present a number of avenues for academic exploration concerning branding, crisis management, and mission communication from the social responsibility perspective.

References

Brint, S. (2001) 'Gemeinschaft revisited: A critique and reconstruction of the community concept', *Sociological Theory*, 19, 1–23.

Built Strong (2010) *Built Strong: Measuring LIVESTRONG's revenue, spending, followers, and reach.* Available at: http://www.fastcompany.com/magazine/150/built-strong.html (accessed: January 15, 2012).

Carr, A. (2011) *Lance Armstrong, Doug Ulman thought the LIVESTRONG wristband would fail.* Available at: http://www.fastcompany.com/article/doug-ulman-didnt-think-the-livestrong-bracelets-would-sell (accessed: January 15, 2012).

Chalip, L. (2006) 'Towards social leverage of sport events', *Journal of Sport & Tourism*, 11, 109–127.

Filo, K., Funk, D., and O'Brien, D. (2008) 'It's really not about the bike: Exploring attraction and attachment to the events of the Lance Armstrong Foundation', *Journal of Sport Management*, 22, 501–525.

Filo, K., Funk, D., and O'Brien, D. (2009) 'The meaning behind attachment: Exploring camaraderie, cause, and competency at a charity sport event', *Journal of Sport Management*, 23, 361–387.

Filo, K., Funk, D., and O'Brien, D. (2011) 'Examining motivation for charity sport event participation: A comparison of recreation-based and charity-based motives', *Journal of Leisure Research*, 43, 491–518.

Filo, K., Groza, M., and Fairley, S. (2012) 'The role of belief in making a difference in enhancing attachment to a charity sport event', *Journal of Nonprofit and Public Sector Marketing*, 24, 123–140.

Filo, K., Spence, K., and Sparvero, E. (In Press) 'Exploring the properties of community among charity sport event participants', *Managing Leisure*.

Funk, D. and James, J. (2006) 'Consumer loyalty: The meaning of attachment in the development of sport team allegiance', *Journal of Sport Management*, 20, 189–217.

Hibbard, C. (2010) *How LIVESTRONG raised millions to fight cancer using social media*, Available at: http://www.socialmediaexaminer.com/how-livestrong-raised-millions-to-fight-cancer-using-social-media/ (accessed: February 6, 2012).

LIVESTRONG: Our history (n.d.) Available at: http://www.livestrong.org/Who-We-Are (accessed: January 12, 2012).

LIVESTRONG: Milestones (n.d.) Available at: http://www.livestrong.org/Who-We-Are/Our-History/ Milestones (accessed: January 12, 2012).

LIVESTRONG: What we do (n.d.) Available at: http://www.livestrong.org/What-We-Do (accessed: January 12, 2012).

McGlone, C. and Martin, N. (2006) 'Nike's corporate interest lives strong. A case of cause-related marketing and leveraging', *Sport Marketing Quarterly*, 15, (3), 184–188.

Rigby, R. (2011) 'The challenge of fundraising fatigue'. *Financial Times*, 2 June. Available at: http://www.ft.com/intl/cms/s/0/cd4e0c4a-8d41-11e0-bf23-00144feab49a.html#axzz286h4X4wa (accessed: September 20, 2012).

Salter, C. (2010a) *How the Lance Armstrong Foundation became LIVESTRONG.* Available at: http://www.fastcompany.com/1698037/how-the-lance-armstrong-foundation-became-livestrong (accessed: January 15, 2012).

Salter, C. (2010b) *Can LIVESTRONG survive Lance Armstrong and a doping scandal?.* Available at: http://www.fastcompany.com/magazine/150/can-livestrong-survive-lance.html (accessed: January 15, 2012).

Salter, C. (2010c) *Meet LIVESTRONG CEO Doug Ulman, the most savvy health care leader in social media.* Available at: http://www.fastcompany.com/1695101/livestrong-ceo-doug-social-media (accessed: January 15, 2012).

Team LIVESTRONG events (n.d.) Available at: http://www.livestrong.org/Take-Action/Team-LIVESTRONG-Events (accessed: January 12, 2012).

6
"GETTING THE TACTICS RIGHT"

Implementing CSR in English football

Christos Anagnostopoulos

Overview

Football clubs in England have a relatively long history of engaging in community-based work, especially since the establishment of the national "Football in the Community" (FiTC) program in the mid-1980s. It does not come as a surprise therefore that, amongst the European football leagues, in English football is where the strongest institutionalized forms of corporate social responsibility (CSR) have evolved. To this end, this chapter draws on findings from a larger empirical study and provides a descriptive account of some of the key issues associated with the way CSR is being strategically implemented in English football. It does so, by using a tactical "line up" analogy in an endeavor to accentuate 11 points that pertain to strategic CSR in this particular context.[1] The aim and its execution are therefore intended as a response to Godfrey *et al.* (2010) call for management scholars studying socially responsible business practices to consider specific manifestations of CSR and take into account relevant industry contexts and forces.

Introduction

The practice of CSR has held a growing appeal for the sport scholarly community over recent years; this holds at least as true for football (soccer) as it does for the rest of the sporting world. Particularly in England, which is perhaps the first nation to have fully embraced commercialization at the highest levels of its football sector, there are frequent criticisms surrounding excessive transfer fees, poor governance, financial instability and ownership controversies. As a consequence, questions concerning the legitimacy of football clubs and their position in society have gained an increased topicality. Although there are no regulatory provisions in existence that require English football clubs to assess their overall social or environmental impact in any detail, or with any degree of formality (James and Miettinen, 2010, Breitbarth *et al.*, 2011), football clubs in England are now heavily engaged in implementing a range of programs designed to improve their local societies and environments.

This, then, is the background to the current chapter. It focuses on the findings of a five-year empirical study into the way CSR is being strategically implemented in English football (Anagnostopoulos, 2013). The discussion proceeds in the following manner. First, it provides a brief historical account of English football and its relationship with the concept of CSR.

This should highlight the contextual parameters to be taken into account when examining the formulation and implementation of CSR strategy. The chapter goes on to give a concise overview of the structural dimensions under which CSR is being implemented, before providing a more detailed discussion of the mechanics of funding these activities. This leads to the core of the chapter, which provides a descriptive account of some of the key issues associated with CSR implementation in English football. This discussion is facilitated by use of a tactical football "line up" analogy, which illustrates the eleven key components of CSR strategy as it is implemented within English football clubs.

Contextual background

Football clubs in England have a relatively long history of engaging in community-based work. This engagement was first formalized by the establishment of the national "Football in the Community" (FiTC) program in the mid-1980s (Russell, 1997). The program was a joint initiative by the Football League and the Professional Footballers' Association through the Footballers' Further Education and Vocational Training Scheme (Walters, 2009). According to Mellor (2005), the reputation of football declined during the mid-1980s with social problems such as hooliganism being sufficiently high profile to demand state intervention. Despite the fact that FiTC schemes around the country have, for years, been recognized as an effective means of improving community engagement (Watson, 2000; McGuire, 2008), it is claimed by Brown *et al.* (2006) that the relationship between football clubs and communities is no longer as close as it once was. Taylor (2004: 48–53) suggests two main contributing factors to this new ambiguous relationship between club and community: shifting economic and social circumstances, and the influence of television. An indirect consequence of these two factors has been increased political pressure from central government.

The first factor has three underlining characteristics: it encompasses the decline of the UK manufacturing base that defined the civil workforce for most of the twentieth century; migration away from inner-city areas; and changes in the cultural and social activities of most UK citizens. As far as the second factor is concerned, while King (2002: 117) believes that the 1992 BSkyB contract was a crucial moment in the transformation of the top level of English professional football because "it linked the game to Thatcherite developments," the "Sky-ification" of football, as Taylor (2004: 50) calls it, has also had a great effect on the way we understand community. Fans are no longer expected to live close to their team's base or to attend matches in order to feel "part of the club" (ibid.) These fans now constitute "fan communities" that require different treatment to the more traditional body of football supporters. The influence of television is obviously crucial to this development, and its use is key to addressing it; as a consequence, football clubs now depend heavily on television revenues.

According to Taylor (2004), the factors of community dispersion and television are the principal reasons for football clubs having come under increasing external pressure to re-consider, and subsequently to re-establish, relations with their communities. At a moment of particularly drastic and rapid transformation within English football, New Labour won a landslide election in the UK. Under the ideological principle of the "Third Way," the party introduced a number of reforms in welfare and other areas of public policy that focused on creating a strong sense of responsibility across society. Hine and Preuss (2009) write that, having assumed government in the wake of the economic liberalization of the 1980s and 1990s, New Labour had to perform a balancing act between the values of their traditional constituencies and the need to be seen as pro- (or at least not anti-) business. For Wilson (2000, cited in Hine and Preuss, 2009: 386), this caused the government to avoid the heavy-handed regulation characteristic of previous Labour administrations by appealing to the logic of the market and fair competition as methods of "regulating" activity.

Mellor (2008) has identified the football sector as part of New Labour's political agenda. His argument is illustrated by the establishment of the Football Task Force (FTF), which was designed to monitor how far the football sector was meeting its "social obligations" (ibid.: 318). Mellor (2008: 319) also observes that, with the arrival of New Labour, the community work in which clubs were expected to engage expanded beyond traditional children's coaching schemes and player appearances. Football clubs were placed in a new position of responsibility, stemming from the fact that the sport was identified by the British Government as potentially being a key deliverer of policy objectives in areas as diverse as health, education, community cohesion, regeneration and crime reduction (Mellor, 2008; Tacon, 2007). The government's creation of the Football Foundation charity was a key part of this agenda (Taylor, 2004). New Labour managed to establish the foundation by securing approximately five percent of the revenue from the Premier League television deals and matched this with funds from the Department for Culture, Media and Sport (DCMS), Sport England and the Football Association (FA).

Structure and organization

The socio-political pressures mentioned above, combined with increasing commercialism within the football sector, prompted Brown *et al.* (2006) to make a number of recommendations. Their report advised, *inter alia*, that FiTC departments should look to gain independence from their football clubs and convert themselves into community foundations or trusts[2] with charitable status, governed by a separate board of trustees. Brown and his colleagues put forward the argument, well received by the football community, that an independent community foundation has more benefits than a community department within a club. These benefits included a greater degree of structural autonomy, responsibility for its own strategic and financial direction, access to a wider variety of funding streams and less need to balance the tension between commercial and community objectives. The above recommendations do not enjoy full empirical support (see Anagnostopoulos and Shilbury, 2013); however, it is unquestionable that a charitable foundation can develop a more open and inclusive approach to community relations than the football club itself. It can also nurture stronger partnerships with local communities, regeneration companies and commercial sponsors committed to CSR as well as enhancing the club's credibility with potential partners and funding agencies (Walters, 2009: 86 referring to Brown *et al.*, 2006). It should be noted however that these recommendations were made on the assumption that the charitable foundation would retain their association with the football club, in order to ensure that CSR-related initiatives continued to have strong significance in the communities involved.[3]

Bingham and Walters (2012) have shown how the foundation model has enjoyed great popularity in the football sector with a total of 89 football clubs from the Premier League and the Football League having a community sports trust/foundation by May 2011. All of the football clubs consulted in the course of this five-year study had established a charitable foundation (see Figure 6.1), although some of these charitable organizations do not necessarily represent anything more than an extension of the football club's overall operational activities.

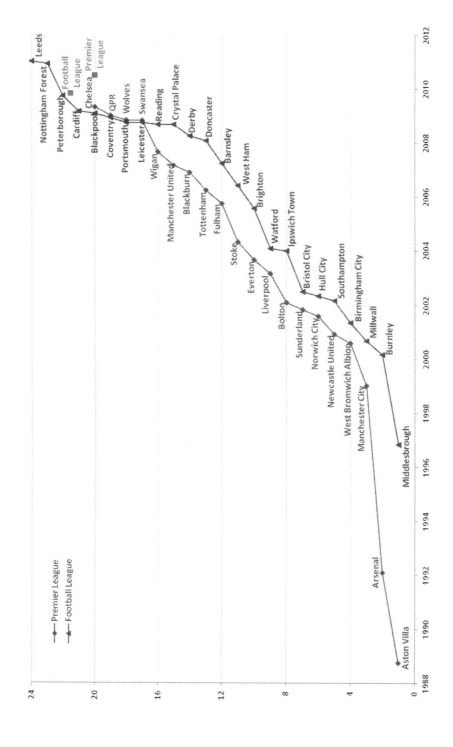

Figure 6.1 Growth of football clubs' foundations in England

Source: http://www.charity-commission.gov.uk.

Although Walters (2009) does highlight this tendency for football clubs to establish charitable foundations, it must also be clarified that this is largely a response to "recipes" provided by football's governing bodies (both the Premier League and the Football League) who provide much of the funding behind CSR strategy. The cases of Aston Villa FC, Liverpool FC, Tottenham FC and Arsenal FC are characteristic. These football clubs have an "independent" charitable foundation, but one could argue that their overall CSR work is being formulated and implemented "in-house." This is either because the established foundation is being run by a small number of trustees who come predominantly from the club, which thus retains control over the foundation, or because the foundation focuses on providing grants or promoting fundraising events and leaves the implementation of more outreach community work to the football club itself. Figure 6.2 provides a simplified illustration of the highly complicated structure within which English football's CSR is currently practiced.

The foundation's relationship with its "parent" football club is an institutionalized one. The latter, at its discretion, supports the foundation by, for example, underwriting losses, providing facilities and equipment and agreeing to player and manager appearances.[4] It is only very

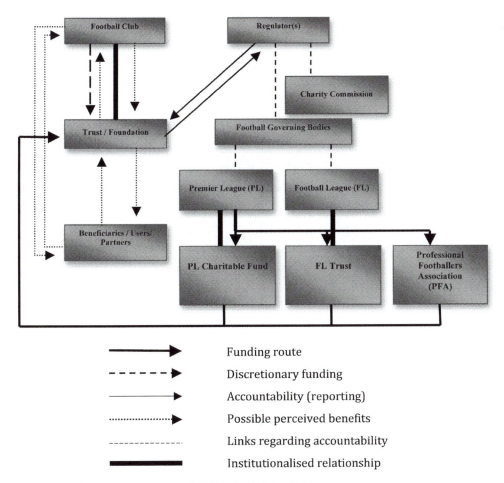

Figure 6.2 Implementation structure of CSR in English football

Source: compiled by the author.

recently that steps have been taken to formalize the relationship between the football club and the charitable foundation through the introduction of a service level agreement. Such additional formalization between the two organizations demonstrates the ever-increasing amount of CSR work being done in English football over the last few years (see Chapter 18 by Simon Morgan that details the work of the English Premier League). Furthermore, as charitable organizations, the foundations are subject to varying degrees of regulation. In 2007 the Charity Commission for England and Wales published a report highlighting the relationship between key stakeholders and good performance. In addition, these foundations are also accountable to football's governing bodies: the Premier League itself and the Football League's charitable arm, the FL Trust. Several studies (e.g., Walters, 2009; Walters and Chadwick, 2009; Brown *et al.*, 2006) have provided a good picture of the perceived benefits the implementation of these CSR programs can secure. The mechanics of funding is, of course, a key (not to mention extremely complicated) factor in this process; the following section offers an explanation of it.

Funding mechanics

Premier League (PL)

The PL has a central Community Development team which dictates policy and strategy, and oversees the operations of all 20 clubs in the league (Morgan, 2010: 16). "Creating Chances" is the community umbrella of the Premier League under which a number of specific projects sit (issues around this extensive CSR program are discussed in more detail in Chapter 18). Figure 6.3 sets out the key themes and projects within the community program of the Premier League.

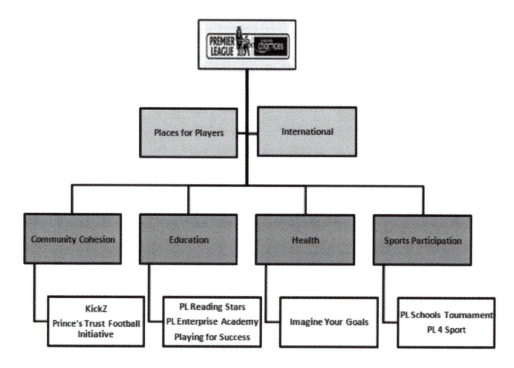

Figure 6.3 The Premier League and Creating Chances: key themes and projects

Source: modified from the 2011 Creating Chances report.

The funding is managed and administered by the Premier League Charitable Fund (PLCF), the PL's registered charitable arm. The PL funding runs on a three-year cycle, following the same pattern as television funding. In order for each club to secure core funding from the PLCF it has to fulfil the "fit-for-purpose" standard (also known as "capability status"). According to Morgan (2010: 17) this criterion mainly serves as the vehicle by which football clubs (or more specifically the established foundations as their charitable arms) meet their legal requirements, particularly in terms of charitable law, financial accounting, the safeguarding of children, workforce development and risk management. The "fit-for-purpose" standard demands that the trustees of the club's charitable foundation provide numerous documents such as employee handbooks, pension schemes, standard contracts, healthcare provisions, public liability insurance and evidence of Criminal Records Bureau (CRB) disclosure processes together with a detailed three-year business plan. Once approved by the PLCF, the foundation qualifies for an unrestricted grant (or core funding) amounting to £45,000 a year for the three-year period 2010–2013 (an 80 percent increase on the period 2007–2010). In addition, there is also an Organisational Improvement Grant (OIG) designed to enhance the overall operations of the foundations. The OIG can provide a maximum amount of £60,000 towards certain needs identified by the foundations regarding, for example, their infrastructure (offices, IT equipment, independent website, etc.) with the proviso that the PLCF acknowledges the value of the investment. The funding is granted over a three-year period: £30,000 in year one, £20,000 in year two and £10,000 in year three. The PLCF stipulates the manner in which these grants are spent.

Beyond these two strands of core funding, the football foundations have the option to apply (or bid) for the Premier League Professional Football Association (PLPFA) community fund. For the 2010–2013 period the total amount available was approximately £12.6 million. Each foundation could bid for a maximum of £200,000, an amount subject to match-funding and investment in the four social themes shown in Figure 6.2. So, a football foundation can bid for a maximum of £200,000 but the PL expects them to match a minimum of 80 percent of this amount (i.e., £160,000), forming a total of £360,000 for the proposed program over three years (£120,000 per year). According to the 2010 Creating Chances report 52 projects were activated through the 2007–2010 PLPFA community fund, generating almost £9 million of matched-funding through various partnerships.

Football League (FL)

The FL Trust operates a different system for allocating the funding that it receives from the Premier League. Since its establishment, the FL Trust has introduced an accreditation system based on criteria (gold, silver or bronze status) its clubs' respective foundations must meet in order to receive available funding.

As yet, no FL foundation has achieved gold status. However, between 2007 and 2010 the FL Trust supported 69 foundations in achieving bronze accreditation and 46 in achieving silver. The foundations received core funding of £24,000 towards fulfilling bronze status, whereas for silver status the core funding amounted to £48,000. With the latest television deal (2010–2013), the total amount of money given to the FL Trust for the implementation of CSR programs dropped from £4million to £2.6 million per year. As a result, all FL clubs (including those with Championship status) receive £25,000 per year as core funding regardless of their accreditation status. Instead, a discretionary pot of money (similar to that which the PL provides for its clubs, albeit on a much smaller scale here) has been introduced for which only foundations attached to a Championship status club can apply. The maximum discretionary funding for which these foundations can bid is £25,000 per year for a three-year project (£75,000 in total). A minimum of 25 percent match-funding is required in order for the foundations to be granted this amount.

With such tight funding procedures to follow as well as institutional "recipes" to conform to, CSR managers in the English football context must now be more strategic in the ways they formulate and implement social and environmentally oriented programs. The next section draws on a tactical formation frequently used in contemporary football as an analogy to outline the strategic foci behind CSR implementation in English football.

Strategic line-up

Tactical formations are recognizable patterns of play resulting from the use of certain players in fairly clearly defined functions on the pitch (Orejan, 2010). The tactical formation seen in Figure 6.4 broadly reflects the key objectives CSR managers in English football try to meet regarding CSR implementation. The "manager's role" here has been given to the foundation's director (referred to hereafter as the "CSR manager"), who is most often the person responsible for setting the strategic CSR agenda.

The importance of the goalkeeper in contemporary football can hardly be overstated. The majority of (if not all) successful football teams in the recent history of the sport owe their achievements to a "safe pair of hands." The positional equivalent for strategic CSR implementation in English football is the facility or venue in which the foundation resides and from which it manages its operations. The "goalkeeping" position has the potential to put CSR managers in a double bind. This is because in most cases such a facility is the football ground (stadium), where the football club has granted the foundation office space for its staff. This eliminates a substantial financial burden (i.e., utility bills and associated costs) from the foundations' shoulders. Such physical integration may also support the argument that the parent club "integrates" the foundation's practices into its overall strategy. On the other hand, the foundation's strategic position would be reinforced if it owned a separate facility. Such an asset would enable the foundation – even taking into account its charitable status – to borrow money in financial difficulties, without relying to the "parent" club to underwrite its losses. Having a solid "goalkeeper,"therefore, by either owning the facility or formally[5] agreeing with the "parent" club regarding the long-term obligations and rights regarding the latter's space is a crucial strategic element upon which the implementation of CSR-related programs is based.

Figure 6.4 Strategic CSR line-up

The back line of defenders for the implementation of CSR in English football consists of the players' health, education, staff and geographical remit. The first two can be seen as the fullbacks, and they are two of the major themes that both the PL and the FL support and promote. A clear overlap has been demonstrated between sport and healthy living (Smith and Westerbeek, 2007). Football, therefore, can be used to deliver positive health impacts through programs and initiatives designed around physical exercise. By way of example, the FL's football foundations engage more than 50,000 participants through over 300 locally-based health projects on an annual basis (FL Trust, 2010). Moreover, very recently the football world has begun to realize that it can play a positive role in the promotion of mental as well as physical health and in the delivery of interventions that impact positively on this (Pringle, 2009). Of equal importance are the educational programs implemented by these football organizations. Initiatives such as "Playing for Success," for example, which is delivered in association with the Department of Education and Skills, use football's magnetism to engage young people with the goal of improving standards of literacy, numeracy and information technology.

The result of these health and education initiatives is to emphasize the geographical remit in which the football club, and by association its charitable foundation, exists and operates. These football organizations have, of course, always been the focal points of certain geographical locations (Anagnostopoulos, 2011) and hence are inextricably linked with local community. At the same time, however, different locations in the same county (or even in the same city) often present their own particular challenges. Such contextual diversities cannot be – and are not – ignored by the CSR managers in English football. For example, the social issues that football clubs such as Chelsea and Fulham need to address in central London differ considerably from those Arsenal and Tottenham Hotspur are dealing with in North London. Apart from a minority of football clubs with an international brand name and field of operations, clubs generally demonstrate a strong locality-focused profile in their overall business practices (see Hindley and Williamson, Chapter 24).

What needs to be stressed, however, is that all the above-mentioned is not "just happening." There are people behind the implementation of those programs and their training and development is seen by CSR managers as an *internal* socially responsible practice. The crucial fact here is that the process of CSR implementation also creates human capital. Wolsey and Abrams (2011: 341) for example point out that, through necessary training, some vocationally oriented skills and knowledge can be applied directly to work-based practice in the short term, whereas personal development can inaugurate the transfer of knowledge into a variety of problem-solving situations in the long term. Staff in these organizations communicate information about healthy lifestyles as well as putting educational messages across through practice (i.e., by keeping themselves active). In this way, notions of education and health are always associated with those people "making things happen." Education and health, therefore, can be seen as fullbacks due to their direct or indirect role behind almost every program these football organizations implement. Staffing and geographical remit complete the line of defence. Before we move on, however, it must be noted that almost all CSR managers reported the charitable organizations they oversee to be under-resourced. This point corroborates findings from McGuire's (2008) ten-year study and as such demonstrates that the issue of staffing has yet to be adequately addressed, despite its significance in the overall CSR implementation process.

The position of the holding midfielder is occupied in our analogy by the "parent" football club. The "parent" club not only deals with the crucial issue of resources (including human resources) but also greatly impacts on the overall CSR implementation process. According to Orejan (2010), the holding midfielders are essential to contemporary football because they can provide better game fluidity by bridging the gap between defence and attackers. This is precisely how CSR managers regard the relationship between the charitable foundation and the football club: it is *the* key link, capable of maximizing any benefits the one can offer the other (Anagnostopoulos and Shilbury, 2013). The benefits an independent community foundation may enjoy over a community department *within* the football club have been mentioned earlier. It seems to be the norm that executive director(s) of the "parent" club (in many cases the Chief Executive Officer or even the owner(s) themselves) are part of the foundation as trustees, and this is often something that CSR managers seek to bring about. The arrangement allows CSR managers to share their strategic agenda with the football club and ultimately strengthens the relationship between them. One could argue that a heavy presence of the "parent" football club in the Board of Trustees undermines the independence of the foundation itself. However, the foundation has its own responsibilities to meet certain charitable objectives and the football club has, in turn, its own legal responsibilities to ensure that this occurs. Whether the kind of "fluidity" Orejan (2010) attributes to the holding midfielder occurs to any great extent between the foundation and the "parent" football club is open to debate. However, it is certainly true that, with a strong buy-in from the club, cross-departmental collaboration has the potential to secure better sponsorship deals and more effective marketing campaigns. For example, by working closely with the football foundation, the "parent" club's marketing department may undertake the difficult task of measuring the impacts of CSR programs through initiatives such as the Customer Relationship Management (CRM) tool. Commercial sponsors, too, are now increasingly looking for well-established delivery mechanisms (such as English football foundations) in order to implement their own CSR agendas in areas such as sports participation and social inclusion (see Downs and Paramio-Salcines, Chapter 9). These issues are the other two "players" to take positions in the middle of the pitch.

Supporting and raising levels of sports participation has always been a key concern for football organizations in England. As Taylor (2011) notes, one of the most enduring problems in the United Kingdom is the substantial fall in sports participation after young people have left school. In football, the decline is from 32 percent of 11–16-year-olds participating to 23 percent of 16–19-year-olds and 12 percent of 20–24-year-olds (Taylor, 2011: 265). Such figures demonstrate why sports participation now has a central role in the strategic CSR agenda of the country's football foundations. Introducing football to the next generation of potential fans/customers via active means (i.e., by playing football) is perhaps more effective, and indeed more in keeping with the principles of CSR, than promoting the sport in a passive way (i.e., watching and supporting football). In 2004, the non-departmental public body Sport England concluded that those engaging least often in sport are from low income groups. Large numbers of English football clubs are located in some of the most deprived areas of the country, and so they are ideally positioned to gain access to and engage with the demographic deemed hardest to reach in terms of sports participation (Mellor, 2010: 34).

As well as targeting them in terms of sports participation, football foundations in England also build on their ability to reach the least well-off communities in their CSR programs for social inclusion. These initiatives target socially marginalized groups, and the work done by foundations in this area is at the core of their CSR implementation strategy (Tacon, 2007); in football parlance, one could argue that social inclusion initiatives constitute the most "experienced" player of the field. The Kickz project, for example, was first launched in April 2006 with just four football clubs taking part across the PL and the FL. Between them, these four clubs reached almost 4,600 young people. Five years later, the same program is now being implemented by 43 football clubs and boasts over 50,000 participants (Premier League, 2011).

The front line of CSR implementation in English football consists of two wingers and one centre forward. The wingers represent areas to which English football foundations and clubs are giving increasing attention: the environment and communication. These issues are being gradually integrated into strategic CSR agendas, although there is still plenty of room for improvement. Until recently the question of environment has been put in the shade somewhat by the foundations' more socially based initiatives. This perhaps is not surprising given the "fit" that issues like participation, social inclusion and health have with sports in general and football in particular. Over the last few years, however, environmental awareness has been growing within the foundations' CSR agendas, most often through their existing education programs. It is largely for this reason that the tactical formation offered in this chapter places education and the environment on same side of the pitch (right-hand side), as a strong collaboration exists between the two "players" (Figure 6.4). As well as promoting awareness of environmental issues to local communities, both the foundations and their "parent" clubs have also started implementing transport planning (thereby reducing the environmental impact of football staff and supporters) and resource management (thereby reducing waste, water and energy use). Both foundations and clubs have specific environmental policies with clear aims and objectives and commitment to the environment (Mellor, 2010: 16).

Another area that has been identified as a key "player" in the overall implementation process of CSR programs is the actual communication of those programs. Morgan (see more details of the communication of CSR programs in Chapters 18, 19 and 20) provides a clear picture not only of how the PL is putting increasing emphasis on communicating its clubs' CSR practices, but also the rationale behind such a decision. This account has an institutionalized context, however; the internal challenges CSR managers often face when trying to incorporate communication into CSR implementation strategy fall outside its remit, and so are worth noting here. For example, despite the fact that official websites serve as the primary communication medium in contemporary football (Kriemadis *et al.*, 2010), only a small number of foundations have launched an independent webpage which allows them to control both the information conveyed and how frequently this information is uploaded (Webster *et al.*, 2011). These two issues are associated with resources (staffing), expertise (training) and priorities (cross-departmental collaboration with the "parent" club) (ibid.). Communication, therefore, is an area recognized by CSR managers as having great potential not only for "repairing the image" (Slack and Shrives, 2008) but also for generating opportunities associated with relationship-building. In addition to this, communication is of course vital to promotional activities which can, in turn, attract sponsorship deals (Webster *et al.*, 2011). Ultimately, more detailed and frequent communication may raise the status of CSR to the salient stakeholder groups of the sector (Walters and Tacon, 2010) and to civil society as a whole as will be analyzed with more detail in Part IV of the handbook. Better communication would help to refute the criticism, encountered among stakeholders and the national community alike, that the CSR programs implemented in English football are a mere "window dressing" exercise.

The place of the centre forward in our tactical formation is given to the concept of the "Big Society." In May 2010, a Conservative–Liberal Democrat coalition government took office in the UK and instigated a change in third-sector policy: this change is referred to somewhat abstractly as "building the Big Society." Alcock (2010) writes that, in essence, this government has been championing community action and sees collective undertakings outside the public realm as the key feature of their third sector model. CSR managers of the football foundations discussed in this chapter regard this political idea as an opportunity to put a clearer strategy in place; the aim of these foundations is to use their revised strategies to help deliver the charitable services that public sector providers may need to relinquish. In order for such aims to be realized in a meaningful way, the centre forward in our analogy needs to be "fed" with quality passes from the rest of the team. Should the other ten "players" underperform, then the goal of a significant contribution to the idea of "Big Society," desired by football organizations and the government alike, may not be met.

Conclusions

The aim of this chapter has been to explain the mechanisms behind the implementation of CSR in English football. It has done so using an analogy of a tactical formation to discuss eleven issues that play a key role in establishing CSR strategy. The aim and its execution are intended as a response to Godfrey *et al.*'s (2010) call for management scholars studying socially responsible business practices to consider specific manifestations of CSR and take into account *relevant industry contexts* and *forces* (emphasis added). Johns (2001), after all, states that one of the most compelling reasons for researchers to pay attention to context resides in its capacity to explain organizational phenomena. Ultimately, however, this chapter draws on a context-specific exercise and this is how it should be regarded and treated.

Notes

1 This chapter largely draws on my doctoral research and I would like to thank all those who agreed to be interviewed for the purpose of that dissertation. I would also like to particularly acknowledge the community scheme director of a South London football club who provided me with the idea of the tactical formation; the suggestion that the tactics put forward within the analogy are "right," as the title implies, is solely the author's interpretation

2 In this chapter the words "foundation" and "trust" are used interchangeably, although preference is given to the former.

3 At the time of writing, the Premier League and Football League have drafted a template service level agreement (SLA) between the club and the foundation that recommends a minimum of two members of the club senior management sit on the board of trustees.

4 Again, this is something that the Professional Footballers Association (PFA) requires from football clubs as part of the broader agreement between the three organizations, the Premier League, Football League and PFA. Therefore, the "discretion" exercised by the club becomes a somewhat abstract notion.

5 This is something that can be potentially achieved after the introduction of a more thorough SLA between the charitable football foundations and their "parent" football clubs.

References

Alcock, P. (2010) 'Building the Big Society: a new policy environment for the third sector in England', *Voluntary Sector Review*, 1 (3), 379–389.

Anagnostopoulos, C. (2011) 'From corporate social responsibility (CSR) to club stakeholder relationship (CSR): the case of football', *Social Responsibility Review*, 3, 14–17.

Anagnostopoulos, C. (2013) 'Examining corporate social responsibility in football: the application of grounded theory methodology', in Söderman S. and Dolles, H. (eds.) *Handbook of research on sport and business*. Cheltenham: Edward Elgar, pp. 418–432.

Anagnostopoulos, C. and Shilbury, D. (2013) 'Implementing corporate social responsibility in English football: towards multi-theoretical integration', *Sport, Business and Management: An International Journal*, 3 (4) (forthcoming).

Bingham, T. and Walters, G. (2012) 'Financial sustainability within UK charities: community sport trusts and corporate social responsibility partnerships', *Voluntas: International Journal of Voluntary and Nonprofit Organizations*. (Online). Available at: http://rd.springer.com/article/10.1007/s11266-012-9275-z (accessed: October 11, 2012).

Breitbarth, T., Hovemann, G. and Walzel, S. (2011) 'Scoring strategy goals: Measuring corporate social responsibility in professional European football', *Thunderbird International Business Review*, 53 (6), 721–737. (Online). Available at: http://onlinelibrary.wiley.com/doi/10.1002/tie.20448/abstract (accessed: August 15, 2012).

Brown, A., Crabbe, T., Mellor, G., Blackshaw, T. and Stone, C. (2006) *Football and its communities: Final Report*. The Football Foundation and Manchester Metropolitan University.

Charity Commission (2007) *The charity commission: Regulating for the future (listening to external views challenging assumptions)*. London: Charity Commission.

Football League (2008) *Football League Newsletter*, June 5.

Football League Trust (2010) *Community matters: the Football League Trust review 2007–2010*. Preston: Football League Trust.

Godfrey, P., Hatch, N. and Hansen, J. (2010) 'Toward a general theory of CSRs: the roles of beneficence, profitability, insurance, and industry heterogeneity', *Business & Society*, 49 (2), 316–344.

Hine, J. and Preuss, L. (2009) '"Society is out there, organisation is in here": On the perceptions of corporate social responsibility held by different managerial groups', *Journal of Business Ethics*, 88 (2), 381–393.

Hovemann, G., Breitbarth, T. and Walzel, S. (2011) 'Beyond sponsorship? Corporate social responsibility in English, German and Swiss top national league football clubs', *Journal of Sponsorship*, 4 (4), 338–352

James, M. and Miettinen, S. (2010) 'Are there any regulatory requirements for football clubs to report against social and environmental impacts?' Working paper as part of the project '*The Social Value of Football*' undertaken by Substance and funded by Supporters Direct.

Johns, G. (2001) 'In praise of context', *Journal of Organisational Behaviour*, 22, 31–42.

King, A. (2002) *The end of the terraces: the transformation of English Football in the 1990s*. 2nd edn. Leicester: Leicester University Press.

Kriemadis, T., Terzoudis, C. and Kartakoullis, N. (2010) 'Internet marketing in football clubs: a comparison between English and Greek websites', *Soccer & Society*, 11 (3), 291–307.

McGuire, B. (2008) 'Football in the community: Still "the game's best kept secret"?' *Soccer and Society*, 9 (4), 439–454.

Mellor, G. (2005) 'Mixed motivations: why do football clubs do 'community' work?', *Soccer Review*, 18–24.

Mellor, G. (2008) 'The janus-faced Sport: English football, community and the legacy of the "Third Way"', *Soccer and Society*, 9 (3), 313–324.

Mellor, G. (2010) *Community matters: The Football League Trust review 2007–2010*. Substance: Manchester.

Morgan, S. (2010) 'Creating Chances: The Premier League's corporate social responsibility programme', *Journal of Sponsorship*, 4 (1), 15–26.

Orejan, J. (2010) 'A descriptive history of major tactical formations used in Football Association from 1863 to the present', in Anagnostopoulos, C. (ed.) *International sport: A research synthesis*. Athens: ATINER, pp. 43–56.

Premier League (2011) 'Kickz 5 Year Publication Report'. (Online). Available at: http://addison.ceros. com/kickz/kickz/5/year/celebration/fiveyearcelebration/page/1/ (accessed: November 23, 2011).

Pringle, A. (2009) 'The growing role of football as a vehicle for interventions in mental health care', *Journal of Psychiatric and Mental Health Nursing*, 16, 553–557.

Russell, D. (1997) *Football and the English: A social history of Association Football in England, 1863–1995*. Preston: Carnegie.

Slack, R. and Shrives, P. (2008) 'Social disclosure and legitimacy in Premier League football clubs: the first ten years', *Journal of Applied Accounting*, 9 (1), 17–28.

Smith, A.C.T and Westerbeek, H.M. (2007) 'Sport and a vehicle for deploying corporate social responsibility', *Journal of Corporate Citizenship*, 21 (1), 43–55.

Sport England (2004) *Driving up participation: The challenge for sport*. London: Sport England.

Tacon, R. (2007) 'Football and social inclusion: Evaluating social policy', Managing Leisure, 12 (1), 1–23.

Taylor, N. (2004) 'Giving something back: Can football clubs and their communities co-exist?' in Wagg, S. (ed.) *British football and social exclusion*. London: Routledge, pp. 47–66.

Taylor, P. (2011) 'Sport and physical activity', in Taylor, P. (ed.) *Torkildsen's sport and leisure management*. 6th edn. London: Routledge, pp. 253–282.

Walters, G. (2009) 'Corporate social responsibility through sport: the Community Trust model as a CSR delivery agency', *Journal of Corporate Citizenship*, 35, 81–94.

Walters, G. and Chadwick, S. (2009) 'Corporate citizenship in football: delivering strategic benefits through stakeholder engagement', *Management Decision*, 47 (1), 51–66.

Walters, G. and Tacon, R. (2010) 'Corporate social responsibility in sport: stakeholder management in the UK football industry', *Journal of Management & Organisation*, 16 (4), 566–586.

Watson, N. (2000) 'Football in the community: what's the score?' in Garland, J., Malcolm, D. and Rowe, M. (eds.) *The future of football: Challenges for the twenty-first century.* London: Frank Cass, 114–129.

Webster, I. Anagnostopoulos, C. and Hudson, K. (2011) 'Getting the message across: website presence and corporate social responsibility in English football', paper presented at the 19th Conference of the European Association of Sport Management, Madrid, Spain, September 7-10.

Wolsey, C. and Abrams, J. (2011) 'Managing people in sport and leisure', in Taylor, P. (ed.) *Torkildsen's sport and leisure management.* 6th edn. London: Routledge, pp. 337–364.

7

CSR AND ENVIRONMENTAL RESPONSIBILITY

The case of NCAA athletic departments

Sylvia Trendafilova, Michael E. Pfahl and Jonathan Casper

Overview

The role and relevance of environmentally sustainable practices, under the umbrella of corporate social responsibility (CSR), have recently received increased attention in the realm of sport. This chapter examines the environmental components of CSR within the context of the National Collegiate Athletic Association (NCAA) and member schools. The primary focus is on the role American intercollegiate athletic department personnel play in the development and implementation of environmentally sustainable practices. The chapter highlights recent research regarding sustainability efforts in Football Bowl Subdivision (FBS) universities (n=97). Athletic department personnel were surveyed with the aim of establishing a foundation to better understand environmental awareness among department personnel and the strategies they used in the decision-making and implementation stages of existing programs. The results reveal that, despite high levels of environmental concern, there are significant challenges associated with a lack of knowledge about sustainability initiatives. In addition, the results raise questions about the coordinated efforts between the athletic department personnel and other units of the university (e.g., sustainability offices). Throughout the chapter, examples of strategic environmental efforts from NCAA universities are provided to augment the research findings. It concludes by providing suggestions for future research for sustainability efforts in the area of CSR and the broader issue of environmental responsibility within intercollegiate athletic departments.

CSR and environmental responsibility in sport

The focus of much of the academic research in the area of CSR has primarily been on identifying the link between financial and social performance (Margolis and Walsh, 2003). CSR is an increasingly pervasive phenomenon on the European and North American economic and political landscape (Doh and Guay, 2006) and has been addressed from multiple angles (Jamali, 2008; Orlitzky, 2008).

CSR practices differ based on the size of the sport entity and the region of the world as cultural differences help determine the relationship between the business and society. The European Commission is one of the major leaders in CSR efforts in Europe, initiating a new strategy called *To Make Europe a Pole of Excellence on Corporate Social Responsibility*. In February

2009, the European Commission hosted a meeting of the European multi-stakeholder forum on CSR with the aim of evaluating the progress of CSR efforts around the world (European Commission, 2009). In response to worldwide initiatives to adopt CSR practices, sports organizations have worked to integrate CSR practices into their operations (Babiak and Wolfe, 2006; Breitbarth and Harris, 2008; Sheth and Babiak, 2010; Walters and Chadwick, 2009).

While there is a growing body of CSR research in general, it has only recently been examined in the sport industry. Consideration is now being given to the unique context in which sport operates, and some scholars argue that the nature and role CSR plays in a sport organization may be different than in other industries (Babiak and Wolfe, 2006, 2009; Smith and Westerbeek, 2007; Walker and Kent, 2009) (see Chapter 1: Babiak and Wolfe offer a detailed analysis of the unique features of sport and CSR). Smith and Westerbeek (2007) for instance, claimed that sport broadly defined has a number of unique factors that may positively affect the nature and scope of CSR efforts including: mass media distribution and communication power; youth appeal; positive health impacts/association; social interaction; and sustainability awareness. These scholars highlight sport's unique imperatives in the realm of social responsibility. In particular related to environmental issues, they ascertain that "sport is demanding on the physical environment. Socially responsible sport acknowledges this burden and develops policies to avoid environmental damage" (Smith and Westerbeek, 2007: 25). Further, sport has emerged as a new platform for the adoption of sustainable development (Coady *et al.*, 2007).

On the surface, the link between the environment and sport may not be immediately obvious. However, upon deeper consideration, a number of relevant connections between sports organizations and the natural environment become clearer. Sport facilities and sport events concentrate large numbers of people in a confined space over a relatively small period, and as a result can pose risks to the natural environment within which they reside (Chernushenko, 1994). Sport initiatives with an environmental connection include sport mega-events such as the Super Bowl, the Olympic Games, and other international sport contests such as World Cup soccer tournaments (see Chapter 8, Zhang and colleagues, for a review of environmental issues on mega-sports events). Specifically, FIFA established a *Green Goal program* to help organizing committees develop a climate-neutral World Cup (FIFA, 2009). The International Olympic Committee (IOC) incorporated the environment as a third *pillar* within the overall Olympic movement alongside sport and culture as foundational Olympic ideals (Cantelon and Letters, 2000). Most, if not all, of these types of events have an environmental responsibility component in their programs or guidelines. Such efforts include tree planting to offset carbon emissions of spectators traveling to events, in-stadia recycling initiatives, recovery and distribution of "prepared food," and the development of environmental guidelines for use by vendors and contractors (Babiak and Trendafilova, 2011; Babiak and Wolfe, 2006; Global Forum for Sport and the Environment, 2010; Mallen *et al.*, 2011; Paquette *et al.*, 2011).

Major league professional and intercollegiate sport in North America are industries in which CSR is playing an increasingly important role, and where increasing attention is given to understanding the impact professional sports teams and leagues have on the natural environment (Babiak and Wolfe, 2006). Corporate focus on the environment and sustainable practices has been an increased interest to sports organizations. This new emphasis has been driven by changing societal values (e.g., environmental care) and increased engagement with and expectations by variety of stakeholders (e.g., return on investment, customer service) (Babiak and Trendafilova, 2011; Horne, 2006).

In the United States, collegiate sport is a complex and thriving enterprise. At the forefront of the business of college sport is the National Collegiate Athletic Association (NCAA) and its member colleges and universities. CSR has been reviewed in the context of professional sports, but scholarship related to CSR and its application in collegiate sports is lacking despite the fact that the role of intercollegiate athletics in environmental management has been addressed (Pfahl and Ott, 2010; Schmidt, 2006; Thibault, 2009). With the rising emphasis in collegiate athletics, there is a need to investigate the constructs linking social and environmental responsibility.

Therefore, the purpose of this chapter is to discuss the concept of CSR and its relationship to college sports in the United States. More specifically, the focus is on the environmental sustainability efforts of collegiate athletic departments as part of the overall CSR goals.

CSR and the NCAA

CSR has been extensively discussed and studied in the traditional corporate world. We argue that the NCAA and its member institutions could be viewed as corporations as well and therefore may be following in the footsteps of other businesses by implementing some CSR initiatives. Historically the NCAA has always been involved with sport as a business and has been defined by scholars as a business cartel comprised of university-firms that have varying desires to restrict competition and maximize profits (Koch, 1973; Rosenthal, 2003). More specifically Koch (1973: 138) argued that the NCAA displays many of the vital characteristics of a cartel including the following functional tasks:

1 Sets the maximum price that can be paid for intercollegiate athletes.
2 Regulates the quantity of athletes that can be purchased in a given time period.
3 Regulates the duration and intensity of usage of those athletes.
4 Occasionally fixes the price at which sports outputs can be sold (e.g., the setting of ticket prices at NCAA championship events which are held on the campuses of cartel members).
5 Periodically informs cartel members about transactions, costs, market conditions, and sales techniques.
6 Occasionally pools and distributes portions of the cartel's profits, particularly those which result from intercollegiate football and basketball.
7 Polices the behavior of the members of the cartel and levies penalties against those members who are deemed to be in violation of cartel rules and regulations.

Millions of dollars are generated within athletic departments via tickets, merchandise sales, media rights, sponsorships, donors, and naming rights. Television companies are locked into bidding wars for the right to own the rights to televise the biggest and best games in college sports. The NCAA has the difficult task of adjusting itself to the continually growing industry of collegiate athletics and the mega-million dollar enterprise. One major indicator that the NCAA and its member institutions have evolved into a "business machine" is compensation of collegiate football and basketball coaches. The budgets of many NCAA Division I athletic departments soar well beyond $100 million annually and some coaches are earning more than $3 million annually (Weir, 2010). College sports have grown from friendly competitions between rivals into big business. The increasing salaries, media/television contracts, and the construction of new sport facilities support the relationship between large corporations and amateur athletics within the NCAA model.

Athletic departments in search of funds are turning to corporate sponsorships, external marketing, and media firms, and are funneling hundreds of millions of dollars into stadiums, thus making the collegiate athletics model begin to resemble the professional athletics model.

Athletic departments have become increasingly commercialized mostly due to their mandate to be self-supporting (Padilla and Baumer, 1994). Evidence for this commercialization is expressed in the efforts to secure property/naming rights. In addition, efforts are made to generate revenue through television and radio rights, stadium boxes, seat licenses, and corporate advertising (Burden and Li, 2003). Those types of activities align with the image of corporate America more than they align with the traditional campus image.

With the rising emphasis on the business aspects of collegiate athletics, there is a need to investigate the constructs towards social responsibility. In fact, initial evidence exists that CSR initiatives in NCAA athletics have been adopted and these practices are influenced by regulatory and institutional policies (Brown, 2012). Regulations put forth by governing bodies strongly influence the emphasis placed on specific CSR practices. Intercollegiate athletic administrators are in a liminal position where they must balance their presence as change agents through CSR efforts with their responsibilities to fulfill university missions and goals (Bohdanowicz, 2006; Rivera and De Leon, 2005; Spaargaren, 2003). However, with this increased responsibility comes increased accountability (Hums *et al.*, 1999; Mascarenhas, 2009). One aspect of CSR revolves around addressing the environment and environmental protection has become an important concern for sports organizations at all levels, including intercollegiate athletics (Jin *et al.*, 2011).

Environmental Responsibility in the NCAA

Intercollegiate athletic departments provide an excellent example of the relationship between sport and the environment. Within the landscape of intercollegiate athletics there are numerous stakeholders including athletic department personnel, university personnel, and students. Athletic departments offer a wide variety of sports and require multiple specialized facilities with a substantial and variable environmental impact. Additionally, athletic departments host large-scale events and spectatorship is a core element of their operations.

As environmental issues are integrated into strategic planning processes of athletic departments, athletics administrators must become more knowledgeable about environmental issues in order to balance (and to satisfy) competing stakeholder requirements. This tension makes examining their awareness and knowledge of environmental issues an important step towards a better understanding of the actions they take in response to environmental issues. Despite the increasing importance of environmental issues in collegiate athletics, a clear understanding of the ways athletic department personnel develop and implement environmental actions remain unclear.

In a seminal study, Casper *et al.* (2012) examined American intercollegiate athletic department personnel in relation to their organization's environmental sustainability practices, organizational strategies, and personal perspectives at NCAA Football Bowl Subdivision (FBS) universities. The study sought to understand the levels of awareness and concern for environmental issues held by key administrators in FBS universities (n=97). In addition, it developed a baseline understanding of environmental actions taken by athletic department personnel.

Casper *et al.* (2012) study chose to focus on Division I athletic departments because department personnel must balance the demands (e.g., winning, budgets, graduation rates) of various stakeholders (e.g., facility management staff, fans, academic administrators, waste management contractors, food and beverage vendors) against strategic natural environmental initiatives. Their environmental actions must be part of their overall strategic planning processes in order to utilize scarce resources in an efficient manner to achieve their strategic goals of all types and to satisfy stakeholder requirements (Hart, 1995; Pfahl, 2010, 2011). A strategic view of the natural environment implies athletic department personnel must take a short- and long-term view when planning environmental initiatives (Pfahl, 2011). At the same time, the costs of operating intercollegiate athletics programs increased substantially in the past twenty years due to significant changes in the sports landscape (e.g., commercialization, professionalization) (Cunningham, 2002; Duderstadt, 2003; Thelin, 2000). Further, strategic planning for environmental initiatives is often complicated by the need to work with University environmental personnel (e.g., sustainability officers) who are responsible for integrating athletic department strategies with broader University ones (Bekessey *et al.*, 2007; Leal Filho, 2000).

In this volatile context, athletic department personnel are now addressing environmental issues. The awareness and knowledge levels of athletic department personnel help to determine the actions they take, especially if they wish to move beyond compliance and into active prevention of environmental problems (Pfahl, 2010; Russo and Fouts, 1997; Shrivastava, 1995). Understanding awareness and knowledge levels allows for a more contextualized view of environmental initiatives (Barney, 1991; Judge and Douglas, 1998).

Casper *et al.* (2012) study found there is high awareness of environmental issues by athletic department personnel, but this awareness is not necessarily resulting in improved planning activities by athletic department administrators. For example, a majority of the respondents believed their university/college viewed environmental and sustainability initiatives as a high priority, while only 43 percent believed these initiatives were a high priority within the athletic department. One important finding was that there appeared to be a disconnect between athletic department and university-led environmental strategies. Additional findings illustrated that most of the high-ranking athletic department administrators did not know whether their president's name was among the signatories of the American College and University Presidents' Climate Commitment (ACUPCC) indicating a lack of clarity and/or mutual understanding of the broader role of sustainability initiatives on campus. The ACUPCC brought together high education leadership to commit to promoting environmentally responsible behaviors on college and university campuses. It also provides a strategic plan to take immediate steps to address environmental issues (e.g., greenhouse gas emissions) on campus. Further, three-quarters of the Athletic Directors (ADs) who responded believed that the emphasis on environmental programs in the athletic department will increase in the future, and while there is recognition of this trend, 89 percent responded that their athletic department does not currently have a sustainability plan in place. Over half of the respondents indicated a plan would come from athletic department personnel, but only a small percentage of departments had even considered developing a strategic plan or had a sustainability team.

The study also measured personal environmental perspective of the ADs. Casper *et al.* (2012) found that most (89 percent) of the key decision-makers held a positive perspective on initiatives, but one-third of them believed they would negatively affect their budget. The most important concerns were related to environmental initiatives having an unclear return on investment and being a distraction to their main organizational goals, whatever those might be. The respondents were also asked to rate their emphasis on 11 environmental initiatives within the athletic department. A majority (72 percent) of the respondents indicated high or very high priority for energy conservation and efficiency. Recycling in the office and at events was also a high or very high priority. Initiatives related to green cleaning, green turf management, green building, and water conservation were viewed as a moderate or high priority with over 50 percent of the respondents. The use of natural/local food vendors and fan transportation initiatives were considered low to very low priorities within the majority of the athletic departments.

Lastly, after gathering information regarding opinions about initiatives, respondents were asked the extent to which implementation of five specific environmentally oriented initiatives were being implemented in their institutions. The first category related to energy equipment. Sustainable lighting equipment and efforts to reduce use of lighting were currently implemented at the institutions surveyed. Conservation based on training behavior, or the environmental actions taken in the athletic department on a personal basis (e.g., recycling) and alternative vehicles were being used in over half of the departments. However, alternative energy solutions, such as solar panels or wind turbines, were not currently being implemented by the majority of the respondents.

The second category was related to buildings and operations. Leadership in Energy and Environmental Design (LEED) certification of new buildings was often reported as environmental issues were taken into account during design and construction (35 percent noted extensive use), but less so for retrofitting existing buildings (13 percent). Green solutions for cleaning and athletic fields were reported to be used moderately often. In the case of green cleaning supplies, 30 percent said they used them moderately compared with 24 percent that said they used them extensively. Green turf management was used minimally (26 percent) to moderately (25 percent). Sustainable event concessions were not or minimally being used by a majority (91 percent) of the schools. To explain, in regard to event concessions offering food composting, 64 percent of the respondents did not do it or only made minimal efforts to do so. Organic food saw 74 percent of respondents say they did not offer it or only minimal offerings.

The third category was related to environmental practices. Purchasing recycled products was implemented by a majority of the respondents. This includes buying recycled content paper for restroom areas (29 percent moderately, 26 percent extensively) and buying recycled paper for office use (31 percent moderately, 20 percent extensively). In addition, athletic department personnel moderately used student volunteer help for their green programs (35 percent) with a small amount reporting widespread use (13 percent). Promotional efforts such as mass transit incentives or efforts to reduce fan travel in addition to employee education programs were being used by some schools, but most reported minimal implementation of these types of initiatives. The fourth category was related to water conservation. A majority of the respondents indicated moderate or extensive use of low-flow water conservation equipment. Respondents indicated moderate reduction through control systems and reduction, but less with outdoor facility efforts such as landscaping or rainwater capture and reuse. The fifth category was related to recycling. Of all categories, recycling was the most commonly used environmental initiative currently implemented in the athletic departments. Over 50 percent of the respondents indicated they recycled both at events and in the office. While recycling was a common occurrence in office contexts (38 percent, 31 percent of which with high to moderate use), and at events (39 percent, 28 percent of which with high to moderate use), athletic department efforts such as in-game announcements about green efforts and collection of recyclable material (e.g., a pass the trash activity) at events were the least implemented initiatives.

Casper *et al.* (2012) also investigated how their findings significantly differed based on the athletic division (BCS division vs non-BCS Division I schools). The most notable difference was athletic department personnel at BCS schools reported the responsibility of environmental initiatives fell to the athletic department, while those at non-BCS schools indicated more campus-wide involvement. Non-BCS school personnel indicated that sustainability initiatives are a bigger distraction for the department's main goals. Additionally, BCS school personnel were found to have more knowledge than their counterparts at non-BCS schools regarding fans' concerns for sustainability and reported greater emphasis on energy conservation initiatives. Non-BCS schools reported more use of pre-planned recycling rate goals (e.g., percentage of waste that was recycled and diverted from landfills).

Overall, this study provided a baseline for assessing the issues facing intercollegiate athletics related to environmental sustainability and provides some directions for future courses of action. Members of the athletic department staff appeared to agree that athletic departments have a role to play in addressing environmental issues. Their responses showed many athletic departments are implementing initiatives (e.g. recycling, water use reduction), but a coordinated effort and actual measurement are needed to determine if their efforts are successful or not. After understanding more about awareness and knowledge of personnel, this chapter provides a few examples of NCAA schools where environmental sustainability has been successfully implemented.

Examples of NCAA schools with well-established environmental programs

Numerous ways exist for NCAA athletic department personnel to implement sustainability initiatives. Casper *et al.* (2012) demonstrated how athletic department personnel are addressing environmental issues. The examples provided here build upon their initial findings and demonstrate specific instances of environmentally related and strategically planned initiatives. The efforts fall into two main categories reflecting the initial findings of the study: recycling efforts and all other environmentally focused efforts.

Examples of recycling efforts

Recycling efforts are among the more visible and simplest to administer environmental initiatives athletic department personnel can take. The following examples provide descriptions of the efforts and illustrate important issues such as collaboration, implementation efforts, and fan engagement (Casper *et al.*, 2012).

University of Tennessee

In 1993, the University of Tennessee (UT) began the recycling program *Good Sports Always Recycle* in an effort to promote recycling at all UT sporting events. The program operates with the assistance of corporate sponsors Eastman Kodak, Coca-Cola, Waste Connections, and Food City. During the football season, 140 55-gallon containers are rolled into Neyland Stadium to collect recyclable materials. Over 100 collapsible bins with blue plastic tops are placed outside the stadium in parking and tailgating areas to give fans opportunities to recycle prior to entering the stadium. There are also recycling containers placed at entrance gates to the stadium in an effort to recycle bottles and cans from fans, as beverages are not allowed to be brought into the stadium. In 2007, small collapsible containers were added to collect newspapers and other types of paper products. Once football season ends, the containers at Neyland Stadium are moved to Thompson-Boling Arena, and the parking areas outside, for use during the basketball season. The recycling efforts from the *Good Sports Always Recycle* program enabled UT to collect over 17 tons of recyclable material during the 2007 football season, and currently roughly 15 percent of the 15 tons of waste generated at each football game is recycled (University of Tennessee, 2012).

Penn State University

In 1996, Penn State University implemented a recycling program inside their football stadium, Beaver Stadium, but expanded their recycling program to include recycling collection in the parking lot and tailgating areas. Inside the stadium, the main recyclables are beverage contain-ers, cardboard, and program booklets, however, the initiatives outside the stadium are where the majority of the recyclables are collected. Penn State places 290 blue, 96-gallon recycling containers and 42 eight-yard dumpsters throughout the parking and tailgating areas. Members of a student volunteer group distribute recycling bags to fans and encourage them to recycle. By including the parking and tailgate areas in their recycling efforts, Penn State tripled their previous recycling record in 2008 by collecting 112 tons of recyclable materials.

Florida State University

Florida State University implemented a recycling program at their football games similar to Penn State's, targeting both the concourses inside Doak Campbell Stadium, along with the tailgate areas and parking lots nearby. Through the program, *Garnet and Gold Goes Green*, vol-unteers arrive on the grounds around Doak Campbell Stadium to collect recyclable materials from 2.5 hours prior to kickoff to well into the time the game is being played. Through the efforts of this program, Florida State University collected over 32 tons of recyclable material during the 2010 football season (Florida State University, 2011).

Moving beyond recycling

The aforementioned recycling efforts are often the first step taken on environmental change pathways. However, some athletic departments in the United States have initiated broader and more strategically oriented efforts. A few of these efforts are described here.

University of Colorado

The University of Colorado (CU) became the first Football Bowl Subdivision (FBS) school to launch a zero-waste program for waste reduction at football games. The program, *Ralphie's Green Stampede*, is an initiative aimed at moving towards zero waste during football season at Folsom Field, CU's football stadium. The program also addresses energy used in powering the stadium, team travel, and other football related activities by investing in local carbon-reduction projects. To help match energy use from both Folsom Field and travel, CU Director of Intercollegiate Athletics Mike Bohn stated CU would invest in local carbon offset initiatives from the Colorado Carbon Fund, which is a program of the Governor's Energy Office, and also through renewable energy credits with assistance from White Wave Foods, who is a zero-waste program partner (Ralphie's Green Stampede, 2011). Other initiatives that are a part of *Ralphie's Green Stampede* include CU's food service provider, Centerplate, Inc., converting almost all of their food and beverage containers to materials that are either recyclable or compostable and the implemen-tation of a bicycle valet service, which is designed to encourage fans to ride their bicycles to football games by providing bicycle parking and storage (Ralphie's Green Stampede, 2011).

University of New Hampshire

The University of New Hampshire (UNH) athletic department partnered with the university's sustainability office to provide fans at UNH football games with eco-friendly products through a program called *Go Green with the Wildcats*. UNH corporate partners set up tables around the football stadium with displays regarding their environmentally friendly products and services. Volunteers are also at the stadium to interact with the fans and to give them reminders to recycle. In addition to the *Go Green with the Wildcats* program, UNH also initiated significant sustainability efforts, including a commitment to reduce carbon emissions to 50 percent by 2020 and 80 percent by 2050, as well as requiring all new construction and renovations of campus buildings be LEED certified (University of New Hampshire, 2011).

North Carolina State University

North Carolina State University (NC State) provides an excellent example of a coordinated effort between the University and the athletic department. Many environmental initiatives in other NCAA member institutions were undertaken by athletic department and university personnel separately and there was no communication or coordination of efforts between them. However, to initiate a more concerted effort, NC State formed the *Sustainability in Athletics Committee*, which included key university and athletic department personnel, campus sustainability office personnel, and professors. One of the first agenda items was an assessment of all current efforts in order to see how they could be better coordinated. An important outcome of this assessment was the decision to use athletic events as a way to help the sustainability office maximize exposure for its events to the non-student Raleigh population. Also, additional evaluations of environmental efforts were conducted by university professors to better understand and to coordinate efforts. Finally, the committee recently incorporated environmental sustainability as part of the university-wide strategic plan. By matching sustainability strategies within broader university strategies, the potential for support, funding, and impact of future sustainability efforts is far greater.

University of California, Santa Barbara and Cal Poly State University

The University of California, Santa Barbara (UCSB) and Cal Poly State University (CPSU) provide an example of inter-campus sustainability efforts. Athletic department personnel from both schools agreed to work together to raise awareness for sustainability issues on campus (e.g., sustainability conferences, events to highlight *Recycle Mania* at athletics events energy savings initiatives). They called their partnership the *Series for Sustainability*, which added a competitive to an otherwise cooperative opportunity. These Big West conference members often compete under a Blue–Green rivalry moniker, but this time, the games are enhanced by an emphasis on environmental awareness and actions. The two athletics programs compete across a number of different sports each year and athletic department personnel on both sides see the rivalry as a means to promote sustainability issues. The partnership is not surprising since both schools have active sustainability programs on campus and UCSB was chosen as one of ten eco-friendly college campuses in the United States in 2011 (Kern, 2011). Such a partnership offers the opportunity for inter-conference and intra-conference cooperation in relation to sustainability initiatives. Further, working together offers athletic department personnel a chance to share resources and costs in reaching out to various stakeholders.

Yale University

Yale University has taken a unique approach regarding sustainability programs at athletic events with the creation of *Bulldog Sustainability*, which is an initiative aimed at positively impacting the environment by educating and encouraging eco-friendly practices and behavior within the Yale community. Bulldog Sustainability has taken a unique approach to communicating their message with the creation of a Facebook page (Yale University, 2011). Educational topics, sustainability news, photographs from sustainability efforts at athletic events, and event announcements are posted on their Facebook page. *Bulldog Sustainability* best practices are shared with the NCAA in an effort to educate athletic departments at other universities (Yale University, 2011).

Evaluation of environmental efforts

These examples highlight the understanding by athletic department personnel that actions can be taken to address environmental issues in collegiate sports. They demonstrate how collaborative efforts with different stakeholders can be used to develop actions to address environmental issues (e.g., with corporations, between universities). Additionally, these examples highlight the complex nature of environmentalism in collegiate organizations. To explain, while the initiative examples are relatively simple to initiate (e.g., recycling), they are also linked with internal processes that holistically address a department's environmental footprint (e.g., usage audits, waste reduction programs) making interconnections between different efforts important to overall success. Finally, the examples demonstrate the need for collaboration and continuous communication across different relationships that are necessary to achieve success (e.g., athletic department, sustainability office, and partners).

Conclusions

This chapter discussed the concept of CSR and its relationship to intercollegiate sport. The primary focus was on environmentally sustainable practices within the athletic departments. The key outcome of the study described in this chapter is to highlight the importance of the environment in intercollegiate athletics. Further, it offers a set of implications for practitioners that emphasize integration, collaboration, strategy, and outreach. Finally, sport scholars and managers are at the beginning of understanding how environmental issues impact the sport world leaving important areas of future inquiry to be addressed.

Implications for practitioners

One of the most significant findings of the study is the disconnection between stakeholders, namely athletic department and sustainability office personnel, despite collaborative efforts on university campuses. Whenever athletic department personnel work with stakeholders, communication and relationship oriented issues come to the foreground. Without these relationships, athletic department personnel will have difficulty developing, administering, and evaluating sustainability efforts.

Second, helping to make certain sustainability efforts are a part of athletic departments' daily routines, issues related to the environment must be integrated into strategic planning. Numerous contextual challenges enable and constrain athletic department personnel (e.g., awareness, financing, time, and labor). Placing sustainability within the strategic web of departmental activities means it will not remain solely in the realm of marketing or community relations nor will it be forgotten entirely. Weaving an environmental focus into strategy continues to keep questions of sustainability in front of planners at each step (e.g., resource allocation) (Hart, 1995). The fact that many environmentally related activities can be measured (e.g., recycling, energy usage, water usage, food waste, recycling tonnage) means that return on investment is calculable and efforts can be evaluated and altered accordingly. In other words, control and oversight systems could be developed.

Third, even if environmental issues are placed in strategic contexts, continued education of all athletic department stakeholders to improve awareness and knowledge is needed. The study highlighted the point that athletic department personnel were aware of environmental issues (some, not all), but were not necessarily moving into the realm of knowledge in terms of how to understand root causes and to develop necessary actions. Operationally, this means there is an additional disconnection between awareness, knowledge, and action because the best solution to a problem might be ignored or left undiscovered. Sustainability office personnel can assist in this area by providing a mechanism to develop and to distribute information and data to athletic department personnel in order to integrate both into strategic actions. The relationship allows information exchange and a platform for education to take place.

Finally, with strategic emphasis on environmental actions, athletic department personnel can include revenue generation opportunities and community outreach into their planning. Strategic partners and sponsors can be developed in relation to community outreach (e.g., a green game) in which revenue is generated or costs offset. For example, it could be a sponsorship of a green game by a local waste management company or engaging in recycling efforts with a campus beverage provider (Pfahl and Ott, 2010).

The digital space is a key component here as well because costs are lower, but developing engaging spaces on athletic department websites related to the environment means sponsors can reach a more targeted and engaged community within the broader fan base. One example of this is from the Big South Conference and a partner with Waste Management that provides a *Sustainability Tip of the* Month (Big South, 2011). This example shows how schools or conferences can utilize (i.e., engagement) and monetize (i.e., branded space, advertising revenue) the digital space. The tips are located at the Big South's website and there is a link to Waste Management's website area that addresses their environmental education and awareness efforts.

The community outreach activities build on strengths of the athletic department because many programs already work in this area (e.g., reading programs). The environmental issues can be woven into existing efforts (e.g., environmentally themed readings, sustainable infrastructure for outreach activities such as recycling). Further, the environmental outreach can be a standalone activity or one that blends service (e.g., recycling campaigns) with departmental needs (e.g., volunteers to collect and to manage recycling at games).

In the end, athletic department personnel must deal with sustainability issues. Sustainability efforts require collective action. In other words, change at the individual level needs to occur first and is necessary but not sufficient for substantial change, unless a large number of individuals act in a similar fashion for the common goal of achieving sustainability. As individuals become more aware and knowledgeable about issues related to the environment and their link to athletic department, then substantive and lasting changes can take place. In the next section, areas of future research, driven by the outcomes of this study, are presented.

Areas of future research

Future areas of research exploring the intersection between the environment and intercollegiate athletics can be found in a number of different areas. First, additional work that identifies motives and driving forces behind the adoption of sustainability practices is needed. While the study discussed in this chapter emphasizes a number of issues related to the environment, it is a baseline. Moving deeper into Division I athletics is a start because of its high media profile and high levels of community engagement. However, additional research within Division II and Division III programs is needed to understand both motivational aspects of environmentally related behavior and contextual elements that enable and constrain them as compared to the larger programs in Division I. Sustainability efforts assist and challenge budgets at all levels, so examining these efforts across the board can elicit a variety of practices, partnerships, and strategies to study.

Second, these contextual studies can help to better understand barriers to adoption. Case oriented studies work well in this situation because they are able to drill deep into issues and allow scholars and practitioners to compare contexts to find answers to relevant questions.

Third, a deeper empirical understanding can help to design systems to measure and to evaluate the success (or lack of success) of the sustainability programs. Scorecards are a good start, but contextual and/or malleable measuring instruments would help move into more actionable results. They would also foster additional partnerships between on-campus offices and researchers and practitioners. Such study can establish a database which could be helpful for schools that are considering, but do not currently have, sustainability initiatives (e.g., held at the NCAA). These studies must also be done over time. There is no end point for environmental issues, so establishing metrics means integrating time into measurement and creating points of comparison to determine success or failure of different efforts.

Fourth, little is known about the NCAA's position on environmental issues. The NCAA is moving forward with sustainability efforts at event such as the men's and women's basketball tournaments (National Resources Defense Council, 2011a, 2011b). Further study of local contexts should help the NCAA better position itself on this issue and begin the process of establishing assistance and oversight to its member institutions. There is no competition regarding the environment because each person has a stake in it, so sharing information and ideas should be encouraged. Perhaps, following in the footsteps of two other sport governing bodies, the IOC and FIFA, the NCAA could work on developing guidelines for sport events and athletic departments to ensure that the environment is addressed and the impact is minimized.

Finally, the numerous and different stakeholders who work with athletic departments and sustainability officials must become part of the strategic planning process of all stakeholders, but especially the athletic departments as they are the driver of most activities in the relationships. Collaborative planning and information sharing will enhance the relationship and positively affect the environmental efforts of the moment. However, little is known about these relationships. Continued examination into the environmental efforts of athletic departments and their stakeholders will help to add depth and breadth to the complicated issue of environmentalism in intercollegiate athletics (and sports in general).

References

Babiak, K. and Trendafilova, S. (2011) 'CSR and environmental responsibility: Motives and pressures to adopt sustainable management practices', *Journal of CSR and Environmental Management*, 18 (1), 11–24.

Babiak, K. and Wolfe, R. (2006) 'More than just a game? Corporate social responsibility and Super Bowl XL', *Sport Marketing Quarterly*, 15 (4), 214–222.

Babiak, K. and Wolfe, R. (2009) 'Determinants of corporate social responsibility in professional sport: Internal and external factors', *Journal of Sport Management*, 23 (6), 717–742.

Barney, J. (1991) 'Firm resources and sustained competitive advantage', *Journal of Management*, 17 (1), 99–120.

Bekessy, S., Samson, K., and Clarkson, R. (2007) 'The failure of non-binding declarations to achieve university sustainability: A need for accountability', *International Journal of Sustainability in Higher Education*, 8 (3), 301–316.

Big South (2011) *Sustainability tip of the month*. Available at: http://www.bigsouthsports.com/ViewArticle. dbml?DB_OEM_ID=4800&ATCLID=205308125 (accessed: November 16, 2011).

Bohdanowicz, P. (2006) 'Environmental awareness and initiatives in the Swedish and Polish hotel industries: Survey results', *Hospitality Management*, 25 (4), 662–682.

Breitbarth, T. and Harris, P. (2008) 'The role of corporate social responsibility in the football business: Towards the development of a conceptual model', *European Sport Management Quarterly*, 8 (2), 179–206.

Brown, L. E. (2012) 'Corporate social responsibility in NCAA athletics: Institutional practices and decision makers'. PhD thesis, The Ohio State University.

Burden, W. and Li, M. (2003) 'Differentiation of NCAA Division I Athletic departments in outsourcing of sport marketing operations: A discriminant analysis of financial-related institutional variables', *International Sports Journal*, 7 (2), 74–81.

Cantelon, H. and Letters, M. (2000) 'The making of the IOC environmental policy as the third dimension of the Olympic movement', *International Review for the Sociology of Sport*, 35, 294–308.

Casper, J., Pfahl, M., and McSherry, M. (2012) 'Athletic department awareness and action regarding the environment: A study of NCAA athletic department sustainability practices', *Journal of Sport Management*, 26 (1), 11–29.

Chernushenko, D. (1994) *Greening our games: Running sports events and facilities that won't cost the Earth*. Ottawa: Centurion.

Coady, L., Snider, S., Duffy, A., and Legg, R. (2007) 'Corporate social responsibility for the Vancouver 2010 Olympic and Paralympic Winter Games: Adopting and adapting best practices', *Corporate Social Responsibility Review*, Autumn, 11–15.

Cunningham, G. (2002) 'Examining the relationship among Miles and Snow's strategic types and measures of organizational effectiveness in NCAA Division I athletic departments', *International Review for the Sociology of Sport*, 37 (2), 159–175.

Doh, J.P. and Guay, T.R. (2006) 'Corporate social responsibility, public policy, and NGO activism in Europe and the United States: An institutional-stakeholder perspective', *Journal of Management Studies*, 43 (1), 47–71.

Duderstadt, J. (2003) *Intercollegiate athletics and the American university: A university president's perspective*. Ann Arbor: University of Michigan Press.

European Commission (2009) *Community social responsibility forum*. Available at: http://ec.europa.eu/enterprise/csr/forum_2009_index.htm (accessed: April 30, 2009).

FIFA (2009) *Green Goal program*. Available at http://www.unep.org/Documents.Multilingual/Default.asp?DocumentID=628&ArticleID=6611&l=en (accessed: November 2, 2012).

Florida State University (2011) *Garnet and gold goes green*. Available at: http://www.sustainablecampus.fsu.edu/Our-Programs/Garnet-Gold-Goes-Green (accessed: October 29, 2011).

Global Forum for Sport and the Environment (2010) *Global Forum for Sport and the Environment 2010*. Available at: http://www.sportenvironment.com/cms/2010/11/global-forum-for-sport-and-the-environment-2010/ (accessed: November 2, 2012).

Hart, S. (1995) 'A natural-resource-based view of the firm', *The Academy of Management Review*, 20 (4), 986–1014.

Horne, J. (2006) *Sport in consumer culture*. New York: Palgrave Macmillan.

Hums, M., Barr, C., and Guillon, L. (1999) 'The ethical issues confronting managers in the sport industry', *Journal of Business Ethics*, 20, 51–66.

Jamali, D. (2008) 'A stakeholder approach to corporate social responsibility: A fresh perspective into theory and practice', *Journal of Business Ethics*, 82, 213–231.

Jin, L., Mao, L. L., Zhang, J. J., and Walker, M. B. (2011) 'Impact of green stadium initiatives on donor intentions toward an intercollegiate athletic programme', *International Journal of Sport Management and Marketing*, 10, 121–141.

Judge, W. and Douglas, T. (1998) 'Performance implications of incorporating natural environmental issues into the strategic planning process: An empirical assessment', *Journal of Management Studies*, 35 (2), 241–262.

Kern, R. (2011) '10 eco-friendly college campuses', *US News and World Report*, June 10. Available at: http://www.usnews.com/education/slideshows/10-eco-friendly-college-campuses/6 (accessed: October 31, 2011).

Koch, J. (1973) 'A troubled cartel: The NCAA', *Law and Contemporary Problems*, 38 (1), 135–150.

Leal Filho, W. (2000) *Sustainability and university life*. 2nd edn. New York: Peter Lang.

Mallen, C., Stevens, J., and Adams, L. (2011) 'A content analysis of environmental sustainability research in sport management literature', *Journal of Sport Management*, 25 (3), 240–256.

Mascarenhas, B. (2009) 'The emerging CEO agenda', *Journal of International Management*, 15, 245–250.

Margolis, J.D. and Walsh, J.P. (2003) 'Misery loves companies: Rethinking social initiatives by business', *Administrative Science Quarterly*, 48 (2), 268–305.

National Resources Defense Council (2011a) *National Collegiate Athletic Association Final Four*. Available at: http://www.nrdc.org/greenbusiness/guides/sports/files/NCAA-Case-Study.pdf (accessed: November 2, 2012).

National Resources Defense Council (2011b) *Sustainability achievements of the 2011 NCAA Final Four*. Available at: http://www.nrdc.org/greenbusiness/guides/sports/files/ncaafinalfoursustainabilitypdf (accessed: November 2, 2012).

Orlitzky, M. (2008) 'Corporate social performance and financial performance: A research synthesis', in Crane, A., McWilliams, A., Matten, D., Moon, J., and Siegel, D.S. (eds.) *The Oxford handbook of corporate social responsibility*. New York: Oxford University Press, pp. 113–136.

Padilla, A. and Baumer, D. (1994) 'Big-time college sports: Management and economic issues', *International Review for the Sociology of Sport*, 18 (2), 123–143.

Paquette, J., Stevens, J., and Mallen, C. (2011) 'The interpretation of environmental sustainability by the International Olympic Committee and Organizing Committees of the Olympic Games from 1994 to 2008', *Sport in Society*, 14 (3), 355–369.

Pfahl, M. (2010) 'Strategic issues associated with the development of internal sustainability teams in sport and recreation organizations: A framework for action and sustainable environmental performance', *International Journal of Sport Management, Recreation & Tourism*, 6, 37–61.

Pfahl, M. (2011) *Sport and the natural environment: A strategic guide*. Dubuque, IA: Kendall Hunt.

Pfahl, M. and Ott, M. (2010) 'Athletic departments and the environment: Environmental efforts & revenue generation on your campus', *Athletics Administration*, 45 (2), 16–19.

Ralphie's Green Stampede (2011) *University of Colorado's Ralphie's Green Stampede*. Available at: http://www.cubuffs.com/ViewArticle.dbml?DB_OEM_ID=600&ATCLID=1549954 (accessed: October 29, 2011).

Rivera, J. and De Leon, P. (2005) 'Chief executive officers and voluntary environmental performance: Costa Rica's certification for sustainable tourism', *Policy Sciences*, 38, 107–127.

Rosenthal, L. (2003) 'From regulating organization to multi-billion dollar business: The NCAA is commercializing the amateur competition it has taken almost a century to create', *Seton Hall Journal of Sports Law*, 13, 321–345.

Russo, M. and Fouts, P. (1997) 'A resource-based perspective on corporate environmental performance and profitability', *Academy of Management Journal*, 40 (3), 534–559.

Schmidt, C.W. (2006) 'Putting the Earth in play', *Environmental Health Perspectives*, 114, 286–294.

Sheth, H. and Babiak, K. (2010) 'Beyond the game: Perceptions and practices of corporate social responsibility in the professional sport industry', *Journal of Business Ethics*, 91 (3), 433–450.

Shrivastava, P. (1995) 'Ecocentric management for a risk society', *Academy of Management Journal*, 20, 118–137.

Smith, A.C.T. and Westerbeek, H.M. (2007) 'Sport as a vehicle for deploying corporate social responsibility', *The Journal of Corporate Citizenship*, 25, 43–54.

Spaargaren, G. (2003) 'Sustainable consumption: A theoretical and environmental policy perspective', *Society & Natural Resources*, 16, 687–701.

Thibault, L. (2009) 'Globalization of sport: An inconvenient truth', *Journal of Sport Management*, 23, 1–20.

Thelin, J. (2000) 'Historical perspective on the political economy of intercollegiate athletics in the era of Title IX, 1972–1997', *The Journal of Higher Education*, 71, 391–410.

University of New Hampshire (2011) *GO GREEN with the Wildcats: Join UNH Football to learn ways to protect the environment*. Available at: http://www.unhwildcats.com/sports/fball/2009-10/releases/09_go_green_fb (accessed: October 29, 2011).

University of Tennessee (2012) *UT Recycling*. Available at: http://fs.utk.edu/Recycle/recycleSpecial.htm#Good Sports (accessed: November 18, 2012).

Walker, M. and Kent, A. (2009) 'Do fans care? Assessing the influence of corporate social responsibility on consumer attitudes in the sport industry', *Journal of Sport Management*, 23 (6), 743–769.

Walters, G. and Chadwick, S. (2009) 'Corporate citizenship in football: Delivering strategic benefits through stakeholder engagement', *Management Decision*, 47 (1), 51–66.

Weir, T. (2010) 'New NCAA president a hard-liner on money for athletes', *US Today*, December 8. Available at: http://content.usatoday.com/communities/gameon/post/2010/12/ncaa-president-jersey-sales-money-athletes/1 (accessed: November 21, 2012).

Yale University (2011) *Bulldog sustainability*. Available at: http://www.yalebulldogs.com/sustainability/index (accessed: October 29, 2011).

8

ENVIRONMENTAL CSR PRACTICES WITHIN THE ASIAN SPORT EVENT INDUSTRY

A case study of the Beijing Olympics

James J. Zhang, Liyan Jin, Minhong Kim and Hai Li

Overview

The objective of this chapter is to consider how the issue of environmental corporate social responsibility (CSR) has been addressed within the context of Asian sport events, particularly in the context of the Beijing Olympics in 2008. One of the ways that Asian economies have demonstrated their emergence onto the world sporting stage has been through the hosting of mega sport events. These have provided a way to highlight the achievement, growth, and potential of Asian countries, such as the Seoul Summer Olympic Games in 1988, the Nagano Winter Olympic Games in 1998, the 2002 World Cup co-hosted by Japan and South Korea, and more recently, the 2008 Beijing Olympics. The chapter begins with a brief overview of how environmental CSR has been implemented within the broader Asian context before setting out the progress made towards understanding and addressing the environmental impact of sport events. The chapter then looks at the increasing prominence of sport events within the Asian sport event industry before detailing the different ways in which the Beijing Olympics addressed environmental concerns. The case shows how the hosting of the Olympic Games provided the Beijing Municipal Government with the impetus to also address environmental issues facing the city and demonstrates that a clear policy, driven by government, the International Olympic Committee (IOC), and the organizing committee can help to mitigate some of the environmental implications associated with the hosting of a mega sport event.

Introduction

CSR has been steadily growing in perceived importance in the corporate sector and there is a rapidly increased attention by academic researchers, consultants, and policy makers in national and international bodies such as the World Business Council for Sustainable Development (WBCSD), trade organizations, and at the central and local levels of government (Frame, 2005). More specifically, research on consumer reactions to CSR has indicated that consumers' beliefs toward CSR are among the primary motives influencing corporations to engage in the practice

(Aguilera *et al.*, 2007). For example, Mohr *et al.* (2001) found that consumers usually preferred to purchase from companies with reputable CSR practices. Sen and Bhattacharya (2001) found that consumers' CSR assessments were moderated by their individual preferences toward specific CSR activities, while Sims (2003) found that nearly 80 percent of their respondents' purchasing decisions were based on CSR. Moreover, Ellen *et al.* (2006) concluded that consumers favored CSR motives that were perceived as value-driven and strategic, yet disliked CSR motives that were regarded as stakeholder-driven or egoistic.

In the sport industry, CSR did not play a significant role in organization governance and operations until approximately 20 years ago (Babiak and Wolfe, 2009) (see Chapter 1 by Babiak and Wolfe for more details). In the modern day sport industry, it is an issue that has been embraced by almost every sport organization (Walker and Kent, 2009). For instance, many teams now use social involvement to leverage new facility construction or stadium expansion to local residents and city officials (Horrow, 2008). While little work (on the consumer side) has been published in sport, Walker and Kent (2009) and Walker *et al.* (2010) indicate that many sport fans believe in the social obligations of sport organizations and feel that most organizations should take active steps to genuinely help local communities. Sheth and Babiak (2010) explained that professional sport franchises are an interesting phenomenon in regard to CSR because, like other businesses, they must maintain a profit to be successful, but unlike other businesses, their financial success largely depends on community support for the team.

Previous academic research has detailed the lengths to which major sports organizations in North America have initiated some forms of CSR programs and activities, such as Nike, Reebok, NBA, MLB, NHL, and NASCAR (e.g., Babiak and Wolfe, 2009; Levermore, 2010; Walker and Kent, 2009). There has also been significant focus on European sports (Levermore, 2010; Pfeiffer, 2008; Walters, 2009). However Godfrey (2009) speculated that CSR may be a luxury good, something that people in the developed world care about but something that those in transition or developing countries care less about given a focus on goals such as economic and industrial development. For example, there is a possibility that prioritizing economic growth over environmental concerns inhibits developing countries from adopting CSR actions. Less is therefore known about how sports organizations in other parts of the world are addressing CSR. The focus of this chapter is on CSR in the Asian sport industry. The Asian continent currently has 51 countries, with over 4.2 billion residents (United Nations Population Division, 2011). Accounting for over 60 percent of the world population, in recent decades Asian countries have experienced a powerful boom in both their economies and their sport industries. According to Bloom *et al.* (1999), Asian countries, particularly those located in East Asia, have nearly tripled income per capita during the last 30 years, which is one of the most extraordinary economic phenomena of this century, although there are still a mixture of developed, developing, less-developed, and least developed countries that are primarily located in South and Southeast Asia, such as Singapore with GDP per capita close to $50,000, Malaysia close to $15,000, India around $2,500, and Burma around $1,000. To a great extent, the "miracle" of this economic growth is attributed to an accumulation of trade and industrial policies, technological progress, savings and capital accumulation, effective governance, investment in education, and improved provision of health care.

It is recognized that CSR in Asia is evolving in different ways, with differences shaping the way Asian companies and leaders define CSR, each with its own priorities and mindsets (Asia Business Council, 2008). While it has been previously argued that social issues linked to labor practices and human rights in the workplace have not received adequate academic attention (e.g., Matten, 2004), it has been suggested that as the consumer behavior of the Asian middle and upper classes is likely to change with their growing sophistication, higher income, and access to information, a range of CSR-related issues will become more prominent. However, one key area that has been of concern is the impact of Asian business on the environment. The objective of this chapter is to consider how the issue of CSR has been addressed within the context of Asian sport events, particularly in relation to environmental aspects. One of the ways that Asian economies have demonstrated their emergence onto the world sporting stage has been through the hosting of mega sport events. These provide a way to highlight the achievement, growth, and potential of Asian countries, such as the Seoul Summer Olympic Games in 1988, the Nagano Winter Olympic Games in 1998, the 2002 World Cup co-hosted by Japan and South Korea, and the 2008 Beijing Olympics. The chapter begins with a brief overview of how environmental CSR has been implemented within the broader Asian context before setting out the progress made towards understanding and addressing the environmental impact of sport events. The chapter then looks at the increasing prominence of sport events within the Asian sport event industry before detailing the different ways in which the Beijing Olympics addressed environmental concerns.

Application of environmental CSR within Asia

The world is facing immense environmental and sustainability challenges in terms of climate change, pollution, and diminishing biodiversity (Greenpeace, 2010; IOC, 2009). As research evidence and practical experience provide a strong rationale that environmental protection can eventually help save financial resources and lead to increased competitiveness, CSR activities associated with environmental protection have received the most attention by Asian countries and their business corporations. For example, China's rise has coincided with growing interest in CSR in Asia; its drive for a "harmonious society" has focused increased government attention on the nation's mounting environmental worries and growing economic disparity. Japanese and Korean multinationals are showing increased interest in the global CSR dialogue. Companies based in these countries have become more actively engaged in looking at supply chain practices and with fellow Korean Ban Ki-moon as Secretary-General of the UN, Korean business may be more inclined to align its energy-saving practices with those of the UN Global Compact, which is a strategic policy initiative for businesses that are committed to aligning their operations and strategies with universally accepted principles in the areas of human rights, labor, environment, and anti-corruption, and provides collaborative solutions to the most fundamental challenges facing both business and society. Japanese business also is well positioned to apply environmental prowess and leadership in an era of resource limitations.

Similar to business entities in other parts of the world, climate change has drawn increasing attention from the Asian business community, including sport businesses. Increasingly, more businesses are now engaged in mitigation and adaptation efforts to offset climate change. While the ultimate solution will almost certainly represent a mixture of public policy, technological innovation, and reduced consumption, the ultimate shape of a de-carbonized economy is still at its early stage, in terms of the need to pursue and achieve massive reductions in carbon dioxide and other harmful emissions while maintaining economic growth. As companies across the globe experience a fundamental shift in how environmental issues and opportunities are understood, one of the growing areas of opportunity in Asia is the application of market-based incentives for environmental performance. This rise of "environmental markets" reflects a potential shift away from a choice between regulation and free markets, towards one where market forces and processes align resource use with their long-term economic value. Today, an expanding set of incentives are emerging for businesses to limit not only traditional air and water emissions, but also to mitigate and even restore the function of ecological systems in areas where environmental markets exist. Engagement in environmental markets may offer greater flexibility to least-cost pathways for meeting regulations within the context of environmental markets. A company can both enhance its brand and address emerging concerns by embedding climate change goals and targets into communications with employees, customers, and other shareholders.

In brief, sustainability strategies are designed in Asian countries to create business approaches to global challenges like economic development, natural resource stewardship, and good public governance. In some ways, sustainability can be considered new or different for business in Asia. It is striking, however, that emerging models for managing sustainability are very similar to the way companies manage traditional business questions. With a sense of purpose, clear priorities, effective implementation and performance measurement, CSR will deliver value for business in Asia and the wider world.

Environmental impact of sport events

Protecting the environment has become an important concern for organizations in the sport industry (see also Chapter 7 by Trendafilova, Pfahl, and Casper). Jagemann (2003) noted that sport can cause considerable damage to the environment due to the use of non-renewable resources, emission of hazardous substances during construction and operation of sport facilities, and production and disposal of sport-related equipment. This holds true for all sport events, especially the Olympic Games, during which venues are built and a large number of people travel across the globe to participate and attend. To reduce the negative impact from sport activities, it is important to integrate environmental concerns into the development of sport events.

Hosting the Olympic Games has significant environmental impacts on the host city, with voluminous resources, activities, and constructions involved, such as waste accumulation, air pollution, and noise pollution. The 1992 Winter Olympic Games in Albertville caused significant environmental damages due to insensitivity to vulnerable alpine ecosystems in venue construction and the lack of any environmental policy and guidelines. The Lillehammer Games in 1994 demonstrated a long-standing and well-developed respect for nature and proved that the environmental damage of staging the games could be minimized. These two games evoked global awareness of the environment and activity within the IOC, and urged the IOC to respond and make effort to repel the adverse environmental impacts of the Olympic Games (Cantelon and Letters, 2000). In an attempt to avoid and eliminate the potential and existing conflicts, the environment was added to the Olympic movement as the third pillar along with sport and culture in 1996 (Beyer, 2006).

Since then, environmental issues have become one of the key factors to choose a host city, and have been considered as essential concerns during the host city's preparatory period. Sydney was the first city to win an Olympic bid with a comprehensive environmental protection plan. Greenpeace originally considered Sydney's "Green Games" as a global showcase of integrating environmental concerns into areas such as transportation, energy, waste disposal, refrigeration, and construction. The concept of Green Games eventually evolved into a mandate from the IOC, and has been a component of every Olympic Games since 2000. However, both Sydney (2000) and Athens (2004) were widely regarded as failures in executing principles of environmental sustainability during the Olympic Games (Chan *et al.*, 2006).

There are three main organizations involved in guiding and supervising the Green Olympics movement, including the IOC, the United Nations Environmental Program (UNEP), and Greenpeace. In 1996, environment protection was added to the Olympic Charter as a new mission for the IOC, where the IOC is responsible for ensuring that the Olympic Games take place in harmony with the environment, encouraging and supporting environmental protection issues, and promoting sustainable development in sport (IOC, 2007). UNEP, established in 1972, is the voice for the environment within the United Nations system. It is considered to be an important entity to educate, advocate, and promote the proper use and sustainable development of the global environment. UNEP is in cooperation with diverse partners, ranging from international organizations, national governments, non-governmental organizations, the private sector, to civil society. It has been working on sports and environmental issues since 1994. The program aims to promote the integration of environmental considerations into sports, raise environmental awareness of and respect for the environment among the public, especially young people, and encourage environmentally friendly sport facilities and sporting goods (UNEP, 2007).

Developmental trends in the Asian sport event industry

According to Rowe and Gilmour (2010), Asia has become a prime target market for the expansionary strategies of some of the world's most powerful professional sports leagues, teams, manufacturing companies, and media corporations. The influence of transnational broadcasters in Asia and the intensive marketing efforts of Western sports organizations provide European and American-based sports leagues, such as the English Premier League and the National Basketball Association, with a significant advantage within the market. Sport consumers in Asia tend to develop a predisposition of choosing globally marketed Western sport leagues, teams, stars, and licensed products over those made in Asia. At the same time, the popularity of Western sports leagues has led Asian corporations, such as Samsung, Air Asia, Chang Beer, Emirates Airlines, Malaysia Airlines, Li-Ning, and Tiger Beer, to sponsor Western leagues such as the Premier League in order to attract customers within Asia, devoting little of their promotional budgets to local Asian professional clubs. There are concerns that this could negatively impact on the development of domestic leagues and sports.

One of the ways to counteract this has been to host mega sport events. Indeed, it has long been believed that hosting mega sport events in Asia would signal the emergence and readiness of Asian cities and countries on the world stage. However, besides the intermittent flourishing of sporting nationalism around such mega sport events, in regional sport competitions such as cricket and hockey, and in some successful professional club competitions such as the soccer A-League in Japan (see more details in Chapter 12 by Harada), there is little evidence of the arrival of a sustained, localized sports culture. Sports culture in Asia still primarily revolves around imported consumption. It still awaits the emergence of a viable system of sports production and locally oriented consumption.

According to Horne and Manzenreiter (2006), there are two central features of mega-events as important for analysis. Firstly, mega-sporting events are deemed to have significant economic, social, and tourism consequences for the host city, region, or nation, and secondly, they will attract considerable international media coverage. Dolles and Söderman (2008) noted that mirroring the trend in other regions, mega sport events in Asia have grown in prominence and are a central stage on which athletes represent their nations. For the host countries, they offer the opportunity to promote their national identities, present their cultures, and utilize the initiatives associated with hosting the event to rejuvenate community and economic development. This is a rather new observable phenomenon in Asia, where sport and recreation have assumed a new relevance in Asian society, attracting attention not just from the residents, but also from political and business sectors. Mega sporting events in Asia are mainly connected with international multi-sport competitions, such as the Summer and Winter Olympic Games, and the FIFA World Cup. There are regional tournaments that can be considered as mega-events, like the Asian Games that are governed by the Olympic Council of Asia (OCA) or the Commonwealth Games governed by the Commonwealth Games Federation (CGF), both of which are overseen by the IOC. Mega sport events may also be elite-level international sports competitions, such as the World Aquatic Championship and the Asian Football Championship.

Olympic Games in Asia

The first mega Olympic Games to be held in the Asian region was the 1964 Tokyo Olympics, at which 5,151 athletes representing 93 countries participated in 163 events from 19 different sporting codes. The 1964 Games can be considered a fulcrum in the global visibility and popularity of the Olympics as it was the first to be televised to the world in color TV. It did not generate significant commercial or broadcasting income however; rather, it was an event used to portray a recovered national prestige and it was used as a symbol of Japan's post-war restoration. South Korea was the second Asian nation to host the Olympic Games in 1988, with the Seoul Games a launching pad for South Korea to boost its international image and diplomacy, promote business and tourism development, and strengthen overall national achievement level. Gaining international prestige has been one of the critical foreign policies for China. Hosting the Olympic Games in Beijing in 2008 was seen as a catalyst for economic growth in Beijing and surrounding areas, and was planned to enhance China's international prestige, and promote a national image of strength and unity among both Chinese and people across the world (Ong, 2004). When the former IOC President Juan Antonio Samaranch announced on 13 July 2001 that Beijing had won the right to host the 2008 Summer Olympic Games, the entire city erupted into a "flag-waving, horn honking, music-jamming, and fire cracker exploding party" (Abrahamson, 2002: 10) and it was also a sleepless night for the whole nation. The Winter Olympic Games have also been held in Asia: in Sapporo, Japan, in 1972 (the first Winter Olympics ever held outside Europe or the United States), and in 1998 in Nagano, Japan.

The Asian Games

With 51 countries currently, over 4.2 billion residents, accounting for over 60 percent of the world population, the Asian Games are a mega sport event by default. The first official Asian Games were held in 1951 in New Delhi, India after the formal foundation of the Asian Athletic Federation in 1949. The founding Asian National Olympic Committees (NOC) agreed that the Asian Games would be held regularly every four years. Due to regional conflicts in Asia, the NOCs decided in the 1970s to revise the constitution of the Asian Games Federation. A new association named the Olympic Council of Asia was created, supervising the Asian Games under the auspices of the IOC, formally starting with the 1986 Asian Games in South Korea. The 15th Asian Games in 2006 was positioned in the host city of Doha, Qatar; with its US$2.6 billion investment into preparing for hosting the event, Qatar intended to be positioned as a leader in destination positioning for major international events, cultural relations, tourism, and investment opportunities. In 2010, 45 nations took part in the Asian Games held in Guangzhou, China. These nations came from the shores of the Mediterranean Sea (Lebanon) to those lying in the Western reaches of the Pacific Ocean (Japan) and with Indonesia in the South and Mongolia in the North.

The Commonwealth Games

The Commonwealth Games are a multi-sport event held every four years, involving the elite athletes of the Commonwealth Nations. For the first time in its 65-year history, the XVI Commonwealth Games was held in Asia in 1998, as Malaysia hosted the event in Kuala Lumpur. A new record of 70 countries sent a total of 5,250 athletes and officials to the Kuala Lumpur Games, featuring 212 events in 15 sports. In 2010, the Commonwealth Games returned to Asia and was held in New Delhi, India. The games were the biggest sport event in New Delhi since the 1982 Asian Games with more than 6,000 athletes from 71 Commonwealth teams participating in the competitions.

The 2002 FIFA South Korea and Japan World Cup

With its historic decision to award hosting the FIFA World Cup finals for the first time to dual host countries (Japan and South Korea) in Asia, football's governing body FIFA moved strategically towards promoting football on a global scale (Baade and Matheson, 2004; Dolles and Söderman, 2005). Japan and South Korea had their own reasons for wanting to host the 2002 FIFA World Cup. While the Koreans aimed at introducing the finals as a "catalyst for peace" (Sugden and Tomlinson, 1998) on the Korean peninsula, the Japanese focused their bid on its ability to advance political stability, high technology, and the country's infrastructure. To date, the 2002 FIFA World Cup was the biggest single-sport world-level sport event in Asia. The 64-game tournament with its 32 participating teams was attended by an unprecedented 2,705,197 spectators in both countries, with an accumulated worldwide TV audience of nearly 50 billion. The co-hosts Japan and South Korea spent a combined $4.4 billion (Japan $2,881 million and South Korea $1,513 million) in building 20 new arenas or refurbishing existing arenas. More recently, Qatar has been selected as the host of the 2022 World Cup. As Qatar is ranked 90th in the FIFA world rankings list and 10th in the Asian rankings (FIFA, 2011), in addition to having a small population of 1.45 million and a modest land mass, it would appear that FIFA is continuing to promote football on a global scale.

Environment CSR within the Asian sport industry: an analysis of the Beijing Olympics

The Olympic Games has been considered as a major opportunity for urban planners and policy-makers to improve the infrastructure and environment of the city even before the environment was added as the third element to the Olympic Movement. Both Tokyo and Seoul made outstanding environmental improvements compared to other games before 1994. They used the Olympic Games as a stimulus to diminish pollution, advance sanitation standards, modernize waste disposal systems, and raise environmental standards (Chalkley and Essex, 1999). In the Tokyo Games of 1964, the city made a number of environmental improvements. For instance, the water supply system of the city that piped water from Kanagawa and other adjacent districts was improved. Its waste management system was ameliorated as a result of three newly constructed sewage disposal plants. Standards of public health within the city were also improved through regulating refuse and garbage collections, renovating public toilet facilities, controlling food hygiene, and cleaning streets and rivers. In the Seoul Games of 1988, various programs were applied to encourage public transportation so as to reduce air pollutions from personal car emissions. South Korea is one of the world's most densely populated countries and by 1988, one half of its over 42 million population resided in the greater Seoul metropolitan area, resulting approximately 17,030 people per square kilometer. Prior to the Games, traffic congestion was of a great concern to the event organizing committee. The renovated public transit system significantly enhanced the event operations during the Games; since then, the public transit infrastructure has remained helpful to the daily life of Seoul residents. Also, an environmental beautification program was carried out to ensure health and hygiene standards throughout the city. The local residents were encouraged to become involved in these projects via conservation awareness campaigns and the formation of local committees for environmental beautification. Also, new programs were introduced to deal with air pollution, garbage control, and water quality preservation (Chalkley and Essex, 1999). On a different note, the 1994 Winter Olympic Games in the French Savoy Region led to widespread environmental damage and urged the IOC to respond and present a strategy for repelling the adverse impacts of the mega event (Cantelon and Letters, 2000). In an attempt to avoid and eliminate the potential and existing conflicts, the environment was added to the Olympic movement as the third pillar along with sport and culture in 1996 (Beyer, 2006). Since then, environmental issues have become one of the key factors to choose a host city, and have been considered as the essential concerns during the host city's preparatory period (Chan *et al.*, 2006).

More recently, sports organizations in Asia have strived to reduce the adverse environmental impact from sport construction by achieving the Leadership in Energy and Environment Design (LEED) certifications. LEED is a rating system initiated by the United States Green Building Council (USGBC) and used to assess a building's environmental performance over its life cycle. LEED building requires 40–49 points for certification in LEED Version 3.0, 50–59 points for silver level, 60–79 points for gold level and 80 points and above for platinum level, which are graded based on five major environmental categories: (a) sustainable sites; (b) water efficiency; (c) energy and atmosphere; (d) materials and resources; and (e) indoor environmental quality. The allocation of points is based on the potential environmental impacts and human benefits due to the design, construction, operation, and maintenance of the building, such as air and water pollutants, fossil fuel use, greenhouse gas emissions, toxins and carcinogens, and indoor environmental conditions. Innovation in design, as another feature of LEED, measures sustainable building expertise as well as design aspects not covered under the five environmental categories. Additionally, regional bonus points evaluate the significance of local conditions in choosing best environmental design and construction practices. All LEED rating systems have 100 base points; innovation in design (or operations) and regional priority credits provide opportunities for up to 10 bonus points. The currently available LEED products include the following: LEED for New Construction, LEED for Core & Shell, LEED for Commercial Interiors, LEED for Neighborhood Development; LEED for Homes; LEED for Healthcare LEED for Retail; and LEED for Schools (USGBC, 2009). Although none of these was specifically developed for sports facilities, to a great extent they are directly all applicable to sport stadium and arena construction and renovation projects.

The Beijing Organizing Committee for the Olympic Games (BOCOG) constructed the first LEED certified Olympic Village. Such initiatives may not only serve to reduce long-run operation and maintenance costs but also help foster enhanced image perceptions of the institution, and raise environmental awareness among the spectators, which can potentially stimulate environment-friendly behaviors. For the 2008 Beijing Olympic Games, BOCOG also worked closely with the IOC, the UNEP, and Greenpeace to stage a "Green Games." New technologies and policies were widely used to improve air quality and energy efficiency in China. Green programs were applied to beautify the appearance of the city, and educational projects were carried out to increase Chinese citizen awareness of environmental problems and stimulate proper behaviors toward a clean environment (Jin *et al.*, 2011). To successfully host the Green Olympics, Beijing made impressive progress in environmental protection. Aiming to improve the air quality, Beijing greatly increased the use of clean and renewable energy, applied a variety of energy saving technologies, expanded public transportation system, and set very stringent emission standards. Wastewater treatment plants, along with sewage and water reuse systems, were improved to satisfy the water needs and increase the efficiency in the use of water. Regulations and laws were enforced to protect water sources and improve water quality in Beijing. A set of "greening" projects was carried out in Beijing to increase the green coverage and beautify the city. As for controlling the industry pollutions, Beijing closed and relocated a large number of polluting companies and set new industrial regulations. Solid waste management systems were improved in Beijing, and recycle projects were initiated to encourage residents to separate waste collection. Furthermore, a series of environmental education programs were implemented not only in Beijing but also across the whole country to raise awareness of environmental problems and increase environmental knowledge within the public (Jin *et al.*, 2011).

BOCOG set three guiding principles for the Games: Green Olympics, High-tech Olympics, and People's Olympics. In the UNEP's environmental review of Beijing Olympic Games, it explains "Green Olympics" as follow:

> The city of Beijing identifies environmental protection and strict environmental standards as a key requisite for the design and construction of the Olympic Games facilities. BOCOG is charged with ensuring that environmentally friendly technologies and measures are applied in the construction of infrastructure and venues, and that urban and rural forestation and environmental protection area carried out. The committee is also responsible for promoting environmental awareness among the general public, and encouraging the citizens of Beijing to make green consumption choices.
>
> (UNEP, 2007: 32)

The "Green Olympics" concept was also reflected in the five Olympic mascots that were designed to promote environmental awareness. Beibei was a flying fish, meaning "clear water"; Jingjing was a panda, representing environmental protection and "Green Hills"; Yingying was a Tibetan endemic protected antelope delivering a "Grass-covered Ground" message; Nini was a flying swallow, referring to the message of "Blue Sky"; and Huanhuan represented the Olympic Flame (UNEP, 2007). In addition, the Green Olympics concept was also delivered through the Green Olympic logo that was composed of people and green trees and used for Green Olympics communication and education (UNEP, 2007).

The environment was prominent in Beijing's original bid, planning, and preparation for the 2008 Olympic Games. In the Green Olympics Program that was formed during Beijing's bid for the Games, Beijing set aside a total investment of $12.2 billion for green initiatives: $5.6 billion for the period of 1998–2002 and $6.6 billion for the period of 2003–2007 (UNEP, 2007). From 1998–2007, Beijing spent a total of ¥120 billion (i.e., $15.7 billion) on environmental initiatives (BOCOG, 2007). According to a report released by UNEP after the Beijing Olympics, Beijing invested over $17 billion on environmental projects. China took a bold step in cooperating with the Greenpeace, the IOC, and the UNEP to participate in the "Green Olympics." Beijing made notable efforts during the preparatory period for the Games in the following environmental areas: air quality, energy, transportation, water environment, ecological conversation and construction, industrial pollution, and solid waste management (UNEP, 2007, 2008; Zhang, 2008). Each of these is described below.

Air quality

Preparation for staging the Games provided the Beijing Municipal Government with the impetus for addressing air quality problems. From 1998 to 2008, the government applied more than 200 environmental measures to reduce air pollution, such as controlling vehicle emission standards, investing in public transportation, increasing energy efficiency, constantly monitoring air quality, and reforming energy structure by increasing the use of other green energy resources. These projects all represented viable long-term solutions for reforming air quality and also represented great policy achievements for Beijing. According to data released by the Beijing Environmental Protection Bureau (EPB) from measurements conducted by 27 monitoring stations in the municipal area, the number of days with air quality equal to or above the National Standard increased from 100 days in 1998 to 241 days in 2006 (UNEP, 2007), to 274 days in 2008 (UNEP, 2008).

Energy

According to the National Bureau of Statistics, in 2007 China consumed 2.65 billion tons of coal equivalents (TCE). Beijing, one of the highest energy consumption cities in China, relies heavily on coal that contributes to large quantities of dioxides and particulate matter air pollution. A variety of methods were applied by Beijing to reform its energy structure, such as increasing the use of natural gas, wind energy, solar energy, and other forms of renewable energy. Also, several projects were developed by Beijing Municipal Government to increase energy efficiency and reduce energy consumption.

With regard to the Games specifically, energy saving design and new technologies were widely incorporated in Olympic venues. Six thousand square meters of direct current tube rooftop solar collectors were installed in the residential units of the Olympic Village, which was capable of providing hot water for all of the residential and supporting buildings. In Peking University, a 300m² solar heating water system was installed to heat all the swimming pool facilities. Solar collectors for bathing facilities were installed in Beijing's shooting range hall and Beijing Olympic Tower. Solar photovoltaic (PV) power generation systems were applied in the National Stadium, Wukesong Stadium, Fengtai Softball Stadium, Chaoyang Park Beach Volleyball venue, and Olympic Forest Park. Geothermal (ground source) heat pump air-conditioning and heating systems were used in Shunyi Olympic Rowing and Canoeing Park, Olympic Forest Park, and Peking University Gymnasium. In addition, renewable energy and energy efficient lighting were widely adopted in the Olympic Green, National Aquatics Centre, and all contract hotels. New techniques and products are currently being encouraged to be adopted in new buildings other than Olympic venues, such as heating preservation/insulation techniques for outer walls and new types of energy saving windows and doors (Zhang, 2008).

Public transportation

Beijing had taken some significant steps toward improving and expanding public transportation, increasing low-emission buses and taxis, and adopting high fuel emission standards for new vehicles. To improve its public transportation system, Beijing started the construction of 77 roads and bridges in the years prior to the opening of the Games (UNEP, 2007). A 16 km long south-middle Bus Rapid Transit line, with a capacity of 100,000 passengers per day, was finished in 2006 (UNEP, 2007). Beijing also built four additional subway lines and an Olympic Branch Line which runs from Line 10 to Olympic venues. According to the official data, the total subway capacity in Beijing was increased from 1.3 million to 3.9 million between 2000 and 2008 (Zhang, 2008). The number of buses reached 20,000 in 2007, twice the number in 1991 (UNEP, 2008). With the new transportation system, Beijing's public ground transportation reached a total of 19 million passengers per day (UNEP, 2007). Beijing also implemented several effective measures to encourage the use of public transportation. During the Olympic Games period, cars with even or odd numbered plates were forbidden to drive on alternative days in Beijing. Also, BOCOG offered people with tickets to the Olympic Games free public transportation throughout the city for 51 days (UNEP, 2007). For visitors during the Games, 200–300 bicycles were available in the Olympic Park and Olympic Village (UNEP, 2007).

Water environment

Beijing, located on a dry plateau in the northern China, struggles with severe water shortages. The water availability per capita of Beijing is just 1/32 of the international average level (Li, 2004). In 2007, Beijing's annual water consumption reached 3.4 billion m^3 (Beijing Water Authority, 2007). Motivated by the Green Olympics, a number of new Olympic venues and refurbished venues, such as the National Stadium (Bird's Nest), Olympic Green, and Olympic Forest Park, applied water saving designs including rainwater collection, water efficiency, water re-use, and water recycling features to reduce water demand during and after the Games. The main water sources of Beijing are the Miyun Reservoir, from which most of Beijing's drinking water comes, and the Huairou Reservoir which provides water for agriculture. The Olympic Games provided a great opportunity to develop the city's water saving techniques and sewage treatment structures.

According to government statistics, 15 projects including the National Stadium (Bird's Nest), Olympic Green, and Wukesong Baseball Field were installed with rainwater collection systems, which were capable of utilizing about one million tons of rainwater. The advanced enclosed water circulation system was installed in the Olympic Forest Park, which meant about 95 percent of rainwater inside the park could be reused for irrigations (Beijing Evening News, 2008). The Olympic Green has a systematic rain gathering water re-use technology that has a collection coverage area of 97 hectares. It can provide $320,000m^3$ of ground water, and also add about $90,000m^3$ to the water system. As a result, 80 percent of the water in the Olympic Green can be re-used which can provide up to $50,000m^3$ of water for irrigation. All wastewater from the Olympic Green can be recycled for landscape irrigations and toilets in the Olympic Green. In addition, the rainwater recycling system installed in the National Stadium is able to process up to 100 tons of rainwater per hour, of which 80 tons can be reused for landscaping, fire-fighting, and stadium cleaning (Zhang, 2008).

The Games also provided Beijing with an opportunity to develop its wastewater treatment system. From 2000 to 2006, Beijing built 600km of new sewage pipes, with a total network length of 2,500km, of which 700km are also used to collect rainwater. Also, 17 new wastewater treatments plants were built in Beijing before 2007, increasing the total treatment capacity by 2 million tons. The rate of wastewater treatment in Beijing city (not including the Beijing suburb areas) increased dramatically from 22 percent in 1998 to 90 percent in 2006 (UNEP, 2007). Wastewater treatment systems were also equipped in some of the Olympic venues including the National Aquatics Center (Water Cube), Shunyi Water Park, Olympic Tennis Center, Olympic Forest Park, and Olympic Center, contributing to a treatment capacity of one million tons in total.

Ecological conservation and construction

BOCOG and Beijing Municipal Government carried out a series of greening projects for both Olympic venues and the city of Beijing. For instance, they increased the forest coverage in mountain areas, established an Olympic Forest Park, and greened five major waterways as well as highways. Aiming to support the principles of the Green Olympics, on May 30, 2006, BOCOG made an official announcement that timber sources from the tropical forests of Indonesia would not be used for Olympic venues, and construction materials with minimal environmental impact would be used instead. Moreover, the Olympic Forest Park was built on the Olympic Green, with an area of 680 hectares that is about 1.5 times the size of Central Park in New York City, with 475 hectares of green space (Zhang, 2008). Green coverage in the urban districts in Beijing increased from 36 percent in 2000 to 43 percent by the end of 2008, which exceeded the Olympic bid goal of 40 percent (UNEP, 2008).

Industrial pollution

Industrial production is economically important for Beijing. Industrial gross product accounts for more than one-third of the city's total GDP. However, it also causes serious environmental problems, such as sulphur dioxide (SO_2) and soot pollution. To reduce and control industrial pollution, Beijing was committed to closing highly polluting companies, relocating factories outside the urban perimeter, adjusting industrial regulations, and developing new industrial zones (Jin *et al.*, 2011). From 1998 to 2006, a dramatic increase in company relocations occurred, and 197 out of 209 companies moved between 2000 and 2006. In the last few years before the Games, 17 major industrial companies were closed or relocated, including the Beijing Second Pharmaceutical Factory, Beijing Dye Factory, and Beijing Coke Plant; some of these were the largest and the most prominent companies that caused major environmental harms.

Solid waste management

According to UNEP (2008), waste classification and recycling services covered 27 percent of the population in Beijing by 2007, which exceeded its Olympic bid goals for waste classification and recycling. On-site composting facilities were encouraged by the Beijing municipality to improve composting rates. In 2006, 270,000 tons of waste was composted, 1.43 million tons were recycled, and the rate of resource re-utilization was increased to 30.6 percent. In 2004 and 2005, two medical waste processing plants were built in Beijing with a total daily processing capacity of 60 tons, meeting the actual needs of the city (UNEP, 2007). On June 1, 2008, the Chinese central government released a policy to forbid the free use of plastic bags and make bags more environmentally friendly (Jinghua News, 2008).

The IOC plays a key role in the process of guiding and ensuring the host city and the organizing committee of the Olympic Games to plan, organize, and implement environmental protection measures. Its influence on Beijing and the BOCOG was no exception. In 1996, the following statement was adopted in the Olympic Charter: "the mission and role of the International Olympic Commission is ... to encourage and support a reasonable concern for environmental issues, to promote sustainable development in sport and to require that the Olympic Games are held accordingly" (IOC, 2007: 15). In 1999, the IOC collaborated with the UNEP to develop Agenda 21 for Sport and the Environment, which is a comprehensive plan of action to be taken by each organization, government, and country where humans negatively impact the environment. According to the outlined description for the Host City Contract (HCC) that needs to be co-signed by the IOC, the host city, and the NOC of the host country, the selected host city for the Olympic Games is required to acknowledge and support environmentally sustainable development when conducting its obligations and activities, as well as during the post-event use of venues and other facilities (IOC, 2009). The host city also needs to consider environmental legislation, promote the concept of environmental protection, and leave a positive legacy in environmental policies and practices related to the Olympic Games (IOC, 2009). The HCC does not specify minimal environmental standards (Greenpeace, 2008); if any dispute arises about the HCC that is governed by Swiss law, it will be resolved conclusively by arbitration (IOC, 2009). A question remains that when a host city of Olympic Games does not implement what has been planned in the HCC, what the IOC can do about the incompliance. Although a precedent has not occurred so far, it is speculated that penalties can be in such areas as apologies to IOC, financial fines, and derivation of hosting future IOC governed events by the host city and/or even country. In order to scientifically measure the impact of an Olympic Games on the host city, its environment, and its residents, the IOC launched the Olympic Games Global Impact (OGGI) study in 2003 (IOC, 2006). The OGGI study covers a period of 11 years. It begins when a city is officially named as an Olympic candidate by an NOC, which is two years before the host city is selected, and terminates two years after hosting the Olympic Games (IOC, 2006). All Organizing Committees for the Olympic Games (OCOGs) are asked to conduct the OGGI study, which regards sustainable development principles as a primary emphasis for all aspects of the mega event, including economic, social, and environmental issues (Furrer, 2002; IOC, 2006).

Sydney was the first city to win an Olympic bid with a comprehensive environmental protection plan and it was regarded as the first "Green Games" (UNEP, 2009). Sydney set an example and created a positive legacy by introducing sustainable solutions in Olympic Games design and planning, applying non-incineration remediation technology for toxic contamination on site and initiating various energy and water saving technologies for Olympic facilities (Greenpeace, 2008). Athens made a strong attempt to host the second "Green Games"; however, according to Greenpeace (2004), green energy usage at the Athens Games was lacking, and the event failed to achieve environmental excellence and sustainability (Chan *et al.*, 2006). Compared to previous Games, the 2008 Beijing Games raised the environmental record-breaking bar (UNEP, 2009). The most recent London Olympic Games in 2012 was the first Olympic Games to measure its carbon footprint over the entire project term, the first Games to commit to a Zero Waste to landfill target (UNEP, 2012).

In early September 2008, the market research company *Ipsos* assisted Greenpeace with conducting a survey in Beijing. According to the survey report, Beijing residents overwhelmingly welcomed the positive environmental changes brought by the Games. About 90 percent of the residents believed that the Green Olympic initiatives contributed to the environmental improvement in the city. Most respondents expressed their support to continuously expand and improve Beijing's public transportation to further improve its air quality. Of the respondents, more than one-third of car owners supported the extension of the odd-even license plate restrictions on car use after the Games. However, Beijing fell short in applying water saving technologies throughout the city, adopting environmentally friendly procurement policies for all constructions, pursuing a zero-waste policy, introducing an internationally recognizable timber procurement policy, fully engaging with third party stakeholders, and making environmental information fully transparent (Greenpeace, 2008; UNEP, 2009). UNEP (2009) recommended that Beijing should make additional efforts to reduce coal consumption and household carbon emissions, and promote greater energy efficiency of industries and buildings. Long-term sustainability of Beijing's water supply should also be considered, since the current long-distance water transfers may become unsustainable (UNEP, 2009).

To strengthen environmental policy-making, planning, and coordinate efforts on major environmental issues, the first meeting of the 11th Chinese National People's Congress decided to establish the Ministry of Environmental Protection (MEP) on March 15, 2008. Major functions of MEP included drafting and implementing environmental protection plans, policies and standards, coordinating efforts to prepare environmental function zoning, monitoring and managing environmental pollution, and solving major environmental issues. The establishment of MEP had great significance for the development of environmental cause and also gave a strong boost to historic transformation of environmental protection (MEP of PRC, 2008). Chinese officials have placed emphasis on continued environmental protections after the Beijing Olympic Games, primarily in the areas of reinforcing energy conservation, reducing major polluting emissions, and protecting the environment. The focus of China's environmental protection in 2009 was on advancing conservation culture and actively exploring a new path to environmental protection in China. Based on the 2009 report on the state of China's environment, the environmental progress was quite effective in improving awareness and putting initiative ideas into practices. In addition, environmental and economic policies, such as green credit, green insurance, and green taxation policies, were developed and used to stimulate environmental protections.

Conclusions

Sports events create a significant impact on the environment and it is necessary for those organizations that are charged with implementing these events to address environmental concerns. This chapter has shown how hosting sport events (particularly mega sport events) have become a way for Asian countries and cities to showcase their emergence on the world stage. However this has led to an increasing awareness of the environmental impact of this hosting policy. It has gone on to show how the Beijing Olympic Games in 2008 provided the impetus for the development of a series of environmental initiatives that were implemented during the preparatory period of the Games to address issues including air quality, energy, transportation, water environment, ecological conversation and construction, industrial pollution, and solid waste management (UNEP, 2007, 2008; Zhang, 2008). The case of the Beijing Olympics shows how the hosting of the Olympic Games provided the Beijing Municipal Government with the impetus to also address environmental issues facing the city and demonstrates that a clear policy, driven by government, the IOC and the organizing committee, can help to mitigate some of the environmental implications associated with the hosting of a mega sport event.

References

Abrahamson, A. (2002) 'Beijing Costs Rise', *Los Angeles Times*, February 10. Available at: http://articles. latimes.com/2002/feb/10/sports/sp-olyioc10 (accessed: November 15, 2012).

Aguilera, R. V., Rupp, D. E., Williams, C. A., and Ganapathi, J. (2007) 'Putting the S back in corporate social responsibility: A multilevel theory of social change in organizations', *Academy of Management Review*, 32, 836–863.

Asia Business Council (2008) *Corporate Social Responsibility: Business solutions to global challenges.* Available at: http://www.asiabusinesscouncil.org/docs/BSR.pdf (accessed: November 15, 2012).

Baade, R. A. and Matheson, V. A. (2004) 'The quest for the cup: Assessing the economic impact of the World Cup', *Regional Studies*, 38, 343–354.

Babiak, K. and Wolfe, R. (2009) 'Determinants of corporate social responsibility in professional sport: Internal and external factors', *Journal of Sport Management*, 23, 717–742.

Beijing Evening News (2008) 'Following natural design: Introduction to the Olympic Forest Park'. Available at: http://2008.sohu.com/20080626/n257762151.shtml (accessed: December 16, 2008).

Beijing Water Authority (2007) *2007 Beijing water projects summary*. Available at: http://www.bjwater.gov.cn/tabid/134/InfoID/13694/frtid/133/Default.aspx (accessed: December 18, 2008).

Beijing Organizing Committee for the Olympic Games (BOCOG) (2007) *Beijing put in big money to improve the environment*. Available at: http://en.beijing2008.cn/26/44/article214084426.shtml (accessed: December 23, 2008).

Beyer, S. (2006) 'The Green Olympic Movement: Beijing 2008', *Chinese Journal of International Law*, 5, 423–440.

Bloom, D. E., Canning, D. and Malaney, P. N. (1999) *Demographic change and economic growth in Asia*. Boston, MA: Harvard University.

Cantelon, H. and Letters, M. (2000) 'The making of the IOC environmental policy as the third dimension of the Olympic Movement', *International Review for the Sociology of Sport*, 35, 294–308.

Chalkley, B. and Essex, S. (1999) 'Urban development through hosting international events: A history of the Olympic Games', *Planning Perspectives*, 14, 369–394.

Chan, C., Koenig, C., and Rajarethnam, S. (2006) 'Beijing 2008: Greening the Games', International Economic Development Program, Ford School of Public Policy, University of Michigan, Ann Arbor, MI.

Dolles, H. and Söderman, S. (2008) 'Mega-sporting events in Asia – Impacts on society, business and management: An introduction', *Asian Business & Management*, 7, 147–162.

Ellen, P. S., Webb, D. J., and Mohr, L. A. (2006) 'Building corporate associations: Consumer attributions for corporate socially responsible programs', *Journal of the Academy of Marketing Science*, 34, 147–157.

FIFA (2011) *FIFA World Ranking*. Available at: http://www.fifa.com/worldranking/index.html (accessed: November 15, 2012).

Frame, B. (2005) 'Corporate social responsibility: A challenge for the donor community', *Development in Practice*, 15, 422–432.

Furrer, P. (2002) 'Sustainable Olympic Games: A dream or a reality?' Available at: http://www.omero.unito.it/web/Furrer%20(eng.).PDF (accessed: November 15, 2012).

Greenpeace (2004) *Athens 2004 disqualified from Green Olympics*. Available at: http://www.greenpeace.org/international/en/news/features/athens-disqualified-from-green (accessed: July 3, 2010).

Greenpeace (2008) *About Greenpeace*. Available at: http://www.greenpeace.org/international/about (accessed: December 26, 2008).

Greenpeace (2010) *Annual Report*. Available at: http://www.greenpeace.org/international/Global/international/publications/greenpeace/2011/GPI_Annual_Report_2010.pdf (accessed: November 15, 2012).

Godfrey, P. C. (2009) 'Corporate social responsibility in sport: An overview and key issues'. *Journal of Sport Management*, 23, 698–716.

Horne, J. and Manzenreiter, W. (2006) 'Sports mega-events: Social scientific analyses of a global phenomenon', *Sociological Review*, 54, 1–187.

Horrow, R. (2008) 'When the game is on the line', paper presented at the 10th Annual Florida State University Sport Management Conference, Tallahassess, FL.

Jagemann, H. (2003) 'Sports and the environment: Ways towards achieving the sustainable development of sport', paper presented at the Conference by the 4th Pierre de Coubertin School Forum Arenzano (MUVITA).

Jin, L., Zhang, J. J., Ma, X. and Connaughton, D. P. (2011) 'Residents' perceptions of environmental impacts of the 2008 Beijing Green Olympic Games', *European Sport Management Quarterly*, 11(3), 275–300.

Jinghua News (2008) *Ban free plastic bags in grocery stores from Jun 1st*. Available at: http://chanye.finance.sina.com.cn/sm/2008-01-09/342772.shtml (accessed: November 29, 2008).

International Olympic Committee (IOC) (2006) *What is the Olympic Games global impact study?*. Available at: http://www.turin2006.com/Documents/Reports/EN/en_report_1077.pdf (accessed: November 29, 2008).

International Olympic Committee (IOC) (2007) *Olympic chapter*. Available at: http://multimedia.olympic.org/pdf/en_report_122.pdf (accessed: November 15, 2012).

International Olympic Committee (IOC) (2009) *Olympic Movement's Agenda 21*. Available at: http://www.olympic.org/Documents/Reports/EN/en_report_300.pdf (accessed: November 15, 2012).

Levermore, R. (2010) 'CSR for development through sport: Examining its potential and limitations', *Third World Quarterly*, 31, 223–241.

Li, J. (2004) 'Project to increase Beijing's water supply'. *China Daily*, 19 August. Available at: http://www.chinadaily.com.cn/english/doc/2004-08/19/content_366665.htm (accessed: November 15, 2012).

Matten, D. (2004) 'The impact of the risk society thesis on environmental politics and management in a globalizing economy: Principles, proficiency, perspectives', *Journal of Risk Research*, 7, 377–398.

Ministry of Environmental Protection of the People's Republic of China (MEP of PRC) (2008) *2008 report on the State of the Environment of China*. Available at: http://english.mep.gov.cn/down_load/Documents/201002/P020100225377359212834.pdf (accessed: July 16, 2011).

Mohr, L.A., Webb, D.J., and Harris, K.E. (2001) 'Do consumers expect companies to be socially responsible? The impact of corporate social responsibility on buying behavior', *Journal of Consumer Affairs*, 35, 45–72.

Ong, R. (2004) 'New Beijing, Great Olympics: Beijing and its unfolding Olympic legacy', *Stanford Journal of East Asian Affairs*, 4, 35–49.

Pfeiffer, C. (2008) 'CSR from Beijing 2008 to London 2012', PhD thesis, University of Geneva, Geneva, Switzerland.

Rowe, D. and Gilmour, C. (2010) 'Sport, media, and consumption in Asia: A merchandised milieu', *American Behavioral Scientist*, 53, 1530–1548.

Sen, S. and Bhattacharya, C. B. (2001) 'Does doing good always lead to doing better? Consumer reactions to corporate social responsibility', *Journal of Marketing Research*, 38, 225–243.

Sheth, H. and Babiak, K. (2010) 'Beyond the game: Perceptions and practices of corporate social responsibility in the professional sport industry', *Journal of Business Ethics*, 91, 433–450.

Sims, R. R. (2003) *Ethics and corporate social responsibility: Why giants fall*. Westport, CT: Greenwood.

Sugden, J. and Tomlinson, A. (1998) *FIFA and the contest for world football: Who rules the people's game?* Cambridge: Polity.

United States Green Building Council (USGBC) (2009) *About USGBC*. Available at: https://new.usgbc.org/about (accessed: November 25, 2012).

United Nations – Department of Economic and Social Affairs, Population Division (2011) *World population prospects: The 2010 revision, Volume II: Demographic profiles*. New York: United Nations Publications.

United Nations Environmental Program (UNEP) (2007) *Beijing 2008 Olympic Games: An environmental review*. Nairobi: UNEP Division of Communications and Public Information.

United Nations Environmental Program (UNEP) (2008) *Independent environmental assessment: Beijing 2008 Olympic Games*. Available at: http://www.un.org.cn/public/resource/f4e0bbec358097eff51675729d8372f3.pdf (accessed: February 26, 2009).

United Nations Environmental Program (UNEP) (2009) *Declaration of the United Nations conference on the human environment*. Available at: http://www.unep.org/Documents.Multilingual/Default.asp?DocumentID=97&ArticleID=1503 (accessed: February 20, 2009).

United Nations Environmental Program (UNEP) (2012) *London 2012 will leave a lasting legacy for the UK and the Olympic Movement: UNEP Executive Director*. Available at: http://www.unep.org/newscentre/default.aspx?DocumentID=2691&ArticleID=9239 (accessed: July 16, 2011).

Walker, M. and Kent, A. (2009) 'Do fans care? Assessing the influence of corporate social responsibility on consumer attitudes in the sport industry', *Journal of Sport Management*, 23, 743–769.

Walker, M., Heere, B., Parent, M. M., and Drane, D. (2010) 'Social responsibility and the Olympic Games: The mediating role of consumer attributions', *Journal of Business Ethics*, 95, 659–680.

Walters, G. (2009) 'Corporate social responsibility through sport: The community sports trust model as a CSR delivery agency', *Journal of Corporate Citizenship*, 35, 81–94.

Zhang, A. (2008) *Greenpeace*. Available at: http://www.greenpeace.org/usa/Global/usa/report/2008/8/china-after-the-olympics.pdf (accessed: November 9, 2008).

9

INCORPORATING ACCESSIBILITY AND DISABILITY IN THE MANCHESTER UNITED CULTURE AND ORGANIZATION AS PART OF THEIR CSR POLICIES

Phil Downs and Juan Luis Paramio-Salcines

Overview

This chapter focuses on the case of Manchester United, one of the most prestigious football clubs worldwide in terms of sporting and financial performance coupled with their long-term national and international fan-base support. However, when explaining the success of the club over the years, less well acknowledged is how they have implemented a wide range of accessibility services and procedures for spectators with disabilities (SwD) and their companions at their Old Trafford stadium which has been a central part of their corporate social responsibility (CSR) policy. This chapter discusses how, over the period 1980–2012, the club has transformed their understanding of accessibility of SwD and disability, who are valued in this process as significant stakeholders of the club, from a charitable and philanthropic activity to their current consideration as a strategic management practice of the club.

Introduction

As in other industry sectors, there is now a great deal of consensus that, in the twenty-first century, all types of sports organizations offer an appropriate context for developing and implementing a CSR approach (Breitbarth and Harris, 2008; Hemsley, 2009; Westerbeek and Smith, 2005; Walters, 2009, 2011). Therefore, football clubs, as the case of Manchester United will show, cannot ignore CSR given that this managerial concept has gradually been integrated with strategic management and corporate governance in most countries (Carroll, 2008). In this vein, as a plethora of authors argue (e.g., Babiak and Wolfe, 2006, 2009; Hamil *et al.*, 2011; Walters, 2009, 2011; Walters and Tacon, 2011), football clubs have to implement CSR within their activities and programs without losing their competitive advantage as Porter and Kramer (2002, 2006), Drucker (1999) and, more recently, Jones (2012) claim.

According to stakeholder theory, a useful framework with which to conceptualize sport and CSR, the point is made that sports organizations should recognize the interests of a wide range of constituents that have a stake in the organization as Walters (2011) suggests. It has gradually been acknowledged that those football clubs, like Manchester United, who want to present themselves as socially responsible organizations should pay greater attention and act responsibly towards a wide variety of issues, including those of human capital, the environment and relations with different stakeholders as in the case of SwD. However, when clubs want to define the range of issues that football clubs should focus their attention in order to translate stakeholders' demands and expectations into practice (Rahbek Pedersen, 2006), the "multidimensional nature of CSR in football clubs" in Europe is widely acknowledged, as a recent study by Walters and Tacon (2011) shows. This makes the issue of CSR complex, and as such there is no universal agreement on what areas professional football clubs in Europe can be involved in when developing and implementing CSR initiatives (Babiak and Wolfe, 2006, 2009; Bradish and Cronin, 2009; Breitbarth and Harris, 2008; Kay, 1993; Johnson and Scholes, 1999; Johnson *et al.*, 2007; Westerbeek and Smith, 2005; Walters, 2009, 2011). As indicated above, promoting accessible environments to SwD to stadiums should not be considered isolated or ad hoc practices (Paramio *et al.*, 2011; Grady, 2010), but instead accessibility and disability must be conceived as fundamental values embedded within the club. Nevertheless, football clubs in the main leagues in Europe do very little to promote access to SwD at their stadiums. This issue is not considered part of the majority of the football industry in Europe-related CSR programs nor is it ranked high on their agendas.

This chapter is organized as follows. In the first section, a brief historical account of the Manchester United approach to the promotion of accessibility by SwD to the Old Trafford stadium is provided which also incorporates a detailed account of the range of activities and policies that the club has promoted to implement accessibility and disability as part of their business operations over the period 1980–2012. In trying to further theoretical development of CSR by incorporating the views of practitioners, as Lindgreen and Swaen (2010) suggest, it was considered pivotal to incorporate the first-hand views and long-term experience of Phil Downs, MBE, one of the pioneers in this area and currently in charge of the operation for all Manchester United events and services for disabled fans at Old Trafford. Downs was also one of the first disabled people to start making proposals to the club as well as observations on the operation of different stadiums in Europe. As Walters and Tacon (2011: 25) argue "there is a need to know more about how sport organizations think about, implement and measure CSR." The following section seeks to fill this need by explaining the reasons why the club decided to address the demands of accessibility and to incorporate this issue into the business operation of the club since the early 1980s. Thereafter, one of the objectives of this chapter is to use CSR as a framework for understanding what has been done for one of their main stakeholders such as SwD by a club like Manchester United over the last three decades. Finally, the expected benefits of the incorporation of accessibility to the business culture and practices of Manchester United are also considered.

Historical background of the Manchester United approach to promoting access for fans with disabilities to the Old Trafford stadium: main milestones

In order to identify and better understand the distinctive characteristics of the Manchester United approach to accessibility and disability, some background points are highlighted below. Founded in 1878 as Newton Heath, it entered the Football League in 1902. However, the club went bankrupt in the same year before it became known by its current name, Manchester United FC. The club survived thanks to a wealthy local brewer, J.H. Davies. One of his aims was to buy the land to build a new stadium, Old Trafford, which is where it still stands today.

This club is probably valued as one of the most prestigious professional football clubs worldwide in terms of sporting performance (by the number of trophies at national and international level), financial performance (the second largest club in Europe as measured by financial turnover) (Deloitte, 2012), as well as national and international fan support over recent decades. Most of these developments have not gone unnoticed by either academics or consultant companies who have focused on the analysis of managerial, sociological and economic themes. In fact, to name a few, themes such as its position and its (successful) business model have increasingly attracted the attention of academics from a wide range of disciplines (Mellor, 2000; Szymanski, 1998), consultant companies or business schools worldwide, and have also inspired the commercial development of other clubs on a global scale. In reality, there are a number of studies that look at the range of distinctive strategies followed by the club to achieve this sporting and financial performance (Johnson and Scholes, 1999; Johnson *et al.*, 2007; Deloitte, 2012; Perry, 2005; Szymanski, 1998) or that focus on the analysis of the range of services provided in Old Trafford to further economic, social and sporting expansion (Paramio *et al.*, 2008, 2009). However, when explaining the success of Manchester United fewer people acknowledge and recognize that the implementation of a wide range of accessibility services and structures for SwD at Old Trafford form an important part of their overall CSR policy. Only in recent years have studies examined the range of services and activities in relation to the promotion of accessibility among their fans with disabilities. The understanding and reasoning of *how* and *why* accessibility has become part of Manchester United's business culture and CSR approach is central to this chapter (Paramio *et al.*, 2008, 2009).

Integrating accessibility and disability in Manchester United's culture and organization as part of their CSR policies

As John Kay (1993: 337) reminds us, "a common view is that the formulation of strategy is easy, but the real issues and problems are those of implementation" (see also Johnson *et al.*, 2007). As stated in the introduction, a plethora of authors such as Walters and Tacon (2011), Rahbek Pedersen (2006) and Maon *et al.* (2009) concur in saying that there is neither one overarching framework, nor a set of guidelines when organizations try to implement CSR activities. Therefore, CSR implementation within the business context requires a tailor-made approach. The implementation process of CSR and the factors that contribute to the process is an area that attracts the attention of academics (similar concern is covered by Anagnostopoulos in Chapter 6). Nevertheless, as Crane *et al.* (2008) note, it is only by engaging in CSR-related activities that an organization will develop a better understanding of this emerging management trend.

Werre (2003: 247) introduces three aspects that must be considered in the effective development and implementation of CSR in organizations: 1) sensitivity to the organizational environments; 2) awareness of values; and 3) clear leadership. In addition, Banerjee (2007: 16–18) adds three other key aspects: 1) some sort of club commitment; 2) those actions went beyond the law and exceed its "minimum obligations"; and 3) activities are discretionary and cannot be enforced in any court of law. Therefore, the approach of Manchester United to accessibility and disability bridged all the main key ingredients mentioned above which certainly seemed to explain the impetus for accessibility at Manchester United from the early 1980s onwards.

Looking in retrospect, one of the key people in this process, Phil Downs, explained how he became involved with Manchester United as a football fan and where his interest originated in promoting accessibility at the club. He also explained how the club initially responded to his proposals and translated his suggestions into actions. Although it took five years for his ambition to be realized, he stated:

It was probably in late 1976 that I first wrote to the club asking to attend the matches as a wheelchair user and I continued writing for five years. One of our local "Bobbies" called to see me one day and we chatted about going to see the games and he took it upon himself to write to the club on my behalf and, behold, I received three postcard-type passes for the last three matches in 1981 ... just before the following season started I received a pass for the entire season which was renewed for many years.

(cited in Paramio *et al.*, 2011: 370–371)

It is interesting to note that in the late 1970s disability and accessibility for SwD to football matches at stadiums, as the proposals of Phil Downs represented, was, according to him, definitely at the bottom of the agenda for most businesses and, by extension, the same would apply to most football clubs (see the whole transcript of his interview in Paramio *et al.*, 2011). In addition, unlike today, promoting access for all people to football matches was neither a social priority nor were there specific laws mandating accessibility to places of public accommodation. Despite this lack of social concern and absence of legal requirements, the initial approach of the club to accessibility and disability may be perceived, drawing on Prakash Sethi (1979), as positive, discretionary and responsive, rather than being reactive or defensive. This is relevant if we bear in mind that the club chose to respond positively to the requests of Phil Downs to promote and implement accessibility practices and services for fans with disabilities, despite the absence of any legal requirements, guidelines or minimum standards in the United Kingdom. Only North America had passed legislation capable of facilitating access for SwD to stadia and arenas (Paramio *et al.*, 2011; Grady and Paramio-Salcines, 2012). More specifically, it can be persuasively argued that, in the United States, the obligation to comply with the Americans with Disabilities Act (ADA) has provided the necessary impetus to ensure that facilities and services are accessible (Grady and Ohlin, 2009). The ADA has been described as "probably the most influential piece of legislation which marked a change of paradigm in North American disability law" (Paramio *et al.*, 2011: 374).

According to Clarkson (1995) a particular society determines what is a social issue and the representative government enacts appropriate legislation to protect social interests (see also Frederick, 2006). Hence, the test is whether an issue like the promotion of accessible environments and services in stadia or any place of public accommodation and services is present in the absence of legislation. If there is no legislation, the issue becomes a "stakeholder issue," which needs to be addressed at the corporate level as was the case of the first approach by Manchester United to accessibility and disability (Clarkson, 1995; Community Business Review, 2007). However this argument has also been criticized for not providing a strong rationale as to why corporations (sports organizations) address some issues at the expense of others.

This situation changed slightly during the 1990s when the legal environment in most countries was becoming more orientated towards addressing the issues faced by people with disabilities. As previously mentioned, one of the most influential pieces of legislation, the Americans with Disabilities Act (ADA), was passed in 1990 and the Disability Discrimination Act (DDA) in Great Britain was finally passed five years later. However, despite the presence of "strong" legislation to protect the rights of people with disabilities, a lack of enforcement by government authorities coupled with conflicting policies and procedures at different sports facilities can often result in a lack of uniformity in providing a high-quality experience for people with disabilities.

Chronologically, and as part of the club's real commitment to the proposals of their SwD, one of the early initiatives was to launch a *Disability Policy* which clearly reflected a social sensitivity of the club to the promotion of accessibility in club strategy. The introduction of the *Disability Policy* led directly to other strategies and actions that the club has been taking as part of the implementation of accessibility and disability into the club organization and culture. Over the last three decades, different supportive strategies have been implemented which have contributed to the effective implementation of accessibility and disability into the club vision. In fact, among other values, Manchester United includes non-discrimination as one of the main values of the club by saying that "Non-discriminatory ... in making Manchester United accessible to all, irrespective of age, race, gender, creed or physical ability" (Manchester United Disabled Supporters Association, 2012).

The foundation of the first disabled supporters' organization of its type in the UK (Manchester United Disabled Supporters Association, MUDSA) in 1989, which owes much to the continuing influence of Downs in the club, was itself another turning point and pivotal to the future development that the club has continued to promote. After setting up MUDSA, the partnership between MUDSA and the club has led to building confidence through a variety of formal and informal relationships, as Rahbek Pedersen (2006) conceptualizes, with "stakeholder dialogue" between both sides having contributed to the involvement of MUDSA in decision-making processes. As the 1990s began, what could have been considered a threat became an opportunity and, as a consequence, an elevated viewing platform, still in use today, was constructed in the Old Trafford Stadium for fans with disabilities. This pivotal action came to fruition as part of the ongoing "stakeholder dialogue" and relationship between club officers and MUDSA. The impact of this action on the operation of Old Trafford and the kind of commitment of the club with this group was huge if we bear in mind that, as Downs notes:

> It's fair to say that a small platform existed in the mid-1980s which held a maximum of 15–20 wheelchair users and their helpers. That was the sum total of people with disabilities apart from a handful of blind people who were sitting in the stadium receiving a commentary from hospital radio. In the first 12 months of me having operational responsibilities, I had managed to contact all the people making enquiries and the numbers had gone to just over 100. That was quite impressive but the facility that held 34 people was expanded to 70 ... We introduced a dedicated email address and telephone number and made a speciality out of my position effectively creating the first Disability Liaison Officer's post.
>
> (Phil Downs, pers. comm., April 30, 2012)

One of the most important aspects of this kind of consideration is what it actually meant to the club in terms of their commitment. In order to provide an elevated viewing position the club lost a total of 13 traditional seats in order to provide one wheelchair place. The additional commitment to providing wheelchair and disabled access amounted to a fairly significant financial commitment but one that they felt had to be made in order to uphold the club's values. One of the most important managerial consequences of this action was to increase and provide the best facilities and opportunities at Old Trafford for SwD of either the home or visiting teams. Table 9.1 gives a picture of the gradual implementation of seats for wheelchair fans and their companions at Old Trafford over the years (see also Table 9.2 for a complete description of the services and facilities provided for people with a range of disabilities at Old Trafford on match and non-match days at the 2012–2013 season).

Table 9.1 Historical evolution of the implementation of seats for wheelchair fans and their companions at Old Trafford over the years

1991 season	37 wheelchair positions with adjacent companion places (during Stretford End redevelopment)
1996 season	70 wheelchair places with adjacent companion places (North Stand 3 Tier development)
2000 season	104 wheelchairs places with adjacent companion places (East and West Stand developments)
2006 season	120 wheelchairs positions with adjacent companion places (NE and NW Quad developments)
2012 season	120 wheelchair positions with adjacent companion places in three wheelchair platforms for general access: 1 104 wheelchair seats plus adjacent companion places (South East) 2 8 wheelchair seats plus adjacent companion places (North East) 3 8 wheelchair seats plus adjacent companion places (North West) In addition, there are 89 wheelchair places (1 place per executive box)

Source: compiled by the authors.

Table 9.1 demonstrates the commitment of the club to providing disabled access as encapsulated in the mission statement. As Kay (1993) argued, this action can be understood by recognizing that the attention of the club was gradually moving from the problems of formulating strategy to the issues of implementation. In addition, strategy can necessarily be incremental and adaptive (Lindgreen and Swaen, 2010). Not long thereafter, in 1993 Phil Downs was recruited on a full-time basis in an emerging and pioneering managerial position at club level as Disability Liaison Officer at Manchester United, a position that he has held since then, a period of 20 years. Moving beyond the quantity to the quality of fan experience, many factors impact the quality of any disabled fan experience when attending a match, as "the holistic journey sequence approach to stadium" describes in much detail. However having a dedicated DLO, as the case of Phil Downs represents at Manchester United, makes a significant contribution to developing a positive and trusting dialogue between SwDs and the club as well as providing input into the gradual implementation of accessibility and inclusion into the club's culture and strategy.

Entering the 2000s, the club set up the Manchester United disability program in line with the FA's Ability Counts campaign. In addition to this, the club decided to build what is known as the Ability Suite in April 2003. This service is unique within the Premier League clubs which provides Manchester United a competitive advantage over other clubs. The Ability Suite aims to cover two objectives: first, a dedicated match day lounge for disabled supporters which provides added benefits to disabled supporters plus frees up concourse congestion; and second, a non-match day Learning Centre forming part of the Manchester United CSR policy. For the latter, the Ability Suite is used on non-match days by a local college, Trafford College, in delivering basic skills courses on areas such as health, well-being, communication and confidence building (Manchester United Disabled Supporters Association, 2012). It is also used by the club to deliver internal training sessions, some focusing on disability awareness.

To understand the relevance of this distinctive and unique educational, social and operational service provided by the club, it is worth emphasizing that still today no other club in the United Kingdom and Europe has managed to replicate this service in its stadium (Downs, 2006; Paramio *et al.*, 2011). Originally, the Ability Suite, which cost £150,000 (around $238,095) to build, was launched with a dual purpose: one as a match-day lounge for home and away SwD and on other days for a wide variety of community and social activities. As Disability Liaison Officer (DLO), Downs is responsible for the whole operation of the activities of the Ability Suite which is a corporate community/social suite funded by Manchester United and Vodafone (currently financially supported by the club and an Arab Telecommunication company). Also, this facility has attracted other partners such as Ability Net, Learn Direct, Heading for Success and Manchester Metropolitan University, who run a range of courses targeted at local disabled people. To understand the value of this distinctive and unique service for the local communities of Manchester and for disabled people in particular, it is extremely relevant to explain in detail how this service came into being, how it was (and is) funded, and how it is operated on match days and non-match days.

Over the last 30 years the club has progressively improved its provisions at Old Trafford. In terms of the provision for SwD the club currently provides 411 seats which represent around 0.53 percent of the total capacity of Old Trafford (76,312). From these numbers, 120 spaces are for wheelchair fans (108 home and 12 away) plus companion seating with clear sightlines for supporters with disabilities. There are also 40 places for people with visual impairments (plus companion seating), who can also listen to commentary (audio description) from MUTV, the official TV channel for Manchester United. In addition, the club has 21 places (plus companion seating) for fans with severe mobility difficulties, which have additional leg room and grab-rails between alternate seats. In addition, the club offers other accessible services such as 300 parking spaces, hospitality areas (such as the Ability Suite) and nine accessible toilets adjacent to the larger wheelchair platform, and a further four accessible toilets allied to the new quadrant facilities. More recently, the club has undertaken an extensive redevelopment program over the last three seasons (2008–11) which has focused on the aging executive areas at the Old Trafford stadium. As a result, all of the existing executive boxes have been upgraded with external seating, which includes provision for one wheelchair per box with adjacent accessible toilets with food, beverages and concessions stands (Table 9.2). Also, the club's commitment to inclusion is further emphasized by offering other accessible services such as the Museum and Tour Centre and the Megastore. Significantly, the official transport partner of the club always offers a minimum of two accessible coaches capable of taking the total of eight wheelchair users to away fixtures with a commitment to providing more accessible coaches on the occasion of semi-finals and finals.

Last but not least, Manchester United continues to extend its CSR credentials in this area by openly re-stating its commitments to employ more disabled people throughout the stadium and developing a clearly defined structure for doing so within the human resources policies of the club. This proactive stance provides tangible evidence of how accessibility and disability continue to be an integral part of the CSR strategy of the club.

Table 9.2 Provision of services and facilities for different kind of SwD at Old Trafford Stadium, season 2012–2013

Website contact and Disability Liaison Officer	Stadium, date of building, capacity	Seats for fans with disabilities (general access)	Other accessible services	Capacity/total seats for SwD (%)
www.mudsa.org Phil Downs	Old Trafford, 1910, 76,312	120 for wheelchairs (108 home and 12 away) (+ companion seating) (240) 21 for severe mobility difficulties) (+ companion seating) (42) 21 for moderate mobility difficulties) (+ companion seating) 20 for visually impaired (+ companion seating) (40)	• Tickets and membership services • Commentary headsets for visually impaired fans • Services for assistance dogs • Induction loop facilities • 300 parking areas • Adapted transport for away matches • Hospitality areas (Ability Suite) and 9 toilets • 89 seats in executive boxes • New food, beverages and concession stands • Museum and Tour Centre, club store and Red Café • Radio headsets and away transport coaches	76,312/411 = 0,53%

Source: compiled by the authors.

Conclusions

Manchester United's Old Trafford stadium is a historic stadium and is, at the time of writing, 102 years old. Despite this fact, most of the stadium has been rebuilt in a piecemeal way over a number of years and complies with every accessible requirement set out in the United Kingdom Building Regulations. The case of Manchester United FC's approach to accessibility and disability serves to illustrate the peculiarities of implementing CSR in small and medium size enterprises as the club represents. Furthermore, through its long-term partnership and stakeholder dialogue with the SwD organization at the club, MUDSA serves to illustrate how what once represented a marginal issue for a professional club like the promotion and the provision of accessible environments in stadia could now be incorporated into the club's culture and strategy over the years. Manchester United's case represents as well the ongoing relationship between the club and different stakeholders such as fans, local communities and employees.

One of the guiding principles for incorporating accessibility and disability in any club culture and organization is to consider this as part of a long-term strategy. As Downs points out:

> I have always said, and still say, that there are no "quick fix" solutions to the overall subject of disability. Each club or national association needs to consider advancements in this area as part of a strategy that is essentially "evolution not revolution."
>
> (cited in Paramio *et al.*, 2011: 371)

Under this philosophy, MUDSA similarly states that:

> since its formation MUDSA has always adopted the view that genuine progress between association and club can only be achieved by "consensus, not confrontation" and the improvements to facilities cannot be expected to materialize overnight; the patience of all disabled supporters is therefore pivotal to developing a process of "evolution, not revolution" and cultivating a good relationship with everyone in football.
>
> (Manchester United Disabled Supporters Association, 2011, 2012)

These are both essential principles for integrating accessibility and disability in any sport organization's culture and operation.

As part of this long-term commitment of the club to promote the best conditions for their SwD, this strategy has also contributed to achieving impressive results over the last decades. For example one of the indicators that can highlight the success of the development and implementation of accessibility and disability into the club's culture can be the large numbers of SwD, estimated by Phil Downs to be around 2,200 (at the time of writing), which also includes some companions that also want to be members, and are able to access football matches and enjoy similar experiences as the rest of the fans. As he states:

> It's my view this personal service with the backing of expertise gave people the confidence to believe that they could start coming to football matches and again the numbers continued to grow. Within five years we were nudging 1,200 people and we now stand at around 2,200 but that number also includes some helpers whom also want to be members. In the case of SwD and People Reduced Mobility it is reasonable to suggest that these numbers are only ever likely to increase. In fact, if we accept that there are growing numbers of disabled people due to improvements in medical technology and couple this with the growing number of elderly people; these figures won't plateau for about 20 years.
>
> (Phil Downs, pers. comm., May 18, 2012)

Another visible outcome of the continuing commitment of the club is the increasing number of children and adults with disabilities that are engaged in different disability programs in the club since its inception in 2000. As the Manchester United Foundation (2012) notes:

> Since 1992, Manchester United has run a Football in the Community scheme that has benefited thousands of people. The scheme became part of the Foundation in 2006. As part of Manchester United we will always deliver football and we are committed to developing the grassroots game in local communities. We run sessions for local youngsters, schools and people with disabilities; giving people of all ages and backgrounds the opportunity to play football.

As Manchester United's Foundation states the disability program was set up in 2000 alongside the Football Association's *Ability Counts* campaign. Since then the program has won numerous awards and has gone on to become one of the largest in the Premier League (Manchester United Disabled Supporters Association, 2012). On average 10 hours of coaching are provided for young people and adults with disabilities every week. Manchester United was also one of the first two disability specific clubs to receive the FA Charter standard award.

The essential message espoused by Phil Downs throughout this long-term process is that managers need to explore the following principle:

There is no doubt that implementing standards has enabled more people with disabilities to enjoy their match experience. What we have found is that if there are good facilities, people will come. The more facilities we've added to Old Trafford, the more oversubscribed we've become.

(Phil Downs, pers. comm., May 18, 2012)

In addition, Downs adds that the Manchester United experience has helped to revolutionize match days for SwD, provide more fans with disabilities access to live football, and also to influence the design and build of other historical and new stadia. With the support of the club:

We have just proved what can be achieved … it simply requires a "can do-will do" approach and a bit of time. I always like to emphasize that that the facilities at Manchester United have not always been like they are now, it took us time to get there and bit by bit it's expanded and become a part of the everyday culture of Manchester United.

(Phil Downs, pers. comm., March 30, 2012)

Drawing on the successful experience of Manchester United, Phil Downs appeals to the CSR policies of football clubs by saying that "We need to generate awareness within football not only in England but also in European clubs to improve their stadium facilities considering the social aspects that accessibility produce" (cited in Paramio *et al.*, 2008: 530). This situation has contributed to identify the experience of Manchester United and MUDSA as one of the best practices in promoting access by fans with disabilities at European football leagues and thus setting standards for other clubs at European level to follow (Manchester United FC, 2009). The conclusion is that any positive development around accessibility depends on the values of the football club and how they incorporate these values into a CSR strategy. The case of Manchester United demonstrates that accessibility and disability are considered part of the values of the club and over the period 1980–2012, the club has steadily addressed these issues as a fundamental part of its CSR strategy.

References

Babiak, K. and Wolfe, R. (2006) 'More than just a game? Corporate social responsibility and Super Bowl XL', *Sport Marketing Quarterly*, 15 (4), 214–222.

Babiak, K. and Wolfe, R. (2009) 'Determinants of corporate social responsibility in professional sport: Internal and external factors', *Journal of Sport Management*, 23, 717–742.

Banerjee, B. S. (2007) *Corporate social responsibility: The good, the bad and the ugly*, Cheltenham: Edward Elgar.

Bradish, C. and Cronin, J. (2009) 'Corporate social responsibility in sport', *Journal of Sport Management*, 23, 691–697.

Breitbarth, T. and Harris, P. (2008) 'The role of corporate social responsibility in the football business. Towards the development of a conceptual model', *European Sport Management Quarterly*, 8, 179–206.

Carroll, A.B. (2008) 'A history of corporate social responsibility: concepts and practices', in Crane, A., McWilliams, A., Matten, D., Moon, J. and Siegel, D. (eds.) *The Oxford handbook of corporate social responsibility*. Oxford: Oxford University Press, pp. 19–46.

Clarkson, M.B.E. (1995) 'A stakeholder framework for analyzing and evaluating corporate social performance', *Academy of Management Review*, 20 (1), 92–117.

Community Business Review (2007) 'CSR and disability: Three case studies', *Community Business Review*, 2, 10–12.

Crane, A., McWilliams, A., Matten, D., Moon, J., and Siegel, D. (2008) (eds.) *The Oxford handbook of corporate social responsibility*. Oxford: Oxford University Press.

Deloitte (2012) '*Fan power Football Money League*'. Sport Business Group. Available at: http://www.deloitte.com/assets/Dcom-Panama/Local%20Assets/Documents/PA_es_dfml_2012.pdf (accessed: May 20, 2012).

Downs, P. (2006) 'Joining forces', *Gazette*, 9, 3.

Drucker, P. (1999) *Management challenges for the 21st century*. New York: Harper Business.

Frederick, W.C. (2006) *Corporation, be good! The story of corporate social responsibility*. Indianapolis: Dog Ear Publishing.

Grady, J. and Ohlin, J.B. (2009) 'Equal access to hospitality services for guests with mobility impairments under the Americans with Disabilities Act: Implications for the hospitality industry', *International Journal of Hospitality Management*, 28 (1), 161–169.

Grady, J. (2010) 'Accessibility doesn't happen by itself: An interview with Betty Siegel, J.D., Director of The Kennedy Center Accessibility program', *Journal of Venue and Event Management*, 2 (2), 69–73. Available at: http://www.hrsm.sc.edu/JVEM/vol2issue2.shtml (accessed: April 10, 2012).

Grady, J. and Paramio-Salcines, J.L. (2012) 'Global approaches to managing the fan experience for patrons with disabilities', paper presented at the 10th Annual Conference of the Sport Marketing Association, Orlando, October 25.

Hamil, S., Walters, G. and Watson, L. (2011) 'The model of governance at FC Barcelona: Balancing member democracy, commercial strategy, corporate social responsibility and sporting performance', in Hassan, D. and Hamil, S. (eds.) *Who owns football? The governance and management of the club game worldwide*. London: Routledge, pp. 133–162.

Hemsley, S. (2009) 'Corporate social responsibility and sports sponsorship: How sport helps business fulfill CSR obligations', *International Marketing Report Publications*. Available at: http://www.imrpublications.com/overview.aspx?sid=22&rid=1 (accessed: May 20, 2011).

Johnson, G. and Scholes, K. (1999) *Exploring corporate strategy: Text & cases*. 5th edn. Harlow: Pearson, Prentice Hill.

Johnson, G., Scholes, K. and Whittington, R. (2007) *Dirección estratégica (Exploring corporate strategy: Text & cases)*. 7th edn. Madrid: Pearson, Prentice Hill.

Jones, D. (2012) *Who cares wins. Why good business is better business*. London: Financial Times Publishing.

Kay, J. (1993) *Foundations of corporate success*. Oxford: Oxford University Press.

Lindgreen, A. and Swaen, V. (2010) 'Corporate social responsibility', *International Journal of Management Reviews*, 12 (1), 1–7.

Manchester United FC (2009) *Manchester United football club policy for disabled supporters*. Manchester United FC, Manchester.

Manchester United Disabled Supporters Association (MUDSA) (2011) *Welcome to MUDSA*. Available at: http://www.mudsa.org (accessed: June 10, 2012).

Manchester United Disabled Supporters Association (MUDSA) (2012) *Disabled Supporters' information booklet 2012–13*. Available at: http://www.mudsa.org (accessed: July 12, 2012).

Manchester United Foundation (2012) *Changing young lives through football*. Available at: http://www.mufoundation.org (accessed: October 17, 2012).

Maon, F., Swaen, V. and Lindgreen, A. (2009) 'Designing and implementing corporate social responsibility: A framework grounded in theory and practice', *Journal of Business Ethics*, 87, 71–89.

Mellor, D. (2000) 'The genesis of Manchester United as a national and international "super-club" 1958–68', *Soccer and Society*, 1 (2), 151–166.

Paramio, J.L, Buraimo, B. and Campos, C. (2008) 'From modern to postmodern: the development of football stadia in Europe', *Sport in Society*, 11 (5), 517–534.

Paramio, J.L., Campos, C., Downs, P., Beotas, E. and Muñoz, G. (2009) 'Disability provision in European stadia within a CSR framework: The case of Primera Division-Spanish football league', *Proceedings of the 17th European Sport Management Congress 'Best Practices in Sport Facility and Event Management'*, Amsterdam, pp. 280–281.

Paramio, J.L, Campos, C. and Buraimo, B. (2011) 'Promoting accessibility for fans with disabilities to European stadiums and arenas: A holistic journey sequence approach', in Trenberth, L. and Hassan, D. (eds.) *Managing sport business: An introduction*. London: Routledge, pp. 267–288.

Perry, B. (2005) 'Manchester United, brand of hope and glory', in Johnson, G., Scholes, K. and Whittington, R. (eds.) *Exploring corporate strategy: Text & cases*. 7th edn. Harlow: Pearson, Prentice Hill, pp. 217–222.

Porter, M. and Kramer, M. (2002) 'The competitive advantage of corporate philanthropy', *Harvard Business Review*, December, 57–68.

Porter, M. and Kramer, M. (2006) 'Strategy and society: the link between competitive advantage and corporate social responsibility', *Harvard Business Review*, 84, 78–92.

Rahbek Pedersen, E. (2006) 'Making corporate social responsibility (CSR) operable: How companies translate stakeholder dialogue into practice', *Business and Society Review*, 111 (2), 137–163.

Sethi, P. (1979) 'A conceptual framework for evaluative analysis of social issues and evaluation of business response patterns', *Academy of Management Review*, 4, 63–74.

Szymanski, S. (1998) 'Why is Manchester United so successful?' *Business Strategy Review*, 9 (4), 47–54.

Walters, G. (2009) 'Corporate social responsibility through sport: The community sports trust model as a CSR delivery agency', *Journal of Corporate Citizenship*, 35, 81–94.

Walters, G. (2011) 'Managing social responsibility in sport', in Trenberth, L. and Hassan, D. (eds.) *Managing sport business: An introduction*. London: Routledge, pp. 412–426.

Walters, G. and Tacon, R. (2011) *Corporate social responsibility in European football*, Report funded by the UEFA Research Grant Program, Birkbeck University of London.

Werre, M. (2003) 'Implementing corporate responsibility: The Chiquita case', *Journal of Business Ethics*, 44, 247–260.

Westerbeek, H. and Smith, A. (2005) *Business leadership and the lessons from sport*. London: Macmillan.

10

CONNECTING WITH PEOPLE

Best practices in Northern Ireland

Richard Smith, Mark Langhammer and David Carson

Overview

This chapter presents two case studies based within the previously fractured communities of Northern Ireland. For 30 years Northern Ireland was headline news throughout the world as a result of civil unrest manifesting in street violence and sectarian murder. A peace agreement was signed by all sections within the community including the British and Irish Governments in 1998 and since then community leaders and local politicians have been striving to repair the years of civil strife and disturbance. This chapter describes two case examples focused upon bringing communities together through sport and promoting good corporate social responsibility (CSR). The case studies are live examples of applying principles of corporate social responsibility, community development and recognition of appropriate business acumen within the context of small business. Case one presents sport as a strategic tool for social inclusion and case two demonstrates cross-community collaboration through sport, eventually leading to a shared stadium and sports complex.

Introduction

The focus of this chapter will be on the ground-breaking new-world context of CSR in sport in Northern Ireland. Perspectives on CSR are, however, firmly founded upon the seminal literature in the area, such as Mintzberg (2008), Vogel (2008), Porter and Kramer (2008), Crane *et al.*, (2008), Carroll (1999), Walters (2009) and Walters and Tacon (2010) (see Part I of the handbook for an extensive overview on theoretical perspectives on CSR in sport).

The civil and political unrest in Northern Ireland was once a regular global headline, much in the same way as the world views similar demonstrations of dissatisfaction, disturbance and revolt in Arab regions of the Middle East and North Africa today.

Situated on Europe's western seaboard, Northern Ireland is a relatively small region of the United Kingdom, the other regions being Scotland, Wales and England. Northern Ireland, with a population of 1.8 million, is what remained part of the United Kingdom after the creation of the independent Irish Free State in 1922. For almost 30 years (within the 1960s to 1990s) Northern Ireland experienced civil unrest. Communities were polarized into two broad sections, those aligned to the United Kingdom and those to Irish Nationalism. These divisions spilled into the sporting world and restricted the access of individuals into particular activities. Since the dawn of a new political dispensation obtained by the significant political agreement in 1998, new initiatives, supported by the principles of equality of opportunity, have involved communities in cross-community activities. A growing number of participants have greater opportunities to be involved in sports which were historically reserved for one section of the community.

Whilst civil unrest occurred in most cities and towns throughout Northern Ireland, the most extreme manifestation of unrest occurred in North Belfast and similarly the regional town of Craigavon. An outline of North Belfast serves to illustrate the depths of polarization, social deprivation and political division. North Belfast has a population of approximately 83,500 with 37.4 percent under 20 years old and a further 17.5 percent between 20–25 years old (NISRA, 2010). In a study into North Belfast, Dunlop and Toner stated that:

> North Belfast is made up of many small, isolated communities. The area is highly segregated along religious lines and has suffered more, as a result, from sectarian violence than any other part of Northern Ireland … As a direct result of its highly diverse and segregated nature, the area has failed to fully benefit from many of the initiatives aimed at economic development, with statutory agencies being widely perceived by the local community as not having supported, nor invested in, the social, infrastructural, economic, educational or recreational development of North Belfast. Without doubt, the image of the area has contributed to North Belfast's inability to attract sufficient resources.
>
> (Dunlop and Toner, 2002: 20)

More recently, the then Social Development Minister Margaret Ritchie stated: "We still live apart, we are educated apart, we mostly socialise apart – and that is just not normal. It may have become our norm, but it is not the behaviour of a normal society" (cited in McAdam, 2009: 12). Unfortunately, North Belfast probably reflects such abnormalities, perhaps most significantly in a chronic lack of common shared sport facilities. Similar descriptions can be applied to Craigavon. In essence, the two regions were and largely remain divided between Loyalist (predominantly "Protestant" religion) and Nationalist (predominantly "Catholic" religion).

In the past few years long-established relationships are being renewed and reinforced. People now engage in ad hoc, informal ways. Networks are interwoven. Stories of connection are abundant. Underlying all of these networks and relationships are elements of social responsibility. People recognize the importance of connections that transgress any political or social divides. Inherent in these connections is an implicit and sometimes explicit sense of community. This sense of community is shared by many in business and not least in sport.

One of the consequences of the "Troubles" – the name given at a local level to the 30 years of political unrest (1969–1999) – was the lack of opportunity for progression in a chosen sport and this resulted in the immigration of sport personalities to the United Kingdom mainland and to other destinations around the world, where they made a significant impression in the sporting world.

The continual exit of residents from Northern Ireland was reversed in 2000 as migrant workers, principally from European destinations, came to the country, given the growing job opportunities and the "settling in" of the peace process. For the first time in history the number of those arriving in Northern Ireland was greater than the number migrating and the arrival of new communities became a challenge to the indigenous population that were not accustomed to dealing with the issue of inward migration. Currently an estimated 88,000 foreign nationals reside in Northern Ireland (NISRA, 2010). It is with this background that the two case studies described later in this chapter are best practice examples of CSR in sport.

Unifying power of sport

The unifying power of sport is well documented in the body of knowledge and elsewhere in this text. For this chapter and in support of the case examples following we recognize that much has been written and support given to community sports initiatives in recognition of the role sport can play in community development. According to Sport for Development and Peace international working group:

> Community sport programs can provide shared experiences between people that "re-humanize" opposing groups in the eyes of their enemies. By sharing sport experiences, sport participants from conflicting groups increasingly grow to feel that they are alike, rather than different.
>
> (Sport for Development and Peace international working group, 2008: 235)

Similarly, Coalter (2005:7) refers to a Sportscotland report by saying that "participating in sport can improve the quality of life of individuals and communities, promote social inclusion, improve health, counter anti-social behaviour, raise individual self-esteem and confidence, and widen horizons." In addition, research studies undertaken at both local and national levels provide evidence of the impact that sport can have in helping to create safe and sustainable communities (Gratton and Henry, 2001; Long and Sanderson, 2001; Scully *et al.*, 1999). In a report entitled *Social benefits of sport*, Coalter (2005: 4) also contends that "sport may contribute to:

- improvements in people's physical and mental health, and well-being;
- the promotion and enhancement of education and life-long learning;
- the promotion of active citizenship;
- programs aimed at combating crime and anti-social behavior;
- economic development."

All of these factors were deemed to be addressed in a positive way by sport initiatives. According to the same author, "Government is increasingly concerned with addressing issues of community cohesion, social inclusion and 'active citizenship' and ... social capital" (Coalter, 2005: 19). Putman (2000: 312) defines communities that are rich in social capital as being those in which there are:

- strong community networks/civic infrastructure, with widespread involvement in the organizational life of the community;
- a sense of local identity/solidarity/equality;
- reportedly high levels of interpersonal trust and reciprocal support.

All of these aspects therefore show that sport and sports clubs are essential to community identity and well-being. In the specific context of football and cross-community initiatives, the Irish Football Association (IFA) is widely recognized by international football governing bodies such as UEFA and FIFA as a best practice example in its *Football for All Project*. In an evaluation exercise Hagen states:

one of the pillars around which the IFA's work will focus is: "That football is fully integrated into the community in every respect," with priorities including "Partnerships" and Good Relations – Celebrating Differences. These elements of development can be directly related to the work carried out by Football For All.

(Hagen, 2008: 5)

It is with this background that this chapter presents two outstanding and in their context unique examples of cross-community initiatives within Northern Ireland.

Best practice in Northern Ireland

The examples of best practice described here have the same underpinning, but address the "shared space" aspects in different ways. Case one focuses upon the use of sport as a strategic tool for a multi-cultural organization to assist their vision of having foreign nationals fully integrated into the local community life. Case two describes a community coming together under the auspices of football. This merging of communities was initially informal and it has manifest as a vision for a *Giants Park Sports Village and Shared Community Stadium*, planned to be built on natural ground on a former landfill site on Belfast Lough's North Foreshore (Crusaders FC, 2007).

Case one: sport as a strategic tool for social inclusion

Craigavon Intercultural Program: sport as a strategic tool to aid integration of foreign nationals in the local community

Immigration is one the greatest challenges facing European societies in the twenty-first century (Kennett, 2005), with citizenship and integration of foreign nationals being key to the development of a new society landscape. One of the areas in Northern Ireland which has witnessed an increase in inward migration is Craigavon, located 30 miles to the west of the capital Belfast. The region was not new to migration for in the 1960s groups of people from Asia settled in the area, however, the opening of European borders brought increasing numbers of migrant workers seeking work in the food producing industry, one of the main sources of employment in the area. According to the latest census around 4,500 foreign nationals are included among the population of 92,000 (Northern Ireland Census, 2011).

In 2006 a group of concerned individuals set up a charitable group to which they gave the title "Craigavon Intercultural Program" (CIP), with the objective to promote the social inclusion of new communities and assist members of these communities to integrate into local community life. It was recognized that migrant workers were largely isolated, had limited access to services, were apprehensive about entry to local facilities due to acts of racism which were targeted at them. All these factors made new communities extremely vulnerable. CIP was determined to address some of these issues through the provision of bilingual support for individuals; development of family support initiatives to address the concerns of growing ethnic families; cultural showcasing events which would promote understanding between communities; and sporting opportunities designed to integrate participants into local sports activities. Realizing the difficulties in engaging with male migrants, the organization developed a strategy which encompasses the realm of social inclusion through the medium of sport. The strategy aimed to cover the following aspects:

- develop interest groups
- deliver sport projects
- identify leaders
- develop groups/teams/clubs
- offer coaching opportunities
- signpost to local clubs
- link with national governing bodies.

Having identified that large numbers of male migrants were employed in Moypark Ltd, one of the region's main food processing companies and largest employer in Northern Ireland, CIP approached the company and secured sponsorship to run an ethnic summer football league, targeting mainly workers from the factory. In all, eight 11-a-side teams became involved in a four-week football competition. Moypark supplied the tee shirts stamped with the company's brand and all remaining costs, i.e. referees and pitch hire were supplied by the local borough council. Groups of migrants workers from Poland, Lithuania, East Timor, Portugal, Africa, Brazil and Ireland participated in the intercultural games and among the outcomes achieved were threefold:

1 Improved levels of cooperation on the factory floor between nationalities.
2 Players became inspired to consider forming teams that would play informally thus reducing isolation.
3 Participants who were facing difficulties were signposted to the support service offered by CIP and leaders among different communities were identified, which proved useful both in developing other on-going sport experiences and connecting with a diverse range of communities.

Building on the experience of the summer league and having secured funding from the Craigavon Borough Council, CIP performed a survey of levels of integration among ethnic communities in 2008. The outcome of the survey, involving 100 participants drawn largely from the Lithuanian, Polish and Portuguese speaking communities, indicated that 57 percent of those surveyed had ceased sport-related activities since arriving in the country for a variety of reasons: lack of opportunity, lack of knowledge of facilities, limited time, finance and a generally remained apprehensive regarding the indigenous response to their inclusion in local sport's activities (Smith, 2008).

Using this survey as a baseline and having identified key personalities within ethnic communities, CIP designed a series of opportunities for male and females. These encompassed a series of sport activities inclusive of basketball, volleyball, indoor soccer and a new sport in Northern Ireland, Brazilian Futsal. These activities were supported by the Sport Department of Craigavon Borough Council and the Regional Health Authority that was anxious to make connections with ethnic communities at a grassroots level. As many migrant men did not register with doctors at health centres, health promotion teams attended ethnic sport days and provided basic health checks which proved to be both popular among participants and resulted in a greater awareness of potential medical concerns.

It also became apparent that certain nationalities had different sporting priorities from those practiced by the indigenous communities. Eastern Europeans had a keen interest in weight lifting and Lithuanians preferred basketball over football. The Asian communities followed badminton with interest and again basketball was popular among the Filipino community.

It is documented in literature that sports opportunities by immigrants is also an opportunity for citizenship, offering some control that may be lacking in other areas of their lives (Kennett, 2005). The sporting activities delivered by CIP laid to the development of individual skills, team competence, access to coaching courses and integration into local clubs and leagues. The pilot basketball opportunities opened the opportunity for the creation of a Lithuanian basketball team which inspired other players in different areas of Northern Ireland to develop similar teams. In a short period of time some of these teams entered the Northern Ireland Basketball League and have made a significant contribution to the sport at a regional level. An interesting outcome in this adventure has been the need for these teams to attract funds from potential sponsors for the development of the clubs.

The preferred delivery method of CIP is the provision of activities that are both cross-community and cross-cultural with the objective to promote increased levels of integration and inclusion. The projects have a strategic fit into the holistic service which the organization offers to ethnic families and communities. Since 2009, CIP has provided a support service for women from ethnic communities and in 2010 increased its staff to include an Ethnic Youth Inclusion worker, which aimed at addressing the issues of growing ethnic family networks that appear to have the intention of settling long term in the country.

Migration implies huge adjustments by the person who leaves his/her familiar environment to settle in a strange new world with different structures and forms of behavior. CIP identified a noticeable change that seemed to be part of the process of migration: a change in eating patterns forced by work patterns, limited finances, different food types and reduced family support networks. A survey conducted by CIP of 50 Portuguese females indicated that most participants had a significant weight gain due to a change of diet. In response to this need, CIP in partnership with the Regional Health Authority delivered a series of initiatives, fitness programs, weight management classes and health awareness sessions which had a measurable success among participants.

Physical activity has played an important role in the integration of ethnic young people and is included as part of personal development programs designed to raise levels of self-esteem and confidence among young people who are located "between cultures." Programs have been delivered in partnership with local sport clubs and teams such as the Belfast Giants, an ice hockey team that is based in the capital. The programs tackle the issues of identity and cross-community relations and have had a significant impact in directing ethnic young people into positive "relationship building" opportunities with indigenous youth clubs.

The political changes in Northern Ireland have opened the local economy to an international audience, while at the same time have attracted new workers to the country from around the globe. With these developments come profound social challenges and responsibilities. Industry is the principal interface between new "work forces" and fresh opportunities, and is ideally placed to enhance integration.

As the workforce in Northern Ireland becomes increasingly "international" and culturally diverse, companies must create structures that raise cultural competence from the shop floor to management. This competence will be driven by employee experiences and relationships developed in their internal and external work environment.

The social impact created can be further maximized if links and partnerships are made between organizations in the public, private and third sectors. It is in this line that CIP will seek to collaborate and partner with major corporations in the local area that are interested in supporting community engagement initiatives that have a track record of enhancing community cohesion and life.

Case two: cross-community collaboration through sport

Towards a shared stadium and sports complex: the journey of Crusaders FC and Newington FC, a cross-community relationship partnership

This case outlines the "coming together" of two football clubs in North Belfast, Crusaders FC a semi-professional club playing in the Irish Premier League and Newington AFC playing in the local amateur league, and shows the progression of this relationship partnership to what it is now and the plans for the future.

History and background

People in North Belfast have always seen themselves as being from North Belfast. In the years of civil unrest the North Belfast community was fractured. Crusaders FC, because of the location of its ground, Seaview became known by association as the North Belfast Protestant club. In some ways Newington was formed out of a void in Catholic North Belfast for youths wishing to play football but who could not relate to Crusaders, not least because of their ground location in a Protestant area.

There was a period when much antagonism existed between the communities and in some cases Crusaders FC's Seaview Stadium was a headline statement of North Belfast troubles; a policeman shot dead at Seaview; a dubious distinction of having the highest recorded police attendance at any football match in the United Kingdom, 1900 police; and numerous arrests for sectarian disturbance. Newington AFC, centered in a predominantly Catholic area or North Belfast, has witnessed a similar catalogue of civil unrest.

The beginning of the Crusaders/Newington relationship partnership: a shared space

Newington has searched in vain for a ground they could call "home" for over 30 years. In recent years serious options at a local public park in North Belfast and at public pitches in the neighbouring borough of Newtownabbey were considered and, for a variety of reasons, proved unsuccessful. Newington AFC is largely homeless and often dependent upon accommodations by other clubs. Since 2002, Crusaders FC have been seeking to develop a new stadium. Seaview Stadium, tightly bordered by housing, roadway and railway, is no longer "fit-for-purpose" as a twenty-first century sports arena.

The Crusaders/Newington relationship partnership began through the football networks, friends and acquaintances. Through these connections, Newington might quietly use Seaview for some games, and help and assistance in both directions was forthcoming in shared coaching and items of equipment. For a time, Newington was able to use Seaview for more games than just a few.

Throughout these informal arrangements, there was a common frustration. On Crusaders part the Seaview stadium and facilities could not be maximized and on Newington's part they simply lacked a place they could relate to as their own. Crusaders, like Newington, were at an impasse, how to progress their shared future and relationship partnership. Friends and acquaintances realized that much more could be shared, exchanged and done together through a shared stadium and sports complex.

Then the realization, at a meeting between Crusaders FC and Newington AFC, the project was about "shared space," good relations, economic development, healthy living, environmental improvement, tackling educational disadvantage and much more. Our dream of a stadium and sports village was only the means – the shared endeavour – through which this could be done.

The formalization of the partnership in October 2007 was the step away from this ad hoc relationship to one going forward together, with common goals. The idea of a shared space that could not only expand the whole football profile for both clubs was also fuelled by the recognition that much more than formal football could be realized in shared space. The opportunity to bring loose groupings of mates together to play five- and seven-a-side football; integration with sport related business and education housed within the stadium facility; a meeting place for community groups; social events; reach out activities shared together.

The progression of the relationship partnership

What initially could have been described as a "marriage of convenience" rapidly moved towards a deeper partnership. What became evident to both clubs was that the success of the "Stadium and Sports Village" project depended upon developing wider governmental, political and civic policy goals.

Based on the immediate need to keep Newington AFC afloat, both clubs signed a ground sharing agreement to allow Newington AFC home games to take place at Seaview. From a community relations perspective, the task of ensuring safe passage to and from the stadium was undertaken with police advice. Likewise a welcoming environment, within the ground and social club, for Newington AFC people was achieved successfully.

Although this facility is owned solely by Crusaders FC, the application to the Sport Northern Ireland, (SportNI) "Places for Sport" grant program, (for the 3G pitch), was clear that the primary purpose of seeking to intensify usage through an artificial surface was to increase cross-community access. Indeed, an updated "facility usage" agreement with Newington AFC was a SportNI condition of offer. As the partnership process deepens, Newington AFC will consider its own governance and the process undertaken by Crusaders FC has been fully shared with Newington AFC to facilitate this.

The role of Seaview Enterprises is to focus fund-raising activities in seeking social grants and corporate donations to sustain and develop cross-community activities. Whilst a core aim of Seaview Enterprises is to promote collaboration and co-operation between Crusaders FC and Newington AYC, all grant revenues and private donations sustained by Seaview Enterprises are independent of the activities, aims and objectives of both clubs. The main objectives of the company are to:

- promote good relations in North Belfast and Newtownabbey by providing good quality and safe facilities and services that are welcoming and accessible to all;
- promote sport and sporting excellence;
- promote vocational training;
- as part of the above, intensify usage of the Seaview Stadium and other venues for the promotion of cross-community activities.

Aspiration for Seaview Enterprises

The main aim for Seaview Enterprises is to become the leading social enterprise organization in North Belfast by developing and demonstrating best practice in all aspects of cross-community collaboration and integration. Seaview Enteprises will expand the scope and range of its functions to incorporate all aspects of cross-community education and training; networks and networking; through sport and wider community events and programs. Seaview Enterprise will seek to secure revenue streams for use in the above programs and activities. Such revenue streams may come from further community grant awards, commercial sponsorships; fee paying programs; local Government and Assembly support. Seaview Enterprises also aims to be the leading and most comprehensive cross-community events and stadium-management company in advance of the proposed Giant's Park Cross Community Sports and Recreation Village. It is envisaged that Seaview Enterprises, with several years' track record in promoting the ethos of the new Village, will be the preferred manager of the complex. In essence, the focus of the partnership, through Seaview Enterprises, has turned to the future.

Launch of the Giant's Park Sports Village and Shared Community Stadium

A public launch event was held at a hotel in North Belfast. At the event, the launch brochure set out the clear cross-community rationale for the project. Key-note speakers included community relations experts from the Community Relations Council (CRC), University of Ulster Institute of Conflict Research and other community organizations. For example, Chief Executive of the Irish Football Association (IFA), Howard Wells said the launch had given him "one of the most exciting hours" since he had taken up his post. "It's created a massive 'wow' factor for me, not least because I think it's highly deliverable – so let's stop talking about it and get it built." From a practical perspective, the tangible gains from the press launch were the public signing of both the Ground Sharing Agreement and the Memorandum of Understanding achieved to formally commit to a working relationship in respect of the new stadium. In addition, the eclectic backgrounds of attendees at the launch, including representatives from all religions, the legal profession, community leaders, politicians and most importantly business corporations, was seen as a commitment from the whole community to the project. All signed on as willing "ambassadors" in support of the project.

Interim progression: opening Seaview for cross-community public access

In order to deepen the cross-community links, the partnership sought to maximize the benefits of a new 3G all-weather pitch at Seaview Stadium facilitating:

- joint Crusaders/Newington mini-soccer
- development of women's football
- inter-school coaching and after schools program
- facilitating Newington FC training and matches
- facilitating IFA Skills Development centre.

Deepening engagement and action planning

By the summer of 2009, through a series of meetings at Committee and Youth Academy level, the two clubs had agreed a five-year action (or engagement) plan, together with a WAGS plan for creating a welcoming environment. In the summer of 2011 it was decided to make Seaview Enterprises solely independent of Crusaders FC. The aims and purpose of Seaview Enterprises was newly stated as: a wholly independent enterprise dedicated to promoting good relations in North Belfast and Newtownabbey by providing good quality and safe facilities and services that are welcoming and accessible to all; promote sport and sporting excellence; and promote vocational training.

In November 2011 Seaview Enterprises secured a PEACE 111 grant (a EU Regional Development funding initiative to promote peace and reconciliation in deprived communities) of £420.000 for a 30-month program of cross-community initiatives involving young people and sport. This program has become the core model for the community stadium which is now Seaview FC. It is envisaged that this model will transfer smoothly to the new cross-community sports village in the North Foreshore planned for 2014. As the partnership between Crusaders FC and Newington AFC is one of the positive stories emerging from North Belfast the idea proposed for a Sports Complex is, in effect, a shared endeavor. Seaview Enterprises is an important trial element illustrated in the next section *Connecting with People* in the context of small business and technology.

Connecting with people: the context of small business and the importance of technology

This section acknowledges the capacity of small local business owners and employees in engaging with local people and enhancing civic pride and engaging CSR as a small business to aid future growth. An important element of connecting with people lies in the business world, in particular, the small business (SB) to medium-sized business (SME) world. The widely accepted broad statistic is that approximately 90 percent of all enterprises in any developed economy are SBs/SMEs. In this context, therefore, small business is a mainstream connection to communities and people. This fact is one of the pillars of future shared and integrated CSR in sport and can be linked in a tripartite Venn diagram in Figure 10.1 as an emphasis of significance.

An inherent pillar of CSR in sport must stem from this new technological age, commonly known as WEB 2.0. The importance of this element cannot be ignored, essentially this construct acknowledges the interaction between human beings and technology. As outlined in Carson and Boone:

> technology in whatever form it develops will increasingly influence business and not least interface infrastructures and performance to the point of being fully integral to business per se. As technology develops so to in tandem will interface competency and skill, based on a foundation of knowledge and expertise.

(Carson and Boone, 2008: 1)

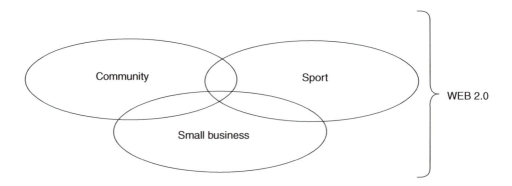

Figure 10.1 A model of shared and integrated CSR in sport

In acknowledgement of this construct, platforms such a YouTube provide an outlet for product stories and events; Facebook and LinkedIn offer networking and discussion platforms; and Twitter provides the daily "noise." A key factor for such communications activity is that it can engage all players within an enterprise and in doing so, most importantly, spread the workload of maintaining it up-to-date and enhancing the market profile. So perhaps, YouTube might be used by entrepreneurs/owners/managers to provide "big" stories; Facebook/LinkedIn may be used by product managers/supervisors/staff for good story profiles; and Twitter may include staff, customers, anybody and everybody in its community.

Seaview Enterprises is a practicing example of the Shared and Integrated CSR in Sport model. A database has been established and segmented in a variety of ways, for example: supporters; schools; clubs; businesses, and so on. Cross-community/Shared Future Ambassadors have been created comprising professional people; business people; religious leaders; politicians, and so forth. A team has been established to roll out YouTube videos stemming from *Soccer Proform*, a system which generates match statistics as well as records highlights. Facebook and Twitter profiles are being created for each of the shared future constituencies outlined above. To date, no conventional "textbook" marketing techniques have been used. The Shared and Integrated CSR in Sport model has been applied from the outset.

Conclusions

This chapter has outlined the elements of the thirty years of conflict in Northern Ireland. In emerging from this civil unrest, previously fractured communities began to resume normality. Through the auspices of CSR a "coming together" of a variety of bodies; local government; businesses; community groups and sporting bodies, has accelerated a return to normality. A key common platform for the "coming together" has been sport.

The chapter has presented two case studies of sporting initiatives that demonstrate a "new beginning." The chapter also illustrates a Connecting with People initiative using business communications, networking, WEB 2.0 and social media, which is linking with "work-in-progress" case involving the two football clubs, Crusaders FC and Newington AFC aspiration for a new shared cross-community sports village, the Giant's Park Community Sports Village. This Village will aim to use many of the successful community engagement events and initiatives developed by Craigavon Intercultural program to fulfil its social mission.

References

Carroll, A. B. (1999) 'Corporate social responsibility: Evolution of a definitional construct', *Business Society*, 38 (3), 268–295.

Carson, D. and Boone, C. (2008) 'Web based marketing for small firms', *paper presented to the AMA/UIC Symposium on Marketing and Entrepreneurship Interface*, University of Orebro, Stockholm, Sweden, June.

Coalter, F. (2005) 'The social benefits of sport: An overview to inform the community planning process', *Sport Scotland Research Report no. 98*. Available at http://www.sportni.net/NR/rdonlyres/F7CA4BE4-9F30-4EF5-879D-2E370ABF9AEE/0/the_social_benefits_of_sport_an_overview_to_inform_the_community_planning_process.pdf (accessed: August 15, 2012).

Crane, A., Matten, D. and Spence, L. (2008) *Corporate social responsibility: Readings and cases in a global context*. London: Routledge.

Crusaders FC (2007) Available at: www.buildingchangetrust.org/download/files/CommunitySharesApril2012.ppt (accessed: August 29, 2012).

Dunlop, J. and Toner, T. (2002) 'North Belfast community action project: North Belfast … A patchwork of communities.' Project Team. Available at: http://www.taristeachnorthbelfast.org/nbcau_dunlop_report.pdf (accessed: August 28, 2012).

Gratton, C. and Henry, I. (2001) (eds.) *Sport in the city: The role of sport in economic and social regeneration.* London: Routledge.

Hagen, C. (2008) 'Evaluation of the Football for All Project'. On behalf of Irish Football Association, October. Available at: www.irishfa.com/the-ifa/community-relations/football-for-all (accessed: August 29, 2010).

Kennett, C. (2005) 'Sport, immigration and multiculturality: A conceptual analysis', paper delivered at the *Foro Europeo: Cultura, Deporte y Proximidad*, Almeria, Spain. Available at: http://olympicstudies.uab.es/pdf/wp103_eng.pdf (accessed: July 12, 2012).

Long, J. and Sanderson, I. (2001) 'The social benefits of sport: Where's the proof?' in Gratton, C. and Henry, I. (eds.) *Sport in the City: The role of sport in economic and social regeneration.* London: Routledge, pp. 187–203.

McAdam, N. (2009) 'Richie calls for steps to tackle segregated society', *The Independent*, September 7, p. 12.

Mintzberg, H. (2008) 'The case for corporate social responsibility', in Crane, A., Matten, D. and Spence, L. (eds.) *Corporate social responsibility: Readings and cases in a global context.* Oxon: Routledge, pp. 32–53.

Northern Ireland Census (2011) *2011 Census.* Available at http://www.nisra.gov.uk/Census.html (accessed: April 29, 2013).

Northern Ireland Statistics and Research Agency (NISRA) (2010) *Registrar General Annual Report.* Available at http://www.nisra.gov.uk/demography/default.asp22.htm (accessed: November 15, 2011).

Porter, M. and Kramer, R. (2008) 'The competitive advantage of corporate philanthropy', in Crane, A., Matten, D. and Spence, L. (eds.) *Corporate social responsibility: Readings and cases in a global context.* London: Routledge, pp. 285–305.

Putman, R. (2000) *Bowling alone: The collapse and revival of American community.* New York: Simon and Schuster.

Scully, D., Kremer, J., Meade, M., Graham, R. and Dudgeon, K. (1999) 'Physical exercise and psychological wellbeing: a critical review', *British J Sports Science*, 32, 11–20.

Smith, S. (2008) *Survey on barriers to sport participation of the BME Community in Craigavon*, Craigavon Intercultural Programme CIP survey on levels of integration of ethnic communities.

Sport for Development and Peace international working group (2008) 'Harnessing the power of Sport for Development and Peace: Recommendations to governments'. Available at: www.un.org/wcm/webdav/site/sport/shared/sport/pdfs/SDP IWG/Final SDP IWG Report.pdf (accessed: July 12, 2012).

Walters, G. (2009) 'Corporate social responsibility through sport', *Social Research*, 35, 81–95.

Walters, G. and Tacon, R. (2010) 'Corporate social responsibility in sport: Stakeholder management in the UK football industry', *Journal of Management and Organisation*, 16 (4), 565– 586.

Vogel, D. (2008) 'Is there a market for virtue? The business case for corporate social responsibility', in Crane, A., Matten, D. and Spence, L. (eds.) *Corporate social responsibility: Readings and cases in a global context.* London: Routledge, pp. 181–209.

11

INTER MOVISTAR FUTSAL

Much more than just indoor football

Carlos Campos

Overview

The aim of this chapter is to analyze the metamorphosis that the Spanish indoor football club Inter Movistar Futsal, one of the most distinguished clubs in the world, has undergone over the last four decades in relation to the implementation of marketing and communication strategies with a marked corporate social responsibility (CSR) focus and to the launching of the Movistar Megacracks Roadshow as an excellent example of a marketing action imbedded with commitment to society. Despite its incredible record of trophies, media and social presence of the club was very low. There were only occasional mentions in the number one Spanish sports newspaper *Marca* after achieving each of their sports successes, but there was no regular communication. The club had to be brought into the limelight, as did the sport as a whole – indoor football. All kinds of marketing and communication activities had to be set in motion. One of the core strategies developed by the club to reinvent their marketing and communication model as part of their CSR approach has been the launching of the Megacracks Roadshow in 2008.

Introduction

In order to better understand the distinctive characteristics of the Spanish club Inter Fútbol Sala, also known as La Máquina Verde (The Green Machine) and their approach in relation to the implementation of marketing and communication strategies and to the launching of the Movistar Megacracks Roadshow as part of their CSR approach, some background points are highlighted below.

Founded in 1977 as Hora XXV ("The Twenty-Fifth Hour"), sharing its name with the nighttime sports show on Cadena Ser, a well-known Spanish radio station, it entered the Honor Division of the Liga Nacional de Fútbol Sala (Spanish Indoor Football League) in 1989. One of the first and main benefactors behind the development of the club was the Spanish radio sports commentator José María García, its soul and driving force, as is commented on the club's own official webpage (Inter Movistar, 2012). The initial aim of the club was to play exhibition and charity matches. Its first lineup of players comprised former football players from Real Madrid and Atlético de Madrid and professionals from the mass media, including García himself. "At first, players for the team were provided by retired players because we never expected to come to anything even remotely serious," remembered one-time team coach Manuel Saorín many years later (Marcos, 1991).

Not long after, and thanks to the partnership of Grupo Zeta, the Spanish mass media group, owners of the magazine *Interviú*, the club changed its name to Interviú Hora XXV and soon after it won its first League championship title. In 1981 El Corte Inglés, the Spanish chain of department stores, sealed a partnership agreement with the club, and thus the team came to be known as Interviú Lloyd's and later Interviú Boomerang – Lloyd's and Boomerang being trademarks of El Corte Inglés. During those early years El Corte Inglés and Grupo Zeta were the team's greatest support. At the end of the 1990s and in the early 2000s it changed its name again to Airtel Boomerang and Antena 3 Boomerang. For the 2002–2003 season, the name was changed back to Boomerang Interviú.

Another name the club has was that of Interviú Fadesa due to the partnership provided by that building company. After Fadesa went bankrupt, the team signed a sponsorship agreement with the mobile telephone company Movistar, which belongs to Grupo Telefónica. Also, after several years of disassociation from the corporation Grupo Zeta, the institution changed its name to Inter Fútbol Sala in October 2010. The club is currently called Inter Movistar Futsal.

José María García, soul and driving force behind Inter Movistar Futsal

As mentioned above, José María García is a Spanish sports journalist, who, after studying journalism, started his professional career with Radio España. Later on, he moved to Radio Madrid and then on to Radio Popular and, in the written press, he worked for the daily newspaper *Pueblo*. In 1964 he was contracted by Televisión Española, where he collaborated on many different programs in different formats. After that he worked in radio on programs like Hora 25, with the radio station Cadena Ser and Supergarcía, where he reached his greatest recognition. The latter program was broadcast firstly by Antena 3 Radio (under the name Supergarcía on the Hora Cero), then by Cadena Cope (Supergarcía on the Cadena Cope) and finally by Onda Cero (Supergarcía on Onda Cero).

García was characterized by his caustic criticism towards anything he considered unfair, or unjust, both in the world of sport and elsewhere. He held harsh arguments with relevant characters from sport, both sportspersons and managers or journalists. He became a phenomenon of Spanish radio broadcasting with a whole legion of imitators. This was due to the fact that García was, for many years, number one in the night-time ratings of Spanish radio. He was also the winner of the Premios Ondas prize in the national category for radio in 1980 with his program El Partido de la Jornada (Match of the Day) with the radio station Cadena Ser and in 1986 with the program Supergarcía in Hora Cero with radio station Antena 3 Radio.

The beginnings of indoor football in Spain

Indoor football in Spain started out as an amateur sport, becoming a professional sport over the years. In fact, the Liga Nacional de Fútbol Sala (National Indoor Football League) was created in 1989. Currently it is made up of a Primera División (Premier League), comprising 16 teams, and a Second Division, also with 16 teams. Below that, there is the Second Division B under supervision of the National Committee for Indoor Football of the Real Federación Española de Fútbol (Royal Spanish Football Federation) (RFEF). Until the founding of the current Liga Nacional de Fútbol Sala, the different indoor football teams took part in their tournaments in association with two federations: The RFEF, which brought together the indoor football teams under the Asociación Española de Clubes de Fútbol Sala (The Spanish Association for Indoor Football Teams) (AECFS), and the split-off Federación Española de Fútbol Sala, whose teams appeared under the name of Asociación de Fútbol Sala (Indoor Football Association) (Asofusa).

Following mediation by the Consejo Superior de Deportes (Spanish Higher Sports Council) (CSD), both parties reached an agreement to create a League Championship, which would bring together the teams of both associations. This tournament would comprise an "Honor" Division (Premier League), with four groups of 12 teams each, and a Primera Nacional (National Premier League) which would unite over 100 squads from all over Spain, although this number would go down quite considerably over the years. The formation of the current Liga Nacional de Fútbol Sala was approved on August 28, 1989, and its first day of competition was held on September 30 of that year, under the auspices of the CSD and the RFEF. Inter Fútbol Sala was one of the founding members, taking part in its first season as Interviú Hora XXV and subsequently becoming its first champion.

The National (Spanish) Indoor Football League (LNFS) is considered to be the best indoor football league in the world and is one of the few professional championships in existence in this sport. Since 2009, and in a particularly troubled period, it has been presided over by Javier Lozano. Lozano, former indoor football player and trainer, holds among his sporting successes two World Championships and three European Championships, and is thus the coach with the most titles to his name with the Spanish national indoor football team.

Thanks to his brilliant hard work as indoor football coach, the Spanish Football Federation asked him to become assistant to the national 11-a-side football team manager José Antonio Camacho in 2002 for the FIFA World Cup of 2002, held in South Korea and Japan. In 2007, Javier Lozano was signed up by Real Madrid as the person in charge of the professional area of the football team, and a year later he became manager of the youth teams of Real Madrid. The chairman of Real Madrid at that time, Ramón Calderón, justified his appointment, saying, "You have the head of a manager and the heart of a sportsman" (Giovio, 2007). Previously and also in management tasks, he had performed as the Director of the Ciudad del Fútbol (Football City) of the Royal Spanish Football Federation. Lozano left the Madrid club in September 2009, when the members of the LNFS at the Assembly of clubs proclaimed him the new Chairman of the Spanish League Championship of this sport.

Management structure of Inter Movistar Futsal: past and present

During the early years after its foundation in 1977, the management of Inter was run by its general manager, Manuel Saorín, but with little structure. Saorín dedicated himself entirely to the club but, while in other sports and clubs such as basketball there was already a clear structure, the key club in indoor football remained in the "old school" style of management. The first major step towards a professional structure in the club took place when Jesús Clavería retired from the pitch and started his career in the club offices as Sports Director, while Manuel Saorín was still at the head of the club. Manolo Saorín unfortunately passed away in 2007 and Jesús Clavería, who had been with the entity for five years by this time, took over management of the club. It was at this point that everything started to take on a professional structure. Another legendary player from within the club, Julio García Mera, retired after 15 years as a professional player, all of them with Inter. Thanks to his preparation and knowledge he took over as Sports Director. And so, the sports facet started to acquire a structure with the creation of the school with professional coaches. The part which was still missing was the Communications and Marketing Office. This is when José Carlos Delgado appeared on the scene, the "Doer" of the "Gira Megacracks" Roadshow, a vital part of the Inter Movistar club strategy and recognized by the club as the star product of its image and communication policy.

Delgado had studied journalism at the Universidad Carlos III de Madrid and after finishing his studies there, he started to work for the number one Spanish sports newspaper, Marca. It was while working at this journal that his connection with the world of sports marketing was forged. Whenever a congress or symposium on sports marketing took place, no one from his publishing team showed the least interest in attending or reporting on them. The same thing happened when some of the Spanish leagues or sports clubs presented any kind of initiative on the matter. "They were a pain in the neck," in Delgado's own words (ManagingSport.com, 2012a). Nonetheless, he enjoyed them. This was something that only happened occasionally. Of the 12 years Delgado spent at Marca, eight of them were spent reporting on indoor football. This is how he was able to get to know the sport so well and the problematic issues facing the sport, and thus a union was created with Inter Movistar. Whilst still with Marca he made an initial proposal to the club: an official magazine, something the club still lacked, which would be run along the lines of the Marca style of journalism. So little by little he got to know the ins and outs of the club. And once the club had the Megacracks Roadshow up and running, the Roadshow service was carried out by an external company; this company did not live up to the club's expectations due to the size of the event – and as a result of the union created by the matter of the magazine, Delgado gave the club advice on how to give more drive to the Megacracks Roadshow and he presented them with a marketing and communication scheme. The scheme was well received and so, in December 2008, the club announced to him that they were thinking of professionalizing the entity under the general management of Jesús Clavería, with Julio García Mera in sports management. He was told that marketing and communication was the only "leg" which had yet to be professionalized and so, in January 2009, he finally joined Inter Movistar Futsal where Delgado gained the position of Director of Marketing and Communication.

Even so, the management structure at Inter Movistar Futsal was still that of a small and medium-size enterprise, but where each person had a clear role with clearly defined and well-established patterns, and where things rarely went wrong. The executive structure was made up of four persons: Jesús Clavería as Chief Executive, Julio García Mera as Sports Director, José Carlos Delgado as Director of Communication and Marketing, who also handled the social facet, and Miguel Ángel Fernández as Press Officer. Between the four of them, with great coordination, they managed to do everything. The FIFA Intercontinental Futsal Cup, which was hosted by Inter itself, was handled by the four men. "And so we rolled up our sleeves and did everything, from communication policies, management, to having to credit the press. We were up to anything, yes sir!" were José Carlos Delgado's words when interviewed for a recent article (ManagingSport.com, 2012a). We feel it necessary to emphasize that the communication and marketing area made its appearance not in an ordinary way, but rather the whole organization has been infused with a marketing philosophy, in the sense of that claim made by one of the greatest academics in the field of management and services marketing, the Finn Christian Grönroos (Grönroos, 1990: 128). Years before, Grönroos had defended the urgent need to move on from the concept of commercial management to market-oriented management. The whole management, not only the marketing and commercial area of the organization has to present the necessary orientation towards the customer, the citizen and society. This is something which Inter Movistar Futsal participates in with great enthusiasm. This is because, although every person in the club has his own area of responsibility within the entity structure with respect to the fields of sports, economics and marketing-communication, everything is carried out accompanied by touches of marketing and communication. And in that respect, he made the following observation on how things are done at his club:

In our club, the first person to enter any meeting is me, and, excuse me for getting personal, but it's just so you can see the philosophy here a little. And why is that? – So that everything is accompanied with the right presentation, with the feeling and meaning we want to give it.

(ManagingSport.com, 2012a)

Inter Movistar Futsal: amazing sports achievements, and a few mentions in the media

Inter Movistar Futsal is, without any doubt, one of the most highly distinguished clubs in sport worldwide: 8 Ligas Españolas (1989/90, 1990/91, 1995/96, 2001/02, 2002/03, 2003/04, 2004/05, 2007/08), 7 Copas de España (1990, 1996, 2001, 2004, 2005, 2007, 2009), 10 Supercopas de España (1990, 1991, 1996, 2001, 2002, 2003, 2005, 2007, 2008, 2011), 4 European Cups (1991, 2004, 2006, 2009), 5 Intercontinental Cups (2005, 2006, 2007, 2008, 2011), 1 Recopa de Europa (European Cup-Winners' Cup) (2008) and 2 Copas Ibéricas (Iberian Cups) (2003, 2005). Also worthy of mention are the 9 League titles from the now-extinct Federación de Fútbol Sala and 3 Copas de España competitions, also part of the Federación de Fútbol Sala – 49 titles in total since its foundation in 1977.

To get an idea of the magnitude of what this Madrid indoor football club has achieved during its short existence, we could bring to the stage the two greatest football teams in Spain: Real Madrid and FC Barcelona. The Madrid team, founded in 1902, has in its showcases 31 Ligas Españolas, 18 Copas de España, 8 Supercopas de España, 9 European Cups, 2 UEFA Cups, 1 European Supercup, 2 Latin Cups and 3 Club World Cups. All together 74 titles since 1902. Meanwhile, Barcelona FC, founded in 1899, has notched up 21 Ligas Españolas, 25 Copas de España, 10 Supercopas de España, 4 European Cups, 4 European Cup-Winner's Cups, 2 Inter-Cities Fairs Cups, 4 European Super Cups, 2 Latin Cups and 1 Club World Cup – 73 titles in total since 1899.

Despite Inter's incredible track record, the media and social presence of the club was quite scarce. There were only the back pages of the newspaper *Marca* when the team reached each one of its achievements and sporting triumphs, but there was no regular press following. They had to bring the club out into the limelight and also indoor football as a sport; they had to initiate all kinds of marketing and communication activities. When Delgado joined the club, all there was a part-time press officer, whose job was to communicate and keep the club webpage up to date (www.intermovistar.com), although it was rather obsolete. He did his best to communicate what the club was doing like a full-time press officer. He used to attend the matches but not all the time. And that was something untenable. Talking about indoor football in general, and about Inter in particular as the reference team in this sport – this was something that had to change.

The club had certain associations with institutions such as the local Alcalá de Henares City Council but very few or no social ties, and no links at all with local industry and businesses. And on top of this, they had to give it content, creating the tools to allow them to grow in their knowledge in each of these areas. The star tool which the new way of doing things at the club revolved around and still does is the Megacracks Roadshow, which we shall explore in detail in the next section. Although the Roadshow is the main tool Inter has at its disposal, it is not the only one. In this respect we should also mention other worthy programs aimed at different social and aged groups:

- The program *Los peques juegan primero* (The kids play first) aims to promote indoor football among kids as well as increase the attendance to the sport facilities on match days.

- The Journalism Workshops organized by the club at schools where schoolchildren examine different styles of journalism.
- The social plan of action *Nuestros mayores, nuestros valores* (Our elderly, our values) aimed at the elderly, whose object is to bring high-performance sport closer to them and create a further activity for the elderly.
- The program *Colegios Amigos de Inter Movistar* (Inter Movistar School Friends), with 30 member schools. A program intended to promote the Inter club and indoor football among schoolchildren through sports and training activities.
- The program *Coles, al Pabellón* (Schools – let's go to the Sports Hall), another of the projects carried out by Inter Movistar to promote indoor football and its image among schoolchildren. This program is divided into two kinds of actions: attendance to games at the sport facilities and attendance to training sessions in those facilities.

But before focusing on the Megacracks Roadshow, we feel it is worth mentioning another circumstance which made it even more complicated in the challenge to gain greater presence in society. That is, until the club decided to settle definitively in Alcalá de Henares, it had been a wandering, stateless club, moving from town to town. Previously, it had played its matches in several locations: Madrid, Alcobendas and Torrejón (both of these being towns in the province of Madrid) until finally ending up in Alcalá de Henares, a city 30 km from Madrid. This is why the club took so long to find an emotional bond or identification. They have only been located in Alcalá de Henares for seven years, and in that short period of time, they have gone from having 700 spectators to over 3,000 today at normal matches. This and other achievements have not gone unnoticed. It is a very significant fact that the Chairman of the National Indoor Football League, Javier Lozano, stated in a recent interview for the portal ManagingSport.com the following: "Inter Movistar FS has gone from being the best team to being the best club. Now they don't win as much as they used to, but they are the best club" (ManagingSport.com, 2010). This was in reference to the fact that in the last two seasons, the number of awards won has waned rather: season 2009–10 – runners-up in the European Cup, semi-finalist in the Spanish Supercup, quarter-finalists in the Spanish League and semi-finalists in the Spanish Cup and in the 2010–11 season, World Champions in the Clubs World Cup, runners-up in the Spanish Cup and runners-up in the Spanish Supercup. Not since the 2007–08 season have they been Spanish League Champions, when they had achieved this title in the seasons 1979–89, 1980–81, 1981–82, 1983–84, 1984–85, 1985–86, 1986–87, 1987–88, 1988–89, 1989–90, 1990–91, 1995–96, 2001–2002, 2002–03, 2003–04, 2004–05 and 2007–08.

A great part of this achievement in terms of supportership may be attributed to the club's new communication strategy philosophy, a philosophy which is expressed perfectly in the words of Communication and Marketing Manager at Inter Movistar Futsal, José Carlos Delgado: "It's not the same thing to have routine communication as it is to set up a routine of communication" (ManagingSport.com, 2012a). And this has brought its fruits and it is something Delgado feels enormously proud of. He told us:

> Both the press officer and myself love being journalists and there are fifty thousand things to be told. Out of the 14,000 direct mail contacts we have, not even ten have asked to be removed, saying we overload their inboxes. And that's aiming high. No one has refused an Inter communication routine.

> (ManagingSport.com, 2012a)

The Megacracks Roadshow: a unique social phenomenon

As mentioned earlier, the Megacracks Roadshow is one of the core strategies developed by the club's Communication and Marketing Manager, Delgado, to boost the marketing and communication model of the club as part of their CSR policy. The Movistar Megacracks Roadshow is an education, sport and integration scheme aimed at children between the ages of 4 and 14. The Megacracks Roadshow has turned into a social reference point and is a sporting event which combines sport with other essential values in life: equality, commitment, teamwork, integration, solidarity, learning, culture – and fun. Since the Megacracks Roadshow was set up in 2008 till now – October 2012 – more than 66,000 schoolchildren and over 4,000 disabled athletes from all over Spain have played and trained with Inter Movistar Futsal; children who have had the opportunity to enjoy themselves while playing and learning side-by-side with the players of the club. Megacracks has visited 70 different locations around Spain and has covered over 36,000 km. The objective for the coming year (2012–13) is to reach the figure of 80,000 schoolchildren and the inclusion of 5,500 disabled children. Furthermore, for the sixth edition, which coincides with the 35th anniversary of the club, a promotional video of Megacracks Roadshow, entitled "The Magic of Megacracks Roadshow" has been issued (see ManagingSport, 2012b).

Some of the best indoor football players in the world, the whole Inter Movistar playing staff, hold a complete training session for over two hours, in which they get the children to take part right from the kick-off. The act is led by the popular Spanish journalist, Iñaki Cano, a master of livening up the event, where fun sparks off and the youngest ones are made to feel part of what's going on. The children attending are taught how to warm up, shoot a goal, dribble … and play lots of mini-games with their idols.

The Megacracks Roadshow is unique in its format because it is a participative event. The kids receive amazing gifts related with the values being transmitted. Not just anything will do. And so each child who attends the sports facilities takes home an incredible set of gifts. One of the core and distinctive elements of this Megacracks Roadshow is the total inclusion of disabled children. Offering young people with disabilities the opportunity to play or coach with some of the best indoor football players in the world, this program has grown into the largest in Spain, with some resemblance to the Ability Count program run by Manchester United, as mentioned in Chapter 9 of this handbook. And their focus is manifold:

1   To transmit to the children the positive messages that indoor football intrinsically holds, encouraging them to practice indoor football in a fun, play-oriented way and put into practice the good sporting habits inherent in it.
2   To make the children aware, in a natural way, of the values of effort and teamwork as pillars of their everyday lives, promoting fair play in all its aspects.
3   Integration: we are all equal regardless of ability, disability, sex, race, and so on.

In this way, the Inter Movistar FC Megacracks Roadshow has become a unique social phenomenon. It has turned into a factory where dreams come true for thousands of children all over Spain. It is a well-oiled machine which gives its all at every act it holds to share out loads of happiness and fun. It is the best school for the kids to learn by playing the values of life and sports, together with their idols. It is a perfect world where disabled children can feel they are the real stars and, what is more important; they feel they are their companions' equals. Integration and involvement is absolute as the excitement fills every corner of the sports halls fortunate enough to host each stage of this tour. Some of the best indoor football players in the world are here, ready to show their condition, ready to give their all, in order to respond to the more than 60,000 hearts which gave them their affection and admiration. Champions of the highest degree, outstanding educators and an example to a society which grows ever more dehumanized, Inter is the only club in Spain which combines sports competition with educational and formative promotion at this level, on this scale.

Origin and spirit of the Megacracks Roadshow

The Megacracks Roadshow started out in early 2008. The first event took place in October 2007, but only became part of the routine in 2008. Not so many events were held that year as today and they didn't have the clear-cut pattern they have currently. It was handled by an external entity as the club did not have the necessary structure; when Delgado joined the club, he was taken on primarily to manage the Megacracks Roadshow, to shape it and reinforce earlier work. It was when Delgado joined the team that the appearance began to change; they started to shape it in consideration of what the team and society needed. Delgado also emphasized the following:

> We started making adjustments in accordance with what we knew was round the bend: a crisis in which local councils were going to find it ever more difficult to help us. I mean help us in the sense of offering us the kind of services the tour needed for everything to work out – there had to be an ambulance, there had to be staff in the sport facilities, the insurance had to be in order …
>
> (ManagingSport.com, 2012a)

And so it was that the tour started to take on the importance it needed to take place and not have to rely on the circumstances of each locality.

"Even so, with the Megacracks Roadshow we have to go one step further, we have to improve it; we don't want to get stuck." With these words Delgado summed up the ever-present intention to improve year after year. For instance, last year the club baptized the tour "Megacracks 3.0," including a series of conferences as part of the tour. This was last year's "one step further." What happens is that the kids enjoy themselves at the Roadshow; they have a great time. But what about all those people from those places the team visits who aren't kids? What about the indoor football coaches or managers from smaller or middle-size teams? Why not reach out to them too? – the club asked – "because they are the ones who are going to bring the children and help them during the event." So a series of conferences has been designed to cater to these people. To this end, Inter Movistar goes to the town councils and says to them:

> We'll bring you the Megacracks Roadshow, which provides you with great impact in the media because you get to appear in the press; because as politicians you are going to identify your town with sports activities – with good habits; because you are going to fill the sports hall for me … but I also propose to train your people in the sports aspect.

And from the city council they say, "How much is all this going to cost me?" We reply, "Nothing! All you have to do is treat the kids well, fill the sport facility for them." And the final step in each and every Megacracks Roadshow, the one which José Carlos Delgado is always a little worried about is to find the work done properly. Why? Because although he plans it from Alcalá de Henares, he cannot previously visit each and every town of the Spanish geography where they hope to visit and explain to the schools what exactly the Megacracks Roadshow is.

In the end, it's the sports coach who is going to have to stay behind, despite the fact that they've just cut his wages by five percent; for him the tour is just extra work; he's going to have to put in extra time that day and stay till 8pm … and to reward them, to show our appreciation, Inter is going to offer them this training activity. In a few hours of training Delgado explains to them how the club is run, or the club physiotherapist comes along and gives them a session on sports injuries, or the manager gives a talk on tactics if more team trainers are attending. That is the "one step further" we have to go to get a greater degree of satisfaction.

As in the previous year, the "one step further" came with the agreement reached with the renown Spanish publishing company, Editorial SM. Inter Movistar presented this scheme to the publisher as the club believes it is vital for there to be some reading as part of the tour. The publishing company liked the scheme, an agreement was reached and this way the children received books as part of the tour … The publisher had books in stock and it got them to the children. It was a major effort. But suddenly Delgado realized that many of the books coming through were in English – a bilingual Roadshow! He thought this was great, although no one had told him anything. He spoke to the warehouse and they told him they had enough books to cover the whole tour. Fantastic! A whole year of bilingual books! And so, they started to incorporate more contents: Editorial SM and Inter Movistar promote schemes to encourage reading and bilingualism on the Megacracks Roadshow. Nonetheless, it is made quite clear to those companies that decide to take part in the Megacracks Roadshow that they cannot make aggressive or lucrative campaigns. That means that SM presents its books and if teachers or head teachers come along, they see the books and say, "Hey, these books are great!" The club does not provide schools', teachers' or children's contact details. They don't even collect data. Inter Movistar always ensures that the Roadshow is as pure as possible, because there is always a lot of suspicion among head teachers. It is made quite clear to these teachers, "You are not going to see one single leaflet for *Movistar*, not one pamphlet for *Joma*, no *Halcón* brochures" – all of these being companies involved in the tour. The only thing they're going to see, obviously, is identification and that thanks to the fact that these companies are taking part, the players can travel and play with the children.

Involvement of the players in the Megacracks Roadshow

In some formative forums Delgado has pointed out that most of the club's budget goes towards players' wages in the first team and nothing is spent on communication and marketing. He has also noted that footballers' jobs include both playing for the team and communication and marketing tasks. And that is something the club makes quite clear when signing up the players. If we take this into account, perhaps we could say there is a budget for your department, insofar as the players are paid to carry out a sporting job and another marketing and communication one.

Having posed this reflection in a personal interview with Delgado, club Communication and Marketing Manager, this is what he replied:

> The interpretation of what you have just done is perfect because it is true. It's quite true that we say most of our budget goes to pay the players, but what you've just pointed out illustrates one of the club's greatest achievements. Today, when a player arrives at the club, he knows that 50 percent of what he earns comes from his playing on the pitch and the other 50 percent comes from his (very active) participation in club communication and marketing activities.
>
> (ManagingSport.com, 2012a)

Proof of this is that, in the reference point in terms of promotion and marketing of the club, the Megacracks Roadshow, the players know they have to combine a very competitive sports schedule with the work required by the Roadshow. They know each event takes two hours and there are at least 15 events a year plus all the consequent traveling. They know it's an event for everyone, and by everyone we don't only mean boys and girls and disabled people, but for everyone in Spain. It's true that we then try to ensure that the localities coincide more or less with the areas the matches are being held in. In any case, they are aware that it is just as important for the club and the partners of the entity to be on the Megacracks Roadshow as it is to compete or win the Super Cup. All of this is explained to the new players when they arrive and also those who were already part of the staff. They are given a dossier where it is made clear, "Who we are. We stress the fact that we are much more than just indoor football" (ManagingSport.com, 2012a). In fact that is the motto which reads across the club dossiers and they are told everything they have to do, so they know they've arrived at a club which is different from the one they've just left.

This is something they had in mind right from the start. As Delgado emphasizes:

> Something we *did* see quite clearly when we did the initial analysis of the club situation is that the player had to be quite mentally prepared when it comes to taking part and it's not enough just to be there; you have to show your best side, because the Megacracks Roadshow is to play with the children, it's about making them happy, the kids are going to admire them, and they can't be there "just passing through."
>
> (ManagingSport.com, 2012a)

And he also added:

> Even though they might be tired or in pain from an injury, they have to give their best and we have achieved that. Indeed, once a tour is over, I congratulate the players personally, because I know it's a great effort but they do enjoy themselves enormously.
>
> (ManagingSport.com, 2012a)

Is players' sports performance affected by their participation in the Movistar Megacracks Roadshow?

Another question we posed to Delgado in the personal interview revolved around certain comments we had heard from several people involved in professional indoor football. They came to say something like "What I don't know is whether the Megacracks Roadshow, with so much travelling all over the country, is taking its toll on the sports side of things" (ManagingSport. com, 2012a). What happens is that the Inter and its players as part of the Roadshow don't only travel to neighboring towns; they have to travel all over Spain.

When it comes to making excuses when the sporting results are not up to expectations, anyone can argue anything. We asked Delgado about this matter and before answering the question, he wished to introduce the following comments:

> When it comes to sports performance, I talk to those "in the know," those who've been here a while. That calms me down because the truth is we're going through a period of change in the sporting aspect. We had been winning practically everything for ten years – we might have let a Cup or a League slip through our fingers. In the season I joined the club, we won the Spanish Super Cup, Spanish Cup and the European Cup and we were on our way to winning the League because we were leaders in the regular season and we

made it to the final against *ElPozo Murcia* and it was because of the fatigue that we didn't win that league. That was the end of a scheme which needed to be renovated and we went on to a season where we didn't win a single thing. Those are the cycles in sports.

(ManagingSport.com, 2012a)

In his view, with the tour the players can indeed get a bit fatigued but underlined that players nowadays are perfectly fit to take on all kinds of things; it's not a matter he worried about – quite the opposite, in fact. And in that sense he declared, "The club has always encouraged me, they have approved ever more projects so the players can take part and it hasn't affected their performance." He summarized his appraisal of this particular issue adding:

When I hear – "Now they do that Megacracks thing, they don't win the way they used to" – we don't share that feeling. Both Jesús and Julio, who have won absolutely everything, have never said anything to me in that respect; so I feel absolutely calm about it.

The Megacracks Roadshow and the main partner of the club: Movistar-Grupo Telefónica

The philosophy the management team wanted to implement in the club was that the day would come when the entity would have such great social presence, it would become a brand so consolidated that it wouldn't have to depend so much on its sports results. "I remember when I joined, speaking to Jesús and Julio, the idea we proposed was: we're going to show Telefónica that we are a key social reference point; we are going to make a commitment for social impact" (ManagingSport.com, 2012a). That's how Delgado expressed it, alluding to his beginnings with the team.

The intention was for the club to go out onto the street, to be on the streets; it would be aware of all social issues; it was to be a key reference point in education. And that is something they have achieved. And it's something that Delgado really congratulates himself on when he introduces the following reflection:

The example I always give is the one of ourselves. And it did me good, although I wouldn't go through it again – I mean not winning anything at all. But it has done me good to see the evidence that everything which at the time seemed to be utopia because here in the club, that had never happened.

(ManagingSport.com, 2012a)

And the consequence of this powerful social involvement has been reflected in the partnership policy at the entity, reflected in many substantial benefits for its main partner, Movistar. As Delgado remembered:

The year we didn't win anything, not even one title, comparing ourselves with the team which did win everything that year, ElPozo Murcia, we got plenty of euros out of it and we were talking about millions of euros of return on their advertising investment in the partnership. And all of that thanks to the Megacracks Roadshow, to our presence in the media, to the events, to the fact we were constantly in the public eye, getting our image around. We obtained nearly €7 million in sponsorship return – two and a bit or three millions more than the team that had won absolutely everything. Despite not having won anything.

(ManagingSport.com, 2012a)

And he also added:

> our partner, Movistar was highly satisfied. The year we didn't win anything and which was ridiculous sports-wise, we had an amazing return thanks to the Megacracks Roadshow. Our partner was very satisfied and didn't have to take a cup back to their office to renew our partnership. And that shows that socially we're doing the right thing – at least with a will and with enthusiasm.
>
> (ManagingSport.com, 2012a)

Winning titles is tremendously important because it helps the club to sell its image and because success is always the best traveling companion, but there is no doubt that if the partner is conscious of the fact that thanks to the tour, over 60,000 kids all over Spain are now wearing the Movistar t-shirt, that must have a value.

One of the greatest gurus of organization management, the North American Tom Peters, states that in companies "What gets measured gets done" (Peters, 1987: 486–488). We enter the matter of measurement, a subject not unknown in the analysis of return on investment in partnerships/sponsorships. The multinational Kantar Media is the company in charge of carrying out media presence studies for Inter Movistar resulting from all their actions and mainly from the Megacracks Roadshow. Right, but can everything be measured? What about that little girl or boy from that small town who got an Inter Movistar Futsal t-shirt and gets to play with the footballer from Inter Movistar Futsal? That should be an unforgettable memory. How do you quantify that? At what point does that necessarily have to have greater value than media presence?

We posed those issues to Delgado and this is the evaluation he gave us:

> Indeed, what Kantar gives you is an evaluation which is necessary. What happens is that these things are so difficult to assess. Like I say, that's where my battle with the partner or the institution lies – to make them see that the unforgettable memory of a child playing with an Inter footballer, although it's not possible to measure, is very important. The easy bit is when you go to the partner with a few "audited" figures. I say "audited" because there are no absolute truths; you turn up there and say to them so much return on your partnership investment as measured by Kantar Media.
>
> (ManagingSport.com, 2012a)

He stresses the idea, repeating:

> But that's the easiest bit, because in the end, they're just numbers. The second part of the meeting is, for, me, my World Cup final. That's when I have to sit down and make them understand that the fact of that kid keeping that memory of the time he played football with a footballer from Inter, even though it can't be measured, is the most important thing we've been able to do thanks to the implementation of their partnership. And that calls for us to be the best when it comes to that meeting.
>
> (ManagingSport.com, 2012a)

Conclusions

The central objective of this chapter has been to offer a case study which illustrates perfectly how an organization's strategic management is infused with CSR. With the actions and philosophy which impregnate the actions carried out by Inter Movistar Futsal, they distance themselves completely from that dominant trend which Porter and Kramer referred to in the following terms when they spoke about corporative philanthropy:

> Most companies feel compelled to give to charity. Few have figured out how to do it well. But what passes for "strategic philanthropy" today is almost never truly strategic, and often it isn't even particularly effective as philanthropy. Increasingly, philanthropy is used as a form of public relations or advertising.
>
> (Porter and Kramer, 2002: 57)

This distinguished Spanish sports club does not have a department or functional area with the heading "CSR" but it does impregnate all its areas – sports, financial, marketing, communication and so on – with a marked sense of responsibility and commitment toward the community. What's more, we have always held that it is not at all necessary to have a specific department to implement CSR culture in the heart of an organization. To establish a kind of parallelism, one is reminded when we hear in marketing that "the establishment of a Marketing Department in an organization is the perfect excuse for everyone else to wash their hands of the matter." Or also taken to this theme, so that the Management Team of the organization might "wash its conscience" with actions that Porter and Kramer (2002) would dismiss as corporative philanthropy, rather than true CSR.

Everyone, absolutely everyone, not just a few, in this case the management team, has to participate in CSR. And this takes us on to another issue with an obvious connection. In service company marketing – and a sports club is one of them – commercial power does not fall directly on the marketing department and the professionals who comprise it, but rather on those employees with direct contact with customers. In the case of a sports club which offers a show, thanks to another kind of employee, the star employees are the players, the sportsmen and women. And everyone is aware that the emotional connection between these people and the fans and their community is absolutely vital. Thus, the leading actors of the Megacrack Roadshow are the first team players; a team of players to whom it is made quite clear from the day they sign up for the club, that are paid not only for their sports performance but also for their social commitment, that is to say their participation in this Roadshow called Megacracks.

To conclude, it is worth emphasizing the fact that the partnership relationship between Inter and its title and main partner, Movistar, is not sustained by sports results. We could even go so far as to say that it is not sustained by the fact that Inter is a sports club, but rather by the social project it carries out; a social program which finds its maximum and prime example in the Megacracks Roadshow. For some time now, it has been suggested to sports clubs that they incorporate ever greater doses of CSR in order to make their partnership proposals more attractive to companies. Well the Megacracks Roadshow is purely and wholly CSR. And that is something the leading figures of this outstanding club are always reminding us of: "Inter Movistar Futsal is much more than just indoor football."

References

Giovio, E. (2007) 'Cabeza de gestor, corazón de deportista', *El País*, September 11. Available at: http://elpais.com/diario/2007/09/11/deportes/1189461610_850215.html (accessed: September 11, 2007).

Grönroos, C. (1990) *Service management and marketing. Managing the moments of truth in service competition.* Lexington: Lexington Books.

Inter Movistar (2012). Available at http://www.intermovistar.com (accessed: May 20, 2012).

ManagingSport.com (2010) 'Interview with Javier Lozano'. Available at: http://www.managingsport. com/entrevista_con_javier_lozano_presidente_liga_nacional_f%C3%BAtbol_sala_por_carlos_campos (accessed: July 1, 2010).

ManagingSport.com (2012a) 'Interview with Jose Carlos Delgado'. Available at: http://www. managingsport.com/entrevista_con_jos%C3%A9_carlos_delgado_director_comunicaci%C3%B3n_y_marketing_inter_movistar_fs_por_carlos_ca (accessed: January 1, 2012).

ManagingSport.com (2012b) 'La magia de la gira Movistar Megacracks' (The magic of Megacracks roadshow). Available at: http://www.managingsport.com/vdo/inter_movistar_f%C3%BAtbol_sala_presenta_el_v%C3%ADdeo_la_magia_de_la_gira_movistar_megacracks (accessed: October 5, 2012).

Marcos, C. (1991) 'Vivir de éxitos', *El País*, July 3. Available at: http://elpais.com/diario/1991/07/03/deportes/678492010_850215.html (accessed: July 3, 1991).

Peters, T. (1987) *Thriving on chaos: Handbook for a management revolution*. New York: Knopf.

Porter, M. E. and Kramer, M. R. (2002) 'The competitive advantage of corporate philanthrophy', *Harvard Business Review*, December, 57–68.

12

SPORT AND CSR IN JAPAN

Munehiko Harada

Overview

The philosophy of corporate social responsibility (CSR) is widely understood in the Japanese sports industry. The purposes of this chapter are twofold: (1) to take a general look at CSR in Japan; and (2) to discuss sports-related CSR from the perspectives of how Japanese companies connect their support of sports to fulfilling their CSR, and how professional teams that operate as business and leagues are enhancing their value by promoting and implementing CSR activities. In Japan, the widely practiced unique system of "corporate sports," in which corporations hire athletes as regular employees and own sport teams, helped companies to understand the significance of utilizing sports in their CSR activities. On the other hand, the Japan Professional Football League (J League) is using CSR activities as a tool to improve the brand value of the league. Clubs of the J League are incorporated sports businesses and are required to engage their players in social contribution activities in order to deepen relations with the local area, to improve the brand value, and to build a fan base. Clubs and the league must continue the specific philanthropic activities to meet their "discretionary" responsibility, as well as reinforcing the league's moral standards to meet its "ethical" responsibility, improving the services and hospitality demanded by fans to exercise "economic" responsibility, and adopting the AFC club licensing regulations to enhance league and team governance to carry out "legal" responsibility.

Introduction

Interest in CSR is growing affront a backdrop of increasing globalization, developments in information technology, and particularly harsh criticism of corporate behavior from general consumers, customers, and society at large. Many Japanese companies have created departments specifically for overseeing CSR and are constructively addressing legal compliance, environmental protection, employment and workplace environments, considerations for human rights, and so on (Mizuo and Tanaka, 2004). This same interest in CSR is rapidly growing in the sports world as well.

An overview of the current relationship between sports and CSR in Japan reveals two basic trends. One trend is corporate sports in which a company owns a team and the players are hired as regular employees of the company. This has been widely practiced in Japan as a way of providing corporate welfare to employees and doing advertising and publicity. Until recently teams have been used as a catalyst for CSR activities. These companies are using their teams to fulfill their CSR through various community outreach programs, sports clinics, etc.

The other trend is the professionalization of sports. An example would be Japan's J League, launched in 1993. The league is a mix of teams that have spun off from corporate sports and incorporated as clubs (e.g., Toyota and Panasonic), and municipal clubs that went professional without any backing by corporate interests.[1] Whichever the case, the J League is directing efforts, as set out in the league's 100 Year Vision, at fostering community-based teams, therefore the common strategy is to constructively promote CSR as a means for building up the fan base. As such, today in Japan, companies are using sports as a means for fulfilling their CSR, while the incorporated clubs are contributing to society through the CSR of the sports business.

Though interest in what companies are doing in terms of CSR is growing worldwide, those involved with sports understand little what CSR is about. While aiming to prevent corporate misconduct on the one hand, CSR activities are being developed to constructively contribute widely to society via human rights, labor, environments, community projects, and more (Mizuo and Tanaka, 2004). Therefore, even professional sports that operate with corporate sponsors cannot disconnect themselves from CSR activities. Companies and sports are being pressed to establish a new business model founded on the principles of coexistence and co-prosperity amongst stakeholders (consumers, employees, shareholders and investors, customers, local communities, and NPOs) and respectful of the concept of bilateral cooperation and satisfaction for all. This chapter takes a general look at CSR in Japan in recognition of the aforementioned issues, then examines sports-related CSR from the perspectives of how companies connect their support of sports to fulfilling their CSR, and how professional teams that operate as businesses and leagues are enhancing their value by promoting and implementing CSR activities.

CSR in Japan

It is said that the term "social responsibility" was first used in the USA to argue the importance of CSR in management philosophy in *The Philosophy of Management* by Sheldon (1924). Later, after much discussion, CSR has come to mean "activities that businesses should do for communities such as local contributions, donations, etc." Kotler and Lee (2005: 3), for example, define it as a "commitment to improve community well being through discretionary business practices and contributions of corporate resources." In other words, in the USA, the underlying thought of corporate social responsibility is the concept that a business, too, is a citizen. Here, the emphasis is placed on doing well for society via social contribution activities, local community support, considerations for environmental issues, donations, and so forth (Mizuo and Tanaka, 2004). Accordingly, those actions are spearheaded by employees, but those actions are not targeted at internal aspects of the company but at society in general, i.e., external environments, local communities, etc.

In Japan, on the other hand, the topic of CSR did not formally appear until after the Second World War. In 1956, the Japan Committee for Economic Development proposed that "businesspeople be aware of and practice social responsibility." After that, the argument for CSR came to the forefront with pollution problems in the 1960s and during the First Oil Crisis in the 1970s when businesses were cornering the market and holding back on supply. In the 1990s, society began to outright question CSR as an issue of business ethics, because of the frequent back-scratching between the banking and securities industry and organized crime. Since then, CSR has been increasingly discussed as a responsibility issue when scandals hit the business world. Accordingly, CSR in Japan is often looked at beyond the meaning of "doing good for society" as it was defined in the USA, to include within the scope of CSR the pretext of "preventing" harm to society via corporate misconduct.

In the coming discussions of corporate sports in Japan are frequent cases of sports teams being disqualified because of the misconduct of a company that has sports within their scope of business activities. In contrast to that is an example of a local community coming to the aid of a corporate sponsor caught up in a scandal because local residents recognize the support the company provides to the team as a sponsor, as a "social contribution activity." In this particular instance, sports sponsorship has the same meaning as risk management.[2]

Corporate sports and CSR: Japan's unique style

The philosophy of CSR is widely understood in the Japanese sports industry, where the amateur spirit has always been strong. In Japan, the widely practiced system of "corporate sports," in which corporations hire athletes as regular employees and own sport teams, helped companies to understand the significance of utilizing sports in their CSR activities. These companies began to use sports as a "platform" from which to communicate their message to the consumer (Breuer, 2012).

Corporate sports serve as a means of corporate welfare, advertising tool, and platform for uniting the workforce. Making money is not the objective. It is a system unique to Japan in which the company bears all operational costs of the team and personnel costs. Throughout the 1970s and into the 1980s, having a sports team elevated the status of listed companies as the team's activities functioned directly as corporate advertisement and publicity because of widespread media coverage. There were over several hundred corporate sports teams in Japan and, though athletes practiced as a general rule after their work was done, it was permitted to excuse top athletes from work and let them just practice.

Nevertheless, the circumstances changed completely in the 1990s. Corporate performances fell because of the recession and corporate sports teams became a cost burden for their owners. Moreover, owing to media advancements, it became possible to watch overseas professional sports, which diluted interest in Japan's top leagues, spurred soccer and basketball teams to go professional, and drained the popularity of amateur sports in general. As a result, over 300 teams folded or were suspended, with ice hockey and basketball being dealt a crushing blow. In contrast, rugby and volleyball still maintain their position as the top amateur sports, but popularity is down and they are having trouble drawing fans.

In the meantime, there are an increasing number of cases of businesses who are taking a forward-looking approach to team survival by injecting new meaning into their teams – they view owning a team is part of their CSR activities. For example, Coca-Cola West Co., Ltd. raises "customer satisfaction," "quality assurance," "compliance," "risk management," "respect for human rights and worthwhileness of working," "coexistence with local communities," and "environmental promotion" as the seven key points of their CSR, but they are directing efforts and resources at cultural and educational support activities and community outreach via sports within their coexistence with local communities. They own the Red Sparks men's rugby and women's hockey teams, both of which play in top leagues. The players are full-time employees. Players from both teams constructively take part in local events, presentations, local clinics, and activities to promote sports, as the company is dedicated to giving back to society. They successfully turned what was a cost center into a CSR profit center and reaffirmed these activities are diversified profit streams for the company.

Sports and the significance of CSR

The general perception of CSR in sports would most likely be the kind of philanthropic activities performed by sponsoring companies, sporting associations, or professional athletes. While not mistaken, this perception does not show the entire picture, as the concept of CSR is not as simple as philanthropy. Rather, CSR is a four-dimensional model of business responsibility: economic, legal, ethical, and discretionary (Carroll, 1991).

"Economic" responsibility refers to the company manufacturing and selling products and/or services in response to consumer or customer demand. In the case of sports, this would translate into professional sports that provide the high quality games and hospitality that fans demand. Moreover, as a business, a team or club must pay dividends to shareholders as a means for distributing results, pay wages and rewards to employees in compensation for their labor, and pay taxes to the national and local governments.

"Legal" responsibility is compliance with laws and regulations; companies are expected to carry out their business activities within that framework. In terms of sports, there is a movement toward better governance and legal compliance by sporting associations and professional sport teams, so as not to disappoint their sponsors, the media, and the fans. Even if a sporting association was to provide the kind of business that consumers of sports are demanding (popularization and promotion of the sport, educating and training youth teams, improving competitiveness, holding competitions, etc.), that sporting association would be shunned by society if there were to be illegal activity in the day to day operations – misuse of subsidies, for example, or doping.

On the other hand, it is impossible to draw a clear distinction between "ethical" and "discretionary" responsibility. The former refers to acting in accordance to the moral expectations of society, although doing so may not be explicitly set forth by law. The latter refers to voluntary activities in line with the company's business strategy; not doing those activities does not mean the company is seen as being unethical. When CSR is mentioned in the context of sports, the aspect of "philanthropy" tends to take on a life of its own, with those types of activities attracting all of the attention. However, this is but an adaptation of philanthropy in the original sense, and we must not forget that genuine CSR includes economic and legal responsibilities.

Even in that sense, for a corporate sports team to switch over to new values, they must fulfill their economic responsibilities by showing their best game and offering the best hospitality to their stakeholders, namely their customers and consumers. By making the excellent-grade car the Prius and offering it to consumers, Toyota is meeting its economic responsibilities under CSR and, though products and performance are different by nature and economic responsibilities are not demanded of sports like at Coca-Cola West, Toyota's rugby team giving their best performance is just as an important part of forming a brand image.

As for legal responsibilities, teams that are owned by companies that conduct their economic activities within the bounds of laws and regulations are freed from compliance issues. For that reason, corporate sports teams in Japan shoulder the difficult task of maintaining a brand image by elevating their game in order to function as a catalyst for implementing CSR and playing an essential role in corporate management.

On a side note, Japan is refraining from hosting the Rugby World Cup in 2019, as the sport is far less followed than soccer and there is little hope of the home team even making it through the qualifiers. In the background of that is the fact that all of the teams in the top domestic league are corporate sports teams and not professional. Though they are a part of social contribution activities and efforts to form a brand image in Japan, they are exempt from the economic responsibilities of an international business. The likelihood of the national team losing in the qualifiers would result in a slump in ticket sales and the possibility of the tournament running a serious loss.

J League and CSR: corporate social activities of clubs

With the exception of one club (Montedio Yamagata) that operates as a non-profit corporation, the clubs of the J League are incorporated sports businesses and are required to engage their players in social contribution activities in order to deepen relations with the local area and build a fan base.[3] As an aside, it is clearly stated in Article 87, Clause (6) of the J League Statutes that players are required to "partake in public relations activities, fan services and social contribution activities designated by the J League."

Over January and February 2009, a survey was conducted of all 36 clubs of the J Leagues J1 and J2 divisions on the social contribution activities that players, coaches, and general managers took part in (J League, 2009). Results showed that players and coaches participated in a total of 2,417 events, which was more than the 2,220 of 2008 and far more than the 1,672 in 2007. Moreover, the average number of activities per club was 67.1, and the average activities per month were 5.6, which were far more than the 53.9 activities per club and 4.5 activities per month of 2007. A total of 1,078 players took part, for an average of 10.1 events per player and an average of 17.3 hours of activities per year. A breakdown of activities showed the highest to be soccer clinics and events at 18.2 percent, followed by fan services (15.1 percent), autograph sessions (12.6 percent), and local community events (11.7 percent). These activities were based on the J League's 100 Year Vision and organized to increase the fan base and enhance the overall quality of the league through community outreach efforts by the teams. In terms of objectives and approaches, nothing differs from the CSR of ordinary businesses.

High corporate sponsorship ratio within income in the J League

The J League gains a higher percentage of its income from corporate sponsorship compared to its counterparts in the UK, Germany, Italy, Spain, and France, where leagues earn vast incomes from broadcast rights. As Figure 12.1 indicates that income from corporate sponsorship as a ratio of total income is 23.4 percent on average in the five major leagues, compared to 45.0 percent in the J1 League. As this figure indicates, strengthening the league's relationship with corporate sponsors is a task of the highest priority. Therefore, investigating why businesses want to sponsor the J League should provide key information for gaining sponsors.

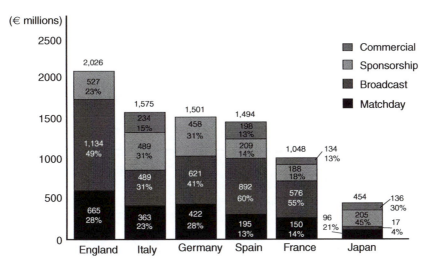

Figure 12.1 Revenue breakdowns for European leagues and J League 2008/09

Onishi (2008) asked 114 corporate sponsors of the J League to rate how important their reasons for sponsoring club uniforms were in 2006 on a 10-point scale from "1: Not important at all" to "10: Extremely important." Of the eight listed reasons, the highest average was scored by "Contribute to the society/local community" at 8.50, followed by "Responsibility to the society/local community" at 8.31. The third and subsequent reasons were "Improve brand loyalty" at 8.298, "Improve awareness and visibility" at 8.179, and "Improve image" at 8.070, all of which were reported as primary motivations and goals in studies done in other countries. The lowest three reasons were "Networking amongst sponsors" at 4.456, "Sell to sponsors" at 3.589, and "Personal preference of directors" at 3.536.

A comparison was then made against the IEG Sponsorship Report (IEG, 2006) to determine whether this trend was peculiar to J League uniform sponsors or not. The numbers in Figure 12.1 indicate the percentage of businesses that responded either "10: Extremely important" or "9: Very important" for the various reasons. Results showed that 59 percent of the businesses in Japan felt that "Contributing to the local community" was an important reason for sponsoring a professional sports team, which was the only reason that far exceeded the IEG Report (35 percent). With all of the other reasons, the IEG Report topped the J League sponsors, clearly indicating a trend towards emphasizing reasons directly connected to business: "Promote use/sales of products or services," "Promote business with dealers," and "Show or supply products or services."

Figure 12.2 highlights the peculiar motivation of J League sponsors, but behind this is a history in which the J League has since its inception in 1993 focused on a mission of community-oriented club management and building good relations with business who endorse that concept. As part of the strategy to gain corporate sponsors, the clubs and league as a whole have had to function as a platform or catalyst for companies to improve their CSR activities.

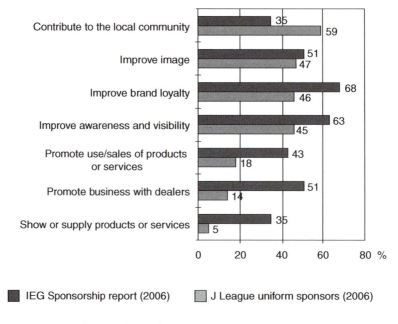

Figure 12.2 Comparison of sponsorship goals

What effect does community outreach conducted by J League teams have on club management? Roy and Graeff (2003) found that local residents have high expectations for community outreach programs of their local team, but also showed that this did not lead to increased ticket sales as compared to the case of the ordinary businesses. This resulted that charity or public-interest activities by the sporting associations have no positive impact on the sales of tickets or merchandise. From these standpoints, it was revealed that community outreach activities conducted by clubs enhanced team identity and, as a result thereof, enhanced spectator intention. In other words, community outreach by clubs does not directly stimulate spectator intention, but indirectly has a positive impact on ticket sales by way of team identity (Onishi and Harada, 2008). This relationship agrees with findings of many studies that spectator intention and actual game attendance are strongly affected by team identity (Fisher and Wakefield, 1998; Matsuoka *et al.*, 2003; Murrell and Dietz, 1992; Wakefield, 1995).

Catalytic value of CSR demanded of sports

As was previously said, the J League made it mandatory in 2002 for its players to perform philanthropic activities so as to further strengthen its ties with the community. The football players visited nursing homes and seniors' facilities, acted as visiting teachers at schools, practiced environmental conservation, and participated in hometown events. In these ways, the league provides visible proof of the "contributions to the local community," which is important to sponsoring corporations. In the meantime, the J League has undertaken various other social contribution activities in order to improve the brand value of the league as a whole. For instance, in 2007, the league began the "Heart Project" based on visit-teaching at elementary schools in collaboration with the Japan Football Association.

This program places emphasis on aiding the healthy mental development of children. To foster sportsmanship and charitable feelings, current and former players on the men's and women's national teams and from the J League stand in front of classes at elementary schools as "dream teachers" and espouse the wonderfulness of having dreams and goals, and the importance of working hard to achieve them. A so-called "dream class" is offered mainly to sixth graders. The class consists of a "game time" component in which the importance of everyone working together to achieve a common goal and playing by the rules is taught while doing physical exercise, and a "talking time" component in which the dream teacher talks about their life, the setbacks they had to overcome, and the moment when they attained their dream. On a side note, this program was staged 247 times across the country and involved the participation of 7,902 students. The dream teachers were expanded from soccer to baseball, track and field, volleyball, and other sports with athletes who support the program, thus broadening the significance of community outreach by athletes.

Conclusions

This chapter has looked at CSR in Japan and examined the current state and issues of CSR activities of corporate sports and professional sports. What began as corporate sports for the purpose of corporate welfare and advertising is today being used strategically as a corporate platform for CSR. With professional sports as well, clubs that want to enhance their team identity and connect that to ticket and merchandise sales are constructively using their players in community outreach programs. Corporate sponsors of the J League feel that community outreach is the most important reason for sponsoring a team; therefore teams are pressed to meet the needs of sponsoring businesses.

Into the future, the clubs and the league must continue the specific philanthropic activities to meet their "discretionary" responsibility, as well as reinforcing the league's moral standards to meet its "ethical" responsibility, improving the services and hospitality demanded by fans to exercise "economic" responsibility, and adopting the AFC club licensing regulations which starts in 2013 and fortifying league and team governance to carry out "legal" responsibility. In these ways, the clubs and league must work to further enhance their value as platforms and catalysts for upgrading their own CSR and supporting the CSR activities of sponsors.

Notes

1 Launched in 1993, the J League replaced the moderately successful Japan Soccer League (JSL). It was the first professional football league in Japan, and aimed to move away from the corporation teams which had characterized the JSL. Conditions of membership encouraged clubs to develop local links, invest in youth development and develop qualified coaches and contracted players (Deloitte, 2005).

2 In 2007, copper wire was discovered in a "multi-grain rice" product made by Hakubaku, a corporate sponsor whose name appears on the jersey front of J League team Venforet Kofu. The company voluntarily recalled 220,000 bags of the product and suffered serious damage. To repay their sponsor who supported them in bad times, the club put on their website a request to fans to buy Hakubaku's products. This example shows how a business made a good impression on a local community by sponsoring a team as part of their social contribution activities and, as a result, led to risk management.

3 Following the AFC club licensing regulations, J League decided the introduction of this system in 2013. The main object of the licensing regulations is to increasing the level of management and organization within the clubs and to protect the credibility and to monitor the financial fair play in the competitions.

References

Breuer, C. (2012) *How could the value of Bundesliga sponsoring be increased: Insights of the model used in the Bundesliga*, paper presented to the Global Center of Excellence Symposium, Waseda University, February 24.

Carroll, A. B. (1991) 'The pyramid of corporate social responsibility: Toward the moral management of organizational stakeholders', *Business Horizons*, 34 (4), 39–49.

Deloitte (2005) *Annual review of football finance*. Manchester: Deloitte & Touche LLP.

Fisher, R. J. and Wakefield, K. (1998) 'Factors leading to group identification: A field study of winners and losers', *Psychology & Marketing*, 15, 23–40.

IEG Sponsorship Report (2006) '06 activation spending to match all-time high'. *IEG Sponsorship Report*, 25 (5), 1–6.

Japan Committee for Economic Development (1956) *Business people be aware of and practice social responsibility*. Tokyo: Report of the Special Committee on Management Guideline, Ministry of International Trading and Industry.

J League Official Website (2009) *Results of Home Town Activity Survey*. Available at: http://www.j-league. or.jp/100year/report/investigation.html (accessed: September 26, 2012).

Kotler, P. and Lee, N. (2005) *Corporate social responsibility: Doing the most good for your company and your cause*. Hoboken, NJ: John Wiley & Sons.

Matsuoka, H., Chelladurai, P., and Harada, M. (2003) 'Direct and interaction effects of team identification and satisfaction on intention to attend games', *Sport Marketing Quarterly*, 12, 244–253.

Mizuo, J. and Tanaka, H. (2004) *CSR Management* (in Japanese). Tokyo: Seisansei Shuppan.

Murrell, A. J. and Dietz, B. (1992) 'Fan support of sport teams: The effect of a common group identity', *Journal of Sport & Exercise Psychology*, 14, 28–39.

Onishi, T. (2008) 'Corporate social responsibility in sport sponsorship: Antecedents and consequences of the perception of CSR', PhD thesis, Waseda University.

Onishi, T . and Harada, M. (2008) 'Antecedents of consumer perception of corporate social responsibility in sport sponsorship', *Proceedings of the 4th Asian Association for Sport Management Conference*, Bangkok, Thailand, pp. 96–100 .

Roy, D. P. and Graeff, T. R. (2003) 'Consumer attitudes toward cause-related marketing activities in professional sports', *Sport Marketing Quarterly*, 12, 163–172.

Sheldon, O. (1924) *The Philosophy of Management*. London: Sir Isaac Pitman and Sons Ltd.

Wakefield, K. L. (1995) 'The pervasive effects of social influence on sporting event attendance', *Journal of Sport and Social Issues*, 19, 335–351.

PART III

STAKEHOLDER ENGAGEMENT IN CSR IN SPORT

13

DELIVERY OF LARGE-SCALE CSR EFFORTS THROUGH CORPORATE COMMUNITY INVOLVEMENT

Lessons from Major League Baseball's Reviving Baseball in Inner Cities program

Lisa A. Kihl and Scott Tainsky

Overview

Many professional sports organizations' corporate social responsbility (CSR) initiatives are part of a broader movement of corporate community involvement (CCI) where companies are moving toward strategically investing in community projects aimed at addressing a social problem. Strategic CCI typically involves aligning an organization's social initiatives with their core competencies and long-term strategies. Major League Baseball's Reviving Baseball in Inner Cities (RBI) is an example of such an initiative. Organizational partnerships (i.e., boys' and girls' clubs, city parks and recreation departments, and local sport associations) are formed to assist with program delivery. However, various challenges in terms of managing these RBI partnerships and delivery of the program can occur. Drawing from the partnership literature we aim to raise students' and practitioners' awareness of certain challenges organizations and their partners might encounter in developing and managing CSR programs delivered via partnering with service organizations. Specifically, we highlight challenges relating to program management, developing and writing effective partnership agreements, effective program marketing and branding; and, in terms of addressing barriers to participation, recruiting and retaining minority male volunteers. Recommendations are also offered where practical considerations in developing partnership plans delineating partnership roles and responsibilities, marketing strategies, program branding with multiple brands, and volunteer recruitment and retention practices.

Introduction

Corporate community involvement (CCI) has become a focal aspect of professional sport CSR's initiatives where programs are strategically implemented to address vital social problems in the community (Selsky and Parker, 2005; Harley and Warburton, 2008; Seitanidi and Crane, 2009). Strategic CCI generally entails aligning an organization's social initiatives with their core competencies and long-term strategies. For example, Major League Baseball's RBI program strategically uses the organization's core competencies (i.e., expertise in the sports of baseball and softball) to address specific social issues in the urban community (i.e., increasing youth physical activity, teaching youth life skills, and enhancing education). Organizational partnerships between several Major League Baseball (MLB) clubs and non-profit organizations (i.e., boys' and girls' clubs, city parks and recreation departments, and local sport associations) have been formed to assist with program delivery because these nonprofit organizations provide the necessary infrastructure to deliver the RBI program. The implementation process of profit–nonprofit sport CCI partnerships in delivering large scale CSR efforts, such as RBI, are not well understood and present certain challenges. It is our intent to highlight some of the challenges and offer practical considerations in managing these types of cross-sector partnerships. We first provide an overview of the RBI program, followed by a summary of related partnership literature. Next, we highlight some of challenges organizations and their partners might encounter in managing a sport related CCI partnership, and conclude with recommendations for consideration in delivering the program.

History

RBI was conceived in 1989 in South Central Los Angeles (LA) by John Young, a former Major League Baseball player and scout. In the late 1970s, Young was concerned about the decline in the number of professional baseball players South Central LA was developing along with the increased drop-out rate of youth participating in baseball. The decline in participation was due to several factors but in particular related to the ineffective organization of area baseball programs. As a result, area youth joined other activities including street gangs. Young strategized to revive the development of professional players and participation in South Central LA through the creation of a 13–16-year-old youth baseball program. The main goal was to use baseball as a tool to challenge youth mentally and physically and lead them away from street life.

Young later added the Academy of Excellence program to emphasize the importance of academics and community responsibility. In 1991, the RBI concept was endorsed by MLB, which has been committed to providing financial support (e.g., start-up grants, equipment, and coaching education) and to serving as the central administrative office for the RBI program. KPMG (an accounting firm based in the United States) was the program's corporate sponsor from 2007–2010 (PRNewswire, 2012). KPMG did not renew their sponsorship beyond 2010. The sponsorship involved awarding US $1 million per year and assistance with managing local RBI programs and the RBI World Series. Help was provided by KPMG in the way of volunteers to coach teams, academic tutoring, and financial and administrative support.

Program philosophy: participation

RBI is an MLB outreach initiative for children and youth aged 5 to 18 years. The program philosophy is participation-oriented, where the aim is to increase minority baseball and softball participation, player development, and teach teamwork (Major League Baseball, 2011a). The RBI program has expanded to include life skills and educational programs (e.g., through partnerships with nonprofit organizations such as *Sport Smart!* and *Breaking Barriers: in Sports, in Life, and Partnership for a Drug-Free America*), and to provide scholarships to assist youth in pursuing secondary education.

Administration and financial support

Major League Baseball's Community Affairs office is responsible for managing the RBI program across the country. The director and the department staff centrally oversee operations, administration, programing, and events. The program is delivered in each of the 30 cities where an MLB team exists. MLB and its clubs have provided over $30 million worth of resources to the various RBI programs. Each individual club typically allocates a certain amount of funding to organizations to help off-set the costs of program delivery. For example, the Minnesota Twins provide approximately $60,000 per year to both the Minneapolis Park Board and the City of Saint Paul Division of Parks and Recreation plus each city receives an additional $10,000 per year to assist in renovating baseball and softball fields.

To optimize maximum participation, leagues operate throughout the year and are organized into divisions: Jr. RB (5–12 years), Freshman boys (13–14 years), Junior boys (15–16 years), Senior boys (17–18 years), and girls' softball (14 years and under and 15–18 years). An all-star program is also offered where teams participate in regional qualifying tournaments for advancement to the RBI World Series. In 2012, over 200 cities sponsored RBI leagues in 37 states, the District of Columbia, and in nine countries, including the United Kingdom, the United States Virgin Islands, Puerto Rico, Dominican Republic, Japan, Venezuela, Argentina, Curacao, and Canada (Major League Baseball, 2012a). In 2012 RBI served over 210,000 baseball and softball participants (Major League Baseball, 2012b). Participation statistics for the 2012 season (see Table 13.1) show the majority of participants were in the 13–18-year-old baseball league with 124,143 players. RBI was comprised of 306 leagues including Jr. RBI (n=118), baseball (n=139), and softball (n=74). The leagues were racially diverse (see Table 13.2) where minority youth represented 80 percent of Junior RBI and RBI baseball and softball leagues.

Table 13.1 2012 RBI League participation breakdown

Leagues	Number of leagues	Participant numbers
JR. RBI: Age 5–12	118 Leagues	75,177 participants
Baseball: Age 13–18	139 Leagues	124,143 participants
Softball: Age 11–18	74 Leagues	12,483 participants
	Total: 306	Total: 211, 783

Source: adapted from Major League Baseball (2012b).

Table 13.2 2012 RBI League demographics

Race	JR. RBI	RBI
African American	41%	41%
Hispanic	27%	28%
Caucasian	25%	25%
Asian	4%	3%
Other	2%	2%
Native American	1%	1%

Source: adapted from Major League Baseball (2012b).

Delivery of program and program partners

All 30 MLB clubs and four Minor League clubs (i.e., Memphis Redbirds, West Michigan Whitecaps, San Jose Giants, and Charleston (SC) River Dogs) support RBI programs. Ten MLB clubs and the minor league clubs deliver RBI independently through their own operations, while the remaining clubs provide either substantial support (financial and/or in-kind) and oversight to RBI in their market or lower level support (financial and/or in-kind) in their market. Several MLB clubs (e.g., Chicago White Sox RBI, Minnesota Twins RBI, and Philadelphia Phillies RBI) that do not deliver RBI programs, partner with a local organization that is responsible to administer and deliver the program. Partners include boys' and girls' clubs of America, parks and recreation departments, local youth sports and youth associations, and Police Athletic Leagues. Some programs, however, are administered without a MLB club affiliation (e.g., Birmingham Police Athletic League, Boys and Girls club of Central Arkansas, North American Amateur Sports Association, and Sedalia, MO). Due to the nature of the different programs and partners, RBI programs are administered differently but within MLB's governing parameters. MLB provide guidelines on league administration (e.g., program development, facilities, sponsorship and finance, managers and umpires, and program administration and responsibilities) (Major League Baseball, 2011b). However, each chapter has autonomy to develop their own processes in terms of promotions and public relations, recruitment, registration, scheduling, human resource management, acquiring equipment and uniforms, and securing sponsorships and managing finances.

Why partnerships?

The evolution of social expectations placed on corporations is one of the impetuses that led to an escalation of cross-sector partnerships. Among these partnerships are nonprofit organizations' collaborations with commercial partners (Hodge and Greve, 2007) and private firms engaging in activities with other commercial entities, the latter in the form of strategic alliances, joint ventures, contracting agreements, and, often in the case of CSR endeavors, sponsorships (Menon and Kahn, 2003). Oliver's (1990) conceptual exploration of the conditions under which partnerships are formed consists of asymmetry, reciprocity, necessity, legitimacy, efficiency, and stability as the underlying bases for interorganizational relationships. These are akin to the preconditions phase of partnership development framed by Wood and Gray (1991) – the combination of organizational and environmental factors that lead to the association with another organization. In all cases of interorganizational collaboration, the goal of the partnership is to further the firm's access to resources or knowledge, skills, and abilities that the organization does not itself possess (Pfeffer, 1987).

One such resource that corporate partners find in sport is visibility. In Eisenhardt and Schoonhoven's (1996) consideration of partnership development via the resource-based view, among the intangible bundles of resources brought to a partnership is the reputation of the firm. Indeed visibility is a rare, albeit imitable, value-added resource even in the summits of the corporate world. Thus, in viewing these strategic alliances as fitting with organizational goals and manifested through formal support and control facilities between partners (Kouwenhoven, 1993) such as memoranda of understanding and guidelines, the link to a sport organization uniquely supplies that awareness.

Nonprofit–corporate partnerships

The landscapes of both for-profit and not-for-profit institutions are evolving. Businesses realize the social pressure to behave in a more socially responsible manner (McWilliams and Seigel,

2001) while nonprofit organizations face increasing pressure to assume a more fiscally practical approach in their dealings (Boyne, 2002). Stereotypes of the profit-driven enterprise and community-oriented nonprofit have thus been blurred. What has followed is an escalation of partnerships between corporate and nonprofit firms in practice and a parallel reflection among academics as to the antecedents of these cross-sector collaborations (Austin, 2000). It is reasonable to posit that this movement in the mindset and functions of corporate and nonprofit firms has resulted in a relative ease of bridging the narrowing gaps in cultures and practices and therefore the usefulness of these cross-sector partnerships in reaching firm objectives.

Research on collaboration between nonprofit and corporations identifies acquisition of resources as one of the principal motivations to build a partnership (Stone *et al.*, 1999). In the case of CCI programs, one of the primary competencies lacking in major professional sports organizations is the technical capacity to run the day-to-day activities involved with a youth program. As a result, even though the sport organization–nonprofit dynamic falls squarely into the prototypical rich–poor imbalance that often leads to an unhealthy power disparity (Kanter, 1989), this is perhaps tempered by the practical competencies that bolster the standing of the nonprofit in the exchange.

Multi-organization partnerships and partnership management

An emergent area in the research of business practice is the nexus of partnerships involving multiple organizations. Researchers may view the relationship between firms in a multi-organization partnership as dictated by the organization serving as the focal point (Sydow and Windeler, 1998). First and foremost, the focal organization initiates the network and directs the level of involvement of all of the participating organizations. In so doing, it also acts as a moderator of the relationships between the ancillary organizations after the initiation stage. The long-term sustainability of the partnership is predicated on effective partner management (Kaplan and Hurd, 2002) including persistently monitoring the vision and creating a solid rapport among the organizations' representatives in order to manifest the stated goals. Definition of roles and tasks and especially the processes shared by the organizations serve as the foundation on which the interorganizational culture is built. However, in practice organizations may place too much emphasis on this phase, as the construction of the relationships receives a disproportionately high level of attention relative to the effective maintenance of the partnership (Kanter, 1989). This is absolutely pertinent in CCI-based partnerships, where research notes the challenges to partnership management at every stage long after partnership selection (Drucker, 1999). These encompass "experimenting with adapting agreements, objectives, reporting mechanisms and other systems, managing crises to the benefit of the partnership, and balancing the necessary personal relationships with needs for ongoing organizational institutionalism" (Seitanidi and Crane, 2009: 422).

In sustaining the partnerships of organizations across sectors, it is vital that each organization assume and embrace certain postures of its partners. For example, Kouwenhoven (1993) recommended nonprofits adopt the corporate mindset in partnering with commercial organizations, despite the fact that this may create new difficulties. One such difficulty is the alignment of organization and partnership outcomes. In the case of the nonprofit–corporate–sport organization partnership triad, where competing values are a given, this is of particular importance. The straightforward detailed articulation of the partnership's goals suggested by academicians (Dussauge *et al.*, 2000) may aid in achieving program goals, but these still require additional intraorganizational scrutiny to identify whose goals have been stated and what is the cost borne internally. The usefulness of the partnership is measured not only by the effectiveness of the community and network, but also the organizations (Provan and Milward, 1995).

At the worker level, multiparty partnerships typically involve high-level staff at the boundary spanning positions, defined as roles that link the organization to the external environment (Aldrich and Herker, 1977). As a consequence, whereas such a staff member may serve in a high post of his/her organizational hierarchy, and thus adopt a traditionally rigid position in dealing with workers at that firm, in interactions with individuals who have achieved a similarly high stature at partnering organizations, a shift to more democratic posture is required. Beyond the skills and responsibilities that workers bring the partnership, they must also adopt the cooperative approach in order to create and effect an operative partnership. Moreover, as important as any aspect of the interaction is the presence of trust underlying the interorganizational dynamic (Gulati, 1995) as well as in autonomous actions undertaken by individual partners (Huxham and Macdonald, 1992).

When partnerships fail

Kanter (1989) cautions that there is a predisposition of individual actors during the nascent stages of an association to not fully embrace the relationship until trust has formed. Consequently, sometimes only much later on, when the technical details of the arrangement are fully understood and the actors trusting in the relative commitment of the organizations involved, moving the partnerships beyond this vulnerable stage, that it becomes truly successful as arranged.

At the firm level inter-organizational partnerships are complex relationships that necessarily come with the relinquishment of absolute organizational autonomy. The loss of control is one among many of the pitfalls of collaboration experienced by partners (Huxham and Macdonald, 1992), oftentimes ending in a failed relationship. Others include lack of communication and lack of collaboration (Huxham, 2000; Linden, 2002). Kanter (1989) further identified uneven levels of commitment, undermanagement, insufficient integration, lack of a common framework, and premature trust as susceptibilities of interorganizational exchanges. To these, Park (1996) added the pursuit of disparate goals as the primary barrier in the success of partnerships between multiple organizations. The extant research has noted the particular challenge faced by partnerships featuring organizations with dissimilar management styles (Prasad, 2001) as well as the divergent motives and cultures between the public and private sectors (Klijn and Teisman, 2003). Environmental factors may also contribute to ongoing changes in the interorganizational dynamic. For example, the social pressures to activate the collaboration may become less important given a change in economic conditions. Accordingly, even if all of the preconditions for partnership formations are suitably met, a shift in the economic environment could conceivably deemphasize the significance of social efforts in the corporate culture.

In the case of CSR, one of the many motivations for corporations and sports organizations to engage in these efforts is often a desire to improve its reputation. This is consistent with legitimacy, one of Oliver's (1990) determinants of partnership formation and one that often is motivated by external norms. What then results when industry norms change? The consequent result is the absence of a mandate by external stakeholders to maintain any specific partnership in order to be viewed as a genuine actor. So too it follows that the sustainability of the partnership is not an imperative. What is more, the success of many CSR programs hinges on the idea of social capital, individuals acting voluntarily in the spirit of institutional arrangements to better society (Coleman, 1988). Again the long-term sustainability of the program is then predicated on individuals' self-interest as much as the formal arrangement of the partners.

RBI delivery challenges

The implementation of large-scale professional sport CCI initiatives, specifically through partnerships with multiple organizations, poses various challenges. Partner administrators involved in program implementation need to be aware and be prepared of the potential challenges in delivering programs, particularly in this case as it relates to RBI delivery. Based on our ongoing research exploring a variety of RBI focused partnerships in the US, we next present some of these challenges.

Undermanaged partnerships

The perceived benefits of MLB clubs entering into a cross-sectoral partnership with a local delivery organization (e.g., the municipal parks and recreation departments) relate to an enhanced ability (i.e., pre-existing infrastructure) to deliver baseball and softball leagues, offer increased exposure to, community appreciation for, and access to the target population – inner-city youth. In turn, the partner delivery organizations' mutual gains include enhanced resources and increased legitimacy by association with a MLB team. Based on our research, established partnerships between respective MLB clubs and delivery organizations were based on trust and mutual respect. In general, each organization was confident that their partner would uphold their responsibilities and obligations. This included either providing resources or delivering the RBI program, both not taking advantage of each other, and appreciating the value of each others' contributions (i.e., financial resource support, delivery of leagues, and human resources). Partnership formation based on mutual respect and trust, however, influences the initial partnership development and can lead to undermanaged partnerships. Situations where both partners trust each other to fulfill their obligations, the relationship agreement is not always formalized and, as a result, tends to reflect informal collaborations. Consequently, limited partnership planning and policy guidelines about the nature of the partnership are included in the partnership agreement. Partners might possess a general understanding of the partnership obligations (i.e., MLB club – financial responsibilities, equipment, uniforms, and facilitating the attendance of RBI teams at an MLB game; delivery organization – program delivery, staffing, maintaining records, and field maintenance), yet a formal partnership agreement delineating the respective partner's roles and responsibilities (e.g., marketing, branding, and staff knowledge of recruitment and registration practices) are in some cases nonexistent and/or partners' awareness of the nature of the agreement can be vague.

In instances where informal collaborations exist, each partner may not fully understand their roles and responsibilities relating to fulfilling the agreement and thus expectations are inconsistently met. For example, a MLB team might assume that in return for providing the delivery organization various resources to deliver the program, the delivery organization's marketing and branding of both the partnership and the RBI program would use similar strategies employed in the professional sport (i.e., corporate) world. In many cases, partner delivery organizations do not possess the resources and/or expertise to carry out corporate marketing and branding strategies. Thus, both partners can become frustrated and annoyed because expectations are not understood or cannot be met. Ultimately, the informal nature of the partnership agreement limits each partner's ability to hold one another accountable for performing tasks and/or at a certain quality. Given each partner's resources and expertise, it is important that both partners communicate what roles and responsibilities each partner can perform and at what level.

Compounding this issue is the insufficient time and human resources devoted to cultivating the partnership. In many cases, both MLB and partner organizational administrators lack the time and staff to foster a relationship between them. Administrators from both parties are generally focused on fulfilling their individual administrative roles to complete the baseball or softball season. Partner organizations at the conclusion of a season are also challenged to find the time to engage in program assessment and strategic development because they are preparing for the next sport/activity season. Rarely do discussions occur throughout the year where program stakeholders (i.e., partner staff and administrators, MLB administrators, and coaches) share information, assess challenges, review strategies, reevaluate partnership agreements, and determine how the MLB club/MLB league office can assist the delivery organization (Kihl, 2009).

Limited marketing and branding

RBI is an important program that provides opportunities for minority youth to participate in baseball and softball, develop life skills, and enhance their education. Its success with these notwithstanding, limited program marketing and brand management at both the MLB and local levels unfortunately has led to a lack of brand equity (Kihl, 2009). That is, potential participants and MLB consumers are unaware of these efforts and therefore the marketing value of MLB's involvement with the RBI program does not come into being.

Despite RBI being an MLB initiative, most people in and outside of the baseball and softball communities are generally unaware of the program. In part, because of the cross-sector partnerships, MLB's overall branding and marketing strategy entails MLB clubs and the partner organizations to advertise and promote RBI in their local communities. Consequently, the marketing strategies are varied. In many cases, MLB clubs' RBI advertisements and promotions are developed from the community relations department where the program is mostly marketed alongside the other CCI initiatives using various marketing techniques (i.e. websites, Facebook, limited television advertising, and some public service announcements). Partner organizations are generally constrained by resources and tend to use marketing activities (e.g., online registration and seasonal brochures) that will reach the greatest number of youth. Limited resources for marketing has resulted in varied promotional activities including presenting the logos on a website, acknowledging the local MLB team or MLB as a sponsoring partner, identifying the league as "RBI" without explaining the program and its objectives on a website or in a seasonal brochure, or failing to mention the brand or the sponsoring partner (Kihl and Babiak, 2008). At the local level, the nominal brand management and marketing can be linked back to the trend of informal partnership agreements and delineation of expectations.

The branding of RBI is relatively new and the negotiation of different partner brands (i.e., MLB, MLB clubs, delivery organizations (e.g., parks and recreation departments and boys' and girls' clubs)) has created challenges in establishing a distinct RBI brand identity. The multiple brands associated with RBI have created challenges in brand management and marketing. The program possesses a central brand yet RBI has failed to draw attention to their sponsorship of the activity. A premise to enhancing brand image, establishing brand credibility, evoking brand feelings, creating a sense of brand community, and eliciting brand engagement is building brand awareness (Hoeffler and Keller, 2002). Limited brand awareness of the RBI program at the local itself exists, much less the association between RBI at the MLB level. Potential and current program participants, parents, and in some cases staff of partner organizations are unfamiliar with the RBI brand (Kihl and Babiak, 2008; Kihl, 2009). These stakeholders (i.e., participants, parents, and staff) do not hold a strong association with RBI, MLB, MLB clubs, and local delivery organizations. In some cases, individuals external to the program (e.g., high-school coaches and local youth baseball and softball association coaches) perceived the program as inferior because it is not connected with a more recognized baseball or softball brand (e.g., American Legion, Babe Ruth, and American Softball Association) (Kihl and Babiak, 2008). The lack of overall brand management and marketing strategies of the respective partner organizations has limited value creation in terms of enhanced brand, addressing a social issue, and competitive respect.

Insufficient human resources

Human resource challenges in program delivery range from insufficient time to invest in administering and delivering the program to non-staffing issues (Kihl and Babiak, 2008; Kihl, 2009). MLB club staff typically has a multitude of duties and responsibilities related to administering the team. Duties related to administering the professional team understandably take priority over RBI duties. The nature of MLB business places staff in an unfortunate time commitment dilemma. Staff must devote the majority of their time to fulfilling their responsibilities with administering the MLB team rather than undertaking RBI duties. Within a MLB team's public relation's office, RBI is not perceived strategically and thus not the priority among operations.

The RBI program's involvement of volunteers (as coaches and administrators) subjects it to many of the institutional challenges being addressed nationally by the Edward M. Kennedy Serve America Act of 2009. Chief among those are the level of volunteerism and the difficulty of mobilizing volunteers from minority and disadvantaged populations (Nesbit and Brudney, 2010). A generation of urban adults of color has not grown up playing baseball, and thus feels reluctant to serve as coaches (Kihl and Babiak, 2008; Kihl, 2009). Volunteers impact participation (Wiersma and Sherman 2005) and therefore assumed an increase in volunteer minority adults would positively impact minority youth participation rates (Cornelli-Sanderson and Richards, 2010).

The failure to renew KPMG's sponsorship may also have additional ramifications with respect to human resources. While the program's creation of social capital is evident via the many former KPMG sponsor employees who have remained involved with RBI, the lack of a formal partnership necessarily terminates the worker incentives to donate their time to RBI. This certainly will steadily and drastically reduce the number of corporate volunteer hours donated to the program in various forms, principally in the non-programmatic benefits such as education and delinquent behavior prevention. These in-kind donations may at times seem tangential to the stated goal of increasing opportunities for inner-city youth to play baseball. Nevertheless the absence of this aspect of the program moving forward means less exposure to role models from outside the players' communities, which had become a valued aspect of the program. Whether MLB seeks to preserve this complementary part of the program themselves or through a new partner is a compelling question.

Need for evaluation

Whilst the MLB asserts that RBI promotes positive youth development and participation of minority youth through participating in baseball and softball, available data to substantiate these claims are limited (Kihl, 2009). Furthermore, evaluation of the various programs and cross-sector partnerships to assess the quality of program delivery or the merits of the respective partnerships is sporadic. MLB's Community Affairs office conducts focus groups at their annual baseball academy to assess the challenges experienced by partnering organizational stakeholders and as an outcome of these meetings determines strategies for improvement. Community Affairs officials have used the information to assist programs to address their respective challenges via the provision of training, consultation, or resources. Evaluations across local RBI chapters are however infrequent and in some cases non-existent, which is partly due to a lack of available resources and expertise to conduct the evaluations (Kihl, 2009).

Strategies for enhancing RBI partnership implementation and management

To assist sport managers of profit–nonprofit CCI partnership such as MLB's RBI program, we have highlighted specific challenges involved in its implementation. Addressing these types of CCI partnership challenges are important as they can impact subsequent interactions throughout the life of the partnership. Austin (2000) argued that partnership viability is contingent on the capacity to create value for each partner. In this case, MLB clubs benefit from delivering RBI programs by enhancing their community image, developing brand/team loyalty from fans, and by building community capacity and access to sport, while partner organizations gain value through receiving different resources, enhanced legitimacy, and increased participation in the programs they deliver. To ensure that both parties are realizing these benefits it is recommended that a partnership plan be developed (James, 1999; Austin, 2000; Frisby *et al.*, 2004). A plan delineates the overall objectives of the partnership and stipulates the set of tasks each party expects the other to perform to fulfill these objectives, and thus create value (Mohr and Spekman, 1994).

Prior to developing the plan, each partner should be clear about their mutual goals and expectations for collaborating. Roles, responsibilities, expectations, evaluation procedures, and how the partnership will operate should be clearly stipulated. Each party can assess their core competencies and resources to determine if they match their partners' expectations. At this point, the analysis may uncover capability gaps in one of the partners (e.g., in our example, the delivery organization's lack of marketing expertise). This could lead to a readjustment of expectations to more effectively address any gaps that arise (e.g., MLB clubs might address gaps in partner competencies by altering or adjusting staff training or providing additional (unplanned) resources from the MLB club (e.g., marketing and branding)). These expectations can be formalized in a partnership agreement. For example, marketing and branding expectations of both partners can be written in the agreement. MLB might also consider communicating to their clubs and the partner organizations regarding their overall marketing and branding plan. MLB clubs and partner organizations can use the league's plan to help formulate and guide their goals and expectations regarding program marketing and creating brand equity at the local level. Moreover, despite the deep appreciation for program benefits among KPMG employees who got involved with the program, because each program is administered at the local level with little guidance on how to incorporate the sponsor, the former sponsor's core competency was not capitalized on at every site or at the macro level. If MLB determines that a sponsor is indeed a benefit to the program beyond the funds associated with the partnership, ideally that partner's competencies would directly serve the program goals. Forming a new corporate partnership could provide a unique opportunity to address the aforementioned gaps, enhancing the program via the unique skills already possessed by the organization, especially those unrelated to participation numbers seemingly well-covered by the service-related partners. With respect to the corporate and service partners, a formal partnership agreement can assist in providing stability and accountability for both partners (James, 1999).

Partnership plans can also map out human resource needs for both partners relating to staffing and non-staffing concerns. Strategies can then be developed to ensure sufficient personnel are available to assist with program delivery. For example, MLB clubs experiencing staffing challenges can assign interns to assist with program coordination and managing partnership roles and responsibilities. Recruiting and retaining former RBI participants to serve as volunteer coaches is another possible strategy. Formulating collaborations with urban community groups and securing a corporate sponsor can also assist in recruiting and retaining volunteers, in particular minority male volunteers.

Evaluating is critical in assessing the extent a community oriented CSR program is both meeting the needs of the recipients and providing benefits to the partners. Building an evaluation component into the partnership agreement allows for continued development and improvement of the partnership (James, 1999) through information sharing between partners and participation in ongoing planning and goal setting. Environments in which these partnerships occur are fluid. Internal changes within partner organizations and MLB clubs will require adjustments for long-term partnership viability. Hence, it is recommended that MLB clubs and delivery organizational partners conduct regular evaluations to assess what goals and objectives are being achieved and the quality of these achievements.

Conclusions

This chapter provided an example of the current trend in large-scale CSR initiatives to engage in strategic CCI where corporations are utilizing their core competencies to address a social issue. We used the case of MLB's RBI youth outreach program that aims to increase baseball and softball participation of urban youth (i.e., in particular, minority youth), to enhance academic achievement, and to develop team work. The majority of MLB clubs use partners to deliver the program. Drawing from the partnership literature, we have highlighted key challenges MLB clubs and their partners may encounter in delivering the program. These challenges include undermanaged partnerships, limited marketing and branding, insufficient resources, and the need for regular evaluation. In order for RBI partners to realize the value in creating these partnerships, we suggest the development of a partnership plan delineating partnership objectives, tasks, and stipulating who is responsible for carrying out respective tasks.

References

Aldrich, H. and Herker, D. (1977) 'Boundary spanning roles and organization structure', *Academy of Management Review*, 2 (2), 217–230.

Austin, J. E. (2000) *The collaboration challenge: How nonprofits and businesses succeed through strategic alliances*. San Francisco, CA: Jossey-Bass.

Boyne, G. A. (2002) 'Public and private management: What's the difference?' *Journal of Management Studies*, 39 (1), 97–122.

Coleman, J. S. (1988) 'Social capital in the creation of human capital', *American Journal of Sociology*, 94, S95–S120.

Cornelli-Sanderson, R. and Richards, M. H. (2010) 'The after-school needs and resources of low-income urban community: Surveying youth and parents for community change', *American Journal of Community Psychology*, 45, 430–440.

Drucker, P. F. (1999) *Management challenges for the 21st century*. New York: Harper Business.

Dussauge, P., Garrette, B. and Mitchell, W. (2000) 'How to get the best results from alliances', *European Business Forum*, 3, 41–46.

Eisenhardt, K. M. and Schoonhoven, C. B. (1996) 'Resource-based view of strategic alliance formation: Strategic and social effects in entrepreneurial firms', *Organization Science*, 7 (2), 136–150.

Frisby, W., Thibault, L. and Kikulis, L.M. (2004) 'The organizational dynamics of under-managed partnerships in leisure service departments', *Leisure Studies*, 23 (2), 109–126.

Gulati, R. (1995) 'Does familiarity breed trust? The implications of repeated ties for contractual choice in alliances', *Academy of Management Journal*, 38 (1), 85–112.

Harley, M. and Warburton, J. (2008) 'Risks to business in social involvement: An Australian case example', *The Journal of Corporate Citizenship*, 29, 49–60.

Hodge, G. A. and Greve, C. (2007) 'PPPs: The passage of time permits a sober reflection', *Public Administration Review*, 67 (3), 545–558.

Hoeffler, S. and Keller, K. L. (2002) 'Building brand equity through corporate societal marketing', *Journal of Public Policy and Marketing*, 21 (1), 78–89.

Huxham, C. (2000) 'The challenge of corporate governance', *Public Management*, 2 (3), 337–357.

Huxham, C. and Macdonald, D. (1992) 'Introducing collaborative advantage: Achieving inter-organizational effectiveness through meta-strategy', *Management Decision*, 30 (3), 50–56.

James, K. (1999) 'Understanding successful partnerships and collaborations', *Parks and Recreation*, 34 (5), 38–47.

Kanter, R. M. (1989) *When giants learn to dance*. New York: Simon and Schuster.

Kaplan, N. J. and Hurd, J. (2002) 'Realizing the promise of partnerships', *Journal of Business Strategy*, 2 (3), 38–42.

Kihl, L. A. (2009) *Reviving baseball in inner cities program: Evaluating the effectiveness of gaining inner city participation in baseball and softball phase II*. Unpublished report. Minneapolis, MN: Author.

Kihl, L. A. and Babiak, K. (2008) *Reviving baseball in inner cities program: Evaluating the effectiveness of gaining inner city participation in baseball and softball phase I*. Unpublished report. Minneapolis, MN: Author.

Klijn, E. and Teisman, G. R. (2003) 'Institutional and strategic barriers to public-private partnership: An analysis of Dutch cases', *Public Money and Management*, 23 (3), 137–146.

Kouwenhoven, V. (1993). 'The rise of the public private partnership: A model for the management of public-private cooperation', in Kooiman, J. (ed.) *Modern governance: New government-society interactions*. London: Sage Publications, pp. 119–130.

Linden, R. (2002) 'A framework for collaborating', *Public Manager*, 31 (2), 3–7.

Major League Baseball (2011a) *Reviving baseball in inner cities*, MLB. Available at: http://mlb.mlb.com/mlb/official_info/community/rbi.jsp (accessed: May 1, 2012).

Major League Baseball (2011b) *RBI Administrative handbook: Includes JR. RBI handbook*. New York: Major League Baseball Properties, Inc.

Major League Baseball (2012a) 'Reviving baseball in inner cities: Local leagues', MLB. Available at: http://mlb.mlb.com/mlb/downloads/community/rbi_local_leagues_20120417.pdf (accessed: November 17, 2012).

Major League Baseball (2012b) 'Reviving baseball in inner cities'. Unpublished report. New York: Major League Baseball Properties, Inc.

McWilliams, A. and Seigel, D. (2001) 'Corporate social responsibility: A theory of the firm perspective', *Academy of Management Review*, 2 (1), 117–127.

Menon, S. and Kahn, B. E. (2003) 'Corporate sponsorships of philanthropic activities: When do they impact perception of sponsor brand?' *Journal of Consumer Psychology*, 1 (3), 316–327.

Mohr, J. and Spekman, R. (1994) 'Characteristics of partnership success: Partnership attributes, communication behavior, and conflict resolution techniques', *Strategic Management Journal*, 15 (2), 135–152.

Nesbit, R. and Brudney, J. L. (2010) 'At your service? Volunteering and national service in 2020', *Public Administration Review*, 70, S107–S113.

Oliver, C. (1990) 'Determinants of interorganizational relationships: Integration and future directions', *Academy of Management Review*, 15 (2), 241–265.

Park, S. H. (1996) 'Managing an interorganizational network: A framework of the institutional mechanism for network control', *Organization Studies*, 17 (5), 795–824.

Pfeffer, J. (1987) 'A resource dependence perspective on intercorporate relations', in Mizruchi, M. and Schwartz, M. (eds.) *Intercorporate relations: A structural analysis of business*. Cambridge: Cambridge University Press, 25–55.

Prasad, B. (2001) 'What management style is considered best for a team-based organization and why?', *International Journal of Value-Based Management*, 14 (1), 59–77.

PRNewswire (2012) 'Major League Baseball properties announces KPMG as an official sponsor of Major League Baseball: KPMG becomes presenting sponsor of Reviving Baseball in Inner Cities (RBI)'. Available at: http://www.prnewswire.com/news-releases/major-league-baseball-properties-announces-kpmg-as-an-official-sponsor-of-major-league-baseball-58525842.html (accessed: November 19, 2012).

Provan, K. G. and Milward, H. B. (1995) 'A preliminary theory of interorganizational network effectiveness: A comparative study of four community mental health systems', *Administrative Science Quarterly*, 40 (1), 1–33.

Seitanidi, M. M. and Crane, A. (2009) 'Implementing CSR through partnerships: Understanding the selection, design and institutionalization of nonprofit-business partnerships', *Journal of Business Ethics*, 85 (2), 413–429.

Selsky, J. W. and Parker, B. (2005) 'Cross-sector partnerships to address social issues: Challenges to theory and practice', *Journal of Management*, 31 (6), 849–873.

Stone, M. M., Bigelow, B., and Crittenden, W. (1999) 'Research on strategic management in nonprofit organizations: Synthesis, analysis, and future directions', *Administration and Society*, 31 (3), 378–423.

Sydow, J. and Windeler, A. (1998) 'Organizing and evaluating interfirm networks: A structurationist perspective on network processes and network effectiveness', *Organization Science*, 9 (3), 265–284.

Wiersma, L. D. and Sherman, C. P. (2005) 'Volunteer youth sport coaches' perspectives of coaching education/certification and parental codes of conduct', *Research Quarterly for Exercise and Sport*, 76 (3), 324–338.

Wood, D. J. and Gray, B. (1991) 'Toward a comprehensive theory of collaboration', *Journal of Applied Behavioral Science*, 27 (2), 139–162.

14

ENGAGING COMMUNITIES THROUGH SPORT

Sustainability as a means of enacting CSR

Laura Misener, Stacy-Lynn Sant and Daniel S. Mason

Overview

The purpose of this chapter is to examine the ways in which sustainability is manifested in social responsibility through the hosting of large-scale sporting events. We utilize a case study of the 2010 Vancouver Winter Olympic and Paralympic Games to demonstrate how sustainable development is being adopted as a means of social responsibility and corporate community involvement in the Games. Two distinct organizations, the Vancouver Olympic Organizing Committee and 2010 Legacies Now, adopted the principles of sustainability in their efforts to stage the Games, and to leverage the event for broader community benefits. The efforts demonstrate how a greater focus on the values associated with socially responsible development is attracting prominent corporations seeking to invest in sustainable development programming.

Introduction

Civic leaders are concerned with the quality of life of local residents. Attempts to improve quality of life have typically involved the provision of amenities and services, but increasingly other activities traditionally viewed as opportunities for economic and tourism development are now seen as occasions to engage local communities through community development while simultaneously engaging the corporate community. Part of the appeal of festivals and large-scale sporting and cultural events such as the Olympic Games is in enhancing community engagement through volunteering and participation in the festival atmosphere. While this agenda is still secondary to the larger economic imperative tied to the hosting of the events, it is nonetheless a means of focusing some of the efforts and resources associated with the events on enhancing communities and community development (Misener and Mason, 2010). As part of this agenda, the notion of corporate social responsibility (CSR) has emerged as a means to focus attention on the need to ensure sustainable and responsible practices in communities associated with events. While the International Olympic Committee (IOC) has not officially adopted any policy specifically related to social responsibility, it encourages host cities to engage in socially responsible practices. According to the IOC Olympic Charter, its role is "to encourage and support a responsible concern for environmental issues, to promote sustainable development in sport and to require that the Olympic Games are held accordingly" (IOC, 2011: 14).

The concept of sustainability or sustainable development has come to the forefront as a means of enhancing environmental and social responsibility (Moon, 2007). According to the United Nations' definition, sustainable development is a balanced development between people's economic and social needs and the ability of the Earth's resources and ecosystems to meet present and future needs. For the Vancouver 2010 Winter Olympic and Paralympic Games, the host Organizing Committee for the Games adopted a focus on sustainable development that centered upon six principles: accountability, environmental stewardship and impact reduction, social inclusion and responsibility, Aboriginal participation and collaboration, economic benefits, and sport for sustainable living (VANOC, 2010). In addition, a separate and independent organization called 2010 Legacies Now was set up to leverage the Games to create lasting social legacies in communities throughout the province of British Columbia. We examine the efforts of VANOC and 2010 Legacies Now in this chapter to demonstrate the ways in which social responsibility is being adopted and articulated in large-scale sporting events. We have focused our discussion on how events can be part of broader community agenda of social responsibility and sustainable development practices. To do so, we begin with an overview of the concept of sustainability to situate this discussion in the context of social responsibility. As Sheth and Babiak (2010) have argued, CSR in the sport industry appears to manifest differently and is distinctive. In this way, we utilize the notion of sustainability to address the way that CSR is manifested in the values of the Olympic Movement and is being adopted by host cities. Next we examine the principles undergirding sustainability within the Olympic movement and in particular through the 2010 Vancouver Olympic and Paralympic Games. We draw specifically upon the case study of the 2010 Vancouver Winter Olympic and Paralympic Games to demonstrate how social sustainability can be incorporated into the broader framework of events in order to positively impact communities.

Connecting sustainability to corporate social responsibility

The origin of the term "sustainability" can be linked to the more general concept of sustainable development and concerns of equity. It is related to an important shift in understanding relationships between nature and people where typically the dominant view has been based on the separation of the environment from socio-economic issues. Sustainable development was brought to the forefront of the social and political agenda in the World Commission on Environment and Development (WCED) report entitled "Our Common Future," also known as the "Brundtland Report" (WCED, 1987). In this report, sustainable development was defined as "development that meets the needs of the present without compromising the ability of future generations to meet their own needs" (WCED, 1987: 43). Specifically, "sustainable development" refers to an initiative of the United Nations (UN) called the UN Sustainable Development Agenda 21 (known simply as "Agenda 21"). This initiative was unveiled in 1992 during the United Nations Conference on Environment and Development (UNCED), also commonly referred to as the Rio Earth Summit.

Sustainability refers to a theory and practice focused on problems associated with development and considers three major points of view: environmental, economic, and social (Holtz, 1998). According to Girginov and Hills (2008), despite its widespread adoption, the concept of sustainable development has been highly contested for two key reasons: 1) there is the lack of agreement on the meaning of the two principal constructs of the concept – "needs" and "development"; and 2) achieving sustainability requires a substantial capacity to predict the future and deal with uncertainty. Hunter (1997) found that the emergence of the concept of sustainable development has led to a complex debate on how best to distribute the social, economic, and environmental costs and benefits which emanate from the utilization of resources.

The concept of equity has been employed as an intermediary to help deal with the distribution of efforts towards the social aspects of sustainability but also fairly encompasses environmental and economic dimensions. According to Jabareen (2008), equity is associated with various other concepts such as social and economic justice, social equity, equal rights for development, quality of life, equal economic distribution, public participation, and empowerment. Haughton (1999) summarized the ideas of sustainable development using five principles based on equity: inter-generational equity refers to the fairness in allocation of resources between current and future generations; intra-generational equity refers to fairness in allocation of resources between competing interests at the present time; geographical equity refers to the notion that environmental responsibility should be attended to both locally and globally; procedural equity refers to the fact that regulatory and participatory systems should be devised to treat people fairly and equitably; and interspecies equity refers to the maintenance of ecosystem integrity and upholds the value of biodiversity. These principles help give clarity to the ideas of sustainable development, link human equity to the environment and provide a useful basis for evaluation of the different trends of sustainable development. The literature on sustainability highlights two types of equity, inter-generational and intra-generational, as being particularly salient in understanding social and community development concepts (Hopwood *et al.*, 2005; Jabareen, 2008). The Brundtland Report emphasized that inter-generational equity in particular could not be achieved unless the environmental impacts of economic activity were being attended to. Although equity factors prominently in sustainability discourse, social sustainability has been largely ignored as a wider debate has focused on environmental and economic issues (Littig and Griessler, 2005).

From a business perspective, the concept of sustainability is a central component of social responsibility for corporations whose fundamental imperative is profit. As Porter and Kramer (2006) noted, sustainability emphasizes environmental and community stewardship as key components of a social responsibility agenda. Further, with CSR there is the tension of balancing different economic, legal, ethical, and social responsibilities with a range of stakeholders, each bringing different values and expectations. Sustainability is not simply the question of finding the means to equitably balance seemingly contradictory principles, but doing so in a context that extends well beyond the human actors concerned. Thus the sustainability agenda, by definition, addresses the implications of ecological dependency and global social impacts of local behaviors (Moon, 2007). A focus on environmental ethics and social responsibility has led to the adoption of this agenda within the context of events.

Sustainability and the Olympic Movement

The IOC adopted its own version of Agenda 21 in 1999. The Olympic Movement's Agenda 21 initially set up three objectives which focused primarily on environmental sustainability: 1) improving socio-economic conditions; 2) conservation and management of resources for sustainable development; and 3) strengthening the role of major groups. Although the IOC has highlighted the main objectives of its Agenda 21, the emphasis has been in the area of environmental sustainability and includes the adoption and promotion of energy saving practices, use of renewable energy sources, and environmental education programs (see also Chapter 8: Zhang, Jin, Li and Kim on environmental impact of major sports events on Asian cities). The IOC's policies regarding sustainability have been geared toward the regular activities of the members of the Olympic Movement, and were voluntary rather than explicit regulations. These policies also did not address the bidding and organizing of the Olympic Games (IOC, 1999). In 2000, the IOC implemented the Olympic Games Global Impact (OGI) initiative in order to measure the impact of the Olympic Games on the host city and region. The OGI encompasses a framework for standardizing the measurement of the economic, social, and environmental impacts of the Olympic Games through a series of indicators (IOC, 2006).

Hosting an Olympic Games is often expected to yield significant economic and tourism benefits (Getz, 1997; Hall, 1992) as well as improve the host city's infrastructure (Hiller, 2006). However, staging the Games has resulted in negative impacts such as underutilized sport facilities (Lenskyj, 2000), massive public debt (Burbank *et al.*, 2002), and the displacement of residents (Burton, 2003; Hall and Hodges, 1997). The literature on the impacts of the Olympic Games on the host city/region and citizens focuses mainly on the economic and tourism effects of the Games (Chalip and Leyns, 2002; Crompton, 1995, 2004), while the long-term social and environmental impacts do not feature as prominently. Recently, there has been an increase in studies which identify mega-events' potential to generate positive social impacts such as increasing civic pride, raising awareness of disability, and increasing voluntarism (Misener and Mason, 2006; Smith, 2009). Recognizing the growing interest in the social impact of hosting the Games, in 2011 the IOC amended its Olympic Charter to include "social responsibility" as part of its fundamental principles of Olympism, stating that:

> Olympism is a philosophy of life, exalting and combining in a balanced whole the qualities of body, will and mind. Blending sport with culture and education, Olympism seeks to create a way of life based on the joy of effort, the educational value of good example, social responsibility and respect for universal fundamental ethical principles.
>
> (IOC, 2011: 10)

Despite the recent attention to social impacts, social sustainability is still regarded as the least explored element in the widely accepted definition of sustainable development (Smith, 2009). There continues to be much criticism over the ability of an event embedded in neoliberal philosophies of development such as the Olympic Games to enhance the social well-being of communities. In fact, critical scholars have argued that few benefits from hosting Olympic Games accrue to the most disadvantaged in communities, and that these events only serve to further marginalize communities (i.e., Hiller, 2006; Olds, 1998). However, an alternative perspective suggests that events can act as interventionist levers to influence public sector activities and increase the potential for social sustainability (Black, 2008). We subscribe to a similar theoretical positioning as Smith (2009) and Black (2008) by arguing that these events offer the potential that create opportunities for social sustainability through socially responsible investments and sustainable development opportunities. As Lenskyj (2008) has also argued, social responsibility should be added to sport, culture, and the environment as the "fourth pillar" of the Olympic Movement. Vancouver, host of the 2010 Winter Olympic and Paralympic Games, committed to planning and hosting the world's first sustainable Olympic Games. The host's commitment to sustainability was in line with a locally held vision of a sustainable city and region. Thus, we utilize the following case study to examine the ways in which CSR is embedded in the hosting of the 2010 Olympic and Paralympic Games through the ethos of sustainability. We begin by examining the rhetoric of the Games philosophy, and then provide some specific examples of how this manifestation of multiple forms of sustainability has been played out in the process of hosting the event.

Case study: the 2010 Vancouver Olympic and Paralympic Games

Vancouver's quest to host the 2010 Winter Olympic and Paralympic Games began in February 1998 when a group of Vancouver citizens approached the Vancouver City Council for approval to launch an Olympic bid. Quebec City and Calgary were also in contention to be Canada's bid city. In late 1998 the Canadian Olympic Committee selected Vancouver to represent the country's bid for the Games and in 2002 the IOC Executive Board selected Vancouver to be one of the four finalist cities. A public referendum was held in Vancouver in February 2003, with 64 percent of the voters approving the city's Olympic bid. In July 2003, Vancouver was selected to host the 2010 Winter Olympic and Paralympic Games and committed to hosting the world's first sustainable Olympic Games (VANOC 2010, 2006). As a result, two separate organizations were formed: 1) The Vancouver Olympic and Paralympic Organizing Committee (VANOC); and 2) 2010 Legacies Now. VANOC was the entity responsible for planning, organizing, and staging the Games. In the early stages VANOC's main aims were to secure millions of dollars in local sponsorships and to develop and implement the sustainability program, which included a focus on environmental planning, community programs, and investment in Vancouver's inner-city. 2010 Legacies Now was considered the social development arm of VANOC; its mandate included the promotion of sport development, arts, literacy, volunteering, as well as accessibility and inclusion. As a not-for-profit organization 2010 Legacies Now was intended to help broker the opportunities presented by partnering with various levels of government, other non-government organizations (NGOs), and the Vancouver 2010 corporate sponsors to create sustainable legacies in the Province of BC and the host communities. Sustainability was a key feature in both VANOC's and 2010 Legacies Now's vision, mission, and value statements (see Tables 14.1 and 14.2).

Table 14.1 VANOC's vision, mission, and value statements

Vision	A stronger Canada whose spirit is raised by its passion for sport, culture, and sustainability
Mission	To touch the soul of the nation and to inspire the world by creating and delivering an extraordinary Olympic and Paralympic experience with lasting legacies
Values	Team: fair play, respect, compassion, accountability, and inclusion
	Trust: integrity, honesty, respect, fairness, and compassion
	Excellence: recognition, compassion, and accountability
	Sustainability: financial, economic, social, and environmental
	Creativity: innovation, flexibility, and adaptability

Source: *Vancouver 2010*. Available at: http://www.vancouver2010.com/en/aboutvanoc/organizing-committee/-/32756/129v23m/index.html (accessed: October 11, 2012).

Table 14.2 2010 Legacies Now's vision, mission, and value statements

Vision	To create sustainable legacies that will benefit all British Columbians as a result of hosting the 2010 Olympic and Paralympic Winter Games
Mission	To work in partnership with community organizations, non-government organizations, the private sector, and all levels of government to develop sustainable legacies in sport and recreation, healthy living, arts, literacy, accessibility, and volunteerism
	To actively assist communities to discover and create unique and inclusive social and economic opportunities leading up to and beyond the 2010 Olympic and Paralympic Winter Games
Values	Trust and respect
	Innovation and creativity
	Collaboration and teamwork
	Celebration
	Integrity

Source: *2010 LegaciesNow*. Available at: http://www.2010andbeyond.ca/media/pdf/Catalyst_Collaborator_Connector_The_Social_Innovation_Model_of_2010_Legacies_Now.pdf (accessed: October 11, 2012).

VANOC was the first Organizing Committee of an Olympic Games (OCOG) to integrate sustainability into its mission, vision, and value statements and to apply sustainability principles in the Olympic Games' planning, organizing, and delivery (VANOC, 2006). VANOC's working definition of sustainability was "managing the social, economic and environmental impacts and opportunities of our Games to produce lasting benefits, locally and globally" (VANOC, 2010: 2). The host city contract signed by the IOC and VANOC detailed the expectations for the delivery of social, economic, and environmental benefits to the city. With its commitment to hosting the first sustainable Games, VANOC had to deliver these outcomes with minimal negative impact on the city, its citizens, and the region.

2010 Legacies Now was established in 2000 by the province of British Columbia (BC) and the Vancouver 2010 Bid Corporation in support of Vancouver's bid for the 2010 Olympic and Paralympic Winter Games. In 2002, the society was registered as an independent, not-for-profit organization. Its vision was "to create sustainable legacies that will benefit all of BC and Canada as a result of hosting the 2010 Olympic and Paralympic Winter Games" (2010 Legacies Now, 2012). 2010 Legacies Now sought to leverage opportunities in key areas of its mandate, such as funding and promoting sport development from playground to podium, advancing physical activity and healthy living, and building community capacity leading up to and beyond 2010 (2010 Legacies Now, 2012). The organization employed three central strategies: 1) to create mutually beneficial partnerships; 2) to be a highly engaged funding organization, and 3) to use innovative methods to broaden its reach (Weiler, 2011). Key partners involved in the programs included all three levels of government (federal, provincial, and municipal) as well as companies such Coca Cola Corporation, Ronald McDonald House, RBC Financial, Bell Canada, 3M Corporation, CTV, and Rona.

Vancouver, like many major cities worldwide, has a number of growing social issues. In order to promote social sustainability the Vancouver Bid Corporation (and later VANOC) attempted to incorporate these issues into their plans in order to leverage the Games to promote improvements in areas such as social inclusion and low-income housing. One of the most publicized problems in the city was the high level of mental illness, drug, addiction, poverty, and prostitution in the inner-city neighborhood known as the Downtown Eastside (DTES). The DTES is also home to one-third of the city's First Nations people, who represent 30 percent of the homeless population (Cardinal, 2006). In response to problems in the DTES, the Vancouver Agreement was signed in March 2000. The Vancouver Agreement is an urban development initiative through which the governments of Canada, British Columbia, and Vancouver collaborate and coordinate resources for projects and initiatives to make the city a healthy, safe and sustainable place to live and work for all residents.

A social sustainability statement entitled the *Inner-City Inclusive Commitment Statement* (ICICS) was included in Vancouver's bid for the 2010 Winter Olympic Games. The ICICS outlined the goals and objectives in the planning for and hosting of an inclusive Winter Olympics Games. The statement specifically promised to ensure DTES residents would have meaningful input into the processes and planning of the 2010 Winter Olympics, would not experience hardship or displacement as a result of the event, and would benefit from affordable housing and other social legacies. Since the statement was included as part of the winning bid submitted by the then Vancouver Bid Corporation, it was adopted by VANOC and 2010 Legacies Now after winning the bid. As a result, VANOC became accountable for fulfilling the ICICS to the IOC, the City of Vancouver, and to its partners to reach the goals outlined in the ICICS. Vancouver was therefore considered the first Olympic Games host city to embody the principles of social and economic sustainability in all activities leading up to and during the Games (Vancouver Agreement, 2005). The work of the VANOC has been recognized through an Institute of Public Administration of Canada award in 2004 for innovative public service management (Vancouver Agreement, 2004) and the United Nations Public Service Award in 2005.

2010 Legacies Now relied heavily on corporate involvement in its effort to create sustainable social legacies for the city of Vancouver and the Province of British Columbia. Table 14.3 highlights some of the programs initiated by 2010 Legacies Now and the corporate partners involved in the sustainable management of these legacies. Many of these corporate partners utilized their partnership with 2010 Legacies Now as part of their own CSR agendas. For example, Bell Canada, a leading Canadian telecommunications company, highlighted its extensive involvement in 2010 Legacies Now programs such as the Accessibility and Inclusivity and the development of the Squamish Lil'Wat (First Nations) Cultural Centre, in its annual CSR report (BCE Inc., 2009, 2010).

Here we are able to see a distinct focus on the ways in which environmental, economic, and social sustainability intersect in order to create a sustainable development opportunity. While there are numerous critiques regarding Aboriginal involvement in the Games, the creation of the Cultural Centre demonstrates how corporate involvement is supporting sustainable development activities, but also ensuring sound value creation for the company through its branding and sustainable reporting efforts.

Table 14.3 Areas of social engagement/sustainability employed by 2010 Legacies Now

Areas of social engagement	Examples of programs	Corporate partner involvement
Literacy and lifelong learning	Heroes Live Here, Parents As Literacy Supporters (PALS), RBC 2010 Legacies Now Speaker Series, Leap BC	Royal Bank of Canada (RBC), CTV, The Vancouver Sun
Sport and healthy living	B.C. Sport Participation Program, Chill, Inner–City Sport Court Project, SportFit, ActNow BC Tours, Zero Ceiling, Game Plan BC, Hosting BC Grants, Action School BC	CTV, Vancouver Canuks (NHL), Bell Canada, Coca Cola, Sport Canada
Aboriginal engagement	Aboriginal Youth Sport Legacy Fund, Aboriginal Sport Participation Bilateral Program, Aboriginal Sport Gallery	Four Host First Nations, Province of BC, and Vancouver Organizing Committee for the 2010 Olympic and Paralympic Winter Games (VANOC)
Arts	Innovations, Catalyst, Explorations, Arts Partners in Creative Development, Infusion: Arts in Education	Canada Council for the Arts, City of Vancouver, Vancouver Foundation, and VANOC
Accessibility	Measuring Up, Virtual Voices Village, AccessWORKS	Ronald McDonald House Charities of Canada, Rick Hansen Foundation

Source: *About us.* Available at: http://www.2010legaciesnow.com/about-us (accessed: October 11, 2012).

VANOC's sustainability management and reporting

VANOC was the first OGOC to create *a sustainability governance model for organizations under-taking the delivery of large sporting events*. A Sustainability Management and Reporting System (SMRS) was also established which served "to foster organization-wide, cross-functional responsibility and public accountability for performance on sustainability commitments and objective" (VANOC, 2010: 28). This transformed the three elements of sustainability – social, economic, and environment – into six main performance objectives, which were included in its strategic and business plans. These objectives were: 1) accountability, 2) environmental stewardship, 3) social inclusion and responsibility, 4) sport for sustainable living, 5) Aboriginal participation, and 6) economic benefits (VANOC, 2010: 23).

The SMRS was the mechanism used to put the organization's bid commitments and sustainability performance objectives into action. In order to develop its reporting system, VANOC incorporated the Global Reporting Initiative (GRI), which is an international method for evaluating economic, environmental, and social performance. Also guiding the SMRS were the AA1000 Accountability Principles Standard (AA1000APS) and the AA1000 Stakeholder Engagement Standard (AA1000SES) for identifying stakeholder groups for engagement, selecting issues on which to address in the sustainability reports, and in ensuring responsiveness to feedback. VANOC has produced five sustainability reports; the first was released in 2005 and the last in 2009. The sustainability reports were VANOC's attempt at encouraging accountability and transparency in the planning, organizing, and staging of the 2010 Winter Olympic Games. This reporting system established a framework for mega sporting events to monitor and evaluate their CSR performance.

Vancouver's pledge of hosting the most sustainable Olympic Games was met with some criticism. For example, Eby (2007) questioned whether VANOC's self-regulation of its commitments was a realistic approach to social sustainability. The author identified VANOC's need for more precise commitments to social sustainability, difficulty in measurement as well as the absence of any enforcement mechanisms in the event that there was a disregard of the commitment statements to achieving social sustainability. Although the Vancouver Agreement was considered to be an effective framework for intergovernmental cooperation by VANOC, it was also heavily critiqued, as the organizational infrastructure was simply not in place to facilitate horizontal monitoring and evaluation (Mason, 2007). Further, critics also argued that despite VANOC's early efforts to encompass and encourage sound principles of equity in its sustainable development agenda, these went by the wayside as economic restraints were imposed in the wake of the recession (Lee, 2009). Despite these criticisms, VANOC's emphasis on sustainability in its strategic and business plans as well as the collaboration of the federal, provincial, and municipal governments through the Vancouver Agreement have set a benchmark in relation to social responsibility for future hosts of the Olympic Games. They also demonstrate the increasing emphasis being placed on social responsibility in sport and events through targeted initiatives and corporate involvement.

Conclusions

As the notion of CSR has become more salient and increasingly important to businesses, sports organizations have also made efforts to demonstrate socially sustainable activities (Babiak and Trendafilova, 2011; Sheth and Babiak, 2010). While there has been little focus in the academic literature on the use of events to focus attention on CSR efforts save some primarily theoretical discussions (Misener and Mason, 2010; Smith, 2009), it is clear that increasingly events are being used to serve a broader agenda of social responsibility and sustainable development. The recent efforts by Vancouver stakeholders involved in the preparations and hosting of the 2010 Winter Olympic and Paralympic Games described above presents some interesting implications for future opportunities to leverage major event hosting for community development purposes. As sustainability and community development are increasingly becoming a targeted agenda of the Olympic Movement and the cities hosting the events themselves, there will be opportunities for companies more interested in engaging in CSR to formally link to the IOC and specific games.

The result of this increased attention on social responsibility and community development surrounding events also suggests that potentially some of the longstanding partners of the IOC might see weaker associations with the Games if they do not also adopt the principles of social responsibility; meanwhile, other companies may find that this new focus on sustainability may link their products and services more credibly to the Olympic Movement than previously. Regardless, these changes in the mindset of the IOC and the communities bidding for and hosting the Games will result in companies adapting to the new opportunities that a focus on sustainability presents. We believe that this interventionist approach to development through the Games creates opportunities for social sustainability through socially responsible investments and sustainable development opportunities. However, we echo Lenskyj's (2008) comments that if we are to truly believe that the Games should enhance social sustainability and community development, then social responsibility should be added to sport, culture, and the environment as the "fourth pillar" of the Olympic Movement.

References

Babiak, K. and Trendafilova, S. (2011) 'CSR and environmental responsibility: motives and pressures to adopt green management practices', *Corporate Social Responsibility and Environmental Management*, 18 (1), 11–24.

BCE Inc. (2009) *Putting the spotlight on corporate responsibility*. Available from http://www.bce.ca/assets/Uploads/Documents/archivesCRReports/Bell_2009_CR_report_accessible_format_en.pdf (accessed: March 10, 2012).

BCE Inc. (2010) *Lets talk about sustainability*. Available from http://www.bce.ca/assets/Uploads/Documents/archivesCRReports/Bell_2010_CR_Report_en.pd (accessed: March 10, 2012).

Black, D. (2008) 'Dreaming big: The pursuit of 'second order' games as a strategic response to globalization', *Sport in Society*, 11 (4), 467–480.

Burbank, M. J., Andranovich, G., and Heying, C. H. (2002) 'Mega-events, urban development, and public policy', *Review of Policy Research*, 19, 179–202.

Burton, R. (2003) 'Olympic Games host city marketing: An exploration of expectations and outcomes', *Sport Marketing Quarterly*, 12 (1), 35–45.

Cardinal, N. (2006) 'The inclusive city: Identifying, measuring, and drawing attention to aboriginal and indigenous experiences in an urban context', *Cities*, 23, 217–228.

Chalip, L. and Leyns, A. (2002) 'Local business leveraging of a sport event: Managing an event for economic benefit', *Journal of Sport Management*, 16, 132–158.

Crompton, J. L. (1995) 'Economic impact analysis of sports facilities and events: Eleven sources of misapplication', *Journal of Sport Management*, 9, 14–35.

Crompton, J. L. (2004) 'Conceptualization and alternate operationalizations of the measurement of sponsorship effectiveness in sport', *Leisure Studies*, 23 (3), 267–281.

Eby, D. (2007) *Still waiting at the altar: Vancouver 2010's on-again, off-again, relationship with social sustainability*, paper presented at the COHRE expert workshop on protecting and promoting housing rights in the context of mega events, Geneva, Switzerland, June. Available at: http://intraspec.ca/EbyJune2007.pdf (accessed: November 15, 2012).

Getz, D. (1997) *Event management and event tourism*. New York: Cognizant.

Girginov, V. and Hills, L. (2008) 'A sustainable sports legacy: Creating a link between the London Olympics and sports participation', *The International Journal of the History of Sport*, 25, 2091–2116.

Hall, C. M. (1992) *Hallmark tourist events: Impacts, management, and planning.* London: Belhaven Press.

Hall, C.M. and Hodges, J. (1997) 'Sharing the spirit of corporatism and cultural capital: The politics of place and identity in the Sydney 2000 Olympics', in Roche, M. (ed.) *Sport, popular culture and identity.* Verlag, Aachen: Meyer & Meyer, pp. 95–112.

Haughton G. (1999) 'Environmental justice and the sustainable city', *Journal of Planning Education and Research,* 18, 233–243.

Hiller, H. (2006) 'Post event-outcomes and the post-modern turn', *European Sport Management Quarterly,* 6, 317–332.

Holtz, S. (1998) 'Integrating environmental, social and economic policies', in Schnurr, J. and Holtz, S. (eds.) *The cornerstone of development.* Ottawa: IDRC, pp. 283–293.

Hopwood, B., Mellor, M., and O'Brien, G. (2005) 'Sustainable development: Mapping different approaches', *Sustainable Development,* 13, 38–52.

Hunter, C. (1997) 'Sustainable tourism as an adaptive paradigm', *Annals of Tourism Research,* 24, 850–867.

International Olympic Committee (IOC) (1999) *Olympic movement's agenda 21: Sport for sustainable development.* Lausanne: Sport and Environment Commission.

International Olympic Committee (IOC) (2006) 'What is the Olympic Games global impact study?' *Focus Olympic Review,* 6, 1–2.

International Olympic Committee (IOC) (2011) *Olympic Charter.* Lausanne: International Olympic Committee. Available at: http://olympic.org/Documents/olympic_charter_en.pdf (accessed: November 15, 2012).

Jabareen, Y. (2008) 'A new conceptual framework for sustainable development', *Environment, Development and Sustainability,* 10, 179–192.

Lee, J. (2009) 'Potential 2010 profits eaten up'. *Vancouver Sun,* April 2. Available from: http://www.vancouversun.com/Potential+2010+Winter+Olympics+profit+eaten/1453598/story.html (accessed: November 15, 2012).

2010 Legacies Now (2012) *About us.* Available from http://www.2010legaciesnow.com/about-us (accessed: March 15, 2012).

Lenskyj, H. J. (2000) *Inside the Olympic industry: Power politics and activism.* Albany, New York: SUNY Press.

Lenskyj, H. (2008) *Olympic industry resistance: Challenging Olympic power & propaganda.* Albany, New York: SUNY Press.

Littig, B. and Griessler, E. (2005) 'Social sustainability: A catchword between political pragmatism and social theory', *International Journal for Sustainable Development,* 8, 65–79.

Mason, M. (2007) 'Collaborative partnerships for urban development: a study of the Vancouver Agreement', *Environment and planning A,* 39, 2366–2382.

Misener, L. and Mason, D. S. (2006) 'Creating community networks: Can sporting events offer meaningful sources of social capital?' *Managing Leisure,* 11, 39–56.

Misener, L. and Mason, D. S. (2010) 'Towards a community centred approach to corporate community involvement in the sporting events agenda', *Journal of Management & Organization,* 16 (4), 495–514.

Moon, J. (2007) 'Responsibility to sustainable development', *Sustainable Development,* 15, 296–306.

Olds, K. (1998) 'Urban mega-events, evictions and housing rights: The Canadian case', *Current Issues in Tourism,* 1, (1), 2–46.

Porter, M. E. and Kramer, M. R. (2006) 'Strategy and society: The link between competitive advantage and corporate social responsibility', *Harvard Business Review,* 78–93.

Sheth, H. and Babiak, K. (2010) 'Beyond the Game: Perceptions and practices of corporate social responsibility in the professional sport industry', *Journal of Business Ethics,* 91, 433–450.

Smith, A. (2009) 'Theorising the relationship between major sport events and social sustainability', *Journal of Sport & Tourism,* 14, 109–120.

Vancouver Agreement (2004) *Vancouver agreement wins highest award for innovative public service management.* Available at: http://www.vancouveragreement.ca/wp-content/uploads/award_public_service.pdf (accessed: November 15, 2012).

Vancouver Agreement (2005) *The Vancouver agreement.* Available at: http://www.vancouveragreement.ca/wp-content/uploads/2005_VA-UrbanDev-cn-bc-van.pdf (accessed: November 15, 2012).

VANOC (2006) *Vancouver 2010 sustainability report 2005–6.* Available at: http://wiki.sustainable-sport.org/@api/deki/files/163/=VANOCsustainability_report_2005-06.pdf (accessed: November 26, 2012).

VANOC (2010) *Vancouver 2010 sustainability report 2009–10*. Available at: http://www.2010legaciesnow. com/fileadmin/user_upload/About_Us/VANOC/SUS-1261_Sustainability_Report_09-10.pdf (accessed: November 26, 2012).

World Commission on Environment and Development (WCED) (1987) *Our common future. World Commission on Environment and Development*. Oxford: Oxford University Press.

Weiler, J. (2011) *The evolution of 2010 LEGACIES NOW: A continuing legacy of the 2010 Winter Games through venture philanthropy*. Available at: http://www.liftpartners.ca/wp-content/uploads/IOC-case-study-2_2011_The-Evolution-of-2010-Legacies-Now_A-Continuing-Legacy-of-the-Games.pdf (accessed: August 29, 2012).

15

OLYMPICS, SOCIAL RESPONSIBILITY AND STAKEHOLDERS

Milena M. Parent and Jean-Loup Chappelet

Overview

The International Olympic Committee (IOC) is the rights holder of the Olympic Games. It is also arguably at the top of the international sport governance system. Just like Organizing Committees of Olympic Games (OCOGs) need multiple stakeholders to host a given edition of an Olympic Games, so too does the IOC interact with different stakeholders in its corporate social responsibility (CSR) activities. Here, stakeholders are those individuals, groups, and organizations that can impact, or be affected by the actions of, the focal organization, the IOC in this case (Freeman, 1984; Parent, 2008). What is unclear however, is how do Olympic stakeholders affect the IOC in its CSR activities and how are they impacted by the IOC's activities at the Games and beyond? The purpose of this chapter is to explore the relationships between the IOC, OCOGs, and other stakeholders in relation to the IOC's CSR activities. We first provide an overview of the IOC and its stakeholders and propose a stakeholder map which reveals seven key stakeholders for Olympic CSR. We then discuss the IOC's CSR activities, contrasting them with other sport organizations' CSR initiatives. We end the chapter with concluding remarks and future directions.

The IOC and its stakeholders

In its charter, the IOC sets out the rules, regulations, and responsibilities for itself and the key stakeholders involved in the Olympic Games (Chappelet, 2009; IOC, 2011a). As such, the IOC's primary sphere of activity is the Olympic Games, and it has a number of stakeholders with whom it deals in this regard: OCOGs, National Olympic Committees (NOCs) and their national team athletes, International Sports Federations (IFs), sponsors, the media, host governments, and IOC and OCOG paid/volunteer staff. Other stakeholders who are part of the Olympic Games though may indirectly deal with the IOC include the general public (i.e., the ticket buyers/consumers) and other community groups/organizations (e.g., activist groups). Figure 15.1 provides an overview of the IOC's myriad of stakeholders.

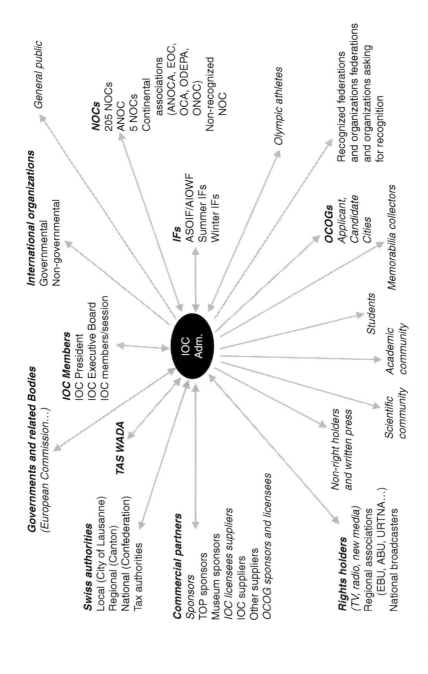

Figure 15.1 The IOC and its stakeholders

Source: International Olympic Committee (2005)

Such a simplistic view, however, is not very helpful for understanding the IOC's social responsibility to each of these groups and the interactions in which they engage. Following Post *et al.* (2002) who propose three concentric rings for classifying stakeholders, we suggest a new "Olympic Stakeholder View" which we believe is useful for the strategic analysis and management of the extended enterprise into which the IOC is evolving and which is known by the name the "Olympic Movement." This Movement is "the concerted, organised, universal and permanent action, carried out under the supreme authority of the IOC, of all individuals and entities who are inspired by the values of Olympism" (IOC Olympic Charter fundamental principle 3, 2011a: 10).

In this new view, stakeholders are drawn in a three-ring concentric diagram to demonstrate the degree of closeness to the IOC (and conversely, the IOC's sense of responsibility towards these stakeholders) following Post *et al.*'s (2002) resource-based, industry structure-based, and socio-political arena-based stakeholder classification system (see Figure 15.2). Post *et al.*'s system differs from past classifications such as Clarkson's (1995) primary/secondary stakeholder groups or Mitchell *et al.*'s (1997) power–legitimacy–urgency approach (Chappelet, 2009; Parent, 2008). However, Post *et al.*'s system does allow for Carroll's (1991) pyramid of responsibilities (1. economic, 2. legal, 3. ethical, and 4. philanthropic/discretionary) to be considered. We therefore used Post and colleagues' and Carroll's models to build our IOC stakeholder classification map.

What we see is that the OCOGs, IOC members, and staff, as well as sponsors and media rights holders form those stakeholders most closely engaged with the IOC as they have a resource-based relationship (mainly financial), as well as a legal relationship. For example, the IOC holds the rights to the Olympic Games, which are entrusted to an OCOG for a given edition of the Games; the IOC members or staff are its trustees or employees and have legal rights and obligations toward the IOC. The IOC has contracts with The Olympic Partners (TOP) program sponsors and media rights holders, in particular broadcasting organizations, where these organizations can use the Olympic symbols in return for a financial contribution; and the Olympians (i.e., the athletes who participate in the Olympics) sign an entry form which specifies their moral right and obligations as participants. In a similar fashion, we could draw a stakeholder map for OCOGs who have resource-based stakeholders such as their own trustees and staff, sponsors, providers, and ticket holders. All these resource-based stakeholders are generally closely associated with the IOC's CSR strategy and involved the delivery of the CSR-based activities.

The second ring of Figure 15.2 regroups the stakeholders that are part of the Olympic and sport industry structure. All the actors in this ring can play an important role in the organization of the Olympic Games, but they are not bound by exclusive legal or financial relationships. The NOCs and the IFs traditionally receive a share of the Olympic Games sponsoring and broadcasting rights although the principle of these payments are not mentioned in the Olympic Charter. But these stakeholders have other revenues and activities apart from the Olympic Games, such as organizing the sport movement in their own countries, participating in regional games, organizing international competitions, and establishing rules for their sport. By sending Olympic teams and providing judges and referees respectively, the NOCs and IFs are an essential part of the Games, but are legally independent entities and not the main resource base of the IOC. Other stakeholders on this second ring are even less bound to the IOC: National Sport Federations (NFs), clubs, professional sport leagues, sport ministries, the Association of NOCs (ANOC), and the Association of IFs (SportAccord). The World Anti Doping Agency (WADA) and the Court of Arbitration for Sport are now essential for the regulation of the sport industry. They are mostly financed by the IOC, the NOCs, and the IFs (and the governments for WADA), but pride themselves in being independent. All these industry structure-based stakeholders can be associated with the IOC's CSR activities but can also have their own CSR activities.

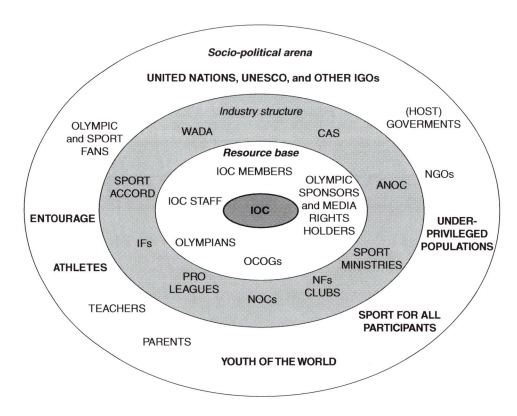

Figure 15.2 The Olympic stakeholder view

The IOC also engages in a second sphere of activity, one not directly associated with the hosting of an Olympic Games. Given that philanthropic responsibilities come at the top of Carroll's pyramid (once the other responsibilities have been met), it is perhaps not surprising that the typical IOC stakeholder map (see Figure 15.1) does not reflect the presence of other stakeholders from the socio-political arena who do engage (directly or indirectly) with the IOC. The third ring of Figure 15.2 provides an overview of the stakeholders towards whom the IOC's CSR activities are directed. Seven stakeholders emerge from this circle as important:

1 *Athletes*: the IOC feels a responsibility towards athletes to ensure fair and ethical competition, even if they are not Olympians. However, it feels a responsibility towards athletes not only during their competitive career, but also after their retirement from competition. This is why the IOC has developed, since 2003 with a sponsor (Adecco), an athlete career program focusing on education, life skills, and employment (see IOC, 2011b).
2 *Youth*: the IOC has identified the youth of the world as a key stakeholder, creating the Youth Olympic Games to inspire young people around the world to participate in sport and adopt and live by the Olympic values in order to build and maintain the Olympic philosophy and brand identity in an important segment of the population (see IOC, 2009a). Further to Recommendation 54 of the 2009 Olympic Congress, the Olympic Movement is to develop and implement programs to explain to families and parents that helping their children choose a career path in competitive sport is highly worthwhile for their overall development and well-being. Further to Recommendation 50, the IOC has established a strategy and operational

team to: attract young people to and retain them in competitive sport; help to actively engage young people in sport and physical activity as a way to reduce sedentary behaviour; promote the benefits of Olympism as a philosophy of life among young people; identify ways to put young people's aspirations and needs at the heart of the organization; develop young people's interest in the broadcast of the Olympic Games (IOC, 2011c, Recommendations 46 and 54).

3   *Entourage*: recently, the IOC created an entourage commission to examine the (sometimes negative) influence of (often young) athletes' entourage members, who can include coaches, trainers, nutritionists, other medical support staff, equipment/service providers, high-level training centers, government, school/universities, unions, lawyers, managers and agents, among others (see IOC, 2009b). However, these stakeholders are arguably not as important for the IOC as the athletes themselves and/or the youth, as the former are those who could participate in the Olympic competitions and the latter are the IOC's future clients.

4   *Sport for All participants*: the IOC has had, since the 1980s, a Sport for All commission and regularly organizes Sport for All congresses. Since 2005, this sector has been reinforced to ensure that other aspects of sport, beyond elite sport, are taken into consideration to promote health, fitness, and well-being through sporting activities adapted to people of all ages, both genders and various social and economic conditions. One of the main activities in this CSR area is the Olympic Day Run (see IOC, n.d.), which is organized by many NOCs in one or several cities of their respective countries and which is based on popular road races, targeted especially to children and young people.

5   *Underprivileged populations*: the IOC, in partnership with various international governmental organizations (IGOs, see below) and non-governmental organizations (NGOs, see below), implement Sport for All, development, education, women, peace, and environment through sport programs in third world countries. These programs allow the IOC to promote the Olympic values and put them in action within underprivileged populations (see IOC, 2011d).

6   *IGOs*: in their interactions with underprivileged populations of the world, the IOC engages with key international IGOs to put its Olympic values in action. The CSR actions/activities are led by the IGOs (in contrast to the point above where the IOC leads the actions/activities). Some notable IGO examples include:

a   The United Nations (UN) and its Millennium Development Goals (MDGs) focus on fostering maternal health, gender equality, education, environmental sustainability, and global partnerships, while reducing child hunger, mortality and disease, and poverty (see United Nations Office on Sport for Development and Peace, 2011). In addition, the UN General Assembly granted in 2009 an observer status to the IOC, which facilitates its contacts with the UN system of organizations.

b   The United Nations Education, Scientific and Cultural Organization (UNESCO) is interested in education, youth, peace, mutual respect, sustainable development, gender equality, and reducing poverty. It undertakes the UN's MDGs through their spheres of activity in the sciences, education, information, and cultural and communication (UNESCO, 2011). In 1979, UNESCO adopted the International Charter for Physical Education and Sport; and in 2005, it adopted the international convention against doping in sport. Other IGOs, such as the World Health Organization (WHO) and the United Nations Environmental Program (UNEP), have undertaken some actions with the IOC in their domains of interest. For example, the IOC cooperates with the UNEP on the environmental assessment of the Olympic Games and with the WHO on the promotion of healthy lifestyles and grassroots sport activities worldwide.

7   *NGOs*: The IOC has partnered with a few NGOs, such as The International Committee
    of the Red Cross (ICRC), Generation for Peace, and Olympic Aid, to provide rehabilita-
    tion through sport programs and safe children's playgrounds in war-torn countries. The
    IOC, being itself a NGO, does not want its message to be hijacked by other NGOs. This
    policy is based on its very first CSR activities which began when Johann Olav Koss, a
    Norwegian skier, became an IOC member and created Olympic Aid in 1992, an organiza-
    tion led by Olympic athletes acting as fundraising ambassadors for humanitarian programs
    in war-torn regions (e.g., Sarajevo hospital, Eritrea schools, and Afghanistan refugee sup-
    port). When Koss left the IOC, the organization changed its name to Right To Play (in
    part because the IOC did not want the organization to use the word Olympic) and was less
    and less involved in partnerships with the IOC (see Right To Play, 2010).

Figure 15.2 therefore demonstrates in its outer ring the often neglected, forgotten or removed
stakeholders from the typical IOC stakeholder map depicted in Figure 15.1.

The IOC's CSR-related activities

While not explicitly stated as being CSR activities, today, the IOC has six main spheres that
could be associated to CSR, each with different activities (IOC, 2011d):

1   *Sport for All*: activities, such as the Sport for All conference and the funding of Sport for
    All projects, promote the idea that sport belongs to everyone. At the September 2011
    Sport for All Conference in Beijing, China, "participants called for increased collaboration
    between the various entities involved in promoting the benefits of Sport for All activities,
    the use of tools such as social media to get the message out and promote dialogue, and
    the organization of Sport for All events wherever possible" (IOC, 2011e: 1). Another key
    initiative is Olympic Day. Each year around June 23, the IOC calls on the world to get
    active and reach their sporting goals. In 2011, millions of people participated in worldwide
    educational, cultural, and sports events. Those who used social media sites like Twitter
    and Facebook could also win a trip to the 2012 London Olympic Games. Future Olympic
    host cities, namely Sochi and Rio, leveraged Olympic Day to also promote their event and
    sport participation (IOC, 2011f).
2   *Development through sport*: activities such as the Giving is Winning solidarity campaign try
    to put human beings first. The IOC partners with the UN's High Commissioner for
    Refugees and OCOGs (currently London 2012) in this endeavour. As well, the IOC
    heads certain international humanity calls, such as providing $100,000 to the UN's High
    Commissioner for Refugees and the World Food program to aid famine relief efforts in
    Somalia where an estimated 9.6 million are desperate for food. The Association of National
    Olympic Committees of Africa (ANOCA) matched this contribution (IOC, 2011g).
3   *Education through sport*: activities such as the Olympic Values Education Program (OVEP)
    are created to develop the body, mind, and will. "OVEP is a tool to maintain young
    people's interest in sport, encouraging them to get moving, and promoting the Olympic
    values" and includes a reference tool (i.e., teaching manual) and a network platform (i.e.,
    interactive database) (IOC, 2010: 1). UNESCO is involved with the IOC at this level as
    well as the International Pierre de Coubertin Committee. OCOGs also offer education
    through sport initiatives, such as London 2012 (London Organizing Committee for the
    Olympic Games or LOCOG) setting up a program encouraging United Kingdom school
    kids to learn about the athletes and cultures of teams coming to the Games (IOC, 2011h).

4   *Women and sport*: the IOC has the Women and Sport Award that promotes women's participation in sport. However, the IOC wishes to go beyond increasing the number of women participating in the Olympic Games; it also believes in the importance of encouraging women to get involved in the management side of sport. As part of this initiative, the IOC, in conjunction with a NOC, hosts the World Conference on Women and Sport. These conferences are held every two years and include plenary and dialogue sessions on various aspects of women and sport (e.g., media, medical issues, attitudes, and sustainability). The last one took place in February 2012 in Los Angeles (IOC, 2011i). These conferences have kept the issue of women and sport on the Olympic Movement's agenda. At the London 2012 Games, half of the new elected IOC members were women (2 out of 4), all Olympic summer sports were open to women (including boxing), and all NOCs had female team members. But much progress should still be made as the IOC barely fulfils its own quota of 20 percent of members in the Olympic Movement's organizations and, in many sports, there are more male than female participants.

5   *Peace through sport*: activities such as the Sport for Peace and Development Forum hope to forge friendships between athletes of all levels. The IOC partners with the UN's Office on Sport for Peace and Development in this endeavor. Before every edition of the Olympic Games, the IOC also asks the UN General Assembly to approve an Olympic Truce resolution. For the 2012 edition of the resolution, a certain Lord Michael Bates walked from Olympia (Greece) to London to encourage individuals to demonstrate "their commitment to the London 2012 Olympic Truce resolution" (IOC, 2011j: 1). The IOC has also funded the organization of a few "Peace Games" by UN peace-keeping missions in Africa. Despite these efforts, wars and conflicts around the world continued through recent Olympic Games.

6   *Environment and sport*: activities such as the World Conference on Sport and the Environment hope to foster the preservation of the world's precious resources. The IOC partners with UNEP for this conference. However, much of the sustainability efforts demonstrated by the Olympic Games stem from OCOGs' efforts to have sustainable buildings and processes such as was the case for Vancouver and is the case for London, Sochi, and Rio (IOC, 2011k).

Throughout these activities, the IOC tries to engage its OCOGs, NOCs, IFs, athletes, sponsors, and other members of the Olympic Movement. In fact, many activities are driven and even paid for by these stakeholders, not (solely) by the IOC.

Olympic Solidarity is the IOC Administration Department which can help the NOCs, in cooperation with IFs, fund activities for some of the Olympic stakeholders such as athletes and their entourage (coaches, physicians, officials, etc.). The large budget for Olympic Solidarity ($311 million for 2009–2012) comes from the NOCs' share of the broadcasting and sponsoring revenues of the Olympic Games. Since 2001, Olympic Solidarity's budget is mostly spent at the continental level under the supervision of the five continental associations of NOCs. Nineteen programs are still run on a worldwide basis from Lausanne in four main areas: athletes, coaches, NOC management, and promotion of Olympic values. The later area focuses on seven activities which can be considered as part of the wider Olympic social responsibility and which more or less match the six main spheres of CSR activities described above: Sports Medicine, Sport and the Environment, Women and Sport, Sport for All, International Olympic Academy, Culture and Education, and NOC Legacy. Fifteen million dollars was earmarked for these seven activities over the years 2009 to 2012 (Olympic Solidarity, 2009).

Unlike the IOC, SportAccord, the association of Olympic and non-Olympic IFs, has recently developed multiple formalized documents about CSR. SportAccord has an interactive social responsibility map depicting its various members' CSR programs and policies associated with the UN's MDGs, child/youth development, health, peace, gender, persons with disabilities, and the environment. Moreover, though, SportAccord incorporated CSR in 2010 within its formal statutes (notably Articles 2.1.1 and 2.1.3, see SportAccord, 2010, 2011) thanks to a partnership with the UN's Office on Sport for Development and Peace. SportAccord also has a dedicated CSR office, called the Sports' Social Responsibility Department (which is managed by a former staff member of the UN's Office on Sport). This department offers services for its members within six special projects: sport and child and youth development; sport and the environment; sport and gender; sport and health; sport and persons with disabilities; and sport and peace. What is interesting is that, for these six projects, SportAccord offers not only advocacy, facilitation, knowledge sharing, and training services/tools, but it also assists in the creation of common standards for these CSR areas.

OCOGs are also doing their part of CSR as members of the Olympic Movement and in cooperation with the IOC, although the OCOGs usually limit their CSR actions to the local or national communities while the IOC addresses communities outside the host country. The Vancouver Organizing Committee for the 2010 Olympic Winter Games (VANOC) was active in two broad areas: sustainability and worker health and safety (see also Misener, Sant and Mason, Chapter 14). In fact, sustainability was one of VANOC's organizational values so it pervaded all functions and was reflected in the annual sustainability reports published demonstrating VANOC's various sustainability and CSR-related activities. For example, VANOC ensured that all its new buildings were LEED (Leadership in Energy and Environmental Design) certified, an independent designation provided to facilities which demonstrate green processes in energy and water efficiency/conservation, reduction of CO_2 emissions, indoor environment quality, and appropriate stewardship of resource use and their impacts. VANOC's flagship venue, the Richmond Olympic Oval, demonstrated this stewardship by being constructed from Stanley Park trees (a Canadian National Historic Site, of 400 hectares of West Coast rainforest) damaged/destroyed following a major windstorm. During the Games, workforce and clients were encouraged to recycle all their drinking bottles with the help of Coca-Cola's recycle bins. Together with the Canadian Standards Association, VANOC launched the Z2010 sustainable event management standard, a first in Canada (The Vancouver Organizing Committee for the 2010 Olympic and Paralympic Winter Games, 2010). With the IOC and the International Academy for Sport Science and Technology, VANOC developed the Sustainable Sport Event toolkit for mega sports events (IOC, 2011l). VANOC also focused a good deal of attention on worker safety, building programs, and setting new standards for the province of British Columbia in partnership with WorkSafeBC. These programs included venue construction health and safety training programs, as well as Games-time health and safety awareness training for the VANOC workforce (Mora, 2010).

Together with the IOC and UEFA, LOCOG developed the Global Reporting Index (GRI) – Event Organizers Sector Supplement, which provides guidelines for sustainability reporting (see Global Reporting Initiative, 2011). LOCOG is also involved in the development and awarding of ISO 26000/ISO 20121 sustainability and social responsibility standards (Pelham, 2011). The follow-up report of the Olympic Congress fully recognizes the GRI Event Organizers Sector Supplement as a relevant standard for reporting on the sustainability and social responsibility of the Olympic Games (IOC, 2011c: 39). The LOCOG implemented this new standard as it was also part of the Event Organizers Sector Supplement working group with the IOC.

While the IOC and its OCOGs are involved in CSR activities, one would expect they are doing this as good global citizens. As Walker and Kent (2009: 743) noted, CSR is "viewed favorably by most fans, and is an important aspect of the overall business strategy of a sport organization," with CSR having a positive impact on sports teams' reputation and consumers' patronage (here, word-of-mouth and merchandise consumption) of the teams. However, a more cynical perspective may argue that these organizations undertake such activities for more strategic and/or economic reasons. When examining consumers' perceptions of the IOC's CSR activities, Walker *et al.* (2010) found that increasing consumers' awareness of stakeholder-driven (society, community focused) and values-driven (socially motivated) CSR activities had an impact on consumers' perceptions, which therefore had a positive impact on outcomes, that is reputation and patronage (here, word-of-mouth, Olympic merchandise consumption, and repeat purchase). However, increased awareness did not seem to impact strategic-driven (i.e., self-interest, instrumental, egoistic) perceptions. In fact, consumers who viewed the IOC's CSR activities as being strategic or instrumental in nature reinforced the negative view these consumers had, that the IOC was not undertaking these activities for purely altruistic reasons, and resulted in a negative impact on repeat patronage.

We therefore see that the IOC's CSR activities can be well perceived and have a positive impact on their organization if their intentions are thought to be more altruistic. However, these actions need to be analyzed to determine their true intentions, whether they are indeed altruistic, or are they perceived to be more strategic or instrumental. For example, a positive step towards altruism is the IOC's association with recognized altruistic organizations such as UNESCO and the ICRC, as well as creating a strategy and team within the IOC dedicated to youth (see the earlier point on the youth). Although the IOC also dedicates a portion of its website to describing how Olympism is put into action within six spheres (sport for all, women, environment, peace, development, and education), the degree to which CSR pervades the organization in more than an instrumental manner can be questioned as long as the formalization of such CSR activities remains lacking and IOC funding for these activities remains unclear. In other words, it is not clear how much money (and therefore importance) the IOC dedicates to its CSR activities with respect, for example, of its broadcasting and sponsorship revenues.

Many other sport organizations of the Olympic Movement have had for several years or have recently started their own CSR programs, such as the Fédération Internationale de Football Association (FIFA) and the United States Olympic Committee (USOC) (Chappelet, 2009). Many national and local sport organizations' raison d'être and DNA are about social activities and integration through sport. Recommendation 40 of the 2009 Olympic Congress recognizes the need for cooperation and coordination with all these organizations inside or outside the Olympic Movement. In its follow-up report, the IOC states that, under its leadership:

> a global strategy with all stakeholders (IFs, NOCs, OCOGs, the International Olympic Academy, National Olympic Academies, the Olympic Museum, the Olympic Museums Network, the Commission for Culture and Olympic Education, the Olympic Values Education Program, Olympic Solidarity, the Youth Olympic Games and their Culture and Education Program and public authorities) will be defined.
>
> (IOC, 2011c: 39)

While waiting for this grand strategy, the IOC relies on three solid pillars: 1) its own activities within the six spheres described above, which are run by its International Cooperation and Development Department; 2) the NOCs' activities partly funded by some Olympic Solidarity world programs; and 3) the OCOGs that have CSR activities mostly for their own local and national communities and sometimes for a wider audience, such as the London 2012 International Inspiration program that aims to use sport as a positive force to enrich the lives of over 12 million young people around the world in partnerships with UK Sport, the British Council, and

UNICEF (LOCOG, 2011). In doing so, the IOC has singled out the OCOGs, the NOCs, and its grassroots audience (the youth of the world, the athletes and their entourage, the Sport for All participants, and underprivileged populations) as their main partners in CSR activities.

Conclusions

In summary, the IOC undertakes CSR-related activities within six main spheres: Sport for All; development through sport; education through sport; women and sport; peace through sport; and sport and environment. They are detailed in a section of its website entitled "Olympism in action." It has become a new frontier for the IOC and the Olympic Movement despite the reticence of the IOC to formally name these activities as CSR. The IOC undertakes these activities with the help of a number of stakeholders including: athletes, the youth of the world, athletes' entourage, Sport for All participants, underprivileged populations, IGOs, and NGOs. However, the IOC does not always foot the complete bill for these activities.

What is unclear is how much money is really being spent on all these CSR activities; there is a need to compare this information to annual budgets, as well as to investigate the actual impacts of these activities. In addition, why is the IOC so reticent to publicly formalize its activities as CSR (such as is the case with SportAccord)? Moreover, research should examine the emerging guidelines and reporting frameworks (such as the GRI and ISO standards) to determine their effectiveness, efficiency and breadth/depth of impact in the organization and on its stakeholders. Such an analysis could only but help the IOC, OCOGs and other Olympic System stakeholders undertake more successful CSR initiatives.

Finally, it is worth exploring the possible conflicts between CSR activities/ideals and sponsorships. For example, fast-food chain McDonald's sponsors the Olympic Day Run (part of the IOC's Sport for All sphere of CSR activities). Is this a good fit? What message does this send to different stakeholders? In addition, Dow Chemical is a TOP sponsor, and thus a LOCOG sponsor; LOCOG was pushing many CSR activities (such as those associated with education and sustainability/environment); but, Dow Chemical does not want to repair the damages caused by its Bhopal plant in India. Likewise, BP (British Petroleum) sponsors the USOC but created the largest environmental damage in the United States with its Gulf of Mexico oil spill in 2010. These are but a few examples of organizations with questionable CSR track records being/becoming associated with the IOC, OCOGs, NOCs or other key Olympic System stakeholders. Knowing that sponsors are an important part of the Olympic System's funding structure, and an essential element of the resource-based ring, which is closest to the IOC (Figure 15.2), a critical analysis of these situations is needed.

References

Carroll, A. B. (1991) 'The pyramid of corporate social responsibility: Toward the moral management of organizational stakeholders', *Business Horizons*, 34, 30–48.

Chappelet, J. L. (2009) 'Corporate social responsibility: A new frontier for the International Olympic Committee', in Rodriguez, P., Kesenne, S. and Dietl, H. (eds.) *Social responsibility and sustainability in sports*. Oviedo: Universidad de Oviedo, 17–29.

Clarkson, M. B. E. (1995) 'A stakeholder framework for analyzing and evaluating corporate social performance', *Academy of Management Review*, 20, 92–117.

Freeman, R. E. (1984) *Strategic management: A stakeholder approach*. Boston, MA: Pitman.

Global Reporting Initiative (2011) 'Event organizers'. Available at: www.globalreporting.org/ReportingFramework/SectorSupplements/Events (accessed: November 29, 2011).

International Olympic Committee (n.d.) *Sport for All – Sport pour tous*. Available at: http://www.olympic.org/Documents/Reports/EN/en_report_26.pdf (accessed: November 29, 2011).

International Olympic Committee (2005) *BOOST building on Olympic strength to transition to a state-of-the-art*. Lausanne: International Olympic Committee internal document.

International Olympic Committee (2009a) *It's a high level sport and much more*. Available at: http://www.olympic.org/content/yog_/yog-2/page/its-a-high-level-sport-and-much-more/?sortby=1&p=1 (accessed: November 29, 2011).

International Olympic Committee (2009b) *Entourage commission*. Available at: http://www.olympic.org/entourage-commission?tab=mission-objectives (accessed: November 29, 2011).

International Olympic Committee (2010) *OVEP ready to go global*. Available at: http://www.olympic.org/education-through-sport/ovep-ready-to-go-global (accessed: November 29, 2011).

International Olympic Committee (2011a) *Olympic Charter*. Available at: http://multimedia.olympic.org/pdf/en_report_122.pdf (accessed: November 26, 2011).

International Olympic Committee (2011b) *IOC Athlete Career Program*. Available at: www.olympic.org/content/Olympic-Athletes/Elite-Athletes/Programme (accessed: November 29, 2011).

International Olympic Committee (2011c) *XIII Olympic Congress Copenhagen follow-up*. Lausanne: International Olympic Committee.

International Olympic Committee (2011d) *Olympism in Action*. Available at: http://www.olympic.org/olympism-in-action (accessed: November 29, 2011).

International Olympic Committee (2011e) *14th World Conference on Sport for All issues call for action*. Available at: http://www.olympic.org/content/Olympism-in-Action/sport-for-all1/14th-World-Conference-on-Sport-for-All-issues-call-for-action (accessed: November 29, 2011).

International Olympic Committee (2011f) *Record participation at Olympic Day 2011*. Available at: http://www.olympic.org/ioc?articlenewsgroup=-1&articleid=132823 (accessed: November 29, 2011).

International Olympic Committee (2011g) *IOC heeds UN call for Somalia assistance*. Available at: http://www.olympic.org/content/Olympism-in-Action/Development-through-sport/IOC-heeds-UN-call-for-Somalia-assistance (accessed: November 29, 2011).

International Olympic Committee (2011h) *UK schools to support London 2012 teams from around the world*. Available at: http://www.olympic.org/content/olympism-in-action/education-through-sport/uk-schools-to-support-london-2012-teams-from-around-the-world/ (accessed: November 29, 2011).

International Olympic Committee (2011i) *The 5th World Conference on women and sport – Don't miss out on registering to attend*. Available at: http://www.olympic.org/losangeles2012 (accessed: November 29, 2011).

International Olympic Committee (2011j) *Walking for the Olympic truce*. Available at: http://www.olympic.org/content/olympism-in-action/peace-through-sport/walking-for-the-olympic-truce/ (accessed: November 29, 2011).

International Olympic Committee (2011k) *Sustainable major sport events*. Available at: http://www.olympic.org/content/Olympism-in-Action/Environment/Sustainable-Major-Sport-Events (accessed: November 29, 2011).

International Olympic Committee (2011l) *Factsheet: Vancouver facts and figures*. Available at: http://www.olympic.org/Documents/Games_Vancouver_2010/Factsheet_Vancouver_legacy_February_2011_eng.pdf (accessed: September 2, 2012).

London Olympic Organising Committee (LOCOG) (2011) *International inspiration. Annual review 2009–2010*. Available at: http://www.london2012.com/mm%5CDocument%5CPublications%5CAnnualreports%5C01%5C24%5C08%5C83%5Clocog-annual-report-2009-10.pdf (accessed: September 2, 2012).

Mitchell, R. K., Agle, B. R., and Wood, D. J. (1997) 'Toward a theory of stakeholder identification and salience: Defining the principle of who and what really counts', *Academy of Management Review*, 22, 853–886.

Mora, M. (2010) 'Vancouver 2010 passes on safety torch for future Olympics'. *Canadian Occupational Safety*. Available at: www.cos-mag.com/Training/Training-Stories/Vancouver-2010-passes-on-safety-torch-for-future-Olympics.html (accessed: November 29, 2011).

Olympic Solidarity (2009) *Where the action is. 2009–2012 Quadrennial Plan*. Available at: www.olympic.org/Documents/PDF_files_0807/os_2009_2012_en.pdf (accessed: November 26, 2011).

Parent, M. M. (2008) 'Evolution and issue patterns for major-sport-event organizing committees and their stakeholders', *Journal of Sport Management*, 22 (2), 135–164.

Pelham, F. (2011) 'Sustainable event management: The journey to ISO 20121', in Savery, J. and Gilbert, K. (eds.) *Sustainability and sport*. Champaign, IL: Common Ground, pp. 43–49.

Post, J. E., Preston, L. E., and Sachs, S. (2002) *Redefining the corporation: Stakeholder management and organizational wealth*. Stanford, CA: Stanford University Press.

Right To Play (2010) *History*. Available at: http://www.righttoplay.com/International/about-us/Pages/History.aspx (accessed: November 29, 2011).

SportAccord (2010) *Sports' social responsibility map*. Available at: http://sportaccord.com/en/services/index.php?idIndex=33&idContent=14523 (accessed: November 29, 2011).

SportAccord (2011) *SportAccord Statues*. Available at: http://www.sportaccord.com/multimedia/docs/2011/05/2011_-_SPORTACCORD_STATUTES_-_ENG_.pdf (accessed: November 29, 2011).

The Vancouver Organizing Committee for the 2010 Olympic and Paralympic Winter Games (2010) *Vancouver 2010 sustainability report: 2009–2010*. Vancouver: The Vancouver Organizing Committee for the 2010 Olympic and Paralympic Winter Games.

United Nations Education, Scientific and Cultural Organization (UNESCO) (2011) *Physical Education and Sport*. Available at: www.unesco.org/new/en/social-and-human-sciences/themes/sport/physical-education-and-sport (accessed: November 29, 2011).

United Nations Office on Sport for Development and Peace (2011) *Achieving the Objectives of the United Nations through Sport*. Available at: www.un.org/wcm/webdav/site/sport/shared/sport/pdfs/Achieving%20the%20Objectives%20of%20the%20UN%20through%20Sport_Sep_2011_small.pdf (accessed: November 29, 2011).

Walker, M., Heere, B., Parent, M., and Drane, D. (2010) 'Social responsibility and the Olympic Games: The mediating role of consumer attributions', *Journal of Business Ethics*, 95 (4), 659–680.

Walker, M. B. and Kent, A. (2009) 'Do fans care? Assessing the influence of corporate social responsibility on consumer attitudes in the sport industry', *Journal of Sport Management*, 23 (6), 749–76.

16

A FOUNDATION FOR WINNING

Athletes, charity and social responsibility

Kathy Babiak, Kate Heinze, Seung Pil Lee and Matthew Juravich

Sport and notoriety increase our capacity for impact. We do this because of personal experiences and passions, and we just have the bigger platform because we're athletes.

(Steve Nash, 2012)

Overview

The professional sport industry in North America has increasingly focused on social responsibility over the past ten years, and sport philanthropy has emerged as a key element of these activities (Babiak and Wolfe, 2009; Sheth and Babiak, 2010; Sports Philanthropy Project, 2007). Athletes are an important resource that professional sport businesses (teams, leagues, governing bodies) utilize to both make a significant impact on social issues and to garner positive associations for their organization (Babiak *et al.*, 2012; Tainksy and Babiak, 2011). In addition to the charitable work athletes perform for their teams via community outreach and team philanthropy, athletes frequently also engage in their own personal philanthropic endeavors. Athlete philanthropy might take the form of direct support of a cause or established organization, such as the American Diabetes Association or a local hospital; or the establishment of a personal charitable organization, such as a public or private foundation or donor advised fund. Much of the research in the area of sports philanthropy, including team and league charitable foundations, community outreach, or cause-related marketing efforts has been at the organizational level (i.e., professional sport teams and leagues or governing bodies) (Babiak and Wolfe, 2006, 2009; Brietbarth and Harris, 2008; Sheth and Babiak, 2010; Walker and Kent, 2009). Little academic attention has been paid to the professional athletes themselves as philanthropists and social entrepreneurs.

The purpose of this chapter is to examine charity in the sport industry, specifically related to charitable foundations established by professional athletes. We discuss how social entrepreneurship in sport plays a role in formalizing philanthropy through the establishment and management of charitable organizations. Dees (1998: 4) defined a social entrepreneur as someone who:

adopts a mission to create and sustain social value, recognizes and relentlessly pursues new opportunities to serve that mission, engages in a process of continuous innovation,

221

adaptation, and learning, acts boldly without being limited by resources currently in hand and exhibits heightened accountability to the constituencies served and for the outcomes created.

Therefore, the main objective of the chapter is to shed more light on athlete philanthropy as one form of social entrepreneurship. We then offer four examples of athlete initiated and managed foundations, highlight their missions and foci, and their financial information. We then discuss potential challenges and opportunities related to athlete philanthropy in these cases. Lastly, we consider the potential impact of sport-related charity and offer suggestions for effective evaluation of the impact of athlete-formed foundations – a key issue in research and practice in this area.

This chapter will lay the groundwork for ongoing research on strategic philanthropy in sport-related foundations, and their social value; it will provide a better understanding of the nature of sport philanthropy and the potential social impact that may ultimately help to encourage this behavior. The conversation around philanthropy will explore the cultural norms about the role of sport and athletes in our society, the way that wealth is accumulated in this "entertainment" business, and the moral and ethical obligations of athletes who benefit from this wealth. This chapter may challenge academics and practitioners to think about our own behaviors related to helping others; as well as engender a dialogue about the value and rewards of giving, and whether the motives (or only the outcomes) matter.

Background on athlete philanthropy

Individual athlete foundations continue to grow in terms of their prevalence and their financial impact on society. For example, National Football League quarterback Tim Tebow's foundation, which aims to provide hope to orphans and kids battling life threatening diseases, raised more than $4 million in its first year of operation. Unique to Tebow's foundation is a membership system whereby contributors can join "Team Tebow" by making a $25 donation. Once this donation is made, members are given the first opportunity to volunteer at foundation-sponsored events. This example demonstrates both the increasing influence and financial reach of individual athlete foundations as well as the entrepreneurial ways in which revenues are being generated (Tim Tebow, 2012).

The significance of athlete philanthropy is rooted in the role of sport in the cultural fabric of our society. Sports are played and watched by millions across the globe – inspiring, entertaining, and uniting the masses. The popularity of sport and the positive traits it promotes, including discipline, passion, teamwork, excellence, sportsmanship, and dedication, make sport a vehicle for social good. In particular, the athletes who embody these traits and excel at the highest levels of sport have a platform to make a difference in important social causes and issues. These individuals are not only extremely skilled in their respective sports, but also highly visible and often very wealthy. Elite athletes can leverage their celebrity status and resources to inspire and motivate others, and create positive social change (Tainsky and Babiak, 2011). They might do so through a variety of specific philanthropic activities, from donating to causes to creating their own charitable foundations.

The expectations and opportunities for athletes to engage in meaningful philanthropy are increasing. Professional athletes today are increasingly expected to demonstrate their charitable involvement and good deeds (Roy and Graeff, 2003). These expectations may come from a variety of stakeholders, including coaches, owners, professional organizations, fellow teammates, fans, family and friends, surrounding communities, and society at large. In addition to these external pressures, ethical and moral motivations and perceptions related to "doing the right thing" may also play a key role in the decisions of athletes to be philanthropic (Babiak *et al.*, 2012). Regardless of their reasons for engaging in philanthropy, "many (athletes) may not be aware of the value – to both their community and their teams – of exercising philanthropy through carefully and strategically structured foundations and programs" (Sports Philanthropy Project, 2007).

Philanthropic practices of sport teams, leagues, athletes, and independent sport-related organizations have evolved over the past five decades. There are now a range of interactions and options available, including: simple benefaction, patronage, cause sponsorship, cause-related marketing, celebrity endorsement, and integrated strategic partnerships. Increasingly, these practices are becoming more deliberate and intentional, with considered use of all possible assets available to leverage processes, impacts, and outcomes. For example, an individual athlete possesses social and cultural assets, such as his or her access to media, celebrity cachet, and corporate sponsors and endorsement relationships. In addition, the athlete has access to resources from his or her team, league or sport, as well as his or her own knowledge, skills, and time. All of these assets can be leveraged to attract additional resources, volunteers, donors, and media attention to causes the athlete cares about. These resources can also be used to help the athlete formalize his or her charity through the creation of a foundation. Today, both professional and "amateur" athletes in particular are using philanthropy and charity as one vehicle to establish and develop their off-field personas (see Chapter 5 by Filo, Funk and O'Brien that details the work of the Lance Armstrong Foundation).

Athlete charity today is a growing and vital force in the philanthropic landscape. Athlete-related charities are bringing increasing and significant material and human resources to bear on social problems, through donations of time, energy, materials, and money. Two recent articles explored the field of athlete philanthropy, detailing the type of athlete who is likely to form a charitable foundation (i.e., older and longer tenured athletes are most likely to have philanthropic foundations (c.f., Tainksy and Babiak, 2011); and the motives underpinning charitable actions, such as personal experiences with a disease or a desire to contribute to the greater good of society (Babiak *et al.*, 2012). However, little else is known about the nature of athlete charity. The cases in this chapter shed a bit more light on this growing trend.

Types and structures of charitable efforts and organizations (US) in sport

There are a number of avenues for an athlete to become engaged in philanthropic work. Perhaps the simplest in terms of formalization is direct giving, where an athlete makes a lump sum donation to a charitable organization. Another approach is for an athlete to align him or herself with a particular cause. This alignment – or endorsement – by a celebrity can take the form of a nonprofit organization partnering with an athlete (e.g., NASCAR driver Danica Patrick and the Chronic Obstructive Pulmonary Disease (COPD) Foundation) to raise awareness for a cause. Patrick's grandmother died from COPD; and her role as ambassador is to educate people about COPD, understand their risks, and encourage them to get screened.

Another avenue for an athlete to become involved in charitable work is through a donor advised fund or to establish a fund under the auspices of a community foundation. This type of vehicle offers the opportunity to create an easy-to-establish, low cost, flexible approach to charitable giving as an alternative to direct giving or creating a private foundation. The fund offers donors relief from complicated administrative concerns. From a financial standpoint, this approach is less costly (than formalizing a charitable foundation) and also offers tax advantages. Perhaps one of the largest and most well-known donor advised funds for celebrities and athletes in the U.S. is the Giving Back Fund. This organization provides philanthropic consulting and foundation management to high-profile individuals and others committed to philanthropy (Giving Back Fund, 2012). The organization provides support to numerous well-known athletes from various sports including for example NFL quarterback Ben Roethlisberger (Ben Roethlisberger Foundation), NBA player Gerald Wallace (Gerald Wallace Foundation), and NHL player Scott Mellanby (Mellanby Autism Foundation).

The most legitimate, formalized, and official form of philanthropy is to start one's own charitable foundation, via the establishment of a public or private charity. To be eligible for tax-exempt status, the organization must be formed for a purpose that has been determined to serve the public good, such as for a charitable, scientific, religious or educational purpose. The organization must also be nonprofit, which means that any extra money cannot go to private interests but must be reinvested to advance the mission of the charity. There are two main classifications of 501(c) (3) charitable organizations – public charities and private foundations. Organizations that qualify as public charities do so by having significant public influence, such as a third or more of their income coming from the public. Due to the fact that they have this public "oversight," the laws that govern these organizations are less restrictive. Private foundations, on the other hand, have little public influence. They are typically funded by a single source (an individual, family, or business) and usually derive their income from investments. Private foundations make grants to others as their main activity, except in the case of a private operating foundation which operates its own programs.

Athlete foundation profiles

Below we highlight four examples of athlete-formed charitable foundations. We gathered information, including documentation from athlete foundations (e.g., 990 tax forms, websites, press releases, news clipping, and so on) to explore written evidence of the mission and focus of the athletes' foundations, and their charitable efforts. We offer these cases to help frame a discussion around issues and opportunities associated with athletes and their charitable efforts.

Previous investigations (Tainksy and Babiak, 2011; Babiak *et al.*, 2012) that assessed the presence and scope of athlete foundations in the United States found that approximately 1,122 charitable foundations were established, or purported to be established, by athletes. The athletes who formed these foundations spanned a range of sports, and included athletes from professional sport leagues (National Football League (NFL), National Basketball Association (NBA), National Hockey League (NHL), Major League Baseball (MLB), Major League Soccer (MLS), and Women's National Basketball Association (WNBA)); professional associations (Professional Golfers' Association (PGA), Ladies Professional Golf Association (LPGA) or Association of Tennis Professionals (ATP)); as well as Olympic athletes, and those from boxing and auto racing. The scope of this initial exploration included athletes who were both active and retired and was limited to only US athletes and/or foreign athletes who have established their foundation in the United States (e.g., Dikembe Mutombo, Steve Nash). From this broad analysis, we selected four examples of athlete charity, ranging in size and scope, and the athlete's sport and gender.

Jimmie Johnson Foundation (JJF)

Jimmie Johnson, a five-time NASCAR Sprint Cup Champion, and his wife, Chandra, established the Jimmie Johnson Foundation (JJF) in 2005. Coming from small towns, the Johnsons were motivated to create this charity by a desire to give back to these communities (Jimmie Johnson Foundation, 2012). Jimmie Johnson was born in El Cajon, California, and began racing motorcycles at the age of five. Upon graduating from high school, he moved to the Midwest to continue his auto-racing career. Chandra Johnson is a native of Muskogee, Oklahoma. The Johnsons current reside in Charlotte, North Carolina.

With the mission "to assist children, families and communities in need throughout the United States," the JJF focuses on supporting K–12 public schools and education through partnerships with various organizations in the Johnsons' hometowns and where they currently reside. A primary way in which the JJF provides support is through the Champions Grant Program. This program has been a major channel of funding allocation to K–12 public schools in these focal areas since 2009. In partnership with Lowe's, the Champions Grant (worth more than $5 million) was awarded to 53 schools located in California, Oklahoma, and North Carolina for the past three years. Other than the Champions Grant, the JJF contributes to the Hendrick Marrow Program, Make-A-Wish Foundation, and Ronald McDonald House of Charlotte (Jimmie Johnson Foundation, 2012).

A unique initiative undertaken by the JJF is known as the "Helmet of Hope" program. Through this program, twelve charities are nominated by fans and the media each year to be featured on the specially-designed helmet worn by Johnson in the NASCAR Sprint Cup Series. The charities also receive a grant of $10,000. This program offers tremendous free visibility to the charities selected. Recently, some of the charities featured on his helmet have included Victory Junction, the Zepp Children's Foundation, the National Multiple Sclerosis Society Mid Atlantic Chapter, and Special Operations Warrior Foundation. In addition to these featured charities, the foundation has many different funding partner corporations, including Lowe's, Sprint, Samsung, IMG, Callaway, and SUNOCO, that are also featured on Johnson's uniform and racing car.

As for organizational structure, the JJF is a 501(c) (3) Private Nonoperating Foundation. As illustrated in Table 16.1, it has raised over $5 million in revenues since 2005. About 70 percent of revenues go to contributions, gifts, and grants, while the remaining of 30 percent goes to administration. In 2009 and 2010, more than 80 percent went to program service including grants. This is a positive trend as many charity watchdog groups evaluate charitable foundations based on the ratio of administration costs (operating expenses, rents, salaries, etc.) and programs and giving expenditures. The JJF has two full-time employees and 10 volunteers. Johnson's total career earnings are $110,902,861 from NASCAR.

Table 16.1 Jimmie Johnson Foundation selected financials

Year	Revenues	Expenses	Assets	Liabilities	Program services	Administration	Fundraising (*as a private foundation, JJF does not engage in fundraising)
2005	6,827	500	6,330	0	0	500	NA
2006	296,025	238,380	68,464	1,923	113,653	124,727	NA
2007	1,474,912	939,235	4,790	12,732	575,590	363,645	NA
2008	998,745	1,053,759	2,790	13,285	690,685	363,074	NA
2009	1,238,536	1,500,774	790	102,219	1,186,101	314,673	NA
2010	1,156,278	1,428,043	133,516	126,087	1,102,503	325,540	NA

Source: compiled by the authors.

Dikembe Mutombo Foundation

The Dikembe Mutombo Foundation (DMF) was started by former professional basketball player Dikembe Mutombo in December 1997. The foundation's mission statement recognizes a "dedication to improving the health, education, and quality of life for the people of the Democratic Republic of the Congo" (Dikembe Mutombo Foundation, 2012). To achieve this mission, the foundation emphasizes primary health care and disease prevention, while promoting health research and health education for people in the Congo. The DMF is recognized by the US Internal Revenue Service as a 501 (C) (3) public charity and it has raised over $32.1 million since 1998 (see Table 16.2).

Mutombo was born in Kinshasa, the capital city of the Congo. Through his upbringing in a family of 10 children, Mutombo recognized the need for healthcare facilities to be built in his native land. In 1987, he accepted an academic scholarship to study at Georgetown University. Upon his arrival in the U.S., he tried out for the basketball team and became a major contributor to a program that was recognized as a national power in NCAA Men's Division 1 basketball. In 1991, he was drafted fourth overall by the Denver Nuggets of the NBA. He went on to earn $144 million during the span of a 20-year professional career, while playing for six different franchises. Mutombo retired at the conclusion of the 2008–2009 season.

The primary focus of the DMF is to build, support, and sustain a hospital and research center in Kinshasa, Democratic Republic of Congo. Initial groundbreaking for these facilities occurred in 2001. The facilities were officially dedicated in 2007. Mutombo contributed $15 million of his own money to cover half of the $30 million cost to build the hospital and research center (Nance, 2006). Other foundation activities include the shipment of medical and pharmaceutical supplies, hospital beds, vaccinations, and purchasing an ambulance; as well as the creation of a new computer lab (all in Kinshasa).

The structure of the organization is such that an executive director oversees all operations. Mutombo himself serves as the chairman of the foundation and is intimately involved in all decisions made impacting operations. Throughout the 12-year history of the foundation, other officers have changed but both Mutombo and his wife Rose have remained on the board of directors.

The DMF publicizes several partnerships with organizations including Qualcomm, Lenovo, Palomar, the NBA, and several healthcare organizations. It appears that some of these partners were utilized to provide supplies or services during the construction of the hospital, while others garner financial support from the DMF as they pursue initiatives related to improving healthcare.

Mutombo has received numerous awards for his charitable work, including the President's Service Award from President Clinton (2000); the J. Walter Kennedy Citizenship Award from the NBA (2001); the American Public Health Association's International Health Section award (2002); the Helen Hayes MacArthur Award (2003); the Jackie Robinson Humanitarian Award (2007); and the Steve Patterson Award for Sport Philanthropy (2010).

Table 16.2 Dikembe Mutombo Foundation selected financials

Year	Revenues	Expenses	Assets	Liabilities	Program services	Administration	Fundraising
1998	180,384	177,125	6,788	3,529	157,615	15,610	3,900
1999	410,989	408,083	9,485	3,320	371,383	28,841	7,859
2000	804,306	695,550	119,651	4,730	670,397	19,402	5,751
2001	3,515,921	467,160	3,164,375	693	394,052	47,265	25,843
2002	1,559,936	735,417	3,988,951	3,988,201	673,690	35,881	25,846
2003	1,736,001	346,253	5,379,892	5,377,949	269,502	46,524	30,227
2004	3,065,127	497,397	15,950,296	8,004,614	404,425	29,742	63,230
2005	5,145,159	329,561	17,325,483	4,564,206	127,568	31,560	170,433
2006	5,210,517	2,220,420	16,921,787	1,170,413	1,766,186	98,684	355,550
2007	4,227,657	2,695,510	17,623,305	339,784	2,324,038	58,534	312,938
2008	2,805,887	3,509,491	16,845,450	274,533	3,235,861	62,887	210,743
2009	2,070,263	3,075,862	16,042,055	467,737	2,920,685	39,718	115,459
2010	1,849,844	2,764,038	15,185,846	525,722	2,519,694	47,106	197,238

Source: compiled by the authors.

Women's Sports Foundation

Although the trend among athletes to form charitable foundations appears to be more recent, the creation of foundations by athletes is not new. The Women's Sports Foundation (WSF), established in 1974 by tennis legend Billie Jean King, is an example of a foundation that has not just stood the test of time, but grown in size and influence over its almost 40-year history. It also represents one of the few charitable foundations established by female athletes. It is now one of the most prominent athlete-created foundations; not to mention, a key foundation for women's issues and sports, in general, in the United States. The mission of the WSF is to advance the lives of girls and women through sports and physical activity. It works for equal opportunity for girls to play sports, "so they, too, can derive the psychological, physiological and sociological benefits of sports participation" (Women's Sports Foundation, 2011). The foundation sees itself as "the voice" of women's sports – serving and speaking for all ages and skill levels.

The creation of the WSF dates back to a critical time in the history of women in sport and in the life of its founder, King. King is now a retired tennis champion, although when she created the foundation she was in her athletic heyday, consistently winning Grand Slam and Wimbledon titles. She was also solidifying her role as an agent and symbol of the women's movement. Most visibly, in 1973, when the WSF was founded, King defeated Bobby Riggs in the famous Battle of the Sexes. The following year she founded the Women's Tennis Association and *Women's Sports Magazine*. These events coincided with the passing of Title IX in 1972. Thus, change was taking place in the United States in the 1970s that was empowering to women, including in the domain of sport. The WSF benefited from that wave of change and at the same time helped further it.

The foundation is involved in a number of different activities that follow from its mission. The focus is on grant-giving and advocacy. The WSF is one of the top five public grant-giving women's funds in the United States, awarding more than $50 million over 34 years to advancing participation, research, and leadership in sports and physical activity for girls and women. For example, the WSF distributes $10,000 to $20,000 per week from operating dollars to provide opportunities for disadvantaged and inactive girls to participate in sports and physical activity through their "Go Girl Go" program. In terms of advocacy, the foundation's efforts include those directed at increasing scholarship dollars for female student-athletes and supporting national laws prohibiting sex discrimination. Finally, the WSF serves as an "information clearing house," through funneling information and research on women's sports and physical activity to the public. The impact of the WSF is evident by the media it generates with 1.5 billion media impressions annually on women's sports and health issues (Women's Sports Foundation, 2011).

In terms of financial structure, the WSF is an educational nonprofit organization and a public charity. It has a $3 million operating budget with funds coming from foundations, individuals, the federal government and corporations. Corporate sponsors include Gatorade, ESPN W, AthleticLink.com, Playtex Sport, and The Hershey Company. Gatorade is the main national partner, with a sponsorship spanning a period of 12 years. Most of the WSF's sponsors have a clear connection to women and sport with their product and target market. Other funders, outside of corporations, include family and sport foundations. Most of the WSF's operating budget (80 percent) goes towards programming with less than 20 percent spent on fundraising and administrative costs (see Table 16.3 for more financial details).

Table 16.3 Women's Sports Foundation financials

Year	Revenues	Expenses	Assets	Liabilities	Program Services	Administration	Fundraising
1997	3,229,321	2,581,334	3,307,862	495,044	1,984,280	368,412	228,642
1998	3,888,848	3,303,072	4,017,839	441,134	2,505,657	456,212	341,203
1999	3,682,073	3,148,397	4,609,344	512,986	2,312,504	481,438	354,455
2000	3,931,381	3,512,452	4,904,391	404,684	2,638,258	480,297	393,897
2001	4,993,893	4,323,476	5,307,908	288,360	3,446,224	504,476	372,776
2002	3,778,141	3,732,757	4,982,502	204,738	3,068,721	399,784	264,252
2003	4,515,712	4,370,568	5,517,332	452,363	3,403,520	495,541	471,507
2004	5,114,399	4,998,814	5,848,356	568,277	3,629,975	626,539	742,300
2005	4,821,171	5,273,806	5,878,467	877,830	4,337,061	315,286	621,459
2006	5,681,698	5,667,489	5,671,494	649,667	4,525,461	488,720	653,308
2007	15,671,451	7,920,762	14,618,688	1,622,645	6,237,828	790,115	892,819
2008	7,004,396	8,844,075	12,458,466	1,577,181	7,312,150	597,252	934,673
2009	3,832,553	5,923,072	9,045,658	2,092,844	4,699,982	452,340	770,750
2010	4,504,624	4,308,545	7,710,391	1,362,305	3,445,414	293,292	569,839
2011	2,878,708	5,000,848	4,412,110	508,455	3,869,868	354,154	776,826

Source: compiled by the authors.

There is a large and visible leadership body governing the WSF, with women and athletes at the core. In particular, the WSF is led by a board of trustees, including a nine-person executive committee and sixteen other board members. These trustees include champion female athletes, prominent businesspersons, major benefactors, and leaders of women's sports organizations. The role of the board is to "establish fiscal policy, assist in the acquisition of adequate financial and human resources and oversee the accomplishment of the Foundation goals and objectives" (Women's Sports Foundation, 2011). The size of the foundation is represented in its staff of 20 part-time, five full-time, salaried employees, and 100 volunteers.

Both the WSF and King have been recognized by numerous awards and honors. The Women's Sports Foundation is seen as a credible and successful foundation, winning accolades from such institutions as the United Nations, the International Olympic Committee, and the Women's Funding Network. And over the years, King's athletic fame has been matched by her renown as a social activist. Most notably, in 2009, she was awarded of the Presidential Medal of Freedom, the highest honor for a civilian.

PeyBack Foundation

As discussed above, superstar athletes often use their fame and popularity to promote and support social causes. One of the most famous and prosperous active athletes of the past decade, NFL star Manning created the PeyBack Foundation in 1999, shortly after the start of his professional career, and continues to be actively involved in its day-to-day activities.

The mission of the foundation is somewhat broad: "To promote the future success of disadvantaged youth by assisting programs that provide leadership and growth opportunities for children at risk" (PeyBack Foundation, 2012). PeyBack argues that this breadth allows it to help as many children as possible. Although the mission is expansive, the activities of the foundation are limited by geography. PeyBack originally focused on a three-state region, including Indiana, Tennessee, Louisiana, and added Colorado in 2013. The first three states make up the region where Manning played for the Indianapolis Colts. Now, Manning plays for the Denver Broncos, so PeyBack is also focused on Colorado. The foundation asserts that it has become a consistent and viable part of the communities of these regions.

The work of the PeyBack Foundation includes grant-giving and operating and funding several of its own programs for underprivileged children. One of the goals is to reach out to children of all different backgrounds with the belief that "children need opportunities through which they can grow and learn" (PeyBack Foundation, 2012). In terms of its activities and support, particular attention is paid to abused and neglected children, boys and girls clubs, after-school programs, summer camps, and foster children. PeyBack has distributed more than $4.3 million in grants to groups like these since 2002. Corresponding to the broad mission, PeyBack's activities can be as disparate as buying and delivering groceries and toys, assisting in disaster relief, and supporting children's hospitals. These are examples of the foundation's direct approach to interacting with their target group. Also in line with this approach is operating its own programs so the foundation can "control the environment and content for the children" (PeyBack Foundation, 2012).

Financially, PeyBack is funded by Manning himself and donations. Manning earns about $30 million per year, with a career total upwards of $250 million (including sponsorships, etc.). Other money for the foundation comes from donations from organizations such as NFL Charities (which gives money to player foundations) and individuals. The latter is often acquired through fundraising events, such as the PeyBack Bowl (a celebrity bowling event). Although there is no evidence that PeyBack has corporate sponsors, Manning has many endorsements, including with Gatorade, Reebok, Mastercard, Sprint, and ESPN that presumably allow him to help fund the foundation's efforts. Structurally, the PeyBack Foundation is a public charity.

In terms of leadership, it is a family affair. Manning's role is President of the foundation. He supports the foundation financially, but is also active in major decisions concerning initiatives and identifying new opportunities for the foundation. According to his website, Manning strives to grow the foundation stronger each year. His approach is to "proceed slowly so programs are done professionally with maximum benefit to the children" (PeyBack Foundation, 2012). The other foundation officers include two family members: Manning's wife, Ashley Manning, who is Vice President; and his father, Archie Manning, who serves as Treasurer. The PeyBack Foundation officers also work with the Resource Council, a foundation that includes 14 business and community leaders from Indianapolis, Knoxville, and New Orleans. The council provides guidance and assistance with respect to connecting with local agencies that could use financial support from the foundation.

The PeyBack Foundation has earned several awards from regional youth and charitable organizations, including the National Pathfinder Award in 2010 that recognizes individuals for their contributions and dedication to youth. The economic results are summarized in Table 16.4.

Table 16.4 PeyBack Foundation selected financials

Year	Revenues	Expenses	Assets	Liabilities	Program Services	Administration	Fundraising
1999	81,041	39,387	41,654	0	N/A	N/A	N/A
2000	247,312	169,885	119,081	0	113,860	10,702	45,323
2001	531,871	108,667	433,987	74	63,079	10,683	34,905
2002	506,782	360,210	580,703	218	284,962	17,267	57,981
2003	557,201	218,860	918,933	107	167,302	17,167	34,391
2005	923,908	546,316	1,424,631	0	503,806	30,193	12,317
2006	1,101,301	567,732	1,958,200	0	508,780	39,122	19,830
2007	937,026	788,334	2,119,292	12,400	729,947	26,703	31,684
2008	874,432	904,428	2,076,896	0	835,934	40,494	28,000
2009	670,821	1,031,982	1,715,735	0	949,665	43,600	39,692
2010	1,774,074	902,964	2,586,845		812,244	46,020	44,700

Source: compiled by the authors.

Discussion

The four examples above demonstrate similarities and differences across athlete foundations and help illustrate key issues and themes related to social entrepreneurship. First, we can infer some of the motivations for establishing foundations. There are a number of reasons why athletes might form a foundation. They may be motivated more intrinsically by morals or ethics to do "what is right," particularly given their position and resources, an enjoyment of helping others, or a desire to create a difference in an area that is of personal significance to them. Athletes may also be motivated by extrinsic factors – they may be urged by professional contacts (e.g., coaches, teammates, leagues) or personal ones (e.g., family), particularly given the increasing focus on social responsibility (Babiak *et al.*, 2012). Athletes who create sustainable and visible foundations, like the ones profiled above, seem to be motivated, at least partially, by intrinsic factors. For example, Billie Jean King's personal experiences appear to be a driver in her desire to make positive social change. She started the Women's Sports Foundation during a period in history when she and other women had limited opportunities to participate in sports. Family encouragement or pressure may also be a motivator – the leadership of athletes' foundations is often populated by family members. In the examples above, both Jimmie Johnson's and Peyton Manning's wives are partners and Manning's father is also involved in decisions and administration of the foundation.

Athletes that are more intrinsically motivated may be likely to be more involved in the running of the foundation. Manning's foundation website claims he is involved in major decisions. Both King and Mutombo have earned numerous, individual awards for their charitable work, suggesting they are active leaders in their foundations. In general, though, it can be difficult to tell why athletes form foundations and the extent of their involvement. Most likely, they are motivated for a variety of reasons and their involvement may change over time. It is also unclear whether the type of motivation and the extent of involvement matter in terms of the ability of the foundation to make a difference. Future research might more closely examine athletes' motivations for engaging in philanthropy and what affect these have on the type and success of their initiatives.

The motivations for creating foundations are often closely tied to the missions of the athletes' foundations. The Women's Sports Foundation's mission follows from King's experience as a female athlete who lacked access to opportunities and resources that male athletes had. Similarly, Mutombo's foundation's mission is to help improve the health of those who share a similar experience growing up in the Democratic Republic of Congo. In these examples, the missions are directly connected to personal experiences and are somewhat narrower. For other foundations, the missions appear to be less clearly tied to personal experience. In these cases, the missions are often broader. One that is common is around helping children. We see this with the missions of both the PeyBack Foundation and the Jimmie Johnson Foundation. The PeyBack Foundation, however, has narrowed its focus, and made it more personal, by concentrating on the specific geographic region where Peyton has played football. Mutombo's foundation and the Jimmie Johnson Foundation are also geographically focused. Thus, both geography and personal experience can be used to develop and focus a mission. Geographic positioning, in particular, can be important for the athlete and the foundation for other reasons. It makes sense to enhance the athlete's brand, reputation, and image by engaging and connecting with the communities in which they play. This has the potential to attract more fans to games; encourage more purchases of athlete-related merchandise; and foster stronger linkages between athlete, endorsers and sponsors, and consumers. It is also a logistical concern, as an athlete who wants to be actively engaged (managing, fundraising, etc.) is most likely to do so in the community in which he/she spends the most time.

The extent to which the mission is connected to sport is another source of variation. Some athlete foundations strive to increase sport participation as one outcome, like the WSF. Others may use sport as a tool to benefit a social group, like the PeyBack Foundation with their charity bowls, yet not include sport directly in their mission. And then there are athlete foundations that have little direct connection to sport, such as DMF that focuses on broader issues around health. More work is needed to understand variation in athlete foundation missions, how they are formulated, and what makes them effective. Drawing on the field of strategy, research could examine the implications of broad versus narrow missions. A broader mission may have the advantage of allowing the foundation to go in a lot of different directions, but a narrower mission could create more of a distinctive niche for a foundation and allow the foundation to specialize and develop a core competence in an area. And what is the role of personal experience in developing a mission? Is it the case that personal experience makes athletes more passionate and/or better able to tackle the needs of their focal beneficiaries, and thus leads to more effective foundations?

The mission, in theory, guides the actions of the foundation, but even with a narrower mission, there are a variety of activities that athlete foundations can choose to pursue. As illustrated by the examples above, foundations may give grants, host charity events, donate money to causes, create their own programs, and generate public awareness for causes, among other activities. The WSF, for example, focuses on grant-giving and advocacy. The PeyBack Foundation focuses on grant-giving and running some of its own programs for children. DMF was primarily working on building a health facility. Like any organization, athlete foundations must choose which activities to pursue and how to spend their resources. The question is: how do they make these decisions? In particular, how involved are the athletes themselves in the decision-making process; what is the effect of their particular skills, resources, and backgrounds? Beyond how the decisions are made, what actually makes an effective portfolio of activities? Are there strong connections between the missions of these foundations and their activities? Are the activities connected in a way that allows the foundation to realize potential synergies? How do the actions of the foundation change over time? These are all questions ripe for investigation.

Another decision foundations have to make is with respect to partners, including other charities, community organizations, and sponsors. Most of the more prominent athlete foundations have corporate sponsors. We see in the examples that the WSF has five corporate sponsors, with Gatorade serving as the main national partner; the Jimmie Johnson Foundation has a variety of funding partner corporations – from Lowe's to SUNOCO; and DMF's partners include several corporations, such as Qualcomm. These corporate partnerships provide financial resources to foundations in exchange for meeting social responsibility goals. They also provide important financial resources to the athletes' charities. Foundations might also partner with other non-corporate organizations, such as healthcare organizations or sports organizations (e.g., NBA) in the case of the DMF; or other charities, like the Jimmie Johnson Foundation's partnerships with the Make-A-Wish Foundation and the Ronald McDonald House. These types of partnerships may provide resources such as supplies, services, expertise, or channels through which to disperse support to beneficiaries. A key set of questions for future investigation is around how athlete foundations decide on partner organizations and what leads to effective relationships. Often, athletes' own personal sponsorships translate to foundation sponsorships. What is the process by which this happens? Also, is there congruence between the foundation's mission and the types of organizations they partner with? What makes for an effective portfolio of partners across different sectors – corporate/private, governmental/public, and nonprofit?

Given the potential of athletes to make a difference and the increasing pressure on them to behave philanthropically, the question some may have is: when is the appropriate time to start a foundation? Some athletes start early in the careers, like Peyton Manning. Others form their foundations soon before or after retiring. And many begin their charitable work after they have had some professional success – in the middle of their careers. All three paths seem to offer some advantages. An early start at developing community relationships and a reputation can help an athlete build a base that can be leveraged and expanded as his or her resources grow. A risk to early formation is that there are unknowns about career length – which determines earnings, as well as visibility. On the other hand, a retired athlete has more time and energy to devote to charitable work and is more experienced in a lot of ways. Finally, the height of one's professional career is when athletes have the most visibility to influence others, and they are generating significant resources. Along these lines, the typical longevity of athlete foundations is not known. There is a highly focused window of opportunity for athletes to capitalize on their command of the media and the interest of fans and customers. As social entrepreneurs, these athletes often use their celebrity and fame to generate awareness and raise funds for causes and issues that are important to them.

As the potential pressure and motivation to engage in philanthropy and create foundations grows, more work can be done to help athletes be effective social entrepreneurs. In particular, research that looks at mission formation, strategic focus, and effective decision making around foundation activities can inform athletes' charitable work. Understanding these variables would be a good starting point to encourage others to establish and manage similar individual charitable foundations for both their own strategic purpose such as revenue generation, image or personal brand enhancement, and/or the ethical, moral, and social welfare value contributed by social entrepreneurs.

Evaluating philanthropy effectiveness

A prevailing question in the charitable sector is to define and refine metrics around how foundations are evaluated. Often foundations – not only sport based or focused foundations – engage in limited evaluation activities. Assessment variables may include key financial indicators, for example, how the funds raised are actually being used, for either salaries and administration costs (running the charity) or on actual charitable work like grants and program service costs. How much is the charity spending on additional fundraising (amount spent on fundraising vs. amount raised) (Better Business Bureau Wise Giving Alliance; American Institute of Philanthropy) (the age and cause focus of the foundation may be factors in the organization's ability to fundraise effectively). These could be considered as measures of charity efficiency. Other assessment criteria may include the extent to which a foundation has a strong and active board (if so, a foundation is likely to have fewer problems), and how transparent the organization is (i.e., do they tell their stakeholders how the money is spent, especially the salaries of the executives). How much money in reserve does charity have (ideally, it should have between three months and three years of assets to support operations in case of financial hardship (Charity Watch, 2012). Some suggest that if a charity has beyond three years' worth of expenses in their financial reserves, the charity may not be in urgent need of a donation (Charity Watch, 2012). Other challenges with these charitable organizations are that regulation and oversight are more concerned with tax evasion than the outcomes of charitable programs, and this potentially sets the stage for mismanagement and charitable scams. Finally, and perhaps importantly, a key indicator of charity effectiveness is how valid is the organization's mission and how successful it is in accomplishing its goals. These factors are difficult to measure through hard numbers, however independent evaluations need to be made of programs and charity initiatives through assessment studies and program evaluations.

In athlete philanthropy in particular, metrics for evaluation (used by the Robert Wood Johnson Foundation (one of the largest US based health focused foundations) to select awardees of their Steve Patterson Award for Excellence in Sport Philanthropy) include the extent to which they distinguish their impact from that of others in sports philanthropy, the degree to which they have sustained, comprehensive, and far-reaching outcomes, how they use all their unique assets to advance the charity's goals, and how effectively they demonstrate leadership within the field of sports philanthropy.

Conclusions

The trend of charitable giving in sport relates to a broader emphasis on using sport, athletes, teams, and other sport-related assets address pressing social and cultural dilemmas. As we have demonstrated in this chapter, the nature of athlete philanthropy can vary based on the focus on a particular social cause, the type of sport played by the athlete, the age and longevity of the charitable organization established, the strategic and active integration of partners and other supporters, and the time at which the foundation was established in the athlete's career.

The athletes profiled in these cases can be considered to be social entrepreneurs. They have each adopted a mission to create and sustain social value through their charitable endeavors, they have recognized and pursued new opportunities to serve that mission through the programs and support their foundations offer, they adapt, innovate, and act boldly in their efforts to make positive social change and are accountable to their constituencies and beneficiaries. These cases highlight the potential power of sport to make positive change around the world. We have identified some key practical challenges such as evaluating and assessing the effectiveness of the organization (including managing and structuring the foundation as well as demonstrating sustained impact on the populations and communities served). This chapter also offered needed areas to explore in future empirical investigations.

References

Babiak, K. and Wolfe, R. (2006) 'More than just a game? Corporate social responsibility and Super Bowl XL', *Sport Marketing Quarterly*, 15(4), 214–224.

Babiak, K. and Wolfe, R. (2009) 'Determinants of corporate social responsibility in professional sport: internal and external factors', *Journal of Sport Management*, 23, 717–742.

Babiak, K., Mills, B., Tainsky, S., and Juravich, M. (2012) 'An investigation into professional athlete philanthropy: why charity is part of the game', *Journal of Sport Management*, 26 (2), 159–176.

Brietbarth, T. and Harris, P. (2008) 'The role of corporate social responsibility in the football business: towards the development of a conceptual model', *European Sport Management Quarterly*, 8 (2), 179–206.

Charity Watch (2012) *Criteria*. Available at: http://www.charitywatch.org/criteria.html (accessed: October 11, 2012).

Dees, J. G. (1998) 'The meaning of "social entrepreneurship"'. Available at: http://www.caseatduke.org/documents/dees_sedef.pdf (accessed: October 11, 2012).

Dikembe Mutombo Foundation (2012) *Dikembe Mutombo Foundation, improving health, education and quality of life*. Available at: http://www.dmf.org (accessed: October 11, 2012).

Giving Back Fund (2012) *The Giving Back Fund. Integrity and innovation in philanthropy*. Available at: http://givingback.org (accessed: October 11, 2012).

Jimmie Johnson Foundation (2012) *Champion Grant Program*. Available at: http://jimmiejohnsonfoundation.org (accessed: October 11, 2012).

Nance, R. (2006) 'Mutombo helps Congo take a big step forward with new hospital'. *US Today*, 16 August. Available at: http://www.usatoday.com/sports/basketball/nba/2006-08-14-mutombo-cover_x.htm (accessed: October 11, 2012).

Nash, S. (2012) 'Steve Nash & Sports Philanthropy', Available at: http://www.tacticalphilanthropy.com/2009/12/steve-nash-sports-philanthropy (accessed: January 14, 2012).

PeyBack Foundation (2012) *Providing leadership and growth opportunities for children at risk*. Available at: http://www.peytonmanning.com (accessed: October 11, 2012).

Roy, D.P. and Graeff, T.R. (2003) 'Consumer attitudes toward cause-related marketing activities in professional sports', *Sports Marketing Quarterly*, 12 (3), 163–172.

Sheth, H. and Babiak, K. (2010) 'Beyond the game: Perceptions and priorities of corporate social responsibility in the sport industry', *Journal of Business Ethics*, 91 (3), 433–450.

Sports Philanthropy Project (2007) *About SPP*. Available at: http://www.sportsphilanthropyproject.com/ (accessed: October 11, 2012).

Tainsky, S. and Babiak, K. (2011) 'Professional athletes and charitable foundations: an exploratory investigation', *International Journal of Sport Management and Marketing*, 9, 133–153.

Tim Tebow (2012) 'Tim Tebow Foundation raises more than $4 million in first year', *The Huffington Post*, 27 July. Available at: http://www.huffingtonpost.com/2012/07/27/tim-tebow-foundation-fundraising_n_1710748.html (accessed: October 11, 2012).

Walker, M. and Kent, A. (2009) 'Do fans care? Assessing the influence of Corporate Social Responsibility on consumer attitudes in the sport industry', *Journal of Sport Management*, 43 (6), 743–769.

Women's Sports Foundation (2011) *Women's Sports Foundation*. Available at: http://www.womenssportsfoundation.org (accessed: October 11, 2012).

17

STAKEHOLDER ENGAGEMENT IN EUROPEAN FOOTBALL

Geoff Walters and Richard Tacon

Overview

This chapter looks at the issue of stakeholder engagement in European football and argues that there are both normative and instrumental reasons that underpin the need for football clubs to engage with stakeholders. It presents findings from a survey aimed at those football clubs playing within the top division within the 53 leagues across Europe. The survey focused on a range of corporate social responsibility (CSR)-related issues: this chapter sets out, in a descriptive manner, what it is that football clubs within Europe are doing to engage with different stakeholders. The results show that a large majority of these clubs are involved in a variety of stakeholder initiatives for the community and employees. However, the research found that a majority of clubs consider making connections with the community a significant challenge, demonstrating that clubs are not automatically embedded within their communities. The results also show that clubs' engagement with a variety of environmental initiatives is less prevalent. Given the increased attention on environmental issues in recent years, this may be an area to which football clubs need to devote more attention.

Introduction

The concept of CSR is multi-dimensional, so providing a succinct definition has proved challenging. One key debate is whether CSR should refer only to activities and motivations that extend beyond an organization's direct economic interest and legal obligations, or whether it should refer to these as well (e.g., Carroll, 1979, 1999). Notwithstanding this debate, an important commonality across most, if not all, conceptual discussions is that CSR is closely associated with how an organization interacts with, and how business activity has an impact upon, a wide range of stakeholders (Carroll, 1991; Wood, 2010). An important organizational consideration in the context of CSR, therefore, is how to manage stakeholders. Stakeholder management, it has been argued, consists of three key elements, namely stakeholder identification, stakeholder engagement, and stakeholder participation (Low and Cowton, 2004). Stakeholder identification concerns who or what can be considered a stakeholder. It should be noted that this is itself a contested process – there are important debates around legitimacy and saliency (see, e.g., Phillips, 2003). Stakeholder engagement is about how organizations communicate and enter into dialogue with stakeholder groups. According to Low and Cowton (2004), engagement does not provide decision-making powers: stakeholders are kept at arms-length from decision-making and are only able to exert influence on an organization. A commitment to engagement, therefore, does not necessarily constitute a commitment to collective, democratic decision-making involving stakeholders (Friedman and Miles, 2006). By contrast, stakeholder participation, the third element of stakeholder management, explicitly involves providing opportunities to integrate stakeholders into the governance structure of an organization.

Interest in CSR and stakeholder management within the sport industry has grown rapidly in recent years. Indeed, specific guidelines have been produced to assist sporting organizations in implementing a stakeholder management strategy. For example, the *Governance Guide* for national governing bodies of sport, produced by UK Sport, the strategic lead body for high-performance sport in the UK, highlights four principles on how to manage stakeholders: accountability of decision makers to stakeholders; participation so that all stakeholders are represented when decisions are taken; responsiveness of the organization to its stakeholders; and transparency about the information on which decisions have been based, the decisions themselves, and the way those decisions are implemented (UK Sport, 2004: 3). These broadly map onto stakeholder engagement and participation strategies. Academic research on CSR and stakeholder management in sport, discussed at length elsewhere in this book, has also grown rapidly. Within this broad literature, recent studies have argued that sports organizations need to work harder to understand the needs of an increasing range of stakeholders (Ferkins *et al.*, 2005).

This chapter investigates CSR in sport by focusing on one of the three elements of stakeholder management discussed above – stakeholder engagement – in the context of European football. As mentioned, there is a growing body of literature on stakeholder engagement in sport; however, to date, much of it has been case-based research on individual sports organizations (e.g., Walters, 2011). This chapter considers stakeholder engagement from a broader pan-European perspective, in order to get a better sense of what it is that professional football clubs are doing to engage with stakeholders. The chapter is based on survey research conducted in 2011 across all top division football clubs in the 53 member associations of the Union of European Football Associations (UEFA).[1] It is structured as follows. The first section discusses the context around stakeholder engagement in sport, focusing particularly on the football industry. The second section discusses the methods used in the survey research. The third section presents key results from the survey: it looks at how European clubs engage with stakeholders through various reporting mechanisms and focuses on three specific stakeholder groups – communities, employees, and the environment. It also considers what institutional support exists to encourage football clubs in Europe to address different CSR-related issues. The fourth section provides a summary discussion, and the fifth, a conclusion.

Stakeholder engagement in sport

The importance of engaging with a variety of stakeholders has been recognized in a number of countries, with guidelines produced to assist sporting organizations. In the UK one of the key recommendations in the *Governance Guide* discussed above was the need for national governing bodies of sport (NGBs) to communicate effectively with members, participants, and wider stakeholder groups (UK Sport, 2004: 4). And recent survey research in the UK has shown that a high proportion of NGBs are taking definite steps to engage stakeholders by reporting and providing information to stakeholders through their website and/or annual report and seeking to engage in dialogue and get feedback from stakeholders on particular consultations (Walters *et al.*, 2010). Elsewhere, Sport and Recreation New Zealand (SPARC) (2010) produced guidelines for sports organizations on how to develop a strategic plan to communicate with stakeholders. The document, *Creating a Stakeholder Communications Plan*, states that an effective stakeholder communications plan will support an organization in achieving its stated goals and objectives; support or improve operational effectiveness; support or improve relationships with those who are important to ensuring success (often called key stakeholders or target audience); and deliver measurable results to an organization. It is clear from this latter set of guidelines that stakeholder engagement is often seen in instrumental terms, as a way to improve the effectiveness of an organization.

The growth and commercial development of the football industry in Europe, notwithstanding national variation, has led to increasingly complex stakeholder environments: football clubs have to manage the demands of a multitude of stakeholders such as supporters, local communities, the football authorities, government, local authorities, sponsors, broadcasters, and players. Part of this can be done through engagement strategies; and, as discussed, there are instrumental benefits to engaging with stakeholders. For example, engaging with local community stakeholders and supporters can help engender a sense of attachment to a club; an attachment that is critical for business performance and long-term sustainability. Nevertheless, there are concerns that football clubs have difficulties engaging with different types of community stakeholders (Brown *et al.*, 2006) while there have been concerns that many supporters have been disenfranchised (see, e.g. Conn, 2005). This is particularly important given that there are normative justifications for putting in place a stakeholder engagement strategy (Walters and Tacon, 2010). For example, it has long been recognized that football clubs have a significant socio-economic function; that there is a need to fully understand the role of a football club as both a business and a social institution; and, in particular, a need to understand the relationships between football clubs and stakeholders such as local communities and supporters (Morrow, 2003). The concept of "fan equity" refers to the high levels of loyalty that many supporters demonstrate which reduces the likelihood of switching allegiances and therefore reduces their "voice" or their bargaining power (Hirschmann, 1970). However, it is because of the strong levels of loyalty, commitment, solidarity, and emotional attachment that supporters demand a specific form of accountability over and above financial accountability. Therefore both instrumental and normative reasons underpin the need for football clubs to engage with stakeholders.

Method

As is stated within other chapters of this book, measuring CSR is a complex task. To date, a variety of methods have been used, including the use of reputation indices and databases, single- and multiple-issue indicators, content analysis of corporate publications, scales measuring CSR at the individual level, and scales measuring CSR at the organizational level. Previous reviews of CSR measurement have concluded that there is no one best way to measure this contested, multi-dimensional concept (Turker, 2009). The main objective of the research reported here was to examine and directly compare several aspects of CSR at organizational level across a large number of organizations in a large number of different countries (Walters and Tacon, 2011). As such, it was felt that a questionnaire survey, incorporating several scales and closed- and open-response items, was most appropriate. Due to the pan-European nature of the research, the questionnaire was translated into nine different languages. It was then administered online, due primarily to issues of time and cost, two key reasons underpinning the use of web surveys as opposed to mail surveys (Kaplowitz *et al.*, 2004). The questionnaire included a previously developed CSR measurement scale that had been piloted and tested to confirm its validity and reliability (Turker, 2009) and included a series of items on stakeholder engagement, the primary area of interest in this chapter.

Data collection

The sample included all 730 top division clubs in the 53 national federations that are members of UEFA. A database was created containing an email address for each club, except in the case of 14 clubs where a follow-up with UEFA and website analysis failed to yield an email address. Following the initial electronic administration of the survey to the revised sample of 716 clubs, it was found that there were an additional 101 clubs for which we did not have the correct email address. Following further website analysis, a total of 24 different email addresses were identified. Therefore from the original population of 730 we were able to contact 639 football clubs directly. We followed the initial email with further email follow-ups and were assisted in survey administrations by UEFA, the national federations, 30 of the professional leagues in Europe, and the European Club Association. In total, we received 112 responses from football clubs in 44 different countries across Europe. From the revised population of 639 clubs, this represents a response rate of 17.5 percent. The data from the online questionnaire were entered into SPSS. This preserved the individual detail of the responses and, where relevant, allowed direct quotations from the open questions to be identified.

Describing the respondents

Of the 112 European football clubs that responded to the survey, 48.5 percent had a turnover of less than €5m; 29 percent had a turnover of between €5m and €50m; and 22.6 percent had a turnover of over €50m (see Table 17.1). The survey also found that 30 percent had made a profit in the previous financial year, 37 percent had made a loss, and 29 percent had broken even (4 percent of respondents did not know). In addition, the mean number of full-time staff at the clubs in the survey was 78; only four clubs had more than 250 employees.

Previous research has suggested that, when it comes to CSR, there may be important differences between large and small enterprises (e.g., Jenkins, 2004; Fassin, 2008). Our research sought to explore this, by examining differences in stakeholder engagement strategies between large and small football clubs. The size of an organization can be assessed in several ways, but two of the most common are turnover and number of full-time staff. Analysis of our survey findings found a very strong correlation between these two variables (Spearman's rho = +.726 ($p<0.01$)). There was a higher response rate to the question on turnover ($n = 93$) than the one on number of full-time employees ($n = 87$), so we decided to use turnover as a proxy for organizational size.

Table 17.1 Football Club respondents' turnover

Turnover	Percentage of clubs
More than €50m	22.6
€5m – €50m	29
€1m – €5m	19.4
€200,000 – €1m	22.6
Under €200,000	6.5

We recoded the club respondents into two groups, based on turnover, using €5m as the dividing line.[2] As can be seen in Table 17.1, there were 48 clubs (51.6 percent) with a turnover greater than €5m and 45 clubs (48.5 percent) with a turnover of €5m or less. In our analysis, we ran Chi-squared tests on all questions to see whether there were statistically significant differences between large and small clubs. Where relevant, the results of these tests are reported below.

Results

For the purposes of this chapter, we present analysis of responses around stakeholder reporting before looking at various initiatives used to engage with specific stakeholder groups.

Stakeholder reporting

One particular method of stakeholder engagement is reporting or communicating to stakeholder groups. To do this, many organizations utilize reporting tools such as annual reports, CSR or sustainability reports, newsletters, websites, and press releases. These are common mechanisms of engaging with broad groups of stakeholders although the lines of dialogue here are one-way and stakeholders have little input or chance to respond. There are concerns that this type of engagement could be manipulative and misleading (Friedman and Miles, 2006). Formal CSR/sustainability reports are less common within sport than in other sectors, although analysis of the first ten years of the English Premier League found that football clubs were taking their social reporting more seriously (Slack and Shrives, 2008).

Our survey found that very few top division clubs in Europe formally report their CSR activities. As Figure 17.1 shows, 29.3 percent produce an annual social report and 14.3 percent report their environmental activities. The survey also found that those that do formally report CSR activities (either through a social or environmental report) were more likely to have a dedicated CSR strategy, a budget for CSR activities, and an individual working on CSR. Figure 17.1 also shows that the majority of European football clubs (72.5 percent) have a code of conduct in relation to supporters. Whilst not necessarily a traditional type of CSR report, this does show that many clubs set out supporter rights and the responsibilities that the club has towards this particular stakeholder group. Moreover, 39.8 percent of clubs have employee newsletters – a means of reporting and communicating to employees. Statistical analysis showed that large clubs were more likely to do this than small clubs. Given the difference in the average number of employees (128 at the large clubs; 22 at the small clubs), these results are unsurprising.

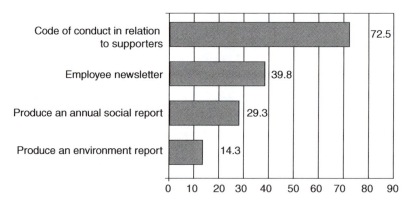

Figure 17.1 Stakeholder reporting (percentage of football clubs)

Stakeholder-specific engagement

The survey also explored methods of engagement with specific stakeholder groups, namely communities, employees, and the environment.

Communities

It has been argued that football clubs play a significant role in the development of local identity and a sense of place and that this underpins the on-going relationship between clubs and their communities (e.g., Morrow, 2003). However, detailed research on the football club–community relationship has found that the notion of "community" is complex (Brown *et al.*, 2006) and involves a variety of different stakeholder groups. This was reflected in the survey. Figure 17.2 shows various community-related initiatives that football clubs undertake and, as can be seen, these involve multiple stakeholder groups.

A very high percentage of clubs (89.1 percent) work with local schools and a high percentage (81.2 percent) provide support for youth programs. In addition, 72.7 percent of football clubs are involved in community engagement projects and 70.6 percent employ people from the local community, whilst 41.8 percent and 39.4 percent respectively provide time for employees to work in the community and support local homeless people. Figure 17.2 also illustrates that 37.8 percent of clubs in the survey are involved in community projects in developing countries, demonstrating that the notion of "community" can span national borders. Notwithstanding the range of community-led forms of engagement, the survey found that 62.7 percent of clubs considered making connections with the community either a significant or a very significant challenge. This finding is interesting, because it has sometimes been assumed that clubs are naturally embedded within their communities. The fact that a majority of clubs find community connections a challenge likely reflects the complex global and local community environments within which modern football clubs operate.

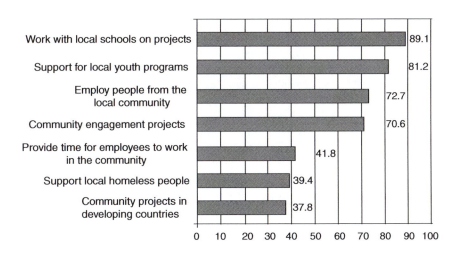

Figure 17.2 Percentage of football clubs involved in community initiatives

As discussed above, we tested for statistically significant differences between large and small football clubs. Analysis showed that there were significant differences between these groups in relation to some of the community initiatives. For example, large clubs were more likely to work on community projects in developing countries than small clubs (Chi-squared = 10.386; p <0.01). This is understandable given that small clubs tend to lack the levels of international awareness and organizational resources necessary for undertaking CSR activities in developing nations. Large clubs were also more likely to work with local schools (Chi-squared = 4.785; p<0.05) and to be involved with community engagement projects (Chi-squared = 10.510; p<0.01).

Employees

The survey also explored clubs' involvement in a range of employee-related initiatives. Figure 17.3 shows that a large majority of clubs provide training and development programs for members of staff (75.8 percent) and run social events (82.2 percent). It also shows that a majority of clubs are committed to equality and diversity, with 64.7 percent employing older and disabled staff members. More than half of clubs (51 percent) indicated that they have one-to-one mentoring schemes in place and just under half (47.5 percent) have family friendly employment initiatives.

The analysis showed, with one exception, that there were no statistically significant differences between large clubs and small clubs in relation to employee engagement strategies. The one exception was around employment of older and disabled people, with larger clubs more likely to do this than small clubs.

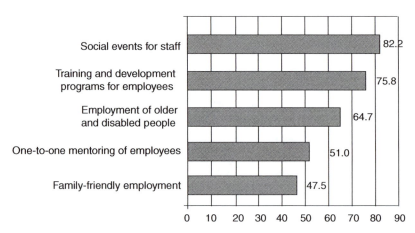

Figure 17.3 Percentage of football clubs involved in employee initiatives

Environment

The survey found that stakeholder engagement was less common in relation to the environment than in relation to communities and employees. The results in Figure 17.4 set out the variety of environmental initiatives that the club respondents are involved in.

As can be seen, around half of all clubs (50.5 percent) are involved in recycling. In addition, 46.6 percent have waste minimization schemes and 41 percent are involved in pollution prevention schemes. Clubs were also asked if they invested in environmental technology or used energy from renewable sources, and 29.3 percent and 29 percent respectively indicated that they do. Significant differences were found between large and small clubs in relation to a number of environmental initiatives. Large clubs were more likely to use energy from renewable sources (Chi-squared = 10.924; p <0.01), invest in environmental technology (Chi-squared = 17.346; p <0.01), implement pollution prevention (Chi-squared = 18.059; p <0.01) and undertake recycling schemes (Chi-squared = 10.177; p <0.01).

Figure 17.4 also shows that only 15.2 percent of European football clubs are members of an environmental organization and just 14.3 percent have signed up to environmental certification schemes, such as the ISO 14001 standards on environmental management. These findings are entirely consistent with broader research that illustrates that small and medium-sized enterprises (SMEs) are less likely to sign up to CSR standards and codes of conduct than large, multi-national organizations (Spence, 2007).

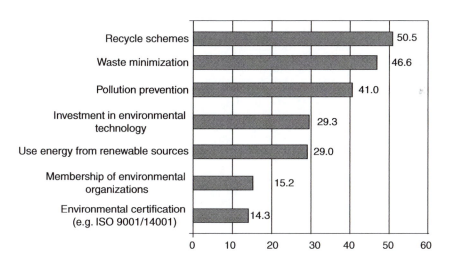

Figure 17.4 Percentage of football clubs involved in environmental initiatives

The institutional context

Institutional pressures can influence the extent to which organizations address CSR. The extent to which a football club engages with different stakeholder groups can be influenced by the institutional environment and the weighting given to stakeholder engagement and the social role of the football club. Nevertheless, running a professional football team and achieving sporting success is often seen as the main objective of a football club and, in the context of the resulting financial pressures, it is understandable that CSR may not be a high priority at many clubs. Figure 17.5 appears to bear this out as it reveals that 55.6 percent of club respondents have a formal CSR strategy; 53.2 percent have an individual dedicated to working on CSR; and 45.5 percent have a CSR budget. There are many clubs therefore for which CSR has not been formalized within the organizational structure. Figure 17.5 also shows that many football clubs are funding CSR activities internally as only 24.5 percent receive funding assistance through government funds and 34 percent from other sources of funding. It was also found that 31.3 percent also have an association with a separate charitable organization that delivers CSR. Football clubs were also asked to identify the additional sources of funding. It was revealed that of the 25 clubs that responded to this question, 10 of these received funding from sponsors to deliver CSR-related projects. From this it suggest that there exists the potential for football clubs to leverage their community/CSR work into sponsorship deals to align with the commitment that many commercial organizations have to CSR and to ensure that there is funding for the football club to deliver CSR programs. However, we found that there were differences between large and small clubs: it is more likely that larger clubs will have a formal CSR strategy; a dedicated budget for CSR activities; receive government funding; receive funding from other sources; and be associated with a charitable organization that delivers CSR on behalf of the club.

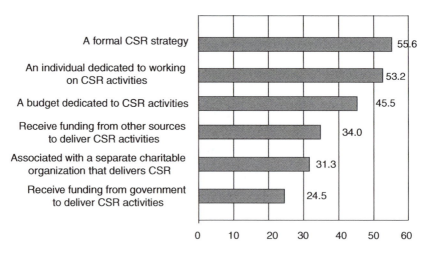

Figure 17.5 Percentage of football clubs reporting varieties of support for CSR

Further analysis of the data revealed that there was a strong positive correlation between having a formal CSR strategy and generating funding from government sources and from additional sources.[3] This finding suggests that if a football club wants to further its commitment to CSR then having a formalized strategy could be a potential first step. Having such a strategy could be a factor in helping a football club to generate increased funding to deliver CSR initiatives, perhaps demonstrating to funders a strong level of commitment to CSR.

Figure 17.6 illustrates the different factors that determine which CSR activities football clubs are involved in. It shows that the most important factor was the seriousness of a social need, with 63 percent stating that this was either important or very important. Matching a social need to corporate skill, need or ability to help was the second most important factor, demonstrating that clubs prefer to identify their own strengths and use these to address CSR. This helps to explain why the main CSR activity at many football clubs is usually the delivery of community football schemes. The public relations value of a particular social action was also an important or very important factor at 41.4 percent of football clubs although only 14 percent stated that the profitability of the venture was important with just 4 percent answering that it was very important.

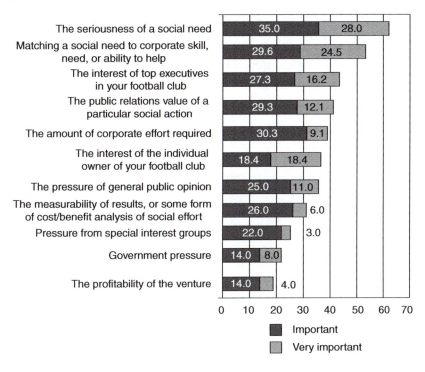

Figure 17.6 Percentage of football clubs reporting factors that influence social involvement

Discussion

This chapter has presented just a brief, descriptive overview of the results from the survey of European football clubs. However, there are three points that can be discussed. First, the results suggest that reporting on CSR activities is not common amongst European football clubs. This may be due in part to a lack of resources, both human and financial, and to a concomitant lack of CSR reporting culture. However, we have seen an increasing trend within the corporate sector for the reporting of social activities and it is likely that the sport industry will face similar pressures to do so in the future. We can already see that this has been the case within the context of the Italian sport system sport, with sports federations encouraged to engage in social reporting (see Chapter 20 by Buscarini and Mura). It is highly probable, therefore, that in the future we will see more football clubs (and more sports organizations in general) producing a formal social or environmental report.

Second, although environmental issues are increasingly a fundamental aspect of CSR, it appears that, at present, only a minority of football clubs engage in environmental initiatives. Football clubs are much more likely to engage with community and employee stakeholder groups. There are perhaps historical reasons for this. Football clubs have often been considered as part of the community and policy makers have increasingly seen football clubs as a means of delivering on broader policy objectives around health, crime, education, and social cohesion. As such, the majority of external funding available for CSR-related activity in football clubs has been for community-focused schemes. Moreover, it has been recognized that employees are very important stakeholders, particularly in small firms or SMEs (Spence, 2007). This can perhaps help to explain the fact that many football clubs in Europe are engaging with employees through a variety of means. However, given the increased focus on the issue of environmental sustainability in sport, it could be predicted that in the future more clubs will engage with these types of initiatives. This is particularly true where there are clear instrumental reasons, for example if they are found to reduce costs.

Third, as noted above, while a large majority of the football clubs in the survey were found to be involved in community-focused CSR initiatives, a majority of clubs also reported that they found making connections with the community a significant challenge. This suggests that, contrary to certain views of football clubs as "community institutions," clubs are not automatically embedded within their communities. This highlights the fact that football clubs should not take the local community for granted and underpins the need for football clubs in Europe to implement a considered engagement strategy with community stakeholders.

Conclusions

The issue of CSR within the professional sport industry is gaining currency. However, more research could usefully focus on sector-level analyses in different geographical regions, in order to understand how different sports organizations engage with stakeholders. The research project on which this chapter is based took one step in this direction, by surveying all top division football clubs in Europe and considering the issue of stakeholder engagement. Whilst this chapter has been predominantly descriptive, it is the first comprehensive, comparative survey in the football industry and therefore serves a purpose as a broad initial overview. Further detailed analysis of the survey, which will be undertaken in forthcoming publications, will examine some of the reasons underpinning aspects of stakeholder engagement. In addition, more in-depth, longitudinal research should help to uncover the organizational processes involved in CSR within sport.

Notes

1 The research was kindly funded by UEFA through the Universities Research Grant Scheme.
2 In fact, the dividing line between large and small enterprises has been drawn in several different ways. For example, the European Union defines an SME as a firm with less than 250 employees and either a turnover of less than €50m or less than €43m of assets on the balance sheet. The division employed here was pragmatic: using €5m as the dividing line enabled us to group respondents into sufficiently large categories (N >30) to make statistical analysis of differences between large and small clubs meaningful.
3 We used the Phi coefficient, a non-parametric correlation coefficient, to identify the strength and direction of the correlation between formal CSR strategy and government funding (+.502; 0.0000 significance) and other funding (+.704; 0.000 significance).

References

Brown, A., Crabbe, T., Mellor, G., Blackshaw, T., and Stone, C. (2006) *Football and its communities: Final Report*. The Football Foundation and Manchester Metropolitan University.

Carroll, A.B. (1979) 'A three-dimensional conceptual model of corporate performance', *Academy of Management Review*, 4 (4), 497–505.

Carroll, A.B. (1991) 'The pyramid of corporate social responsibility: Toward the moral management of organizational stakeholders', *Business Horizons*, 34 (4), 39–48.

Carroll, A.B. (1999) 'Corporate social responsibility: Evolution of a definitional construct', *Business and Society*, 38 (3), 268–295.

Conn, D. (2005) *The beautiful game: Searching for the soul of football*. London: Yellow Jersey Press.

Fassin, Y. (2008) 'SMEs and the fallacy of formalising CSR', *Business Ethics: A European Review*, 17(4), 364–378.

Ferkins, L., Shilbury, D., and McDonald, G. (2005) 'The role of the board in building strategic capability: Towards an integrated model of sport governance research', *Sport Management Review*, 8, 195–225,

Friedman, A.L. and Miles, S.V. (2006) *Stakeholders: Theory and practice*. Oxford: Oxford University Press.

Hirschmann, A. O. (1970) *Exit, voice and loyalty: Responses to decline in firms, organizations and states*. Cambridge, MA: Harvard University Press.

Jenkins, H. (2004) 'A critique of conventional CSR theory: An SME perspective', *Journal of General Management*, 9 (4), 55–75.

Kaplowitz, M., Hadlock, T., and Levine, R. (2004) 'A comparison of web and mail survey response rates', *Public Opinion Quarterly*, 68 (1), 94–101.

Low, C. and Cowton, C. (2004) 'Beyond stakeholder engagement: the challenges of stakeholder participation in corporate governance', *International Journal of Business Governance and Ethics*, 1 (1), 45–55.

Morrow, S. (2003) *The people's game?: Football, finance and society*. Hampshire: Palgrave Macmillan.

Phillips, R. (2003) 'Stakeholder legitimacy', *Business Ethics Quarterly*, 13 (1), 25–41.

Slack, R. and Shrives, P. (2008) 'Social disclosure and legitimacy in Premier League football clubs: The first ten years', *Journal of Applied Accounting Research*, 9 (1), 17–28.

Spence, L.J. (2007) 'CSR and small business in a European policy context: The five "C"s of CSR and small business research agenda 2007', *Business and Society Review*, 112 (4), 533–552.

Sport and Recreation New Zealand (2010) *Creating a stakeholder communications plan*. Available at: http://www.sportnz.org.nz/Documents/Partners/Stakeholder-Comms-Planning.pdf (accessed: June 30, 2012).

Turker, D. (2009) 'Measuring corporate social responsibility: A scale development study', *Journal of Business Ethics*, 85 (4), 411–427.

UK Sport (2004) *Good Governance: A Guide for National Governing Bodies of Sport*. London: Institute of Chartered Secretaries and Administrators.

Walters, G (2011) 'The implementation of a stakeholder management strategy during stadium relocation: a case study of Arsenal football club's move to the Emirates Stadium', *Managing Leisure*, 16 (1), 49–64.

Walters, G and Tacon, R (2010) 'Corporate social responsibility in sport: Stakeholder management in the UK football industry', *Journal of Management and Organization*, 16 (4), 566–586.

Walters, G. and Tacon, R. (2011) *Corporate social responsibility in European football*. Birkbeck Sport Business Centre Research paper, 4 (1), 1–101. Available at: http://www.sportbusinesscentre.com/research/researchpapers/UEFA%20Report (accessed: October 11, 2012).

Walters, G., Trenberth, L., and Tacon, R. (2010) *Good governance in sport: A survey of UK National Governing Bodies of Sport.* Birkbeck Sport Business Centre Research Paper Series. Available at: http://www.sportbusinesscentre.com/images/NGBGovernanceReport (accessed: October 11, 2012).

Wood, D. J. (2010) 'Measuring corporate social performance: A review', *International Journal of Management Reviews*, 12 (1), 50–84.

PART IV

COMMUNICATING CSR
IN SPORT

18

THE PREMIER LEAGUE

A commitment to social responsibility

Simon Morgan

Overview

The Premier League has established itself as one of the most popular and entertaining football competitions in the world. The interest that has been generated by the exciting on-field action has been converted into considerable commercial success. A key strand of the Premier League's business model is to ensure that those revenues are distributed equitably to provide a balance between commercial success and a clear commitment to social responsibility. This ethos manifests itself in considerable investment into the "Creating Chances" program, which uses the power of football to make a positive social difference to the local communities in which the clubs are located. The success of Creating Chances can be proven by the myriad of participants and partners that are involved, the successful outcomes of flagship programs such as Kickz, the way it helps to shape policy, and the fact that it offers a blueprint for the delivery of community sport.

Introduction

The Premier League is well renowned as one of the most popular and successful football competitions in the world. Across nine months of every year, 380 matches are beamed out to over 720 million homes in 212 territories. An estimated global adult audience of 4.7 billion watched the 217,000 hours of coverage broadcast last season, while in England, domestic television viewing figures set new records. As well as being the world's most watched league the Premier League has also enjoyed attendance growth inside the stadiums with utilization at 92.6 percent. Research shows that the Premier League has 935 million worldwide followers with 615 million supporting a specific club (Sport+Markt, 2012).

On the field the Premier League's 20th season proved to be the most exciting and competitive so far. Manchester City claimed the title with Sergio Aguerro's last gasp winner to leapfrog their neighbors, Manchester United, in a record breaking season for goals scored – 1,066 in total with 19 hat-tricks. Marc Albrighton recorded the 20,000 goal in Premier League history and Chelsea's Champions League win ensured England was top of the UEFA League coefficient for the fifth season in a row. The home grown player criteria is starting to deliver results as clubs look to develop talent through their Academy and into the top end of the professional game. In 2011/12 55 percent of Premier League players were home grown, a 24 percent increase on 2009/10.

These successful statistics are produced through a Premier League business model based on a "virtuous circle" of reinvesting all income for the overall benefit of the game. The starting point is to stage the best possible competition, with the teams made up of the world's best playing talent taking to the pitch in some of the finest stadiums around. The Premier League generates huge public, commercial and political interest. That interest is then converted into commercial success and political space free from excessive regulation. The revenues are then distributed equitably and responsibly, balancing commercial success with a socially responsible outlook. This redistribution covers a staggering 15 percent (£189.4m) of Premier League revenue to external organizations. Around 4 percent is reinvested into Social Responsibility (SR) community programs, good causes and charity projects. Compare that figure with the industry standard of commercial organizations committing around 1 percent into SR programs and it shows how embedded this work is within the Premier League's ethos and culture. However, this off-the-field commitment is not so well recognized and the huge investment and dedication shown to developing innovative community programs both in the UK and overseas is regarded as one of football's best kept secrets (Morgan, 2010).

The League works closely in partnership with key agencies, including national and local government, to ensure the funding is invested wisely where it can make a socially beneficial contribution. With most of the Premier League clubs located in inner-city areas, where deprivation is often at its worst, the clubs bear a huge responsibility to all groups within their community regardless of their age, gender or ethnicity, or which team that person supports. As a result the Premier League has developed a SR policy that links directly to the overall objectives of the organization and mirrors the local to global appeal.

The Premier League's approach to CSR is based upon using the power of football as a vehicle for development. The interest that people have in the Premier League and its clubs has the ability to engage, motivate and inspire and can reach out and touch people of all ages and backgrounds. Its vision is to place clubs at the heart of their community and to affect positive social change that responds to local need. The entire CSR program is entitled "Creating Chances" and this brand is adopted across domestic and international activity.

Creating Chances

The objectives of the program "Creating Chances" are:

- To increase the quality and broaden the reach of good cause activity.
- To channel funding through clubs to raise the quality of their community programs, improve the visibility and recognition of their good cause work and emphasize their position as centres of their community.
- Consolidate governance standards across all funded partners.
- Streamline the efficiency, management and administration of Premier League funding.
- Develop consistent branding and PR strategy for Premier League recognition and reputational enhancement.
- Develop relationships with key partners and align delivery for shared value.

Funding is distributed to effect change and development in five key thematic areas:

- Community cohesion – to bring communities together, create inclusive environments and opportunities that channel the energy and potential of hard to reach young people into positive activities that contribute to safer and stronger communities for all.

- Education – to provide inspirational learning and personal development opportunities that motivate, improve skills and enhance self-esteem, encourage educational and entrepreneurial achievement.
- Health – to promote healthy lifestyles, increase physical activity, tackle sensitive health issues and improve well-being, change lives for good in our communities.
- Sports participation – to widen access to sport and provide pathways that enable young people to realize their full potential, experience the sheer enjoyment of taking part and benefit from a more active lifestyle.
- International – to develop overseas projects that train tomorrow's coaches and provide opportunities for the development of young people in learning and personal growth across the world.

Centrally the League has a Community Development team within the Public Policy and Communications department. This team dictates the CSR policy and strategy and much of the recent work has been to create an effective mechanism for distributing the good cause funding, raising standards of club community organizations, building relationships with key partners and developing ground-breaking sport for development programs. Creating Chances is a key strand of the League's communications and public affairs strategy so engaging and informing politicians, policy makers, opinion formers and journalists of the good cause activity is vitally important.

Distribution mechanism

Governance of the good cause investment is provided by the Premier League Charitable Fund (PLCF) set up in 2010. The PLCF task is to administer a modernized grants process that incorporates applications, distribution of funding, performance, monitoring and evaluation. Funding is generally distributed through club community organizations. The League's trump card (or 20 trump cards to be precise) is the clubs themselves. Each member club has a legally constituted community operation delivering high-quality, innovative and socially beneficial activity. The clubs collectively employ over 1,600 skilled staff to deliver innovative programs that engage with local people. The inclusive nature of these programs can be shown by 32 percent of participants being female and 28 percent from black or ethnic minority (BME) backgrounds.

The Premier League also cascades its community funding down the football pyramid with significant donations to the 72 Football League clubs and 68 Football Conference clubs to create a wider reach and scope for Creating Chances. Quality assurance is provided by a capability status kite mark that is consistently applied by the PLCF across all clubs and ensures high governance standards. Funding is not distributed to the clubs until they have reached this standard. This distribution mechanism underpins the local to global nature of Creating Chances. Clubs are able to access funding that allows them to develop projects that work with local partners to meet local needs. Clubs also deliver central projects that use the collective power of the Premier League to meet national objectives – Kickz and Premier League 4 Sport are two such examples that we shall examine shortly. The success of the strategy in implementing local and national initiatives has empowered the Premier League to replicate these sustainable models and partnership approach to enable growth on a local to global basis. Examples of this will be covered in the international section.

Funding is not solely focused on project delivery. Sustainability and legacy are built on combining revenue projects with the opportunity to build new facilities through the Premier League Community Facilities Fund. The players have also contributed, with each club squad donating £25,000 to a Premier League Players Kit Scheme that provides kit and equipment for the under-16 teams most in need. In addition, club staffs are supported through a workforce development program that ensures they are all highly skilled and fully qualified. This joined-up approach helps to support grass roots football, uses sport as a development tool and places the club at the hub of their local community.

Projects

These strategies are only successful if the correct partnerships are created and developed; if funding is set at the required levels; if there is a proven need for a project; and if the clubs have the staff with the necessary skills to deliver a high quality program. Two UK projects are now highlighted to show the power and scope of Creating Chances (Premier League, 2011a).

Kickz

A prime example of how Creating Chances successfully operates is the flagship community cohesion program, Kickz. The Premier League provides the funding, management support and club delivery operations for this ground-breaking, award-winning scheme that has just celebrated its fifth anniversary and has now engaged over 70,000 young people. The Kickz vision is to use football to "create safer, stronger, more respectful communities through the development of young people's potential." In particular, Kickz aims to target some of the most challenging and disadvantaged communities which suffer from higher rates of crime and anti-social behavior and use the power of football to engage young people aged 12–18 in a range of positive activities. The Kickz model adopts a consistent format which engages youngsters three nights a week, 48 weeks of the year with two sessions involving football and one flexible session where the young people can decide the activity from a wide variety of sports, music, arts or workshops.

The success of Kickz has been built on key partnerships and investment between the Premier League, the Government and the Metropolitan Police. The strategic lead from these organizations has developed a national program that can be delivered on a local basis and this cascade effect has now engaged over 650 local partners, 44 professional football clubs, over 70,000 participants, 100 projects, 19 different police forces and 64 local authorities. Additionally, 91 percent of Kickz projects are delivered on a Friday or Saturday night when anti-social behavior is at its peak. Compare and contrast that figure with average local authority provision of 4 percent on a Friday and 1 percent on a Saturday evening.

A central Kickz project management team are based within an external organization to provide a network of support, particularly concentrating on quality assurance. The target beneficiary group is often high risk so the club coaches are required to be highly trained and skilled in dealing with any potential incidents. The quality of the coaches is imperative in breaking down any barriers with the youngsters, building their confidence, encouraging volunteering within projects and steering them towards routes into employment, training or education. Independent research shows how successful Kickz has been in meeting its myriad objectives:

- 75 percent of participants live in the top 30 percent most deprived areas.
- Reductions in anti-social behavior of up to 60 percent have been reported in areas where Kickz takes place, along with crime decreases of up to 28 percent in criminal damage and 19 percent in violence against the person.
- Over 8,300 volunteers have been created, an impressive one in nine of all participants.

- Over 400 young people have progressed to employment within clubs following a pathway from participant to role model.
- There has been a total of 129,578 positive outcomes and over 8,600 qualifications achieved by young people attending Kickz sessions.

There is much external evidence to back up the success of Kickz. An evaluation report carried out by Laureus Sport for Good Foundation, published in 2011, entitled *Teenage Kicks: The Value of Sport in Tackling Youth Crime* highlighted the success of Kickz. The report showed that for every £1 invested into Kickz £7.35 of value was created for society across the Police, Criminal Justice System and the local community. The report also said that Kickz is doing more than just diverting young people from crime to football. It's also improving their behavior at other times by teaching the dangers of crime and changing attitudes and aspirations (Nevill and Van Poortvliet, 2011). Kickz was highlighted by Brooke Kinsella as an example of best practice in her Home Office report "Tackling Knife Crime Together – a review of local anti-knife crime projects" issued after the tragic killing of her brother Ben (Kinsella, 2011).

A report into the 2011 summer riots in various parts of England praised the Kickz project. The Independent Riots Communities and Victims Panel, commissioned by the Home Office, identified Kickz as a "particularly compelling" example of good practice (Home Office, 2011). A Kickz five-year celebration event was held at the Houses of Parliament at which the Home Secretary, the Right Honourable Theresa May, praised the work of Kickz saying:

> We all know how many supporters enjoy watching football, but the idea of using its strength to help young people in this way is fantastic. I congratulate Richard Scudamore (Chief Executive, Premier League) and Tim Godwin (Acting Commissioner, Metropolitan Police) for coming together and making this idea work, because it is obviously having a tremendous impact across the whole country.
>
> (Premier League, 2011b)

The Home Secretary added:

> Kickz is a wonderful project and the number of young people involved is great. It's doing really good work enabling them to not just be taken out of situations in which they might get involved in gangs or crime, but actually giving young people a voice and enabling them to be heard. All those involved in it deserve a great deal of praise, especially those that volunteer, as they make it what it is.
>
> (Premier League, 2011b)

Kickz, and other Premier League programs, are more than just a football community project. Football is the hook to engage them in constructive or educational activities. From there we can increase the playing, coaching and officiating opportunities for participants. We can create routes into education, volunteering, training and employment. We can help address social issues such as breaking down perceived barriers between young people and the police. And we can use the universal language of football to help build stronger and safer communities. Based on the old saying that imitation is the sincerest form of flattery then it's a huge compliment to Kickz that it has been used as the model for similar inclusion programs involving rugby, cricket and athletics.

Figure 18.1 The Secretary of State for Education Michael Gove presenting an award at the 4th National
Kickz Awards held at the Etihad Stadium

And this work can be exported. During the last year three "Inspired by Kickz" projects
have been set up in partnership with the British Council in Brazil, India and Indonesia. In Rio
de Janeiro there are now over 280 young people taking part in the Esporte Seguro (Safe Sport)
project in the Morros dos Prazeres favela, an area with high levels of deprivation and crime.
A delegation of participants and coaches from the Rio project visited London in April 2012.
When asked to describe the impact of Kickz in Rio, one of the coaches, Orlando Data, said
"You cannot put into words something that is immeasurable."

Premier League 4 Sport

The focus of football clubs' work is not just about getting people to play more football. Another
national project, Premier League 4 Sport (PL4S), is the Premier League's contribution to the
legacy of the London 2012 Olympics. The UK Government wanted more people participating
in sport and identified a drop-off rate among secondary school pupils. PL4S was set up to use
the power and brand of football to address this drop-off and encourage secondary school pupils
to take up four particularly under-represented sports – judo, badminton, table tennis and volleyball. The project, run in partnership with Sport England, works with the national governing
bodies for each sport and is delivered by Premier League clubs through the development of new
satellite and hub clubs to boost the school to club link.

Launched in 2009, the pioneering sports participation program exceeded its initial target
of engaging 25,000 young people in the Olympic sports to such an extent that four additional
sports have already been added to the program – netball, basketball, hockey and handball.

Figure 18.2 Participants in the Premier League 4 Sport program

Over 43,000 young people have already engaged in PL4S with more than 2,300 sports leaders and sports coaching qualifications achieved. The initiative has provided a blueprint for the Conservative Government strategy idea of turning secondary schools into community sports clubs. PL4S has already created over 400 such new clubs, with over 80 percent of them situated within schools, to help drive the PL4S participation strategy to engage, retain and sustain. PL4S is having a positive impact on sports participation figures. Since the start of the initiative there has been an overall increase of 80,000 young people playing the four sports of badminton, judo, table tennis and volleyball. A quarter of these 80,000 are directly attributable to PL4S. And it's not just the total participation figures that are bucking the national downward trend – 34 percent of the participants are female, nearly three times the national average and 14 percent are from a black and minority ethnics (BME) backgrounds.

Due to this huge uplift the PL4S program expansion will take Premier League investment to £5.8m and there has been £1.24m additional investment in the program via Sportsmatch funding. Using the power of football to attract young people, the aim is for PL4S to be providing a legacy long after the 2012 Olympic Games in London. Secretary of State for Culture, Olympics, Media and Sport, Jeremy Hunt said:

> Football can be incredibly powerful in engaging young people. The Premier League 4 Sport scheme has already involved tens of thousands of young people, and has given a huge boost to grassroots sport. The extra funding announced today by the Premier League means that the project will be able to offer even more sports. Initiatives like this will do a huge amount to help deliver the Government's plans to encourage young people to develop a sporting habit for life.
>
> (Premier League, 2011e)

Olympic Gold Medallist Darren Campbell has witnessed PL4S at first hand. He said:

> I fully appreciate how the power of the Premier League name, in association with the commitment of the clubs, can provide real inspiration and motivation for young people to participate in these sports. This is clearly the "magic dust" that is working to great effect through the delivery of this program. Who knows one day we may well see an Olympian or Paralympian whose first opportunity to play the sport was created through the PL4S program, but along the way many thousands will have been inspired to participate. That will be a powerful legacy for sport.
>
> (Premier League, 2011e)

The success of this has proven the power that football possesses to engage, inspire, develop and motivate young people in a multi-sport arena. Using football for development can be the catalyst to provide a sporting participation, and career, pathway that then acts as a catalyst to help sustain programs such as PL4S. In the post-Olympic period, when the euphoria of Team GB's success has faded, so projects like PL4S will become even more important to the sporting legacy of 2012.

International projects

With the Premier League now broadcast in 212 territories around the world, and hundreds of millions of people tuning in to watch Barclays Premier League matches over a season, having an international element to our off-pitch work is now a crucial, and growing, part of the Creating Chances program. Our international development work is well defined: it is about using the power of football and the appeal of the Premier League around the world, to inspire people to make a difference to their own lives and those around them. We take coaches and referee trainers from the Premier League and our clubs to help build up a network of community-level coaches and referees in countries where there is a major interest in football, but often without the footballing infrastructure to help support people to work at the community level. We deliver this in partnership with people and organizations with an intimate knowledge of what is needed in each country, and help support inspiring projects and individuals to use football to bring about positive change in the communities in which they live.

This ethos manifests itself on the ground through a variety of initiatives. Our flagship project is Premier Skills, which we are actively involved in delivering with our lead partner the British Council, in the many countries in which it exists around the world. Alongside this are a series of projects that we support to deliver work that fits with our ethos. Detailed below is an overview of all of this work, concentrating mainly around Premier Skills itself, looking at how it works on the ground, with feedback from those involved and those closest to be able to judge the impact it is having.

Premier Skills

Premier Skills is the Premier League's lead international project. A multi-strand partnership between the Premier League and the British Council, it combines the Premier League's global appeal and experience in delivering football-based community projects with the presence and experience of the British Council in education and culture. Through this multi-strand approach, Premier Skills involves an innovative grassroots coach and referee development initiative, a select number of pilot projects "inspired by" the hugely successful UK Kickz project, as well as an element devoted to producing Premier League-related resources for teachers and learners of English around the globe. Premier Skills is active in 20 countries around the world, and has already helped train over 1,500 local community coaches and referees, who our research has shown have gone on to work with over 400,000 young people (Premier League, 2011c).

Comic Relief

Through our long-term sponsorship tie-up with the UK charity Comic Relief, we support two international development projects working in Sub-Saharan Africa. The first is Grassroots Soccer's "Generation Skillz" HIV education and prevention project working with over 30,000 young people in South Africa and Zimbabwe. The second is to support the UK charity Motivation, who are working in Uganda with two local organizations called The Kids League and Gulu Disabled Peoples' Union, to give young disabled children more access to sport (Comic Relief, 2011).

Magic Bus

The Premier League is now one of the major strategic funding partners for the Indian sports development charity Magic Bus. The Premier League acts as a key funding partner for the organization's three year expansion project 2010/11–2012/13, with funding from the Premier League devoted to expanding the innovative Magic Bus coaching program out from Mumbai State into Delhi, Hyderabad and Maharashtra States. Over these three years Magic Bus expects this expansion to help radically improve the lives of over 80,000 young people living in poverty (Magic Bus, 2011).

International Small Grants Fund (ISGF)

The ISGF was launched in 2007 as an opportunity for the Premier League to support a range of charitable organizations that use sport as a tool for development around the world. The ISGF has a maximum grant level of £15,000 per project, and has enabled us to work with a range of different agencies in countries as diverse as Guatemala, Indonesia, Lesotho and Sri Lanka (Premier League, 2011d).

Premier Skills

Premier Skills started life in 2006, focusing back then entirely on creating community coaches in various countries around the world. Pilots initially ran in Egypt, using three or four coaches drawn from Premier League clubs to deliver week-long intensive classroom and pitch-based activities to around 50 male and female Egyptian coaches. This core element to Premier Skills is still active today, helping coaches drawn from a wide range of day-to-day roles – some school teachers, some amateur coaches, others working in sport for development charities – to develop their understanding of innovative coaching techniques. Known now as Phase 1 to the project, it provides participants with an introduction to some of the skills used by Premier League community coaches to engage young people from a wide range of backgrounds.

The Phase 1 coaching model is followed up in each country by Phase 2, delivered between three and six months later. This is aimed at the 30 most promising coaches from that first phase, who the British Council have continuously monitored, and have subsequently shown the greatest acumen for further learning. Phase 2 is another week-long session, again delivered by different Premier League coaches, and whilst continuing to blend practical and theoretical learning, it focuses more on developing the participants' understanding of how to create specific projects, how they might engage volunteers and staff, and how to apply for funding to support these initiatives.

Using case studies of projects delivered by Premier League clubs in the UK, as well as seeking examples from the participants themselves, Phase 2 also aims to take the coaches to a new level of understanding of how to use football as a tool to tackle whatever social issues may be prevalent in their community. These could be health issues, or cultural differences between ethnic groups, or a lack of opportunity to access an education. Instilling an understanding of how football can be used to make a positive difference to some of these issues is a core element to Premier Skills, and leads on to how we seek to ensure the project remains sustainable in each country through Phase 3.

Phase 3 targets again a smaller core group of these coaches, between 12 and 15, and those who the British Council and the Premier League coaches feel have got the best potential to be able to pass on what they have learnt to others: in other words, become Premier Skills mentors themselves, and go on to run their own Phase 1 courses in each country, using the methodology and curriculum they had learnt from themselves. This is a difficult skill, hence why Phase 3 focuses on a smaller number of participant coaches. But the benefits are enormous. Should these coaches, over the course of a three-staged Phase 3, show the skills needed to become Premier Skills coach mentors themselves, the end result is a legacy in the country far beyond the need for Premier League coaches to be there each time.

Botswana is a country which has been through all of these stages, and thanks to a memorandum of understanding signed with the Botswana Football Association, Premier Skills hub sites are being set up in a number of different towns in the country, where coaches who have taken part in all Phase 3 of Premier Skills so far, are now about to embark on passing on their knowledge to hundreds more coaches, who in turn will work with thousands of young people. Fatima Sidomo, from Francistown in the North East of Botswana, is one of the coaches who have recently undergone Phase 3 training. She had this to say:

> I am one of those people that Premier Skills is all about; I go back into my community to teach others what I have learned. I am a teacher and coach and I work with vulnerable people with a disability aged between six and 30 years old. If the purpose of Premier Skills is to train the trainers then the Premier League is doing a good job as we are developing a lasting legacy for football in Botswana. This has had a direct benefit for my community. I have since offered six coaches formal training. I still have to recruit more coaches, especially those who work with disabled people. What I do know is that the life skills they learn from Premier Skills has uplifted their spirits and they feel included in society.
>
> (Premier League, 2011a)

Alongside developing coaches such as Fatima, the project has also moved to help create community referees since 2010. Feedback from countries during the first three years of Premier Skills was that there was a need for better trained referees at the grassroots level. And so, using the expertise of former FIFA referees such as Keith Hackett and Alan Wiley, and a number of current professional referee trainers, the Premier Skills referee course was developed. It revolves around a three day training intervention which is often run as an add-on to a Phase 1 coaching course. Twenty referees in each country undergo this first phase of training, and in some countries such as Malaysia, there has been a focus on rolling out back-to-back courses due to a particular need for greater numbers of referees there.

As well as face-to-face work, Premier Skills also utilizes an innovative website with download-able materials available free of charge to anyone in the world interested in learning or teaching English. Using football-based content and the British Council's world class expertise in English, a range of materials have been created for teachers and learners of English, complementing the British Council's wider global offer in English, and furthering the reach and impact of Premier Skills considerably. Andy Hansen, Senior Advisor, Sport in Education, British Council, states:

> As partnerships go they don't come much better for the British Council than the Premier League. Working with the Premier League helps to open up new doors for the UK. We know the benefits of working with the Premier League and its clubs. They have fantastic experience of using football to tackle issues in communities, and this is often a new concept for many of overseas partners – it adds value to what they are trying to achieve for young people and creates a new strand in the relationship we have with them.
>
> (Premier League, 2011a)

Premier Skills: key facts

- Premier Skills' face-to-face activities take place in 20 countries around the world. These are: (in Africa) Egypt, Morocco, Tunisia, Ethiopia, Cameroon, Senegal, Nigeria, Sudan, Uganda, Kenya, Botswana and Malawi; in India four different areas have hosted separate Premier Skills activity: New Delhi, Kolkata, Goa and Kerala; (in South East Asia) Malaysia, South Korea, Indonesia and Vietnam; and in China (across a multitude of cities and regions). We have also launched in 2011 in Mexico and Brazil.
- The impact of the coach development project is forever growing as more activity takes place. Through monitoring it has been ascertained that it has trained over 1,500 new coaches, who have been monitored to have gone on to improve the lives of over 400,000 young people. There is a new element to Premier Skills which is still in its infancy, whereby we have launched three projects "inspired by" the Kickz program, run by 40 professional football clubs in England.
- The projects – in Jakarta, Kolkata and Rio de Janeiro – are based on the Kickz model, but are each distinct in their own right, tackling the issues prevalent in each city. The one thing they have in common is what is at the heart of Kickz – giving young people from disadvantaged backgrounds the opportunity to express themselves in a positive fashion.

Conclusions

Football is an integral part of millions of people's lives from attending matches, watching on television or being the social glue that binds together conversations in workplaces, pubs and social media forums on a daily basis. Through Creating Chances the Premier League is now reaching out to millions more people every year, using football and sport for positive develop-ment and transformed the community development landscape. Partnerships have been formed that have enabled clubs to address such diverse and wide-ranging issues as anti-social behavior, men's health, participation drop-off in teenagers, educational standards and youth unemploy-ment. The conclusion is a clear one: Creating Chances has created a best practice template that can offer government departments, local authorities, charities, National Governing bodies and other community agencies the opportunity to work with professional football clubs to meet their own strategic objectives and achieve lasting legacy.

References

Comic Relief (2011) *Comic Relief*. Available at: http://www.comicrelief.com/home (accessed: April 30, 2013).

Home Office (2011) *After the Riots – Independent riots communities and victims panel*. Available at: http://www.homeoffice.gov.uk/publications/effective-practice/community-effective-practice/After-the-Riots-IRCVP (accessed: August 23, 2012).

Kinsella, B. (2011) 'Tackling knife crime together – a review of local anti-knife crime projects', *Home Office*. Available at: http://www.homeoffice.gov.uk/publications/crime/tackling-knife-crime-together (accessed: August 23, 2012).

Laureus Sport for Good Foundation (2011) *Teenage Kicks: The value of sport in tackling youth crime*. Available at: http://www.laureus.com/publications (accessed: April 30, 2013).

Magic Bus (2011) *Magic Bus*. Available at: http://www.magicbus.org (accessed: April 30, 2013).

Morgan, S. (2010) 'Creating Chances: The Premier League's corporate social responsibility programme', *Journal of Sponsorship*, 4 (1), 15–25.

Nevill, C. and Van Poortvliet, M. (2011) 'Teenage kicks: The value of sport in tackling youth crime', *New Philanthropy Capital Blog*, March. Available at: http://www.philanthropycapital.org/publications/education/sport.aspx (accessed: August 23, 2012).

Premier League (2011a) *Premier League Creating Chances*. Available at: http://addison.ceros.com/premier-league/creating-chances-2011/page/1 (accessed: August 21, 2012).

Premier League (2011b) *Kickz 5 Year publication report*. Available at: http://addison.ceros.com/kickz/kickz/5/year/celebration/fiveyearcelebration/page/1: (accessed: November 23, 2011).

Premier League (2011c) *Premier Skills English*. Available at: http://premierskills.britishcouncil.org/ (accessed: August 21, 2012).

Premier League (2011d) *International Small Grants Fund*. Available at: http://www.premierleague.com/en-gb/creating-chances/2011-12/small-grants-fund.html (accessed: August 22, 2012).

Premier League (2011e) *Premier League initiative exceeds expectations*. Available at: http://www.premierleague.com/en-gb/creating-chances/2011-12/premier-league-4-sport-initiative-exceeds-expectations.html) (accessed: November 7, 2012).

Sport+Markt (2012) *Premier League Season Review 2011/12*. Available at: http://www.premierleague.com/en-gb/about/season-review-2011-12.html (accessed: November 7, 2012).

19

"STREET VIOLENCE RUINS LIVES"

Communicating CSR initiatives

Steve Sutherland

Overview

This chapter presents a case study of the "Street Violence Ruins Lives" initiative launched by the Charlton Athletic Community Trust in 2008. The aim of the initiative is to teach young people about the dangers of carrying a knife and of gang membership. Based on a personal account given by the former Commercial Director of Charlton Athletic Football Club and the founder of the Community Trust, the case study highlights the ways in which the initiative has been communicated in order to raise awareness of the campaign. It argues that it is important for sports organizations to effectively communicate corporate social responsibility (CSR) initiatives as it can raise awareness amongst those individuals that can potentially benefit from a particular scheme but that it can also potentially lead to increased funding from the commercial sector that can be used help to expand the delivery of CSR initiatives.

Introduction

It has been argued that there are two broad motivations, or reasons, for implementing CSR activities (Bhattacharya and Sen, 2010). Intrinsic reasons place emphasis on the importance of a particular social or environmental issue and are underpinned by normative justifications: i.e., there is a sense that these issues are important enough in their own right to be addressed. Extrinsic reasons consider that CSR can be a way to add value to a business through improved reputation or increased customer loyalty (e.g., Dean, 2003; Porter and Kramer, 2006), demonstrating instrumental, performance-oriented motivations for CSR. Research has shown that consumer awareness of CSR activities is generally low (Bhattacharya *et al.*, 2008), demonstrating that a key challenge faced by organizations is to communicate their CSR activities. This is an important aspect whether your motivation is to raise awareness of a particular CSR program amongst those individuals or groups that could potentially benefit (intrinsic) or as a way to position the brand of an organization (Lindgreen and Swaen, 2010) to gain business benefits (extrinsic). However, there are concerns that marketing CSR activities can be perceived as a form of public relations and lead to increased skepticism and cynicism (Mohr *et al.*, 2001).

Within sport, CSR initiatives can also be motivated by intrinsic and extrinsic factors. There are many different types of sports organizations that are involved in implementing CSR including sport leagues, governing bodies, professional athlete foundations, and professional teams (see Part II of the handbook for a much more detailed discussions on this area). For a professional sports team, CSR initiatives may help to create goodwill within the community that the club is based; they may help to attract commercial sponsors to a club that want the association with community-based schemes; and initiatives around sport involving young children may identify potential future players. These can be seen as extrinsic motivations. However, in the professional football (soccer) industry in the UK, the vast majority of community work associated with football clubs is delivered by community trust organizations (see also Chapters 6, 24, and 25). These are a particular type of organization that uses sport as the vehicle with which to deliver a range of community-oriented initiatives. These organizations were formerly Football in the Community schemes that were an internal part of the organizational structure of a football club. However, research showed that football clubs were failing to understand what was meant by the concept of community and how they should respond to different stakeholders (Brown *et al.*, 2006). The move to independent charitable status was seen as a way to overcome this issue and provided strategic and financial decision-making authority, allowing these organizations to focus on the implementation of CSR activities. It can be argued that the initiatives implemented by community trust organizations are fundamentally driven by intrinsic motivations and a firm belief that sport can be a mechanism with which to enact positive social change.

This chapter focuses on the Charlton Athletic Community Trust (CACT) and in particular, the groundbreaking initiative "Street Violence Ruins Lives." The aim of this initiative is to teach young people about the dangers of carrying a knife and of gang membership. The case study highlights the ways in which the CACT has communicated the aims and objectives of the "Street Violence Ruins Lives" initiative in order to raise awareness of the campaign. The chapter is based on my own personal experience and account of my involvement with the initiative. I enjoyed a 22-year career in the game that included two spells at Charlton Athletic, a brief but enjoyable period at Swindon Town, and eight very successful years as Marketing Executive of The Football League during the most impactful period of change in The League's history. After leaving Swindon Town in 1999, I returned to Charlton Athletic FC in January 2000, first as Assistant to Peter Varney, the Club's respected CEO, and then in 2006 as Commercial Director. During my time as Commercial Director I played an important role in helping to establish the Community Trust. Although I left my position as Commercial Director at Charlton Athletic FC at the end of the 2008/09 season, I am still involved with the CACT and continue in my roles as Chairman of CACT's Women's and Girls' football department and of the "Street Violence Ruins Lives" committee, which I co-founded with my long-time associate, Jason Morgan, the CEO of the CACT.

The Charlton Athletic Community Trust

The Charlton Athletic Community Trust is the charitable organization associated with Charlton Athletic Football Club. The football club is based in the Borough of Greenwich, south-east London and play at The Valley stadium. The club spent the best part of the last decade competing in the Premier League, although was relegated to the Championship in 2007 and League One in 2009. They have since achieved promotion back to the Championship in 2012. The club has a proud history of developing projects that can deliver positive messages, that are sustainable, and that get results and contribute to the community from which they draw their support. This close association with the community dates back to the 1980s and 1990s when the club spent seven years in exile from The Valley and played their home matches first at Selhurst Park, home of Crystal Palace football club (where I spent my first period with the club as Commercial Manager), then at West Ham United's Upton Park ground. During this period fans formed The Valley Party and in 1990 contested 60 out of the 62 seats in the local Greenwich Borough Council elections. The Valley Party received 14,838 votes, a total of 10.9 percent of the vote (Everitt, 1991: 218) on the strength of their single-issue campaign to return the club to The Valley. As a result of the election success Greenwich Borough Council granted planning permission to upgrade The Valley allowing the club to return in December 1992. The community therefore played a key role in helping the club return to The Valley which provided Charlton with a level of stability lacking in the previous seven years with which to take the club forward.

The community program (Football in the Community) at Charlton Athletic Football Club was first established in 1992 on the club's return to The Valley. Under the stewardship of Jason Morgan, who literally started the program with just a "bag of balls," the community program went from strength to strength and by 2003 had become one of the most respected schemes in English football. It was at this point that it was decided that the work of the Football in the Community scheme needed to be to ring-fenced and the decision was taken to re-launch the community program as a formal charity under the auspices of trustees led by prominent Charlton fan, Roger Godsiff MP and with core-funding from Sir Maurice Hatter's Hatter Foundation, under the new name of the Charlton Athletic Community Trust (CACT). As a not-for-profit charitable organization the board of trustees has the responsibility of setting the strategic direction of the trust, while implementing strategy is the responsibility of the chief executive of CACT. He oversees a total of 37 full-time staff supported by an additional 139 part-time, casual coaches. These coaches deliver a variety of programs that are designed to fit within one or more of five key aims: raising education achievement; creating pathways to employment; building healthier lifestyles; bringing communities together; and reducing crime. CACT's ground-breaking and innovative programs are delivered through a regular presence in schools, and working with disadvantaged or socially excluded groups in society, through crime reduction initiatives and community based football coaching sessions. In total the coaches engage with approximately 7,500 young people on a weekly basis, with over 55 separate strands of work delivered by CACT each year.

CACT is highly regarded for the way that it engages with different stakeholder groups. In particular, the work that the club does within its local community has earned Charlton a reputation within the football industry and the broader business domain as a community club.

The work being undertaken by CACT has received recognition within its local communities, nationally, as well as internationally through the ground-breaking, ongoing, project in the township of Alexandra in Johannesburg, South Africa that was established in 2002 to break down the barriers between the South African Police and young people and to discourage young people from engaging in criminal activities. CACT has received numerous prestigious industry awards over recent years. For instance, in November 2005, Charlton Athletic Football Club was voted as one of the top 10 organizations at the National Business Awards in the CSR category in recognition of the impact that the football club and Community Trust have in their local community. More recently they have received the Silver Jubilee Award for Community Engagement, the Football League Championship Community Club of the year, and the Football League Family Excellence Award.

The "Street Violence Ruins Lives" campaign

I have always believed that a club's commercial department should work hand in hand with its community scheme, and accordingly I had a very close working relationship with Jason

Morgan, the Chief Executive of CACT. It was this close working relationship between Jason and I that led to the creation of the "Street Violence Ruins Lives" campaign in 2008. This campaign was created in response to increasing concerns over violent street stabbings. During the summer of 2008 it seemed that every day a young person lost their life by being the victim of a violent street stabbing and the headlines in the national press reflected this blight on society. The knife problem was then to come close to home as we heard the terribly sad news that a talented young actor and Charlton Athletic fan called Rob Knox, who had just finished filming the latest Harry Potter film, had been stabbed to death outside a bar in Sidcup. I remember that moment vividly: on hearing the sad news of Rob's tragic death Jason and I sat in my office at The Valley and said to each other that the club and the Trust must try to do something to address the growing problem of youth violence in our catchment area of South London and Kent. We had a track record in these types of projects: for example the renowned "Kick Racism out of Football" campaign had started at Charlton some 10 years earlier. In addition, CACT was also the first to pilot a project warning children of the dangers of playing near railway lines, a hugely successful initiative that went on to be implemented nationwide.

Jason and I decided to call a meeting, which was held in the boardroom at The Valley, to voice our concerns and to try and get support for our idea to launch a separate strand of work by CACT to combat knife crime. We invited representatives from the Greenwich, Bexley and Kent Police Forces, Greenwich Council and Bexley Council to attend – no one declined. At the meeting, Jason and I highlighted the problem and we distributed a selection of press cuttings relating to knife crime that had appeared in the media that very week. We explained that our idea was to put together an educational program that CACT officers would deliver at every school in Greenwich and Bexley and longer term, in Kent. The thinking behind this was that a "tracksuit" will be able to relate to at risk and vulnerable children far better than a "suit" or a police uniform could ever do. Our idea received unanimous support. Initially Jason and I felt that our program would be an anti-knife campaign but at that same meeting it was made very clear that there was also a growing gun problem in London and we should position our program as an anti-street violence campaign. After a short discussion the title of CACT's latest campaign was agreed: "Street Violence Ruins Lives." The aim of the initiative is to teach young people about the perils of carrying a knife and of gang membership. The program is delivered in schools, on estates-based provisions and with young people identified as being involved or at risk of becoming involved in crime or violence. Specialist work is also carried out with repeat offenders who are at risk of custodial sentences or who have been released from custody on licence.

Both Jason and I felt very strongly that if we were to make a real difference we would need the co-operation of Colin and Sally Knox, Rob's parents, and with the support of Kevin Taylor, the family's Police Liaison Officer. It was agreed that we would contact Colin and Sally to seek their support for our program and to invite them to join our "Street Violence Ruins Lives" Committee. Both Colin and Sally could not have been more supportive and their commitment to the work of CACT has been instrumental in the success of the "Street Violence Ruins Lives" campaign.

Figure 19.1 Left to right: Jason Morgan, CEO, CACT, Sally Knox, Colin Knox and Bob Bolder, former CAFC player and now CACT Officer

Communicating the campaign

There are different ways in which "Street Violence Ruins Lives" has been communicated to raise awareness of the campaign. The following three ways are discussed: the launch of the campaign, which helped to raise national awareness of the initiative; a co-ordinated public relations and media campaign to continue to promote the initiative; and the on-the-ground delivery of the projects that helped to raise awareness amongst young people within the local communities of South London and Kent.

The campaign launch

It was agreed that we would formally launch "Street Violence Ruins Lives" at the club's forthcoming live Sky TV match with Reading at The Valley, and The Football League and Football Association gave Charlton permission for the club's players to wear a specially produced logo, proclaiming that "Street Violence Ruins Lives," on their shirts during the televised Championship fixture. It is at this point that I must acknowledge the fantastic support that Jason and I received from Sky's Dickie Davies. When Dickie heard of our plans he immediately offered to do a news piece on the launch of "Street Violence Ruins Lives" for Sky Sports. Jason and I asked Colin and Sally whether they would be prepared to do an interview with Dickie in support of the campaign and they readily agreed. Without a doubt, the support of the Knox family and the impact of Dickie's coverage on Sky Sports were the major factors in the successful launch of the campaign. However, the role played by the Government Office

Figure 19.2 Launch at the Valley

for London was also critical in that it provided some core funding to cover the formal launch. The then sponsors of Charlton Athletic, JD Sports, were also extremely supportive of the campaign and their staff at local branches wore specially produced "Street Violence Ruins Lives" t-shirts supplied by the club's kit suppliers, Joma, on the day of the Reading match to promote the campaign. Jason and I were also extremely pleased when then Government Minister Tony McNulty MP accepted our invitation to attend the launch as this graphically highlighted that our campaign had full government approval.

Public relations and media campaign

In line with the launch of the initiative, CACT was able to secure the services of a PR company (on a pro-bono basis) to help raise further awareness of the initiative. This enabled the initiative to receive a significant amount of press coverage within national newspapers in the build up to the launch. Moreover, the "Street Violence Ruins Lives" initiative has received a significant amount of coverage on the internet through partner websites and through media support for the campaign. The CACT website has a section on the initiative whilst there is a dedicated campaign website that provides details of the objectives of the initiative and the partners involved and provides information on annual charity events that draw on celebrity support to keep the campaign in the public eye and to raise funding.

Program delivery

The "Street Violence Ruins Lives" initiative is delivered by CACT officers who visit schools and estates across Greenwich, Bexley and Kent to talk to children and educate them about the dangers of knives and guns and of the perils of gang membership. CACT delivers programs into 80 estates per week where it reaches the most at risk and vulnerable young people. As well as delivering programs in estates, the campaign has been promoted in schools in line with the national curriculum. The delivery of the programs is in partnership with a range of different partners such as local authorities (Greenwich Council; the London Borough of Bexley), central government, the Metropolitan Police and Kent Police, and the Safer London Foundation. Some of these partner organizations provide funding to help the delivery of the program. Central to the delivery is that the power of sport, and football in particular, has the potential to reach out to young people in a way that more traditional delivery approaches find challenging.

The communicational impact of "Street Violence Ruins Lives"

Since launching "Street Violence Ruins Lives," I am proud to say that, with the total support of Rob's parents Colin and Sally, our work in this important area has gone from strength to strength; so much so that everyone connected with Charlton Athletic and CACT were delighted to receive in March 2009 the accolade of Community Club of the Year from The Football League, thanks in the main to this important project. Moreover, in 2009 CACT was the regional winner for the South East for the Tilley Award – an annual award from the Home Office that recognizes innovative partnership projects aimed at crime reduction. The "Street Violence Ruins Lives" initiative was central to this. Part of the reasoning behind the award was the 25 percent reduction in reports of anti-social behavior within the areas in which the initiative was in operation. In 2012, the work of the project has been further recognized as having an impact on knife crime: recent figures compared the period of April 2011 to May 2011 with April 2012 to May 2012 and demonstrated a 28 percent reduction (66 offences in 2011 compared to 47 offences in 2012). Moreover, youth violence was reduced by 40 percent with 48 fewer crimes. The work of the police in Greenwich in collaboration with CACT and the "Street Violence Ruins Lives" initiative is one factor that has been recognized as contributing to this decline.

However, while these awards have been given for the impact of the "Street Violence Ruins Lives" initiatives on crime reduction, it can be argued that there are two additional impacts that have resulted from the extensive communications surrounding the scheme. First, the various means of communication have helped to raise awareness of the scheme and this, in turn, has encouraged partner organizations to sign up to support the initiative. A number of partner organizations were noted above that contribute to the initiative. The example of collaboration with government and private sector organizations is critical for charitable organizations such as CACT given the financial uncertainty and instability across the third sector following cuts to local government budgets. The issue of financial sustainability is critical and affects community sport trusts as any other charitable organization: seeking alternative sources of revenue and working in partnership is a way to address this challenge. However, an important aspect of this is the visibility of community initiatives and therefore communicating CSR initiatives is of critical importance to raise awareness and in particular to attract corporate sponsors. The involvement of multiple partner organizations with the "Street Violence Ruins Lives" initiative, attracted in part due to the high-profile nature of the campaign and the extensive media coverage, has helped to provide sustainability and longevity.

The second impact resulting from communicating the initiative to raise awareness of the issue of weapons related violence amongst young people is that it has led to the development of the acclaimed Crime Reduction program run by CACT. Under the supervision of Nick Darvill, a former policeman with over 30 years' experience, CACT's Crime Reduction program works at three levels: first, through awareness programs within schools and on estates-based provision, with young people identified as being involved or at risk of becoming involved in crime; second, in the area of violence and radicalization, including specialist work with repeat offenders who are at risk of custodial sentences or who have received sentence but are released on license; third, the Crime Reduction program has spent considerable time working with 16 of the most at risk young people on Bexley Council's U Turn 1 Program. This comprises a five-day intensive program and is presently followed up by one day per week over a 12-week period. The work has also extended to encompass the victims of anti-social behavior. This program is the first one of its kind delivered by a football club community program in the UK and the hope is that it will be adopted as a model of best practice by other clubs.

This CACT Crime Reduction program has a focused approach and works in very close partnership with CACT's key stakeholders in Bexley, Greenwich, Dartford and Gravesham. Engaging, supporting and challenging some of the most at risk young people in terms of offending and becoming the victims of crime are the key objectives of the program. The Greenwich Crime Reduction program has made sound progress working alongside The Youth Crime Prevention Panel, 18–25 Intervention Management Group, Serious Youth Violence Offender Management Group and The Deter Panel. CACT will have an integral role working with 'The Top Ten' at risk young people, providing support and development opportunities. Work within The Kent Program is still in its early stages of development. The program has also begun work under the preventing violent extremism agenda. This area of work is at an early stage and CACT is now ready to take referrals from The Channel Project after formalizing its own information sharing agreement with the Metropolitan Police Service.

Conclusions

This chapter began by discussing the extrinsic and intrinsic motivations for implementing CSR initiatives and how, in both cases, communicating CSR programs can be important. The main section of the chapter has focused on CACT and in particular the "Street Violence Ruins Lives" initiative and it has discussed different ways in which this initiative has been communicated. It has been made clear that the fundamental motivation for the implementation of this initiative was intrinsic in that it developed out of a genuine concern surrounding a particular issue: in this case it was in regard to the dangers of carrying a knife and of gang membership and the need to raise awareness of this issue. This, it could be argued, is the main motivating factor underpinning the work that the CACT trust is involved in given that it is a charitable organization with the clear objective to work in partnership with local communities to empower individuals to improve their lives and their environment. This is also the case for community trust organizations more broadly that are associated with professional football clubs where there is a firm belief in the power of sport as a mechanism to enact positive social change.

Nevertheless, this is not to dismiss the fact that there are also extrinsic benefits that arise from communicating CSR initiatives such as "Street Violence Ruins Lives." For example, I have always believed that the commercial department from a football club should work hand in hand with its community scheme. During my time as Commercial Director of the football club I had a very close working relationship with Jason Morgan and the largest ever sponsorship deal signed by the club with Spanish property giants Llanera (a deal worth £1.5m a year to the club) also included title sponsorship of CACT demonstrating the potential for community/CSR work to also have commercial value for a football club. Indeed, I believe it is vital for football to attract sponsors who want to do more than just place perimeter boards around the pitch and enjoy fine-dining in the match day restaurants and projects such as CACT's "Street Violence Ruins Lives" campaign help to highlight this point. In this sense, communicating CSR programs has an extrinsic benefit in that it can help to raise awareness amongst potential commercial partners and lead to closer working relationships in which sports organizations such as CACT can act as the delivery vehicle as part of a commercial organization's CSR strategy. In doing so, it will hopefully unlock other important sources of funding for sporting organizations and their community operations. Although this can be seen as an extrinsic benefit for communicating CSR schemes, ultimately the motivation is intrinsic in that it allows CACT to generate funding for delivering additional community projects. The Crime Reduction program that emerged from the success of the "Street Violence Ruins Lives" initiative is testament to this.

Although research has been skeptical about the claims made of the impact of social initiatives (Coalter, 2007) (see also Chapters 2 and 3) it can be argued that football, and sport in general, has the potential to play an important role in combating social ills. However, this is dependent upon the required level of funding and corporate support to enable community trust organizations and indeed other sporting bodies, to address issues such as reducing crime, improving health, raising educational attainment and increasing pathways to employment. CACT has come a long way since the launch of "Street Violence Ruins Lives" in 2008 and we have achieved a great deal in establishing such a groundbreaking initiative. I am extremely proud to be Chairman of the "Street Violence Ruins Lives" Committee and of the important work that is undertaken in South London and Kent. Sadly though, knife crime continues to blight our lives and although communicating initiatives such as "Street Violence Ruins Lives" help to raise awareness of this issue and can play a considerable part in helping to educate young people, much more needs to be done to eradicate this problem.

References

Bhattacharya, C.B. and Sen, S (2010) 'Maximizing business returns to corporate social responsibility (CSR): The role of CSR communication', *International Journal of Management Reviews*, 12 (1), 8–19.

Bhattacharya, C.B., Sen, S. and Korschun, D. (2008) 'Using corporate social responsibility to win the war for talent', *Sloan Management Review*, 49, 37–44.

Brown, A., Crabbe, T., Mellor, G., Blackshaw, T. and Stone, C. (2006) *Football and its communities: Final Report*. The Football Foundation and Manchester Metropolitan University.

Coalter, F. (2007) *A wider social role for sport: Who's keeping the score?*. London: Routledge.

Dean, D.H. (2003) 'Associating the cooperation with a charitable event through sponsorship: Measuring the effects on corporate-community relations', *Journal of Advertising*, 31 (4), 77–88.

Everitt, R. (1991) *Battle for The Valley*. Avon: Formatvisual Ltd.

Lindgreen, A. and Swaen, V. (2010) 'Corporate social responsibility', *International Journal of Management Reviews*, 12 (1), 1–7.

Mohr, L.A, Webb, D.J and Harris, K.E (2001) 'Do consumers expect companies to be socially responsible? The impact of corporate social responsibility on buying behavior', *The Journal of Consumer Affairs*, 35, 45–72.

Porter, M.E. and Kramer M.R. (2006) 'Strategy and society: The link between competitive advantage and corporate social responsibility', *Harvard Business Review*, December, 78–92.

20

ITALIAN SPORT FEDERATIONS

Communicating CSR through the social report

Cristiana Buscarini and Rita Mura

Overview

The aim of this chapter is to highlight recent trends in the field of social accounting and reporting involving Italian sport federations. The social report can be considered as an important tool of corporate communication. This chapter considers the factors that affect the adoption of social reporting, and the effects that this has on Italian sports federations. It is based on a research project initiated in 2004 with the aim of outlining specific guidelines for the compilation of the social report in Italian sports federations (Buscarini, 2006). The chapter shows how Italian sports federations use the social report to confirm the social utility of their activities with specific reference to the development of sports, educational and social welfare. In particular, social reporting activates a "virtuous circle" of planning–management–accounting–control, which can increase accountability throughout the organization in order to achieve social and institutional goals and to enable external stakeholders to assess the federation's performance.

Introduction

There has been a growing interest in the issue of social responsibility in the area of sport management (e.g., Godfrey, 2009; Bradish and Cronin, 2009) with focus on specific areas such as professional sport (Babiak and Wolfe, 2006), cause-related sport marketing (Irwin *et al.*, 2003; Lachowetz and Gladden, 2003; McGlone and Martin, 2006; Roy and Graeff, 2003), sport events (Babiak and Wolfe, 2006; Filo *et al.*, 2009), corporate citizenship (Mallen *et al.*, 2008), and sport and environmental sustainability (Babiak and Trendafilova, 2011; Ioakimidis, 2007). There has been less focus on the issue of communicating corporate social responsibility (CSR) initiatives however. The aim of this chapter is to consider CSR communication by focusing on the issue of social accounting and reporting. Social accounting and reporting are tools of communication that can legitimize the role of the organization in both structural and moral terms and in the perceptions of stakeholders within the community in which the organization exists. They can be used to highlight its links with the region in which it exists and can show how the organization, by pursuing its core interests, can contribute to improving the quality of life of the members of the community it is part of. Social accounting enables organizations to give an account ex-post to its social partners through its final product (the social report) and to show how it can contribute to developing and pursuing the corporate mission. Social reporting in particular has become commonplace within large multinational organizations. For example in 2005, over 80 of the FTSE 100 listed companies in the UK produced a CSR/sustainability report separate from the annual report (Owen, 2005).

Within sport, it can be argued that the social report for a sport federation will provide evidence of its ability to carry out projects coherent with its mission and the pursuit of which can highlight the organization's social utility. However, there has been little focus on social accounting and reporting within sport. The aim of this chapter is to consider, within the context of Italian federal sports organizations, the factors that lead to the implementation of accountability instruments and also the impact that social reporting has on these organizations. The implementation of accountability models in sport organizations belonging to the nonprofit sector has been looked at previously in Italy (Marano, 2001) and within Italian sports federations (Buscarini *et al.*, 2006). The chapter begins with an account of the Italian sporting system with a focus on the specific role of sports federations. The research methodology used in this study is briefly set out before analyzing the reasons why reporting in Italian sports federations took the form of a social report and the factors that determined this choice. We then consider the impact that the social report has had on the federal system.

The role of Italian sports federations within the national sport system

The Italian sport system has a unique organizational structure (see Figure 20.1). Italy has developed a peculiar mixed model of organization, characterized by the simultaneous presence of public and private financing. Figure 20.1 demonstrates how the Italian sports system is drawn towards the Italian National Olympic Committee (CONI). CONI is a centralized public organization that is financed by the Italian government. Italian Sports Federations, Sporting Associated Disciplines, Sporting Promotion Organizations, Honorary Associations and Military Clubs receive financing from CONI.

According to recent legislation, there are two fundamental divisions within CONI: CONI and CONI Services Ltd. The political body, the CONI-Public Authority, remains unchanged and is responsible for the development of sports in Italy and for coordinating with the International Olympic Committee (IOC). CONI Services Ltd is a new operational body of the organization through which the CONI-Public Authority carries out its tasks.

As a consequence of the absence in the Italian system of direct intervention of the central government to manage sport, many important functions have been assigned to the CONI. These include:

- to provide the organization and strengthening of the national sport, and particularly the preparation of the athletes and the organization of the suitable means for the Olympics and all other national sporting events;
- to promote the widest possible dissemination of the sport;
- to promote and to take appropriate action against all forms of discrimination and violence;
- to adopt measures of prevention and suppression of the use of substances which alter the natural physical performance of athletes in sport events, in conjunction with the Italian Commission for the supervision and control over doping and health in sport.

The financing of all Italian sport system is guaranteed by the State through the Ministry of Economy and Finance (€410 million in 2011). CONI, in turn, provides the bulk of the fees assigned to the functioning of sport organizations. Figure 20.2 provides an illustration of the sport financing process. The relationship between the CONI and CONI Services Ltd is based on an

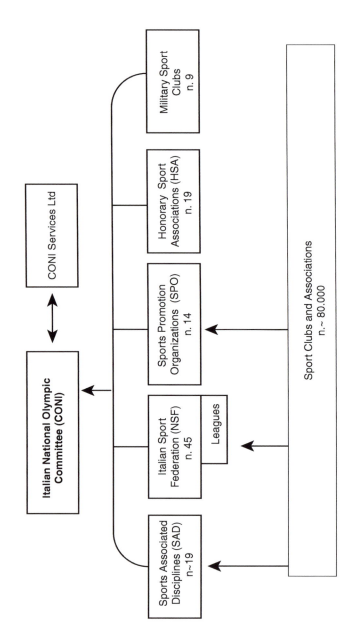

Figure 20.1 The Italian sport system

Source: our elaboration on CONI data.

annual contract of service (the amount of which is €134 million in 2011). CONI Services Ltd assists CONI with economic activities and business, and the operation of its "sports–real estate assets." However, the financing of CONI has been an ongoing issue. In 1997 the revenue forecast of sporting competitions (on all the Totocalcio) constituted about 90 percent of the sources of income of CONI, which had exclusive jurisdiction on competitions related to the sporting events that it organized. However, since the mid-1990s there has been a decline in revenue and the creation of CONI Services Ltd is in response to the need for economic and financial management based on the criteria of economic efficiency and greater functionality for Italian sport (Valori, 2005: 52).

As outlined in Figure 20.2, Italian sports federations receive the bulk of available funds by virtue of the important role they play within the sport system. In particular, Italian sport federations are associations endowed with legal personality under private law. They are legally recognized by the National Council of CONI and pursue their goals of organizing and promoting their sports in accordance with national law and international sports. In general, they are designed, in relation to their specific discipline, to organize, regulate, develop, and promote their sports through regional sport clubs and associations. They are also responsible for organizing their sports at an amateur and professional level where relevant.

Research methods

Social reporting guidelines

This chapter is based on a research project initiated in 2004 that had the aim of outlining specific guidelines for the development of the social report in Italian sports federations (Buscarini, 2006). Those guidelines were initially formulated by GBS, the research group that was set up in 2001 with the aim of codifying a set of principles to be included within the social report. This social reporting model consisted of three sections: a) corporate identity; b) generation and distribution of added value; and c) social report (GBS, 2001). Within each of these sections organizations would be required to provide a minimum amount of mandatory information.

With respect to the GBS model, the guidelines developed for Italian sports federations included the three sections above in addition to two further sections: one defining corporate efficiency and the other measuring, through a numeric index, the federation's degree of social responsibility. In brief, the guidelines we have formulated contain the following five sections.

- *Section 1*: the first section of the social report must provide an account of the identity of the organization. This includes governance arrangements and the vision and values of the organization. The description of the corporate identity sets out the structural aspects that enable it to implement in a coherent way its mission, strategic plan and policies.
- *Section 2*: this second section relates to the definition and sharing of added value. It represents the main link with the annual accounts, in particular with the profit and loss account, which is reclassified so as to highlight the economic impact of the federation's activity on the principal groups of stakeholders. The "value added assessment table" is the accounting aggregate showing how economic value for the year is generated. The "net value added distribution table" indicates how value added was shared among several stakeholders including: a) employees; b) the public administration, to which direct and indirect taxes are paid for the general services provided to the federation; c) financial backers or sponsors; d) the community of associations and affiliated sports societies; and e) the federation itself, to which, ideally, the eventual accumulation of generated wealth is due (Gabrovec Mei, 2006).

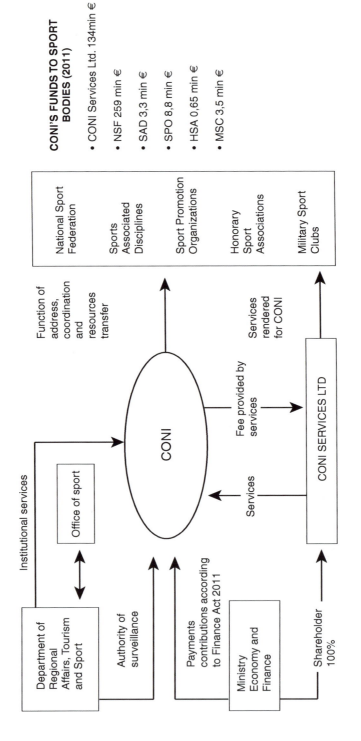

Figure 20.2 The sports financing process in Italy

Source: our elaboration on CONI data.

- *Section 3*: the third section focuses on the federation's performance and in particular provides an account of the federation's activities to its social stakeholders. These activities are grouped in seven macro areas: sporting results; dissemination of the sporting discipline; federal structure; promotional and development activity; communication and marketing; education and research; and sporting facilities. For each of these macro areas, a number of indicators have been defined expressing in quantitative terms the organization's activities and structure.

- *Section 4*: this section provides an accurate report of the organization's action vis-à-vis its principal stakeholders. These are defined by CONI as members, payroll staff, collaborators, suppliers and business partners, the local community, public administrators, and the environment. Several specific parameters have been defined (corporate practices and indexes) with a view to measuring the federation's ability to meet the expectations of its stakeholders.

- *Section 5*: a key feature of this section is the application of a specifically created system of measurement that can, on the one hand, compare the social performance over time of an organization and, on the other, create the conditions for broader comparison between all sports federations. From this a social responsibility index has been developed.[1]

Sampling

The guidelines for the social report described above were tested by six Italian "pilot" sports federations. The six were selected from the 43 sports federations that existed in Italy at the time of the pilot. In recent years two additional federations have been established: the Italian Dance Federation and the Italian Squash Federation. The pilot federations were divided into three groups: large, medium, and small. The classification based on size related to the number of individual members that each federation had. More specifically, the large-sized group concern federations that had a membership ranging from 101,714 to 1,050,695; the medium-sized group from 17,058 to 95,312; and the small-sized group from 1,813 to 14,573. On the basis of the relations existing with the Economic and Management Unit at the Foro Italico University of Rome, purposive sampling was carried out for each of the groups. In the end the decision was taken to pilot the guidelines on the following federations: the Italian Federation of Volleyball and the Italian Federation of Motor Cycling were selected to represent the large federation group; the Italian Federation of Sailing and the Italian Federation of Gymnastics represented the medium-sized group; and the Italian Federation of Triathlon and the Italian Federation of Rowing were part of the small-sized group. The purpose of the pilot was to consider whether the social reporting model could be applicable to all sized federations in Italy.

Data collection

The study involved the participation of the researchers at two levels: first as facilitators for the application of the guidelines they themselves had developed for the drawing up of a social report on the part of the federations; and second, as evaluators of the degree of social responsibility through the calculation of the index of social responsibility the researchers themselves have developed. In connection with this initial phase of the work, the research focused on the initial effects produced by the implementation of the social report on sports federations by identifying the factors that influence the implementation of accountability instruments and of the consequences that the social report has on the sports federations in the pilot study.

At a methodological level, the research relied on a survey tool of the qualitative kind based on semi-structured interviews (Corbetta, 1999). The utilization of this type of survey method was deemed to be the most appropriate because it enabled the researchers to gather a large amount of information that could be used to provide a better understanding of the issues surrounding social accounting and reporting. Semi-structured interviews were undertaken with top-ranking officials within each of the six federations, namely the chairman, general secretary and heads of department (in the areas of administration, sports, participation in Olympic Games and high-level events, marketing, and external relations). In total 39 interviews were carried out. The information gathering process through interviews took place within a time period of four months (between January and April 2010). The first step was to develop an open communication with the interviewees so as to create a relaxed environment that would allow them to respond as naturally as possible to the questions. In some cases this task proved to be particularly difficult, notwithstanding the involvement of a network of relations that facilitated access to the interviewees.

The interview strategy applied by the researchers involved two areas of questioning. First, there were a number of key questions common to all federations. This was necessary to ensure a satisfactory degree of coherence within the interviews (Patton, 2002). Interviewees were first asked to describe their operational roles and the tasks they were assigned in these roles as well as set out how long they have been working within the federation. This information was crucial because it allowed researchers to find out if the interviewee was present at the time the social report was compiled. There were also key questions that focused on better understanding the management's degree of attention for social responsibility themes and to find out to what extent the interviewees were involved in the drawing up of the social report. The second area of questioning focused on the five sections of the social report. The duration of each interview was approximately 50 minutes. All interviews were recorded and successively transcribed to aid analysis and the transcriptions were sent out to interviewees for approval. The analysis involved an initial categorization of the factors leading to the decision to draw up a social report and the effect this has on the federation being studied.

Reasons for implementing the social report

There were a number of reasons underpinning the federations' decision to implement a social report. The main reasons were linked to the acknowledgment on the part of the management of the functions of the social report in terms of communication with the federation's stakeholders, and the interpreting and assessment of appropriate indicators within strategic controlling activities. It also was important for the organization in that it was found to strengthen the process through which the federations were able to identify the stakeholders involved in the activities of the federation. This was found to strengthen the levels of democratization within the institutions. Among the three functions listed above, communication played a key role and involves all stakeholders.

The interviews also revealed that the social report is in fact a useful instrument to ensure transparency in the relations with internal stakeholders as well as a tool to guarantee accountability of the federation's external relations. In addition, a number of other factors have facilitated the adoption of the social report. These are the federation's high propensity to communicate the results achieved on the playing field; awareness on the part of the organization of the value of the social dimension of its action; involvement of those responsible for the governance of the federation in the compilation of the social report; and acknowledgment by the top management that the social report is a tool for strategic management and to set out distinctive competencies.

Consequences of the adoption of the social report

The interviews also considered the impact of the social report within the pilot federations, with a focus on each of the sections that make up the document. The first section of the social report, focusing on the distinctive identity of the federation, showed that the definition of the mission, vision, values, history, and international makeup were important aspects that were acknowledged and shared by interviewees. For example, it was clear that the federations valued this section as it gave them the opportunity to set out the mission and values of the organization:

> passion, courage, freedom, tradition, respect, competitiveness, equality, loyalty, integrity are values that distinguish our federation and form the base of our formative and educational project.
>
> (Chairman, large federation, pers. comm., March 18, 2010)

> Our mission is above all to pursue excellence according to one's own abilities, sound values and sporting desires.
>
> (General secretary, medium federation, pers. comm., February 2, 2010)

However, it was found that there was some apprehension regarding the implementation of policies and the future strategies of the federation that reflected concerns about a managerial culture that failed to consider holistic aspects of the organization due to the technical and sporting background of the management.

The second section of the document dealt with the determination of added value. The federations focused above all on the way the economic wealth produced can be distributed. In fact the social reporting model was considered useful to assess ex-post the contractual role of stakeholders, and to whom the added values should be distributed. The merit of this approach is that of having communicated to the outside besides fully gauging the degree in which the results of the activity carried out during the year contribute, in terms of economic value, to defined categories of subjects. This has led to a reflection not only on the potential of the federation but also on its ability to develop policies capable of ensuring over time a suitable distribution of economic value among various stakeholders, and in the process defining an approach capable of producing a degree of satisfaction amongst stakeholders. The following citation provides evidence of the benefits of this approach: "I consider this section of the document as being crucial because it allowed us to single out the economic wealth that was created by the activity of the federation to be distributed among our principal stakeholders" (General Secretary, small federation, pers. comm., April 13, 2010).

In regard to the third section of the social report concerning the effectiveness of the organization, all federations agreed on the importance of adopting the proposed model because it enabled the federation to highlight its performance in the seven macro areas concerning the most salient aspects of the organization. The impact of the fourth section, dedicated to underlining the relations with social partners and the environmental policies, was also found to have been significant. Notwithstanding the ease with which stakeholders are identified and the awareness of the role played by each one of them within the organization, the federations all stressed the fact that not enough effort has been made to foster a more intensive dialogue with some of them. This has led to the implementation of policies that had never before been considered with a view to meeting stakeholder needs. Some examples of policies included the managerial training of payroll staff; the federation's involvement in cultural and/or value creation initiatives in local communities through its sporting activities; the environmental and social certification of its suppliers; and the involvement in activities aimed at protecting the environment and at fostering sustainability. In some of the federations surveyed, these issues had previously been developed and were further pursued while in others these types of initiatives were established as a result of the social report. The following quotes demonstrate this:

> Through the social report we realized we simply hadn't been paying enough attention to some of our stakeholders. Thanks to the renewed awareness arising from the implementation of this tool we developed actions aimed at offering our members broader and improved online action.
>
> (General Secretary, medium federation, pers. comm., April 20, 2010)

> We felt it would be useful for the Italian volleyball federation to compile a manual containing regulations aimed at protecting the environment during indoor and outdoor sporting events.
>
> (Head of Department, large federation, pers. comm., January 28, 2010)

Finally, the fifth section concerning the social responsibility index acted as a stimulus for the federations as a whole to improve performance with regard to stakeholders. The social responsibility index was the outcome of a series of specific assessments that were used to describe, through a qualitative judgment, the nature of the relationships with stakeholders that were revealed in the fourth section of the social report. The social responsibility index was favorably received by the federations in this research and it triggered a virtuous cycle through which the management of the federations were able to consider the challenge of continually improving social performance:

> We are planning training and retraining programs for our staff with a view to developing their skills within the organization.
>
> (General Secretary, small federation, pers. comm., April 20, 2010)

> We would like to initiate cooperation with institutions such as the ministers for education, culture and environment in a bid to showcase what our federation is doing for society.
>
> (Chairman, small federation, pers. comm., March 4, 2010)

However, it should be observed that the managements' high expectations in terms of social responsibility were often not met to the extent that four out of six federations did not publish the social report although there was a view that they would do so in the future to provide an account of improved social performances.

Conclusions

The increased societal focus on issues of social responsibility and the drive by many organizations to communicate what it is that they do has stimulated scholars within the field of sport management to investigate the ways in which social responsibility can also be implemented. However, there is less focus on the issue of social responsibility communication in sport. This is an important managerial challenge if sports organizations are to meet the legitimate expectations of different stakeholders. This chapter has focused on the issue of social accounting and reporting – key tools of social responsibility communication – within the context of six Italian sports federations. It is argued that social reporting is important to ensure that these organizations are in a position to meet all institutional demands and that they will only be able to survive if they are able to meet stakeholder demands.

This study has been conducted by the authors over a number of years. It involved an initial phase aimed at formulating guidelines for the drafting of the social report of sports federations (2004–2005) and a successive phase in which assistance was provided to the federations chosen as a sample (2005–2011). This has generated awareness of the importance of providing information on the quality of the targets set by the organizations and on their performance with a view to strengthening their image and to justify their existence. The social report in particular emerges as an information document aimed at rationalizing governance while facilitating communication and interaction with internal and external stakeholders such as associates, athletes and players, employees, local communities, sport government entities, local entities, and sponsors.

For a number of years, Italian sports federations have manifested the need for an accurate management assessment with a view to highlighting, on an annual and/or multi-annual basis, the internal dynamics of the amateur or professional sport system and to be able to compare such dynamics with the management standards, values and strategic guidelines set by CONI. Although Italian sports federations have shown and continue to show reluctance in applying this approach, the few that have done so have acknowledged the strategic and organizational relevance of the social report.

The systematization of data, a key step for the disclosure of the information contained in the document, has in many instances brought about significant impacts such as the implementation of the organization's information system; enhanced dialogue between the organization's principal areas; awareness that the information flow from the centre to the periphery (regional and provincial committees) is often inefficient; and the development of social and environmental themes that had been previously ignored. The Italian volleyball federation, for example, has compiled a code of conduct for the organization of indoor and outdoor events that did not exist previously simply because it had never before tackled environmental issues. To this end, a reflection, we feel, should be solicited: federations could offer a significant contribution in enhancing environmental concern within the community. What has emerged thus far shows that writing a social report is necessary for organizations of this kind. The social report of a federation can be considered as a further step in the organizational process leading to the implementation, alongside traditional accounting methods, of new accountability instruments that enables management to provide information to stakeholders about the nature of the organization's activities and social results. Moving forward it is hoped that social accounting will become an innovative way to communicate the effectiveness and efficiency of a sport federation, and in the process triggering what we hope is a virtuous cycle in other sports organizations.

Note

1   The social responsibility index is the outcome of the methodological application stemming from a series of specific assessments that describe and synthesize, through a qualitative judgment, what was revealed in the fourth section in connection with each stakeholder. Such assessments, expressing a judgment regarding the social responsibility of the federation, were made by interposing within the assessment range (0, 100), a symbol indicating, in the form of a score, the result of the judgment expressed for each sub-theme considered. When all assessments have been gathered within a table (social indicator assessment table), an average of all interim scores attributed to each parameter within each single sub-theme is calculated in order to arrive at an overall score. All the values expressed in the social indicator assessment table, entered in the scores column, are then transferred to the calculation of the social responsibility index in correspondence with each of the sub-themes investigated. All scores are successively weighted in relation with each sub-theme with respect to the theme investigated so as to obtain a result. The total sum of the results relating to each sub-theme provides

an indicative parameter of the social responsibility of the federation. When all the results of each sub-theme have been calculated they are added together to give an overall social responsibility index indicating the federation's degree of social awareness (on a scale from 0 to 100).

References

Babiak, K. and Trendafilova, S. (2011) 'CSR and environmental responsibility: Motives and pressures to adopt green management practices', *Corporate Social Responsibility and Environmental Management*, 18, 11–24.

Babiak, K. and Wolfe, R. (2006) 'More than just a game? Corporate social responsibility and Super Bowl XL', *Sport Marketing Quarterly*, 15, 214–222.

Bradish, C. and Cronin, J.J. (2009) 'Corporate social responsibility in sport', *Journal of Sport Management*, 23, 691–697.

Buscarini, C. (2006) 'Il ruolo della rendicontazione sociale nelle Federazioni Sportive nazionali. Proposta di Linee Guida per la redazione del Bilancio Sociale', in Buscarini, C., Manni, F. and Marano, M. (eds.) *La responsabilità sociale e il bilancio sociale delle organizzazioni dello sport*. Milan: Franco Angeli, pp. 82–130.

Buscarini, C., Manni, F. and Marano, M. (2006) (eds.) *La responsabilità sociale e il bilancio sociale delle organizzazioni dello sport*. Milan: Franco Angeli.

Corbetta, P. (1999) *Metodologia e tecniche della ricerca sociale*. Bologna: Il Mulino.

Filo, K., Funk, D. and O'Brien, D. (2009) 'The meaning behind attachment: Exploring camaraderie, cause, and competency at a charity sport event', *Journal of Sport Management*, 23, 361–387.

Gabrovec Mei, O. (2006) 'Responsabilità sociale d'Impresa, sviluppo sostenibile e rendicontazione sociale', paper presented at *IV Simposio Europeo dei Docenti universitari*, Rome, June.

GBS – study group for the social reporting (2001) *Social reporting standards*. Milan.

Godfrey, P.C. (2009) 'Corporate social responsibility in sport: An overview and key issues', *Journal of Sport Management*, 23, 698–716.

Ioakimidis, M. (2007) 'Green sport: A game everyone wins', *The Sport Journal*, 10 (2). (Online). Available at: http://www.thesportjournal.org/article/green-sport-game-everyone-wins (accessed: August 1, 2009).

Irwin, R.L., Lachowetz, T., Cornwell, T.B. and Clark, J.S. (2003) 'Cause-related sport sponsorship: An assessment of spectator beliefs, attitudes, and behavioral intentions', *Sport Marketing Quarterly*, 13 (3), 131–139.

Lachowetz, T. and Gladden, J. (2003) 'A framework for understanding cause related sport marketing programs', *International Journal of Sports Marketing and Sponsorship*, 4, 313–333.

Mallen, C., Bradish, C. and MacLean, J. (2008) 'Are we teaching corporate citizens? Examining corporate social responsibility and sport management pedagogy', *International Journal of Sport Management and Marketing*, 4, 204–224.

Marano, M. (2001) 'Implementing management control and performance measurement systems in large non-profit sport organizations', paper presented at *9th Congress of the European Association for Sport Management*, Vitoria, Spain, September.

McGlone, C. and Martin, N. (2006) 'Nike's corporate interest lives strong: A case of cause related marketing and leveraging', *Sport Marketing Quarterly*, 15, 184–188.

Owen, D. (2005) *CSR after Enron: A role for the academic accounting profession*. Working Paper 33, International Centre for Corporate Social Responsibility, University of Nottingham.

Patton, M. (2002) *Qualitative evaluation and research methods*. 3rd edn. Thousand Oaks, CA: Sage Publications, Inc.

Roy, D.P. and Graeff, T.R. (2003) 'Consumer attitudes toward cause-related marketing activities in professional sports', *Sport Marketing Quarterly*, 12, 163–172.

Valori, G. (2005) *Il diritto nello sport*. Turin: Giappichelli.

PART V

MEASURING CSR
IN SPORT

21

CAUSE-RELATED MARKETING/ SPONSORSHIP IN SPORT

Dae Hee Kwak and T. Bettina Cornwell

Overview

Cause-linked marketing is one of the fastest growing sectors of sponsorship spending in North America. Aligning a brand with a meaningful cause is not only socially responsible but also potentially profitable. While cause-linked marketing is a marketing strategy to communicate the organization's corporate social responsibility (CSR) effort, relatively little is known about its impact on consumers. The purpose of this chapter is to provide a brief overview of cause-linked marketing in the sport context. The definition and the implementation strategies of cause-linked marketing will be discussed. The benefits and drawbacks of implementing cause-linked marketing along with directions for future research will be discussed in this chapter.

Introduction

Despite the global economic recession, sponsorship spending has continued to increase. According to the IEG Sponsorship Report (2010), the total estimate of global sponsorship spending has steadily increased from 2007 to 2010. In particular, the estimated expenditure on sponsorship increased from \$37.9 billion in 2007 to \$46.3 billion in 2010. In North America, corporate sponsorship on *causes* is the fastest growing sector. The IEG Sponsorship Report estimates sponsorship spending on causes by North American companies at \$1.64 billion in 2009 with an increase of about 6.7 percent to \$1.75 billion for 2010. Meanwhile, sponsorship expenditure on the four major professional leagues and their teams increased by 3.4 percent during the same period (IEG Sponsorship Report, 2010). Thus, the investment trend suggests that cause-related sponsorship and promotion is an increasingly common form of marketing and is a key strategy for signifying a firm's social responsibility effort (Sheikh and Beise-Zee, 2011).

Early in the development of cause-linked marketing, it was thought of as a purchase incentive tactic, whereby an organization makes a financial or non-financial contribution to a designated cause each time consumers engage in revenue-producing transactions with the firm (Varadarajan and Menon, 1988). As cause-linked marketing campaigns evolve, sport properties are also actively engaged in cause-related promotions to become more socially responsible and to build emotional bonds with fans. According to Babiak and Wolfe (2006),

285

sports organizations provide unique advantages of initiating socially responsible campaigns. For instance, strong allegiance with events, leagues, team, and athletes can be transferred to the property's supported cause.

Fans tend to have more favorable attitudes toward athletes and teams that are engaged in cause-linked marketing than nonfans (Roy and Graeff, 2003). Further, the media exposure opportunity allows sport properties to communicate their cause-linked marketing efforts to a broader audience. Therefore, sport properties (e.g., events, leagues, teams, or athletes) seem to have advantages in linking with a cause or a nonprofit organization in delivering socially responsible messages. For instance, corporations may partner with sport organizations to sponsor a cause or sporting event while sports organizations may partner with a charitable organization to support a cause. The aim of this chapter is to provide an overview of cause-linked marketing and how it is applied in the sport context. This chapter focuses on both corporations and sport properties linking their entities with a cause. In particular, this chapter is organized as follows: definition of cause-linked marketing, implementation strategies of cause-linked marketing, benefits and risks associated with cause-linked marketing, and challenges and directions for future research.

Definition of cause-linked marketing

Several researchers have defined the similar term cause-related marketing (CRM). According to Varadarajan and Menon (1988: 60), CRM is defined as "the process of formulating and implementing marketing activities that are characterized by an offer from the firm to contribute a specified amount to a designated cause when customers engage in revenue providing exchanges and satisfy organizational and individual objectives." Varadarajan and Menon's definition specifies that a revenue-generating transaction is involved in the process. For instance, purchasing a ticket for a fundraising sporting event (e.g., Roger Federer Foundation's "The Match for Africa") or buying merchandise that supports a designated cause or a foundation (Nike's "**LIVESTRONG** wristband"), as discussed in Chapter 5, are some sport-related CRM examples that involve transaction processes.

In turn, Cui *et al.* (2003: 310) define CRM more broadly as "a general alliance between business and non-profit causes that provide resources and funding to address social issues and business marketing objectives." Following Cui and colleagues, we coin the term cause-linked marketing to avoid confusion from other marketing terms (i.e., customer-relationship management) and to move away from the early narrow definition of CRM. According to Cui *et al.*'s definition, an alliance between a sport property and a nonprofit organization and the entire array of cause-promoting activities in which it engages (e.g., donation, fundraising, sales of licensed merchandise) are considered as cause-linked marketing. For instance, NFL has partnered with the American Cancer Society since 2008 and has been donating revenue generated from various sources, including auctions for player-worn jerseys and equipment, sales of breast cancer-themed licensed merchandise (see www.nflshop.com), and donations. In 2010, NFL donated over $1 million to the American Cancer Society as a result of "A Crucial Catch" campaign (NFL, 2010). In addition, the league has been promoting breast cancer awareness by having players, coaches, and referees wear pink-themed equipment and gear during the month of October – breast cancer awareness month. Such financial and non-financial effort allows the league to communicate their effort of supporting the cause and the designated organization (i.e., American Cancer Society).

Cause-linked sponsorship refers to linking the brand to an event or property that promotes socially responsive causes. For instance, becoming a corporate sponsor of an event that supports a cause (e.g., Susan G. Komen's "Race for the Cure," PGA Tour's "Children's Miracle Network Hospital's Classic") would be an example of cause-related sponsorship. Cornwell and Coote (2005) distinguished sponsorship of causes from transaction-based cause-related marketing. They argue that in sponsorship-linked marketing, the donation (or sponsorship fee) comes before the event and that it is this fee that, in part, makes the event possible. Thus, the funding for the sponsored nonprofit organization is fixed prior to sponsorship and cause-linked sponsorship does not hinge on the consumer's behavior to support the cause (Cornwell and Coote, 2005).

However, in cause-linked marketing, contribution to a nonprofit an organization is often not limited to a sponsorship fee but also includes additional revenues generated from ticket sales (or participation fees), donations, merchandise sales, and so on. Thus, in cause-linked marketing the success of an event is also an important factor that benefits both sponsoring company and the benefactor (i.e., nonprofit organization). For instance, the more NFL sells its pink merchandise, the greater the proceeds will go to the partnering organization (American Cancer Society). Ultimately, from a marketing communication standpoint, the purpose of cause-linked marketing and cause-linked sponsorship remains similar in that both are marketing activities that emphasize a cause.

Difference between cause-linked marketing, cause-linked sponsorship, and CSR

While CSR incorporates a wide range of corporate citizenship behaviors, cause-linked marketing is often employed as a form of CSR that involves: (1) a partnership with a nonprofit organization; and (2) financial support for a specific cause. In this regard, some scholars contend that cause-linked marketing is a signifier that communicates cause-specificity of CSR (Sheikh and Beise-Zee, 2011). According to Polonsky and Speed (2001), key market outcomes for sponsorship and cause-linked marketing involve attitudinal and behavioral changes that lead to support of the sponsoring organization. As such, cause-linked marketing/sponsorship differs from general corporate philanthropy (altruistic giving) since it is part of a firm's marketing activities. However, cause-linked marketing is different from cause-linked sponsorship in that its support for a cause is often directly tied to actual consumption behavior (e.g., purchase). On the other hand, cause-linked sponsorship could be utilized to enhance brand image and goodwill but not necessarily tied to purchase behavior (e.g., every time a Detroit Tigers pitcher throws a strikeout, Trader Joe's will make a donation of $25 to a local food bank). Therefore, key market outcomes vary across CSR, cause-linked marketing, and cause-linked sponsorship. For cause-linked marketing, the amount of funding for a nonprofit organization is contingent upon the revenue-generating process. Although in many cases the total donation amount is capped at a certain maximum (Polonsky and Speed, 2001), the volume of sales has a direct impact on the amount of funding given to a nonprofit organization. In turn, there is no direct sales impact for corporate philanthropy and cause-linked sponsorship. However, since one of the primary objectives of all cause-linked marketing campaigns is to generate revenues, various forms of marketing promotions (e.g., advertising, sales promotion, etc.) are activated to leverage the association with the nonprofit organization. In this regard, it has been suggested that cause-linked marketing can be strategically integrated into regular sponsorship programs. For instance, Cornwell and Maignan (1998) highlighted the potential of combining cause-linked marketing with sponsorship and leveraging sponsorship through a cause-related campaign. A company may partner with a sport organization to support a meaningful cause (cause-linked sponsorship) and further implement a revenue-generating process to enhance both market performance and donation amount to support the cause.

Various implementation strategies of cause-linked marketing

In the marketing and management literature, researchers have attempted to classify cause-linked marketing implementation strategies (Gupta and Pirsch, 2006; Liu and Ko, 2011). Based on the existing literature, the current chapter classifies cause-linked marketing implementation strategies in two main forms: transaction-based and joint promotion (see Table 21.1 for summaries and examples).

To qualify as cause-linked marketing, the activation plan (i.e., sales promotion) should include an offer to the customer by the firm (i.e., sponsor) to contribute a dedicated amount to the nonprofit organization. For instance, a partnership between the property (e.g., sport entities or corporate organizations) and nonprofit organization is a common formation of a social alliance that reflects a cause-linked marketing campaign (Berger *et al.*, 2004). This partnership allows each organization to access a resource that is available for its partner. Once the partnership is established, various forms of implementation strategies take place to benefit both parties. Table 21.1 summarizes each implementation strategy and corresponding examples.

First, the transaction-based cause-linked marketing implementation strategy refers to corporations donating a portion of their profits generated from each transaction (e.g., products or services) to a designated charity. For instance, MasterCard, a long-term sponsor of MLB, decided to activate their association on a charitable platform. MasterCard made a donation to "Stand Up 2 Cancer" every time cardholders used their MasterCard when dining out, including spending at ballpark concession stands. This cause-linked marketing campaign was a part of the larger "Eat, Drink and be Generous" campaign. As a result of the entire campaign, the credit card sponsor donated more than $4 million for the campaign. The donation presentation ceremony took place during Game 4 of the 2011 MLB World Series, which was aired on Fox television (see more details in Stand Up 2 Cancer, 2011). In this case, MasterCard, a sponsor of MLB, activated their sponsorship on a charitable platform to promote cardholders' card usages by donating to a designated nonprofit organization.

The other approach involves joint promotion. A joint promotion initiative involves cooperation with regard to the communication efforts of promoting the link between the two entities. It focuses on the messages that entities want to deliver to consumers. For instance, the National Association of Basketball Coaches (NABC) in the United States partnered with the American Cancer Society to promote the annual "Coaches vs. Cancer Suits and Sneakers" awareness weekend. Participating NABC member coaches and staffs wear sneakers instead of dress shoes with their suits during weekend games to demonstrate their support for the American Cancer Society and its vision of a world with less cancer. Fans can support this initiative by texting "COACH" to a designated number from any wireless phone to make a $5 donation. Since 1993, the joint promotion between NABC and the American Cancer Society has raised more than $70 million to fund cancer-related research (see American Cancer Society, 2012).

Sponsorship activation often involves joint promotion between the sponsoring and sponsored properties. For instance, in order to promote the awareness of the link between the credit card company and the nonprofit organization, MasterCard donated $1,000 for each of the 63 home runs hit during the 2009 playoffs and World Series. As a result, MasterCard donated $63,000 in addition to the amount indicated earlier to the designated charity organization – Stand Up 2 Cancer (Stand Up 2 Cancer, 2011). Additionally, there are some cases where sport properties initiate a joint promotion with nonprofit foundations. For instance, Kansas City's new stadium partnered with **LIVESTRONG** Foundation to name the complex as "**LIVESTRONG** Sporting Park." Instead of paying for the naming rights, a portion of all stadium-related revenues (e.g., ticket sales and concessions) will go to the foundation to fight cancer (Paylor, 2011).

Similarly, FC Barcelona's partnership with UNICEF also exemplifies the sport team-initiated joint promotion effort.

Table 21.1 Examples of transaction-based and joint promotion cause-linked marketing

	Partnership	Transaction-based	Joint-promotion
Description	Refers to the alliance between a property with a nonprofit organization or a cause.	Giving a percentage for every single transaction when someone makes a purchase or uses a corporation's product or service.	Refers to the cooperation in promotion effort between a for-profit corporation and a cause.
Example 1: Professional sport league (NFL's "A Crucial Catch" campaign)	NFL and the American Cancer Society	Sales of pink-themed licensed merchandise and player-worn pink items will be donated to the American Cancer Society.	Players, coaches, referees, and cheerleaders wear pink-colored uniforms. Some areas in the stadium (field, goal posts, walls, etc.) are decorated in pink.
Example 2: Individual athlete (Roger Federer and "The Match for Africa")	Roger Federer and Roger Federer Foundation	Ticket sales for a fundraising match against Rafael Nadal were donated to the foundation. Telephone line donations were accepted during the telecast of the event (Every call was charged CHF 2.5 and 80% of these revenues were forwarded to the foundation.	Two fundraising matches (The Match for Africa) were held in Spain and Switzerland in 2010, to help underprivileged kids in Africa. The event raised $2.6 million.
Example 3: Corporate organization (MasterCard and "Stand Up 2 Cancer" campaign with MLB)	MasterCard and Stand Up 2 Cancer	Each use of MasterCard at restaurants (including ballpark concessions stands), a penny is being donated by MasterCard to Stand Up 2 Cancer.	MasterCard donated $1,000 for each of the 63 home runs hit during the 2009 playoffs and World Series to Stand Up 2 Cancer (Mastercard. com, 2009). MasterCard donated $63,000 to Stand Up 2 Cancer.
Example 4: Corporate organization (Anheuser-Busch and "Here's to the Heroes" campaign with MLB)	A–B and Folds of Honor Foundation	Budweiser donated five cents for every case sold from June 6–July 10 to the organization	A–B donated $100 for every home run hit during the 2011 MLB regular season

Source: compiled by the authors.

Individual athletes also actively engage in cause-linked marketing campaigns. For example, Roger Federer has his own charity foundation (for more discussion about individual athletes and philanthropy and more details around this phenomenon, see Chapters 5 and 16 in this book) and generates revenues from a variety of sources. According to the foundation's annual report, revenue sources include general donations from corporate sponsors and public accounts. In 2010, the foundation held its first fundraising event – The Match for Africa – which was a tennis match between Roger Federer and Rafael Nadal (then numbers 1 and 2 in the world ranking). The revenue generated from the event (e.g., ticket sales, merchandise sales, corporate sponsor donations, phoneline donations, etc.) brought in over $2.6 million, which doubled the entire income the foundation generated the past year (Roger Federer Foundation, n.d.). The funds raised from this purpose-specific event were forwarded to multiple projects in Africa to improve the quality of early learning and basic education.

Although Table 21.1 discusses only two strategies – transaction-based and joint promotion – there are other implementation strategies that an entity can further utilize. One such is an in-kind donation. The donation in-kind refers to a non-financial contribution towards the improvement of a targeted cause (Liu and Ko, 2011). Hellenius and Rudbeck (2003) suggest that the in-kind gift's market value is more than double the value of a cash donation, since the cost of the gift is only the marginal costs associated with the product. Thus, corporations are usually more willing to donate their products and services than to give cash to the cause. For instance, after the devastating earthquake and tsunami which struck eastern Japan in March, 2010, Fédération Internationale de Football Association (FIFA) donated a total of $6.4 million to Japan, which was used for the reconstruction of the football stadiums and facilities damaged by the disaster. In an effort to support Japan's restoration, FIFA's partner Adidas donated 15,000 football kits to the Japan Football Association (JFA) for distribution to the areas with most need after the disaster. At the same time, FIFA also donated 15,000 Adidas Goal balls (FIFA, 2012).

The abovementioned cause-linked marketing implementation strategies represent distinct ways of initiating a cause-linked marketing campaign. However, this does not mean that only one particular strategy should be used for a campaign. As seen from Table 21.1, a combination of several implementation strategies might be used. For example, MLB's brewing sponsor, Anheuser-Busch, has combined both transaction-based and joint promotion strategies to communicate the company's commitment for military support. Since 1987, Anheuser-Busch has donated nearly $11 million to military organizations to support veterans and dependents of military families. In March 2011, the brewing company launched the "Here's to the Heroes" Home Run program as a part of their sponsorship activation with MLB. The program included a $100 donation for every home run hit during the 2011 MLB regular season to benefit the Folds of Honor Foundation, which provides post-secondary educational scholarships for families of U.S. military personnel killed or disabled while serving their country. Additionally, Anheuser-Busch launched "Walk-Off a Hero" program in 2012 and raised $2.5 million. For each of the 205 walk-off wins during the 2012 regular MLB season, Budweiser donated $5,000 to the Folds of Honor Foundation and contributed a portion of all retail sales from May 20 through July 7 (Broughton, 2012). In this case, Anheuser-Busch activated its sponsorship right on a cause-platform by tying the performance of the MLB players to military support foundation.

Overall, transaction-based approaches provide sport consumers with a chance to engage in good citizenship behaviors and sponsoring organizations can gain visibility by various forms of joint promotion and activation. In-kind donation allows companies to be financially more flexible than a cash donation. Therefore, by supporting a specific cause (e.g., breast cancer) a property (e.g., NFL) can build an association between itself and that cause through various implementation strategies, thereby gaining favorability and receptivity among the segment of society that supports the cause. The following section will discuss the potential benefits and risks associated with cause-linked marketing activities.

Benefits of cause-linked marketing

Academic literature on cause-linked marketing suggests that cause-linked marketing is a versatile marketing tool to achieve a broad range of marketing objectives (see Varadarajan and Menon, 1988 for a review). We classified a broad range of managerial dimensions of cause-linked marketing into three sub categories – public relation-related, brand-related, and sales-related (see Figure 21.1).

Increasing sales is one of the most basic objectives of a firm to engage in cause-linked marketing campaign. Successful cause-linked marketing campaigns are reported to have led to incremental purchases and uses among consumers. Lachowetz *et al.* (2002) found that participants attending a cause-related sporting event believed that cause-linked marketing enhances their likelihood of using a sponsoring company's services. In the spectator sport context, fans recognizing their favorite team's cause-linked marketing initiatives were more likely to re-attend the game in the future (Kim *et al.*, 2010). Therefore, cause-linked marketing appears to have had a positive effect on initiating and repeating purchase decisions, which directly impacts the organization's financial performance.

Another important benefit of cause-linked marketing campaigns is brand-related. An extensive body of cause-linked marketing research has documented the positive effect of cause-linked marketing on a brand's image and perceptions of its corporate citizenship (e.g., Irwin *et al.*, 2003; Webb and Mohr, 1998). For instance, Irwin and colleagues (2003) found that a nonprofit organization involved with cause-linked marketing had a positive influence on sport consumers' attitudes, beliefs, and purchase intentions toward the sponsoring company (such as a sport team or league). Particularly, the study found that event participants at the FedEx St. Jude Classic professional golf tournament showed favorable attitudes, beliefs, and purchase intentions toward the sponsoring company (FedEx).

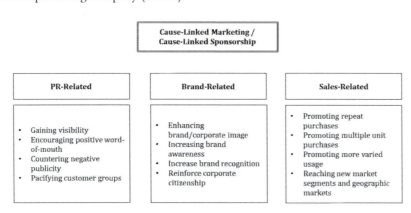

Figure 21.1 Managerial dimensions of cause-linked marketing/cause-linked sponsorship

Lastly, engaging in cause-linked marketing activities can also be very effective in encouraging positive publicity and negating negative images. Supporting popular and pressing social causes (e.g., child obesity or breast cancer in the United States) can help increase the stature of a sponsoring organization as a result of the association (Varadarajan and Menon, 1988). For instance, NFL's "Play 60," NBA's "Fit," MLS' "W.O.R.K.S." programs teamed up with federal government effort to fight against child obesity and promote health and physical activity programs for children and youth. Utilizing the leagues' players, the programs share important health and fitness tips with kids and parents, informing, educating, and engaging children and families in healthy living practices. As discussed in detail by Babiak and Wolfe (2006), sports organizations' investment in cause-related initiatives can help building the organizations' image as a socially conscious organization. By doing the "right thing," leagues can benefit from positive publicity associated with CSR programs and establish an emotional bond with its consumers (Babiak and Wolfe, 2006).

Additionally, a firm may benefit from cause-linked marketing by repairing its negative images from scandals. As an official sponsor of the U.S. Olympic Committee, British Petroleum (BP) launched an augmented reality campaign featuring U.S. Olympic and Paralympic athletes in the exclusive trading card series (BP, 2012). When the company was involved in the disastrous oil spill on the U.S. Gulf Coast in 2010, BP received strong public criticism. BP quickly attempted to repair negative images of the company and established a $20 billion repair fund. Although much more time is needed for BP to fully recover its public image, the company is actively utilizing various sponsorship relationships as part of their image repair strategy. For instance, BP title sponsored the 2011 Crosstown Cup, the interleague game between the Chicago Cubs and Chicago White Sox. Given that BP's headquarter is located in Chicago, the company used its sponsorship as a key element of post-disaster promotional plans (Fisher, 2011). BP focused heavily on local activation by supporting local charities and community service projects. While the long-term effects of cause-related sponsorship or cause-linked marketing on repairing negative images for BP's case remain to be seen, cause-linked marketing can be an effective image repair strategy (Harlow *et al.*, 2011). Taken together, cause-linked marketing or cause-linked sponsorship can be seen as potentially generating a competitive advantage for those organizations involved by enhancing sales, brand images, and positive word-of-mouth.

Potential risks of cause-linked marketing

Although it is a generally accepted notion that consumers will positively view firms engaging in social initiatives, there is some evidence to the contrary. A counter-position has been taken by several researchers who argue it is unlikely these social initiatives always lead to favorable consumer evaluation (Becker-Olsen *et al.*, 2006; Mohr *et al.*, 2001). For instance, corporate motives for cause-linked marketing (cause-oriented vs. profit-oriented) may have differential outcomes on the effect of cause-linked marketing on consumers (Ellen *et al.*, 2006). Simply put, cause-linked marketing can jeopardize the organization and the cause if not implemented properly.

Previous studies on consumers' responses toward cause-linked marketing have been mixed. Consumers may perceive the firm's cause-linked marketing efforts as either cause-beneficial or cause-exploitative. For example, Ross *et al.* (1992) measured consumer attitude toward a real-life cause-linked marketing campaign that was communicated via a Proctor and Gamble advertisement. This ad stated to the public that Proctor and Gamble would donate 10 cents to the Special Olympics for every coupon redeemed for Proctor and Gamble products. In this study, participants did not perceive the campaign to be exploitative of the cause; most participants perceived the firm was executing the campaign in a socially responsible manner. Conversely, Webb and Mohr (1998) found a split-decision with their participants regarding cause-linked marketing. Herein, half of their respondents attributed an egotistic interest to firms engaged in cause-linked marketing, while the other half recognized that at least some part of firm motivation was altruistic.

While communicating the genuine, cause-friendly attributes or policies of a brand can be a powerful way of distinguishing itself in the market place, more consumers are also becoming aware of potentially cause-exploitive nature of cause-linked marketing. Recently, the Susan G. Komen for the Cure Foundation has come under fire for its affiliation with Kentucky Fried Chicken (Black, 2010). The fast-food chain changed the traditional red color of its buckets to pink during the campaign and donated 50 cents for every bucket sold in what is being billed as the "Buckets for the Cure" campaign. However, critics pointed out that high-fat diet is a contributor to higher risk of breast cancer. From the eyes of the public, this particular alliance may portray KFC as cause-exploitive and also alienate the foundation's most ardent supporters. Consumers may find it difficult to associate a fast-food chain with a foundation that supports cancer prevention. In sports, NFL has recently been criticized for profiting from "A Crucial Catch" campaign, a breast cancer awareness campaign to support the fight against the disease (Gaines, 2012). While NFL has launched pink-themed merchandise to increase sales and promote breast cancer awareness, there is no information on the website as to how much is being donated to the American Cancer Society. Some critics pointed out that only a small margin of the sales are being donated to the nonprofit organization and NFL is keeping 90 percent of the profit from sales of pink merchandise (Gaines, 2012). Such lack of transparency would discourage some fans from supporting the cause. Therefore, monitoring how consumers and fans respond to various cause-linked marketing campaigns can help design effective strategies for sport properties and corporate sponsors to benefit both entities.

Challenges and future directions

Undoubtedly, there is a growing demand for corporate citizenship behaviors. According to a recent survey, for instance, Americans now expect businesses to not only support social causes as part of being good corporate citizens, but also expect them to be transparent and communicate the result of cause-related programs. In fact, a 2012 Cone Communications Corporate Social Return Trend Tracker reported that 86 percent of American consumers are more likely to trust a company that reports its CSR results. In addition, 40 percent reported that they will not purchase a company's products or services if CSR results are not communicated (Cone Communications Corporate Social Return Trend Tracker, 2012). Therefore, there remain some challenges in the marketplace regarding the application of cause-linked marketing or cause-linked sponsorship in sport.

Increased clutter

As a greater number of corporations associate themselves with causes, the resulting clutter makes it harder for firms to stand out. For instance, in the past decade, breast cancer has been an overtly marketed cause in the U.S. and has become a "dream cause" for many American corporations, politicians, and institutions (King, 2006). Although such widespread use of pink ribbons across industry may have increased the public awareness of the cause, it remains challenging if market-driven objectives for the firms are met with the increased clutter. As La Ferle *et al.* (2011) noted, not all cause-linked marketing offers necessarily enhance the sponsoring company's sales or image. In order to break through the increased clutter, sponsoring organizations should demonstrate strong and genuine commitment toward the cause. Adding specific examples of how corporate funds help people and/or communities could provide transparency as well as more personal connections with the cause. Furthermore, more creative implementation and communication approaches should help an organization to distinguish itself from other competitors tied to similar causes.

Considerations for contextual factors

As discussed previously, causes found in sport alliances range from environmental issues, health-related issues (e.g., cancers, obesity, AIDS) to issues of racism, poverty, and education (e.g., fighting for literacy). The most pressing causes in society may differ from region to region and from culture to culture. Finding and aligning with an appropriate cause within a marketplace is also important for a successful cause-linked marketing campaign. For instance, breast cancer is one of the most frequently diagnosed cancers among Caucasian women but the incidence rate is far less in Asian and African countries. Therefore, global sport organizations and/or multinational brands might want to consider leveraging different causes that are most important in specific target markets. Recent studies have shown that consumer acceptance toward cause-linked marketing differs based on culture and other contextual factors (Becker-Olsen et al., 2011; La Ferle et al., 2011). For example, consumers have different views against the origin of the organization (multinational vs. domestic; La Ferle et al., 2011), nature of organizations (profit-driven vs. nonprofit; Svensson and Wood, 2011), and charity proximity (local vs. national; Ross et al., 1992), indicating that various forces influence how consumers respond to cause-linked promotions and campaigns. Future research should explore how these various contextual factors impact sport consumers' perception toward cause-linked marketing and cause-linked sponsorship.

Conclusions

This chapter has presented a brief overview of cause-linked marketing in the sport context. This chapter cannot be considered a comprehensive overview of cause-linked marketing as the focus was made to provide relevant examples pertaining to cause-linked marketing and cause-linked sponsorship. In addition to defining the term, several cause-linked marketing implementation strategies as well as benefits and drawbacks of this emerging marketing tool are presented. Lastly, future challenges that need to be considered in practicing cause-linked marketing are briefly discussed.

Cause-linked marketing and cause-linked sponsorship are commercially driven marketing tools that involve revenue-generating process while promoting corporate citizenship behavior. Cause-linked marketing signifies the organization's core identity as a socially responsible entity. Various cause-linked marketing implementation strategies allow an organization to actively communicate its CSR value in the marketplace. Cause-linked marketing begins with a partnership with a designated nonprofit organization (e.g., American Cancer Society), which will be the benefactor of various fundraising activities. Implementation strategies include: transaction-based (a small portion of incentives given to the cause from each purchase), joint promotion (collaborative promotion efforts between sponsor and sponsored entities), and in-kind donation. Sponsoring organizations use one or multiple approaches in an effort to increase cause awareness as well as to drive profit. Several examples discussed in this chapter highlight the combination of various implementation strategies to increase awareness of the cause as well as revenue.

Commonly stated intended outcomes and benefits of cause-linked marketing include incremental sales, enhanced brand images and attitudes, and positive publicity. Although a line of research generally supports the idea that cause-linked marketing has a positive effect on consumers' acceptance toward the firm engaged in cause initiatives, organizations need to be cautious as they can face criticisms of being cause-exploitive and opportunistic rather than cause-supportive and genuine. Future challenges include increased clutter as cause-linked marketing is becoming a popular marketing tool. Simply pairing with a cause alone would not provide the organization an increased market performance over many other similar cause-related offerings. Additionally, there are various contextual factors that might moderate the effect of cause-linked marketing on consumers. Some examples include the characteristics of organizations (e.g., origin, nature, etc.) and charity proximity (e.g., local vs. national). As previously discussed, same causes might have different social importance or meanings depending on the culture or region. Overall, sport – either as a form of spectator sport or as a participant sport – provides a unique opportunity for an organization to make a strategic alliance with a cause to promote a cause-linked marketing campaign.

However, compared to general sponsorship research, there are far fewer empirical studies on cause-linked marketing's effectiveness in the sport context. Certainly, more research in this area should be conducted to further our understanding of the effectiveness of cause-linked marketing in sport. First, well-controlled experimental studies should be conducted to better understand when and how cause-linked marketing campaigns work. Given that a typical cause-linked marketing campaign involves two partnering entities (e.g., NFL and American Cancer Society) with a specific cause (e.g., breast cancer); there are multiple context-specific variables that could influence outcome variables. One area for future research is the complexity of the cause landscape. When a sport holds a cause relationship and a brand sponsors this sport, what values and images transfer to the brand? Do cause-related images mainly stay with the sport? With this complexity in mind, a well-designed experiment might be a starting point to understand under what conditions the brand also benefits from existing cause relationships of the sport. Second, a comparative analysis of the effectiveness of various cause-linked marketing implementation strategies (transaction-based vs. joint promotion vs. donation in-kind) is also warranted. Understanding differences and similarities across various implementation strategies may provide empirical insights on how to design and activate a cause-linked marketing campaign. For instance, if an organization is facing a PR crisis and wants to utilize a cause-linked marketing campaign, what type of implementation strategy would be most effective to negate negative publicity? On the contrary, can cause-linked marketing act as a buffer against future negative publicity? Empirical studies along these lines would provide additional insights on the effective use of cause-linked marketing and cause-linked sponsorship in sport.

References

Babiak, K. and Wolfe, R. (2006) 'More than just a game? Corporate social responsibility and Super Bowl XL', *Sport Marketing Quarterly*, 15, 214–222.

Becker-Olsen, K.L, Cudmore, B.A and Hill, R.P. (2006) 'The impact of perceived corporate social responsibility on consumer behavior', *Journal of Business Research*, 59, 46–53.

Becker-Olsen, K.L, Taylor, C.R., Hill, R.P. and Yalcinkaya, G. (2011) 'A cross-cultural examination of corporate social responsibility marketing communications in Mexico and the United States: Strategies for global brands', *Journal of International Marketing*, 19 (2), 39–44.

Berger, I., Cunningham, P. and Drumwright, M. (2004) 'Social alliances: Company/nonprofit collaboration', *California Management Review*, 47 (1), 58–90.

Black, R. (2010) 'Eat fried chicken for the cure? KFC's fundraiser with Susan G. Komen group raises some eyebrows', *NY Daily News*, April 22. Available at: http://articles.nydailynews.com/2010-04-22 (accessed: December 28, 2011).

British Petroleum (2012) *BP supports U.S. Olympic hopefuls. BP team USA.* Available at: http://www.bpusathletes.com (accessed: November 22, 2012).

Broughton, D. (2012) 'In a first for survey, MLB completes the sweep', *Street & Smith's SportsBusiness Journal*, November 19, p. 16.

Cone Communications Corporate Social Return Trend Tracker (2012) Available at: http://www.conecomm.com/stuff/contentmgr/files/0/b2481c3a38bbac7c659ca5f4f1cb9a4a/files/2012_corporate_social_return_press_release_and_fact_sheet_final.pdf (accessed: November 26, 2012).

Cornwell, T.B. and Coote, L.V. (2005) 'Corporate sponsorship of a cause: The role of identification in purchase intent', *Journal of Business Research*, 58, 268–276.

Cornwell, T.B. and Maignan, I. (1998) 'An international review of sponsorship research', *Journal of Advertising*, 27 (1), 1–21.

Cui, Y., Trent, E.S., Sullivan, P.M. and Matiru, G.N. (2003) 'Cause-related marketing: How generation Y responds', *International Journal of Retail & Distribution Management*, 31 (6), 319–320.

Ellen, P.S., Webb, D.J. and Mohr, L.A. (2006) 'Building corporate associations: Consumer attributions for corporate socially responsible programs', *Journal of the Academy of Marketing Science*, 34 (2), 147–157.

Fédération Internationale de Football Association (FIFA) (2012) *Activity Report 2011.* Available at:http://www.fifa.com/mm/document/affederation/administration/01/62/06/21/fifa_ar2011_e_gesamt.pdf (accessed: November 25, 2012).

Fisher, E. (2011) 'BP will ramp up activation behind Cubs-White Sox series', *Street & Smith's Sports Business Journal*, 17 January, p. 7.

Gaines, C. (2012) 'Is The NFL profiting off of Breast Cancer?' *Business Insider*, October 10. Available at: http://www.businessinsider.com/why-is-the-nfl-profitting-off-of-breast-cancer-2012-10 (accessed: October 27, 2012).

Gupta, S. and Pirsch, J. (2006) 'A taxonomy of cause-related marketing research: Current findings and future research directions', *Journal of Nonprofit and Public Sector Marketing*, 15 (1), 25–43.

Harlow, W.F., Brantley, B.C. and Harlow, R.M. (2011) 'BP initial image repair strategies after the *Deepwater Horizon* spill', *Public Relations Review*, 37, 89–83.

Hellenius, R. and Rudbeck, S. (2003) 'In-kind donations for nonprofit', *McKinsey Quarterly*, 4, 55–60.

IEG Sponsorship Report (2010) 'IEG Sponsorship briefing: Special edition for cause marketing'. Available at: http://sponsorship.com (accessed: November 15, 2011).

Irwin, R.L., Lachowetz, T., Cornwell, T.B. and Clark, J.S. (2003) 'Cause-related sport sponsorship: An assessment of spectator beliefs, attitudes, and behavioral intentions', *Sport Marketing Quarterly*, 12 (3), 131–139.

Kim, K.T., Kwak, D.H. and Kim, Y.K. (2010) 'The impact of cause-related marketing (CRM) in spectator sport', *Journal of Management and Organization*, 16 (4), 515–527.

King, S. (2006) *Pink ribbons, INC: Breast cancer and the politics of philanthropy.* University of Minnesota Press, Minneapolis, MN.

Lachowetz, G., Clark, J., Irwin, R. and Cornwell, T.B. (2002) 'Cause-related sponsorship: A survey of consumer/spectator beliefs, attitudes, behavioral intentions, and corporate image impressions', *American Marketing Association Educators Proceedings*, 13, 14–20.

La Ferle, C.L., Kuber, G. and Edwards, S.M. (2011) 'Factors impacting responses to cause-related marketing in India and the United States: Novelty, altruistic motives, and company origin.' *Journal of Business Research*. Available at: http://www.sciencedirect.com/science/article/pii/S0148296311002943 (accessed: March 28, 2012).

Liu, G. and Ko, W. (2011) 'An analysis of cause-related marketing implementation strategies through social alliance: Partnership conditions and strategic objectives', *Journal of Business Ethics*, 100, 253–281.

Mastercard (2009) *Groundbreaking live "Standing Up 2 Cancer: Priceless MasterCard spot to air during game three of the World Series.* Available at: http://www.mastercard.com/us/company/en/newsroom/standing_up_to_cancer.html#ld (accessed: November 26, 2012).

Mohr, L.A., Webb, D.J. and Harris, K.E. (2001) 'Do consumers expect companies to be socially responsible? The impact of corporate social responsibility on buying behavior', *Journal of Consumer Affairs*, 35 (1), 45–72.

NFL (2010) *NFL donates more than $1 million to American Cancer Society.* Available at: http://www.nfl.com/news/story/09000d5d81d45907/article/nfl-donates-more-than-1-million-to-american-cancer-society (accessed: July 28, 2012).

Paylor, T.A. (2011) 'Sporting KC's stadium name: Livestrong Sporting Park', *Kansascity.com Blog*, March 8. Available at: http://www.kansascity.com/2011/03/08/2707798/sporting-kc-teams-with-armstrong. html (accessed: July 28, 2012).

Polonsky, M.J. and Speed, R. (2001) 'Linking sponsorship and cause related marketing: Complementarities and conflicts', *European Journal of Marketing*, 35 (11/12), 1361–1385.

Roger Federer Foundation (n.d.) Available at: https://www.rogerfederershop.com/en/foundation.html (accessed: July 29, 2012).

Ross, J.K., Patterson, L. and Stutts, M.A. (1992) 'Consumers' perceptions of organizations that use cause-related marketing', *Journal of the Academy of Marketing Science*, 20, 93–97.

Roy, D.P. and Graeff, T.R. (2003) 'Consumer attitudes toward cause-related marketing activities in professional sports', *Sport Marketing Quarterly*, 12 (3), 163–172.

Sheikh, S. and Beise-Zee, R. (2011) 'Corporate social responsibility or cause-related marketing? The role of cause specificity of CSR', *Journal of Consumer Marketing*, 28 (1), 27–39.

Stand Up 2 Cancer (2011) *This is where the end of cancer begins*. Available at: www.standup2cancer.org/ (accessed: July 29, 2012).

Svensson, G. and Wood, G. (2011) 'A model of cause-related marketing for "profit-driven" and "non-profit" organizations', *European Business Review*, 23 (2), 203–214.

The American Cancer Society (2012) *Coaches vs Cancer*. Available at: http://coaches.acsevents.org/site/ PageNavigator/CVC_FY12_Home.html (accessed: November 22, 2012).

Varadarajan, P.R. and Menon, A. (1988) 'Cause-related marketing: A coalignment of marketing strategy and corporate strategy and corporate philanthropy', *Journal of Marketing*, 52 (3), 58–74.

Webb, D.J. and Mohr, L.A. (1998) 'A typology of consumer responses to cause-related marketing: From skeptics to socially concerned', *Journal of Public Policy and Marketing*, 17 (2), 226–238.

22

ASSESSING SOCIAL IMPACT OF SPORT-INDUSTRY PHILANTHROPY AND CSR

Yuhei Inoue and R. Aubrey W. Kent

Overview

This chapter aims to explain how sports organizations can assess the impact of their corporate social responsibility (CSR) initiatives on society, or social impact. To achieve this end, the chapter starts by pointing out the growing importance of evaluating social impact for companies including sports organizations. This is followed by the discussion of the uniqueness of sports organizations in terms of their potential to implement a highly impactful CSR program. Moreover, in order to address the lack of agreement about what the term "social impact" entails, this chapter proposes a framework of the social impact of CSR initiatives ("CSR impact") based on existing literature. More specifically, along the two dimensions, the unit of analysis dimension and the timing of impact dimension, this framework classifies CSR impact into four types: (1) intermediate individual impact, (2) intermediate community impact, (3) long-term individual impact, and (4) long-term community impact. The remainder of this chapter is devoted to provide a detailed explanation of each type of CSR impact through a case study of the "Get Fit with the Grizzlies" program launched by the Memphis Grizzlies in 2006. This chapter concludes with suggestions on how sport executives overseeing CSR programs can perform the assessment of the programs' social impact based on the developed framework.

Introduction

While CSR initiatives have been conventionally assessed in terms of their impact on business-related outcomes such as financial performance (Inoue *et al.*, 2011) and corporate reputation (Walker and Kent, 2009), growing academic attention has been given to the impact of these initiatives on society, or social impact (e.g., Forester, 2009; Inoue, 2011; Inoue and Kent, 2012; Irwin *et al.*, 2010). Within industry, companies such as Nike (2009) and Intel (2010) have started to discuss the social impact of their CSR activities in their CSR reports. In 2010, the European Commission established a consortium of 16 research institutions to conduct a comprehensive research project named "The IMPACT Project" that aims to develop measurements for assessing the social impact of CSR (IMPACT, 2011). This increasing attention to the social impact of CSR can be explained from the following three perspectives. First, while a traditional CSR approach was to simply offer monetary donations to charitable organizations, companies are now expected to make actual impact on society by putting more concerted effort on their CSR activities (Kotler and Lee, 2005). Second, some companies, such as Nestlé and Cisco, have demonstrated that making positive social impact through CSR can actually improve the long-term competitive advantage of businesses (Porter and Kramer, 2002, 2006). Finally, it is de rigueur to suggest that the onus is on companies to bring the corporate world and society "back together" by redefining success in their business to be the creation of shared value (Porter and Kramer, 2011).

Uniqueness of sport-industry CSR

In this context, sport-industry CSR is thought to be unique because the celebrity status of sports organizations may enable them to implement a highly impactful CSR program that effectively promotes social ideas and behavior to a large number of people (Alexandar *et al.*, 2011; Chalip, 2006; Loakimidis, 2007; Smith and Westerbeek, 2007). For example, a senior communication officer of the Robert Wood Johnson Foundation, the largest charitable organization devoted to public health in the U.S., states that "professional sports, as a corporate partner, could be a force for social change like no other ... sports teams have such cachet in the community, such market power, and so many other resources" (Diehl, 2007: 4). Smith and Westerbeek (2007: 25) further support the distinctiveness of CSR in sport by pointing out that "sport, more than any other potential vehicle, contains qualities that make it a powerful force in effecting positive social contributions." One of such qualities is proposed to be the large communication power of sport resulting from valuable resources it possesses, such as venues, events, signage, corporate sponsors and access to media; this power should allow sport organizations to effectively reach various segments of the population in communicating their CSR messages (Babiak and Wolfe, 2009; Smith and Westerbeek, 2007) (see Chapters 18, 19 and 20). In addition, a high level of identification and passion that sport generates would likely increase the effect of sport-industry CSR on one's attitudes and values to adopt socially responsible ideas and behavior (Babiak and Wolfe, 2009).

Given the expected high impact of sport-industry CSR, a growing body of research has assessed CSR programs of sport organizations in terms of their benefits accruing to society (e.g., Forester, 2009; Inoue, 2011; Inoue and Kent, 2012; Irwin *et al.*, 2010). Forester (2009) examined a CSR program of a golf management company that was designed to introduce golf to local elementary and middle school students and to further help their character building through the sport. Based on the analysis of interviews with program participants, this study found that the program provided both physical and educational benefits to the students (Forester, 2009). Inoue (2011) and Inoue and Kent (2012) conducted a series of studies examining the effectiveness of environmental programs by professional sport teams, showing that these programs could effectively promote pro-environmental behavior among consumers. Irwin *et al.* (2010) investigated the effectiveness of Get Fit with the Grizzlies, a program implemented by the Memphis Grizzlies to promote health-related behavior among students at local elementary schools. By examining behavior change before and after the implementation of the program, the researchers found that this program significantly increased the nutritional knowledge, healthy eating practices and physical activity of the students (Irwin *et al.*, 2010). In relation to Irwin *et al.* (2010), Walker and Kent (2009: 747) identified "youth health initiatives" as a major CSR category in their framework of professional sport team CSR initiatives. Sport franchises further help address the issue of youth health by providing charitable donations to local youth sport/fitness programs, which have consistently been shown to provide a variety of positive outcomes for their participants (e.g., Fraser-Thomas *et al.*, 2005; Lerner *et al.*, 2005).

Definitional issues

While extant research has advanced our understanding of the social impact of CSR (hereafter called "CSR impact"), there is consensus among neither academics nor practitioners regarding the definition and scope of CSR impact. For example, Du *et al.* (2010: 11), in their research on Crest's oral health program, define CSR impact as "the actual benefits that have accrued ... to the target audience of a social cause," suggesting the narrow scope of this concept. On the other hand, IMPACT (2011) proposes that CSR impact is a much broader concept that entails the benefits of CSR activity to social, economic and environmental welfare. The confusion surrounding the definition of CSR impact is further expressed by Nike in their 2007–2009 CSR report:

> In our work to develop better metrics for our community investments, we sought the counsel of NGOs, academics and other experts in the field. Many offered valuable suggestions. Nevertheless, from our work and these meetings we realized that there is to date no common methodology that we could adopt and apply to our work. As we continue to wrestle with the best ways to define and capture our social impact, we believe that our investment in tracking systems and ongoing work with our partners and grantees during FY07–09 will ultimately yield fruit and increased understanding as we measure results over time.
>
> (Nike, 2009: 138)

Given the lack of consensus over the definition and measurement of CSR impact, this chapter develops an integrative framework of this concept based on previous works on the social impact assessment (SIA) of public/private development programs (Burdge, 2003; ICGPSIA, 1994) and on the assessment of philanthropic programs (Lim, 2010; McLaughlin *et al.*, 2009). In turn, this framework is further explained through a case study of Get Fit with the Grizzlies, a CSR initiative by the Memphis Grizzlies of the National Basketball Association (NBA).

An integrative framework for understanding impact

In 1993, a group of scholars from various social science disciplines formed the Interorganizational Committee on Guidelines and Principles for Social Impact Assessment (ICGPSIA) to address a growing need to evaluate the social impact of policies, programs and projects (ICGPSIA, 1994). In their 1994 report, the ICGPSIA (1994): 1) defined social impact as "the consequences to human populations of any public or private actions that alter the ways in which people live, work, play, relate to one another, organize to meet their needs and generally cope as members of society" and "cultural impact involving changes to the norms, values, and beliefs that guide and rationalize their cognition of themselves and their society." As implied in this definition, social impact entails the impact of a given action on both *individuals* and *communities* they make up (Burdge, 2003). At the individual level, the social impact of a program is assessed in terms of how people change their values and behavior due to their involvement with the program. At the community level, SIA involves the assessment of how the program influences the collective actions of community members, which results in more longstanding cultural change in the community.

Furthermore, the assessment of social impact involves an additional consideration for the timing of impact. This is because the direct impact of an action may lead to further individual and community impact in the long run (Goodlad *et al.*, 2002). This point is clearly illustrated by the Center for High Impact Philanthropy's report on the bednet (i.e., netting used to protect against mosquitoes) distribution program for malaria prevention (see Lim, 2010; McLaughlin *et al.*, 2009). Based on logic modeling (Cooksy *et al.*, 2001), a dominant framework for program assessment, this report discusses that the performance of a philanthropic program can be evaluated from four aspects: activities, outputs, outcomes and impact. *Activities* refer to preliminary actions taken at the implementation of the program, such as training of staff, purchasing of related goods and communication with community leaders, and *outputs* refer to actual services delivered by the program. While the first two are related to what the program has done, the last two are concerned with actual benefits and changes accrued from the program. Specifically, *outcomes* are the *intermediate* changes or benefits directly resulting from the activities and outputs of the program, and impact is *long-term* consequences that lead to improved quality of life (Lim, 2010; McLaughlin *et al.*, 2009). Capturing the business processes that can create impactful outcomes is the main reason that the non-profit world heavily utilizes the concept of logic modeling when engaged in the strategic planning process. Traditional logic models explicitly separate the outputs and outcomes of a business process in order to clearly demonstrate "impact" that can result from its programming and business practices. For the purpose of providing a clear framework of CSR impact, the remainder of this report refers to outcomes and impact, as defined by McLaughlin *et al.*, (2009), as *intermediate* and *long-term* impact respectively.

The ongoing discussion suggests that the social impact of CSR activity can be better understood along the two dimensions: the unit of analysis dimension and the timing of impact dimension. The unit of analysis dimension is concerned with the beneficiaries of CSR activity, an individual at one end of this continuum and a community at the other end. In our context, an individual refers to each participant of a CSR program, and a community refers to a geographical area where the majority of the participants reside. The timing of impact dimension, on the other hand, is related to when the impact of CSR programs are observed, ranging from intermediate to long term.

An integrative framework

As shown in Figure 22.1, a two-by-two matrix can be formed by using these two dimensions, categorizing CSR impact into four types: (1) intermediate individual impact, (2) intermediate community impact, (3) long-term individual impact, and (4) long-term community impact.

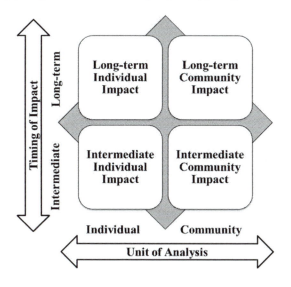

Figure 22.1 An integrative framework of CSR impact

First, *intermediate individual impact* is concerned with the extent to which individual participants acquire desired knowledge, values and/or behavior due to program participation. For example, if a CSR program aims to promote physical activity, the intermediate individual impact of this program can be assessed based on whether each participant increases his or her engagement in physical activity after the program when compared to his or her original physical activity level. The level of this impact can also be quantified as either the percentage of individuals who have significantly changed their behavior or the average level of behavior changes among the participants. Thus, for the CSR program described earlier, the level of its intermediate individual impact can be described using such statements as "60 percent of the program participants increased their physical activity levels due to the program," or "the participants on average engage in one more hour of physical activity per day as a result of the program participation." In short, the assessment of this impact often involves the comparison of related knowledge and behavior of each participant before and after the implementation of the program by conducting a pre/post experimental study (Lim, 2010). An example of such an assessment is Irwin *et al.*'s (2010) study of the Get Fit with the Grizzlies program, which is explained in detail in a later section of this chapter.

Second, *intermediate community impact* refers to an aggregate of the intermediate individual impact of a program on the community where it is implemented. One way to estimate this impact of a given CSR program is to obtain the product of the level of its intermediate individual impact and the number of participants in the program. For example, if a CSR program has reached a total of 1,000 participants in the community, and 60 percent of the participants have significantly increased their physical activity levels due to the program participation, the intermediate community impact of this program is the enhanced physical activity levels of 600 participants in the community. In another example, if a CSR program has influenced 1,000 participants to recycle an average of three more plastic bottles a week, then the intermediate community impact of this program is an additional 3,000 plastic bottles recycled in the community every week (see more details on the environmental programs in Chapters 7 and 8).

Third, *long-term individual impact* is the desired state of physical, psychological and/or living conditions that individual participants would achieve by continuously engaging in the behavior promoted in a CSR program. This type of CSR impact may be further classified into two subcategories: direct and indirect impacts. Direct impacts refer to the intended long-term outcomes of a program directly produced by participants' engagement in the promoted behavior and practices. For example, continuous involvement in physical activity for a certain period of time should likely allow participants to increase their fitness and maintain a healthy physical condition. Furthermore, such direct impacts may result in some supplemental indirect impacts, such as mental health and the reduction of medical costs in the case of improved physical fitness. It should be noted, however, that the formal evaluations of long-term individual impact tend to require a rigorous experimental study that compares the status of program participants with the status of a control group consisting of non-participating individuals (Lim, 2010). While such evaluations can provide precise information about the long-term effectiveness of a program and enhance the program credibility, they could be complex, expensive and time-consuming (Lim, 2010).

Finally, *long-term community impact* entails cultural and infrastructural changes and improved quality of life in the community due to the combined effects of the long-term individual impact of a CSR program. That is, as individual participants achieve desirable physical, psychological and/or living conditions by performing the behavior promoted by the program, and also directly or indirectly influence other community members surrounding them to engage in that behavior, the culture of the community would eventually be transformed into the one that values that behavior. In addition, such cultural changes should encourage local government and community organizations to establish new infrastructure that provides individuals with more opportunities to engage in the behavior. Moreover, these cultural and infrastructural changes should result in satisfying the needs of community members, enhancing the quality of life in the community.

Enhancing CSR impact

The above descriptions of the four types of CSR impact provide insights into how sport organizations can increase the effectiveness of their CSR initiatives. First, since intermediate individual impact is evaluated based on the level of behavior changes among participants due to involvement in the program, it is essential that organizations choose to promote behavior in which members of their community have the greatest areas of need and/or to select program participants from a population segment performing the target behavior to a lower extent than the other segments of the community. This should ensure that participants have enough room to improve the performance of the intended behavior, increasing the program's potential to generate high intermediate individual impact. Second, given that intermediate community impact captures the aggregated benefits of the intermediate individual impact of a program, this impact should increase as the program reaches more individuals in the community, under the condition that the level of its intermediate individual impact is consistent. Third, as noted, long-term individual impact refers to desirable conditions achieved through continuous involvement with the behavior promoted in a CSR program. Therefore, in order to enhance this impact, sport organizations need to provide participants with additional support after the conclusion of the program, such as access to a facility and supplemental materials and information, that help them continuously engage in the behavior by themselves. Finally, since long-term community impact is the ultimate product of the other three impacts, increases in this impact should be achieved when: (1) the program influences participant behavior to a great extent (i.e., high intermediate individual impact); (2) the program reaches a large number of people in the community (i.e., high intermediate community impact); and (3) the majority of the participants are continuously committed to engaging in the promoted behavior (i.e., high long-term individual impact).

Case study of the Memphis Grizzlies Get Fit with the Grizzlies program

To further explain the framework of CSR impact described above, this section provides specific examples for each impact type through a case study of the Get Fit with the Grizzlies program, a CSR initiative of the Memphis Grizzlies. While the assessment of the program's effectiveness has been reported in other studies (Irwin *et al.*, 2010, 2012), this chapter expands on them by offering a more comprehensive understanding of the program's CSR impact based on the developed framework.

Overview of the program

The NBA's Memphis Grizzlies launched Get Fit with the Grizzlies in 2006 in an attempt to address childhood obesity – which is a growing epidemic in the city of Memphis (Irwin *et al.*, 2010, 2012). The organization became involved in this program due to the strong interest in this issue of a team executive. Given the trend of increasing obesity rates among children in Memphis, the executive discussed the issue with the administration of Memphis City Schools

(MCS) in order to find a way to improve the situation. This discussion eventually led to the establishment of the Get Fit with the Grizzlies program (Irwin *et al.*, 2010, 2012).

With the cooperation of MCS, the Get Fit program was implemented at all 110 elementary schools in the MCS district, reaching approximately 17,000 students during its first year (Irwin *et al.*, 2010, 2012). The program consisted of a six week instructional curriculum that was designed by veteran physical education (PE) teachers within MCS to teach the fourth and fifth grade students about nutritional knowledge and fitness. For each week, PE teachers at the elementary schools had a 30–45 minute lesson during their regular PE classes, covering basic knowledge on nutrition and healthy eating practices, muscular endurance and strength, flexibility and cardiovascular endurance. As part of the program, students were assigned to keep track of their diet for each meal and total weekly minutes of physical activity using a program log under the supervision of their parents.

While PE teachers within MCS took charge of the design and delivery of the Get Fit program, the Memphis Grizzlies were responsible for the funding of the program through sponsorship fees and other operating activities, such as providing incentive prizes, conducting schools visits by the team mascot and staff, and developing the program website (Irwin *et al.*, 2012). In addition, the organization hosted an annual "Achievement Day with the Grizzlies" at their home arena, FedExForum, inviting students who successfully completed their log assignments and further educated them on fitness and nutrition through lessons with Grizzlies players, coaches and dancers. Along with supporting the program financially and operationally, the Grizzlies' involvement was essential to enhance the program's impact on the community due to their unique status as the only major league franchise in the city. This point was highlighted by the following statement of a team's operations staff member: "We felt it was of value to lend our name and brand recognition … we want to use our star power to get kids moving and change the way that kids behave when it comes to healthy eating" (Irwin *et al.*, 2012: 58). The Get Fit program was continued for the next three years until 2010, when it was replaced with a new "Health Home Court" program that expanded the former program by adding breakfast assemblies at local high schools that encourage students to eat a healthy breakfast every day.

Evaluating the social impact of the program
Intermediate individual impact

This type of CSR impact addresses the extent to which individual participants adopt promoted behavior due to the program participation. Therefore, this impact of the Get Fit program can be evaluated by comparing participating students' health-related knowledge and behavior before and after the implementation of the program. In fact, the Memphis Grizzlies commissioned local universities to conduct the evaluations of the program's intermediate effects on the students for each of the four years between 2006 and 2009 (Irwin *et al.*, 2010). To this end, the research team designed a pre/post test consisting of 18 questions that asked students' knowledge and behavior relating to nutrition and exercise, and administrated the test to 11 schools randomly chosen from the 110 elementary schools in MCS. Irwin *et al.* (2010) reported the results of the assessment conducted during the 2006–2007 school year. By collecting data from 888 students, their results showed that the percentage of the students who answered correctly increased significantly for all but one knowledge-based questions. For example, in one question asking the definition of the term "calorie," 71.1 percent of the students had the correct answer in the post-test when compared to 53.8 percent in the pre-test, increasing by approximately 16 percent. In addition, with respect to the behavior-based items, students showed positive behavior change for 7 of 10 questions relating to the consumption of vegetables, fruit, grains and meat/protein and engagement in both moderate and vigorous exercises. Most notably, the percentage of the students who had adequate amounts of fruits increased by 10 percent from 56.6 percent to 66.1 percent as a result of the program. These results thus provided evidence for the intermediate individual benefits of the Get Fit with the Grizzlies program (Irwin *et al.*, 2010).

Intermediate community impact

The second type of CSR impact, intermediate community impact, refers to an aggregate of the program's intermediate individual impact, computed as the extent of this impact multiplied by the number of participants in the program. In the ongoing example, Irwin *et al.* (2010) indicated that about 16 percent of the students at the randomly selected schools acquired correct knowledge about the definition of a calorie due to the program. Therefore, if this number is applied to schools that were not included in the assessment, then it can be estimated that the program enhanced the knowledge of roughly 2,720 students (i.e., 16 percent of the total 17,000 students who participated in the program) in MCS schools in 2006. Moreover, since this program has been conducted for the recent five years till the 2010–2011 school year (as noted above, the program was conducted under the new name in 2010), a simple calculation suggests that a total of 13,600 (2,720 students × 5 years) obtained the correct understanding of a "calorie" from the program over the five-year period. In a similar vein, it is estimated that about 1,700 MCS students (i.e., 10 percent of the 17,000 students) improved their eating habits by increasing the intake of fruits annually, resulting in a total of 8,500 students over the five years. These figures suggest that the Get Fit program has produced substantial intermediate community impact for the city of Memphis.

Long-term individual impact

The major goal of the Get Fit program is to reduce childhood obesity among students in Memphis. Therefore, the intended direct outcome of this program is that individual participants maintain, or reduce to, an adequate body weight after the intervention through continuous involvement in physical activity and healthy eating practices promoted by the program. In addition, this direct outcome should allow the participants and their families to enjoy associated indirect benefits, such as high fitness levels and healthy physical conditions, high psychological well-being and reduced medical costs. Furthermore, given empirical evidence on a high association between academic performance of students and their fitness and physical activity levels (Dwyer *et al.*, 2000), these participants would generally achieve high academic standings as a result of the program. Although the evaluation of the long-term effect of the Get Fit program was not included in the formal assessment of the program commissioned by the Grizzlies (Irwin *et al.*, 2010), this can be done by comparing indices of an adequate body weight, such as the body mass index (BMI), and other measures of physical fitness and health, psychological well-being and academic performance, between students who previously participated in this program and non-participating students from other regions that share similar demographic, socio-demographic and geographical characteristics with Memphis.

Long-term community impact

The long-term community impact of the Get Fit program should be realized when most participants continue to engage in healthy eating and physical activity after the program and further encourage others to adopt such practices. This impact would be most directly reflected in a reduction in obesity rates in Memphis. Along with this, the culture of Memphis should gradually be changed in a way that places greater importance on health-related activities, which may be manifested in increases in the number of fitness facilities, the number of sport events, public investment in parks and recreation, youth participation in sport programs, and the number of restaurants and grocery stores that offer healthy options. In addition, the indirect effect of the program on students' academic performance as discussed above could result in improving the quality of education in the city. Ultimately, these long-term benefits of the Get Fit program could collectively lead to the enhanced quality of life among residents in Memphis.

Conclusions

This chapter started by pointing out the growing importance of assessing the social impact of CSR. This is due to increasing social expectations that corporations make an actual impact on communities through their CSR activities (Kotler and Lee, 2005) as well as anticipated linkage between the creation of social impact through a company's CSR and its sustainable competitive advantage (Porter and Kramer, 2002, 2006). Sport-industry CSR is uniquely positioned in this regard because the so-called "star power" of sport organizations and athletes is thought to allow sport organizations to implement highly impactful CSR programs (Alexander *et al.*, 2011; Chalip, 2006; Loakimidis, 2007; Smith and Westerbeek, 2007). However, one problem associated with the assessment of the social impact of sport-industry CSR is that there has been no agreement about what the term "social impact" entails.

In order to address the definitional issue, this chapter developed a framework of CSR impact based on extant literatures on SIA (Burdge, 2003; ICGPSIA, 1994) and on the evaluation of philanthropic programs (Lim, 2010; McLaughlin *et al.*, 2009). The framework explained that the CSR impact of a given program can be understood along the two dimensions: the unit of analysis dimension and the timing of impact dimension. The former refers to the beneficiaries of CSR activity, ranging from an individual to a community, whereas the latter refers to when CSR impact is observed, ranging from intermediate to long-term. Furthermore, these two dimensions led to the formation of a two-by-two matrix (Figure 22.1) that classifies CSR impact into four types: (1) intermediate individual impact, (2) intermediate community impact, (3) long-term individual impact, and (4) long-term community impact. The definition and assessment of each impact is summarized as follows.

- *Intermediate individual impact* addresses the extent to which individual participants of a CSR program acquire intended knowledge, values and/or behavior due to the program participation. The assessment of this impact involves the comparison of related knowledge and behavior of each participant before and after the implementation of the program.
- *Intermediate community impact* is an aggregate of the intermediate individual impact of a program on the community where it is implemented. This impact can be estimated as the product of the level of its intermediate individual impact and the number of participants in the program.
- *Long-term individual impact* is the desired state of physical, psychological and/or living conditions that individual participants would achieve by continuously engaging in the behavior promoted in a CSR program. The formal evaluations of this impact require rigorous experimental study that compares the status of program participants with that of a control group consisting of non-participating individuals.
- *Long-term community impact* entails cultural and infrastructural changes and improved quality of life in the community due to the combined effects of the long-term individual impact of a

CSR program. For example, in the case of a program that promotes health-related behavior, this impact may be reflected in reduced obesity rates, increased number of fitness facilities and sport events, and increased public investment in parks and recreation in the community.

The second part of this chapter explained each type of CSR impact through a case study of the Get Fit with the Grizzlies program launched by the Memphis Grizzlies in 2006. This case study highlighted the results of a commissioned study that assessed the short-term impacts of the program (Irwin *et al.*, 2010), and also described the program's anticipated long-term impacts. It should be noted that the empirical assessment of the social impact of sport-industry CSR is still at its very early stage. Hence, it is hoped that the framework and the case study provided in this chapter will serve as a basis for future investigation.

This chapter concludes by providing sport executives overseeing CSR programs with suggestions on how they can perform the assessment of the programs' social impact based on the proposed framework.

- Conduct a pre/post-evaluation of attitude and behavior change with at least a portion of the program participants and record the precise number of individuals served by the program to demonstrate both intermediate individual and community impacts.
- For the assessment of the long-term individual impact of the program, obtain data on the extent of continued involvement with the promoted behavior and state of physical, psychological and/or living conditions among selected participants by implementing a follow-up study.
- In order to further provide evidence for the long-term community impact of the program, gather relevant secondary data, such as obesity rates in the community, and observe changes in these data over a period of time.
- Carefully examine the results of these assessments to continuously improve program design and hence enhance the effectiveness of the program.

References

Alexandar, L., Eavey, L., O'Brien, K. and Buendia, M.T. (2011) 'Sports teams and social impact: An analysis of recent developments and best practices', unpublished manuscript, The University of Pennsylvania. Available at: http://www.wharton.upenn.edu/socialimpact/files/Social_Impact_of_Sports_Report_Final.pdf (accessed: November 25, 2011).

Babiak, K. and Wolfe, R. (2009) 'Determinants of corporate social responsibility in professional sport: internal and external factors', *Journal of Sport Management*, 23, 717–742.

Burdge, R.J. (2003) 'The practice of social impact assessment – background', *Impact Assessment and Project Appraisal*, 21, 84–88.

Chalip, L. (2006) 'Toward a distinctive sport management discipline', *Journal of Sport Management*, 20, 1–21.

Cooksy, L.J., Gill, P. and Kelly, P.A. (2001) 'The program logic model as an integrative framework for a multimethod evaluation', *Evaluation and Program Planning*, 24, 119–128.

Diehl, D. (2007) 'The sports philanthropy project', *The Robert Wood Johnson Anthology*, 11, 1–15.

Du, S., Bhattacharya, C. and Sen, S. (2010) 'Maximizing business returns to corporate social responsibility (CSR): The role of CSR communication', *International Journal of Management Reviews*, 12 (1), 8–19.

Dwyer, T., Sallis, J. F., Blizzard, L., Lazarus, R. and Dean, K. (2001) 'Relation of academic performance to physical activity and fitness in children', *Pediatric Exercise Science*, 13, 225–237.

Forester, B.E. (2009) 'The social impact of corporate social responsibility: A case study', PhD thesis, The Florida State University.

Fraser-Thomas, J., Côté, J. and Deakin, J. (2005) 'Youth sport programs: An avenue to foster positive youth development', *Physical Education and Sport Pedagogy*, 10, 19–40.

Goodlad, R., Hamilton, C. and Taylor, P.D. (2002) 'Not just a treat: arts and social inclusion', University of Glasgow. Available at: http://www.gla.ac.uk/media/media_7761_en.pdf (accessed: November 25, 2011).

ICGPSIA (1994) *Guidelines and Principles for Social Impact Assessment*, U.S. Department of Commerce National Oceanic and Atmospheric Administration National Marine Fisheries Service. Available at: http://www.nmfs.noaa.gov/sfa/social_impact_guide.htm (accessed: November 25, 2011).

Inoue, Y. (2011) 'Investigating the role of corporate credibility in corporate social marketing: a case study of environmental initiatives by professional sport organizations', PhD thesis, Temple University.

Inoue, Y. and Kent, A. (2012) 'Sport teams as promoters of pro-environmental behavior: an empirical study', *Journal of Sport Management*, 26 (5), 417–432.

Inoue, Y., Kent, A. and Lee, S. (2011) 'CSR and the bottom line: analyzing the link between CSR and financial performance for professional teams', *Journal of Sport Management*, 25 (6), 531–549.

IMPACT (2011) *Impact measurement and performance analysis of CSR*. Available at: http://www.csr-impact.eu/documents/documents-detail.html?documentid=2 (accessed: November 25, 2011).

Intel (2010) *2010 Corporate responsibility report*. Available at: http://csrreportbuilder.intel.com/PDFFiles/CSR_2010_Full-Report.pdf (accessed: November 25, 2011).

Irwin, C.C., Irwin, R.L., Miller, M.E., Somes, G.W. and Richey, P.A. (2010) 'Get fit with the Grizzlies: a community-school-home initiative to fight childhood obesity', *Journal of School Health*, 80, 333–339.

Irwin, R. L., Irwin, C. and Drayer, J. (2012) 'Get fit with the Grizzlies: application of entrepreneurship on sport sponsorship,' in Ciletti, D. and Chadwick, S. (eds.) *Sports Entrepreneurship: theory and practice*, Morgantown, WV: Fitness Information Technology, pp. 51–64.

Kotler, P. and Lee, N. (2005) *Corporate social responsibility: Doing the most good for your company and your cause*. Hoboken, NJ: Wiley.

Lerner, R.M., Lerner, J.V., Almerigi, J., Theokas, C., Phelps, E., Gestsdottir, S., Naudeau, S., Jelicic, H., Alberts, A.E., Ma, L., Smith, L.M., Bobek, D.L., Richman-Raphael, D., Simpson, I., Christiansen, E.D. and von Eye, A. (2005) 'Positive youth development, participation in community youth development programs, and community contributions of fifth grade adolescents: Findings from the first wave of the 4-H Study of Positive Youth Development', *Journal of Early Adolescence*, 25 (1), 17–71.

Lim, T. (2010) 'Measuring the value of corporate philanthropy: social impact, business benefits, and investor returns'. New York: Committee Encouraging Corporate Philanthropy. Available at: http://www.corporatephilanthropy.org/pdfs/resources/MVCP_report_singles.pdf (accessed: November 25, 2011).

Loakimidis, M. (2007) 'Green sport: a game everyone wins', *The Sport Journal*, 10 (2).

McLaughlin, C., Levy, J., Noonan, K. and Rosqueta, K. (2009) 'Lifting the burden of malaria: An investment guide for impact-driven philanthropy'. Philadelphia, PA: The Center for High Impact Philanthropy, University of Pennsylvania. Available at: http://www.impact.upenn.edu/our_work/Malaria-ExecutiveSummary.html (accessed: November 25, 2011).

Nike (2009) *Corporate Responsibility report FY07–09*. Available at: http://www.nikebiz.com/crreport/content/pdf/documents/en-US/full-report.pdf (accessed: November 25, 2011).

Porter, M.E. and Kramer, M.R. (2002) 'The competitive advantage of corporate philanthropy', *Harvard Business Review*, 80, 56–69.

Porter, M.E. and Kramer, M.R. (2006) 'Strategy and society: The link between competitive advantage and corporate social responsibility', *Harvard Business Review*, 84, 78–92.

Porter, M.E. and Kramer, M.R. (2011) 'Creating shared values: How to reinvent capitalism – and unleash a wave of innovation and growth', *Harvard Business Review*, 1–17.

Smith, A.C.T. and Westerbeek, H.M. (2007) 'Sport as a vehicle for deploying corporate social responsibility', *Journal of Corporate Citizenship*, 25, 43–54.

Walker, M. and Kent, A. (2009) 'Do fans care? Assessing the influence of corporate social responsibility on consumer attitudes in the sport industry', *Journal of Sport Management*, 23, 717–742.

23

THE PARADOX OF CSR MEASUREMENT

Putting the "responsibility" back in CSR through program evaluation

Matthew Walker, Bob Heere and Chiyoung Kim

Overview

The advancement of empirical research into the antecedents, correlates, and consequences of corporate social responsibility (CSR) has been hindered by a lack of CSR impact measures, and by a myopic view of the purpose of social responsibility. While a number of empirical studies have investigated CSR at the consumer level, research on the beneficiary and societal impacts are lacking. To illuminate this phenomenon and build on the existing body of scholarship, this chapter discusses the current trends and future directions of measuring CSR. By initially focusing on the strategic "payback" from behaving socially responsible, we segue to the argument that research has not holistically determined what societal benefits actually accrue from CSR engagement. The paradox is that, although it is a "responsibility" of modern business, little attention has been paid to understanding the true benefits of CSR. In this chapter, we not only shed light on this idea but maintain that many organizations have developed a fear of program evaluation – what we call "evaluation-phobia." Many organizations shy away from evaluating the effectiveness of CSR and instead rely on generic public relations and marketing messages to convey CSR strategies.

Introduction

The NBA's *Read to Achieve* was one of the longest running programs of its kind in professional sport. The year round program has been supported (and endorsed) by all 30 NBA teams, 13 WNBA teams, and six NBDL teams with the sole purpose "to help young people develop a life-long love for reading and encourage adults to read regularly to children" (NBA, 2012a). According to the program website, the *Read to Achieve* reaches more than 50 million children each year and donates in excess of 200,000 reading material for reading events and book fairs. Unfortunately, there is no mention of program outcomes such as reading literacy itself, which indicates that the NBA has never measured the impact of the program on youth literacy in the United States. This lack of evaluation has given ammunition to critics depicting many sport organizations as purely self-interested. Therefore, the emergence of a climate fraught with heightened scrutiny toward socially responsible behavior underscores the idea that CSR programs are being viewed largely as strategic communication mechanisms. In the case of the

NBA, this view can be problematic because it could negate any positive image effects garnered from the *Read to Achieve*, while at the same time preventing the NBA from improving the program to better serve its intended mission.

Segueing to the larger industry context, it is easy to see that sports organizations serve a mixture of private and public interests. Private interests are maintained through sponsoring companies and organizations that associate themselves with various sport entities. Public interests represent the moral, ethical, and social concerns connected through a continuous and evolving process that is intimately tied to the sports organization's self-interest, as any sport organization's lifeblood is (for the most part) associated with the emotional bond with their fan base. As a result, the interests that many sports organizations serve derive from legitimate social and ethical claims on the organization by others. While a number of phenomena have been investigated within sport, the concept of corporate social responsibility (CSR) has risen to the forefront of the public–private interest debate. However, CSR scholarship is still in its infancy and measurement of the concept has remained stagnant due to the focus increasingly being placed on the reciprocal (i.e., strategic) benefits for the firm. This focus, unfortunately for society, stands in stark contrast to whether the goals of CSR actually yield socially beneficial returns, and not just create strategic value for the firm. This is a slippery slope that could be damaging for businesses if they fail to transparently acknowledge all the intents and purposes of CSR. For example, Walker *et al.* (2010) noted that the search for a strategic organizational advantage from CSR ultimately alienated consumers and negated any positive effects that might have resulted from CSR programming.

Much of the research on CSR in sport has examined the manner in which consumers and organizational stakeholders perceive and react to so called "responsible" initiatives. On the surface, these studies show that the perception of CSR is indeed reality – as consumers tend to react to CSR often times with very low awareness levels of the actual social initiatives performed (Walker and Heere, 2011) (see Kwak and Cornwell, Chapter 21). Taking a step back from these findings, it is easy to see why the simple perception of CSR is more beneficial for businesses, over and above any potential benefit for society. In the modern sport industry, CSR has become an ever-present concept assuming a key role in most organizational planning. This reason behind this CSR push is twofold: (1) organizations have become increasingly aware of the strategic "payback" that CSR can provide; and (2) there has been a steady rise in consumer demand for CSR programs and socially and environmentally responsible products. The first point makes sense since these businesses are bottom-line driven and showing profits that exceed expenses is what keeps them operational. The second point also makes sense since most organizations listen to the wants and needs of their consumers, who (by and large) agree that the companies they support should act ethically, produce less waste, and give back some of their profits to those who are less fortunate. In a perfect world, most sport businesses would heed these calls and use their status to impart positive social change. However, this has traditionally not been the case, and the marketing of CSR seems to supersede the reporting of how, or even if, the programs are working for the intended beneficiary.

What the empirical data show is that the perception of CSR can benefit sport businesses in a number of ways. Tracing the chronology of scholarship in this area, Walker and Kent (2009) first found that CSR programming by two NFL teams resulted in purchase intentions and an elevated perceived reputation of the teams. Sartore-Baldwin and Walker (2011) demonstrated that the image of NASCAR was directly influenced by their perceived response to a lack of diversity in and around stock-car racing. Walker *et al.* (2010) examined the effects of perceived social responsibility performed by the International Olympic Committee (IOC) during the 2008 Beijing Olympic Games. The results confirmed that CSR was subject to the perceptions (i.e., attributions) of the IOC, which had a direct influence on several areas of consumption intentions. In addition, Kent and Walker (2010) demonstrated that perceived philanthropy performed by the PGA tour significantly influenced both the reputation of and patronage intentions directed towards the PGA Tour. More recently, however, Walker and Heere (2011) showed that the relationship between what consumers know about CSR, coupled with their feelings about CSR, resulted in a significant, but very marginal effect, on actual consumer spending.

This latter finding illustrates that although the sport consumer acknowledges that CSR might influence how they feel about the organization, this does not automatically translate to actual behavior. This gap between attitude and behavior signals a primary weakness in CSR-related survey research and perhaps a positive bias from respondents to agree with statements regarding CSR. Yet, the marginal variance explained on behavior by Walker and Heere (2011) might nonetheless indicate that CSR, despite the positive perceived connotations of consumers, still is an afterthought for the consumer when purchasing based on CSR attributes.

While the aforementioned results show that CSR can be financially and perceptually beneficial for sport businesses (albeit to a marginal extent), they nevertheless help to beg the question – is CSR also beneficial for society? This chapter discusses the growing phenomenon of CSR being viewed as nothing more than a business strategy to increase profits, shape public perception, and grow a larger consumer (i.e., fan) base. We argue that the ubiquity of CSR reporting is all that has been required to render the practice meaningful in the prevailing discourse articulated in and around the market. And, that corporations believe the guise of CSR is enough to demonstrate legitimacy and business transparency beyond any tangible/actual impact on society or the beneficiaries of the practice. We propose that implementing evaluation methods to assess the effectiveness of CSR would ultimately yield more influential programmatic outcomes. These outcomes, coupled with awareness of social activities, could send a much stronger message to the consumer about the power of CSR, thereby increasing the effect of these efforts on actual consumer behavior.

The guise of CSR – societal or strategic?

The manner in which consumers perceive and react to CSR is directly tied to how the organization has marketed the initiative. However, it is important to distinguish "perceived awareness" from "actual awareness" because the relationship to consumer attitudes will, unfortunately, be linked to the former and not necessarily the latter. This is where the opportunistic marketing manager and public relations staff takes advantage of the consumer. By using imperfect information, the organization is able to craft the most desirable (and often vague) message to the intended recipient, as illustrated by the opening paragraph about *Read to Achieve*. Nearly every team, league, and sport business has a website dedicated to their own brand of social responsibility. However, much of the information on these pages simply points to the program's focus, with little attention paid to its impact on society, or if the program is meeting its goals or the needs of the community. On its website, for example, the National Football League (NFL) discusses the *Hometown Huddle* and *Play 60* initiatives in very broad terms with no information on how the programs have influenced youth health or youth fitness. One could argue, based on this description alone, that sending players out in into their local community and encouraging children to get active is simply a way of connecting more and less fortunate fans to the core product of football. In 2005, the NBA refocused its attention on their *NBA Cares* initiative stating:

> The NBA Cares Community Caravan is a year-long community and fan engagement program through which the NBA Family has raised $175 million for charity, provided more than 1.8 million hours of hands-on service, and built more than 675 places where kids and families can live, learn or play in communities around the world.
>
> (NBA, 2012b)

While this message does present actual spending data, the program's impact on the supported charities is not mentioned, the hands-on service component is not discussed, and the construction project impact is not detailed.

The debate of who benefits from a CSR strategy is also apparent outside the United States. In the Netherlands, for example, Ajax Amsterdam (professional soccer club) founded a professional football team in South Africa (Ajax Cape Town). Initially, this project was undertaken as a strategy to gain access to the most talented youth players in South Africa (Ajax Cape Town, 2012a), who could then be acquired and relocated to Amsterdam. Over the years, however, criticisms of colonialism (i.e., exploiting the natural resources of a former colony) against Ajax Amsterdam were levied. These criticisms pushed Ajax Amsterdam to reframe the program as a CSR initiative that would benefit the youth in South Africa. Accordingly, the revised mission of Ajax Cape Town is to "lift the standard of the South African football industry" (Ajax Cape Town, 2012b). As part of this mission, the "Ajax Cape Town Community Scheme" was developed to provide opportunities to South African youth to participate in football, regardless of race, class, gender, social status or disability. According to the program website, the *Scheme* has been implemented in more than 120 schools, reaching more than 8,000 children. Similar to their United States counterparts, there is no mention of benefits or impact on the program's intended beneficiaries.

Arguments in the business literature have maintained that CSR initiatives should only be undertaken if the cause ultimately benefits the organization, and should not be forwarded in response to societal pressure or business ethics, but in response to demands from stakeholders that directly benefit the firm (Siegel, 2009). Based on the preceding examples, the passive orientation in professional sport is not altogether unexpected. And, based on our commentary, it appears that these instrumental (i.e., strategic) sentiments have been adopted by sport practitioners, which unfortunately obscures the value of CSR espoused by some of the early pioneers of the practice (see Bowen, 1953). This myopically strategic philosophy could yield negative trickle-down effects on the true intents and purposes of CSR for organizations that have the power to enact true societal and community change. In addition, the sport industry might also adopt CSR for more strategic, as opposed to a social change, tool.

Sport, by its very nature, is a socially constructed phenomenon built on the notions of fair play, teamwork, and inclusion. On the other hand, sport also enables some less than meritorious qualities such as a winning at all costs mentality and social imbalance. In much the same way, CSR has been understood as a means of "doing good" and giving back, but is also fraught with self-serving and pejorative underpinnings. Somehow, these latter ideals have grossly overshadowed the former with business strategy assuming a key role in the operationalizing and fostering of socially responsible initiatives. As a concept, CSR has resided under the broad umbrella of business ethics. While the ethical arm of sport has been around for decades, a more synergistic aspect of ethics is being supported in terms of how CSR can be embedded in sport business strategy. Quazi (2003: 882) maintained that, "growing demands on business to address and respond to social concerns is an important component of the modern business landscape." These demands are critical to the deployment of CSR initiatives since many organizations only support initiatives that have a high degree of affinity to their direct consumer base and which also align with their core product. These demands also underpin the growing number of research studies aimed at identifying the strategic consequences of CSR, rather than social impact. Therefore, as businesses increasingly recognize the duties of accountability implied by their stakeholders' (non-financial) expectations, the role of CSR will continue to assume an elevated profile in the strategic positioning of sport business products and services rather than the seemingly altruistic intentions of the practice.

The CSR paradox

What gets lost in the view of CSR is what the term "responsibility" is intended to convey. The issue is that social responsibility, as a concept, is often intended to simplify some complex arguments between society and businesses – that is – who is responsible, and for what? Are businesses responsible for helping to cure societal ills; are they responsible for generating profits that exceed expense; are they responsible for helping the communities where they conduct their operations? Consequently, managers implementing CSR fail to acknowledge the trade-offs between the organization's financial health and the social impact of the initiatives (Doane, 2005). Thus, when CSR policy decisions are made, organizational profit might undoubtedly win out over any societal benefit (Baron, 2001). Therefore, since the current emphasis has been on organizational benefits that derive from the initiatives, CSR no longer seems like the correct term. Instead, we argue that the term corporate social strategies (CSS) better reflects the concept – since social leveraging has been the primary focus and is seemingly better aligned with the misinterpretation of what CSR is supposed to be.

When looking through the CSS lens, corporations seemingly have little use for program evaluation. This might be a reflection of the fact that it does not matter to the organization whether the beneficiaries of CSS are actually impacted. What is more is that the organization is able to effectively communicate its social initiatives through public relations channels and only measure the impact of the program based on the tangential view of their stakeholders. As long as the prevailing sentiments are positive, the organization can tout the effectiveness of their campaign, regardless of program effectiveness. Based on this logic, we argue that many organizations have developed "evaluation-phobia," since their programs are not evaluated, and their ineffectiveness cannot be tangibly proven. Therefore, organizations touting "responsibility" will continue to proclaim that they are meeting the demands of society.

Clearly a paradox exists between the role that businesses should assume in remedying societal ills and business strategy. It is also clear that the focus of CSR has been obscured since profitability is an anticipated outcome of behaving responsibly. It goes without saying that the value of social responsibility has been a much-debated topic because measuring the costs and benefits of these activities on organizational stakeholders can be difficult. Within this cost-benefit discussion resides a number of factors related to social engagement, which have mainly been grounded in business pragmatism discussions centered on the correlation between "doing good" and financial performance. While research on this connection has tangentially shown that little financial benefit is realized from CSR, Orlitzky *et al.*'s (2003) meta-analysis suggests that a positive effect of CSR on financial performance does indeed exist (albeit quite small). On the surface, these data bring some closure to the debate about whether it is in an organization's best interest, at least financially, to engage in CSR (Aguilera *et al.*, 2007). However, actual societal impacts have been empirically ignored and more alarming still, is the lack of business reporting regarding the outcomes of CSR investments.

Program beneficiaries

The preceding sections of this chapter illustrate that both corporate and research foci of CSR have been somewhat one-sided, with the majority of attention being paid to the strategic outcomes of CSR policy and practice. Consequently, little (if any) consideration has been given to program beneficiaries. Some years ago, Porter and Kramer (2006) noted a gap in the CSR conversation with the phrase "social impact" assuming just a cursory role in the deployment and presentation of CSR. Based on the historical and definitional evolution of CSR, which dates back decades, the underpinning element is the social contract between society and business. It, therefore, stands to reason that organizations who are fully engaged in CSR should (at some level) be inclined to fulfill their implied obligation to society.

Table 23.1 Social impact and anticipated outcomes

Social impact	Outcome
Way of life	Live, work, play, and interact
Culture	Shared beliefs, customs, values, etc.
Community	Cohesion, local stability, services, and facilities
Political system	Life affecting decisions and democratization
Environment	Air, water, food, noise, sanitation, safety, etc.
Health and well-being	Physical, mental, social, and spiritual well-being
Personal and property rights	Personal disadvantage and violations of civil liberties
Fears and aspirations	Safety, community fears, and future aspirations

Much like CSR, the discussions of social impact have been mired in an amalgam of ideas as to what constitutes an actual outcome. Nevertheless, the International Association of Impact Assessment (IAIA) does provide some direction in the area of impact assessment (IA). They state that an IA is the processes involved in identifying any future consequences of a current or proposed action, with the "impact" being the difference between what would happen with or without the action (IAIA, 2012). In a similar vein, Vanclay (2003) noted that social impact should be viewed as changes that affect people, directly or indirectly, and are pertinent to social impact assessment (see Table 23.1).

The role of program evaluation

As previously mentioned, organizations are increasingly reluctant to evaluate their CSR programs, as such evaluative processes could potentially illustrate ineffectiveness, thereby fostering negative publicity. Additionally, smaller organizations often lack the resources and expertise to conduct a proper evaluation. Yet, as the field of CSR continues to advance, the role of program evaluation will likely become a central force within the sport industry. As criticisms of CSR as marketing, communication, and public relations tools grow, organizations will find themselves searching for ways to counter the claims of their naysayers. More importantly, many CSR initiatives of smaller (or even non-profit) organizations are funded through grant dollars, and recent developments within these programs have signaled a marked increase in the demand for evaluation. Sport management scholars could assume a key role in this process. For example, graduate programs could begin to offer courses that cover aspects of program evaluation providing graduates with the requisite skills to and knowledge to assist both the for-profit and non-profit sport organizations. Additionally, one of the emerging disciplines within sport management is the idea of Sport for Development; a sub-aspect of the discipline devoted entirely to exploring and identifying the positive effects sport programs on society. While the corporate perspective of CSR within this field has yet to be addressed, we argue that combining these areas could provide critical insights on the impact of CSR – particularly for the program participants and beneficiaries.

Program evaluation is a technique to examine the effectiveness of a program in obtaining their objectives (Fitzpatrick *et al.*, 2004). Accordingly, evaluative questions should address issues such as which programs work best, which parts of the program are most effective, how the parts relate to each other, and what can be done to improve certain areas. Looking at program evaluation from a systems view (see Chelladurai, 2005), researchers could examine the input (e.g., donations in time, money, materials, etc.), the throughput (e.g., how the inputs are being utilized), and the subsequent outcomes of these processes. A program makes an impact when the variance in outcomes (e.g., reading skills) cannot be explained by input variables (e.g., demographics).

To measure program impact, researchers have a wide array of methodological instruments to choose from. One of the most used approaches is a (quasi-) experimental approach where program participants would answer questions before and after participating in the program. The response patterns could then be compared with people from the same population who did not participate in the program (i.e., to control for the causality between input and outcomes). While this approach could demonstrate program effectiveness, the quantitative approach limits one's ability to understand the reasons behind the lack of success. Based on this inherent problem, researchers often opt for a mixed methods approach where the above-mentioned experimental survey approach is combined with qualitative methods (e.g., observations, interviews, or secondary data collection). In most cases, the researcher would integrate these differing qualitative methods within an ethnographic approach. This process would foster personal involved with the researcher in order to gain a full understanding of the programs working dynamics. Qualitative approaches are perhaps the best mechanisms to clarify why certain programs are successful and why others are not.

Ultimately, these evaluation techniques provide program organizers with a multitude of informational opportunities. If the program is effective, the organization would be able to communicate this to their stakeholders, providing evidence of CSR value to the community or society more broadly. This information would help assuage concerns that the organization is just "playing the game" for their own benefit, and would also allow the organization to better showcase the beneficiaries of the program. If the program is ineffective, the evaluation should provide recommendations and knowledge on how to alter the program (or certain parts) for further improvement and refinement. If organizations start addressing these failures publicly, then there could possibly be little to no image issues since they are communicating what was done incorrectly and propose remediation. In fact, they would be able to communicate this learning curve as positive to show that the resources are being used in an effective manner.

Putting the focus back on responsibility

The sections of this chapter bring to light the question of who exactly social responsibility is intended to serve. We show that, from a bottom-line perspective, CSR is to some extent regarded as good for business, since the prevailing trend has been to serve organizational interests above and beyond the interests of society. Even under this strategic umbrella, the importance of accounting for multiple levels of analysis and actors to understand the holistic impact of CSR is required. We, therefore, contribute to the debate by narrowing the public-private interest divide. In particular, we show that the interactions within and across levels of business and societal interests can both facilitate and impede CSR. Based on this, we suggest transposing CSR from the consumer-oriented domain viewed as a business strategy (i.e., self-serving) to include the much needed society-oriented domain. We also add a prescriptive layer to this debate by suggesting that scholars and business practitioners should begin to provide the necessary tools and metrics for program evaluation. By doing so, organizational managers might actually gain a more thorough understanding of how beneficiary impacts can also serve both business and societal interests.

This discussion of CSR as an antecedent to social change is intended to show that the power of the relationship between business and society can be more synergistic than previously conceptualized. Rather than the one-way application of CSR as a business strategy, organizations should work to facilitate two-way interactions where both the societal actors and the bottom-line returns are synergistic outcomes. We assume that when CSR practices are diffused at the beneficiary level, they can be adjusted to the local conditions and be geared toward the societal ills that organizational stakeholder deem critical. Implementing CSR in this manner will allow for the adaptation to the different actors, expand the motives of the practice, and help to facilitate relationship building in and around the community.

References

Aguilera, R. V., Rupp, D. E., Williams, C. A., and Ganapathi, J. (2007) 'Putting the "S" back in corporate social responsibility: A multilevel theory of social change in organizations', *Academy of Management Review*, 32, 836–863.

Ajax Capetown (2012a) *Club history*. Available at: http://www.ajaxct.com/the_club.htm?category=club+history (accessed: January 28, 2012).

Ajax Capetown (2012b) *Mission and values*. Available at: http://www.ajaxct.com/the_club.htm?category=mission+and+values (accessed: January 28, 2012).

Baron, D. P. (2001) 'Private politics, corporate social responsibility, and integrated strategy', *Journal of Economics and Management Strategy*, 10 (1), 7–45.

Bowen, H. R. (1953) *Social responsibilities of the businessman*. New York: Harper and Row.

Chelladurai, P. (2005) *Managing organizations for sport and physical activity: A systems perspective*. Holcomb Hathaway: Scottsdale, AZ.

Doane, D. (2005) 'The myth of CSR', *Stanford Social Innovation Review*, Fall, 23–29.

Fitzpatrick, J.L., Sanders, J.R., and Worthen, B.R. (2004) *Program evaluation: Alternative approaches and practical guidelines*. New York: Pearson Education Inc.

International Association for Impact Assessment (2012) *Mission, vision, and values*. Available at: http://www.iaia.org (accessed: January 15, 2012).

Kent, A. and Walker, M. (2010) 'Testing a schema for strategic corporate philanthropy in the sport industry', *International Journal of Sport Management*, 11 (3), 1–26.

NBA (2012a) *Read to Achieve*. Available at: www.nba.com/features/rta_index.html (accessed: January 31, 2012).

NBA (2012b) *NBA Cares Overview*. Available at: http://www.nba.com/caravan (accessed: January 30, 2012).

Orlitzky, M., Schmidt, F.L., and Rynes, S.L. (2003) 'Corporate social and financial performance: A meta-analysis', *Organizational Studies*, 24 (3), 430–441.

Porter, M. E. and Kramer, M. R. (2006) 'Strategy and society: The link between competitive advantage and corporate social responsibility', *Harvard Business Review*, December, 78–92.

Quazi, A. M. (2003) 'Identifying the determinants of corporate managers' perceived social obligations', *Management Decision*, 41 (9), 822–831.

Sartore-Baldwin, M. and Walker, M. (2011) 'The process of organizational identity: What are the roles of socially responsive behaviors, organizational image, and identification?' *Journal of Sport Management*, 25 (5), 489–505.

Siegel, D. S. (2009) 'Green management matters only if it yields more green: An economic/strategic perspective', *Academy of Management Perspectives*, 23 (3), 5–17.

Vanclay, F. (2003) 'International principles for social impact assessment', *Impact Assessment and Project Appraisal*, 21 (1), 5–11.

Walker, M. and Heere, B. (2011) 'Consumer attitudes towards responsible entities in sport (CARES): Scale development and model testing', *Sport Management Review*, 14 (2), 153–166.

Walker, M. and Kent, A. (2009) 'Do fans care? Assessing the influence of corporate social responsibility on consumer attitudes in the sport industry', Journal of Sport Management, 23 (6), 743–769.

Walker, M., Heere, B., Parent, M.M., and Drane, D. (2010) 'Social responsibility and the Olympic Games: The mediating role of consumer attributions', *Journal of Business Ethics*, 95 (4), 659–680.

24

MEASURING AND EVALUATING COMMUNITY SPORTS PROJECTS

Notts County Football in the Community

David Hindley and Doug Williamson

Overview

The objective of this chapter is to advance the understanding of corporate social responsibility (CSR) in English professional football through a case study analysis of the Football in the Community program at Notts County, a League One football club in the English Football League. Specifically this chapter considers some of the challenges that arise when trying to measure and evaluate the social impact of their community projects. The conclusions from the case study are that more robust evaluation is necessary that documents the importance of practitioners playing a more influential role in designing and measuring the social impact of sport. It also argues for a stronger dialogue between policy-makers/funders, practitioners and researchers, which potentially can help to develop a greater sense of ownership and understanding. The chapter also raises a number of broader questions relating to community programs such as: what is the extent of the social obligations to the diverse and complex communities in which football clubs operate? What are they capable of doing and achieving, and are these required? In addition, and as a corollary to that question, is there a danger that by heightening expectations of their "good works" is this actually setting up community departments for failure?

Introduction

Although CSR has been thoroughly articulated, the social responsibilities implicit to sport remain underdeveloped (Smith and Westerbeek, 2007). In the context of English professional football (soccer), concerns about the game's "new commercialism" (Hamil *et al.*, 2000), spiralling player wages and questionable player behavior, growing evidence of overseas ownership and the increased public scrutiny of football's governance have meant that there are "significant questions about the legitimacy of football clubs and their position in society" (Slack and Shrives, 2008: 25). This leads them to suggest that in response football clubs are looking to engage with their local communities and greater social disclosure (see Chapters 6, 18 and 19).

Wagg (2004) notes that there is evidence of widespread adoption of the word "community" in official football discourse, designed to invoke feelings of identity and belonging, and providing a barrier against the rigors of an increasingly global and competitive market. Richard Scudamore, Chief Executive of the Premier League claims that "community engagement is now woven into the fabric of football … the size and scope of that commitment is something of which the Premier League and our clubs can be proud" (Premier League, 2007: 1). The Football Foundation's Community program talks about operating at the intersection of football's three key priorities: "quality participation, social cohesion and corporate social responsibility" (The Football Foundation, 2008: 17). The Football Association (FA) meanwhile is keen to stress that football has a unique place in British society and that it is able to act as a power for good off the pitch across different areas of policy (FA, 2004)

Against this backdrop it is understandable why the potential of CSR has become attractive. The Sport Business group at Deloitte who are responsible for an annual review of football finance recommend that clubs integrate CSR management to ensure healthy relationships with the community. Put simply, "a strong relationship between club and community is … good for business" (Deloitte and Touche, 2004: 55). Taylor observes that

> in a period of public debate about corporate governance and social responsibility the more forward-thinking and/or publicity-conscious clubs see some merit in acting as good "local citizens," whether by establishing good relations with their neighbours on issues such as redevelopment of their grounds, or as a means of attracting new sponsors.
>
> (Taylor, 2004: 53)

This perspective is reinforced by Babiak and Wolfe (2006) who assert that strong relations with the local community are essential for a sport organization's success, citing that it will help to attract supporters, sponsors, and to have effective relations with the local authorities. In this sense CSR may be deemed to be a rational management response on social or instrumental grounds.

According to Breitbarth and Harris (2008: 200) CSR if implemented and managed rightly "can create specific sources of value among stakeholders" which in turn can lead to a range of benefits, including increased participation, greater institutional relevance, (financial) profits, and thus strategic advantages in terms of competitiveness. They go on to herald that "the professionalization and commercialisation of professional football and its high profile create a demand to integrate CSR into the game" (Breitbarth and Harris, 2008: 200). While it could be contested that there is a danger of amplifying the persuasiveness of CSR, it is undeniable that CSR in the football context has the potential to deliver a range of benefits, including fostering goodwill amongst supporters and the local community, enhancing their public image and countering negative scrutiny – all of which add weight to the belief that "doing good is good business" (Mintzberg, 1984). As Slack and Shrives (2008) assert football clubs are likely to report on their social activities to distract the "relevant publics" away from negative issues and any adverse media reporting by focusing on more positive issues.

Despite the term "community" being mobilized by the game's governing bodies – as evidenced by the platitudes above – the process for achieving a social return from sport is as yet unclear (Levermore, 2011) (see Chapters 2 and 3 for a more detailed discussion). Furthermore, the deployment of CSR within the football industry remains a mixed picture, with many clubs continuing to separate out "community" based activities from their core, everyday business operations and practices. Critics have also argued that "although this sporting, educational and other community activity is important, it is possible to see this as just PR work for rich businessmen's playthings" (Bishop *et al.*, 2004: 13).

Hence, this chapter aims to advance the understanding of CSR in English professional football through a case study analysis of Notts County Football in the Community. Specifically our examination will consider some of the thorny challenge of trying to measure and evaluate the social impact of their community projects. It is noteworthy that from this enquiry a number of broader questions also arise. What is the extent of the social obligations to the diverse and complex communities in which football clubs operate? What are they capable of doing and achieving, and are these required? In addition, and as a corollary to that question, is there a danger that by heightening expectations of their "good works" is this actually setting up community departments for failure? As Taylor (2004: 65) observes "football clubs themselves have entered a vicious circle: they have created and perpetuated myths of community ties, and then been surprised when others seek to hold them to the commitments that these myths imply."

Football and social responsibility: a brief history

The election of the Labour administration in 1997 can be defined by a new "third way" political discourse about social inclusion, which emphasized the cosy language of community, stake-holding and social cohesion. Sport has been promoted as a potential instrument in the pursuit of these diverse social policy agendas including enhancing health, engaging disaffected youth, combating anti-social behavior and helping to build stronger and safer communities (Bloyce and Smith, 2010; Coalter, 2007a; Collins and Kay, 2003). New Labour's approach and its subsequent funding initiatives stem from a report by Policy Action Group 10 (DCMS, 1999: 23) which stressed that "sport can contribute to neighborhood renewal by improving communities' performance on four key indicators – health, crime, employment and education." The belief that sport can extend to spheres that are hard to reach through more traditional political activities has had important ramifications for the football industry, with central government increasingly keen for football clubs to play a role in tackling social exclusion. Indeed, the promotion of football in a public policy context is rooted largely on the contribution it could make to social exclusion. Within the UK, government-backed national programs of education through football (such as "Playing for Success") have reinvigorated aspects of the civic functions of stadium spaces, utilized as sites for learning, healthcare, social enterprise and neighborhood renewal. This is encapsulated by Perkins' (2000: 113) observation that "what football ... can be *used for* almost has no bounds these days given the huge public interest in the sport."

Thus, football provides an attractive terrain for delivering the government's wider social outcomes due to its widespread popularity both at the elite level and at the "grassroots" (see Morgan, Chapter 18). Of course the notion of clubs as "community" institutions is not a new phenomenon. For more than a century professional football clubs in towns and cities across England have been recognized as playing a key role in their local communities, helping to reinforce a sense of place and local identity (Bale, 2000). During the late Victorian and Edwardian era clubs were commonly established as sporting and community entities, often by churches and enlightened employers. Manchester United, for example, was conceived as Newton Heath in 1878, with the stated aim of providing opportunities for workers from the Lancashire and Yorkshire Railway to play association football (Gibbons, 2001). Neighbors Manchester City meanwhile grew out of a team formed in 1880 by the vicar's daughter at St Mark's Church, Gorton – a deprived industrial area of Manchester – to steer young working men away from drink and fighting.

More recently the labeling of clubs as "community" institutions has largely taken place under the banner of the national Football in the Community (FITC) initiative. The latter has its antecedents in the late 1970s when the Sports Council encouraged football clubs to combat the spectre of hooliganism by establishing formal schemes with the intention of attracting supporters and improving fans' behavior. Notably the scheme was launched principally in response to football's problems rather than those of its communities (Mellor,

2005). The schemes had limited success, receiving fresh impetus in the mid-1980s from the Professional Footballers' Association who piloted six FITC schemes in the North-West of England. Their aim was to build bridges between football clubs and their local communities primarily through the provision of sporting opportunities and player appearances (Mellor, 2001; Reade, 2000). Since then the "community brand" has generally been reflected in managerial practice, responding to the national anti-racism (Kick-it-Out) campaign, demonstrating greater awareness of disabled supporters (see Chapter 9) and, in some cases, becoming more sensitive to those living near grounds.

Notts County FC: Football in the Community

Notts County Football Club has an illustrious history being one of the founder members of the Football League, but in more recent years has experienced a turbulent time. The oldest professional football club in the world (established in 1862) has languished in the lower reaches of the Football League, and less than a decade ago faced the very real threat of extinction due to ongoing financial difficulties and mismanagement (Conn, 2004). Despite these struggles, the club has doggedly held on, and plays an important role in the community. Notts County's Football in the Community program was established in 1989 with the aim of providing direction – especially in hard-to-reach, disadvantaged and marginalized communities – through sport and education. The community team works directly with targeted groups to deliver a beneficial impact: improving opportunities to people who are in educational, social and economic disadvantage, which results in better health, confidence and life skills. Their focus is manifold:

• increase the numbers participating in sport and physical activity, and develop innovative projects;
• encourage healthier, active lifestyles and positive behaviors;
• re-engage young people in learning maximize their potential;
• develop programs to reduce youth offending;
• encourage social inclusion by targeting specific demographics;
• promote Notts County FITC as a community resource; and
• create employment and volunteering opportunities.

As the world's oldest professional Football League club, Notts County is deeply rooted in the local community, and through using the club brand, and the effective "hook" of football, the community department is able to engage people from a diverse range of ages, backgrounds, ability and disability across Nottingham. The city has a large number of social and health-related problems and the work of FITC has been designed to address these. They aim to use the transformative capacity of sport-based intervention programs to inspire people to become more active, positive and healthier.

FITC delivers an extensive and diverse range of innovative, community and grassroots projects, typically working in challenging inner-city areas, where it is difficult to engage "hard-to-reach" groups, for example older men, teenagers, excluded young people, and those at risk of committing crime. Their community out-reach projects are designed to be inclusive and accessible, offering a supportive environment to encourage and assist those individuals, and are often positioned in areas of Nottingham that have high incidences of obesity, deprivation, crime, low educational attainmentand low employment.

The program is considered to be an example of best practice nationally, recognized by the Football League Trust to be a Silver accredited scheme (the highest level) as well as a recipient of a number of awards. The Football League Trust is a charitable body established in 2007 to oversee youth and community development by the 72 clubs which make up the Football League (see also Chapter 6).

In 2008, On the Ball (a football-based project aimed at young men with mental health issues) won the Football League Trust's Best Community Initiative. In 2010 their Active School's initiative which is aimed at years five and six and delivered in all 81 inner-city primary schools (working with over 10,000 participants) won Best Community Project for Health. Notts County FITC has an excellent reputation within the city, acknowledged as a key partner by the two major public sector funders, working closely with both Nottingham City Council and National Health Service (NHS) Nottingham who have identified FITC as an important element of their agenda.

Sport for social good: where is the evidence that sport works?

While this snapshot of Notts County FITC's work clearly serves to promote the positive contribution sport, and football in particular, can make to deliver a range of social agendas, the need to evidence the impact of the community projects, and to measure and evaluate the effectiveness of the various projects against their specific objectives, is imperative. However, this is easier said than done. Whilst sport's potential to contribute positively to a multitude of societal outcomes is widely celebrated, empirical evidence for such benefits is limited. Numerous authors argue there is a lack of robust evidence of the direct impact of sport and physical activity, calling for more rigorous and sustained testing (Coalter, 2007a; Collins and Kay, 2003; Spaaij, 2009a, 2009b; Tacon, 2007). More broadly, Coalter (2008: 48) contends that "sport in any simple sense rarely achieves the variety of desired outcomes attributed to it" going on to state that "issues of process and context … are key to understanding its developmental potential."

It is necessary to position this debate in the current political and economic context. While unprecedented amounts of public and private money in recent times have been targeted at Football in the Community departments, this has since been replaced by an age of public spending austerity with the likelihood of cuts in such levels of funding and scrutiny on the impact of this investment likely to intensify. It is probable therefore, that critical questions will be asked about what should and shouldn't be funded. Core to this is the necessity to be more circumspect about the claims – what Coalter (2007a: 172) calls "a rhetorical fudge that seems to keep policy-makers, practitioners and some researchers happy" – that sport can achieve broader welfare policy objectives (see Chapters 1, 2 and 3 for a much detailed overview of the role of CSR in sport).

One possible scenario is that as the current economy weakens, public sector funding for initiatives is clawed back, and competition for limited resources intensifies, community sports programs will have little choice but to set inflated targets. As Weiss observes:

> because of the political processes of persuasion and negotiation that are required to get a program enacted, inflated promises are made in the guise of programme goals. Furthermore, the goals often lack clarity and intellectual coherence that evaluation criteria should have.
>
> (Weiss, 1993: 96)

This is a view shared by Coalter (2007a: 30), who argues that even when desired outcomes and aims are set out by initiatives, they are often very vague and/or far too ambitious to be fulfilled. Moreover, despite the strong political commitment to the social inclusion agenda, there remains no definitive and rigor analysis of the rationale underpinning sport-based interventions, while the evidence gathering has been piecemeal, uncritical and without standardization. This picture is slowly changing, as illustrated by the comprehensive and expanding monitoring and evaluation of the UK Kickz initiative, which has developed since its inception to incorporate quantitative and qualitative, participatory and user-friendly tools, whilst the Football League Trust's championing of the Substance model of reporting means that they can pool together common data (see http://www.substance.coop). Nevertheless, it is customary practice for the attention of community schemes to focus more on delivery rather than on evaluation, with consequently, inadequately designed and resourced research, as well as a serial lack of research expertise within FITC programs.

Against this backdrop, Notts County FITC has identified the requirement for a more strategic and robust approach to monitoring and evaluation. As stated, this isn't an isolated need but reflects a wider demand on not only sport-based organizations to demonstrate in a more evidence-based way the impact of their work. Sport England in recent years have stressed the need for "evidence, insight and understanding," emphasizing "we want to understand what does and doesn't work ... so we can invest our time, money and expertise wisely" (Sport England, 2012). At the same time there is a burgeoning literature examining the potential social impact of sport, which repeatedly argues that the cumulative evidence base for many claims for sport is relatively weak (Coalter, 2007a, 2007b; Collins and Kay, 2003; Long and Sanderson, 2001; Crow and Nichols, 2004).

As a consequence, there is a pressing need for a far greater methodological understanding of how to "capture" the potential contribution that sport makes. This formed the basis and rationale behind an application to Nottingham Trent University's Stimulating Innovation for Success (SIS) program. The SIS initiative specifically aims at building on the University's existing contract research and consultancy work, by providing funding to help foster new relationships with public, privateand third sector organizations. The SIS application was timely for Notts County FITC in that they had recently allocated new resources to look at how they consider "impact," further reflecting the importance of having to "prove" their value and being able to demonstrate the outcomes and effectiveness of the community programs they deliver.

The challenge of measuring CSR

It can be argued that there has been little attempt on the part of football clubs to integrate CSR reporting into their communications function in order to enhance the image or identity of football clubs. Moreover it can be said that few clubs report CSR in a strategic, or even planned, way. This view was strengthened by Slack and Shrives (2008) who found that, while clubs are beginning to take social reporting more seriously, there remained great disparity over the level of disclosure. What this serves to illustrate is that the economic and societal value of a club's community activities, and in turn the potential to leverage and use the "brands" of professional football clubs, is currently unfulfilled. Thus, the communication of CSR in the football industry has been, at best, mixed. On the one hand there is some evidence that clubs are trading heavily on its community involvement, keen to stress their vital role as community institutions, particularly when looking for support from local authorities. On the other hand, community work is seen as a superfluous "bolt on," perceived to be a potential drain on resources and crucially at odds with the "win at all costs" mentality. It is to some of these issues that this chapter will now turn.

Within professional football certain basic operating systems are customary and well understood. The importance and functioning of aspects such as ticketing, marketing, facilities management, media relations, fan relations, as well as the sports side have become entrenched. The same, however, cannot be said when it comes to CSR. What is becoming evident is that some football clubs have deemed CSR to be applicable to specific areas of work and not to others. Frequently, clubs have designated community departments which are primarily involved in the delivery of community-based initiatives, while other areas of the club are responsible for dealing with "customers" (Mellor, 2008). Indeed in recent years a number of community departments have sought independence from their host clubs, most commonly by adopting charitable status. Mellor (2008) suggests there are a number of benefits of such a strategy, citing a level of autonomy will enable clubs to overcome some of the potential tensions between commercial and community motivations. However, in doing so there may be a danger that the "add on" mentality will persist, helping to perpetuate a general lack of understanding of the function and activities FITC schemes are involved in.

Taking this a step further there are clearly underpinning questions with regards the business of football clubs. Commonly, football clubs in England are incorporated, mostly as companies limited by shares operating within the Companies Act, and exist as commercial entities with an operational need to maximize income. And yet perversely they rarely make a profit with their owners seemingly focused on either investment to strengthen the team to challenge, or servicing debt payments. Since its inception the combined Premier League clubs have never made a collective pre-profit in any one season – in 2006/07 the 20 clubs made a combined loss of £285 million. During the same period, despite dramatic increases in revenue, nearly 50 out of 92 English Football Leagues' clubs have been in administration. From this it could be concluded that football clubs are preoccupied by "on the pitch" concerns, leaving community work a mere distraction. Holt and Shailer confirm this aspect by stating that:

> The irony is, of course, that when clubs need support from local authorities on planning issues, they are not slow to stress the role of the football club as a community institution, a vital part of social and economic fabric of the town and region.
>
> (Holt and Shailer, 2003: 159).

However, irrespective of their corporate format, football clubs are much more than businesses. As Bishop *et al.* (2004: 4) contend "their status in the community makes them very different to other small businesses – the extra activities make them more akin to a school or hospital than a local employer." Supporters invest not only their financial capital in clubs, but also their human and emotional capital. Football evokes strong personal identification and draws on the emotional attachment by supporters described as "fan equity" (Salomon Brothers, 1997). However, football is different from more conventional businesses and it can be argued that the concept of the customer is inadequate to describe supporters, who fundamentally consider issues of identity and attachment to their football clubs rather than one of economics. Supporters are, in economic terms, irrational customers, with such a fierce brand loyalty that they do not exercise the main characteristic of "ordinary" consumers – that of choice. In addition, football clubs have a deep rooted identification with particular regions and hence with communities.

In summing up, there is little evidence to suggest that CSR is more than just an activity marginal to the core objective of achieving success on the field of play. Such an approach downplays the unique resources that clubs possess, something that is inimitable and non-transferable. At a simplistic level, the "power of the club badge" shouldn't be underestimated and can enhance credibility when utilized to support a whole range of targeted schemes. Players equally enjoy iconic status making them a potentially powerful asset in helping to access traditionally hard-to-reach groups in society. It is these unique resources which if used strategically by football clubs may enhance their reputation.

The "holy grail" of developing a monitoring and evaluation toolkit

As previously discussed there remain major challenges when it comes to measuring the impact of community sport programs. As Nichols (2007: 58) elucidates "evidence from programs is scant because they do not have the funds or skills to conduct their own evaluation, and a higher priority is to assure next year's funding to allow them to continue." In the past the monitoring of programs has been relatively simplistic, which typically has comprized some simplistic quantitative data (e.g., monitoring attendance) and is founded on a cause and effect relationship between sports initiatives and their intended outcomes. Part of the difficulty is that those working in community sports development know intuitively the positive contribution that sport can make, but find it difficult to articulate these outcomes beyond anecdotal evidence.

From working in partnership with Notts County FITC on the SIS project, a number of key issues have emerged. First, is the research challenge – namely, how to ensure that the monitoring and evaluation is embedded in the actual design and delivery of a project, and not simply at the end. Related to this is the need to develop a meaningful and constructive dialogue with the funding sponsor/stakeholders so that their views and expectations can be incorporated into the program development. By gaining a deeper understanding of what sport can and cannot achieve, and in turn what realistically can be measured, this will help ensure that there is a clear agreement at the beginning on identifying appropriate indicators to monitor programs, the interim outputs and the final outcomes, as well as balance between initial expectations (of sports organizations and funders) and what realistically can be achieved. It is hoped that this will also lead to monitoring and evaluation gaining greater recognition, and not an after thought whereby programs often receive finite short-term funding that covers running costs (where the central focus is on delivery) but rarely leaves additional resources for evaluations, or for setting up effective monitoring processes to measure outcomes.

Second is the cultural challenge of how to contest and change coaches and practitioners' views towards monitoring and evaluation, which can be negative, seen as being part of an audit trail, potentially intimidatingand a distraction from the core business of delivery. As McGuire and Fenoglio (2004) note, officers working in FITC schemes often have little or no training in research and evaluation. Here, there is a need to up-skill and empower staff so that they are actively involved in reflective practice. As Coalter (2001: 1) points out in order "to address the current information deficit will require the development of a culture in which output and outcome definition, monitoring and evaluation are regarded as central components of planning, management and service delivery."

Third is the need for learning and development, so that staff have a greater understanding of what can be measured, as well as the necessary skills and expertise to record evidence using a variety of quantitative and qualitative techniques. These could form a participatory approach, which blends a range of methods with the aim of incorporating recipients in the monitoring and evaluation process. These may include:

- detailed questionnaires/life histories to provide a profile of the participant;
- structured observations using a standardized recording matrix to determine the extent to which sport-based activities match the process components of the program aims;
- face-to-face semi-structured interviews; and
- follow-up interviews post-program to assess longitudinal personal/behavioral changes.

Put simply, organizations such as Notts County FITC need to have the skills to be able to tell their own stories. Furthermore, just as sports-based programs need to be tailored to meet the needs of local problems and be oriented towards different social groups (and the diverse range of individual needs that exist), we need to also design bespoke evaluation methods that are based on the specific aims and objectives of the initiative.

Underpinning all of the above is the need to embed a "theory of change" approach in the design, delivery and monitoring of community sports programs (Astbury *et al.*, 2005). Here the *process* is as important as the desired outcomes, exploring the complex processes involved in such projects by identifying the contexts, mechanisms and outcomes through which they operate. Green (2008: 131) notes that "it is not sport per se that is responsible for particular outcomes; it is the ways that sport is implemented." It is not sufficient to assume that a program alone will achieve an assumed outcome or behaviour change without some careful planning. In turn, the focus shifts to cast a critical gaze on the interaction between the participant (and their predispositions) and the project, as well as needing to understand not only what influence the sports-based intervention has, but *why* it had that effect. In this way, researchers and practitioners can gain an understanding of the necessary conditions where positive social outcomes can be derived, and in turn will be able to use these insights to inform the design and delivery of future projects and their evaluation.

Conclusions

As this chapter has highlighted, while CSR in a sporting context is increasingly being recognized as a vehicle for fostering social and economic development, there remains a paucity of research on evaluating CSR through sport (Levermore, 2011). To that end, the conclusions presented here corroborate key themes and ideas drawn from the growing literature on the social impact of community sports development. As stated previously, it is widely believed that sport provides an effective hook for engaging with traditionally hard-to-reach, socially disadvantaged and excluded groups. In turn, it is assumed that a number of positive and observable by-products (e.g., enhanced confidence and self-esteem; empowering marginalized groups; improving health and well-being) can be derived from sport-based interventions, although proving the link between sport participation and these broader social objectives remains problematic (Bloyce and Smith, 2010; Coalter, 2007a). The case study project with Notts County FC Football in the Community has attempted to grapple with some of these thorny issues, representing a tentative step towards answering the call for more extensive evaluation. What this partnership demonstrates is the need to clear the mist of sport's mythopoeic nature (Coalter, 2007a) and to be more circumspect about the presumed benefits of sport. It has also helped to make stark some of the inherent methodological issues. This leads the authors to conclude that more robust evaluation is necessary, and documents the importance of practitioners playing a more influential role in designing and measuring the social impact of sport. It also argues for a stronger dialogue between policy-makers/funders, practitioners and researchers, which potentially can help to develop a greater sense of ownership and understanding.

References

Astbury, R., Knight, B. and Nichols, G. (2005) 'The contribution of sport-related interventions to the long-term development of disaffected young people: an evaluation of the Fairbridge programme', *Journal of Park and Recreation Administration*, 23 (3), 82–98.

Babiak, K. and Wolfe, R. (2006) 'More than just a game? Corporate social responsibility and Super Bowl XL', *Sport Marketing Quarterly*, 15, 214–222.

Bale, J. (2000) 'The changing face of football: stadiums and communities', in Garland, J., Malcolm, D. and Rowe, M. (eds) *The future of football: Challenges for the twenty-first century*. London: Frank Cass, 91–101.

Bishop, D., Breeze, J., Danczuk, S. and Bailey, G. (2004) *Funding football from the grassroots to the championship*, Research paper on behalf of the All Party Football Group, Manchester.

Bloyce, D. and Smith, A. (2010) *Sport policy and development: An introduction*. London: Routledge.

Breitbarth, T. and Harris, P. (2008) 'The role of corporate social responsibility in the football business: towards the development of a conceptual model', *European Sport Management Quarterly*, 8 (2), 179–201.

Coalter, F. (2001) 'Realising the potential of cultural services: The case for sport'. London: LGA Publications. Available at: http://www.lga.gov.uk/lga/culture/researchagenda.pdf (accessed: August 22, 2012).

Coalter, F. (2007a) *A wider social role for sport: Who's keeping the score?* London: Routledge.

Coalter, F. (2007b) 'Sports clubs, social capital and social regeneration: "Ill-defined interventions with hard to follow outcomes"?' *Sport in Society*, 10 (4), 537–559.

Coalter, F. (2008) 'Sport-in-development: Development for and through sport?' in Nicholson, M. and Hoye, R. (eds) *Sport and social capital*. Oxford: Elsevier Butterworth-Heinemann, pp. 39–67.

Collins, M. and Kay, T. (2003) *Sport and social exclusion*. London: Routledge.

Conn, D. (2004) *The beautiful game? Searching for the soul of football*. London: Yellow Jersey Press.

Crow, I. and Nichols, G. (2004) 'Measuring the impact of crime reduction interventions involving sports activities for young people', *The Howard Journal*, 43 (3), 267–283.

Deloitte and Touche (2004) *Annual review of football finance*. Manchester: Deloitte and Touche Sport.

Department for Culture, Media and Sport (DCMS) (1999) *Policy Action Team 10: Report to the social exclusion unit – Arts and Sport*. London: HMSO.

Football Association (2004) *FA Annual Review 2003–2004*. London: The F.A.

Gibbons, P. (2001) *Association football in Victorian England: A history of the game from 1863 to 1900*. Leicestershire: Upfront Publishing.

Green, B.C. (2008) 'Sport as an agent for social and personal change', in Girginov, V. (ed.) *Management of sports development*. London: Butterworth-Heinemann, pp.130–145.

Hamil, S., Michie, J., Oughton, C. and Warby, S. (eds) (2000) *Football in the digital age: Whose game is it anyway?*. Edinburgh: Mainstream.

Holt, M. and Shailer, L. (2003) 'The role of the stadium in building good corporate governance at football clubs', in Trenberth, L. (ed.) *Managing the business of sport*, New Zealand: Dunmore Press, pp. 143–162.

Levermore, R. (2011) 'The paucity of, and dilemma in, evaluating corporate social responsibility for development through sport', *Third World Quarterly*, 32 (2), 551–569.

Long, J. and Sanderson, I. (2001) 'The social benefits of sport: where's the proof?' in Gratton, C. and Henry, I. (eds) *Sport in the city: The role of sport in economic and social regeneration*. London: Routledge, pp. 187–203.

McGuire, B. and Fenoglio, R. (2004) *Football in the community: Resources and opportunities*. Manchester Metropolitan University, Department of Exercise and Sport Science.

Mellor, G. (2001) *'Can we have our fans back now? Football, Community and the Historical Struggles of small-town clubs'*. Singer and Friedlander Football Review 2000/01 season.

Mellor, G. (2005) 'Mixed motivations: Why do football clubs do "community" work?' in Murphy, P. and Waddington, I. (eds) *Soccer Review 2005*, pp. 18–23. Available at: http://www.supporters-direct.org/docs/Soccer%20Review%202005.pdf#page=23 (accessed: August 24, 2012).

Mellor, G. (2008) 'The janus-faced sport': English football, community and the legacy of the 'third way', *Soccer and Society*, 9 (3), 313–324.

Mintzberg, H. (1984) 'Power and organisation life cycles', *Academy of Management Review*, 9 (2), 207–224.

Nichols, G. (2007) *Sport and crime reduction: the role of sports in tackling youth crime*. London: Routledge.

Perkins, S. (2000) 'Exploring future relationships between football clubs and local government', in Garland, J., Malcolm, D. and Rowe, M (eds) *The future of football: Challenges for the twenty-first century*, London: Frank Cass, pp. 102–113.

Premier League (2007) *Premier League Community Report 2006–07*. London: The Premier League.

Reade, R. (2000) 'Football in the Community'. Singer and Friedlander Football Review 2000/01 season.

Salomon Brothers (1997) *UK Football Clubs: Valuable assets? Global Equity Research: Leisure*. London: Salomon Brothers.

Slack, R. and Shrives, P. (2008) 'Social disclosure and legitimacy in Premier League football clubs: The first ten years', *Journal of Applied Accounting Research*, 9 (1),17–28.

Smith, A.C.T and Westerbeek, H.M. (2007) 'Sport and a vehicle for deploying corporate social responsibility', *Journal of Corporate Citizenship*, 21 (1), 43–55.

Spaaij, R. (2009a) 'The social impact of sport: diversities, complexities and contexts', *Sport in Society*, 12 (9), 1109–1117.

Spaaij, R. (2009b) 'Sport as a vehicle for social mobility and regulation of disadvantaged urban youth: lessons from Rotterdam', *International Review for the Sociology of Sport*, 44 (2–3), 247–264.

Sport England (2012) *Research*. Available at: http://www.sportengland.org/research.aspx (accessed: November 9, 2012).

Tacon, R. (2007) 'Football and social inclusion: evaluating social policy', *Managing Leisure*, 12, 1–23.

Taylor, N. (2004) 'Giving something back: Can football clubs and their communities co-exist?' in Wagg, S. (ed.) (2004) *British football and social exclusion*. London: Routledge, pp. 49–54.

The Football Foundation (2008) *Community programme: Strategy 2008*. London: The Football Foundation.

Wagg, S. (ed.) (2004) *British football and social exclusion*. London: Routledge.

Weiss, C. H. (1993) 'Where politics and evaluation research meet', *Evaluation practice*, 14 (1), 93–106.

25

IMPLEMENTING "MONITORING AND EVALUATION" TECHNIQUES WITHIN A PREMIER LEAGUE FOOTBALL IN THE COMMUNITY SCHEME

A case study involving Everton in the Community

Dan Parnell, Gareth Stratton, Barry Drust and David Richardson

Overview

Football in the Community (FitC) schemes have been operating within football clubs in the UK for a number of decades. The rise of corporate social responsibility (CSR) within the broader societal context has resulted in these schemes being championed as a delivery arm for CSR through community engagement. Alongside this, FitC schemes (and community sport) have received unprecedented funding and support for sport based social change projects (i.e., crime, social inclusion and health). This enthusiasm to champion (and fund) football as a key vehicle to tackle social agendas has not been matched with funding to support research and evaluation. Across FitC schemes very little is known about day-to-day working practice and the effectiveness of their work tackling social issues. This case study explores a unique collaborative research project between a Premier League Football Club (Everton Football Club), a corporate funder and a higher education department. The chapter aims to explore the process of monitoring and evaluation within this collaborative environment to effectively improve working practices and the effectiveness of the FitC scheme. It also aims to provide the reader with an understanding of the realities of developing and delivering monitoring and evaluation within an FitC scheme. The chapter concludes with some key recommendations for practitioners seeking to develop effective monitoring and evaluation within their organization.

Introduction

Football clubs, via the development of CSR strategies and/or FitC schemes, have a relatively long history of working with the "community" (Breitbath and Harris, 2008; Russell, 1997; Walters and Chadwick, 2009). As CSR has become more widely used to capture corporate social "good," FitC schemes have been placed within the scope of CSR to better understand this community engagement work within football clubs. The launch of the national FitC program (highlighted within Chapter 24) sought to attend to social and sporting changes and build greater links between clubs and their communities, in part as a result of football's conscience in response to football hooliganism (Brown *et al.*, 2006). These FitC schemes had an initial focus on traditional children's coaching schemes to widen access (Mellor, 2008). Sport, and societies expectation for sport, has evolved remarkably since the introduction of the FitC national program (for further insight into this see Chapter 24 by Hindley and Williamson).

In one of the first detailed insights into FitC schemes, Watson (2000) sought to explore the purposes of individual FitC schemes, the positioning of these schemes within football clubs and how they reconcile such different agendas (i.e., club and community) with which they are confronted. To highlight difficulties and perhaps allude to the hostile culture of football (Parker, 2001), Watson detailed an account of a National FitC scheme manager:

> When I started, 12 years ago, one of the six pilot scheme clubs would hardly let me through the door. When I did get in he [the club secretary] gave me five minutes to describe what the scheme was going to do for his club. I remember him saying: "If this involves one more piece of paper crossing my desk I will stop it."
>
> Watson (2000: 117)

At this time Watson (2000) stated that the majority of community officers reported that they understood the role of FitC schemes within the football club, but that "community" was not a high priority. Watson (2000) also highlighted that FitC was at a critical stage of change in terms of the scope and future of the programs. The same author recommended clubs create charitable arms under which FitC schemes would sit. Such a financial divorce would thus reduce the influence of the football club on the strategic "social" agenda of the community arm and allow for the inclusion and/or shared ownership with other stakeholders, including local authorities and the public sector. It was argued that this had the potential to enable FitC schemes to grow, independently, with more social purpose, develop and become more influential within the community that they serve (Watson, 2000; Brown *et al.*, 2006).

The importance of FitC schemes' independence and subsequent financial security is critical in aligning to social agendas (and subsequently attracting social funding). Recently, Jenkins and James (2012) found that in a sample of 23 clubs that had been involved in the Premier League, only three FitC schemes were located within the organizational structure of the football club (i.e., managed internally). The other 20 Premier League clubs for the 2011/2012 season, including the three newly promoted clubs, and the three clubs relegated at the end of the 2010/11 season, adopted a community trust or foundation model of community engagement (Jenkins and James, 2012). Despite this financial, structural and strategic independence from the football club, the majority of schemes maintain association in name with the football club. This relationship highlights that the football club recognizes the value of such an alliance, whilst also allowing the community scheme to use the brand of the football club, as a "hook" for community engagement (Vigor *et al.*, 2006).

Since the development of FitC schemes and the early scepticism of football clubs (highlighted by Watson, 2000), there has been a huge shift in the social role of sport, and football in particular, beyond simply using football as a "hook" to address a range of societal ills (detailed in Chapter 24). Essentially, FitC schemes have been (politically and corporately) re-positioned in order to address broader and more complex social agendas (including social inclusion, crime and health). During this time (1997–2006) FitC schemes were undergoing a significant period of organizational development. Hindley and Williamson (see Chapter 24) suggest that FitC schemes were in the midst of receiving "unprecedented amounts of public and private money," prior to the emergence of "an age of public spending austerity" and subsequently without the accompanying risk of reduced funding and increased scrutiny over investment. In this regard, there has been little or no recognition of evaluation or the adoption of evidenced based practice. Jackson *et al.* (2005) reportedly found no studies to demonstrate the effects of sport-based policy interventions on increasing participation and/or promoting healthy behavior. Similarly, Tacon (2007) reinforced such frustrations by calling for a need for more rigorous evaluation of FitC schemes. Such calls for more supporting evidence to substantiate the use of football as a vehicle for social change highlights the fact that current monitoring and evaluation processes do not fairly reflect the true nature, complexity and subsequent outcomes of the numerous interventions. It was around this time (2005/06) that this case study began, with the aim to better understand the implementation of monitoring and evaluation within the Everton in the Community (EitC) scheme.

Everton in the Community

Everton Football Club has an illustrious history spanning back as far as 1878. Indeed, the club was one of 12 featured in Peter Lupson's acclaimed book: *Thank God for FOOTBALL* (2006). Lupson's work tracks the origins of 12 Premier League clubs who owe their existence to church and religion. Similarly, Bale (2000) also portrayed clubs as "community" institutions playing key roles in their local communities, helping to reinforce a sense of place and local identity and by extension the local community.

Everton were founded in November 1878 when the St Domingo's Church held a meeting at the Queen's Head Hotel, Village Street. They already had a cricket team but wanted to find another sport for the winter months. Moving forward, the newly established St Domingo team played in Stanley Park and won their first game, against St Peter's Church. The following year the club were renamed Everton Football Club after the surrounding area. Since then the club have accumulated the highest number of years in the top flight (highest division) of English football, experiencing their most successful period during the mid-1980s. The club flirted with relegation in the mid-1990s before seeing more recent (relative) success with a number of appearances in European competitions and regular finishes in the top half of the Premier League table under manager David Moyes. Moyes joined Everton on March 14, 2002 and at his unveiling press conference, he acknowledged Everton as a club with a long-standing community attachment. He said: "I am joining the people's football club in Liverpool. The people in the street support Everton (http://www.youtube.com/watch?v=h-JwkqKbTOo).

From then on both the club and fans alike have taken the banner "The People's Club on Merseyside" forward with pride. At this point the club already had a community program in place. EitC became an independent registered charity in 2004. This suggests that EitC was a part of the more organized FitC schemes and aligned with the recommendations of both Watson (2000) and Brown *et al.* (2006).

The initial focus of EitC was in the facilitation of public player appearances to support local causes and to provide sporting opportunities in hard to reach, deprived and marginalized communities. Such communities come in abundance across Liverpool, a city of historic deprivation with ensuing riots in the 1980s, and more recently retaining the title of most deprived local authority within England in 2004, 2007 and 2010 (see Liverpool City Council, 2010). EitC quickly moved forward from the initial *loose* remit of the national FitC scheme and school-based development activities to embrace other social agendas, including disability awareness and empowerment, social inclusion, and women and girls' development.

It is difficult to calculate the local, national and international acclaim credited to EitC and its respective practitioners and community coaches (especially when trying to avoid the "game" of stating engagement figures in the tens of thousands per year). At present there are few tools available to compare FitC schemes achievements and success. However, Responsiball, a European platform developed with a purpose to "support the progress of social responsibility with football clubs" recently completed a benchmarking exercise, which compared website data from nearly 270 clubs in the top divisions of those nations competing in the UEFA EURO 2012 (Responsiball, 2012). Encouragingly, the Premier League ranked highest, with the highest scores for community and governance (Responsiball, 2012). While this research is web-based, it helps to position FitC schemes within Premier League football clubs as leaders in community football in Europe. For those involved in FitC schemes and those that work in the aligned development work it is common knowledge that EitC have a forward thinking approach, highly skilled practitioners and successful programs. A selection of awards achieved between 2010 and 2012, pay tribute to the high acclaim that EitC is held:

- Runner-up "Everyday Impact Award – Long Term Enterprises," Everton in the Community
- MBNA Northern Football Award, Community Scheme of the Year
- North West Public Health Award, Imagine Your Goals Mental Health Program
- MBNA Northern Sports Award, Best Grassroots Club Program
- Stadium Business Awards, Best Community Scheme in Europe
- Sport and Recreation Alliance Awards (London), "Highly Commended" in the category of Professional Sports Club Community Program of the Year
- National Sports Industry Awards, Community Program of the Year – Disability Program
- Kickz (Youth Inclusion), Outstanding Police Contribution.

(Everton FC, 2012)

Despite these and past awards, EitC recognized that they could be doing more and that monitoring and evaluation could help them improve their effectiveness. The following section aims to take the reader on a journey through the realities of a FitC scheme, attempting to capture their impact with "real" monitoring and evaluation during a time of "unprecedented funding," however very little scrutiny regarding the social impact of such funding.

Improving quality of life through community football

The relatively simple engagement and participation agenda renowned within traditional football development activities (and the roots of FitC) (Mellor, 2008) was a major part of the core work of EitC up until 2004. At the time EitC was a highly regarded FitC scheme having been the first English Premier League football club to be awarded the prestigious "Community Mark" national standard from Business in the Community (patron HRH Prince of Wales). Their vision was: "To motivate, educate and inspire by harnessing the power of football and sport, improving the quality of the lives of all within our community, locally and regionally" (Parnell *et al.*, 2008).

It was during this time that EitC began communication with a local higher education (HE) department (School of Sport and Exercise Sciences, Liverpool John Moores University).

Through informal discussions between both the EitC and the HE department there was a consensus to develop an understanding of the "real" impact of EitC through monitoring and evaluation. It was Taylor (2004) that highlighted the danger of committing to highly favorable outcomes and the risks of someone actually holding them to their commitments. In this regard, EitC were claiming to improve quality of life. However, there was no evidence to support such a claim and no prior intention (understanding or ability) to begin to measure whether such a claim was valid.

By 2005/06 EitC were beginning to enter into more complex agendas including those concerning behavior change, health promotion and quality of life echoing the conclusions of Watson (2000). Given the major deprivation and health concerns in Liverpool (Liverpool City Council, 2010) it was important for a FitC scheme (and any program) that was being funded to tackle such health issues to begin to monitor and evaluate their impact.

It is important to note that this occurred at a time where there was no requirement by funders for EitC to consider measuring the "real" impact of their work. Hindley and Williamson (see more details in Chapter 24) conclude that at the time of writing there is still a need for more robust monitoring and evaluation and dialogue between practitioners and researchers across FitC schemes (and community sport), to develop and understand the impact of the community work. EitC's early movements in the pursuit for "real" evidence adds further weight to the suggestion that EitC, was (and still is) a forward-thinking FitC scheme.

Case study: Everton in the Community

In 2006, a collaboration was developed in a bid to tackle the need for monitoring and evalua-tion with FitC. Within this section the challenges to monitoring and evaluation, and aligning theory and practice, are set out within the context of the case study. This formal collabora-tion was developed between EitC, the HE department and Greggs North West Plc (Greggs). Greggs, a well-known bakery outlet, emerged during the 1930s in north-east England, with a long established community philosophy and a socially responsible approach to business, high-lighted through the development of the Greggs Foundation in 1987. The main focus of the Greggs Foundation was to "give something back" to the communities in which it operates (Greggs, 2012). It appears that Greggs, like both EitC and the HE department, were com-mitted to their social responsibility in giving something back to the community. In this case, funding by Greggs enabled the formation of a strategic alliance (i.e., Greggs, EitC and the HE department) in order to evaluate the effectiveness of the EitC community coaching program in promoting health in primary school children.

Methodological considerations to the research

When beginning to consider the process of measuring the impact of FitC schemes, many major challenges are raised. The collaboration was funded by Greggs, who helped overcome a major challenge of funding for both the delivery and monitoring and evaluation (Nichols, 2007). At the time very little was known about the day-to-day working practices within FitC schemes (Watson, 2000) and/or the culture in which these schemes operated. For example, the world of professional football clubs has been characterized by traditional and ruthless culture (Parker, 2001) and have evolved more recently into major business enterprises (Relvas *et al.*, 2010) concerned with entertainment and profit. FitC schemes are aligned to the professional football club but are (typically) required to adopt a more social not-for-profit approach to business.

Any work that attends to a behavior "change" agenda (whether practitioner and/or participant related) requires buy-in from the target for change. Within this case study there was an overt willingness to examine, change and improve the effectiveness of existing practices that operated within EitC. Finally, it should also be recognized that, at this time, there was a real lack of understanding of what constitutes *robust* "monitoring and evaluation" (McGuire and Fenoglio, 2004). The requirement to collate credible data (Nichols, 2007) meant that it was important that any monitoring and evaluation was collaborative in nature and aimed towards skilling up, empowering and engaging those involved (i.e., practitioners and community coaches) to ensure learning and development takes place.

The approach

This case study was framed within a longitudinal collaborative action research oriented methodology that engaged a series of "reflective cycles" (Gilbourne, 1999; Richardson *et al.*, 2004). Action research is associated with addressing practical problems in the workplace (Gilbourne 1999, 2001; Richardson *et al.*, 2004), and seeks to encourage practitioners to reflect on existing working practice with a view to evolving new and/or refining existing working strategies (Richardson *et al.*, 2004). Action research is intended to stimulate thinking towards an action or *change strategy*, which is reflective in nature (McFee, 1992). The reflection on current practice can act to encourage debate among practitioners and facilitates ideas relating to practice, which can be shared (Gilbourne, 2001). As the process of action research opens and the reflective cycle(s) begin, positive changes in working practice become more likely. The research surrounding this case study consisted of three studies, which developed within the action research framework (see Figure 25.1).

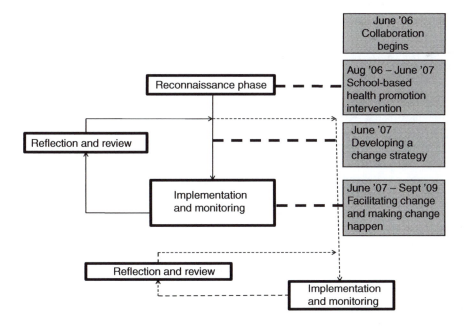

Figure 25.1 The action research cycle

Source: adapted from Richardson, Gilbourne and Littlewood (2004).

Familiarization and continued engagement required the researcher (first author) to go "native" by submerging himself into the culture of the practitioner's environment. The principal researcher adopted an ethnographic approach to undertake prolonged fieldwork with extensive observation in the natural setting (typically two days per week between August 2006–September 2008 and five days a week September 2008–November 2009) (Hammersley and Atkinson, 1995; Eder and Corsaro, 1999). The researcher attempted to develop a clear understanding of what daily life was like for the practitioners and community coaches, become accustomed to and understand the physical and institutional settings in which they lived, the daily routine of activities, the beliefs that guided their actions and the linguistic and other semiotic systems that mediated all their contexts and activities (Eder and Corsaro, 1999). Participant observations were utilized in a variety of settings throughout the project (Hammersley and Atkinson, 1995, Parnell *et al.*, 2013) in order to balance the notions of engagement and trust, whilst adopting an (initially) objective lens, the researcher then actively engaged in both observation and participation and participant-observation (Hong and Duff, 2002).

Data representation

Verbatim citations (*in italics*) are utilized to illustrate the contextual features of the participants. The first author's field note extracts and personal reflections are evidenced as indentations, single spaces within the text. Staying close to the data is the most powerful means of telling the story, while also ensuring that data interpretation, where possible, is undertaken using the participant's (i.e., children's, practitioners or coaches) language, rather than that of the researcher (Janesick, 1999). However, a first-person writing style was adopted in order to help contextualize the data and move the story on for the reader (Tierney, 2002). Again, the themes discussed are those that have emerged from the cursory content analysis undertaken throughout the research. Pseudonyms are used for all involved.

The effectiveness of a community coaching program in promoting health in primary school children

The reconnaissance phase (see Figure 25.1) spanned across a 10-month period (August 2006–June 2007), which included the researcher delving into the complexities of a 16-week long community based football-oriented coaching initiative (targeting primary school children) to ascertain the effectiveness of such initiatives delivered by EitC. This multi-method evaluation adopted throughout the reconnaissance phase and specifically within the 16-week long community based coaching initiative (including attendance at each one hour coaching session per week) across four schools allowed the researcher to adopt a range of informal, open and relaxed approaches (e.g., conversations) to data collection. Such an approach enabled the researcher to explore issues as they evolved "on the ground." Additionally, the researcher's personal reflections and observations were recorded through informal field notes and a reflective diary. The informal field notes were continually developed in an attempt to capture the context, culture and practice of EitC and the preceptions of all involved (McFee, 1992; Krane and Baird, 2005). Additionally, semi-structured interviews were conducted with practitioners and community coaches within EitC (Krane and Baird, 2005).

Did the community coaching program promote health?

The data suggested that the initiative was unable to promote positive health changes in the children involved, but was able to maintain activity in already active participants. The fun and enjoyable nature of the initiative and the hype and excitement within the children, teachers and schools involved in the program seemed to be an important aspect of keeping the children engaged/participating in physical activity (Figure 25.2). For instance the children reported that they "look forward to the sessions all weekend and all day" (Steven, aged 11 years) and that they were taught "lots of skills and played big matches" (Jonas, aged 10 years). Even the children's teacher (Mary) described the coaches as "wonderful." However, despite the overwhelming approval of the majority of children there were some negative comments, reported during the child focus groups that concerned the demeanour of the coach:

> Charlie (aged 9): If he (the coach) turned up on time we could get started straight away and have more time for a match.
> Titus (aged 10): The coach told me to shut up!

While such comments are not a wholesale representation from all of the children, they do allude to possible negative memories of the intervention and specifically the community coach. Further contextual information from the researcher, children and teachers suggests that this coaching initiative provided excitement, enjoyment and fun for (the majority of) those involved (Craig *et al.*, 1996; Butcher *et al.*, 2007). However, issues emerged that suggested

Figure 25.2 Delivering community programs: Everton in the Community

ineffective practice adopting traditional football coaching practices aimed at child football-ers, rather than adopting a health promotion remit working with mixed (i.e., football) ability groups. Coaches evidencing such practice throughout the initiative (and on specific occasions) limited the potential effectiveness of this initiative.

One of the first issues to surface within the initiative was the declining participation figures in the data. Of the original 57 children that were involved prior to the intervention, 14 chil-dren dropped out before the first session had even taken place. The total dropout rate for the entire intervention was 54 percent (n= 31). This relatively high attrition rate appeared to go unnoticed, unrecognized or even investigated by the coaches or the teachers. Although poor adherence isn't uncommon within interventions its presence was a cause for concern especially given that the children were apparently already "active" in their school football team (therefore you would expect them to be less likely to drop out!) (Van Sluijs *et al.*, 2007). The lack of a recruitment criteria and problems that emerged with coaching a diverse (i.e., ability) group of children is evident in a conversation with Ibrahim below:

> Ibrahim (a 9-year-old boy) said *"the sessions aren't challenging enough."* I explored this com-ment further with Ibrahim, specifically seeking his expectations and his perceptions before speaking with other children. It appeared that the sessions were in some cases *"too chal-lenging"* and *"too structured,"* which frustrated the children, specifically Ibrahim who didn't want to admit this given his normally confident and outgoing character. In essence, I knew that all that these kids wanted was to *"just play football and have fun."*

Maintaining adherence and participation should be the cornerstone of interventions seeking to promote positive health changes (Parnell *et al.*, 2013). These ineffective working practices appeared within the delivery of the intervention surrounding the role of "the coach" and their respective coaching practice. The following discussion explores the role of the coach, alluding to coaching practice, coach recruitment, aspirations and skill base.

The coach and coaching practice

It was evident that (generally) the children did not want to engage in long sessions that were focused on improving technical skills or tactical play. Overly prescriptive approaches to coach-ing have been reported as a factor in reducing participation (Dwyer *et al.*, 2006). In this regard, the researcher was able to empathize with the children's frustrations as throughout the inter-vention I witnessed a number of situations where the coaches attempted to deliver *routine* or *traditional* (performance oriented) football drills. This approach opposed that espoused by child development practitioners that allude to the importance of play (Packer Isenberg and Quisenberry, 2002), fun and enjoyment (Craig *et al.*, 1996; Butcher *et al.*, 2007).

One such example is Alan, a community coach with a number of years of experience working with young people in a range of roles. Alan had accrued his "badges" (required by the English Football Association and *Football* in general to coach children) through his role within the EitC. There were concerns here that although Alan had appropriate accreditation, it would appear that he was less able to translate his skill set to fulfil and meet the needs and requirements of a community oriented (i.e., predominantly recreational) session. In effect, the FA's accreditation program did not equip Alan, the "community coach," with a full skill set to work across such complex situations such as this (i.e., health promotion) (Borrie and Knowles, 2003). In this sense, while Alan was able to demonstrate high-level technical instruction, he failed to give (positive) feedback, reinforcement and supportive behavior, which has been associated with higher player (and child) perceptions of competence, enjoyment, self-esteem and self-confidence (Smoll and Smith, 1993; Spencer, 2001). Such inadequacies suggest that Alan was falling short in his attempt to encourage participation and/or the promotion of physical activity. His coaching practice typically failed to directly embrace a health promotion remit and appeared detrimental to the self-worth that these kids may have had. Despite this, when Alan was asked informally, about what he thought the sessions were all about, he replied:

> Enjoyment, it's the taking part that we (EitC) try to look at; we don't want to go into the schools and spot the next Stephen Gerrard or Tim Cahill. We want to look to get everybody involved, so the enjoyment is the main part. If they are enjoying it you've obviously achieved what you have gone in there to do.

While coaches obviously understand the need to make sessions fun, it appears that, in this instance, Alan could not deliver to this agenda as the children that he was coaching were not skilled enough to cope with his coaching strategies. Somewhere between Alan becoming a regular "community coach," completing his coaching qualifications and joining the FitC scheme, he developed some negative working practices. In this sense, his interpretation of a "fun and enjoyable" session would typically involve a (performance-based) pass and move drill. Importantly, it has been highlighted that situational factors such as national (the Football Association) and organizational culture (of the FitC scheme) may have played an influence on the behavior of the coach (Cote *et al.*, 1995). This may in part be a result of the coach adopting (performance) coaching norms or expectations. It would appear that the expectations of a coach were typically grounded in a performance model rather than a positive healthful behavior change model. Despite being aligned to a community based environment, it is the performance model of coaching that is the dominant template for football coaches (for further details on the role of the coach see Parnell *et al.*, 2013).

Using the findings to "move forward"

It is evident that this coaching initiative provided excitement, enjoyment and fun for (the majority) of those involved. In particular, the initiative provided an opportunity for the majority of (active) children to engage in further physical activity opportunities. While this positive experience is highly laudable, it appears that due to the deficiencies (or gaps) in the coaches' skill base, and subsequent inappropriate working practices. The potential effectiveness of this initiative has been limited to "keeping active children active, through fun and enjoyable sessions" (such findings are echoed within by Hindley and Williamson, Chapter 24). FitC schemes should be encouraged to adopt a clearer approach to the strategic targeting of more "at risk" population (i.e., including inactive, overweight and/or obese). Moreover, in order to better attend to the needs of such populations it is incumbent on the respective national coaching bodies and FitC schemes to equip their coaches with an appropriate skill base beyond that of a technically driven performance coach (i.e., including health agendas, and an ability to offer fun and enjoyable sessions to a diverse range of age groups and populations). Such a skill set must be seen as a prerequisite to addressing the increasingly complex social and health agendas that they are being asked to tackle (Parnell *et al.*, 2013). The findings from this initial phase of the research were discussed with senior management with a view to moving forward and improve practice.

Moving forward and developing a *change strategy*

In line with the action research process the researcher worked with senior management at EitC (within action meetings) to create a *change strategy*. It was within these action meetings the researcher disseminated the reconnaissance phase findings including the outcomes and concerns. Therefore, any *change strategy* would address the findings and work towards improving the effectiveness of EitC's working practice. The initial *change strategy* chosen by EitC senior management (Phil and Barry) was the development of a quality assurance (QA) model for practitioners and community coaches. There was an acceptance within senior management within these action meetings that the staff (community coaches) "*could only do so much*," echoing findings relating to limited practitioner skill base and lack of time highlighted by Nichols (2007).

Facilitating change

When facilitating this *change strategy* the researcher began to experience some barriers presented by senior management. For example, when asked about the progress made and the next step with regarding the facilitation of the QA model the researcher was met with the following response, "I am too busy to deal with this …" (Barry). Barry appeared too busy to deal with developing change, as the majority of time was spent busy with just getting coaches to turn up in time to deliver sessions rather than concern themselves with "what" they were delivering. Barry was the "key change person," the (agreed) nominee, responsible for seeing through the change, and also a senior manager at EitC. This reluctance to follow up with the change, despite initial senior management agreement, typified the complex meetings of cultures. In this case the monitoring and evaluation, evidence-based practice culture associated with academic research (and HE) met with the performance/outcome oriented and/or just "doing" culture present within football. The *change strategy* had been agreed between the researcher and senior management (including Barry). Following this, further political and organizational barriers to the *change strategy* began to emerge. For example, in one instance Barry explained that he now needed to discuss the agreed changes with the club's human resource department. To be fair to Barry, he did appear to want to facilitate the change strategy over a number of months but with no real success. Barry continued to claim that he couldn't get hold of the HR representative and in essence, was passing the blame on, "I cannot get hold of him [HR representative]. I have called, emailed, but have had no response …" Allegedly, Barry made several more failed attempts, "I will get this done. I need to get this done …" Despite the initial agreement stated in the action meeting, it appeared that Barry lacked the requisite authority to make this *change* across departments and organizations (EitC and the football club). The lack of success and pressure created through attempting to implement the *change strategy* raised ethical issues around Barry's ability to see through the *change* and also highlighted the incongruence between the FitC scheme and football club.

It was not until August 2008 (14 months into the *change strategy*) that *finally* some real action (change) was about to take place. However, as this change was about to come to fruition a different member of the senior management team was dismissed. This prompted both concerns by the researcher and EitC practitioners and community coaches. The principal researcher reflected:

> most staff within the charity seemed happy to be rid of Phil [senior manager], with some people showing genuine pleasure. However, Martin [new senior manager] had a HR background and carried a fierce reputation [and track record especially for dismissing staff].

This created a new anxiety amongst the staff, who were concerned about their job security. Whilst I empathized with my collaborators, colleagues and [now] friends, I also realized that, from a research perspective, we had lost a critical friend. Phil was a key ally and this was a major blow given the complex issues I was experiencing with Barry. I had established rapport and acceptance amongst EitC staff, but I needed someone to drive the change strategy forward from within ...

Making change happen

Remarkably, in September 2009 Martin the new senior manager (amicably) departed EitC adding to the extensive period of "turmoil" or "revolving door" culture. This played a major role in further embedding insecurity and anxiety across all of the practitioners (senior management included) and coaches within EitC. It was during this period of uncertainty that the researcher found that the more respected and influential practitioners (and community coaches) with a shared vision had led the other practitioners through the senior management and job security crisis. EitC community coaches commented, "as soon as we start getting somewhere and begin to settle, they [senior management] leave and we [the staff] are left to steady the ship ..."

> I had at this point met with Mike [a community coach with shared aspirations for better practice] and we "informally" decided to "make things happen," otherwise [we agreed] we wouldn't get this [or anything of any worth] done. Barry wasn't doing anything; he wasn't empowered or respected to do anything. Besides, he was also fretting over his future. Mike [and I] proposed that the new QA model should be ready prior to any new senior manager appointment. Mike's assertiveness was a welcome relief. He appeared to have the respect and support of the other coaches. Mike had "stepped up" as the new key change person and I felt comfortable that he would be more able to help see through the change ...

Mike and a number of other community coaches began to share their beliefs and maintained focus. Ultimately, these characters, especially Mike, had driven the organization forward (despite the absence of continuity in senior management). The researcher reflected:

> the "change" didn't happen overnight. I spent many long meetings, both formally and informally with Mike debating and discussing the role of EitC. We discussed strategic and operational targets, how they could be achieved and ways in which "we" [EitC and I] could be innovative and lead the way in best practice. It was during these meetings that we both recognized our shared aspirations and visions to take EitC forward. The emergence of such a character was indeed fortuitous. The ability to create rapport and closeness with him enabled such visions to be shared. It must be recognized that this was only realized as a result of prolonged engagement. In a place that is entrenched in doing the same thing because it's what's always been done, such aspiration and enthusiasm was refreshing to hear. Interestingly, people listened, took interest in and wanted to be involved in what Mike was talking about ...

The adoption of new philosophies and aspirations to improve by practitioners and the subsequent positive shift in culture created by this "new way of doing things" highlighted that both the practitioners and community coaches believed that this was "more than just a job." The process of reflection on practice had created a sense of accountability to their clients (people within the community they serve). By November 2009 (29 months into the *change strategy*) given the on-going senior management uncertainty we (researcher, practitioners and community coaches) did not manage to roll out the QA model. However, we had all contributed to towards making changes happen affecting recruitment, the philosophy of coaches, the utilization of evidenced based practice and the development of a culture of monitoring and evaluation.

Conclusions

It is important to highlight that although many FitC schemes are independent organizations, they are inextricably linked to their host club. This often involves more than just an association by brand and extends to shared departments including HR, communication, press relations (PR) and marketing functions. Often, requests for support from the FitC scheme to the club go unnoticed, as clubs do not see the value that FitC schemes offer (Slack and Shrives, 2008), unless an opportunity arises where there is "something in it for the club." Perhaps evidence to feed critics who argue that "although this sporting, educational and other community activity is important, it is possible to see this as just PR work for rich businessmen's playthings" (Bishop *et al.*, 2004: 13). With the notion of CSR being relatively new to football, both FitC schemes (i.e., practitioners and community coaches) and researchers could (and should) help reconcile such distinct agendas and advocate the importance of FitC schemes to their respective clubs. Given the argument that true CSR needs to be embedded with the fabric of the organization, to do this football clubs need to see FitC schemes as a strategic interest and vehicle to deliver CSR (and not simply used for to one-off projects).

FitC schemes possess a number of potentially positive factors that may provide a backdrop for such initiatives to deliver positive changes in, and through, community based football projects, such as fun and enjoyable sessions (for all ages and all types) and a passionate group of practitioners and community coaches. However, it is apparent that FitC schemes may require a number of positive organizational changes to maximise the *potential* impact they can have. Specifically, there is a need to develop and utilize effective working practices that specifically relate to the individuals (i.e., the practitioners and community coaches) who are involved in the direct delivery of the programs (Parnell *et al.*, 2013).

How to develop a monitoring and evaluation toolkit

As opposed to a specific evaluation tool, a change is needed in the philosophy of the practitioner and culture of the organization to aspire to doing things better, understanding what works and evidencing their impact (Coalter, 2001). This is not something that can happen overnight, but something that requires sustained long-term commitment alongside rapport and trust that creates "real" change in practice (i.e., it affects the "people" and their day to day practice).

The engagement provided through a collaborative (i.e., industry and academic department) action research oriented methodology (alongside the utilisation of relevant quantitative and qualitative data collection techniques) along with extensive immersion by the research enabled a thorough understanding of the characters and political landscape within a workplace (i.e., EitC). This permitted the researcher to successfully gravitate towards an appropriate key change person. This closeness, rapport and detailed individual and organizational understanding enabled the researcher to identify the "key change person" (i.e., a more respected, empowered person better able to see-through change).

Acceptance and familiarization within the host organization by senior management and practitioners is imperative to allow the researcher to realize and uncover the subtle intricacies of working practice, cultures and philosophies. This, alongside such an intimate relationship between the researcher and practitioner (and community coaches), played a crucial role in "making change" happen. It is clear that collaborations of this nature, especially in cultures prone to "regular" changes in senior management require continued and extensive engagement. In this sense the adoption of collaborative action research oriented methodology played a critical role in the "success" of the facilitation of *change* and should be considered as a tool to help create sustainable positive behavioral change in working practice. It is important not to underestimate the role of independent academic/theoretical voice that is not contaminated by, or a hostage to, the existing culture and practice. The independent body is in a position to challenge, where appropriate and where required, the existing status quo.

Key messages for football clubs: community engagement

- There is a need to have a clear purpose and strategic objectives (which are relevant to the skill base of their practitioners).
- There is a need to provide relevant continued professional development (CPD) opportunities to coaching staff and practitioners.
- It is important to promote a culture of research and evaluation (i.e., understanding what works and making practice more effective).
- Create and develop meaningful partnerships with relevant higher education departments with a clear focus on helping practitioners improve their practice (i.e., engage in action research).

References

Bale, J. (2000) 'The changing face of football: Stadiums and communities', *Soccer & Society*, 1 (1), 91–101.

Bishop, D, Breeze, J, Danczuk, S, Vision 21 and Bailey, G. (2004) 'Funding football from the grassroots to the championship', research paper on behalf of the 'All Party Football Group', Manchester.

Borrie, A. and Knowles, Z. (2003) 'Coaching science and soccer', in Reilly, T. and Williams, A. M. (eds.) *Science and soccer*. 2nd edn. London: Routledge, pp. 187–197.

Breitbarth, T. and Harris, P. (2008) 'The role of corporate social responsibility in the football business: Towards the development of a conceptual model', *European Sport Management Quarterly*, 8 (2), 179–201.

Brown, A., Crabbe, T., Mellor, G., Blackshaw, T. and Stone, C. (2006) *Football and its Communities: Final Report*. The Football Foundation and Manchester Metropolitan University.

Butcher, Z., Fairclough, S., Stratton, G. and Richardson, R. (2007) 'The effect of feedback and information on children's pedometer step counts at school', *Pediatric Exercise and Science*, 19, 29–38.

Coalter, F. (2001) *Realising the potential of cultural services: The case for sport*. London: LGA Publications.

Cote, J., Salmela, J.H., Trudel, P., Baria, A. and Russell, S.J. (1995) 'The coaching model: A grounded assessment of gymnastics coaches' knowledge', *Journal of Sport and Exercise Psychology*, 17, 1–17.

Craig, S., Goldberg, J. and Diet, W.H. (1996) 'Correlates of physical activity among fifth and eighth graders', *Preventative Medicine*, 25, 506–513.

Dwyer, J.J., Allison, K.R., Goldenberg, E.R., Fein, A.J., Yoshida, K.K. and Boutilier, M.A. (2006) 'Adolescent Girls' perceived barriers to participation in physical activity', *Adolescence*, 41, 75–89.

Eder, D. and Corsaro, W. (1999) 'Ethnographic studies of young children and youth', *Journal of Contemporary Ethnography*, 28 (5), 520–531.

Everton Football Club (2012) *Everton in the Community*. Available at: http://community.evertonfc.com/ (accessed: October 17, 2012).

Gilbourne, D. (1999) 'Collaboration and reflection: Adopting action research themes and processes to promote adherence to changing practice', in Bull, S. (ed.) *Adherence issues in sport and exercise*. Chichester: John Wiley, pp. 239–263.

Gilbourne, D. (2001) 'Developing a culture of change in the workplace: Applying processes and principles from action research to sports injury settings', in Crossman, J. (ed.) *Coping with sports injuries: Psychological strategies for rehabilitation*. Oxford: Oxford University Press, pp. 174–191.

Greggs (2012) *Greggs Foundation*. Available at: http://www.greggs.co.uk/greggs-foundation (accessed: October 17, 2012).

Hammersley, M. and Atkinson, P. (1995) *Ethnography principles and practice*. London: Tavistock.

Hong, L.K. and Duff, R.W. (2002) 'Modulated participant-observation: Managing the dilemma of distance in field research', *Field Methods*, 14, 190–196.

Jackson, N., Howes, F., Gupta, S., Doyle, J. and Waters, E. (2005) 'Policy interventions implemented through sporting organisations for promoting healthy behaviour change'. *Cochrane Database of Systematic Reviews*, 2. Available at: http://www.ncbi.nlm.nih.gov/pubmed/15846732 (accessed: October 17, 2012).

Janesick, V.J. (1994) 'The dance of qualitative research. Design, metaphor, methodolatry and meaning', in Denzin, N. K. and Lincoln, Y.S. (eds.) *Handbook of qualitative research*. London: Sage, pp. 209–219.

Jenkins, H. and James, L. (2012) 'It's not just a game: Community work in the UK Football industry and approaches to Corporate Social Responsibility', The ESRC Centre for Business Relationships, Accountability, Sustainability and Society, Cardiff University.

Krane, V. and Baird, S. M. (2005) 'Using ethnography in applied sport psychology', *Journal of Applied Sports Psychology*, 17, 87–107.

Liverpool City Council (2010) *The index of multiple deprivation 2010: A Liverpool Analysis*. Available at: http://liverpool.gov.uk/council/key-statistics-and-data/indices-of-deprivation (accessed: October 17, 2012).

Lupson, P. (2006) *Thank God for FOOTBALL*. London: Azure Press.

McFee, G. (1992) 'Triangulation in research: Two confusions', *Educational Research*, 34 (3), 173–83.

McGuire, B. and Fenoglio, R. (2004) *Football in the community: Resources and opportunities*. Manchester Metropolitan University, Department of Exercise and Sport Science.

Mellor, G. (2008) '"The janus-faced sport": English football, community and the legacy of the "Third Way"', *Soccer and Society*, 9 (3), 313–324.

Nichols, G. (2007) *Sport and crime reduction: The role of sports in tackling youth crime*. London: Routledge.

Packer Isenberg, J. and Quisenberry, N. (2002) 'A position paper of the association for childhood education international PLAY: Essential for all children', *Childhood Education*, 79 (1), 33–39

Parker, A. (2001) 'Soccer, servitude and sub-cultural identity: Football traineeship and masculine construction', *Soccer and Society*, 2, 59–80.

Parnell, D., Drust, B., Stratton, G. and Richardson, D (2008) 'Football in the Community: Effective community engagement', paper presented to the *European Association of Sports Management 16th Annual Conference*, Heidelberg, Germany, September 11.

Parnell, D., Stratton, G., Drust, B. and Richardson. D. (2013) 'Football in the Community schemes: Exploring the effectiveness of an intervention in promoting positive healthful behaviour change', *Soccer and Society*, 14, 1, 1–17. Available at: http://www.tandfonline.com/doi/abs/10.1080/14660970.2012.692678 (accessed: October 17, 2012).

Relvas, H, Littlewood, M, Nesti, M, Gilbourne, D. and Richardson, D. (2010) 'Organizational structures and working practices in elite European professional football clubs: Understanding the relationship between youth and professional domains', *European Sport Management Quarterly*, 10 (2), 165–187.

Responsiball (2012) *Responsiball. The first point of reference for responsible football clubs*. Available at: http://community.responsiball.org (accessed: October 17, 2012).

Richardson, D., Gilbourne, D. and Littlewood, M. (2004) 'Developing support mechanisms for elite young players in a professional soccer academy: Creative reflections in action research', *European Sports Management Quarterly*, 4, 195–214.

Russell, D. (1997) *Football and the English: A social history of Association Football in England, 1863–1995*. Preston: Carnegie.

Slack, R. and Shrives, P. (2008) 'Social disclosure and legitimacy in Premier League football clubs: the first ten years', *Journal of Applied Accounting Research*, 9 (1), 17–28.

Smoll, F.L. and Smith, R.E. (1993) 'Educating youth sport coaches: An applied sport psychology perspective', in Williams, J. M. (ed.) *Applied sports psychology: Personal growth to peak performance*. Mountain View: Mayfield Publishing, pp. 36–50.

Spencer, A.F. (2001) 'A case-study exemplary American College physical educator-tennis coach', *International Journal of Sport Pedagogy*, 3, 1–27.

Tacon, R. (2007) 'Football and social inclusion: Evaluating social policy', *Managing Leisure*, 12 (1), 1–23.

Taylor, N. (2004) '"Giving something back": Can football clubs and their communities co-exist?' in Wagg, S. (ed.) (2004) *British football and social exclusion*. London: Routledge, pp. 47–66.

Tierney, G.W. (2002) 'Get real: representing reality', *International Journal of Qualitative Studies in Education*, 15, 385–398.

Van Sluijs, E.M.F., McMinn, A.M. and Griffin, S.J. (2007) 'Effectiveness of interventions to promote physical activity in children and adolescents: Systematic review of controlled trials', *British Medical Journal*, 355 (703), 703–715.

Vigor, A, Hallam, K. and Jackson, M. (2006) 'A good game? The role of sport in society: a scoping study', Draft report presented to Football Association.

Walters, G., and Chadwick, S. (2009) 'Corporate citizenship in football: Delivering strategic benefits through stakeholder engagement', *Management Decision*, 47 (1), 51–66.

Watson, N. (2000) 'Football in the community: what's the score?' *Soccer and Society*, 1, 114–125.

CONCLUSION

Trends, challenges and the future for CSR in sport

Juan Luis Paramio-Salcines, Kathy Babiak and Geoff Walters

Societies around the world face significant challenges in the twenty-first century: a growing global population, changing demographics and an ageing population in certain countries, the effects of global warming, as well as continuing global poverty (Blowfield and Murray, 2008). It can be argued that the fundamental role that organizations play in addressing these trends and issues is, and will continue to be, an ongoing concern. At the same time, it can also be argued that societies will expect businesses to continue to demonstrate greater responsibility, accountability and transparency; that they will seek to ensure that corporate irresponsibility, greed and excess is minimized; and that they will treat employees in a fair and responsible manner. The expectation, therefore, that companies do more than simply generate wealth and shareholder profits by demonstrating a commitment to societal issues through social and environmental activities will remain a central and fundamental issue for organizations in the future. Will, as Burchell (2008) considers, these ongoing challenges ensure that CSR in the long term will lead to a fundamental shift in organizational behavior towards more sustainable ways of operating, or will it be seen as a management fad that is of less concern when more immediate issues present themselves?

This latter point is particularly poignant when considering the current issues affecting global economies. At the time of writing, many economies have endured significant economic and financial uncertainty. There have been periods of recession, rising unemployment and an increased number of firms that have gone out of business. In response, stimulating economic growth has been at the top of many government agendas during this recent period. The wider state of the global economy raises fundamental questions as to how organizations (and more broadly governments) will address the issue of CSR. Within such an environment to what extent will organizations consider CSR activities to be core to their business strategy? Will, and have, organizations cut their commitment to CSR in order to reduce costs and have they prioritized financial performance in order to stay in business rather than engage in activities that as Carroll (1979) argued can be considered discretionary? What has been the effect on consumers and their consumption of sustainable and ethical products? Will consumers continue to pay a premium for these types of product? Or given that many face increasing costs, stagnant wages and the threat of unemployment, will they turn to cheaper alternatives that are perhaps sourced from less ethical producers? Will we see organizations responding by integrating CSR into their strategy as a way to control costs, maintain reputation, build consumer trust and expand into new customer markets? What impact will codes and standards that increase awareness of what organizations are doing and encourage uptake of CSR through peer pressure and activism (Waddock, 2008) have in the future given these concerns around the current state of the global economy?

These issues are central to the evolving nature of the relationship between business and society and are fundamental to understanding the implications for corporate social responsibility in the future. What these questions demonstrate is that the future of CSR is open for debate (Burchell, 2008). The same can be said for the future of CSR in the sport industry. We cannot isolate sports organizations from trends affecting the broader economy and while sport may be somewhat more recession-resistant, it is not recession-proof. A struggling economy may impact sport organizations, manifest through a fall in attendances at live sport events or a reduction in spending on sporting goods and equipment as consumers face the prospect of a fall in disposable income. Therefore, sport organizations may also face financial pressures that could impact how they address the issue of CSR. At this point in time, the future approaches that sport organizations will take is unclear. What this book – the first to focus on sport and CSR – has done is set out the current status of the field by taking an organization-focused approach through the use of case studies to better understand what sport organizations are doing. It has provided an understanding of how sport organizations have implemented CSR programs and initiatives and how CSR has been integrated into organizations' cultures and strategies; it has considered ways in which sport organizations engage with stakeholders and manage stakeholder relationships; it has looked at the ways in which sport organizations communicate their CSR activities; and it has also considered how sport organizations measure CSR.

This book has shown the extent to which sport organizations are addressing CSR and for this there are reasons to be optimistic about the future of CSR and sport. Given that some CSR-related activities have been around for many years within certain sectors of the sport industry, in addition to the general increased level of awareness of CSR across the sector all suggest that CSR is not necessarily a management fad. However, two key issues remain. First, to what extent is CSR considered by sport organizations to be a marketing or PR tool? By itself this is not necessarily problematic: if a sport organization is able to realize business benefits from engaging in CSR, whether through an enhanced reputation that translates into increased attendance, improved levels of loyalty from fans, or through larger sponsorships deals then it can benefit both the sport organization and those stakeholders that benefit from the CSR initiatives. However, the point is that this comes back to the long-standing issue of why organizations engage in CSR and the concerns that if it is simply to deliver business-benefits then the level of engagement will perhaps be at a superficial level and that sport organizations are only moved by the issues that they perhaps feel will enhance their brand. Burchell and Cook (2006) also make the argument that the narrow focus on justifying CSR based on the business-case places too great an emphasis on the role of organizations at the expense of interactions between the private sector, public sector and civil society. In some ways we see this happening in the sport industry: many organizational reports, peer-reviewed articles, and academic and professional conferences on sport and CSR tend to be on the benefits to the business and not on stakeholder benefits. This is where academic research has an important role to play in shifting the focus of attention. While this book has focused on CSR from the perspective of the sport organization in order to set the scene, we would argue that future academic research should look to engage at a more critical level and in particular, to consider issues from multiple stakeholder perspectives.

This leads to the second inter-related issue: how should sport organizations structure CSR to have the most significant impact? There are many cases where CSR could be argued to be seen as an add-on to the main activity of the sport organization, for example through the formation of partnerships between professional sport teams and charitable foundations (see Chapter 25, which looked at Everton Football Club and their link with the Everton in the Community Sports Trust). In the US this partnership model often involves team owners providing funding for charitable foundations. However, to what extent is this outsourcing CSR and is this the best way to structure CSR? Is there a need to better integrate CSR across all aspects of the organization rather than consider it the role of a particular department or a specialized function? In this respect perhaps a key future challenge that CSR faces within the sport industry is to encourage sport organizations to develop an approach that involves integrating CSR throughout the whole of the sport organization. Such an approach would ensure that CSR is an issue that is embedded within the organization, through strategy, policies and processes, and would encourage socially responsible behavior to become the norm across organizations.

References

Blowfield, M. and Murray, A. (2008) *Corporate responsibility: A critical introduction*. Oxford: Oxford University Press.

Burchell, J. (2008) *The Corporate Social Responsibility Reader*. London: Routledge.

Burchell, J. and Cook, J. (2006) 'Confronting the "corporate citizen": Shaping the discourse of corporate social responsibility', *The International Journal of Sociology and Social Policy*, 26 (3/4), 121–137.

Carroll, A. B. (1979) 'A three-dimensional conceptual model of corporate performance', *Academy of Management Review*, 4 (4), 497–505.

Waddock, S. (2008) 'Building a new institutional infrastructure for corporate responsibility', *The Academy of Management Perspectives*, 22(3), 87–108.

INDEX